MAGILL'S GUIDE TO

Science Fiction and Fantasy Literature

MAGILL'S GUIDE TO

Science Fiction and Fantasy Literature

Volume 1

The Absolute at Large – Dragonsbane

Consulting Editor
T. A. Shippey
St. Louis University

Project Editor
A. J. Sobczak

Hillsborough Community College LRC

Salem Press, Inc.
Pasadena, California   Englewood Cliffs, New Jersey

Editor in Chief: Dawn P. Dawson
Consulting Editor: T. A. Shippey   *Project Editor:* A. J. Sobczak
Research Supervisor: Jeffry Jensen   *Production Editor:* Joyce I. Buchea
Proofreading Supervisor: Yasmine A. Cordoba   *Layout:* William Zimmerman

Library of Congress Cataloging-in-Publication Data
Magill's Guide to Science Fiction and Fantasy Literature / consulting editor, T. A. Shippey; project editor, A. J. Sobczak.
    v. <1   > : cm.
    "A Magill Book"
    Includes bibliographical references and indexes.
    ISBN 0-89356-906-2 (set : alk. paper) — ISBN 0-89356-907-0 (vol. 1 : alk. paper)
    1. Science fiction—History and criticism—Bibliography.   2. Fantastic literature—History and criticism—Bibliography.   I. Shippey, T. A.
Z5917.S36M24   1996
[PN3433.8]
016.80883'876—dc20
                                                                                                96-26261
                                                                                                CIP

Second Printing

PRINTED IN THE UNITED STATES OF AMERICA

PUBLISHER'S NOTE

The four volumes of *Magill's Guide to Science Fiction and Fantasy Literature* provide descriptions of hundreds of famous and well-regarded works of science fiction and fantasy, summarizing plots and analyzing the works in terms of their contributions to literature and the effectiveness of various literary devices employed. This four-volume set is the only work of its kind in print. Arranged alphabetically by title, entries in this set discuss long-recognized classics as well as books published recently. The 1980's and 1990's, for example, saw a resurgence of fantasy literature and innovations in science fiction, with the advent of cyberpunk fiction among the most prominent of them. Of the 791 entries on individual books or sets of related books, 238 include discussions of books published during the 1980's and 1990's. These entries introduce the work of writers who emerged as important and influential during that period, such as William Gibson, Charles de Lint, Ellen Kushner, Connie Willis, Iain Banks, Tim Powers, Angela Carter, and David Eddings, as well as showing the further development of the careers of such established writers as Marion Zimmer Bradley, Stephen King, and Lois McMaster Bujold.

The entries in *Magill's Guide to Science Fiction and Fantasy Literature* discuss individual books and series as self-contained as well as putting them into context. Out of the total of 791 entries, 155 discuss pairs of books, trilogies, and longer series. This approach allows contributors to discuss overarching themes and styles within a series. Each entry, whether on an individual book or on multiple books, contains a section, headed "Analysis," that describes the themes, meanings, and literary devices in the work as well as setting it in the context of other works by the author or related works by other authors.

Entries on a single book are approximately 1,000 words in length; entries discussing two or more books are approximately 1,500 words. The ready-reference information at the top of each entry lists titles; provides brief, one-sentence descriptions of the books; gives the authors and their dates of birth and death; identifies the books as fantasy or science fiction and assigns one of thirty-seven genre categories; identifies works as novels, novellas, sets of novels, stories, drama, or collected works; provides the time and physical location of the plots; and identifies the dates of first publication.

The main body of each entry consists of two sections of approximately equal length, headed "The Plot" and "Analysis." "The Plot" provides the primary plot points of the work and identifies major characters. "Analysis" provides criticism of the work. This section also places the work within any trends or movements in science fiction or fantasy as a whole as well as in the author's body of work. It identifies the literary devices employed and the themes that emerge. Any major awards won by the work are also listed. Each entry is signed by the contributor. This format of top matter and section headings ensures that the same basic types of information are present in each entry, while allowing contributors scope to emphasize various aspects of different works.

The 791 entries composing the bulk of these volumes are supplemented by an extensive annotated bibliography of critical works on science fiction and fantasy as well as by a list of major awards and their winners. Both of these features appear in volume 4, which also includes three indexes. The Genre Index lists titles according to the genre identified in the top matter of the entry, allowing users to identify all the books of a particular type. The thirty-seven genres are identified and described in the List of Genres appearing at the beginning of volume 1. The Title Index lists all the works covered by their primary titles as well as cross-referencing alternate titles and titles of individual works that appear within a series. The Author and Title Index lists all titles, under the name of the author of the work.

Magill's Guide to Science Fiction and Fantasy Literature recognizes the emergence of critical studies of both science fiction and fantasy as important forms of literature. The decision was made to incorporate analyses of both science fiction and fantasy for several reasons. Lines between the two fields have blurred. Magic, for example, in some cases is treated as a form of technology or science and in others as a mysterious fantastic element. In addition, increasing numbers of writers have chosen to write both science fiction and fantasy, blurring the distinctions between the two types of literature. Comprehensive discussion of works by these authors therefore necessitates examining both types of literature together.

Works that may be classified as science fiction emerged from the background of nineteenth century "scientific romance" but came to prominence in the 1920's, when "pulp" magazines popularized the form. Although the pulps emphasized action and adventure stories, they also were prepared to develop social and political themes arising from scientific change, arguably among the most important topics to be treated in modern literature. Beginning in the 1960's, science fction also was increasingly open to sophisticated and imaginative literary development. Fantasy literature, which has older roots, also evolved, from primary emphasis on myths and legends to an expanded scope of the fantastic. It made an unexpected and electrifying comeback after the 1950's and the "Tolkien revolution." Hundreds of fantasy titles now are published every year, including some work that is at once the most popular and the most challenging of contemporary fiction. Both science fiction and fantasy are literatures of the imagination, and authors in both fields can claim to have created new worlds of the imagination for their readers to explore. Consulting editor T. A. Shippey examines developments in both fields in his introductory essay in volume 1.

We believe that the entries in *Magill's Guide to Science Fiction and Fantasy Literature* will aid scholars, researchers, and students in appreciating the contributions made in each of these forms. In addition, the plot summaries provide introductions to the works, so that the entries can be used as guides to potential readers looking for books that will provide entertaining reading. With usefulness to users in mind, the decision was made to include discussions only of books originally published in English or translated into English. These are the most accessible to readers and are the primary focus of researchers and scholars.

We would like to thank the many academicians and other writers who contributed to this set. A list of their names and affiliations appears at the beginning of volume 1.

CONTRIBUTING REVIEWERS

Amy Adelstein
Independent Scholar

Walter Albert
University of Pittsburgh

A. Owen Aldridge
University of Illinois

Emily Alward
Greenwood, Indiana, Public Library

Steve Anderson
University of Arkansas at Little Rock

Ronnie Apter
Central Michigan University

Stanley Archer
Texas A&M University

Gerald S. Argetsinger
Rochester Institute of Technology

Mike Ashley
Independent Scholar

Bryan Aubrey
Independent Scholar

Charles Avinger
Washtenaw Community College

Mary Bagley
Missouri Baptist College

Jim Baird
University of North Texas

Barbara L. Baker
Central Missouri State University

Neal Baker
Dickinson College

James J. Balakier
University of South Dakota

Jerry L. Ball
Arkansas State University

Paul J. Baltes
Brigham Young University

Henry J. Baron
Calvin College

David Barratt
Independent Scholar

Martha A. Bartter
Northeast Missouri State University

Margaret W. Batschelet
University of Texas at San Antonio

Elizabeth H. Battles
Texas Wesleyan University

Margaret D. Bauer
Texas A&M University

Paulina L. Bazin
Loyola University

Karen S. Bellinfante
Independent Scholar

Cynthia Breslin Beres
Independent Scholar

Donna Berliner
Southern Methodist University

Cynthia A. Bily
Adrian College

Margaret Boe Birns
The New School for Social Research

Nicholas Birns
The New School for Social Research

Russell Blackford
Independent Scholar

Tim Blackmore
York University

Franz G. Blaha
University of Nebraska—Lincoln

Pegge Bochynski
Salem State College

Edra C. Bogle
University of North Texas

Janice M. Bogstad
University of Wisconsin—Eau Claire

Bernadette Lynn Bosky
Independent Scholar

Wendy Bousfield
Syracuse University

Kevin Boyle
Elon College

C. K. Breckenridge
Independent Scholar

John P. Brennan
Indiana University-Purdue University at Fort Wayne

Peter Brigg
University of Guelph

Wesley Britton
Grayson County College

David Bromige
Sonoma State University

Carroll Brown
Independent Scholar

Siobhan Craft Brownson
University of South Carolina—Columbia

Sam Bruce
Independent Scholar

Paul Buchanan
Biola University

Mary A. Burgess
Borgo Press

Edmund J. Campion
University of Tennessee

Peter Cannon
Independent Scholar

David B. Carroll
California State University, Los Angeles

Shawn Carruth
Concordia College

Erskine Carter
Black Hawk College

Sonya Cashdan
East Tennessee State University

Jeffrey Cass
Texas A&M International University

Christine R. Catron
St. Mary's University

Karen Rose Cercone
Indiana University of Pennsylvania

Edgar L. Chapman
Bradley University

Danièle Chatelain
University of Redlands

Amy Clarke
St. Mary's College of California

Daryl R. Coats
Northwestern State University of Louisiana

David W. Cole
University of Wisconsin Center—Baraboo/ Sauk County

Tammy S. Conard
Texas Tech University

Gary William Crawford
Independent Scholar

Peter Crawford
Independent Scholar

C. K. Breckenridge
Independent Scholar

Shira Daemon
Independent Scholar

Susan Jaye Dauer
Austin Community College

Clark Davis
Northeast Louisiana University

Mary V. Davis
Independent Scholar

Radford B. Davis
Independent Scholar

Frank Day
Clemson University

Dennis R. Dean
Independent Scholar

Mary Jo Deegan
University of Nebraska—Lincoln

Bill Delaney
Independent Scholar

Paul Dellinger
Independent Scholar

Francine Dempsey
College of St. Rose

Mike Dickinson
Independent Scholar

Frank Dietz
Independent Scholar

Gene Doty
University of Missouri—Rolla

Catherine Doyle
Christopher Newport University

H. L. Drake
Millersville University

Lawrence Driscoll
University of Southern California

Thomas DuBose
Louisiana State University—Shreveport

Joyce Duncan
East Tennessee State University

Stefan Dziemianowicz
Independent Scholar

Bernard J. Farber
*Illinois Institute of Technology,
    Kent College of Law*

Jo N. Farrar
San Jacinto College

James Feast
Baruch College

Tom Feller
Independent Scholar

John Fiero
University of Southwestern Louisiana

David Marc Fischer
Independent Scholar

James O. Foster
Baylor University

Ronald Foust
Loyola University in New Orleans

Diana Pharaoh Francis
Ball State University

D. Douglas Fratz
Independent Scholar

June M. Frazer
Western Illinois University

Kelly Fuller
The Claremont Graduate School

Jean C. Fulton
Maharishi International University

Robert Galbreath
University of North Carolina at Greensboro

Robert L. Gale
University of Pittsburgh

Jeffery Galle
Northeast Louisiana University

Charles Gannon
Fordham University

Ann D. Garbett
Averett College

Tanya Gardiner-Scott
Mount Ida College

Gayle Gaskill
College of St. Catherine

Victoria Gaydosik
East Central University

Diana L. Gerow
Niagara County Community College

Craig Gilbert
Portland State University

Marjorie Ginsberg
William Paterson College

Beaird Glover
Independent Scholar

Marc Goldstein
Independent Scholar

Lewis L. Gould
University of Texas

Carla Graham
University of Wisconsin—La Crosse

Charles A. Gramlich
Xavier University

Kenneth B. Grant
*University of Wisconsin Center—
    Baraboo/Sauk County*

David Griffin
Carnage Hall Magazine

John L. Grigsby
Tennessee Technological University

Elizabeth A. Hait
McNeese State University

James C. Hall
University of Illinois at Chicago

Peter C. Hall
Independent Scholar

Paul Hansom
University of Southern California

William H. Hardesty III
Miami University

Betsy P. Harfst
Independent Scholar

Michael Harper
Scripps College

Gregory Harris
Independent Scholar

June Harris
East Texas State University

Maverick Marvin Harris
East Texas Baptist University

Darren Harris-Fain
Shawnee State University

Katie Harse
University of Calgary

Donald M. Hassler
Kent State University

A. Waller Hastings
Northern State University

Gary Layne Hatch
Brigham Young University

Len Hatfield
*Virginia Polytechnic Institute and State
    University*

John C. Hawley
Santa Clara University

Robert W. Haynes
Texas A&M International University

Charles Heffelfinger
Independent Scholar

Karen Hellekson
University of Kansas

Terry Heller
Coe College

CONTRIBUTING REVIEWERS

Suzette J. Henderson
University of South Florida

Karin U. Herrmann
University of Arkansas

Richard A. Hill
Taylor University

David Hinckley
University of California, Riverside

Joseph W. Hinton
Independent Scholar

Arthur D. Hlavaty
Independent Scholar

James L. Hodge
Bowdoin College

W. Kenneth Holditch
University of New Orleans

John R. Holmes
Franciscan University of Steubenville

Joan Hope
Indiana University at Bloomington

Kenneth L. Houghton
Independent Scholar

Mary Hurd
East Tennessee State University

Susan Hwang
Independent Scholar

Earl G. Ingersoll
State University of New York College at Brockport

Archibald E. Irwin
Indiana University Southeast

Charles Israel
Columbia College of South Carolina

John Jacob
Northwestern University

Jeff Johnson
Independent Scholar

Eunice Pedersen Johnston
North Dakota State University

Paul Joseph
Nova Southeastern University Law Center

Donald P. Kaczvinsky
Louisiana Tech University

Anne K. Kaler
Gwynedd Mercy College

Daven M. Kari
California Baptist College

Cynthia Lee Katona
Ohlone College

U. Milo Kaufmann
University of Illinois at Urbana-Champaign

Philip E. Kaveny
University of Wisconsin—Madison

James D. Keeline
Prince and the Pauper Collectible Children's Books

Kara K. Keeling
Christopher Newport University

Richard Keenan
University of Maryland—Eastern Shore

Fiona Kelleghan
University of Miami

Richard Kelly
University of Tennessee

Howard A. Kerner
Polk Community College

Paul Kincaid
Independent Scholar

Jeff King
University of North Texas

Susan S. Kissel
Northern Kentucky University

Katharine Kittredge
Ithaca College

E. Laura Kleiner
Indiana State University

Kim G. Kofmel
University of Western Ontario

Grove Koger
Boise Public Library

David C. Kopaska-Merkel
Independent Scholar

Dennis M. Kratz
University of Texas at Dallas

David Lampe
State University College at Buffalo

Douglas Edward LaPrade
University of Texas—Pan American

David H. J. Larmour
Texas Tech University

Eugene Larson
Los Angeles Pierce College

William Laskowski
Jamestown College

Dianna Laurent
Southeastern Louisiana University

William T. Lawlor
University of Wisconsin—Stevens Point

Benjamin S. Lawson
Albany State College

L. L. Lee
Western Washington University

Steven Lehman
John Abbott College

Elisabeth Anne Leonard
Kent State University

Leon Lewis
Appalachian State University

Rania Lisas
Virginia Polytechnic Institute and State University

Janet Alice Long
Independent Scholar

Steven R. Luebke
University of Wisconsin—River Falls

R. C. Lutz
University of the Pacific

Janet McCann
Texas A&M University

Robert McClenaghan
Independent Scholar

Jean McConnell
New Mexico Military Institute

Andrew Macdonald
Loyola University, New Orleans

Gina Macdonald
Loyola University, New Orleans

Ron McFarland
University of Idaho

James M. McGlathery
University of Illinois at Urbana-Champaign

Edythe M. McGovern
West Los Angeles College

S. Thomas Mack
University of South Carolina—Aiken

Edgar V. McKnight, Jr.
John A. Logan College

Kevin McNeilly
University of British Columbia

Willis E. McNelly
California State University, Fullerton

Samuel Maio
San Jose State University

Daryl F. Mallett
Angel Enterprises

Edward A. Malone
University of Missouri—Rolla

CONTRIBUTING REVIEWERS

Carl Rollyson
Baruch College, City University of New York

Natalie M. Rosinsky
Independent Scholar

Franz Rottensteiner
Independent Scholar

Nicholas Ruddick
University of Regina

Willard J. Rusch
University of Southern Maine

Todd H. Sammons
University of Hawaii at Manoa

Donna D. Samudio
Tarrant County Junior College

Scott Samuelson
Ricks College

Joe Sanders
Lakeland Community College

W. A. Senior
Broward Community College

Roberta Sharp
California State Polytechnic University, Pomona

Agnes A. Shields
Chestnut Hill College

T. A. Shippey
Saint Louis University

R. Baird Shuman
University of Illinois at Urbana-Champaign

Charles L. P. Silet
Iowa State University

Carl Singleton
Fort Hays State University

Amy Sisson
Independent Scholar

George Slusser
University of California, Riverside

Pamela J. Olubunmi Smith
University of Nebraska at Omaha

Ira Smolensky
Monmouth College

Jean M. Snook
Memorial University of Newfoundland

A. J. Sobczak
Independent Scholar

George Soule
Carleton College

Thomas D. Spaccarelli
The University of the South

Hartley S. Spatt
State University of New York Maritime College

Maureen Speller
Independent Scholar

William C. Spruiell
Western Carolina University

Andrew Sprung
D'Youville College

Brian Stableford
Independent Scholar

Barbara C. Stanley
Independent Scholar

Isabel B. Stanley
East Tennessee State University

Joshua Stein
University of California, Riverside

Eric Sterling
Independent Scholar

W. D. Stevens
Independent Scholar

Louise M. Stone
Bloomsburg University

Sue Storm
Independent Scholar

Sherry Stoskopf
Minot State University

Gerald H. Strauss
Bloomsburg University

Michael Stuprich
Ithaca College

C. W. Sullivan III
East Carolina University

Rŏy Arthur Swanson
University of Wisconsin—Milwaukee

Christina Sylka
University of British Columbia

Marcelle Thiébaux
St. John's University

Raymond H. Thompson
Acadia University

John C. Tibbetts
University of Kansas

John H. Timmerman
Calvin College

Michael J. Tolley
The University of Adelaide

Tony Trigilio
Northeastern University

Samuel J. Umland
University of Nebraska—Kearney

Jeff VanderMeer
Council on Literature of the Fantastic

Scott D. Vander Ploeg
Madisonville Community College

J. K. Van Dover
Lincoln University

Dennis Vannatta
University of Arkansas at Little Rock

Susan A. VanSchuyver
Oklahoma City Community College

Mary E. Virginia
Independent Scholar

G. A. M. Vissers
Independent Scholar

Jaquelyn W. Walsh
McNeese State University

Kathryn A. Walterscheid
University of Missouri—St. Louis

Janeen Webb
Australian Catholic University

Quinn Weller
Independent Scholar

Earl Wells
Independent Scholar

James M. Welsh
Salisbury State University

John T. West III
University of Arkansas at Pine Bluff

Gary Westfahl
University of California, Riverside

Robert Whipple
Creighton University

Thomas Whissen
Wright State University

Clyde Wilcox
Georgetown University

Bettye J. Williams
University of Arkansas at Pine Bluff

Donna Glee Williams
North Carolina Center for the Advancement of Teaching

Philip F. Williams
Arizona State University

Judith Barton Williamson
Sauk Valley Community College

John Wilson
Independent Scholar

Michael Witkoski
Independent Scholar

Susan Wladaver-Morgan
Independent Scholar

Lynn Wolf
Nova Southeastern University

Milton T. Wolf
University of Nevada—Reno

Tim Wolf
Middle Tennessee State University

Gary K. Wolfe
Roosevelt University

Martin Morse Wooster
American Enterprise Institute

Clifton K. Yearley
State University of New York—Buffalo

Carl B. Yoke
Kent State University

Beth Rapp Young
University of Alabama in Huntsville

Mary Young
The College of Wooster

Gary Zacharias
Palomar College

Marc Zaldivar
Virginia Polytechnic Institute and State University

Alan Ziskin
Independent Scholar

INTRODUCTION

The urge to tell tales of wonder is at least as old as any records human beings possess, and almost certainly older. Although modern literary criticism tends to downplay that urge, or to assign it a lower seniority than other narrative forms, one could properly claim that there are in essence three different provinces of the realm of story, all of equal value and all of equal age. Most obvious is the urge to record what actually happened, or what people believe actually happened. This is called not story but "history." Next is the urge to make up stories about events that did not actually happen, and about people who may be complete inventions of the storyteller. This we call "fiction," a genre that extends from the anecdotes people still tell about things that (allegedly) happened to their (perhaps imaginary) friends all the way through to the great and developed complexity of the written novel.

Third and last in this progression is the urge to tell stories not only about invented events and invented people but also about invented creatures, such as werewolves and vampires, or invented worlds, such as Middle-earth or Atlantis or the Earthly Paradise, or to tell any kind of tale that invents not only the people who exist in it but also the conditions under which they exist. Perhaps it is significant that there is no generally accepted label in our culture for this final category of story. One might suggest the word "fantasy," a word related to both "phantom" and "fancy" and having a root meaning of "making (something) visible," specifically imagining or making images of something that is not actually there. Fantasy, however, has an established meaning in the parlance of modern literary marketing, as well as in the title of *Magill's Guide to Science Fiction and Fantasy Literature*. Part of that meaning is "not the same as science fiction," a difference further discussed below. The International Association for the Fantastic in the Arts has proposed "the fantastic" as a broader label to set against the very large categories of "history" and "fiction." This label covers both modern fantasy and modern science fiction, taking in as well the ancestor genres of fairy tale, romance, myth, legend, ghost story, and many others. Stories of "the fantastic" may be defined as including any set in a world different from our own or that include elements recognized as alien to our own, things that are not true or not yet true. The dominant modern branches of the fantastic are those covered in *Magill's Guide to Science Fiction and Fantasy Literature*—fantasy and science fiction—but the fantastic includes genres older than either of them.

These three very broadly defined types of story—history, fiction, and the fantastic—did not, as far as is known, develop out of one another. All three were present at the dawn of European literature more than two thousand years ago and no doubt existed earlier on other continents. As an example of history, one can point to Herodotus' *The History of the Persian Wars* (c. 430 B.C.), an account of the Greek and Persian wars and all that led up to them in the fifth and sixth centuries B.C. For fiction, one could cite Homer's epic poem *The Iliad* (c. 800 B.C.), an account of an even older war between Greeks and Trojans, possibly with a historical basis but clearly composed to tell a story of adultery and revenge, not to list dates and events. Finally, Homer's *The Odyssey* (c. 800 B.C.) is in many ways a classic example of the fantastic, with its much loved and still much imitated tales of one-eyed, man-eating giants and witches who can turn people into beasts.

These three cases should provide a salutary reminder that there is no seniority in literary modes and that the fantastic, far from being a junior partner to history and fiction, is as old as either of them. The examples also show how difficult it is to keep the basic distinctions between story types absolutely clear. Many historians, Herodotus included, have been called liars and writers of fiction. By contrast, much fiction has been, and sometimes still is, thought by many people to be literally true. To switch from early Greek to early British literature, Geoffrey of Monmouth, the author of *History of the Kings of Britain* (1718; first published as *Historia regum Britanniae*, c. 1136), was dismissed as a total fabricator by some of his contemporaries, and most modern scholars have agreed with that assessment. Geoffrey's retelling of the legend of King Arthur, however, was accepted as absolute fact by many readers from the twelfth century to the early sixteenth, when the first historian to cast serious doubt on Arthur's reality was dismissed by English patriots as a crazy and jealous Italian. At present, books about King Arthur may be produced by professional historians, by writers of historical fiction, and by writers of the fantastic such as T. H. White, author of *The Once and Future King* (1958). One of the earliest references to the Arthur story is an incident that crept into real history when, in 1113, a Frenchman visiting Cornwall told a local resident that his belief that King

Arthur was not dead but would return again was utter nonsense, or as one might now say, "completely fantastic." A fracas began when the Cornishman defended the truth of his belief, and it was the fracas, not the legend, that found its way into recorded history.

Arguments about literary genres usually are not taken as far as that, but the incident serves to demonstrate that one person's fantasy may be another person's history. Just the same, although figures such as King Arthur, Odysseus, and Beowulf may be very hard or even impossible to categorize, the basic idea of the three modes, with their different relationships to literal truth, remains valid. It also can be said that as time has gone by, the differences generally have become more marked and the distinctions have become clearer. One of C. S. Lewis' characters, the scholarly Dr. Dimble in *That Hideous Strength* (1945), the last work of Lewis' Space Trilogy, says at one point:

> if you dip into any college, or school, or parish—anything you like—at a given point in its history, you always find that there was a time before that point when there was more elbow-room and contrasts weren't so sharp; and that there's going to be a point after that time when there is even less room for indecision and choices are more momentous. . . . The whole thing is sorting itself out all the time, coming to a point, getting sharper and harder.

Dimble says this only to excuse his own side's resurrection of Merlin from the past and its use of a kind of magic that would now be unlawful but in the old days was not yet categorized, not yet ruled out. What he says has a kind of force, however, for literary genres as well. Even the well-publicized efforts of modern avant-garde writers to mix literary genres depend for their effect on awareness of what the genres are. When it comes to fiction and the fantastic especially, and beyond them to the modern division of the fantastic into fantasy and science fiction, the tendency of present-day readers to draw sharp lines of distinction has become very strong.

This is a result of the major social and psychological development that marks off modern times from all previous eras and that (however much one may complain about it) most people see as a process of continuous acceleration: The rise of science. It entirely confirms Dr. Dimble's theory to note that although "science" is a word of great age—*scientia* is only the Latin word for "knowledge"—the highly specialized meaning now given to the word has been traced by the *Oxford English Dictionary* no further than 1725, and then not very convincingly. As late as 1834, that dictionary recorded objections to the use of the newly invented word "scientist." Only in the later nineteenth century does one find the words "science," "scientist," and "scientific" being given their modern meaning. From then on, however, one can see the ideas of science and scientific method taking hold in more and more minds, with ever increasing power, as tools for establishing human control over nature and as particularly reliable guides for systematizing some kinds of knowledge. This immense physical, mental, and semantic change has had its effect on literature, in particular on the whole realm of the fantastic and on its two major modern divisions of fantasy and science fiction.

* * *

To consider first the history of science fiction alone, one may say in brief that as human beings began to do things in sober reality that no human being had ever done before, storytellers began to wonder what limits on novelty there were and what in the world might happen next. This impulse intersected with the ancient urge toward telling tales of wonder but also tended radically to alter it. For example, stories had been told for countless generations about raising the dead. In Homer's *The Odyssey*, Odysseus calls up the ghost of Achilles to give him advice. In the Bible, one reads of Jesus' raising of Lazarus. The first is a matter of magic, the second of religion. In *Frankenstein* (1818), however, Mary Wollstonecraft Shelley imagines the creation of new life from the dead by scientific method, by means of a kind of electricity. The speculation nowadays would be classified as fantasy, because scientists are fairly sure that her method would not work. In Mary Shelley's time, this cannot have been so obvious. Scientists had made the legs of dead frogs react by stimulating them electrically. Who was to say that the method could not be extended and perfected? In exactly the same way, but eighty years later, H. G. Wells in *The Island of Dr. Moreau* (1896) put forward the idea that human beings could create not life but intelligence, by taking animals and altering them surgically through "vivisection." After his book was published, Wells carried on an indignant correspondence designed to show that his idea was not impossible but had a basis in scientific fact. Although nowadays it appears certain that he was wrong, as with Mary Shelley this was not so obvious at the time. Michael Crichton's *Jurassic Park* (1990), with its dinosaurs revived from blood samples, probably will pass into the same area of "disproved theses" in even less time than Mary Shelley's or Wells's speculations, but for the moment at least a few of his conjectures appear plausible. The point is that science fiction in particular, whether *Frankenstein* or *The Island of Dr. Moreau* or *Jurassic Park*, tends to follow the frontier of scientific possibility. This frontier, effectively static for hundreds if not thousands of years, expanded with growing acceleration all through the nineteenth and twentieth centuries. Its expansion has created an ever increasing area of speculation and possibility in which science fiction can flourish.

Most modern definitions of science fiction accordingly make some reference both to the need for novelty and the use of the imagination (an ancient requirement of all forms of the fantastic) and to the need for logic, rigor, and control by the strict requirements of science (a distinctively modern demand). Robert Heinlein thus declared, in an essay printed in *The Science Fiction Novel* (1969), edited by Basil Davenport, that science fiction is:

> a realistic speculation about possible future events, based solidly on adequate knowledge of the real world, past and present, and on a thorough understanding of the nature and significance of the scientific method.

One notes, on one hand, words such as "speculation" and "possible," but on the other, the words "realistic," "adequate," "thorough," and "scientific." Kingsley Amis, another distinguished practitioner in the field, asserted in his *New Maps of Hell* (1961) that:

> Science Fiction is that class of prose narrative treating of a situation that could not arise in the world that we know, but which is hypothesized on the basis of some innovation in science or technology, or pseudo-science or pseudo-technology, whether human or extraterrestrial in origin.

There is a sense in this definition that Amis is rather "hedging his bet" by careful use of the term "pseudo," and one can see why. Who is to say that the science of *Jurassic Park* is not as unreal as that of *Frankenstein*? Nevertheless, one sees once again the element of "not-truth" ("could *not* arise in the world that we know," emphasis added), qualified and even opposed by "science," "technology," "innovation," and "hypothesized." One can sum up both Heinlein and Amis, and most other definitions of the genre, by saying that science fiction takes place in a world or setting that its contemporary readers know for certain is not true but that they are also prepared to accept as not impossible.

It may seem that this last requirement acts as a kind of restraint on the imagination, but to think that is to ignore the deep and powerful effect that real scientific innovation has had on the lives and attitudes of many modern readers. It is, after all, still possible for living memory to reach back to a time when it was generally accepted that human beings would never be able to fly. Many old people of the late twentieth century, as well as most of the early writers of American science fiction, grew up in a world that swept with unbelievable speed from the Wright brothers' flight in 1903 to dueling fighter planes in 1915, to transatlantic flights in 1919 and thousand-bomber raids in 1943, and then on to the *Enola Gay* and the dropping of the atomic bomb, the Strategic Air Command, everyday commercial traffic, and supersonic passenger jets. In the same way, the very idea of "wireless" transmission seemed in its beginnings eerie, almost ghostly, in the way that radio waves could be transmitted invisibly, impalpably, and apparently with nothing for them to transmit through. Technological advance led in quick succession to the radio becoming a normal household appliance, followed in turn by television and satellite links, accompanied by all the innovations of film technology from the first "cinema" to modern video.

It has been remarked often by science-fiction writers themselves that although many of them had imagined the first flight to the moon, none of them had ever thought that the first flight would be watched live on television by a mass world audience. In such cases, the progress of science outstripped even the range of imagination. One result has been the creation of a mass audience sensitized to the idea of unpredictable but nevertheless possible, or plausible, technological change. The modern subgenre of "cyberpunk" could not exist without an audience aware of the progress from vacuum tube to transistor to silicon chip, and from the giant computers of older science fiction, such as John Brunner's *Stand on Zanzibar* (1968), to the personal computers of today, the Internet, and the "hacker culture" that technology instantly if inadvertently created.

Science fiction thus differs from its ancestor forms of the past, such as the "utopia" or the "imaginary voyage," in containing within itself an element of belief, or at any rate something stronger than the "suspended disbelief" of older theories of ordinary fiction. Many, if not most, science-fiction readers firmly believe that there are alien intelligent races, simply because of what astronomy seems to say about the number of stars and planets in the real universe. It does not follow that one needs to believe that any of these races has contacted humans, and many popular stories of UFOs would be met with some scorn as scientifically implausible. One might note the way in which intelligent Martians have drifted slowly out of the area of plausibility, or possible belief, as astronomy and space probes have increased knowledge of the planet Mars. Wells's *The War of the Worlds* (1898) drew on the theories of his own time, which saw Mars as an Earth-like but ancient and hence further evolved planet. Edgar Rice Burroughs' Barsoom series, beginning in 1917 with *A Princess of Mars*, added to that the idea of reduced gravity and hence greater strength and speed for his Earth-born human hero. By the time of Kim Stanley Robinson's Mars trilogy (1992-1996), both these scenarios had become untenable, and the Mars of Robinson's imagination (which is also that of contemporary knowledge) is a different, less populated, but not less fascinating place. Scientific progress once again has ruled out some speculations and at the same time created completely different ones. Although these too may one day be ruled out in their turn, the Mars trilogy, like *The War of the Worlds* or *A Princess of Mars*, will remain science fiction as originally conceived, drawing on a deep well of belief and real knowledge, though such knowledge is always known and admitted to be incomplete.

* * *

Science fiction's modern companion genre, fantasy, has been less obviously but no less deeply affected by the triumph of rationalism and the accelerating awareness of science. It might seem that stories about dragons could be much the same in the twentieth century as in the tenth. Indeed, Smaug, in J. R. R. Tolkien's *The Hobbit* (1937), has an ancestry that stretches back to the Norse Fafnir and the nameless dragon that is the bane of Beowulf in the epic that carries his name, dating from about the eleventh century. Even if the creatures are the same, however, the context of belief in which they are embedded cannot help being different. To put it simply, although people find it much easier now to believe in voyages to Mars, they find it much less easy to believe in the existence of dragons on Earth. To the audiences of Old Norse or Old English poems, it might not seem at all impossible that dragons existed, perhaps somewhere outside the rather small patch of territory they had explored. The *Anglo-Saxon Chronicle*, a work every bit as historical in its intentions as Herodotus', and one that remains highly respected by modern historians, nevertheless records the appearance of flying dragons in Northumbria in the year 793 and shows no sign of intending to be "fantastic." The case is quite different now. It is reasonably certain that there are no canals on Mars, but it is 100 percent certain that there are no dragons (as traditionally described) on Earth. The world is too well explored to leave a place for them. In any case, the sheer mechanics of imagining a beast that could breathe fire, somehow insulate its own internal organs, and also find a means of ignition appears impossible. This has not prevented author after author from trying to create a situation in which the impossible dragon of tradition could become possible, whether through Tolkien's device of distancing the creature into a far-past world where all kinds of things appear to be different or Ursula Le Guin's method of creating "a world where magic works," governed, it seems, by a different set of physical laws. Both Tolkien and Le Guin were well aware that they could not simply bring a dragon into the story and expect the skeptical and well-informed modern reader to accept it as a fact. If one wishes to continue to use the creatures of humanity's oldest fears and imaginings—such as dragons, elves, werewolves, and vampires—these creatures have to be given some kind of explanation, some kind of apparently rational setting. At the very least, the challenge of rationality has to be faced, not ignored.

One can say, then, that if science fiction deals with what is known not to be true, but not known to be beyond possibility, fantasy in its modern sense deals with what is known or very generally thought to be impossible. A common method of doing this is to set the tale in a different universe or an alternative reality, as is done in Stephen Donaldson's Chronicles of Thomas Covenant (1977-1983). One should note that this is not the same as setting it on an alien planet within this universe, for in that case the laws of physical causation as understood would still apply. In a different universe, the world and the characters may be ruled by magic, not science, and the problem (as, for example, in L. Sprague de Camp and Fletcher Pratt's Incomplete Enchanter series, 1941-1954) may be for the characters to understand the different logic of magic. Despite the appearance of Norse gods, giants, enchanters, werewolves, and other such beings, de Camp and Pratt's universe does run on logic: It is only the premises of the logic that have changed. Works of this nature demonstrate at once both the urge to escape from the confines of the real and accepted and an inability to let go of the cause-and-effect beliefs so thoroughly part of modern everyday life.

Modern definitions of fantasy accordingly often find difficulty in being both broad enough to take in what is an extremely prolific genre and narrow enough to say anything useful. It is hard to improve on Kathryn Hume's statement, in her book *Fantasy and Mimesis* (1984), that "*Fantasy is any departure from consensus reality*, an impulse native to literature and manifested in innumerable variations." This definition, however, needs to be filled out by a long discussion of the "variations" and leaves open the distinction between ancient examples of the fantastic such as *The Odyssey* and its modern mutations.

To understand the latter point, one needs only to look at some of the works discussed within *Magill's Guide to Science Fiction and Fantasy Literature*. The fantastic is an ancient mode; fantasy (at least as defined by bookstores) is a modern genre. As a result, one often can find pairs or comparisons, with a traditional work of a kind that goes back to antiquity on one hand, and on the other a self-conscious modern version of the same thing. Thus, ghost stories are as old as literature, and no doubt older, but in the nineteenth century M. R. James (a famous classical scholar) still was capable of exploiting the ancient fears from his great depth of learning. Kingsley Amis' *The Green Man* (1969) also is very clearly a ghost story, but one that cannot rely on old assumptions about the afterlife and one whose agnostic hero finds it hard to have any belief in the afterlife at all. Argument about the very nature of ghosts and of religious belief becomes, accordingly, a vital part of Amis' tale. In a similar way, *Baron Münchausen's Narrative* (1785) represents the old "traveler's tale" or "tall story." These are re-created in Sterling Lanier's Brigadier Ffellowes stories (collected in 1972 and 1986), made plausible not only by their far-off settings but also by the cool and matter-of-fact narrative of the brigadier himself. Both *Dracula* (1897) and *Frankenstein* are rewritten by Brian Aldiss; Kenneth Grahame's animal fable of *The Wind in the Willows* (1908) is reshaped by modern knowledge of ecology and animal behavior in Richard Adams' *Watership Down* (1972); Angela Carter, Tanith Lee, and Jane Yolen have created among them a new genre of modern (and often both feminist and Freudian) fairy tale, related but also ideologically opposed to old tales like those of the Brothers Grimm; the almost contextless romance narratives of William Morris and E. R. Eddison are pulled firmly into shape with maps, calendars, languages, and appendices by Tolkien; traditional ballad is made into realistic narrative by Ellen Kushner's *Thomas the Rhymer* (1990) and Diana Wynne Jones's *Fire and Hemlock* (1985). In all these cases, one can see a sense of argument, of explanation, one might almost say of discipline, falling on the old genres that once had no need to justify themselves. That sense of discipline parallels the growth of science fiction, as *Unknown* was for a while the partner fantasy magazine to science fiction's *Astounding* (note the implications of the two adjectives), and as joint audience interest created twin-track publications such as *The Magazine of Fantasy and Science Fiction* (still in existence) and *Science Fantasy* (unfortunately extinct).

* * *

The considerations discussed above had an effect on the scope and plan of *Magill's Guide to Science Fiction and Fantasy Literature*. Modern fantasy authors in particular are often eager to model their work on, to rewrite, or to reply to works of the past in which they see some element of the fantastic. John Gardner's *Grendel* (1971) is a retelling of the Old English epic of *Beowulf* from the point of view of the monster, not the hero; T. H. White's *The Once and Future King* passionately rehandles the story of Sir Thomas Malory's Middle English romance *Le Morte d'Arthur* (c. 1469); the medieval Welsh anthology of wonder-tales known as *The Mabinogion* provides the basis for Alan Garner's *The Owl Service* (1967) and for several other modern works; and the de Camp and Pratt Incomplete Enchanter series works its way through settings as diverse as the Icelandic *Prose Edda*, the Finnish *Kalevala*, Irish mythology, and English and Italian romantic epic. No attempt has been made, however, to include in this guide the old models as well as their modern rehandlings. For one thing, the guide would too readily have expanded into a general survey of early literature; modern authors have cast their nets very widely indeed. Even more important, although all the works above may contain some element of the fantastic, this often may be more in the eye of the modern beholder than in that of the ancient author. *Beowulf* contains as much apparent history as apparent fantasy, and Sir Thomas Malory may well have believed that he was writing about real people and real events. *Magill's Guide to Science Fiction and Fantasy Literature* accordingly restricts its field deliberately to more modern literature.

For similar reasons, one further ancient/modern parallel has for the most part not been pursued, namely the move from "gothic novel" to "horror story." Once again, one has to note the immense number of works that would have a good case for inclusion, demanding coverage at the expense of concentration. There is, moreover, a strong case for considering horror as a separate genre, with its own history and its own conventions. Accordingly, although such evident masters of the field as H. P. Lovecraft and Stephen King are included here, the attempt has not been made to cover horror to the same extent as fantasy or science fiction.

The existence of horror stories does, however, indirectly raise an interesting question. Why are so many people prepared to write and to read pure fantasy in the modern day, when "consensus reality" is so strong and readers in a way have to be coaxed outside it? The answer, in the case of horror stories, is clear. These stories have an obvious motivation, which is to frighten their readers, duplicating in literary form the controlled fear of, for example, a fairground ride. Science fiction also can justify itself easily, as an "early warning system" or education in possibility. But fantasy? Is it not a kind of nostalgia, a reluctance to let go of old images, perhaps learned and loved in childhood, before the defenses of skepticism were raised? Arguments against this "escapist" accusation are common and powerful. It has been pointed out that authors as different as J. R. R. Tolkien and C. S. Lewis, Kurt Vonnegut, Jr., and Ursula Le Guin, and Stephen Donaldson and Gene Wolfe are all clearly addressing through their fantasies (just as much as through their works of science fiction) such grim and vital issues for the twentieth century and beyond as the origins of evil, the nature of war, and the future of the planet—topics that seem to be outside the scope of mere realistic fiction. It is also possible that "heroic fantasy" in particular—a mode that seemed dead until revived by Tolkien, but now perhaps is the most commercially successful and popular form of writing to be found in America—draws its impetus from deliberate rejection of the prevailingly unheroic, ironic, self-doubting attitudes of much realistic fiction: It is not an escape so much as a defiance.

What cannot be denied is the present competitiveness, one might almost say dominance, of the current fantasy/ science fiction field. Hundreds or thousands of titles are published each year in each genre. Some authors—among them Greg Bear, Gregory Benford, David Eddings, and Terry Brooks—figure consistently in best-seller lists. Both science fiction and fantasy have made the transition to film and television, with series as popular as *Star Trek* and *Star Wars*. In a more academic mode, authors such as Angela Carter are recognized subjects of study in universities across the world. Science fiction especially has been an immensely influential vehicle for feminist thought, through authors such as Joanna Russ, Suzy McKee Charnas, Marge Piercy, and James Tiptree, Jr. (the pen name of Alice Sheldon). Experimental writing is represented by such tours de force as Russell Hoban's *Riddley Walker* (1980). Furthermore, in this situation of commercial success and commercial exploitation, although the line between fantasy and science fiction remains in most cases clear, there is a sense of continuous probing of the boundaries of both forms by several authors, prominent among them Tim Powers, Michael Swanwick, and Gene Wolfe. At the same time, if there is a shift of weight discernible, it is on the whole from science fiction toward fantasy. A number of established "hard science fiction" authors, among them Gordon Dickson, Orson Scott Card, and Piers Anthony, have shown themselves ready to move sideways into the writing of fantasy. Commercial considerations likely play a part in this move, but one may well believe that in the same way that science fiction earned public respect and won its way to literary favor through the middle of the twentieth century, so practitioners of fantasy have shown the world what can be done within that genre toward the end of the century, making their case not by argument but by example.

There is a further and final point that may be made about the nature of both modern genres, fantasy and science fiction, and about their joint relationship to the dominating principle of science. This is that there are many disciplines that aspire to the dignity of being scientific. The core disciplines remain, no doubt, physics, chemistry, biology, and mathematics: No one doubts that these, and their modern offshoots or specializations such as genetics and astronomy, are sciences in every sense of the term. At the other extreme, traditional humanities subjects such as history and literary study have ceased, after a sometimes brief flirtation with "scientificity," to make any claims of this nature. There remain what are often described as the "soft sciences," which include sociology, political science, economics, anthropology, and others. It is not often realized how fertile some of these fields have been for creative writers, nor how radically new they may be, developing over much the same relatively short period as the "hard sciences." Just as one could see an "epistemic break" or major transformation between, say, medieval alchemy and modern chemistry, or medieval astrology and modern astronomy, so there are clear developments from the ancient habits of treasure hunting and grave robbing to systematic archaeology; from dilettante ethnography to modern anthropology; from belletristic philology to the nineteenth century science of comparative philology and through it to computational linguistics; from the antiquarian sketching of stones and monuments to the recovery of hieroglyphs, cuneiform, and the code-breaking ability to read totally lost and forgotten scripts such as Cretan "Linear B." All these "soft sciences" have provided major inspiration for creative writers. The dream of inventing the mathematical hard science of "psychohistory" is at the heart of Isaac Asimov's famous Foundation series. Ursula K. (for Kroeber) Le Guin is herself the daughter of two of the most prominent American anthropologists of the twentieth century, Alfred and

Theodora Kroeber. Tolkien has a fair claim to being one of the most influential ancient philologists of the twentieth century, even disregarding the effect of his fantasies. The power and lure of archaeology (a subject that filled the nineteenth and twentieth centuries with glittering discoveries from Mycenae to Babylon to Ur and Egypt's Valley of the Tombs) have given inspiration to authors as different as H. P. Lovecraft, Gregory Benford, and Larry Niven.

Perhaps the most dramatic development of recent years has been the sudden interest taken in the idea of "alternate history," an idea that goes back at least as far as 1931, when Winston Churchill wrote his provocatively titled essay "If Lee Had Not Won the Battle of Gettysburg," and that has led to such complex works as Philip K. Dick's *The Man in the High Castle* (1962), Ward Moore's *Bring the Jubilee* (1953), and Kingsley Amis' *The Alteration* (1976). At present, more than a dozen well-known authors are working busily in the field, including at least one prominent American politician (Newt Gingrich) and the prolific Harry Turtledove, once a professional historian. Is this particular subgenre fantasy or science fiction? If one looks at Mark Twain's *A Connecticut Yankee in King Arthur's Court* (1889) or L. Sprague de Camp's *Lest Darkness Fall* (1941), one would probably decide for fantasy: Neither work makes any serious effort to explain how the modern-day heroes find themselves suddenly "back in the past." Both of them, however, and Turtledove's stories as well, show a keen interest in the history of technology that gives them a claim to "not impossible" status. In cases such as these, the distinctions between fantasy and science fiction, between hard and soft sciences, lose their usual force. One may add that such works also are a powerful argument against a kind of ethnocentrism that could be called "chronocentrism," the belief that the way history did happen is the only way it could have happened, that the arrow of time points unerringly and inevitably to the world as it stands.

Both science fiction and fantasy have functioned during the twentieth century, and will continue to function during the twenty-first, as major explanatory tools that have provided meaning and insight to millions of readers, often about vital issues such as the origins of war and the nature of humanity, and often to readers who have been failed by or who have proved inaccessible to all older and more traditional forms of writing (such as history and mainstream fiction). They also can be seen as the main indicators of radical shifts of attitude and understanding in the population at large. In the process, they have acted as powerful if unrecognized forces against prejudice and ethnocentrism, and they have served as guides to and recruiters for both hard and soft sciences. It has been acknowledged many times that there would have been no ventures into space, no moon landings or planetary fly-bys, without the stimulus of decades of space fiction. Both fantasy and science fiction have opened unexplored territories of the imagination.

Magill's Guide to Science Fiction and Fantasy Literature acts as a chart of this immense adventure of the mind, covering 791 of the most significant works of both genres from their modern beginnings to the present. In addition and above all, the guide introduces readers to an inexhaustible well of delight. There are few experiences more productive of lasting pleasure than coming upon a previously unknown but soon-to-be-favorite author or favorite work. The guide contains such favorites that have enthralled, collectively, tens if not hundreds of millions of readers during the last two centuries. There is no material more likely to create a lasting taste for reading than that expounded and discussed in these pages.

— *T. A. Shippey*

LIST OF GENRES

The ready-reference top matter of each entry in this guide includes identification of a primary genre—science fiction or fantasy—and a secondary classification into a more specific genre. Definitions of works that fall within each of the secondary categories are provided below.

Alien civilization: Centers on an attempt to present an alien (nonhuman, nonartificial) intelligence or civilization.

Alternate history: The fictional world corresponds to the real world in many respects, but its history has been altered at some crucial point, such as having the South win the American Civil War. In some cases, more than one change may take place as various factions seek to change history in their separately desired ways; most such stories are better classified as **time travel**.

Animal fantasy: A genre going back to Aesop, sometimes called "beast fable." It often functions as allegory.

Apocalypse: Deals with the end of the world as known, often but not always through nuclear holocaust. This is a more dramatic form of the **catastrophe** story. **Post-holocaust** fiction, in contrast, discusses the aftermath of the apocalyptic event more than the event itself.

Artificial intelligence: Plots deal with human-created forms of intelligence such as "thinking" computers, robots, androids, and cyborgs.

Catastrophe: Usually set on Earth, involving various natural disasters and attempts to deal with them.

Cautionary: Attempts to warn of some current or extrapolated danger, seriously and without amusement. May overlap with **apocalypse** fiction.

Closed universe: Protagonists are in some type of closed environment that they perceive as natural and complete; they discover the "outside" during the plot action.

Cosmic voyage: Begins with early "voyage to the moon" stories and continues through longer space travels.

Cultural exploration: Works affected by anthropological theory. Cultures are different because of different cultural decisions, not different physical characteristics.

Cyberpunk: Characterized by extensive use of computers or artificial intelligences, often with a state of streetwise anarchy among the protagonists.

Dystopia: The opposite of **utopia**; an imagined world that is horrific rather than ideal. Differs from **cautionary** works through an element of relish or deliberate exaggeration.

Evolutionary fantasy: Concerns attempts to demonstrate, disprove, or modify evolutionary theory. Some works deal with mutations. Overlaps to some extent with **superbeing** stories.

Extrapolatory: Takes a feature of contemporary society and projects it into the future as increasingly dominant. May overlap with the **cautionary** story.

Extrasensory powers: Characters possess some form of ESP. The society may be based on control and development of such powers. Overlaps with **superbeing** stories.

Feminist: Characterized by a concern for altered female roles or by future gender war.

Future history: Extensive histories of the future, often in series form and often cyclic.

Future war: Central interest is on the nature of war rather than war as a threat or as part of the background.

Galactic empire: The plot is interstellar. A **future history** may contain a galactic empire; the galactic empire story will not be as encompassing in its span of time.

Heroic fantasy: Set in a fantasy world in which characters approach the scale of epic or romance; encompasses "sword and sorcery" plots.

High fantasy: Little or no connection with the current world, set "elsewhere." Many works of **heroic fantasy** are also high fantasy, but not all high fantasy is **heroic fantasy**.

Inner space: Stresses internal alterations of consciousness rather than external technological control.

Interplanetary romance: Like **planetary romance**, an old category of fiction motivated by a desire to extend the travels and adventures of nineteenth and twentieth century adventurers into space. This genre perhaps is the most recognizable as science fiction to readers who are relatively unfamiliar with the field.

Invasion story: Alien beings attack a planet.

Magical Realism: A relatively realistic plot is disturbed by figures of myth or fantasy.

Magical world: A type of **heroic fantasy** with emphasis not on characters' quests but instead on social organization based on a technology that does not conform to current science.

Medieval future: A future era reverts to medieval social structures, which then are exposed to change. These works often are set on an alien planet with civilizations of some medieval type.

Mythological: Depends on the characters and settings of some established system of mythology.

New Wave: Imagistic and highly metaphoric, inclined toward psychology and the soft sciences, and often similar to works of **dystopia**. The New Wave, largely contained in works of the 1960's, attempted to turn science fiction more toward mainstream literature. New Wave overlaps to a large extent with **inner space** fiction, and **cyberpunk** can be seen as a resurgence of the New Wave.

Occult: A mode of fantasy characterized by interest in the practices of magic and the supernatural, often with an element of the macabre.

Planetary romance: A type of **heroic fantasy** but with scientific trappings, often set on Venus or Mars.

Post-holocaust: Set in a world recovering from a (usually nuclear) holocaust, often characterized by anarchy, mutations, and an attempt to struggle toward some form of civilization. Differs from **apocalypse** stories in dealing with the aftermath of the holocaust rather than the holocaust itself.

Superbeing: Conjectures on the next stage of evolution, usually rejecting the idea of greater intelligence in favor of some exaggerated physical characteristic or a new form of mental power; the latter type overlaps with **extrasensory power** stories.

Technocratic: A technological object or idea is the dominant plot element. Much of science fiction has technocratic elements, particularly that known as "hard" science fiction, but if these elements do not dominate the plot, the work falls into another classification.

Theological romance: Often involves a divinely ruled universe within the framework of a postscientific society. Such works are seen as "antiscience" fiction.

Time travel: Characters are able to move forward or backward in time and often attempt to use this power to create or maintain an acceptable stream of history.

Utopia: Describes an ideal society.

LIST OF TITLES IN VOLUME 1

MAGILL'S GUIDE TO

Science Fiction and Fantasy Literature

THE ABSOLUTE AT LARGE

The unleashing of nuclear power leads to merciless religious wars on a global scale, each sect identifying the new power as justification for its dogmas

Author: Karel Čapek (1890-1938)
Genre: Science fiction—extrapolatory
Type of work: Novel
Time of plot: 1943-1953
Location: Primarily Czechoslovakia
First published: *Továrna na absolutno* (1922; English translation, 1927)

The Plot: Karel Čapek published *The Absolute at Large* at the beginning of his career, showing early his fascination with futurology. The interest manifested itself in several other works. The story concerns a young Czech engineer, Rudolph Marek, who invents a machine called the Karburator, which uses atomic energy without any residue, which he calls the Absolute. A manufacturer, G. H. Bondy, inspects the machine and is overcome by a strange euphoria resembling that of religious ecstasy. This absolute, godlike power of the machine made the inventor anxious to sell it. Whatever it is—an intoxicating, stimulating gas developed by the process of complete combustion, a form of X ray, or some hitherto unknown power—it affects everyone coming in contact with it and transports them into religious ecstasy. Concerned only with profit and seeing in the Karburator the realization of a centuries-old dream of a cheap, pure source of energy, Bondy buys the machine and sells it worldwide.

After Karburators have been installed throughout the world, their impact becomes evident. Because they enhance religious fervor, people love one another more, factory owners become philanthropists, and religious fanaticism increases everywhere. These developments are offset by opposite effects. Workers protest insane overproduction, the loss of jobs as the machines take over, and the depletion of raw materials. Unnecessary work is undertaken because the machines demand work. Church authorities worry that the "new god" may replace them. Moreover, the Karburators may result in a loss of control, as in the case of the workers on a dredge who are trans-formed into religious zealots and the riders on a merry-go-round who suddenly sense that they are embarking on a flight into an unknown land.

More important, various religious groups identify with the Absolute and use it as a proof that only their dogmas are correct. This leads to rivalry among them and ultimately to full-scale skirmishes. The entire planet becomes engulfed in a war of all against all. The widespread religious war results in tremendous damage and bodily harm. Not only are the two main religions—Protestants and Catholics—at war; so are other religions as well as nationalities. The Chinese fight in Czechoslovakia, Russian Cossacks in the Sahara, Macedonians and Senegalese in Finland, and the French in Tibet. African blacks fight Mongolians in Europe while North America is invaded by Japan. This so-called "Greatest War" lasts from February, 1944, to the fall of 1953. Only thirteen people survive a war that engages 198 million participants.

Years later, several survivors get together and argue about the war, bemoaning the lack of tolerance. Bondy, who along with Marek started it all, finds refuge on a Pacific island. He concludes succinctly that every nation insists on its own absolute truth and each person thinks he or she has the whole of God; when others claim the same, they have to be killed so that God and truth can belong only to one person, or group, or nation.

Analysis: Čapek started his literary career by writing short stories in a pessimistic vein. He would later soften his pessimism and write with humor, even cheerfulness, yet he was always drawn to the dark secrets of human nature. In *The Absolute at Large*, he tried to illuminate some of those secrets on a cosmic scale. Although he often wrote to entertain, he combined entertainment with a warning against the negative impulses of human behavior. In doing so, he was often philosophical in his approach, in the tradition of liberal humanism of European intellectuals between the two world wars.

The Absolute at Large is a satire not only on human mores but also on some of the most pressing dilemmas of the twentieth century. The most obvious satire is on the common belief in steady progress brought on by scientific achievements such as atomic energy. The novel reflects somewhat skeptically on the beneficial effects of the splitting of the atom, treating it as an example of the "genie out of the bottle" syndrome. Instead of bringing only benefits, it creates problems such as how to control the unleashed energy, overproduction, alienation, and ultimately war. Although Čapek did not foresee the horrors of nuclear bombs (he would do that in a 1924 novel, *Krakatit*), he predicted the divisions, enmity, and war among various nations. To be sure, the wars in *The Absolute at Large* are based on religious differences and intolerance dating back thousands of years, but the discovery of atomic energy increased the ferocity of the divisions.

The religious wars serve Čapek only as a pretext for lashing out at fanaticism of any kind. Čapek speaks as a true humanist immediately after World War I, having witnessed a catastrophe involving many nations and causing almost as much suffering as the fictitious wars of his novel. The novel appeared on the eve of the rise of totalitarian systems in Italy and Germany that gave rise to as much intolerance as in *The Absolute at Large*. By musing that if annihilating conflicts can happen in the realm of religion, Čapek warns of dangers in other areas.

Because of its societal and semiphilosophical overtones, the novel is not science fiction in the classical sense. Čapek uses the framework of the genre to hint at, and warn of, possibilities for the future. Although not everything from the novel has come true, Čapek did predict important happenings: the power of the atom, often difficult to control; another world conflagration; and warfare fanned by religious intolerance. In this sense, the novel is a moral story, a parable, a satire, and a fictionalized philosophical essay, with enough science-fiction traits to make it a potential vision of the future.

—*Vasa D. Mihailovich*

ADAM AND EVE

Dialogue, domestic scenes, and another woman combine to reduce Adam and Eve's status from that of biblical icons to that of an average couple

Author: John Erskine (1879-1951)
Genre: Fantasy—alternate history
Type of work: Novel
Time of plot: The origin of humankind
Location: Paradise
First published: 1927

The Plot: The novel's action is limited to the characters' observation of the flora, fauna, and elements that surround them. The plot focuses on the characters' gradual appreciation of the cause-and-effect relationships inherent among all natural phenomena. The main theme is the conflict between carnal and spiritual love, which John Erskine dramatizes by involving the biblical couple in a romantic triangle with the provocative Lilith. Adam's attention vacillates between the sensual Lilith and the more mystical Eve.

In the novel's first of five parts, Adam encounters various animals, including a dog that helps to lighten the tone of this philosophical novel. Adam also observes the beauty of nature and meets Lilith. In part 2, Adam and Lilith milk a cow and learn how to kiss. Part 3 begins with Adam's realization that he has invented love. Adam and Lilith go swimming, and Adam discovers that love alters the physical senses.

The cow bears a calf at about the time Eve appears in the novel. In the same way that part 2 had ended with Adam kissing Lilith, Adam kisses Eve at the end of part 3, and she slaps him in response. In part 4, Lilith assumes the form of a serpent and offers Adam and Eve the forbidden fruit. Adam builds a wall around the garden and teaches Eve to swim. By the end of part 4, Adam has become confused about whether he is happier with Lilith or with Eve.

In part 5, Eve begins to wear clothes for modesty and learns to cook with fire. She becomes pregnant and bears a son. The novel concludes with Adam resolving to teach his son so he will not repeat his father's mistakes. Adam's experiences have taught him that intelligence is fundamental to happiness.

Analysis: Much of the plot of *Adam and Eve* is consumed with Adam's Hamlet-like indecisiveness as he weighs the choice between Lilith and Eve. Despite Erskine's assertion in the novel that actual experience is more important than mere discussion of experience, a large portion of the novel consists of seemingly aimless conversations. Many of these dialogues are characterized by circular logic, as the earth's first inhabitants debate ultimate causes.

As the title suggests, *Adam and Eve* is about the beginning of history. More precisely, the novel is Erskine's attempt to rewrite history by supplementing the biblical story of Adam and Eve. This concept of rewriting history was popular among novelists after World War I, an event that represented the end of history, if not in fact, at least in metaphor.

The revision of the book of Genesis in *Adam and Eve* is also a testament to the influence of pragmatism, the philosophy made popular at the turn of the century by William James, a Harvard professor. When Erskine compiled his "Outline of Readings in Important Books," a list of books to be read by undergraduates at Columbia University, William James was one of the approximately fifty authors included. Erskine clearly considered pragmatism to be a fundamental concept.

Pragmatism is the antithesis of Platonic idealism. Plato suggests that everything on Earth is a shadow of a cosmic ideal, whereas pragmatism holds that there is no ideal because the truth is constantly changing. The only way to stop the truth from changing is to stop time.

It is impossible to stop time in realistic terms, but many writers in the early twentieth century found that one could reverse time in artistic terms by rewriting myths, legends, and the Scriptures. For example, in the years immediately prior to publication of *Adam and Eve*, James Joyce updated Homer's epic as the novel *Ulysses* (1922) and Ernest Hemingway chose a biblical quote from Ecclesiastes as the title for *The Sun Also Rises* (1926), a novel about the social and psychological consequences of World War I. Erskine himself wrote *The Private Life of Helen of Troy* (1925) and *Galahad* (1926), revisions of Greek mythology and Arthurian legend, respectively.

Pragmatism also stresses the importance of experience to the acquisition of knowledge, a phenomenon that is dramatized repeatedly in *Adam and Eve*. In fact, the novel's plot is so rudimentary that it is indefensible unless the reader recognizes that, in narrating such apparently trivial events as the first drink of water and the first kiss, Erskine is illustrating the pragmatist tenet that sensory experience is the source of knowledge. The characters frequently discuss the significance of experience, concluding that actual experience is more important than talking about it.

Besides serving as an exposition of pragmatism, *Adam and Eve* pays homage to several other artistic and philosophical trends of the day. The novel was published two years after the Scopes trial of 1925, which focused on the teaching of evolution in schools. Erskine acknowledges evolution by comparing the novel's characters to animals, albeit humorously, as when he compares the pregnant Eve to a cow. The 1920's were also characterized by a sexual revolution that was best personified by the flappers of F. Scott Fitzgerald's writings. Erskine adapts the Bible to the Jazz Age by involving Adam and Eve in a love triangle with the wily Lilith.

Modernist writers of the time also liked to compare life to art, and Erskine's characters in *Adam and Eve* state at various times that life is a tragedy. Erskine's extensive use of dialogue may have been inspired by the classical Greek model but may also represent Erskine's response to interior monologue and stream of consciousness, techniques that William Faulkner, James Joyce, and Virginia Woolf were pioneering in the 1920's.

—Douglas Edward LaPrade

THE ADVENTURES OF VLAD TALTOS

A wisecracking professional assassin carves out a profitable business in the dangerous underworld of the Dragaeran Empire, despite the fact that he is a human and thus an outsider

Author: Steven Brust (1955-   )
Genre: Fantasy—magical world
Type of work: Novels
Time of plot: Undefined
Location: Primarily the city of Adrilankha, of the Dragaeran Empire
First published: *Jhereg* (1983), *Yendi* (1984), *Teckla* (1987), *Taltos* (1988), *Phoenix* (1990), and *Athyra* (1993)

The Plot: The Vlad Taltos series centers on a wisecracking professional assassin, who is an Easterner—or human—living among a race of beings called Dragaerans. The Dragaerans are humanoid creatures who stand seven to eight feet tall and have a life span of between two thousand and three thousand years. Their empire is built on a class system: Every member belongs to one of seventeen houses, each named for a native creature of that world. Easterners are a much-despised minority. In an effort to assimilate, Vlad's father squandered his life savings on a baronetcy in one of the lower-status houses.

Vlad, who early on became accustomed to the dangers of urban street life, has risen through the ranks of House Jhereg, a criminal organization, to control the gambling and other illegal activities of a small section of the city of Adrilankha. Reflecting the danger of his chosen career, he never leaves home without an arsenal of weapons concealed on his person. One of Vlad's favorite mottoes is "No matter how subtle the wizard, a knife between the shoulder blades will seriously cramp his style."

Vlad also knows some sorcery and witchcraft. He travels with a familiar, a wisecracking jhereg named Loiosh with whom he communicates "psionically," or psychically. A jhereg is a small, poisonous, winged, lizardlike creature. Loiosh often perches on Vlad's shoulder. Loiosh has a humanlike intelligence and stays ever on the lookout for danger, which always seems to be near.

Vlad is married to a fellow Easterner named Cawti. She is also a professional assassin and is known as the Dagger of the Jhereg. Vlad and Cawti met when she was hired to kill him—and succeeded in her task. As Vlad aptly put it, "Some couples fall in love and end up trying to kill each other. We'd done it the other way around." In this world of sorcery and witchcraft, however, death may or may not be permanent. Fortunately, Vlad was revivifiable. The possibility of revivification depends on the manner in which one dies. Even if death is permanent, one's soul may survive to go on to the afterlife, if it is not destroyed by a magical "Morganti" weapon.

The first book in the series, *Jhereg,* introduces Vlad Taltos, his profession, and his world. It centers on his being hired by the Demon, one of five members of the council of House Jhereg, to kill another member of the council, Mellar, who has absconded with council funds. Mellar, however, is no simple thief: He has set in motion a complicated and diabolical revenge plot that Vlad must foil. The next book in the series, *Yendi,* is a prequel to *Jhereg. Yendi* relates the story of Vlad and Cawti's first meeting, when she assassinated him and he was revivified, and how they later teamed with two lords of the House of the Dragon, Morrolan and Morrolan's cousin Aliera, to defeat an enemy of Vlad.

The third book, *Teckla,* picks up where *Jhereg* left off. Cawti joins a revolutionary band of Easterners and Teckla—the peasant class of Dragaerans—whose goal is to overthrow the oppressive Dragaeran Empire. Vlad is opposed to the revolt and does everything in his power to extricate his wife from this group, to the detriment of his marriage. The fourth book, *Taltos,* is chronologically the first. It relates Vlad's early life, how he met and befriended the reticent Lord Morrolan, and how they came to walk the Paths of the Dead. The fifth book, *Phoenix,* follows *Teckla* chronologically. Vlad and Cawti are still suffering from marital problems, as Cawti has become more deeply involved with the band of rebels. His marital problems prompt Vlad to question his life and the direction it has taken. In the end, events conspire to force Vlad into a self-imposed exile.

The sixth book in the series, *Athyra,* differs markedly in style and tone from the previous five. Rather than using Vlad as protagonist, Steven Brust chooses a young Dragaeran peasant named Savn. Set several years after the events in *Phoenix,* this novel centers on Savn and the rural village of Smallcliff, where he lives with his parents and his sister, Polyi. When Vlad appears in Smallcliff, Savn befriends the stranger. Unfortunately for Savn, Vlad's dangerous past catches up with him, forcing Savn to defy his parents and ultimately to commit murder.

Analysis: *Jhereg,* Brust's first published novel, evolved from a tabletop fantasy role-playing game the author played with a group of friends. Perhaps indicative of the series' origins, the book was criticized by reviewers as an unexceptional "sword and sorcery" story with an obnoxious young punk as its protagonist. Vlad Taltos, a cynical assassin, is not the most sympathetic of protagonists. His profession makes for a bloody series of stories, not to mention a narrow worldview.

Although Brust's first attempts at fiction subscribed to the "hack and slash" school of fantasy writing, he began to experiment with tone and style in subsequent novels. One reviewer noted Brust's skillful handling of a triple first-person viewpoint (Vlad's present, immediate past, and distant past) in the fourth book of the series, *Taltos.* In the sixth book, Brust abandoned Vlad as narrator, opting to tell the tale through the eyes of an intelligent but naïve young Dragaeran peasant. This change in point of view led to a greatly diminished emphasis on bloodletting.

Brust went on to publish other books in the science fiction/fantasy genre, including *To Reign in Hell* (1984), *Brokedown Palace* (1986), *Cowboy Feng's Space Bar and Grille* (1990), *The Phoenix Guards* (1991), and *Five Hundred Years After* (1994). *The Phoenix Guards* and *Five Hundred Years After* (known collectively as the Khaavren Romances) are set in the same world as the Vlad Taltos series, with the first book taking place a thousand years before Vlad's birth. Brust also published a book in editor Terri Windling's Fairy Tale Series published by Ace Books, titled *The Sun, the Moon, and the Stars* (1987). This novel, based on a folktale from Brust's Hungarian heritage, marks a departure from the traditional science fiction/fantasy genre.

In his books, Brust acknowledges the help of fellow science fiction/fantasy writers such as Emma Bull, Pamela Dean, and Will Shetterly, all members of a writing group based in Minneapolis, Minnesota. He also greatly admired fellow fantasy writer Roger Zelazny, who provided glowing endorsements for the covers of several of Brust's books. Some of the structure of the Vlad Taltos series is reminiscent of Zelazny's celebrated Amber fantasy-adventure series.

Fantasy as a genre has been defined as imaginative fiction centering on strange settings and characters. It is devoted to making the impossible appear possible or real, and it often draws on folktales and legends. The Vlad Taltos series embodies these notions, with its peasants and nobles, its sorcery and witchcraft, and its medieval castles, dress, and weaponry, combined with a contemporary sense of humor and conflict that appeal to the modern reader.

Brust's fantasy world in many ways mirrors the 1980's society in which it was created. Vlad's psionic communications with his familiar and with his friends and employees could be likened to contemporary society's fixation on cellular telephones. The beings' abilities to "teleport" instantly from one place to another, whether minutes or hours away by foot, reflects modern society's dependence on cars and airplanes to cross long distances quickly. Vlad's nausea when teleporting may arouse sympathy in readers who have experienced similar effects of motion sickness. Even Vlad's marital strife and eventual estrangement from his wife remind the reader of the high divorce rate that plagued American society of the late twentieth century.

Booklist praised the series for its "intelligent world building" and "genuine touches of originality." Over the decade that transpired between the publishing of the first and sixth novels in the series, Brust matured as a writer, as evidenced in not only the Vlad Taltos series but his other published work as well. Negative criticisms notwithstanding, the series was an intriguing first venture into the fantasy genre by a promising newcomer.

—*C. K. Breckenridge*

AEGYPT and LOVE AND SLEEP

Pierce Moffett abandons an academic career to write a quasi-historical book about a kind of magic practiced in the Renaissance

Author: John Crowley (1942-   )
Genre: Fantasy—Magical Realism
Type of work: Novels
Time of plot: The mid-twentieth century and late sixteenth century
Location: The eastern United States and Europe
First published: *Aegypt* (1987) and *Love and Sleep* (1994)

The Plot: It is perhaps easiest to think of *Love and Sleep*, the second novel of a projected four-book cycle, as chronologically wrapped around *Aegypt*, the first in the cycle. *Aegypt* chronicles Pierce Moffett's escape, to a rural life in the Catskills, from the City (New York) and an unsatisfying academic career. *Love and Sleep* takes the reader forward to the next stage in Pierce's various types of research, both into historical accounts and into himself, to understand the "time when the world worked differently." It begins by chronicling Pierce's personal history as a boy growing up on the fringes of a family in the Cumberlands in the early 1950's. Stories are included about historical figures of the late sixteenth century, including Giordano Bruno, who is credited with the discovery of infinity, Queen Elizabeth and her various counselors, Philip of Spain and the Armada, Rudolph II, and the magician Doctor Dee. Although passages in *Aegypt* make reference to each of these periods, the story of each is more fully provided in *Love and Sleep*.

Aegypt mentions Pierce's childhood and Doctor Dee's research with two short prologues. Primarily, however, it narrates the quest begun in Pierce's thirties. He sets out in the first section to interview for a teaching position at a small college in upstate New York. The bus he has taken breaks down, and he skips the interview to stay with Spofford, a former student who is now a shepherd in the small town of Blackbury Jambs. Pierce decides that he wants to stay, then briefly returns to the City to take up his old teaching job and sell a book proposal to a former girlfriend. He can then settle in Blackbury Jambs to write a popular account of the epistemological break between the medieval and the modern periods, a time of religious, magical, and scientific fervor. He meets Spofford's girlfriend, Rosie, and another girl, Rose, both of whom will help him in his quest. *Aegypt* focuses on Rosie; her husband Mike, whom she is in the process of divorcing; their small daughter, Sam; and their uncle, Boney Rasmussen. Rosie hires Pierce to work for Boney's foundation and put in order the papers of a novelist, Fellowes Kraft (an allusion to Fellowescraft, the second level of masonry), a deceased writer who also worked for the foundation. Among Kraft's papers, Pierce discovers an unfinished work that matches his own proposed book. *Aegypt* ends with him having completed his project for the foundation but trying to decide what to do about his own book, close in structure and intent to the unfinished manuscript.

Love and Sleep continues the story of Pierce's book by documenting his motivations. The first thirteen chapters of part 1, titled "Genitor," narrate two years of Pierce's boyhood in the early 1950's, when he lived with his mother, Winnie, in his uncle's house in the Cumberland Mountains. The focus is on his experiences with his cousins, the mountain people alternately endowed and devastated by mining operations, and on his relationship to books and to Catholic doctrine, all equally fantastic to him. The second section, titled "Nati," introduces the sixteenth century through texts of Fellowes Kraft read by Rosie Rasmussen and Pierce himself in the late 1970's. As Rosie and Pierce read, Pierce attempts to use the magical forces of Doctor Dee and his medium, Kelley, for his own purposes. Pierce appears to be a disturbed individual who uses his research for the foundation, which is simultaneously research for his own book, to satisfy lusts of spiritual and physical kinds. His discovery that a lost land of Aegypt may be responsible for the survival of magic in the modern world is confirmed for him (if not for the reader) by his analysis of accumulated personal occurrences. He notes that he "accidentally" ended up in Blackbury Jambs, home of Fellowes Kraft, whose novels he read as a child; that he was sexually involved with a crazy gypsy in the City (he takes "gypsy" as derived from the magical Aegypt); and that he accidentally finds himself editing the manuscript of a book by Fellowes Kraft that corresponds very closely to the book he plans to write.

A third story, of the actual historical figures Giordano Bruno, Doctor Dee, Rudolph II, and a variety of figures from the sixteenth century, carries the reader into Pierce's and Fellowes Kraft's research in an immediate sense. Pierce learns enough of Dee's magic, he believes, to use the sexual energy of "coldly performed love" with the "other" Rose (Ryder) to create for himself a barely corporeal son and an incestuous (if imaginary) relationship, slipping further into his parallel world of magic. This novel ends with a section titled "Valetudo," which can be translated as ill health or health. It is clear that both Pierce and his friends fear for his mental health, as does he. His only solution is to wait for the next big change in "the way the world works" so that his self-created succubus will leave him and he will be merely "crazy," a potentially curable condition.

The reader is left to extrapolate Pierce's or others' accuracy in assessing his quest. The clearest message is that his life has brought him repeatedly to the same questions and the same answers, suggesting that the parallel world was never really there, in ancient Aegypt or Egypt, in sixteenth century magic or in Pierce's own life. This analysis is constantly balanced with the suggestion that accidental childhood experiences set up the framework for the scope of Pierce's adult interests.

Analysis: These novels amply reward reading and re-reading. Their structural details magnificently contribute

to the experience of a story that is never completely told, only inferred. The narrative is in the third person, shifting among several characters and always unreliable, leaving much to delight a careful reader. Upon rereading, one discovers that seemingly unrelated episodes are closely intertwined. This is especially apparent in the juxtaposition of narratives about the early 1580's and the late 1970's and those concerning the lives of Giordano Bruno and Pierce Moffett.

Although one can find many reviews of John Crowley's work, there are few critical articles for an author who has been many times a nominee for the Hugo, Nebula, and World Fantasy awards (won for *Little, Big* in 1981) and the American Book Award (nominated for *Engine Summer* in 1979 and won for *Little, Big* in 1981). *Aegypt* and *Love and Sleep* are his fifth and sixth novels. He has also worked as a screenwriter for documentaries.

These two novels are different in tone from *Little, Big* but share ideas with that book. *Little, Big* also plays off the city of New York and the Catskills, but where that novel validates a magical dimension to the universe, grounded in Rosicrucians and Theosophists, *Aegypt* and *Love and Sleep* sidestep the question while maintaining the tension. These two novels offer a much more sobering and intellectual reading experience that amply repays a reader's attention but also demands much more of it.

Each of the two books is divided into three sections, and each section is given the title of a house of the zodiac, starting with Vita, Lucrum, and Frates in *Aegypt* and continuing with Genitor, Nati, and Valetudo in *Love and Sleep*. Presumably the other six houses will be worked into the projected third and fourth volumes. The houses of the zodiac are explained, in the same provisional sense as everything in these novels, by both the local astrologer, Val, and a writer from the 1620's, Fludd.

The discussion of the zodiac typifies the elaborate game the reader must play if secrets of these books are to be unlocked. These secrets are revealed as Pierce himself searches for some confirmation of his book's theme, that once the world worked differently and that the last time a change occurred was at the cusp of the sixteenth and seventeenth centuries. He believes that the world is in the midst of such a radical change. He also searches for magical powers that were available to historical figures so that he can put them to personal use.

Both novels interleaf contemporary and historical chapters. The historical chapters provide a surprising amount of historical detail. Each gives a nonscientific interpretation of events of the time and is linked to contemporary events. In one example, the defeat of the Spanish Armada is known to have been aided by an unexpected wind, but the narration insists that there are no firsthand accounts of this wind. One of Kraft's books suggests that the wind was caused by demons conjured up by Doctor Dee. This historical occurrence is then mirrored in the cold and winds of 1977-1978 in the Catskills, and by reference in the rest of the modern world. The sum of these carefully crafted illusions re-creates an experience of Pierce's journey.

Love and Sleep was written long after *Aegypt* and provides enough background to be accessible on its own. Readers who finish the second book are likely to want to go back to the first and will await the rest of the sequence. Each of the first two books ends on a note of completion, whetting curiosity about an unpredictable rest of the story.   —*Janice M. Bogstad*

AGAINST INFINITY

Assisted by an older man and a bioengineered "hound," a young boy hunts a mysterious alien artifact on Ganymede

Author: Gregory Benford (1941-   )
Genre: Science fiction—extrapolatory
Type of work: Novel
Time of plot: The twenty-first century
Location: Jupiter's moon Ganymede and Earth
First published: 1983 (sections previously appeared in *Amazing Science Fiction*, February and April, 1983)

The Plot: Closely modeled on William Faulkner's 1942 novella "The Bear," *Against Infinity* is a coming-of-age story developed in six parts. The story begins in Sidon, a frontier settlement on the Jovian moon Ganymede. The settlement has been plagued by a mysterious and elusive alien artifact called the Aleph. Its random burrowings throughout the interior of the moon threaten human efforts to terraform the moon and tame the wilderness.

Manuel López, the son of the settlement's commanding officer, first sees the Aleph when he is thirteen years old and encounters it repeatedly over the next several years. He comes under the tutelage of an aging pioneer named Matt Bohles, whose own coming-of-age story was the subject of Gregory Benford's 1975 novel *Jupiter Project*. The two of them continue over the years to join periodic hunts for the Aleph. Not until Matt and Manuel are joined by a mechanically enhanced, part-human, part-animal "hound" named Eagle, however, are they able to immobilize the mysterious artifact.

Years later, after Manuel has moved from Sidon to the city of Hiruko, he learns that the entire project of space exploration is driven not so much by idealism as by brute economic necessity, to sustain an economy that must forever expand to survive. Learning of the death of his estranged father, Manuel returns to Sidon, where he finds the wilderness replaced by a thriving community of domes. An atmosphere is developing on Ganymede, there is talk of the mechanized animals forming a new underclass in society, and the Aleph has been reduced to an object of scientific study. The Aleph itself remains a mystery, however, forever rebuilding itself at the atomic level. Moreover, the Aleph seems to contain memories of all it has encountered and all who challenged it. At the novel's conclusion, a catastrophic moonquake brought on by the stresses of terraforming nearly destroys the settlement and reasserts the primacy of the wilderness.

Analysis: More than any other writer of hard science fiction, Benford consciously has sought to bring the resources of his own literary and cultural background to bear on the futuristic settings of his work. A Southerner like Faulkner, he is equally concerned with language, with the loss of the past, with the lessons of youth and age, and with archetypal rituals such as the hunt. *Against Infinity* is by far the most successful of his attempts to adapt Faulknerian techniques to science fiction, and it is one of the most direct. The novel displays direct allusions to Faulkner's Ike McCaslin in Manuel, to the bear Old Ben in the Aleph, to the Indian guide Sam Fathers in Matt Bohles, and to the hunting dog Lion in Eagle. Like part 4 of Faulkner's novella, part 4 of Benford's novel is set some years later than the beginning, and in it the protagonist reflects on what was lost in his experience of conquering nature.

The novel is far from a simple transcription of Faulkner's story into science-fictional terms. Benford fills the book with futuristic products of his invention, including terraforming, mechanically reinforced animals with enhanced intelligence, alien artifacts, space colonies, an overpopulated Earth, and new concepts in physics revealed by the Aleph. These inventions are worked out with an extrapolative rigor that matches the best hard science fiction. Benford realizes the novel must work purely on its own terms as a science-fiction narrative, and it does.

Benford's approach is unusual for his thoughtful and ambivalent attitude toward the technology and endless economic expansion that are so often celebrated by hard science fiction. Like "The Bear," *Against Infinity* is at heart a celebration of the wilderness, of the always receding edge of human hegemony, represented not only by the colonization of other worlds but also by the unstable economic systems that accompany such colonization, by the equally unstable geology of newly explored worlds, and finally by the new realms of physics and science opened by the mysteries of the Aleph itself. These discoveries in science suggest that even the fundamental laws that govern the universe may undergo evolutionary change. As an alien artifact of uncertain purpose, the Aleph implies entire worlds as yet undiscovered, and as the moonquake that concludes the novel implies, asserting control over these worlds will not come without a price: The wilderness will always reassert itself and challenge human attempts at conquest. The elegiac tone of the final chapters is complemented by the realization that frontiers forever redefine themselves and that certain individuals such as Manuel—like Matt and Manuel's father before him—will always be drawn to "the wilderness, the opening-outward, the undomesticated, the country of the old dead time."

Against Infinity explores the notion of frontiers in science fiction at every level from economics to physics to the ancient myth of the hunt. It also reflects a unique dual perspective, with Benford drawing equally on his scientific training and on his Southern boyhood traditions of storytelling and mythmaking. Although the Faulknerian style sometimes seems at odds with the hard-edged extrapolation of Benford's future, it lends the novel a poetic depth and mythic power unusual in the genre. In its own way, *Against Infinity* is one of the genre's classic coming-of-age tales.

—Gary K. Wolfe

ALADORE

A weary knight following an unknown "desire" encounters an enchanting lady and, with her help, enters an alternate world

Author: Henry John Newbolt (1862-1938)
Genre: Fantasy—high fantasy
Type of work: Novel
Time of plot: An idealized Middle Ages
Location: Paladore, the magical counterpart of Aladore, and the surrounding countryside
First published: 1914

The Plot: Ywain, the jaded administrator of an unnamed medieval state, is so bored that he renounces his rights,

turning over his lands and office to a younger brother. He becomes a pilgrim, setting out to follow his "desire," a will-o'-the-wisp in the guise of a child. In the wilderness, he encounters a hermit who teaches him the joys of life. Eventually he leaves this solitary paradise and is directed toward the walled city of Paladore. There he encounters the beautiful Aithne, who begs him not to desert her.

The sounds of a nearby battle compel him to join the Eagles, who are attacking the besieged Tower, and he helps them to prevail. The battle is an age-old custom whereby the Eagles (the liberal forces for change) challenge the Tower (the bastion of conservative power). The warring parties converge at the end of the battle, and both sides honor Ywain as a hero and welcome him to the community. An interlude is begun with Aithne, whose powers enable her to travel to the magical city of Aladore, which Ywain is unable to see.

Still longing for fulfillment, Ywain joins a band of knights seeking the City of Saints. Ywain and his companion, Bartholomy, travel to the City, which is both lovely and unusual. It is governed by ringing bells. Both men succumb to the lure of the bells, which lull them into forgetfulness. Ywain stumbles into a garden and encounters Aithne, who asks him to follow her on a new pilgrimage. Suddenly, his memory returns, and he realizes that she is the image of all he desires.

Ywain follows Aithne to a magical kingdom peopled with fauns, who enchant Ywain with their pursuit of earthly pleasures. Although he spends blissful days there in pastoral harmony with Aithne, he gradually comes to fear the fauns and their antics. A vision of Aladore rekindles his longing, and he begs Aithne to aid him in casting off the fauns' influence.

Aithne and Ywain are taken up by a strange winged creature and flown to a city where a race of men carry on the tradition of Daedalus. Ywain is taught the art of flight and flies off, leaving Aithne behind. He falls to the ground and is rescued by the old hermit, who counsels him to return to Paladore. There he temporarily pacifies the Tower and the Eagles, who are still at odds.

One afternoon, Ywain follows the sound of children frolicking and singing and rediscovers the city of Aladore. He is permitted to cross through the mist and sea to its gates and is taken to a chamber. He finds a book containing a picture of Aithne; turning, he finds that the image has become reality. He weds Aithne, and they begin an idyllic existence. Aithne, through magic, shows Ywain all the seekers and lovers of myth and history. He visits scenes of Aithne's childhood and experiences with her all the warmth and love of her youthful years.

With the sounding of the midnight bells, Ywain finds himself in Paladore once more. Aithne follows, and together they are drawn into the final climactic battle for mastery of the city. Ywain elects to sacrifice himself to purchase the salvation of his companions in arms, the Eagles. He sees the child of his desire one last time and follows him to Aithne's sanctuary. Ywain and Aithne depart, hand in hand, through the battle. They are never seen in Paladore again, but the effigies of a knight and his lady are discovered on the tomb of the altar in the sanctuary.

Analysis: *Aladore* is a haunting tale, so limpid and gentle in the telling that one is tempted to read it simply for pure enjoyment. Henry John Newbolt's pastiche of the style made popular by William Morris employs a rich, though archaic, language that contributes to the beautiful flow of this allegorical account of a medieval quest for love and the meaning of life.

Aladore contains many allusions to Christian fellowship and theology. Ywain and the hermit break bread together and bathe in a mountain stream, acts comparable to the rites of communion and baptism. Ywain continually is torn between the fellowship and peace of the hermitage and the lure of his will-o'-the-wisp desire. This tension is reminiscent of the pull between religious life and the knightly quest—"The bird calls 'Come!'; the saint whispers 'Stay!'"—that is depicted so compellingly in "The Knight's Tale" in Geoffrey Chaucer's *The Canterbury Tales* (1387-1400). This problem is never resolved completely in the novel. At one point, the reunited lovers are startled in a garden by a spy slithering away in the grass, like a serpent invading their Edenic paradise. During the climactic battle, Ywain willingly sacrifices himself, in the manner of Jesus Christ, to save his brothers in the final Armageddon.

This deceptively simple allegory is notable for the fact that it is (except for the somewhat juvenile Greenwood tales of G. P. Baker) the only significant medieval fantasy published between the death of William Morris in 1896 and the end of World War I. Newbolt clearly is familiar with Morris' work and uses the same style of language, indefinable time period, and medieval trappings. That such a tale, with its emphasis on brotherly love and Christian fellowship, should appear on the eve of World War I is ironic. Newbolt, who later wrote the official history of the navy in that conflict and was knighted for his efforts, never wrote another novel.

—*Robert Reginald*

ALAS, BABYLON

After a nuclear explosion, Randy Bragg assumes responsibility for the survival of his "family" and takes control of his town to reestablish some semblance of civilization

Author: Pat Frank (Harry Hart Frank, 1907-1964)
Genre: Science fiction—post-holocaust
Type of work: Novel
Time of plot: The mid-twentieth century
Location: Fort Repose, a river town in Central Florida
First published: 1959

The Plot: The time frame of *Alas, Babylon* is limited to a single year following a nuclear war. Randy Bragg is a thirty-two-year-old lawyer and former military officer living in Fort Repose, Florida. He and his small community manage to survive the effects of the war and, through their communal efforts, to preserve a modicum of civilization.

Randy receives from his brother Mark, an Air Force colonel and member of Strategic Air Command Intelligence, a telegram that ends with the phrase "Alas, Babylon." This is their code for disaster, adopted from fiery sermons they heard in childhood. Mark is certain that nuclear attack is imminent, and he entrusts to Randy his wife Helen and his children, Ben Franklin and Peyton.

Mark's prediction proves true sooner than expected. The next morning, two nearby cities are hit by atomic bombs. Randy is awakened by shaking of the house, a loud rumbling, and an orange light. Peyton's temporary blindness from looking at the light is only the first of many crises. Randy, on his way to find his friend, Dr. Dan Gunn, passes an overturned car with a dead woman beside it. Stopping automatically, he realizes that all the rules have now changed and that the days of the Good Samaritan are over. All the roads are jammed with refugees, convicts have escaped from prison, and businesses have closed. In short, chaos reigns. In the next few months, charity loses its moral imperative. As electricity, running water, telephone service, and other amenities become unavailable, filth, squalor, and moral poverty become, for many, the conditions of life.

Randy, governed by enlightened self-interest, does what must be done in a civilized world. He unceremoniously buries the bodies of his fiancée's mother and the selfish politician Porky Logan, putting Logan and all of his contaminated goods in a lead coffin. Randy forms a community made up of Helen and her two children, Lib McGovern, her father, Dan Gunn, two "spinsters," a retired admiral, and Randy's "wards," the Henrys. Through cooperation, the community avoids the degeneracy into which many have fallen. The worst of these are the gangs of "highwaymen," to whom Dan falls victim.

Randy, as a Reserve officer, forms a troop and assumes control of Fort Repose. He imposes martial law and brings order to the town, punishing the highwaymen who beat Dan. He also establishes a means for legal marriage, then becomes the first to take advantage of it, marrying Lib McGovern.

A year after The Day (as it came to be called), one of Mark's friends lands a helicopter in the yard. He reveals that the United States had won the war, that Mark could not possibly be alive, and that Fort Repose is free from radiation. When he offers to take the community to another city, the members all decline, preparing together to "face the thousand-year night."

Analysis: *Alas, Babylon* is one of many post-catastrophe novels written in the era of the Cold War. Like the more highly regarded *A Canticle for Leibowitz* (1960) by Walter M. Miller, Jr., it assumes a return to barbarism after such a catastrophe. Whereas Miller's novel covers some eighteen hundred years after the holocaust, Pat Frank's novel concerns only the first year and shows the process by which such decadence comes to be. Frank's novel is more optimistic than Miller's, ending with the re-establishment of schools, an increase in reading, the return to a more purposeful existence, and the hope that the best people will survive and retain their civility.

One of Frank's last novels, written at a time when America feared and prepared for atomic war, *Alas, Babylon* can be called science fiction only in the sense that the holocaust does occur. At the beginning, Frank makes the setting seem familiar. With careful attention to place, he creates a small river town in Florida, modeled after Mandarin, where his mother lived. As the town becomes strange to Randy, it becomes strange to the reader because of the lack of necessary services, the destruction of such symbols as money and ceremonies, and lack of communication with the outside world. For several months, the characters do not know whether the war is still going on or which side might have won, and they do not know if there is a national government in control. The uncertainty of authority and the necessary barbarism of life caused by the lack of accustomed services unleashes the worst aspects of human nature.

The narrative voice is omniscient, with events seen through the consciousness of several characters. The novel begins with the thoughts of Florence Wechek,

Randy's neighbor. This allows Frank to present a humorous view of Randy before putting the reader into Randy's consciousness. Randy appears at first to be rather purposeless, but the good stock he comes from, his military service, and his intelligence and good character foreshadow his heroic actions.

The novel is dated by its racist and sexist assumptions. The author treats the black characters with condescension, presenting them stereotypically as, for example, a lazy, drunken loafer; an overweight domestic worker; and an industrious manual laborer. Women, too, are presented in shallow terms. Helen momentarily goes mad because of repressed sexual desires, and when the women are left alone, chaos ensues. Randy concludes that women need men around. Despite expression of these dated attitudes, *Alas, Babylon* is well crafted and is instructive as a moral tale. The community members' interdependency shows that civilization is based on ethical behavior rather than on technology and material goods.

—Jo N. Farrar

ALICE'S ADVENTURES IN WONDERLAND
and
THROUGH THE LOOKING-GLASS

A young girl explores a bizarre world that lies underground and an equally strange land that lies on the other side of the looking-glass

Author: Lewis Carroll (Charles Lutwidge Dodgson, 1832-1898)
Genre: Fantasy—alien civilization
Type of work: Novels
Time of plot: Undefined, in dreamlands
Location: Wonderland and Looking-Glass Land
First published: *Alice's Adventures in Wonderland* (1865) and *Through the Looking-Glass* (1871 but dated 1872)

The Plot: *Alice's Adventures in Wonderland* is an outgrowth of Lewis Carroll's earlier and shorter tale titled *Alice's Adventures Under Ground*, which he based on a story he told to Alice Liddell and her two sisters during a boat trip they took in 1862. Carroll completed this story, written in longhand and illustrated with his own drawings, in 1863. In 1864, he gave the manuscript to Alice as a gift. Revised and expanded by Carroll and newly illustrated by John Tenniel, this work evolved into *Alice's Adventures in Wonderland* the following year.

While listening to her older sister reading aloud, Alice

drifts off to sleep and begins her dream adventures. She follows a white rabbit and falls down his hole into Wonderland. Alice is constantly at odds with the creatures who inhabit this alien world and also with her own body, which shrinks when she drinks from a mysterious bottle, then grows to enormous size when she eats a small cake.

She encounters many creatures endowed with wit and cleverness, who confuse her at every turn. She meets the ugly Duchess, whose baby turns into a pig in Alice's arms. Things are not what they seem. It is at the Duchess' house that she first sees the unsettling Cheshire Cat, who sits in the corner grinning, with his eyes fixed on Alice. Later, the Cheshire Cat reappears on a tree branch, from which he demonstrates his ability to vanish, leaving only his eerie smile lingering in the air.

At the Mad Tea-Party, Alice must exchange witty remarks and insults with the Hatter and March Hare, an experience that further challenges her sense of time and logic. It is always six o'clock, always teatime, at this table.

The threatening nature of Wonderland is reinforced in the garden scene, dominated by the raucous Queen of Hearts, who continually shouts "Off with her head!" The threat becomes problematic, however, when the executioner is summoned to cut off the disembodied head of the Cheshire Cat.

Alice's last adventure is at the trial of the Knave of Hearts, who is accused of stealing the Queen's tarts. The Queen calls for the defendant to be sentenced before the jury submits its verdict, and it soon becomes clear that the law itself is on trial. Outraged at the absurd form of justice she witnesses, Alice asserts, "You're nothing but a pack of cards!" With that exclamation, she annihilates Wonderland as if by magic, and she emerges from her strange dream.

In *Through the Looking-Glass* (which carries the subtitle *And What Alice Found There*), Carroll again frames his story as a dreamlike experience, but this time he presents a world that is controlled by the rules of a chess game. Alice enters the geometrical landscape, which is laid out like a chessboard, as a pawn. During her movement across the board en route to becoming a queen, she may converse only with the chess figures on adjacent squares. Among the many memorable characters she engages are the White Queen, from whom she learns the advantages of living backward in time; the battling Lion and Unicorn; the pompous Humpty Dumpty; the bullying Tweedledee and Tweedledum, who tell Alice that she is merely an object in the Red King's dream; and the eccentric White Knight.

After Alice bids farewell to the White Knight, in a scene that may represent Carroll's adieu to Alice Liddell as she reached puberty, Alice goes on to become queen. In terms of the chess game, the pawn has become a queen, and in human terms, Alice's final move suggests her coming of age. It is at this point that she wakes from her dream and is left wondering who dreamed it all, herself or the Red King.

Analysis: *Alice's Adventures in Wonderland* presents a world in which everything, including Alice's own body size, is in a state of flux. She is treated rudely, bullied, asked questions that have no answers, and denied answers to her own questions. Her recitations of poems turn into parodies, a baby turns into a pig, and a cat turns into a grin. The essence of time and space is called into question, and her romantic notion of an idyllic garden of life turns out to be a paper wasteland. In order to escape that oppressive and disorienting vision, she finally denies it with her outcry, "You're nothing but a pack of cards!," and happily reenters the morally intelligible and emotionally comfortable world of her sister, who sits next to her on the green banks of a river in a civilized Victorian countryside.

The assaults on Alice's senses of order, stability, and proper manners wrought by such characters as the Hatter, the Cheshire Cat, and the March Hare make it clear that Wonderland is not the promised land, a place of sleepy fulfillment. Rather, Wonderland stimulates the senses and the mind. It is a *monde fatale*, one that seduces Alice (and the reader) to seek new sights, new conversations, and new ideas, but it never satisfies her. Conventional meaning, understanding, and the fulfillment that comes with illumination are constantly denied her. That is the secret of Wonderland: Its disorienting and compelling attractions make it a Wanderland and Alice herself an addicted, unfulfilled wanderer.

Significantly, she is presented with a stimulating, alluring vision early in her adventures. Alice finds a tiny golden key that opens a door that leads to a small passage. As she kneels and looks along the passage, she sees a beautiful garden with bright flowers and cool fountains. She is too large, however, to fit through the door and enter the attractive garden. Alice's dream garden suggests an adult's longing for lost innocence and youth, and her desire to enter it invests the place with imagined significance. Later, when she goes into the garden, it loses its romantic aspect. In fact, it turns out to be a parodic Garden of Life, for the roses are painted, the people are playing-cards, and the death-cry "Off with her head!" echoes throughout the croquet grounds.

Alice's dream garden is an excellent example of Carroll's paradoxical duality. Like Alice, he is possessed by a romantic vision of an Edenic childhood more desirable than his own fallen world, but it is a vision that he knows is corrupted inevitably by adult sin and sexuality. He thus allows Alice's romantic dream of the garden to fill her with hope and joy for a time, but he later tramples that pastoral vision with the fury of the beheading Queen and the artificiality of the flowers and inhabitants.

Through the Looking-Glass abandons the fluidity and chaos of *Alice's Adventures in Wonderland* for artifice and strict determinism. In the first book, the emphasis is on Alice's adventures and what happens to her on the experiential level. In the sequel, Alice's movements are controlled strictly by the precise rules of a chess game. The giddy freedom she enjoyed in Wonderland is exchanged for a ruthless determinism, as she and the other chess pieces are manipulated by some unseen hand.

Whereas *Alice's Adventures in Wonderland* undermines Alice's sense of time, space, and commonsensical logic, *Through the Looking-Glass* questions her very reality. Tweedledum and Tweedledee express the Berkeleian view that all material objects, including Alice herself, are only "sorts of things" in the mind of the sleeping Red King (God). If the Red King were to wake from his dreaming, they warn Alice, she would disappear. Alice, it would seem, is a mere fiction shaped by a dreaming mind that threatens her with annihilation.

The ultimate question of what is real and what is dream, however, is never resolved in the book. In fact, the story ends with the perplexing question of who dreamed it all—Alice or the Red King? Presumably, Alice dreamed of the King, who is dreaming of Alice, who is dreaming of the King, and so on. The question of dream versus reality is appropriately set forth in terms of an infinite regression through mirror facing mirror. The apprehension of reality is indefinitely deferred, and the only reality may be one's thoughts and their well-ordered expression.

In the final chapter, Alice, having become Queen, asserts her human authority against the controlling powers of the chessboard and brings both the intricate game and the story to an end. In chess terms, Alice has captured the Red Queen and checkmates the sleeping Red King. In human terms, she has grown up and entered that fated condition of puberty, at which point Carroll dismisses his dream child once and for all from his remarkable fiction.

—Richard Kelly

ALL HALLOWS' EVE

The Antichrist seeks to take over the world through magic but is foiled by two young couples whose love and sacrifice stop him and allow for their movement toward happiness

Author: Charles Williams (1886-1945)
Genre: Fantasy—occult
Type of work: Novel
Time of plot: 1945
Location: London, England
First published: 1945

The Plot: Charles Williams' last novel brings together many of the themes of his other five novels. Lester Furnival, who has been married for six months, and her school friend Evelyn Mercer are killed by a plane that crashes near Westminster Bridge. Only gradually does Lester realize that she is dead. As she crosses a strangely quiet but still familiar London, Lester speaks to her living husband, Richard. With Evelyn, she sets out to accomplish something in her "new life" to make up for her incomplete earlier life.

Jonathan Drayton, a painter friend of Richard Furnival, is in love with Betty Wallingford. To impress Betty's mother, he paints a portrait of Simon Leclerc. Lady Wallingford sees in the picture "a ranked mass of beetles" around the face of an imbecile. Offended, she insists that Betty break off her engagement to Jonathan. Jonathan also has painted a remarkable picture of the city of London as a city of light. The painting impresses Richard, who asks how Jonathan came to create it. Jonathan explains that Sir Joshua Reynolds, a famous English painter of the late eighteenth century, once alluded to common observation and a plain understanding as the source of all art. Jonathan is later visited by Simon, who approves of his portrait but dislikes the painting of the illuminated city. He attempts to flatter Jonathan, calling him a genius and insisting that great art is apostolic. A practical artist, Jonathan throughout the novel insists on observation and understanding rather than apostolic excess.

Betty turns out to be the daughter of Lady Wallingford and Simon. She is being used by Simon to enter the world of spirits and bring back information about the future. On one such mission, she meets her former schoolmates Lester and Evelyn, who follow her home. Unknown to Simon, Lester enters the house and intercedes when Simon attempts to sacrifice his daughter.

Later, Evelyn, whose motives are petty and malignant, is called up by Simon at his Holburn meeting place.

After his attempt to sacrifice Betty fails, Simon, in an attempt to control Lester, creates a humanoid figure from his spittle and dust. Both Evelyn and Lester enter into it. Using this figure, Lester places a telephone call to Richard to alert him about what has happened.

Simon is destroyed by his own creations in a final confrontation. Lady Wallingford tries to save Betty at the last moment and survives, to be taken care of by her transformed daughter, who even cures the attendants of Simon. Evelyn consigns herself to the region of the damned. Because of her self-sacrifice and Betty's forgiveness, Lester moves through Purgatory toward final blessing.

Analysis: As in his other novels, Williams is more concerned with the conflict between good and evil than with the depiction of everyday life. To establish this conflict, he uses many of the conventions of the fantasy genre.

The title, *All Hallows' Eve*, suggests the ancient Celtic festival of Samain, when it was believed that the gates between the spirits of the living and the dead opened and allowed easy passage. Williams accepted the Christian transformation of this holiday. In the tradition of Saint Augustine's *The City of God* (413-427), the "hallows," the souls of the blessed dead, take on the form of "the Acts of the City" and support Lester when Simon attempts to destroy her. The world of the dead, in fact, seems more vital and alive than drab wartime London. Although Betty is Simon's daughter, she is saved from his power both by Lester and by the "wise waters" of baptism, the christening given to her by her nurse.

Williams, who was a member of the Mystical Order of the Golden Dawn, also uses magic in the novel. Simon is both a version of Simon Magus (Acts 8:9-24) and the Antichrist. Williams insists that Simon is a Jew not because he is being anti-Semitic but because he is setting Simon in contrast to "that other sorcerer of his race, the son of Joseph, . . . Jesus Bar-Joseph." The scenes of conjuring and magical creation seem authentic but avoid the melodramatic excess of much gothic fiction.

Williams also uses Dante Alighieri's *The Divine Comedy* (c. 1320) in his fiction. Lester moves beyond Hell and through Purgatory. Readers see a hint of Paradise in the martyr's blood and mystic rose of the last chapter, which draws on Dante's portrayal of the blessed in Paradise. The first chapter may owe something to Dante's spiritual autobiography, his *La vita nuova* (c. 1292; *The New Life*, 1867).

The confrontation between good and evil, like the contrast between Jonathan's two paintings of the blessed and the damned, the light and the dark, emerges only through gradual revelation rather than melodramatic announcement. Readers come to recognize that although Simon preaches love, his only interests are himself and the establishment of his own complete power. He sires Betty not out of love or even lust but instead out of his desire and need to create an instrument he can use for his own ends. Simon insists, "I am the one who is to come, not Hitler!" To this end, he has created images of himself that appear in Russia and China. These unreal shadows, parodies of the Christian trinity, finally return to destroy him.

In contrast to Simon's joyless self-absorption, the novel presents the self-sacrifice of Lester, the radiant forgiveness of Betty, and the love that Richard and Jonathan feel for these two remarkable women. As Williams put it in an essay on "The Redeemed City" (1941), "There is no final idea for us but the glory of God in the redeemed and universal union—call it Man or the Church or the City."
                                                    —David Lampe

ALL TIMES POSSIBLE

A dimensionally displaced man foments revolution in an alternate America and briefly serves as director of the Free Democratic State before being ousted by more cynical colleagues

Author: Gordon Eklund (1945-   )
Genre: Science fiction—alternate history
Type of work: Novel
Time of plot: The 1920's to July 4, 1947
Location: Various parts of the United States
First published: 1974

The Plot: On July 4, 1947, in a United States with a governmental regime that appears considerably more authoritarian than the one recorded in history, a political radical named Timothy O'Mara attempts to assassinate General Norton. He fails and is summarily executed by the general. He then finds himself back in the early 1920's, inhabiting the body of a man named Tommy Bloome, whom he once murdered in order to take over his identity.

The main narrative describes, from several points of view, how Tommy Bloome, armed with a mysterious knowledge of things to come, becomes a zealous labor organizer, preparing the way for a general strike that precipitates a new American revolution in the early 1930's. After an extended civil war, Bloome's insurrectionists finally defeat the last remnants of the Nationalist army and secure power, but their rule follows much the same pattern as that of Soviet communism, involving constant internal power struggles within the hierarchy of the party and frequent purges.

Bloome is ousted from his position as director of the new Free Democratic State by his deputy, Arnold Lowrey, a political opportunist who had been the governor of Arkansas before the revolution. Lowrey is helped in this treachery by the sinister John Durgas and is further assisted by the passive but willing cooperation of Bloome's wife, Rachel, a former socialite who became an alcoholic during the difficult years of the civil war.

Once ousted, Bloome retires to secret seclusion, accompanied by his longtime friend Bob Ennis, who is the only person loyal to him. Lowrey's propaganda machine continues to use Bloome's name, claiming that he is fighting heroically in various distant arenas of the world war, which is still grinding on in 1947. After Tommy's death, on July 4, 1947, Ennis and Rachel continue to count the cost of their association with him, knowing that they will be killed as soon as Durgas—now the effective ruler of Free Democratic America—can do so.

At the end, the story reverts to the viewpoint of O'Mara-as-Bloome, who is told by Durgas that he has changed nothing, because this world is not the one he left behind. He already has become aware of slight differences in its history for which he could not have been responsible, and he must accept what Durgas says about that other world continuing along its own terrible path. Durgas also assures O'Mara/Bloome that he will die at exactly the same moment as he died in the other world, claiming to know this because he also is a dimensionally displaced person. As the moment of his death approaches, O'Mara/Bloome indeed finds himself slipping back to the moment of his "first" death, seeing General Norton's bullet heading toward him while the face of John Durgas looks on from the crowd.

Analysis: The flyleaf blurb (presumably written by the book's editor and publisher, Donald A. Wollheim) describes *All Times Possible* as a "uchronian" novel, borrowing that label from *Uchronie* (1876), Charles Renouvier's pioneering exercise in alternate history. In fact, though, the pattern of the plot is an elaboration of the device employed in Ambrose Bierce's famous short story "An Occurrence at Owl Creek Bridge" (1891): The main

narrative is a momentary hallucination experienced at the point of death. This is confused by the fact that by far the largest part of the main narrative is told from viewpoints other than that of the protagonist and that these supposedly objective accounts extend beyond the moment of O'Mara-as-Bloome's death. The conclusion makes it clear nevertheless that the narrative is a hallucination.

All Times Possible also is strongly reminiscent of Philip K. Dick's classic tale of alternate worlds, *The Man in the High Castle* (1962), in that the ordinary world remains outside the scope of the story as the protagonist struggles to adjust psychologically to the fact that he has lost his grip on his own identity and the solidity of his own world. The fact that O'Mara, at the moment of death, finds himself reliving the life of a man whose identity he stole, in a world in which he was never born, must be taken as an expression of his guilt, but he makes it clear that his adventure as Tommy Bloome is an act of revenge against the world rather than an attempt at atonement. Given this, it is not surprising that his career is a catalog of spoliation, in the course of which everyone who loves him is ruined. Nor is it surprising that his personal nemesis, John Durgas, delivers and bears witness to an unrelentingly hard judgment; in Hindu mythology, Durga is a violent and vengeful avatar of Parvati.

What perhaps is surprising is that Donald Wollheim—a man fervently committed to upbeat endings, who is rumored to have rejected Stephen King's first novel on the grounds that he was not interested in "negative utopias"—should have consented to publish such a bleak and politically sensitive book as *All Times Possible*. There is reason for readers and critics to be glad that he did, however, because the novel stands out as a uniquely interesting work in a genre not known for painstaking attention to matters of fine psychological detail or for outstanding bravery in matters of political speculation. Although the novel's account of the second American revolution and its cruel aftermath is sketchy and impressionistic, its condensed biographies of the subsidiary characters—particularly Rachel, Bob Ennis, and Lowrey—are highly effective, and it is entirely apt that the mysterious figure of Tommy Bloome—of whom O'Mara, after all, knows nothing—should be allowed to remain essentially elusive. The judgment passed on O'Mara is harsh and hellish, but it is neither inapt nor unjust. Readers will have to make up their own minds as to whether the judgment implicitly passed on America is equally appropriate.

—*Brian Stableford*

ALRAUNE

Professor ten Brinken engineers the birth of an amoral, semi-supernatural woman who enslaves and destroys all who fall under her influence

Author: Hanns Heinz Ewers (1871-1943)
Genre: Fantasy—superbeing
Type of work: Novel
Time of plot: 1885-1910
Location: Germany
First published: 1911 (in German; English translation, 1929)

The Plot: *Alraune* is an occult fantasy, a modern reworking of the mandrake myth woven together with elements of *Frankenstein* (1818) and played against the background of the decadence and moral collapse that preceded World War I.

Inspired by the legend that mandrakes (*alraunes* in German) are engendered by the semen of hanged criminals, Frank Braun, a dissolute young lawyer, proposes an experiment to Professor Jacob ten Brinken: The creation of a woman through artificial insemination. Nymphomaniacal prostitute Alma Raune is impregnated with the final emission of rapist-murderer Peter Noerrissen, collected at the moment of his execution by guillotine. The experiment succeeds, and the mother is imprisoned until the midnight birth of a female child. The difficult labor kills the mother, who is the first victim of the sensual, amoral, and marginally human Alraune.

Ten Brinken adopts the child, encouraging and observing with delight the development of her evil nature and its effects upon those around her. Like the mandrake of superstition, she brings wealth to the house, along with unhappiness and destruction.

Alraune's manipulation of those who fall into her web causes her expulsion from the convent where she is initially reared; at home she mesmerizes, enslaves, and ultimately destroys a series of men and women whom she encourages while denying herself to them, maddens with jealousy, and goads to destroy one another. She rarely acts directly, but she inspires her admirers to deeds, in their willingness to do "anything" to please her, that will bring about their destruction. She feels nothing for any of them, not even for Wolf Gontram, one of the novel's few decent characters. She tortures him throughout his childhood and finally kills him by enticing him into freezing weather, chilling him so that he dies of pneumonia. Alraune herself is immune to disease.

Although ten Brinken is her creator, he falls under her baleful influence, neglects his shady business speculations, and even molests a child to relieve his sexual frustration. Soon he is faced with prison, and when Alraune tells him that she is leaving him, in desperation he hangs himself. He first alters his will to make Braun his executor, in the hope of drawing him into Alraune's net, thus repaying him for having conceived the poisonous experiment.

Alraune is indifferent to the claims of all who have been ruined by ten Brinken's business and banking ventures, and she amuses herself by enslaving Frieda Gontram and driving Olga Wolkonski to madness. In revenge, financially ruined Duchess Wolkonski, the mother of Olga and godmother of Alraune, reveals to her the secret of her birth, the facts of which are confirmed by Braun.

Initially, Braun is immune to Alraune, and this intrigues her. After she learns her nature, Braun and Alraune drop their defenses, engage in amorous dueling, and become intoxicated with each other. Alraune finally yields herself. Braun finds his finances becoming suddenly and abnormally successful, and Alraune suggests that "It's happening again." Their life together alternates between periods of passionate love and ferocious fighting. He attempts to leave her and even burns the mandrake that gave him the idea for the experiment, but he cannot leave. Finally, he discovers to his horror that Alraune has taken to sucking his blood while he sleeps. He is freed when Alraune falls to her death while sleepwalking on the roof.

Analysis: *Alraune* is one of the most fascinating and yet unpleasant and disturbing of fantasy novels. It was a popular success and has been filmed numerous times. With the exception of Hanns Heinz Ewers' other work—*The Sorcerer's Apprentice* (1907) and *Vampire* (1921), also featuring Frank Braun—there is nothing quite like it. The closest works are Joris-Karl Huysmans' *Against the Grain* (1884) and *Là Bas* (1891) and Valery Bryusov's *The Fiery Angel* (1908). One would be hard pressed to find a less pleasant cast of characters between two covers.

The disturbing quality stems from the author's apparent gusto in portraying decadence, cruelty, and amorality. He seems to delight as much in Alraune's conquests as does Professor ten Brinken. Ewers lovingly dwells upon the sensuality and the perversity of characters and events described, and he excels in exotic description. He, like his Alraune, toys with his reader. For example, the experiment that will result in her conception is much planned and discussed, but the scene itself is entirely passed over. Alraune's death occupies very little space, though the author provides several pages of weirdly perverse comment.

Ewers' technique here, as in his other novels, is to take a superstition, update it in sociological, scientific, or psychological terms, and all but explain it away, leaving only enough of the supernatural and the unexplainable to unsettle his reader. He seems to ask, "What if there really is something to the superstition for which our modern knowledge cannot account?" One may debunk the "mystery" from Alraune's birth, sordid as it is, but how can one account for her ability even as a child to pick winning lottery tickets, locate long-buried treasure, and know which stocks will go up?

The experiment in artificial insemination fails to impress in times when the technique is fairly common, and the book overall is repulsive. Although Braun is meant to be the hero, Alraune is nearly the most sympathetic of the characters. Ewers' attempts to make her seem soulless make it nearly impossible to pity her in the way that they might the Frankenstein monster, for example. Ewers' own life may make his work unattractive to some readers: He worked enthusiastically with the Nazis. A fascination with evil permeates his fiction.

—*Jerry L. Ball*

THE ALTERATION

A boy must choose between manhood and fame in a world in which the Catholic church dominates society

Author: Kingsley Amis (1922-1995)
Genre: Science fiction—alternate history
Type of work: Novel
Time of plot: 1976
Location: England
First published: 1976

The Plot: Hubert Anvil, a ten-year-old choirboy in the prestigious Cathedral Basilica of St. George in Coverley, the most important religious city in England, is faced with a dilemma. Although he may have very little personal control over the decision made, it will seriously affect the rest of his life. Experts brought in from the Vatican have advised Abbot Peter Thynne that the boy's soprano voice is so rare that it would be foolish to allow the child to mature in the normal way. They suggest that emasculating him would give him a distin-

guished musical career as a castrato.

Such a situation might seem irrelevant in 1976, but Kingsley Amis has made a single adjustment in European history. The Protestant reformation is presumed never to have taken place. Martin Luther, rather than leaving the Catholic church, becomes the pope, and Henry VIII does not take Britain out of the Catholic church. Not only is Roman Catholicism the official religion of Europe, but it is the ruling political force, and the aristocracies still reign throughout the continent. Only in North America is there a more benign, partially democratic government in power, and a form of Protestantism is practiced there.

Hubert comes to the conclusion that however famous he may become, he is not willing to reject a normal life. It is not simply a matter of saying no, however; his father, a prominent Catholic layman, is eager to please the powers of the church, particularly when he is called to Rome, where the pope offers to take Hubert into the Vatican choir. Hubert's mother is against the "alteration" of her son, but her efforts to help him are ignored, and the attempt by her personal chaplain (and lover) to thwart both the religious and the civil authorities is met with a swift brutality that marks the nature of the Roman Catholic regime.

The boy attempts to escape with the help of some of his school friends and the American ambassador. He almost succeeds in getting out of the country and making his way to a freer life in America. At the last moment, however, his desire to evade castration is thwarted by a cruel turn of nature that settles the matter. The novel ends, some fifteen years later, with Hubert as the greatest religious singer of his age, but not without some sadness concerning the opportunities and experiences he has missed.

Analysis: Amis uses the simple idea of altering history in more than one way. He employs it, for example, as a serious thematic device to explore how religion—particularly in concert with totalitarian political forces—can exert seemingly benign power and influence against the best interests of the people. In doing so, he accepts the common view of historians that the Protestant Reformation was more than simply a matter of resistance to the overweening power and corruption of the Roman Catholic church in the late Middle Ages and early Renaissance and that it was also the first sign of what later became the gradual movement toward democracy.

The 1976 of this book, though it includes some novel developments in the scientific world, is still far behind the actual world of comfort and convenience, serviced by the best elements of scientific discovery. Electricity, for example, is known, but its use is forbidden in Europe (although, significantly, Americans make use of it). Much of the day-to-day life of the civilized world is not much advanced from centuries before, and there is an implied sense that the backwardness of life, however quaint it may be, is related directly to the church's pervasive dominance over religion, society, and politics. Perhaps most damaging is the tyranny exercised in Europe, whereby the individual, exemplified by Hubert, is simply a tool of the religious and political powers, which are prepared to reward him if he does what they want but to crush him and those who help him if he resists. Those in power argue that it is simply a matter of serving the Christian God, but Amis conveys the impression that those in power have a strong inclination to take care of themselves. He concentrates on the abuses of religious power, but the lesson has wider political implications for any political system in which the wielders of power put self-interest first.

The less serious aspect of Amis' rearrangement of history is the manner in which he plays with minutiae. Making Martin Luther the pope is a wry manipulation of the idea that the best way to deal with an enemy is to bring him or her into one's own camp. Benedict Arnold proves to be an American hero, and various historical celebrities have their reputations and careers altered to meet the pattern of religious dominance. *Gulliver's Travels* (1726) winds up as *St. Lemuel's Travels*. James Bond becomes Father Bond, and there is a popular novel titled *Lord of the Chalices*. Amis thus provides the reader with a modest knowledge of history and art, an amusing bonus, in addition to a serious consideration of the way in which people accept the modern democratic world without fully appreciating what might have happened had things been otherwise.   —*Charles Pullen*

ALWAYS COMING HOME

A complex exploration of the futuristic, feminist, utopian Kesh society focusing on the character Stone Telling

Author: Ursula K. Le Guin (1929-   )
Genre: Science fiction—future history
Type of work: Novel
Time of plot: Several centuries in the future, backtracking to the present
Location: Northern California
First published: 1985

The Plot: Ursula Le Guin's narrator in *Always Coming Home* is Pandora, mistress of ceremonies for the unraveling of a richly complex tale spanning several centuries. Pandora in Greek mythology was the beguiling human upon whom Zeus, king of the gods, bestowed an unquenchable curiosity. Ignoring all admonitions, she opened the forbidden box she received. It contained the world's evils, now loosed upon civilization.

Le Guin's Pandora lives in two worlds separated by centuries. She moves facilely between them as spokesperson for a past civilization and narrator of a future one. Le Guin devotes the last 116 pages of this 525-page book to what she labels "The Back of the Book," an extensive anthropological description of the Kesh people who, ironically, do not yet exist.

Le Guin devotes fifteen tightly packed pages to a glossary of the Kesh language, and she extensively portrays Kesh folkways and dress. Earlier, in five pages, she describes written Kesh, including its alphabet and pronunciation.

Stone Telling relates much of the Kesh story. She is the daughter of Willow (Towhee), a Kesh woman who married Terter Abhao, a Condor invader. The matrilinear, feminist, utopian Kesh society is peaceful. Its members strive consciously to live in harmony with nature rather than to control it. Condor society, on the other hand, is male-dominated and aggressive. When the Condors invade the Kesh in their native Na (Napa) Valley, the societies bewilder each other.

Condors cannot understand people who measure wealth by how much one gives away or comprehend people who eat as little animal flesh as possible and who hold forgiveness ceremonies for taking the life of any chicken, apple, or grape they might consume to sustain themselves. Conversely, the Kesh cannot understand people who can invade and subjugate their culture, which, although retaining such civilized contemporary trappings as electricity, flush toilets, power looms, and computers, eschews many modern conveniences and rejects much of what twentieth century society labels progress. Because they wish to control cultural clutter, the Kesh do not keep voluminous written records and often destroy the few they have made. The invading Condors desecrate the cherished Kesh philosophy of "live and let live."

Stone Telling grows up on her father's land. Eventually she escapes with her infant daughter, Quail. She makes the arduous trip home, calling herself "Woman Coming Home." She recounts her story and, essentially, the story of the Kesh civilization, as an old woman reflecting on a curious past.

Analysis: At the beginning of *Always Coming Home*, in a section titled "A First Note," Le Guin alerts her readers to her book's uniqueness. Its first sentence reads, "The people in this book might be going to have lived a long, long time from now in Northern California." The unusual, conditional verb phrase in this sentence splices together past and future, as Le Guin continues to do throughout the book.

Always Coming Home, richly illustrated by Margaret Chodos and with maps by the author, was marketed originally with an accompanying cassette of Kesh music by Todd Barton. The book generally is called a novel but is so heterodox in structure that it virtually creates a new fictional genre, in the same manner as Truman Capote's *In Cold Blood* (1966) and Rolando Hinojosa-Smith's still-incomplete, multivolume work, the Klail City Death Trip, begun in 1973.

Le Guin, daughter of noted anthropologist Alfred Kroeber and novelist Theodora Kracaw Kroeber, applies the techniques of field anthropology, both physical and cultural, to a future rather than past culture. She drifts easily through nonlinear time, creating a philosophical-fictional world that includes artifacts from two cultures, contemporary and future, unified by Pandora's narration and Stone Telling's story, the four major parts of which are interspersed throughout the novel. Between Stone Telling segments, Le Guin constructs the Kesh culture that has grown up in California's Na Valley. The material between such segments advances readers' perceptions of both the philosophical and the physical constructs that Le Guin concocts in an ascending spiral of elucidating information.

She focuses on feminist, ecological, and mythic concerns. The Kesh's locale, seemingly, was created by either global warming or some cataclysm (hinted at through allusions to uninhabitable, radioactive regions) that has turned San Francisco Bay into a gigantic inland sea and inundated much of the Pacific Coast, swamping its coastal cities. The coastal mountain range has become a peninsula.

Le Guin divides the world of the Kesh into nine venues or "houses," five concerned with earth (material things) and four with sky (spiritual things). Computers in City of Mind control the planet, but the Kesh elect to lead simple lives, leaving City of Mind to the Condors. The Kesh favor City of Man, which revolves around humans.

In *Always Coming Home*, Pandora grapples with the search for answers to existential questions. Le Guin's writing strains the genre in which much storytelling conventionally occurs, ever testing the limits of human communication. In so doing, however, her Pandora, as a self-declared anthropologist of the future, forces readers to think through the cultural constructs within which human beings live and on which they base their philosophical—especially ethical—systems. Is the structure of storytelling, for example, natural or something writers impose?

Le Guin is not alone in her search for new literary means to transmit complex information. In experimenting with Pandora, Le Guin blurs the lines of time and space. Pandora lives in two distinct contexts. Clearly, *Always Coming Home* is at the forefront of a unique, experimental fictional genre that simultaneously presents philosophy and fantasy.   —*R. Baird Shuman*

THE AMBER SERIES

In Amber, a world of magic that can be reached from Earth by "traveling through shadows," members of the royal family fight among themselves for control of the kingdom and the worlds it controls

Author: Roger Zelazny (1937-1995)
Genre: Fantasy—heroic fantasy
Type of work: Novels
Time of plot: Contemporary on Earth and undefined but resembling medieval Earth on a variety of alternate worlds
Location: Earth, Amber, and the lands in between
First published: *The Chronicles of Amber* (1979; two-volume set including *Nine Princes in Amber*, 1970; *The Guns of Avalon*, 1972; *Sign of the Unicorn*, 1975; *The Hand of Oberon*, 1976; and *The Courts of Chaos*, 1978), *Trumps of Doom* (1985), *Blood of Amber* (1986), *Sign of Chaos* (1987), *Knight of Shadows* (1989), and *Prince of Chaos* (1991)

The Plot: The story of Amber is told in two cycles, consisting of ten novels. The tale is extremely complex, written over a span of twenty years, and involves dozens of principal characters who are related in various ways. Amber is depicted as the "real world"; all other worlds, including contemporary Earth, are shadows cast by that reality. It is a world of magic and swordplay ruled by members of a bickering royal family who form temporary alliances and then regularly betray one another.

Outside Amber, the characters "travel through shadows" by creating differences in reality as they walk, ride horses, and occasionally even drive cars. Physical laws are different in the various worlds; a motor vehicle, for example, would be useless in Amber.

The first cycle, contained in *The Chronicles of Amber*, tells the story of Corwin, Prince of Amber. He is the son of King Oberon, who has disappeared. Corwin finds himself in a hospital in New York State, apparently injured in a car accident. He thinks of himself as Carl Corey and has little memory of his past. Gradually, he learns that there is more to his past than an ordinary earthly existence. His first clue is the discovery of a pack of tarot cards that includes trumps with the pictures of Corwin and his brothers and sisters. Eventually, he is contacted by his brother Random and brought back to Amber, where he learns about the Pattern.

The Pattern is a mazelike series of twisting trails that can be walked safely only by a member of the royal family. Corwin learns that he is in great danger. His brother Eric is trying to claim the throne of Amber and has placed Corwin on the Shadow Earth (contemporary Earth) to get him out of the way. Corwin therefore walks the pattern in Rebma, a mirror image of Amber under the sea, as a means of regaining his memory. He then faces Eric, who for a brief period has managed to seize the throne.

The rest of the first cycle is concerned mainly with various intrigues in the Court of Amber and the opposition of the Courts of Chaos, which stand at the opposite end of the shadows from Amber. Along the way, Corwin meets Dworkin, a mad but powerful wizard. It becomes apparent that Dworkin is the oldest member of the House of Amber and creator of the Pattern. The Pattern has been damaged, and Dworkin's madness is a direct reflection of that damage.

The final showdown occurs at the Courts of Chaos, where Brand, the evil prince who has been responsible for much of the bloodshed within the royal family, is killed after wresting the Jewel of Judgment, a powerful charm that Dworkin used to create the original Pattern, from Corwin. Brand falls into a deep abyss still carrying the Jewel. The Unicorn, a mythical symbol of Amber, appears with the Jewel around his horn and presents it to Random, indicating that he, not Corwin, is to be King of Amber.

The second cycle, beginning with *Trumps of Doom*, follows the adventures of Merlin, the son of Corwin of Amber, and Dara, a princess of Chaos. He is one of few who have walked both the Pattern of Amber and the Logrus, its equivalent at the Courts of Chaos. He is a computer programmer in San Francisco on the Shadow Earth and has built a new computer, called the Ghost

Wheel, that will not work. Merlin is content in contemporary Earth but is forced back to Amber when repeated attempts are made on his life.

The second series ends with another visit to the Courts of Chaos, which is seen from the inside. There, Merlin finds the answer to his many questions, and the Ghost Wheel finally is put into operation. The story is left open-ended. Because of the nature of the worlds involved and the differing time schemes in the various shadows, the series could continue indefinitely.

Analysis: The concept of parallel worlds is common in fantastic literature. Isaac Asimov used this idea in *The End of Eternity* (1955), though his method was science fictional rather than magical. C. S. Lewis created an alternate world in *The Chronicles of Narnia* (1950-1956), a series of children's fantasies with an overt Christian message. More recently, Stephen King embarked on an alternate world epic, the Dark Tower series, begun in 1982 and incorporating elements of horror.

Perhaps the most unusual concept in the Amber series is the ability of some of the characters not only to travel freely among the alternate worlds but also to create new ones in the process. When a prince of Amber travels through shadows, he does so by changing reality bit by bit. The characters speak various languages and have various identities in the worlds they choose to inhabit.

It is also possible for a shadow walker to bring materials from one world into another. In Amber, gunpowder is useless. Corwin, however, discovers that in the shadow world of Avalon, there is a type of jeweler's rouge that is benign in that world (and contemporary Earth) but highly explosive in Amber. He travels to a shadow world much like Earth except that South Africa has not been colonized by Europeans. There, he easily collects uncut diamonds, which he uses in the Europe of contemporary Earth to buy automatic weapons. He then has these weapons loaded with bullets propelled by the material from Avalon. With these weapons, he saves Castle Amber from invaders.

Unlike most fantasies, the Amber series is not a conflict between good and evil; rather, the fight is between order, represented by Amber, and chaos, represented by the Courts of Chaos. Underlying this theme is a strong suggestion that both Amber and Chaos are projections of something deeper and that one cannot exist without the other. Certainly, there are many characters who owe allegiance to both places. The most obvious is Merlin, who is searching for his father, Corwin of Amber, but was reared in the Courts of Chaos.

The ultimate reality of the situation remains elusive. At several points, various characters have glimpses of the "True Amber," of which Amber itself seems to be a shadow. There is a mythological assumption that the Houses of Amber and Chaos both spring from Dworkin and the Unicorn. The fate of Amber literally dictates the fate of the universe. All other worlds are shadows of Amber; therefore, if Amber is destroyed, all other places will be destroyed as well.

A final point concerns religious undertones. Although there are no references to gods as such, the Unicorn is more than an ordinary animal, and the princes of Amber themselves appear to be effectively immortal. Like the ancient Greek gods, they can be killed violently, but they do not appear to age as ordinary humans do, and they have amazing powers of regeneration. Corwin was first exiled to Earth during the Middle Ages, where he survived an outbreak of bubonic plague. In modern New York, he is still, to all appearances, a young man.

Amber owes many of its parts to sources from ancient legends and mythology to modern science fiction. The Amber books, for example, incorporate elements of time travel and use fantastic weapons. Sir Lancelot makes a brief appearance in *The Guns of Avalon*, and both Oberon and Merlin have names stemming from ancient legends.

Roger Zelazny has written many stories, varying from "sword and sorcery" tales to hard science fiction involving spaceships and alien worlds. In most cases, the distinctions between reality and fantasy, and between science and legend, are blurred. In the ten books that make up the Amber series, this is especially evident.

—*Marc Goldstein*

ANALOGUE MEN

Persons immune to the mind-controlling analogue machines survive a conflict and plan to rescue and control human society

Author: Damon Knight (1922-   )
Genre: Science fiction—dystopia
Type of work: Novel
Time of plot: 2134, with brief sections in the 1990's and earlier
Location: Various sections of the United States, particularly on the West Coast
First published: *Hell's Pavement* (1955; as *Analogue Men*, 1962; chapter 1 originally in *Astounding Science-Fiction*, 1951; chapters 2, 3, 4, and 8 adapted from the story "Turncoat," 1953)

The Plot: The novel relates a few months in the life of Arthur Bass, born immune to the analogue machines that, via instilled mental imagery, control the behavior of virtually all humans in the year 2134. Unable to function robotically in a world of fanatical capitalistic consumption and ideological indoctrination, Bass is discovered and rescued by a covert society of Immunes. They enlist his aid in bringing to eventual fruition their plan to rescue and control a schizophrenic Earth fallen victim to human greed and machine power.

The analogue machines were created as a means to control the criminally insane by instilling mental images. A prior authority figure in one's life would appear and prevent that person from committing a forbidden act such as striking another human. Soon afterward, American capitalists realized the potential of the analogue treatment as ultimate guarantor of free market consumption and profit. They contractually manipulated consumers to buy only from them, with analogue treatment as guarantee.

The result, after approximately 150 years, was a schizophrenic America, deeply divided ideologically and physically. Consumers and Executives in Umerc (United Mercantile Territory) have the motto "buy," and their sexuality is almost totally suppressed. They are separated by a high wall from the bacchanalian celebration of Weekend, in nearby Darien. The promiscuous mobs there have the motto "live" and attach little significance to consumerism. One section of America, Conind, has returned to the buying and selling of human beings. In each section, the rare appearance of a nonresident results in cries of "demon!" and a quick arrest and dispatch to the Blank, a small, mysterious section of Washington State from which no human has ever returned.

Bass is born a Consumer but promoted to Junior Assistant Salesman in Glenbrook Store. Because he is an Immune, lacking an analogue-created "angel," he cannot control his behavior sufficiently when he witnesses a "possession" (a customer refusing to buy or cursing a salesman). Further transgressions, such as trying to touch his girlfriend, result in pursuit by the Guardsmen and Bass's escape over the wall into Darien. Thus made aware of Bass, the Immunes recruit him for their education project. Subsequently, he becomes an Immune agent, promoting the covert attempt to gain control over and restore sanity to Earth by eliminating the analogue treatments.

Sent to Conind to investigate reports of surreptitious analogue deprogramming in preparation for an attempt to conquer and enslave the rest of America, Bass is captured and dispatched to the Blank. He is able to escape because he is immune to the analogue treatment there that removes all desire to leave. He returns to observe the end of the Conind-incited war, which involves little physical violence. The primary weapons are those of psychological warfare. Enemies are "possessed" by the influence of the "demons" from elsewhere.

Despite his misgivings about the Immunes because of their practice of killing people who become aware of and oppose their plan, Bass stays with them. He supports their plan to eliminate the analogue machines and realizes that he is "unfit for any but an agent's life" and has "nowhere else to go."

Analysis: As a suspenseful and entertaining narrative, *Analogue Men* is of the highest quality. The reader is led to visualize a future America so schizophrenic that Bass is driven by its extremes to one narrow escape after another as he tries to adjust to life in a world gone mad. The novel's dystopian presentation of economic exploitation via capitalism and technology logically extrapolates from economic and political trends, and the psychology of demonism is a realistic extension of class, race, nationality, and religious intolerance.

In its vein of prescient, cynical depiction of the degeneration of modern society into mind control and human homogenization, *Analogue Men* fits well with Aldous Huxley's *Brave New World* (1932) and George Orwell's *1984* (1949). This powerfully satiric, dystopian theme is implicitly and problematically contradicted by 1950's naïveté about both human psychology and covert political action, and even by a simplistic optimism. The leader of the Immunes quotes Friedrich Nietzsche and, apparently without ironic intent, is presented asking, "Can any society be sane and wise if its citizens are neither? If we spend less ingenuity on breeding men than on breeding garden vegetables, do we deserve anything but what we have always got?" The elitist and racist assumptions of this view are not questioned, and the Immunes' murder of opponents is condoned based on this implicit "super race" endorsement.

Equally problematic are the simplistic assumptions that anyone could be truly immune to the psychological controls of modern society and that such a privileged group covertly could direct the vast majority of "normals" to a better life. This is a simplified version of the *Walden Two* (1948) psychological elitism of B. F. Skinner. Skinner's views were adapted by Isaac Asimov in the Foundation trilogy, written in the same era as *Analogue Men*.

Ideas of elitism and control in *Analogue Men* doubtlessly derived from Cold War principles and practices. The Berlin Wall analogy to the walls between societies is instructive. The novel perhaps is most clearly seen as a thinly veiled allegory of Cold War conflict and as intellectually escapist in failing to address directly how to "get down from this tiger." The novel evades the issue of real, immediate improvement finally posed by Bass. The Immunes' leader simply assures eventual success, after enough Immunes are genetically engineered to combat the hopelessly insane masses. Such a perspective smacks of upper-class rationalization for the aggrandizement of power, wealth, and status. Ironically, the ultimate cause of the social schizophrenia in the novel is the very perspective Damon Knight creates for his heroic, rescuing class.

—*John L. Grigsby*

THE ANDROMEDA STRAIN

Deadly organisms from outer space threaten to depopulate Earth while a team of leading scientists searches frantically for a solution

Author: Michael Crichton (1942-   )
Genre: Science fiction—catastrophe
Type of work: Novel
Time of plot: The late 1960's
Location: Arizona and Nevada
First published: 1969

The Plot: With utmost secrecy, the U.S. government has been sending satellites into orbit to scoop up particles from outer space and bring them back to Earth to be studied. This undertaking is known as Project Scoop, and one of its purposes is to see if there are particles in outer space that are unlike anything known on Earth. Retrieval of the satellites poses a problem because no precise method of reentry exists that will bring a satellite to a predetermined landing site. Because landings can occur anywhere in the world, a system has been devised to either recover or destroy satellites, depending on whether they land in friendly or hostile territory.

One night, a satellite is tracked to Piedmont, Arizona, a remote town with a population of forty-eight. The first trackers to get there find dead bodies all over the streets. The trackers hardly have time to react before they, too, are dead. The government has prepared itself for such an emergency by having a Wildfire Alert team on call at all times. This team consists of a group of scientists with credentials in biology, bacteriology, pathology, and surgery. Wearing protective clothing, two members of this team fly to Piedmont, where they find two survivors, a baby and an old man. They also find the satellite and see that it has been pried open.

The satellite and the two survivors are flown to a top secret underground facility in Nevada known as Wildfire. This impregnable complex consists of five levels of research laboratories and is programmed to self-destruct in three minutes should its chambers become contaminated beyond control. One member of the team, Dr. Hall, the only surgeon and the only bachelor, is given the only key that will deactivate the nuclear self-destruct device.

While the scientists of the Wildfire Alert team experiment unsuccessfully with rats and monkeys, news comes that a military plane flying over Piedmont crashed when all of its plastic fittings disintegrated. Piedmont was supposed to have been destroyed by an atomic bomb, but the president held off giving the order. This proves to be fortunate, because the scientists discover that the space organism (now code-named the Andromeda strain) grows fastest when it has a source of energy. They also discover that the organism thrives on carbon dioxide and that people who breathe rapidly, such as the crying baby and Sterno-drinking old man who survived at Piedmont, escape its effects. Soon thereafter, the scientists notice that the organism is mutating. Now, instead of attacking humans, it attacks plastic. This explains the plane crash.

The fittings of Wildfire's chambers begin to disintegrate, and the automatic self-destruct system is activated. Dr. Hall barely manages to deactivate the system. By this time, the organism has dissipated into the atmosphere, where it continues to mutate into something benign and harmless.

Analysis: *The Andromeda Strain* was one of the first science-fiction novels to explore the threat of extraterrestrial biological contamination of Earth. In writing a story of bacteria and organisms, Michael Crichton shifted the focus of science fiction away from physics, chemistry, or advanced technology to an area that surpassed them all in menace. The thought of mutating microbes invading Earth and causing madness and death seemed more frightening than the remote possibility of a planet off its axis or the invasion of aliens from outer space. Germs can be more frightening than guns, and the fear of invisible microbes working in mysterious ways to wreak havoc seized the public imagination.

In this novel, Crichton introduces stylistic tricks that later became the stock-in-trade of science-fiction and thriller writers determined to make their works realistic.

He uses scientific jargon (for which he apologizes) to explain the scientists' work. As an M.D., he is able to dazzle the lay reader with arcane medical terms. As a computer expert, he was one of the first writers to use computer language and format to lend an incredible story an aura of reality.

Another, now-familiar device he uses is to assemble a team of experts, complete with their vanities and eccentricities, yet somehow indistinguishable from one another. Character development is unimportant in a work of this sort. In fact, the only character who really emerges as an individual is the old derelict who drinks Sterno. Crichton prefers to focus on what the characters do—or fail to do.

Human error is an important element in this story, often manifesting itself as oversight or neglect rather than wrongdoing. For example, obliterating Piedmont with an atomic bomb would have spread rather than destroyed the Andromeda strain. Neglecting to do autopsies on the rats that had been given an anticoagulant meant not knowing about how the strain functioned. Failing to recognize the progressive mutations of the strain leaves the team unprepared for the disintegration of the plastic tubes that seal the chambers. Whatever their drawbacks and errors, however, the scientists ultimately behave nobly and selflessly. They remain determined to solve this mystery even as they fear that things are coming apart.

Crichton's novels, entertaining as they are meant to be, are also cautionary tales. In this novel, filmed in 1971, his concern is with biological warfare and the dangerous experimentation that surrounds it. He is less worried about a strain from outer space than he is about an organism sent into outer space that mutates into something lethal before it is returned to Earth. He also is concerned about misguided motives and the perils of human error, especially human inability to control what is created. Ultimately, he presents the Frankenstein syndrome in modern dress.   —*Thomas Whissen*

ANIMAL FARM

The animals of Manor Farm drive off the farmer who owns it and establish a community in which all animals are supposed to be equal, but their ideal state is corrupted when some animals prove to be more equal than others

Author: George Orwell (Eric Arthur Blair, 1903-1950)
Genre: Fantasy—animal fantasy

Type of work: Novel
Time of plot: The mid-twentieth century
Location: England
First published: 1945

The Plot: A prize-winning boar named Major has a dream that he shares with the other animals of Manor Farm one night after the drunken farmer who owns the farm, Mr. Jones, has fallen asleep. Major advises the animals to reject misery and slavery and to rebel against Man, "the only real enemy we have." The rebellion, on Midsummer's Eve, drives Mr. Jones and his men off the farm.

Major draws up Seven Commandments of Animalism to govern the newly named Animal Farm, stipulating that "whoever goes on two legs is our enemy," that "all animals are equal," and that they shall not wear clothes, sleep in beds, drink alcohol, or kill any other animal. The pigs quickly assume a supervisory position to run the farm, and two of them, Snowball and Napoleon, become leaders after the death of old Major. Factions develop, and Napoleon conspires against Snowball after the animals defeat an attempt by Mr. Jones and the neighboring farmers to recover the farm at the Battle of the Cowshed.

Snowball is a brilliant debater and a visionary who wants to modernize the farm by building a windmill that will provide electrification. Two parties are formed, supporting "Snowball and the three-day week" and "Napoleon and the full manger." Meanwhile, the pigs reserve special privileges for themselves, such as consuming milk and apples that are not shared with the others.

Napoleon raises nine pups to become his guard dogs. After they have grown, his "palace guard" drives Snowball into exile, clearing the way for Napoleon's dictatorship. Napoleon simplifies the Seven Commandments into one slogan: "Four legs good, two legs bad." With the help of Squealer, his propagandist, Napoleon discredits Snowball's bravery and leadership in the Battle of the Cowshed and claims as his own the scheme to build a windmill. Every subsequent misfortune is then blamed on Snowball.

Thereafter, the animals work like slaves, with Napoleon as the tyrant in charge. Gradually the pigs take on more human traits and move into the farmhouse. Before long, they begin sleeping in beds and consuming alcohol. Napoleon organizes a purge, sets his dogs on four dissenting pigs who question his command, and has them bear false witness against the absent Snowball. He then has the dogs kill them, violating one of the Seven Commandments, which are slyly emended to cover the con-

tingencies of Napoleon's rule and his desires for creature comforts.

Eventually, Napoleon enters into a political pact with one neighboring farmer, Pilkington, against the other, Frederick, whose men invade Animal Farm with guns and blow up the windmill. Working to rebuild the windmill, the brave workhorse Boxer collapses. He is sent heartlessly to the glue factory by Napoleon, who could have allowed Boxer simply to retire. All the principles of the rebellion eventually are corrupted and overturned. Finally, the pigs begin to walk on their hind legs, and all the Seven Commandments ultimately are reduced to a single one: "All Animals Are Equal, but Some Animals Are More Equal Than Others." The pigs become indistinguishable from the men who own the neighboring farms, and the animals are no better off than they were under human control.

Analysis: Of George Orwell's six novels, the two most famous, *Animal Farm* and *Nineteen Eighty-four* (1949), were both written during the decade preceding his death. This animal fable is a political allegory of the Russian Revolution. The allegory, as various critics have demonstrated, has exact counterparts to the events and leaders of the Bolshevik Revolution, the October Revolution, and the development of the Soviet Union into a dictatorship under the control of Joseph Stalin.

The animals are led by the teachings of old Major, whose historical counterpart is Karl Marx. Snowball, the theoretician, represents Leon Trotsky, and it is Snowball who organizes the rebellion against Farmer Jones, who represents capitalism. Another swine, Napoleon, representing Joseph Stalin, discredits Snowball with the help of his propagandist, Squealer. Napoleon organizes a counterrevolution with the help of his guard dogs (the state police or palace guards, in terms of the allegory) and drives Snowball into exile (as happened with Trotsky), then plays one neighbor, Frederick (Hitler), against the other, Pilkington (a Churchillian Tory), paralleling the events of World War II.

Orwell explained his motive for writing the book in a special preface he wrote for the Ukrainian edition. He intended to expose the transformation of the Soviet Union from Socialism "into a hierarchical state, in which the rulers have no more reason to give up their power than any other ruling class." Ultimately, the democratic principles of Animalism as defined by old Major are redefined as the totalitarian principles of Napoleon, and the Seven Commandments are changed to accommodate Napoleon's reign of terror, particularly the two words added at the end of one central commandment to make it read, "No animal shall kill another animal without cause."

This barnyard fantasy demonstrates how an ideal state founded on humane principles easily can be corrupted by the real world. Brutal tyrants driven by greed and ambition may lie and cheat to achieve their own selfish ends. The novel is distinguished by its clarity of style and the apparent simplicity of its narration, which has made it a classic that can be read on one level by younger readers for its story content and on other, more sophisticated levels by those interested in its political thesis. It has become a model of political allegory, a small masterpiece that speaks eloquently to the turmoil of the twentieth century.

—*James M. Welsh*

ANNO DRACULA

In a nineteenth century England in which Bram Stoker's Dracula is not vanquished by his human foes, he rises to power during the reign of Queen Victoria

Author: Kim Newman (1959-   )
Genre: Fantasy—alternate history
Type of work: Novel
Time of plot: 1888
Location: London, England
First published: 1992

The Plot: *Anno Dracula* merges nineteenth century history and literary fiction in such a way as to blur the distinctions between them. Chapter 1, "In the Fog," opens with Dr. Jack Seward of Bram Stoker's *Dracula* (1897) recording on a phonograph cylinder, as was his habit in that novel, a murder he has just committed. His narrative clearly identifies him as the historical Jack the Ripper. As the novel begins, Stoker's famous vampire nemesis, Dr. Van Helsing, has his head on a pike on the London bridge, and Arthur Holmwood (one of Lucy Westenra's stalwart suitors) is now the up-and-coming vampire Lord Godalming.

Even more surprising is that in the quasi-historical realm, Count Dracula, identified as Vlad Tepes, has become the Queen's consort. All of London is trying to reconcile itself to the changes as more and more people "turn," or become vampires. Dracula has brought the Carpathian guard to Buckingham Palace, where Mina Harker is one of his vampire mistresses. Oscar Wilde has turned vampire but is still shunned for his homosexuality. Robert Louis Stevenson's Dr. Jekyll is studying the dual

nature of vampire existence and physiology. Seemingly every important nineteenth century figure from George Bernard Shaw to Beatrix Potter makes a cameo appearance.

In *Anno Dracula*, Jack the Ripper, first known as The Silver Knife, is at large in London, killing young, female, vampire prostitutes. His activities concern more than the municipal police, because his grisly murders are exacerbating the already dangerous tensions between the "warm" (human) and "turned" (vampire) inhabitants of London at a time when things are increasingly volatile. Various elements of society want Jack caught for their own reasons: the criminal underground because increased police surveillance is making their activities more difficult; Scotland Yard because his continued rampage is making a fool of the law; the ruling cabal, the Diogenes Club, because they serve the interests of the Queen; and Geneviève Dieundonné, a vampire of the pure bloodline of Chandagnac, because he is killing the unfortunate young girls whom she works so hard to save in the charity wards of Toynbee Hall.

Although this clearly seems a case for Sherlock Holmes, he unfortunately is not at liberty to investigate. He is out of favor with the current government and probably locked up in Devil's Dyke, a kind of concentration camp for political prisoners. Most of the novel follows the investigative efforts and burgeoning romance of Charles Beauregard, chief operative of the Diogenes Club, and Geneviève Dieundonné, a formidable and beautiful elder vampire. The novel concludes when Dr. Seward, alias Jack the Ripper, is brought to justice, ensuring Beauregard an audience with the Queen, which was the real goal of the mysterious Diogenes Club all along. In a spectacular final scene, Beauregard tosses the silver knife of Jack the Ripper to Queen Victoria, who commits suicide, liberating herself from Vlad Tepes' tyranny. The same deadly stroke makes Albert Edward, Prince of Wales, the king of England. Charles and Geneviève, with the help of Mr. Merrick (the elephant man), escape the ensuing melee. The novel ends with an inconclusive sense of where their romance will lead them.

Analysis: The clever melding of historical and literary characters in *Anno Dracula* will provide the greatest delight for readers familiar with Stoker's *Dracula*, the Victorian era, and the vampire traditions of nineteenth and twentieth century literature. Kim Newman draws heavily on these sources, but *Anno Dracula* is still enormously original in its inventive alternate ending to the original *Dracula* novel and in its attempt to add to the already large store of sometimes contradictory vampire lore.

Among the innovations Newman fosters are the ideas that vampires can be killed by a stake through any major organ, not only the heart; that they can see in the dark, but not through a dense London fog; that religious symbols, such as crosses, do not do them any harm, although older vampires such as Vlad Tepes still believe they do; that silver is lethal to vampires; that female vampires do not menstruate and consequently are incapable of bearing children in the "natural" way; that vampires do not feel the cold; and that some vampires can absorb a person's memories with his or her blood. Newman even introduces a cadre of Chinese vampires into the novel, giving him a chance to explore traditional Oriental vampire lore.

Like most vampire and occult novels, *Anno Dracula* has a moral point to make. Humans turned into vampires do not act very differently from their unturned counterparts. The poor stay poor, the vicious stay vicious, and the good are always battling evil, at what always seems to be a slight disadvantage. At the end of the book, as London steels itself for the new, disgusting crimes of the notorious Mr. Hyde, it is clear that the passing of the vampires will not end the brutality, crime, and sin that seem such an enduring part of the human experience.

—*Cynthia Lee Katona*

THE ANTHONY VILLIERS NOVELS

Anthony Villiers, a remittance man of noble birth, and his alien traveling companion encounter plots and strangeness all over the universe

Author: Alexei Panshin (1940-   )
Genre: Science fiction—galactic empire
Type of work: Novels
Time of plot: The thirty-fifth century
Location: The planets Star Well, Pewamo, and Delbalso
First published: *Star Well* (1968), *The Thurb Revolution* (1968), and *Masque World* (1969)

The Plot: All the stories involve the adventures of Anthony Villiers, Viscount Charteris, as he wanders the Nashuite Empire, usually in pursuit of his remittances. He travels with a Trog, a large hairy froglike alien, named Torve. Trogs are supposed to be banned from most worlds, but Torve manages to travel.

In *Star Well*, Villiers is on the eponymous gambling planet. There, too, are Norman Adams, a young Imperial

agent passing as a rich tourist, and a couple who attempt to practice the badger game on Villiers. They fail because Villiers finds the woman's performance generally unconvincing.

A spaceship arrives carrying Torve; Augustus Srb, an Imperial Inspector General (superspy) disguised as a priest of Mithra; and five young girls on their way to Miss McBurney's Justly Famous Seminary and Finishing School on Nashua, along with their chaperon, Mrs. Selma Bogue. Two of the young ladies, Alice Tutuila and Louisa Parini, hope to escape Mrs. Bogue's watchful eye and have an adventure. Villiers meets the spaceship and turns out to know Louisa, whose family are swindlers pretending to be gentry.

Godwin, the operator of the casino, and his superior, Hisan Bashir Shirabi, decide that Villiers may be about to find out the secret of Star Well: a hidden underground port used for "thumb running," the exportation of frozen corpses for body parts. They decide to have Godwin challenge Villiers to a duel and kill him that way. The duel takes place, but Villiers kills Godwin. Shirabi had given Godwin a useless weapon because he loathed Godwin and decided that Villiers was not an Imperial agent.

Alice and Louisa, who had sneaked downstairs to see the duel, are captured, frozen, and put aboard a thumb-running ship. Villiers notifies Srb and rescues Adams from the badger game before the "husband" can burst into the bedroom to catch him. They discover the thumb running and revive the girls. Villiers receives his remittance.

In *The Thurb Revolution*, Villiers and Torve start out on the planet Shiawassee. Torve enjoys making throbbing noises, represented as "Thurb" or "Frobb"; he combines them into compositions that he considers musical but Villiers and other humans do not. His Thurbs, however, fascinate three "yagoots" (bored young rich men) who follow Torve and Villiers to the planet Pewamo. They in turn are followed by Admiral Walter Beagle, a retired naval officer who is Chief Censor on Shiawassee and is Ralph's uncle. Admiral Beagle wants to protect the youth from suggestive reading matter in favor of such wholesome works as the children's books of Mrs. Waldo Wintergood. They are also followed by Solomon "Biff" Dreznik, a professional assassin hired to kill Villiers.

By prearrangement, Villiers meets his old friend Fred Fritz. They plan to camp out on Pewamo's main island in accordance with the teachings of the Big Beavers, a Boy Scout-like group in which Fred has attained high status. Fred likes such manly pursuits, but his parents want him to marry Gillian U, whom he has refused to meet. Villiers reads the Wintergood books and finds an obvious, if unconscious, sexual subtext. On the island, they meet a young boy named David Clodfelter and recruit him to the Big Beavers.

The yagoots plan to start a cultural revolution, one element of which will be Torve's Thurbs. Villiers realizes that David is really Gillian U and confronts her. She has come to Pewamo to meet Fred and convince him that she is an outdoor type, not the sort of silly girl he has been fleeing.

They all prepare to put on a musical show that evening. Fred tells Villiers that he fears he is falling in love with David. Villiers sets a trap (part of the Big Beaver training). Claude, a plonk (a talking pink cloud), has been following them. He informs them that he is God. Gillian passes a note to Fred admitting her true identity. Claude attempts to prove his divinity by showing that he is omniscient. He announces that David is really Gillian, but that already is known. He then reveals that Mrs. Wintergood is really Admiral Beagle. As Dreznik is about to attack Villiers, Claude scares him so that he falls into Villiers' trap. Dreznik decides that Claude really is God and gives up the assassin business to follow Claude. Fred and Gillian will apparently live happily ever after. Thanks to an article written by Villiers, Mrs. Wintergood's books attain new heights of popularity as Symbolic Pornography, a development that thoroughly disgusts the admiral.

In *Masque World*, Villiers and Torve land at Castle Rock on Delbalso. They pass inspection by Imperial Customs Officer Jerzy McBe. McBe's superior, Slyne, realizes that McBe should have checked Torve's papers more carefully. Slyne is an Orthodoxou, a sentient alien covered with velvety black fur. Orthodoxous, once in their lives, find the perfect odor and fall in love with it. For Slyne, McBe has that odor. Villiers is coming to Delbalso to see Jules Parini (Louisa's father) to get forged papers for Torve and to find out who had hired Dreznik to kill him. Torve is there to visit his pen pal, Badrian Beaufils, who lives in one of four local Monist monasteries.

One notorious inhabitant of Delbalso is the loathsome Lord Semichastny, who is obscenely fascinated by melons. The local government has passed the Winter-Summer laws, largely in an attempt to get him to leave, though they have driven away many others. Villiers visits Lord Semichastny, meeting the new Administrator of Delbalso, Henry Oliphaunt, and his wife Amita. Lord Semichastny schedules a costume party, and Henry gets

a Trog costume that transforms him. The Monists are invited but decline because they are playing a scavenger hunt type of game called Wonders and Marvels. The Monists try to make Slyne one of their Wonders, but he refuses. Occupants of the different Monist houses claim Torve, Sir Henry (in his Trog costume), and an alleged practitioner of the all-but-forgotten religion of Christianity (who turns out to be merely a historian who studies the religion and has some Christian artifacts). Lord Semichastny moves his party to the public square where the Wonders and Marvels game is being judged. Torve and Sir Henry dance together, and then Torve kicks Sir Henry. Villiers gets Torve's forged papers from Parini just in time for Torve to present them to Slyne, who had attempted to arrest Sir Henry as an illegal Trog. Lord Semichastny likes the party so much that he becomes a Monist. Villiers learns that Dreznik was hired by his hitherto-unmentioned brother Robinet Villiers.

Analysis: The books were originally published as "Anthony Villiers Adventures," but there is relatively little adventure or action in them, and less as the series proceeds. Much of the appeal of the series comes from the voice of its narrator, an omniscient figure (not Claude) who sometimes speaks in the first person but never takes part in the action. The voice is witty and cynical; this omniscient narrator sounds like someone who has seen it all.

The books are rich in references. In the first, Alice and Louise, trying to find out about the duel, "remained in an uncertain world where Villiers might be alive or dead" (a reference to the Schrödinger's Cat experiment). In the second, an encounter between two minor characters is described in the exact words of the first meeting between Isaac Asimov and Harlan Ellison, as described in *Dangerous Visions* (1967), edited by Ellison and published the year before *The Thurb Revolution*. In the third book, the Monist houses have the names of Brooklyn streets. The books have a strong philosophical element, including Torve's view of an acausal world where all entities are monads, following independent "lines of occurrence" that may or may not meet, and a continuing discussion of the medieval doctrines of realism and nominalism.

Star Well appeared shortly after Alexei Panshin had published two highly praised books: *Rite of Passage* (1968), which won the 1968 Nebula Award for best novel of the year, and *Heinlein in Dimension: A Critical Analysis* (1968), a study of one of science fiction's most popular figures. There were to be four more volumes in the

Anthony Villiers series, and at the end of the first edition of *Masque World* was an announcement that the fourth volume, *The Universal Pantograph*, would be published soon.

Panshin instead began writing with his wife, Cory. They did a symbolic fantasy, *Earth Magic* (1978), and some short stories but have mainly written criticism. This work has received mixed reactions. *The World Beyond the Hill: Science Fiction and the Quest for Transcendence* (1989) was widely praised for its close readings of classic stories from *Astounding Science-Fiction* and won a Hugo Award for best nonfiction, but their continuing love-hate relationship with Robert A. Heinlein and their insistence on a quasireligious element of "transcendence" as the essence of science fiction have been condemned. Many readers wish that Panshin had finished the Villiers series instead.   —*Arthur D. Hlavaty*

THE ANUBIS GATES

Brendan Doyle, a poet and historian, joins a jaunt back to the eighteenth century that turns deadly and permanent

Author: Tim Powers (1952-   )
Genre: Fantasy—time travel
Type of work: Novel
Time of plot: 1684, 1802, 1810-1811, 1846, and 1983
Location: London, England, and Cairo, Egypt
First published: 1983

The Plot: In *The Anubis Gates*, Professor Brendan Doyle is hired to give a lecture on Samuel Taylor Coleridge and then attend an 1810 lecture by Coleridge. The book's title refers to a set of holes in spacetime, created by worshipers of Anubis. Doyle and his party, led by millionaire J. Cochran Darrow, use one of these gates to travel to 1810. As they are leaving, Doyle is kidnapped by Dr. Romany, one of two sorcerers who created the gates. Romany takes Doyle to his camp to be tortured, but Doyle escapes.

Penniless and hungry, Doyle discovers that begging is the only employment for which he is fit. Romany has enlisted the beggar and thief guilds, led by Horrabin the Clown, to look for Doyle, but the beggars with whom Doyle falls in hate Horrabin and hide Doyle. Romany nevertheless finds him, and Doyle is forced to flee, escaping with the assistance of a young beggar named Jacky Snapp (actually a woman, Jacqueline Elizabeth Tichy, in disguise).

Doyle hopes to meet William Ashbless, a nineteenth century poet Doyle studied back in the twentieth century, and get some assistance. Ashbless never shows up where his biography claimed he wrote his first published poem, so Doyle angrily writes the poem himself from memory.

Doyle meets Dog-Face Joe, Romany's former partner, who is possessed by Anubis and cursed with ever-growing fur. Joe uses magic to trade bodies when the fur gets ahead of the razor, and he poisons his old bodies so they cannot tell tales. Joe switches bodies with Doyle, but Doyle survives. He realizes that his new body fits the description of William Ashbless, who apparently never existed, so Doyle becomes Ashbless. Doyle goes after Romany but is accidentally carried with the sorcerer through a gate to 1684. Doyle severely injures Romany and returns to 1810 alone.

Meanwhile, Darrow finally finds Dog-Face Joe, which is why he traveled to 1810: He wants to live forever. Joe will transfer Darrow into a succession of bodies, and Darrow figures to secretly own the entire world by 1983. Joe swaps bodies with Darrow, however, killing him. Joe is then killed by Jacky, who has been tracking him to avenge the murder of her fiancé.

Dr. Romany turns out to be a ka, a magical clone. The original, Dr. Romanelli, arrives in England, kidnaps Doyle, and takes him to Cairo. Doyle escapes and flees to England, but Romanelli recaptures him, along with Jacky and Coleridge. Romanelli tortures Doyle but is interrupted by a revolt of Horrabin's "Mistakes," the offspring of magically enhanced vivisection experiments. Romanelli flees with the dying Doyle to the underground river on which Ra sails the Sektet boat each night. Romanelli plans to ride the boat until dawn, when the Sun God is reborn, along with any passengers deemed worthy. Romanelli's soul fails the test, however, and it is Doyle who rides the boat through the healing dawn. He meets Jacky sitting by the Thames and discovers that she is his future bride: Jacqueline Tichy married William Ashbless.

They live happily together for many years, and the book ends when Doyle is attacked by the ka drawn many years before. Doyle kills the ka (which history has assumed was Ashbless) and begins a life that, for the first time in many years, will be a surprise to him.

Analysis: This is perhaps Tim Powers' finest novel to date and won the 1984 Philip K. Dick Award. Its fast pacing, one of Powers' hallmarks, never lets up from beginning to end. Highlights include further insights into the nature of a magical paradigm that was first outlined in *The Drawing of the Dark* (1979) and was used in *On Stranger Tides* (1987). Powers' theory of magic includes some engaging twists on old myths. For example, the power of a mage's real name presumably derives from its reflection of the mage's inner being. Thus, when a sorcerer undergoes a major personality change, his or her true name changes as well.

An important theme in this book is the gradual fading of magic. In Powers' schema, magic fades before the light of Christianity. As the last strongholds of magic-working religions are overwhelmed during the nineteenth century, magic gradually vanishes. As part of this process, the universe is transformed from a magical world to a scientific one. For example, until 1810, the sun actually was carried by Ra underground in a fabulous boat. By the end of the story, however, the underground channel has vanished, and the sun has become the ball of burning gas it is today. This is a delightful way to work the paradigm shift. In Powers' sixth novel, *Last Call* (1992), he uses a different paradigm involving the tarot and nonfading magic.

Powers brought the grotesque simile, another of his trademarks, to fantastic heights in this book. In one example, he describes a character's "blank smile returning to his face like something dead floating to the surface of a pond."

The plot of *The Anubis Gates* is similar to those of some of Powers' other novels. The protagonist encounters a problem, struggles against it, and gives himself up to drugs and denial but pulls himself together in the end. In this book, the "problem" that Doyle cannot face is the death of his first wife, and he is well on the way to becoming an alcoholic wreck in the first chapter. Being dumped into the nineteenth century in the midst of a struggle for mastery of the world seems to be what Doyle needs to take his mind off his misery.

An interesting facet of this book is the treatment of immortality. The Egyptian Master is more than forty-three hundred years old and is senile. His two servants, Romanelli and Amenophis Fikee, millennia old themselves, trudge through the same ruts they seem to have occupied since they reached adulthood. Extended life does not bring enhanced wisdom, and one is compelled to pity the doomed sorcerers even while loathing them. J. Cochran Darrow, the wealthy sponsor of the time trip, has personal immortality as his ultimate goal. This obsession destroys him and leads the reader to pity him. Powers' treatment of immortality strongly resembles that of Barry Hughart in the Master Li series.

—David C. Kopaska-Merkel

APE AND ESSENCE

In a post-apocalyptic future, a scientist discovers a brutal society of scavengers who worship the devil

Author: Aldous Huxley (1894-1963)
Genre: Science fiction—post-holocaust
Type of work: Novel
Time of plot: 1948 and 2108
Location: Los Angeles, California, and the Mojave Desert
First published: 1948

The Plot: *Ape and Essence* begins in 1948, in an office at a Hollywood film studio. Screenwriter/director Bob Briggs is recounting his marital and financial woes to an unnamed narrator. Unconcerned with Bob's troubles, the narrator contemplates the recent assassination of Mohandas K. Gandhi and the relationship art and science have to politics and commerce. The narrator's philosophy holds that the ideals of order and perfection are the aesthetics of tyranny and that nationalism and politics are corrupting forces. Gandhi died, the narrator decides, because he became involved in the "machine" of politics, a machine that destroys what it no longer can use.

When they leave the office, the narrator is nearly run over by a truck carrying rejected scripts to the incinerator. When the truck turns a corner, some of the scripts fall off. One of them is *Ape and Essence* by William Tallis. Curious about the author of this unusual script, the narrator and Briggs go to Tallis' address, a ranch in the Mojave Desert. They discover that Tallis is dead.

The rest of the book is Tallis' script, a surreal vision of Los Angeles after World War III, which involves the use of nuclear weapons. New Zealand, one of the few areas not ravaged by radiation, has sent several scientists to "rediscover" North America. The chief botanist, Dr. Alfred Poole, discovers a group of gravediggers in a Hollywood cemetery. All the diggers wear patches reading "NO" on the clothing over their genitals. Poole is in danger of being buried alive until he offers to improve their crops.

Poole discovers that this society worships Belial (the devil) and that he has arrived on Belial Eve, the night on which deformed babies are sacrificed by the ruling class of castrated priests. During the sacrifices, Poole talks with the arch-vicar, who explains that, in the age of the machine, humanity's self-destruction was inevitable.

The sacrifices are followed by an orgy. Although his prudish upbringing forbids it, Poole joins in the Belial

Day orgy with Loola, a gravedigger with whom he has fallen in love. Belial Day begins a two-week period of mating. Sex at any other time of year is punishable by death. A small percentage of the population, called "Hots," mate all year round. A community of expatriate Hots supposedly has gathered near Fresno, California.

Poole's report on the possibility of returning to agriculture is bleak. He argues that humanity is a parasite of the earth and that such a relationship always leads to the death of the host. Poole and Loola decide to flee Los Angeles and join the Hots. Crossing the Mojave Desert, they discover the grave of William Tallis (1882-1948).

Analysis: Although British by birth, Aldous Huxley moved to California in the late 1930's, partly because the pacifism he expressed in works such as *What Are You Going to Do About It?: The Case for Constructive Peace* (1936) made conditions uncomfortable for him in an England preparing for war. Although critics often generalize that the "American Huxley" was more a religious mystic than a satirist, his novels about Los Angeles— *After Many a Summer Dies the Swan* (1939) and *Ape and Essence*—show that his harshly comic view of modern society had, if anything, grown sharper. *Ape and Essence* is, in part, a critique of a world in which art is disposable (like Tallis' incinerator-bound script), in which scientists are manipulated by politicians into creating weapons of mass destruction (Huxley includes surreal visions of famous scientists led on leashes by baboons), in which sexuality is repressed while violence is not, and in which humanity poisons its habitat with by-products of scientific "progress."

The novel has several obvious contextual relationships to the events of the time. The Holocaust and World War II showed that human beings are willing to destroy one another in massive numbers, and the bombing of Hiroshima and Nagasaki showed that science was providing spectacular means for massive slaughter. Huxley had argued in his essays, especially *Ends and Means* (1937), that nationalism is the basic cause of these problems because it is used by people in power to control the masses. In *Ape and Essence*, the narrator of the prologue makes a similar argument. The assassination of Gandhi is developed as an example of how even a pacifist can be drawn into the cycle of destruction that politics and nationalism create.

The prologue is perhaps primarily an attack on popular culture and the commercialization of art. The maudlin, soap opera life of Bob Briggs obviously mimics the films cranked out by people such as Briggs, and Briggs's con-

cerns, including marital infidelity and tax evasion, are trivial in comparison to the narrator's concerns about the structure and direction of modern societies. Commercial art cannot deal with weighty issues because it must pander to popular opinion. It can serve only to distract people from what is really important.

Tallis' script is focused more on the role of science in the modern world. In the New Zealand scientists, readers see how the segmentation of science into disciplines such as botany, psychology, and geology creates scientists who can see phenomena only from the perspectives of their fields; no one has a broad enough knowledge base to see the big picture. Huxley was a strong advocate of integrated education, which merged different fields rather than treating them as mutually exclusive entities.

Perhaps more important, scientists have been the means by which those in power have gained weapons like the atom bomb. In *Ape and Essence*, armies of baboons slaughter one another with viruses "improved" by science to kill more efficiently. In contrast, science is helpless to restore what has been destroyed. Poole cannot enliven the irradiated soil. Some critics have argued that the escape of Poole and Loola provides the potential for hope.

—*Christian L. Pyle*

ARACHNE

A retelling of the Greek myth of the young Lydian tapestry weaver Arachne and her conflict with the goddess Pallas Athene

Author: Eden Phillpotts (1862-1960)
Genre: Fantasy—mythological
Type of work: Novel
Time of plot: Antiquity
Location: Ancient Greece
First published: 1927

The Plot: For two decades, beginning with *The Girl and the Faun* (1916), Eden Phillpotts wrote allegorical fantasies using Greek mythology to develop themes with contemporary significance. One of the best is *Arachne*, his retelling of the legend of Arachne, whom Pallas Athene transformed into a spider because the young girl challenged the goddess in weaving.

As the novel opens, Pallas Athene, goddess of wisdom, and her sister Hebe come upon Arachne of Lydia, who is creating designs from brightly colored stones but would prefer to make silk tapestries. Athene—known as the first weaver of Olympus—promises to teach the girl the art. Hebe expresses doubts, fearing that Arachne's innate talent could be harmed by Athene's interference and sensing that the girl will be reluctant to take Athene's advice and thus will anger the goddess. Indeed, at the first lessons Arachne is disappointed with the immortal's colors and designs and is bored by her philosophizing, although she acknowledges Athene's perfection, precision, and speed. When the goddess tells Arachne to copy Athene's tapestry, the girl ignores the model and creates from her imagination. A wealthy Roman purchases one of her tapestries, but the goddess says that in it Arachne has "broken from tradition, drawn opposed colours together, created disharmony, challenged elemental axioms and woven deliberate confusion."

The girl thinks that Athene is prejudiced and old-fashioned, and Hebe cannot assuage her sister's subsequent anger and disappointment. Arachne, eschewing marriage to devote herself wholly to art, starts weaving a grand tapestry that may take years to finish. As her father says, she "must do as her demon prompts."

Hebe, visiting when the tapestry is almost done, thinks Athene will delight in the work and appreciate it because, as an artist, she will realize its beauty. When Athene views the tapestry, however, she is uncompromisingly critical, whereas the erstwhile student is proud and disrespectful. This confrontation concludes with a challenge: Each will weave a tapestry for a committee of three gods to judge.

When the tapestries are complete, Zeus, Dionysus, and Hermes announce Arachne as the winner. Zeus explains that Arachne's work displays the treasure, loveliness, and emotion of Earth seen through the eyes of mortality, a vision forever hidden from immortal consciousness. Informed of the decision, Athene has Hecate send a hurricane to destroy the "sacrilegious web." Distraught, Arachne goes to a wood to hang herself.

Hebe, aware of this, saves Arachne but lies to Athene, telling her that where Arachne hanged herself there is a spider clad in her colors, concluding that Zeus metamorphosed the girl into a spider who will spin eternally. Athene accepts the story, and her anger fades. Only millennia later does Hebe tell Athene the truth: Arachne gave up weaving, changed her name to Echo, married, and lived happily as a wife and mother.

Analysis: During a long and prolific career, Phillpotts wrote not only realistic novels of England's Wessex region but also detective and science fiction, thrillers, and mythological fantasies. His short novels of the last category, particularly *Arachne*, demonstrate the narrative and

characterization skills he honed elsewhere, and although the stories come from familiar myths, he creates suspense, imbues his characters and their conflicts with convincing contemporaneity, and develops timeless themes.

At its simplest, the conflict around which the novel's action revolves is between goddess and mortal, but it is more complex. Athene is a straitlaced traditionalist challenged by a youngster's new ideas. Arachne, a precocious girl totally committed to her art, crudely and immaturely rejects the knowledgeable criticism of an acknowledged authority. The goddess lacks interpersonal skills and is quick to anger; she guards her preeminence and is petulant when she does not get her way. This clash of two strong wills propels the action.

By having Arachne surprisingly prevail in the struggle, Phillpotts shows his belief that a touch of hubris is acceptable, at least in a mortal, less so in a god. He also suggests that artists, particularly those with exceptional gifts, should be excused such aberrations of behavior as Arachne exhibits. Geniuses, he implies, must be tolerated and encouraged. Because he focuses on Athene's jealousy, intolerance, and arrogance, the latter two of which she shares with Arachne, Phillpotts seems intent as well on lowering Olympians to the level of mortals, with their failings as well as singular qualities.

Although Arachne eventually forsakes her art for domesticity, she does so only after having accomplished her goal, the creation of an unparalleled tapestry that Zeus and his committee prefer over Athene's effort. Whereas Athene's web may have been technically perfect, Arachne's had a wonderful, wistful beauty that only a mortal artist could produce. Phillpotts' rendering of Zeus's judgment encourages students to rebel against mentors and welcomes youth's rejection of tradition.

From early in the action, Arachne is pursued by two suitors: Polydorus, a patrician intellectual who humbles himself before the goddess of wisdom, and Mopsus, a down-to-earth country boy. Polydorus, who defers to the goddess and wants Arachne to follow Athene's artistic prescriptions, also encourages her to conform to social expectations by marrying, becoming a proper wife, and devoting less time to her art. Mopsus also wants Arachne to wed and settle down to domesticity, but not for reasons of conformity: He loves her and is afraid for her well-being if she continues to provoke Athene.

Although he is the suitor sanctioned by her family, Polydorus withdraws from the fray, concerned that his reputation will suffer if he continues to be involved with one who has rebelled against wisdom. Mopsus, who remains loyal throughout Arachne's trials, gains her love, and they marry. The novel closes, interestingly, with Athene asking Hebe what became of Polydorus. "He founded a School," she replies, "and attained to immense importance. If you think like everybody else, you are always of immense importance." Hebe concludes by noting that although the world is filled with Polydorians, their founder is forgotten. Arachne, the rebellious artist who did not think like everybody else, is immortal.

—*Gerald H. Strauss*

ARTHUR REX

A humorous re-creation of the legend of King Arthur and his knights of the Round Table, based primarily, albeit loosely, on the medieval romance by Sir Thomas Malory

Author: Thomas Berger (1924-   )
Genre: Fantasy—mythological
Type of work: Novel
Time of plot: The Middle Ages
Location: Great Britain
First published: 1978

The Plot: *Arthur Rex: A Legendary Novel* humorously re-creates the legend of King Arthur and his knights of the Round Table, from the king's conception in Tintagel Castle to his final voyage to the Isle of Avalon after his fatal battle against Mordred. Although he draws his material from Sir Thomas Malory's *Le Morte d'Arthur* (1485), supplemented by incidents from other medieval romances, Thomas Berger transforms the story through his exuberantly comic vision.

The novel opens with the account of how Uther Pendragon, king of Britain, falls in love with the fair Ygraine, duchess of Cornwall. With Merlin's aid, he assumes the appearance of her husband and conceives Arthur with her in Tintagel Castle. Reared in secret by humble foster parents, Arthur learns his parentage only when he draws the Sword from the Stone and thereby wins the throne of Britain. Arthur defeats early challenges to his authority from rebel Britons, an alliance of Angles and Saxons, and the Irish king, Ryons, who wants Arthur's beard to adorn his mantle. Arthur then acquires another sword, Excalibur, from the Lady of the Lake, begets Mordred with a lady who turns out to be his own half-sister Margawse, then marries Guinevere and acquires the Round Table.

The knights who sit at this table form a fellowship devoted to bringing about the triumph of virtue. After

describing Merlin's willing confinement by the Lady of the Lake, the middle part of the novel details their adventures: Tristram's ill-fated love for La Belle Isold; Launcelot's rejection of the Fair Maid of Astolat who dies for love of him, his rescue of Guinevere after her abduction by Meliagrant, and his conception of Galahad with Elaine, daughter of King Pelles; Gareth's year of service in the royal kitchens, followed by his rescue of Lynesse from imprisonment; the quest of Percival and Galahad for the Holy Grail; and Gawaine's encounter with the Green Knight, his marriage to the loathsome Dame Ragnell and her subsequent transformation, and his final mortal combat against Launcelot, his best friend.

Also included are the largely ineffectual machinations of those devoted to evil, most notably Morgan la Fey and Mordred. What ultimately dooms Arthur's realm is not assault from outside but failure from within. The story culminates in the discovery of the adultery between Launcelot and Guinevere, and the former's combat with Gawaine; the final, fatal battle between Arthur and Mordred, followed by the return of Excalibur to the Lady of the Lake by Bedivere, Arthur's last knight; and Arthur's voyage, in a barge attended by three veiled ladies, to the mystical Isle of Avalon.

Analysis: Authors familiar with Arthurian legend always have been aware of the potential for irony in it, even during the Middle Ages. Noble aspirations and high-minded ideals, even as they inspire heroic endeavor, do have their comic aspects. This ironic vision dominates a number of modern fantasies that invite the reader to measure not only the heroic achievements of Arthur and his knights but also, more particularly, the gap between expectations and results. Even before he turned to Arthurian legend, Berger had won recognition as one of America's leading satiric writers, winning praise for a series of novels about his character Carlo Reinhart as well as for his best-known work, *Little Big Man* (1964), which is set in the American West. This talent ensured that *Arthur Rex* would prove to be one of the finest ironic novels about King Arthur since Mark Twain's *A Connecticut Yankee in King Arthur's Court* (1889).

Berger demonstrates a keen eye for the ridiculousness inherent in the unrealistic conventions of medieval romance. He remarks, for example, that while the lower classes died from the diseases rampant in that era, knights died only in battle and ladies from love, as the sad fate of the Fair Maid of Astolat demonstrates. The exaggerations of those romances in which the knights perform superhuman deeds of valor are recalled in Launcelot's attack on Mordred's army, skewering foes on his lance ten at a time.

The author is particularly fond of mixing exaggeration with ironic reversal. The attempts of Morgan la Fey to murder her brother all go astray, for God, readers are told, protects the innocent. Moreover, when the would-be assassins are forgiven by the king, as they invariably are, they are released from the spell she had cast over them and thereafter lead lives of exemplary virtue. In disgust, Morgan eventually decides to reform in the belief that corruption is spread more effectively among humankind by the forces of virtue.

Although he undoubtedly relishes the humor of the situations in which he places them, Berger nevertheless retains a warm affection for Arthur and his knights. Despite the unscrupulousness with which evildoers seek to take advantage of their generosity, they struggle valiantly to maintain the right. The author adapts his medieval sources to emphasize the nobility of his characters, particularly Gawaine. Most episodes that reflect badly on his heroes he either changes, so that the heroes emerge with more credit, or omits completely, replacing them with adventures drawn from more favorable sources, such as the story of Gawaine's encounter with the Green Knight. As a result, the knights emerge as heartwarming, if impractical, champions of a better, kinder way of life.

Eventually, however, Arthur and his knights do go down in defeat, mainly because of an inability not only to adhere to their high ideals but even to discern what is the best course of action in a complicated world. Nevertheless, it is their achievements that are emphasized at the end of the novel, and they remain shining examples of how much can be achieved by those prepared to devote themselves to a nobler vision of the world, however foolish it may look to the self-centered.

—*Raymond H. Thompson*

THE ARTIFICIAL KID

Violence and biological and political mysteries of the planet Reverie intrude on the life of a performance artist called the Artificial Kid

Author: Bruce Sterling (1954-   )
Genre: Science fiction—cyberpunk
Type of work: Novel
Time of plot: Undefined
Location: The planet Reverie
First published: 1980

The Plot: Arti, the Artificial Kid, introduces himself and explains his persona and his performance art, which he produces assisted by his gang members and drone cameras. In the Decriminalized Zone, rival youth gangs strut and challenge one another, filming all the while. He and his friend and patron, Mr. Richer Money Manies, produce films for people living off-planet on orbiting platforms called oneills (a pun on Irish migrants and "one ills"). The Kid is recognized as the best of the combat artistes.

When one of the ritualized gang combats turns serious, the Kid suspects involvement by the Cabal, a shadowy group that supposedly rules Reverie. It later emerges that the problems are instigated by the evil professor Angeluce. The Kid, along with Saint Anne Twice-born, a virginal religious fanatic, and Moses Moses, a recently self-resurrected former leader of Reverie, find themselves on the run from enemies. An attack at sea results in the death of Armitrage, one of Kid's closest friends. Before he dies, Armitrage declares his previously hidden love for the Kid.

Saint Anne, Moses Moses, and the Kid tell their life stories while floating in the ocean waiting for death. They are rescued by a vast floating organic multicelled hydrogen balloon that carries rich mud from the ocean bottom to dump it in the biological stew of the Mass on a mysterious closed continent. In the balloon, they discover Professor Crossbow, the gilled neuter who had overseen the conversion of Rominuald Tanglin, who chose brain suicide but whose body is now the Kid's. Crossbow, an exquisite parody of a boring academic, had served as surrogate father to the Kid, who had Tanglin's adult body when he awoke with a child's consciousness. Crossbow and Moses exchange selves, and the former Moses helps Anne and the Kid across the mysterious continent, first through a phantasmagoric jungle and then through the Mass until he falls into it. He then mutates gradually into a tree, exclaiming about the miraculous biological process of which he is a part.

Annex and the Kid are rescued and find themselves heroes of extensive films of their adventures, the influence of which has also aided in the overthrow of the evil Cabal. In the first stage of the denouement, Money Manies explains that there was no Cabal at all but that Reverie replicates in social forms the complex molecular pattern of the Mass; therefore, the planet is its own government. In the second stage of the denouement, the Kid explodes this myth and correctly accuses Money Manies of being the power on Reverie. The Kid and Annex, who have both enthusiastically discovered sex, go off to a retreat where they make films and live in a state of uneasy balance with Manies, coexisting because the Kid can provide Manies with original footage.

Analysis: *The Artificial Kid* is part of the backbone of the first articulation of cyberpunk science fiction, along with Bruce Sterling's novels *Schismatrix* (1985) and *Islands in the Net* (1988), the short-story collection *Mirrorshades* (1986) edited by Sterling, and William Gibson's *Neuromancer* (1984). *The Artificial Kid* features the high-speed action; wild invention mixing media, technology, and biochemistry; witty cynicism; and implicit political criticism of 1980's and 1990's culture that define cyberpunk.

The Kid is himself a classic punk exhibitionist with kohled eyes, green-oiled body, leather jacket, metallic pants, plasticized hair sticking upright from his scalp, a handy repertoire of power drugs, and a cynical, distanced air from the violence in which he participates. Moreover, there is a lighthearted brutality, a sort of game quality, to what he does, even when the games are subverted by real violence.

The technologies created in the novel are various and fascinating. Sterling combines the drone cameras and other devices of futuristic media manipulation with a fascinating broth of biological creations that is a triumph of baroque envisioning. He theorizes that there is a biological gestalt on Reverie, that the swamplike Mass contains the immortality of all the gene-types on the planet, and he populates Reverie with exotic life-forms.

After the Kid and his friends become involved in the deadly struggle, their lives continue to be played out with wit and a self-critical style. The paradox of life as entertainment is near the heart of the novel. In fact, inside the fantastic decor of this novel there is a story of a Kid made to grow up and take on adult responsibilities, a cyberpunk "portrait of the artist" in which sexual maturation takes place when the Kid runs out of hormone suppressants.

In the character of Saint Anne Twiceborn, Sterling savagely satirizes religious enthusiasts. In Moses Moses, he attacks the aged who exert political control; they are sexually "impotent for decades," bored and disillusioned even by power.

The deliberately artificial quality, the comic-book feel, of cyberpunk novels such as this relates them to the times in which they were created. The keys of survival in the cyberpunk world seem to lie in getting by, being cool, and playing heroically but being aware that one hangs over a genuine abyss. The Kid is a gladiator hero as

portrayed by the media, but there is a quality of careless, slightly cynical awareness in his role playing that makes him able to "surf" a complex, fast-moving, and genuinely dangerous society. Political corruption in his world features complications of conspiracy and open exhibitions of wealth-based class.

—*Peter Brigg*

AT THE BACK OF THE NORTH WIND

A little boy named Diamond is befriended by the North Wind and finds in her an escape from poverty and disease into a world beyond pain and suffering

Author: George MacDonald (1824-1905)
Genre: Fantasy—high fantasy
Type of work: Novel
Time of plot: The nineteenth century
Location: London and Kent, England
First published: 1871 (serial form, *Good Words for the Young*, 1868-1870)

The Plot: *At the Back of the North Wind* was first published in installments, with the first appearing in November, 1868, and others from November, 1869, to October, 1870. This work, George MacDonald's first full-length children's story, has been reasonably popular.

The story begins with a little boy named Diamond who is growing up in poverty. He is the son of a gracious coachman named Joseph, who is married to a kindly woman named Martha. Joseph works for the Colemans, who are kind enough in manners but not very generous in paying their employees, who live meagerly in the weatherbeaten room above the coach house. Mr. Coleman's speculation in questionable business matters eventually leads to his ruin and descent into near poverty. This state of hardship improves Mr. Coleman's character but makes life even more difficult for Diamond and his family.

Diamond's family goes through many trials as he is befriended by the North Wind and goes on adventures with her. She first meets him while he is sleeping in his bed in the hayloft. She coaxes him to join her for flights into the night. Diamond is often uncertain whether he has actually been outside during the night or has only been dreaming. On these trips with the North Wind, he meets a little girl named Nanny whom he befriends and later helps.

Diamond learns that the North Wind destroys ships and chimneys as well as rescuing people. He is troubled by her seeming dual nature but learns to accept both sides of her. Diamond's own health is uncertain at times, and he is sent to his aunt's home in Sandwich on the seaside. From this home he takes an adventure all the way to the back of the North Wind, or at least to a picture of it, as he later learns. For seven days, he lingers near death before returning to consciousness.

Some time after Diamond has recovered, he returns with his mother and her new baby to a home in the mews near London. Joseph is working for himself now and using his favorite horse from Mr. Coleman's estate, the horse for whom Diamond had been named. Diamond proves to be a helpful child, even taking over the family business when his father falls ill. While working, he meets Mr. Raymond, a man who loves children and stories and encourages Diamond to learn how to read. With Mr. Raymond's help, Diamond rescues Nanny from sickness and seemingly certain death. Mr. Raymond later gives Joseph the task of watching Ruby, a lazy horse who needs exercising, while Mr. Raymond spends three months on the Continent. When Mr. Raymond returns from vacation, he has a new bride with him and invites Joseph and his family to move to the country in Kent and serve as the Raymonds' hired help. There the family enjoys great comfort and some prosperity. Diamond seems lonely, however, in spite of friends such as Nanny and her friend Jim. Diamond takes a few more trips with the North Wind and finally makes a last journey to the back of the North Wind. He dies in peace.

Analysis: Like many of MacDonald's fantasy works, *At the Back of the North Wind* evolves organically, with many loose ends and an unexplained conclusion. As his first full-length story specifically written for children, this work embodies many small messages for the young, much like his earlier work *Phantastes* (1858), supposedly written for adults. If a distinction between his writings for children and those for adults is difficult to draw, this is so because, as MacDonald declared, he did "not write for children, but for the childlike, whether of five, or fifty, or seventy-five."

Two of MacDonald's later fantasy works for children, *The Princess and the Goblin* (1871) and *The Princess and Curdie* (1882), also proved to be popular for a time. MacDonald's fantasy work bears some resemblance to *Alice's Adventures in Wonderland* (1865) by Lewis Carroll (C. L. Dodgson), an author with whom MacDonald often corresponded.

Throughout *At the Back of the North Wind*, MacDonald introduces themes such as the value of kindness, cheerfulness in spite of poverty, and helping one's parents. The North Wind introduces the little boy Diamond

to the harsh realities of life and leads him to understand that a positive attitude and selfless pattern of living will help everyone to endure the hardships of life more easily. Although they are not mentioned directly, much of this book emphasizes Christian values and Victorian ideals. The values of hard work, honesty, selflessness, and loving patience are all abundantly evident in the life of Diamond. He is sometimes teasingly called "God's baby" because his line of thinking is so different from that of other people. His good conduct makes the other coachmen feel ashamed of their cussing and mean ways.

These qualities of goodness in Diamond are prompted by his trip to the back of the North Wind, where he learns to be gracious and kind. Even Nanny, Diamond's spiteful friend, learns to be kinder by her dream trips guided by the North Wind while she recovers from a serious illness.

The strength of this novel lies in its imaginative presentation of difficult theological problems, such as providence or the hand of God as represented by the North Wind. The trials of daily life are seen as being potentially useful if people are selfless. What is less strong in this novel is the repeated use of lyrics, which are more chatty than interesting and purposeful. These verses do little to convey the beauty of the back of the North Wind, with which Diamond has fallen in love. Another weakness is the use of a lead character, Diamond, who seems too good for life. Like many of MacDonald's works, this one feels overly long, yet it is full of intriguing perspectives and imaginative treatments of the commonplace.

—*Daven M. Kari*

AT THE MOUNTAINS OF MADNESS AND OTHER NOVELS

In the primary novella, an expedition to Antarctica discovers the remains of a great alien civilization; other works describe various horrors

Author: H(oward) P(hillips) Lovecraft (1890-1937)
Genre: Science fiction—occult
Type of work: Collected works
Time of plot: The 1920's and 1930's
Location: New England and Antarctica
First published: 1964 (corrected edition, 1985; contains *At the Mountains of Madness*, 1936; *The Case of Charles Dexter Ward*, 1941; "The Statement of Randolph Carter," 1920; "The Shunned House," 1937; "The Dreams in the Witch-House," 1933; "The Dream-Quest of Unknown Kadath," 1948;

"The Silver Key," 1939; and "Through the Gates of the Silver Key," 1934, written with E. Hoffman Price)

The Plot: *At the Mountains of Madness and Other Novels*, which contains the title novella and several of H. P. Lovecraft's longer tales, was first published in 1964 by Arkham House, the Sauk City, Wisconsin, publishing house created in 1939 by Donald Wandrei and August Derleth for the primary purpose of making Lovecraft's work generally available to the American public. Until then, Lovecraft's tales had appeared only in the pages of such "pulp fiction" magazines as *Weird Tales* and were known to relatively few readers. By the 1950's, however, thanks to the efforts of Wandrei, Derleth, and other loyal members of the Lovecraft "circle," Lovecraft generally was recognized as the finest twentieth century American writer of horror fiction.

Although Lovecraft tried his hand at many kinds of horror story, he is best remembered for his tales of cosmic horror based on the so-called "Cthulhu Mythos." These dozen or so tales, which include both *At the Mountains of Madness* and *The Case of Charles Dexter Ward*, employ a common background: the idea that Earth was inhabited for eons before the appearance of humans by a race of extraterrestrial/other-dimensional beings whose tremendous powers dwarf those of humankind. These beings, which Lovecraft calls the Old Ones, continue to exist both outside the earthly dimensions inhabited by humans and, more threateningly, in crypts hidden deep within the planet's surface or below the oceans' waters. Under the right circumstances, with the aid of forbidden knowledge gained from such books as the dreaded (but wholly fictitious) *Necronomicon*, they can be called back.

Although Lovecraft's linguistic style—with its excessive use of adjectives and arcane spellings—might well be termed idiosyncratic, it is difficult, even among those tales employing the Cthulhu Mythos, to identify any "typical" Lovecraft plot. *At the Mountains of Madness* tells of a scientific expedition sent by Lovecraft's fictional Miskatonic University to explore Antarctica, whereas "The Dreams in the Witch-House" is the story of a college student's macabre dreams while rooming in a reputedly haunted house. *The Case of Charles Dexter Ward* concerns a student in Lovecraft's hometown of Providence, Rhode Island, who is possessed by the malevolent spirit of his ancestor, a seventeenth century wizard.

Certain threads do seem to run through most of Lovecraft's fiction. There is, for example, the nature of the "cosmic" horror on which he so often depends. Rather than being actively evil, Lovecraft's Old Ones are more frequently indifferent, oblivious to such insignificant creatures as humans and completely uncaring. The creatures in *At the Mountains of Madness*, for example, are certainly repulsive—in fact, they very nearly defy description—but what makes them truly horrifying is their seeming disdain for human life. This aspect of his creations sets Lovecraft apart from other writers of horror fiction. The Old Ones' behavior toward humans usually lacks either calculation or ill will. They behave exactly as humans might toward ants: Those that get in their way are crushed, without explanation or apology. Traditional religious symbols offer no protection, nor do prayers or more conventional weapons.

The characters in Lovecraft's tales seem, for the most part, to be cut from similar fabric. With very few exceptions, they are decidedly ordinary and nonheroic. By profession, they are often scientists and antiquarians, who often are stereotyped as cold and emotionless. Whatever victories they achieve seem at best equivocal and temporary. Lovecraft's universe, in which humanity's role is so minor as to be irrelevant, allows for little more.

Analysis: Since Lovecraft's death in 1937, his fiction has gained steadily in popularity and critical prestige. This is hardly surprising, for his work, taken as a whole, possesses a strange but undeniable power, in large part because he avoids the standard horror fare of vampires, ghouls, and werewolves. He concentrates instead on creating a sense of horror that is as much intellectual and spiritual as visceral. There are few "chase" scenes in Lovecraft's work and few of the battles to the death between heroes and monsters readers have come to expect from modern writers of horror fiction such as Stephen King. What readers experience instead is a gradually increasing sense of horror grounded in the awareness that the universe is not at all as people traditionally have conceived it. Humans are not the center of this or any other universe; they are mere specks of sentient matter protected only by their own ignorance and relative insignificance. All that knowledge finally can provide, as several of Lovecraft's narrators explain, is horror too great to bear.

A further strategy Lovecraft employs involves denying his characters the conventional props of religion and science. Lovecraft himself was a professed atheist, and his stories usually are set within a larger framework that might be called existential. The God of Judeo-Christian tradition is wholly absent, rendering moot the question of divine assistance in combating the monstrous creatures of Lovecraft's imagination. His characters neither seek God's help nor seem to expect it. In "The Dunwich Horror" (1929), perhaps Lovecraft's best-known story, several Miskatonic professors turn not to the Bible for help in foiling an evil plan to open the gates between dimensions, but to the *Necronomicon*. Science, constructed as it is from a mistaken view of the universe, is likewise of no real use. In fact, as the scientist-narrator tells readers at the beginning of *At the Mountains of Madness*, science's wisest course might be "to deter the exploring world in general" from uncovering more evidence of humankind's true place in the universe.

—*Michael Stuprich*

THE ATLAN SERIES

Cija, hereditary goddess of a small realm in prehistoric South America, leads a life of perilous adventure and ultimately brings about the downfall of Atlan (Atlantis)

Author: Jane Gaskell (Jane Gaskell Lynch, 1941-　　)
Genre: Fantasy—high fantasy
Type of work: Novel
Time of plot: Prehistory
Location: South America and the continent of Atlan (Atlantis)
First published: *The Serpent* (1963; published in two volumes as *The Serpent*, 1975, and *The Dragon*, 1975), *Atlan* (1965), *The City* (1966), and *Some Summer Lands* (1977)

The Plot: Cija (pronounced Key-a), hereditary goddess of a small realm in prehistoric South America, spends the first seventeen years of her life confined to an abandoned castle tower because it has been prophesied that she will bring about the downfall of her nation. The people of her country have been told that she died shortly after birth. Meanwhile, she has been taught that men no longer exist, so when she first encounters Zerd—the half-man, half-serpent to whom her fate is intimately tied—snooping around her tower, she thinks he is an extremely ugly, and insolent, woman. She is shocked when she learns not only that men exist but also that Zerd has conquered her nation and she is to be handed over to him as a hostage. In addition, her mother tells Cija that she must overturn her birth-prophesy by getting Zerd to fall in love with her, then killing him.

Cija fails in her attempt, escapes from Zerd's entourage, and begins a wide variety of adventures. She is raped more than once, tills fields, works as a cook, and becomes the mistress of a hostage-turned-soldier named Smahill. When Zerd finds her, she flees, in the process discovering that he produces poisonous venom. Cija stows away on a riverboat. Upon being discovered, she is taken to live in the court of a religious government. There she learns that Smahill is her half-brother. Eventually, she finds the way to Atlan, immediately before Zerd invades. She marries Zerd and becomes empress of Atlan.

The marriage soon proves to be loveless. In *Atlan*, Cija gives birth to a boy, Nal, who is Smahill's son, though Zerd does not know this. Zerd's first wife, Sedili, shows up. Zerd sends Cija and Nal to safety, but the accompanying troops are attacked, and Cija is forced into servitude. Zerd rescues her, and she gives birth to Seka, his daughter. After other exploits, including an encounter with a mad scientist who has created an "ectogene" from body parts, the native emperor of Atlan attacks. Cija escapes to the mainland with Seka, whom terror has driven speechless. Nal has disappeared.

At the start of *The City*, Cija is sold into slavery and prostitution in a city ruled by religious dictators. She soon escapes and discovers that this city belongs to her mother's realm. The high priest is her father. She visits the tower, now fallen into disrepair, in which she had been held as a child. She is captured by her father's troops. Because she is proof that he broke his vows of celibacy, he plans to kill her, but she is rescued by Smahill.

A herd of wild apes takes her prisoner and fattens her up with the intent of eating her. One ape, Ung-g, becomes her lover. They fall in love, but their idyllic forest life ends when the high priest's troops kill Ung-g and recapture Cija. Smahill tells Cija that he will rescue her if she will abandon Seka and become his lover. Cija refuses, but before the high priests cut her throat, her mother's troops rescue her. Her mother wants Cija to become reconciled to Zerd. Cija is pregnant with Ung-g's child, however, and does not know if Zerd will want her back.

Some Summer Lands is narrated by Seka, who loyally stands by her mother through kidnapping and forced abortion by Smahill, capture by Sedili, marriage to a cruel farmer in a town run by a warrior-turned-prophet, life with Zerd's serpent family, and various other adventures that lead to a return to Atlan. Seka regains her voice. Cija, Seka, and their traveling companion, Juzd (a priest of Atlan), all experience mystic visions. Atlan then destroys itself rather than be conquered. Zerd, Cija, and Seka turn their backs on what was Atlan, seeking a new land for themselves.

Analysis: The Atlan series, which was especially popular with readers in Jane Gaskell's native Great Britain, contains her later novels, but it is tangentially connected to one of her first, *King's Daughter* (1958), another story about Atlantis. All the books in this series are action-packed; the plot summary above describes only a fraction of Cija's experiences.

Some reviewers consider the Atlan series to be a mixture of heroic fantasy and popular romance, presumably because of the high quotient of sex and adventure, on one hand, and the female hero, on the other. Cija, however, is unlike the typical romance heroine. She never experiences an emotion that she would call "true love"; she either succumbs to an enervating lust for Smahill or passively allows herself to be ruled by Zerd. The closest Cija comes to love is her relationship with Ung-g, and even this began with kidnapping and imprisonment. Cija's life with Ung-g is more of a primitive satisfaction of physical and emotional need than the love that grows between the protagonists of a romance novel.

Furthermore, the romance heroine's ultimate quest is to be joined with another. Cija's quest is the opposite: to stand on her own and to cease being a pawn of others. Rather than seeking out the special personality that will mesh perfectly with her own, one of Cija's most important goals is to give up her personality so that she can become a true companion rather than a clingy lover.

The Atlan series might better be thought of as the inverse of the "sword-and-sinew" subgenre of high fantasy. The books feature the requisite amounts of hand-to-hand combat, explicit sex, and (for the most part) flat characters. The emphasis is on action, not ideas, and the language is matter-of-fact, not lyrical.

Cija, however, is the opposite of the barbarian hero. Although nobly, even divinely, born, she rarely wins her battles. Her sojourns into poverty do not ennoble or strengthen her; instead, they extinguish her beauty, sap her health, and dull her will to survive. The physical magnetism she possesses does not bring her success—it causes her to be raped by nearly every man she meets. Her many adventures do not bring her wisdom. Seka, instead, learns by the experiences that her mother forces on her. Ultimately, Cija must be rescued by Seka, who calls Zerd to them when Cija is ready to be his companion.

These adaptations of well-known forms alone make the Atlan series interesting reading, but Gaskell also seeks to infuse this high-concept, low-intellect genre with comments on Western myths. The ectogene is Frankenstein, tamed by Cija's kindness to him; life with Ung-g is a return to Eden; and the lost continent of Atlantis dominates the entire series. Gaskell lists a bibliography of twenty scholarly volumes on myth for readers who wish to identify strands of other legends in the series. These myths are not included merely for texture; Gaskell uses them to explore important issues such as the nature of love, obligations of parents to their children, the nobility of human character, and the worthiness of various goals.

Gaskell is the great-great-great-great-niece of Elizabeth Gaskell, who wrote novels of Victorian life as well as ghost stories for Charles Dickens' periodicals. Jane Gaskell was a runner-up for the Llewellyn Rhys Award for *Attic Summer* (1963) and received the Somerset Maugham Award (1970) for *A Sweet, Sweet Summer* (1969).
                                        —*Beth Rapp Young*

BABEL-17

Poet Rydra Wong travels in space to find the origin of the superlanguage Babel-17

Author: Samuel R. Delany (1942-　　)
Genre: Science fiction—extrasensory powers
Type of work: Novel
Time of plot: The distant future
Location: Earth, the Alliance War Yards, and aboard the starship *Jebel Tarik*
First published: 1966

The Plot: Rydra Wong, a poet and linguistics expert, is asked to decipher mysterious transmissions in a code called Babel-17. The transmissions are picked up in conjunction with sabotage attacks by the Invaders, who have been at war with the Alliance for twenty years. Rydra determines that Babel-17 is not a code but a language of unusual analytic properties.

She recruits a starship crew to seek the location of the next attack. In Earth orbit, her ship is sabotaged, knocking out all external navigational sensors. Via Babel-17, she solves the problem of fixing the ship's position by using the physics and mathematics implicit in that language's description of great circles. Rydra comes to believe that one of the crew must be an Invader spy.

At their destination, the Alliance War Yards, Rydra and her crew are invited to an elaborate dinner party by Baron Ver Dorco, who is in charge of weapons research. During the party, the baron is assassinated by a genetically engineered spy/saboteur designated TW-55. Rydra and crew escape, but their ship is sabotaged once again. Rydra's crew blacks out.

They wake aboard an interstellar privateer, the *Jebel Tarik*. Again using knowledge of Babel-17, Rydra helps Jebel and his lieutenant, the Butcher, win a battle against an Invader ship. Afterward, she uses the language to discover a plot against Jebel and the Butcher.

Rydra also discovers that the Butcher does not have the concept of the personal pronoun "I" and that her own superhuman ability with languages is in part telepathic. Rydra begins to teach the Butcher the concepts "I" and "you," and she discovers that he is amnesiac. He recalls no childhood, only the exploits of a criminal career.

Rydra and the Butcher defeat another Invader ship, then leave to deliver her report on Babel-17 to Administrative Alliance Headquarters. During the trip, the two merge telepathically into a single being. Rydra makes a tape analyzing Babel-17 and sends it to Dr. Markus T'mwarba, her psychiatrist, on Earth.

When T'mwarba goes to claim the tape, he finds Rydra and the Butcher in custody. General Forester tells T'mwarba of evidence linking the wave of sabotage attempts to the Butcher. Rydra has told T'mwarba that Babel-17 is like a computer language, in which insoluble paradoxes are easily constructed. By being forced to solve the paradoxes, the Butcher is driven to remember his past. He is Nyles Ver Dorco, son of the baron who was killed at the War Yards. He was programmed with Babel-17 by the Invaders. The nature of the language makes anyone who learns it a saboteur; thus, Rydra, after learning it, unconsciously was responsible for sabotaging her own spacecraft. Rydra and the Butcher escape in an Alliance battleship. Using their reprogrammed version of the language, Babel-18, they hope to end the war in six months.

Analysis: In *Babel-17* Samuel R. Delany explores the nature of language and its relationship to thought. The theory of language on which the book is based derives from the work of Benjamin Whorf, who believes that the language people speak defines what they know and how they understand the world around them (the "Whorfian hypothesis"). Delany uses this idea to craft a story around Rydra Wong, a poet, telepath, and linguistic genius who discovers an artificially constructed language, Babel-17, that has been "booby-trapped" to impose certain thought patterns on its speakers.

Specifically, it is designed to turn any speaker into a saboteur of Rydra's government, the Alliance, and to prevent any criticism of this goal by removing the sense of self. Because Babel-17 does not contain the concept of "I," it is impossible for the speakers to conceive of their own identity, needs, or goals. The Butcher, who has been programmed thoroughly by the language, also has had his memory erased in order to ensure that he has no possible external stance from which to criticize his own actions, that is, no remnant of the concept of "I." Delany likens this lack of self-criticism to computer languages such as Algol and Fortran. Not only does Babel-17 program certain behaviors, but it also prevents the speaker from questioning those behaviors.

Like computer languages, Babel-17 also has formidable analytic properties. Simply by thinking about a subject in Babel-17, the speaker instantly is able to comprehend complex situations and choose a course of action. For example, when Rydra wakes aboard a space privateer, the *Jebel Tarik*, she is bound in a hammocklike webbing. Under normal circumstances, it would hold her, but the web as described in Babel-17 is a single word whose vowels and pitch identify the weakest points. With this knowledge, Rydra easily frees herself. Later, she uses the same kind of linguistic reasoning to break up an enemy attack on the *Jebel Tarik*.

The novel also explores social ideas such as alternative sexual arrangements. Rydra's space navigators are Ron and Calli, two men, and Mollya, a woman. Together they form a "triad," a psychic and sexual unit. The arrangement reflects the author's own domestic life at the time, as described in his autobiography, *The Motion of Light in Water* (1988). The other characters on the crew have mythic qualities that, added to Rydra's telepathic and linguistic powers, make her seem like a sorceress. Outstanding among them are the pilot, Brass, who is part man and part lion, and the three "discorporates" who act as the ship's sensors and who are, more or less, ghosts. Rydra's command of Babel-17 and the amazing powers it confers borders on magic anyway. With this cast of familiars, she becomes a futuristic Circe.

—George E. Nicholas

BAREFOOT IN THE HEAD

A European society altered by various psychedelic chemicals creates a cult messiah out of Colin Charteris, who begins to believe the myths about him and attempts to live out the image, unsuccessfully and tragically

Author: Brian W. Aldiss (1925-   )
Genre: Science fiction—dystopia
Type of work: Novel
Time of plot: The near future
Location: Western Europe
First published: 1969

The Plot: Colin Charteris is a nineteen-year-old Jugoslav and an official in the New United Nations Strategic Air Command (NUNSACS). That agency has an ostensible mission of aiding in the rehabilitation of war victims in a Europe maddened by psychedelic bombs. Told in episodic form, the story follows Charteris as he wends his way across the continent, driving a Banshee into repeated auto crashes, moving from the south of France toward England, and eventually returning to his home.

In Metz, his hallucinogenic vision leads him to discover that time is merely a fabrication of matter and that matter itself is merely another hallucination. During the vision, he thinks of himself as God, and he tells the hotel maid, Angelina, who becomes his mistress, that he had wished to experience mystical insights similar to those of Russian philosopher P. D. Ouspenski. Charteris wonders if the vision may have been induced by drugs. Ouspenski's work on Armenian mystic G. I. Gurdjieff provides the novel with its structure. His influence, together with the stylistic inventions of James Joyce, is acknowledged by Brian Aldiss.

During his travels across Europe, Charteris experiences dreams as reality and undergoes other phenomena related by both Ouspenski and Gurdjieff. Soon he comes to think of the two mystics as one and relives some of their psychic visions, such as hearing the crunch of muscles, perceiving the inherent motion of stones, and knowing the multiple "I's" within a person. Charteris comes to think of himself in Gurdjieffian terms as Man the Driver, then eventually as Saint Charteris, leader of the Fourth World System and New Thought. (Aldiss derived the name of his protagonist from Leslie Charteris, the author of the "Saint" detective series.)

A succession of increasingly bizarre incidents leads Charteris to be hailed by various citizens as a saint, and he soon comes to believe their projections. Huge crowds follow him as he leads a virtual pilgrimage or crusade across Europe, accompanied by a vast panoply of hangers-on and camp followers including rock bands and film producers. Angelina, his mistress, remains faithful to him. Her name is significant, symbolizing at once the redemptive aspect of the feminine as well as the angelic. She remains faithful even when Charteris takes several other mistresses and accidentally kills several people as his motorcade proceeds along highways doubled or tripled in width to accommodate speedsters under the influence of psychedelic drugs.

Even though he walks on water and is apparently headed for a crucifixion, he comes to realize that his crusade to find the Christ self, which in turn becomes intermixed with his search for Gurdjieff-Ouspenski, is futile. All the events in the novel become confused in various parodies of the myth of the eternal return. Charteris lives to be ninety years old, and in what may well be a reference to the Buddha sitting in enlightenment under the Boh tree, he inches toward death.

Analysis: *Barefoot in the Head* (subtitled *A European Fantasia*) is a difficult yet rewarding novel. Aldiss intersperses many poems as inter-chapters. The poems augment, reflect, or explain the events of the novel. The stylistic techniques of Aldiss' writing become increasing dense, allusive, elusive, and rewarding.

James Joyce's linguistic experiments, begun in *Ulysses* (1922) and continued in *Finnegans Wake* (1939), are at the heart of *Barefoot in the Head*. The book is also filled with wordplay of all types, including complicated multilevel puns and abstruse figures of speech. Aldiss makes literary references to such diverse writers as William Shakespeare, John Milton, T. S. Eliot, and Joyce himself, as well as references to both Gurdjieff and Ouspenski. Joyce was often concerned with the myth of the eternal return, but Gurdjieff did not advocate the subject, believing that it discouraged striving for change.

In this novel, when everything seems twisted and out of shape, and when the concepts of traditional narrative linearity are often difficult to follow, Aldiss seems to be not only mirroring the psychedelic experiments of the 1960's but also providing some cautionary warnings. Aldiss, however, is never sermonic, and his own beliefs, whatever they might have been, are hidden carefully under the thrust of narrative structure and the complications of plot and character. The novel is written almost in a molecular structure, with the electrons of the various plot elements spinning around one another, intermixing or impinging on the central themes of Man the Driver, Man the Searching, Man the Unpredictable, and Man the Mechanical.

For all the difficulties encountered in reading *Barefoot in the Head*, its abundant humor is not to be overlooked. Aldiss uses an exuberant, almost joyful style, at once deliberative and ecstatic, even considering the nature of the story line. Although baleful in subject matter, the novel is ultimately joyful in both conception and execution and is certainly one of Aldiss' most intriguing works.

—*Willis E. McNelly*

BARON MÜNCHAUSEN'S NARRATIVE OF HIS MARVELLOUS TRAVELS AND CAMPAIGNS IN RUSSIA

A collection of short tales describing the exaggerated and impractical adventures of a celebrated German soldier

Author: Rudolf Erich Raspe (1737-1794)
Genre: Fantasy—alternate history
Type of work: Stories
Time of plot: The eighteenth century
Location: Germany, Poland, Russia, Turkey, and the Moon
First published: 1785 (serial form for the bulk of the first edition, *Vademecum für Lustige Leute*, 1781 and 1783)

The Plot: The original *Baron Münchausen's Narrative of His Marvellous Travels and Campaigns in Russia* was published late in 1785, though its title page bears the date 1786. Published anonymously as authentic reminiscences, this slim volume recounted in fourteen anecdotes of some four thousand words each the preposterous experiences of an old German soldier. As a result of its immediate success, Rudolf Erich Raspe brought out a new edition with five additional "naval adventures," published as *Singular Travels, Campaigns, Voyages, and Sporting Adventures of Baron Munnikhouson, Commonly Pronounced Munchausen; as He Relates Them over a Bottle When Surrounded by His Friends* (1786). At this point, Raspe's influence ends. A host of ambitious editors and authors added to, embellished, illustrated, and amended the original author's work. By the turn of the century, there were at least fifteen editions, and Raspe's humble collection of tall tales had grown ninefold in the hands of inferior writers.

As a picaresque romance, *Baron Münchausen's Narrative* minimizes plot. Each of the stories introduces a separate conflict that bears little or no relation to previous circumstances. Using resources beyond belief and his own supernatural skills, the baron stretches luck to the limit. For example, on a snowy journey from his home to Russia, he ties his horse to a stump in the square of a Polish village. Upon waking, he notices that a "sudden change of weather" has taken place and that his horse is now dangling far above him, tied to the weathercock of the steeple. He quickly resolves the problem, using his pistol to shoot through the bridle, enabling the horse to continue the journey. Only the baron and his resourcefulness remain constant, however. In the very next anecdote, the faithful horse, now pulling a sledge, is eaten by a ravenous wolf that, by virtue of its meal, slips into the harness and carries Münchausen on to his destination.

The original narrative of 1785, comprising chapters 2 through 6 of most modern editions, was restricted to Münchausen's travels in northeastern Europe, a brief period of slavery in Turkey, and an even briefer sojourn to the Moon for the purely practical purpose of retrieving a royal axe that he had flung inadvertently into space. The success of these grand impostures led Raspe to expand the memory of his imaginary hero, who swore that his naval adventures were "equally authentic." These incorporated further improbable adventures in England, France, the Mediterranean, and Turkey, including the story of how Münchausen's friend (or the baron himself in some editions) was conceived in the subterranean apartment of an attractive but promiscuous seller of oysters who attracted the roving eye of Pope Clement XIV as he passed her on a Roman street.

Without copyright provisions, publishers were free to expropriate Raspe's version of what were anyway popular folktales emanating from the human propensity for exaggeration. Various authors led Münchausen on extraordinary adventures farther and farther afield. Whereas the core of Raspe's laconic narrative had been relatively coherent and rooted in eighteenth century events, new anecdotes often were disconnected, ponderously developed flights of pure fancy. In one chapter alone, for example, Münchausen is made to travel through the deserts and forests of North America, where he is scalped and burned in making his way to the Kamchatka peninsula, from there down to Tahiti and over to Panama, where he repeatedly ploughed the isthmian earth with the chariot of Queen Mab before returning to England, "having wedded the Atlantic Ocean to the South Seas."

Analysis: The appeal of *Baron Münchausen's Narrative* is rooted in an unusual combination of understated satirical wit, exotic venue, and legendary tall tale. Obvious models are Lucian's "Voyage to the Underworld," which elevated the value of a lie; the fifteenth century *Arabian Nights' Entertainments*, rich in supernatural and unexpected circumstances; and François Rabelais' *Gargantua and Pantagruel* (1533-1567), exaggerations composed across time and by several hands. Voyages of discovery from Homer's sixth century B.C. *The Odyssey* onward have captivated people's imaginations, the exotic surroundings both entertaining and enlarging the capacity of readers to isolate themselves in unfamiliar surroundings, free from ordinary human constraints.

Like Rabelais and Jonathan Swift after him, Raspe developed his stories around contemporary events. The surname of the hero is taken from a noble family of Brunswick, the hero himself being patterned on a younger son, Captain Hieronymous Karl Friederich,

Freiherr von Münchhausen. Although it is unclear if Raspe and Münchhausen ever met, the author had known Münchhausen's cousin and certainly was aware of the German soldier's legendary exploits in the Russian service. The real baron not only served against the Turks, witnessed the eclipse of German influence at St. Petersburg, and was driven from Russia—events that can be traced in Raspe's narrative—but upon his retirement at the age of forty became known for his hospitality and "narration of palpable absurdities." Added to the real-life adventures of this colorful figure, however, was the residue of a lifetime of eclectic reading, including popular collections of folk stories such as *Scharaffenland*, in which the biggest liar was the king. The substance of many of Raspe's anecdotes can be found in medieval monkish drolleries composed to relieve the boredom of secluded life.

Raspe's narrative is distinctive in taking direct aim at the perpetrators of preposterous memory, though one should not make too much of his achievement. Pompous old soldiers and country gentlemen are easy targets of satire. On the other hand, few have ventured to retell their exaggerations. Raspe succeeded in combining travel fantasy, local tradition, and contemporary gossip in exactly the right proportions, a feat that the lesser hands of the later editions were unable to achieve.

—John Powell

THE BARSOOM SERIES

John Carter, a Civil War veteran, journeys to Mars in a series of out-of-body experiences and establishes himself as one of the most respected warriors on the red planet

Author: Edgar Rice Burroughs (1875-1950)
Genre: Science fiction—planetary romance
Type of work: Novels
Time of plot: The late nineteenth and early twentieth centuries
Location: Earth and Mars
First published: *A Princess of Mars* (1917; serial form, as by Norman Bean, "Under the Moons of Mars," *All-Story Magazine*, 1912), *The Gods of Mars* (1918; serial form, *All-Story Magazine*, 1913), *The Warlord of Mars* (1919; serial form, *All-Story Magazine*, 1913-1914), *Thuvia, Maid of Mars* (1920; serial form, *All-Story Weekly*, 1916), *The Chessmen of Mars* (1922), *The Master Mind of Mars* (1928), *A Fighting Man of Mars* (1931), *Swords of Mars* (1936), *Synthetic Men of Mars* (1940), *Llana of*

Gathol (1948; serial form, *Amazing Stories*, 1941), and *John Carter of Mars* (1964; serial form, *Amazing Stories*, 1941-1943)

The Plot: Although the Barsoom series was written over a long period of time and spans a long time in its internal chronology, Edgar Rice Burroughs sustained his narrative by creating a plot line that chronicled the adventures of a family, not one individual. Through eleven novels, originally serialized in popular science-fiction magazines, the history of Mars is traced from ancient times to the present.

Seeking to recoup his fortunes after the defeat of the Confederacy, John Carter leaves Virginia to prospect for gold in Arizona. While trying to rescue his partner, who has been ambushed by Apaches, Carter is trapped in a cave by the same warriors, undergoes an out-of-body experience, and awakes on Mars.

A Princess of Mars initiates a series of amazing adventures. After being captured by a band of Tharks, the four-armed green men of Barsoom, the native name of Mars, Carter wins their admiration by strength of arms. Accepted into this warrior culture, he masters their language and encounters another captive, Dejah Thoris, Princess of Helium, a beautiful woman of the red Martian race. Carter falls in love with the princess, whom he rescues. They marry, and for nine years their happiness is complete. Then, while trying to save the system that stabilizes the atmosphere of Mars, Carter collapses. When he awakes, he is again in the cave.

After willing himself to return to Barsoom, Carter begins his adventures anew in *The Gods of Mars*. As he reveals the hypocrisy in the Martian religion, Carter encounters carnivorous plant men, vicious white apes, the white race, and finally the black race of Mars. After an absence of a decade, Carter is surprised and delighted to find his son, Carthoris, who is almost grown. They escape death only to discover Dejah Thoris trapped in an impregnable prison.

Having delivered the Martians from the religion that had duped uncounted generations, Carter rescues his beloved in *The Warlord of Mars*. While seeking Dejah Thoris, he encounters the yellow race of Mars, overthrows a tyranny more pernicious than any he had yet encountered, and is proclaimed Warlord of Barsoom.

Thuvia, Maid of Mars is a love story that relates the adventures of Carthoris. Thuvia, princess of Ptarth, is kidnapped by a rejected suitor who frames Carthoris with the crime, but Carthoris proves his innocence and wins his bride after a series of harrowing adventures.

Tara of Helium, the daughter of Carter and Dejah Thoris, is the heroine of *The Chessmen of Mars*. After she lands her damaged aircraft in a violent windstorm, Tara begins a series of adventures that include her capture by the inhabitants of the city of Manator, who play jetan, the Martian version of chess, to the death with living beings. Through the same tenacity shown by the other members of her family, Tara overcomes all difficulties.

Inspired by Carter's example, Ulysses Paxton escapes from the trenches of World War I and awakes in the clinic of Ras Thavas, the title character of *The Master Mind of Mars*, who has perfected a technique for transplanting organs—including the brain—from one human to another. When an evil ruler purchases the body of the woman whom Paxton loves, the Earthman embarks on a successful quest to rescue his beloved.

A Fighting Man of Mars relates the quest of Tan Hadron, who saves Mars while trying to rescue the woman he loves from a power-crazed warlord. Absent from this narrative are the philosophical speculations that form an important part of *The Gods of Mars* and *The Master Mind of Mars*. This tale is pure adventure.

Swords of Mars is fascinating not merely for the swashbuckling exploits found in all the Barsoom novels but also for the introduction of an artificial brain capable of guiding a Martian airborne vessel. After Dejah Thoris is injured in an accident, Carter seeks Ras Thavas, the mastermind of Mars, who is unfortunately the prisoner of his own creations, a group of artificial humans. Following a series of harrowing escapades, *Synthetic Men of Mars* concludes with the treatment and recovery of Dejah Thoris.

In *Llana of Gathol*, Carter encounters a race of white men who have lived in secret for ages in one of the ruined cities of Mars. His discovery of this race sets in motion a number of exploits that lead him across the face of the planet. He ends his adventure by delivering the city of Gathol from Hin Abtol, a would-be conqueror from the frozen wastes of Barsoom.

In the final volume, *John Carter of Mars*, the red planet is threatened by a gigantic white ape that is the creation of a scientist gone mad. The Warlord of Mars once again delivers his adopted home from destruction.

Analysis: With the publication of *A Princess of Mars*, his first novel, Burroughs began a series that would have a profound effect on the development of the genre of science fiction. Each volume originally was serialized in a popular journal, and Burroughs did not alter the episodic quality of his Barsoom stories when they were published as separate works.

The record of the deeds of John Carter and his family have endured partly because the reader encounters ideas and concepts that are usually the purview of philosophers and theologians. Many of the carefully crafted details in the stories might initially shock, but as a whole they become essential ingredients in the creation of a vision of another world that still captures the imagination. Burroughs is as successful as Jules Verne in predicting the shape of things to come, and his vision of the moral dilemmas that haunt his own century is both extraordinary and frightening.

Having deposited his hero on the surface of Mars, Burroughs casually mentions that Carter is naked—in fact, all Martians, male and female, prefer that state. The only accessories they wear are decorative harnesses and belts that provide protection and denote their status and accomplishments. By discarding the external adornments that occupy significant attention in other works of science fiction, Burroughs is able to concentrate on the internal habiliments of his characters. He is more concerned with the psychological than the fashionable. Because Carter accepts nudity as normal, the reader also tolerates this altered state of being. Burroughs also deals with Martian sexuality by revealing the fact that the women of Barsoom do not bear their young alive but instead lay eggs that take years to mature. Sex for the average Martian takes a poor second to the favorite preoccupation of violence.

Peace and tranquillity are almost unknown to the inhabitants of Barsoom. The moment they fight their way out of their shells, they are ready for conflict. It is impossible to exaggerate the importance of brutality in each and every story. Slavery is an accepted part of life. It is nonracial and is the potential fate of both sexes and all ranks, from rulers to commoners.

Carter embraces the life of the warrior and revels in it from the first page to the last; however, gratuitous violence and unwarranted cruelty are punished by Martian hubris because they are not part of the code of the warrior. In his sometimes stirring prose, Burroughs captures a rather unflattering reflection of his own world and its obsession with honor, duty, and war.

The discussion of race and religion is subtle and masterful. Each group of Martians boasts superiority only to be superseded by another. The green race is dismissed by the red as inferior, only to be labeled by the white with a similar epithet. Blacks dismiss whites only to be regarded as mediocre by the yellow inhabitants of Mars.

Each racial division is equally deceived by the ancient religion of Barsoom, which is but a cult of death. The triumph of Carter over the superstition embraced by the inhabitants of his adopted world may well reflect the feelings of Burroughs himself toward the religious establishment of his own time. Carter often seems near to death, but he never surrenders control of his own fate to any power; he is ever the master of his soul. Carter is Everyman, and in that fact lies the enduring quality of the Barsoom series.

—Clifton W. Potter, Jr.

BEAUTY AND THE BEAST
and
SONG OF ORPHEUS

Beautiful, wealthy Catherine Chandler discovers the existence of a secret underworld of outcasts below the subway tunnels of New York

Author: Barbara Hambly (1951-   )
Genre: Fantasy—cultural exploration
Type of work: Novels
Time of plot: 1986-1987
Location: New York City
First published: *Beauty and the Beast* (1989) and *Song of Orpheus* (1990)

The Plot: *Beauty and the Beast* and *Song of Orpheus* are based on the television program *Beauty and the Beast*, which began airing in 1987 and was created by Ron Koslow. The story concerns Catherine Chandler, a beautiful, well-educated debutante whose narcissistic, privileged life has begun to lose its appeal. Her job as junior partner in her father's prestigious corporate law firm has become dull and her performance in that capacity lackluster. While trying to hail a taxi one evening, Catherine is grabbed by a stocky man and forced into a van. Three days later, she is thrown out of the van in Central Park and left for dead. She has been beaten badly, and her face has been slashed.

Catherine awakes Below, in a secret underworld beneath the level of old subway tunnels in Manhattan, having been found by Vincent, a huge half-human, half-lion. She immediately feels a powerful bond with Vincent. She is cared for by Father, patriarch of the secret society of outcasts and refugees from the heartless, profligate society Above.

Despite her own father's efforts to facilitate her return to normalcy by hiring a plastic surgeon and by remaining patient in the face of her flat refusal to discuss the details of her disappearance, Catherine's thoughts are not at all on settling back into her old routine. Searing memories of the injustice done to her and to Vincent, an "accident" horribly discarded at birth but rescued by the Tunnel Dwellers, claim her attention. Although she understands that Above remains as closed to Vincent as Below is to her, she knows also that her life henceforth will never be the same. She leaves her father's corporate law firm and, seeking to aid other innocent victims, becomes a deputy district attorney. She also begins to learn how to defend herself.

Vincent, his thoughts on Catherine, occasionally ventures stealthily into Central Park from the Tunnels, merely to gaze at the light in her room. Neither Vincent's dreams of Catherine nor his visits Above find favor with Father, who insists that by going Above, the Tunnel Dwellers invite their doom. Vincent appears one evening on Catherine's terrace and stays with her until dawn.

At the district attorney's office, Catherine soon discovers information concerning another victim and thereby learns the identity of her assailant, who then sets out to kill her. Vincent, sensing her danger, rushes to her aid with the ferocity of an animal. The book ends as Catherine and Vincent, realizing the strength of the bond between them, bid goodbye for the time being.

In *Song of Orpheus*, Barbara Hambly develops three episodes previously aired in the television series that intertwine the lives and worlds of Catherine and Vincent. Vincent's nightly journeys Above to see Catherine have become more frequent. On one of them he brings her a necklace. It is a gift from Mouse, who has discovered, at the end of a remote tunnel, a buried ship laden with treasures. The treasure produces dissent among the Tunnel Dwellers, turning friend against friend. Against the wishes of others, Cullen takes gold items Above to sell but succeeds only in attracting a rapacious intruder who enters the Tunnels, bent on taking all the treasure. Following a fight, during which the intruder falls into the Abyss, the Tunnel Dwellers finally agree to donate the treasure Above to the St. Regina Shelter for the Homeless.

In the second episode, Father receives a message and mysteriously ventures Above. In the office of Alan Taft, an old friend, Father discovers Taft's body and is promptly arrested for Taft's murder. Vincent appeals to Catherine for help in locating Father. Believing rightly that his disappearance is linked to his past, Catherine and Vincent peruse microfilm at the public library and learn that Father is Dr. Jacob Wells, a physician called before the House Committee on Un-American Activities in 1951 and subsequently blacklisted. Shrinking from sharing his fate, Margaret, his bride, retreated to Paris with his father. Having never remarried and now dying of cancer, Margaret had sent the enigmatic note to Father noting the "wreck of my memories." Catherine discovers the identity of Taft's murderer, and Father returns to the Tunnels. Margaret joins him Below, spending the last seven days of her life with him.

Father recovers slowly from Margaret's death. One day, a Tunnel child falls into the Maze, a labyrinth of echoing caverns and tiny tunnels. In a rescue attempt, rocks collapse upon Father and Vincent. Above, Catherine immediately senses his peril. She descends into the Tunnels, falling headlong into Mouse's Mousehole. With Mouse she finds Vincent and Father pinned in a rockslide, their oxygen rapidly running out. Desperate to save Vincent, Catherine secures a drill and explosives from her former lover, Elliot Burch, an architect and construction magnate. Vincent and Father, who is injured, are rescued. At last a real part of life Below, Catherine realizes how much she loves and needs Vincent.

Analysis: Hambly uses a loose adaptation of the Beauty and the Beast fairy tale to provide an imaginative commentary on problems in modern society. In particular, Hambly targets the 1980's lifestyle, which in her view seems characterized by a general insensitivity to the plight of human beings whose standard of living falls far below that of the book's heroine.

As suggested by the fairy tale, the story's primary concern is the maturation of Catherine, who evolves from "Daddy's little girl" to a woman with selfhood, identity, and integrity. The death of Catherine's mother many years before had placed Catherine solely in the care of her wealthy, doting father, who naturally encouraged attitudes that would ensure her status in the life he enjoyed. He could not protect her, however, from the ugliness and violence rampant in society. That violence appeared, at first, to wreck her life but ironically proves to be the catalyst for her progression from supreme self-centeredness to a higher level of existence. Catherine's discovery of a world inhabited by people who had forsaken the glittering society Above and who had suffered barbarities that had equaled or surpassed those inflicted upon her leaves its impression upon her. This secret, tightly knit community restores her faith in humankind and precipitates her change in attitude.

Catherine's real growth is initiated by her love for Vincent. Like the Beast in the fairy tale, Vincent is dangerous and repugnant only to those who remain unacquainted with his inner qualities. Devotion to her father and the life of refinement he wanted for her required a static condition that would allow no exploration of her own possibilities. Her love for Vincent, whose animality appears revolting, provides Vincent and her father with the love and devotion most beneficial to both. Her father is proud of her hard work and derives pleasure from her dedication, and Vincent, his true nature revealed, is gratified that his faith in her is confirmed. Most important, Catherine understands the division between the animal and the human, as well as the love that heals that division.

Song of Orpheus continues the story of Vincent and Catherine only peripherally, as references to the myth of Orpheus and Eurydice in the Underworld shift the focus to interaction between the worlds of Above and Below. The three episodes explore inherent conflicts between the two worlds, ending with Catherine's commitment to Vincent, which forms a union of the two worlds.

Although the addition of the myth does not remove the probability of a happy ending, it adds tragic aspects that might otherwise be inappropriate in a fairy-tale framework. In the first episode, Hambly demonstrates the susceptibility of humans to the lure of wealth and its profound corrosiveness of spirit. Cullen, who succumbs to gold fever, doing violence to his friend, Mouse, illustrates the effects of greed. He becomes beastly, illustrating an underlying point in both books: Love of money gives rise to inhuman treatment of fellow humans.

In the second episode, Hambly draws on knowledge of the myth of Orpheus and Eurydice. In the myth, Orpheus attempts to lead his wife from the underworld but, through his own error, loses her forever. The association with Orpheus affirms Father's humanity, underscoring years of silent suffering from the knowledge that he has inadvertently caused human misery. The emphasis on the tragic aspects of life adds depth to the story of Margaret and Father, whose happiness was curtailed by Margaret's failure of resolve in coping with the circumstances life had dealt her. Margaret's function as foil, or contrast, to Catherine prepares readers for Catherine's later rescue of Vincent and emphasizes the lesson that Catherine has learned from Vincent: Follow your heart. —*Mary Hurd*

BEGGARS IN SPAIN
and
BEGGARS AND CHOOSERS

An exploration of the effects on society of the release of partly understood technologies and the ways in which different groups respond

Author: Nancy Kress (1948-   )
Genre: Science fiction—future history
Type of work: Novels
Time of plot: The twenty-first and twenty-second centuries
Location: Earth and Sanctuary, a space station orbiting Earth
First published: *Beggars in Spain* (1992; as novella, 1991) and *Beggars and Choosers* (1994)

The Plot: *Beggars in Spain* opens in the year 2008 with the birth of Leisha Camden. The world is prosperous, thanks to the discovery of a cheap energy source by Kenzo Yagai. Roger Camden is a leading Yagaiist, embracing Yagai's philosophy of an individual's responsibility to do the appropriate thing. He is determined to produce a perfect daughter and insists on a modification to ensure that Leisha never needs to sleep, so that she will be more useful to the community.

Leisha is intellectually brilliant and develops rapidly. As she grows older, she is aware of the resentment toward her from her unmodified sister and others. Unable to talk to her family about her feelings, she discovers the existence of other Sleepless, and they form a community, keeping in regular contact. Sleepers become fearful and envious of the achievements of the Sleepless, particularly following the discovery that it is sleep that causes the aging process, so that the Sleepless will not age at the same rate as ordinary people. Some members of the Sleepless community propose building themselves a community apart from the Sleepers, but Leisha believes in the integration of Sleepless and Sleepers and refuses to go into Sanctuary, a space station orbiting Earth.

This first schism among members of the Sleepless community is mirrored by a further schism within Sanctuary when one group, led by Jennifer Sharifi, begins genetic experiments to further enhance the abilities of the Sleepless. Sharifi is ruthless in pursuit of her goal. Adopting a radical definition of community as a group of people whose purpose is to serve the whole, she ruthlessly expels or murders anyone whom she considers incapable of being part of the community, even her own grandson. She also has no sympathy for Sleepers and is keen to form her own nation distinct from the United States. The country benefits from taxing Sleepless technology, so it is unwilling to agree to secession. Sharifi plans to blackmail the United States by threatening to release a plague. When the Supersleepless, who are the product of Sharifi's experiments and already are disturbed by her callousness, learn of her plans, they take control of the space station from her, hand her over to the authorities, and leave for their own hideaway.

On Earth, Leisha has adopted a Sleeper boy, Drew Arlen, a member of the faux-aristocratic Liver faction who is looking for revenge against Sanctuary for killing his grandfather and is determined one day to own it. Unable to settle and unable to adapt to "donkey" ways, in which he would have to work for a living, he is a source of trouble in Leisha's home until he is accidentally crippled by Leisha's great-nephew, Eric, in a fight. Even this does not stop him from continuing on a path to destruction. In a dangerous attempt to save him from a life of waste, Eric forcibly treats him with a drug that unleashes an ability to induce lucid dreams in others, including the Sleepless. Leisha also tries to respond to the increasing divisions among pro-Sleeper organizations that promote their shoddy goods at the expense of superior Sleepless products, on the basis that they are primarily philanthropic in their aims. Society is in upheaval because of a curious division between "donkeys," Sleepers who are prepared to continue working, and Livers, a faux-aristocratic section of the Sleeper population. Their relationship is an uneasy symbiosis, whereby the donkeys provide for the Livers in return for their votes. By the end of the book, the situation is still unresolved, although Leisha remains confident that Sleepers and Sleepless can live in an integrated society.

Beggars and Choosers presents a very different world, partly through the eyes of Diana Covington, a roving agent for the Genetic Standards Enforcement Agency. She is hunting for Miranda Sharifi, who is believed to be performing illegal genetic experiments. As becomes clear, other groups also are performing experiments and are releasing products into the environment in an attempt to return to a time before gene modification was the norm. The effects of unauthorized gene modification are shown through the eyes of Billy Washington, a Liver whose community gradually is disintegrating as services fail.

Drew Arlen's lucid dreaming ability is being employed by the Supersleepless to inspire the Livers to return to the donkey way of life in the face of this disintegration, but Arlen is ambivalent about continued genetic experimentation. Miranda Sharifi argues that in this instance, she does know best. Sharifi is imprisoned for her work, but not before producing an antidote to a plague released by an illegal organization, thus demonstrating her willingness to help Sleepers. The book closes with the certainty that a new order has been established but no certainty as to what shape it will take.

Analysis: Nancy Kress's *Beggars in Spain* first appeared as a novella, and some critics believe that its expansion to novel length was to the work's detriment. It could be argued that the expansion of the novella and the subsequent writing of a sequel obliged Kress to speculate ever more improbably, creating not only the Sleepless but also the Supersleepless. In a novella, space constraints oblige the author to focus on one small fragment of the greater whole; Kress clearly believed she had more to say. There can be no doubt that the future Earth she created raises many fascinating speculative points.

It is rare, for example, for science fiction to deal with the idea that one can never really know what a new invention or technological development will do, except by using it. Extrapolation from experiments always will be insufficient. It often is supposed that cheap energy for all will be the salvation of the world's problems, yet, as Kress clearly shows, there is a downside to the prosperity. People become indolent, working for other people loses its respectability, and society begins to disintegrate as basic community ties are weakened and then severed.

Kress also presents a complex series of ethical arguments for the reader to consider. Kenzo Yagai believed that he was benefiting the world by releasing his cheap energy source to one and all, assuming that people would respond as generously toward one another as he had. The Sleepless are perceived by Sleepers as gods of a sort, but they are divided among themselves as to whether they have any loyalty to outsiders. Having been experiments themselves, they wonder whether they have the right to create yet another super-race. This question is pursued more and more strongly, particularly in the second novel, in which Arlen and Covington, although both working for the Genetic Standards Enforcement Agency, do so for very different motives and, in Diana's case, with increasing doubts.

Kress's presentation of her various arguments is powerful and convincing, although she offers the reader no easy solutions; in fact, she offers no real solutions at all. Her skill lies in showing the myriad different viewpoints, from those who revel in their Sleeplessness through those who have empathy with the Sleepers, along with those troubled by their own alienness. Among the Sleepers, she charts the fascinating sway of emotions as Livers seek to find someone to blame for their predicament, fastening by turns on the Sleepless, the gene enhanced, and the donkeys. She is able to pin down the swirling, contradictory mass of human emotion, which is so easily manipulated and so willing to blame anyone but oneself. She paints a dark picture of a future society, particularly in *Beggars and Choosers*, as the world reaches its breaking point, and she offers only the faintest glimmers of hope. Even then, she seems to suggest that those who seek salvation may want to dictate the manner in which it will come. From this idea comes the title of the second book, derived from the saying "Beggars can't be choosers."

This moral and ethical dimension sets Kress's work apart from much of modern hard science fiction, which is more concerned with parading the wonders to come than with asking how people will live with them and what will happen as a result. More important, she explores what can be done to prevent overly radical changes. Her vigorous prose style and memorable characters ensure that readers will take notice of her vision of the future.

—Maureen Speller

THE BEGINNING PLACE

Two adolescents learn trust and cooperation in an archetypal world in which they must slay a monster and make their way back to reality

Author: Ursula K. Le Guin (1929-   )
Genre: Fantasy—magical world
Type of work: Novel
Time of plot: The late 1970's
Location: The suburbs of an unspecified city and the twilight "ain" country
First published: 1980 (condensed form, *Redbook*, 1979; published in England as *Threshold*, 1980)

The Plot: While running away from his disturbed mother and his empty suburban life, Hugh Rogers discovers a gateway into a magical forest world. There, where it is always twilight, he finds solace and belonging. Although he returns to reality, he crosses the gateway frequently to drink from the river and to recharge his spirit in the natural setting.

On one trip, he meets Irene Pannis, who also discovered the gateway while trying to escape her unhappy home life, which includes the threat of physical assault at the hands of her stepfather. Irene had been crossing over into what she calls the "ain" country for years. Like Hugh, she believes that she belongs here. She has made ties with the inhabitants of the mountain town of Tembreabrezi, who represent family to her and the only real home she has ever known. She also harbors a secret love for the grim mayor of Tembreabrezi, Master Sark.

Irene is enraged to find Hugh in "her" place, but the two soon establish an uneasy truce, for they learn they need each other. Irene sometimes cannot get into the twilight world; Hugh cannot always get out. The townspeople need them too, for there is a goblin or monster haunting them, choking off their livelihood and holding them hostage. When Hugh arrives in Tembreabrezi, its residents take him to be their savior, the knight who will slay this dragon. Hugh is willing—he wants in particular to impress the fair-haired damsel Allia, with whom he is secretly in love. When Irene realizes that Sark would use her as an offering for the monster, she becomes disenchanted with the twilight world and joins Hugh in his quest.

Together, Hugh and Irene track the screaming, gobbling monster. Although in their first encounter with it they hide, cowering in fright, they gather their courage and follow the monster's path to its lair. Irene baits it, and Hugh kills it with a sword. Hugh is seriously injured as the dying monster falls on him, and Irene must aid him as they find a way out of the labyrinthine twilight world and back to reality. In this final journey, they realize that they love each other and that in order to get on with their lives they can and must depend on each other. They vow to reconfigure their lives on the outside and not to return to the twilight world.

Analysis: *The Beginning Place* was published after the huge successes of the Earthsea trilogy (1968, 1970, 1972; collected as *Earthsea*, 1977), *The Left Hand of Darkness* (1969), and *The Dispossessed* (1974), the last of which won both Hugo and Nebula awards. Following publication of those works, Ursula Le Guin reassessed her career. From 1975 until 1985, when another major work (*Always Coming Home*) appeared, she published criticism and some short stories and novels that are generally outside the realm of science fiction or fantasy.

Although well received at the time of publication, *The Beginning Place* has since received little attention from scholars, possibly because, unlike the Earthsea trilogy, it is not pure fantasy. It is instead an ironic thinking through of the necessity of fantasy and of the dangers of overdependence upon it. In critic Brian Attebery's words, it is a "metafantasy," a fantasy about fantasy.

The Beginning Place continues the major themes of Le Guin's fantasy writings, particularly her interest in the theories of psychoanalyst Carl Jung and in the Taoist belief in the need for balance between good and evil, or dark and light elements. Jung's interest in the unconscious mind is reflected in the characters' crossing over from the real, daylight world into a twilight, magical world in which they learn skills to help them cope with life.

Like much fantasy, *The Beginning Place* is essentially a story of the characters' journey to adulthood. In the twilight world, Hugh and Irene initially find security and belonging; the ain country is the only place they can feel sure of themselves. They are able to begin to awaken romantically and sexually, nurturing fantasies of love with the characters they most resemble. The fair, clumsy, and ineffectual Hugh loves the blond, passive Allia; dark, scowling Irene worships dark, cruel Sark.

Part of the journey of these characters is the turning away from these mirror images of themselves and toward each other. The screaming, howling creature—which remains only poorly defined—is an integral part of this maturation process. It is the embodiment of Hugh and Irene's fears, of their negative self-images. In the same way that Ged turns and faces his shadow in *A Wizard of Earthsea* (1968), Hugh and Irene must face the creature and merge with it. This is reflected in Jung's idea of the shadow, the darker part of human nature that must be acknowledged and integrated into the self to form a whole. In slaying the creature and returning to the real world, Hugh and Irene recognize and deal with the darker side of their lives and thereby rob it of the power to rule them. This is also related to Taoist philosophy, which requires a balance of the dark and light aspects of life, symbolized in the union of the blond Hugh and the dark-haired Irene. In recognizing that the ain country is essentially a place of escape, the two agree to stop running away from their problems and accept responsibility for themselves, in effect confronting adulthood.

—Amy Clarke

A BELEAGUERED CITY

A provincial city in nineteenth century France has its fundamental beliefs challenged when the dead return to life

Author: Margaret Oliphant (1828-1897)
Genre: Fantasy—occult
Type of work: Novella
Time of plot: The late 1870's
Location: Semur, a provincial city in France
First published: 1880

The Plot: *A Beleaguered City* is a fantastic, speculative ghost story that takes stock of the changing beliefs of nineteenth century Europeans regarding religion and the supernatural. Very popular in the nineteenth century, it went out of print until late in the twentieth century. It can be seen as one of the first attempts to include within the realm of fantasy stories the areas of inquiry usually associated with religion.

Semur is a rather dreary French provincial city participating in the general malaise of France after that country's defeat by Germany in the Franco-Prussian War. Martin Dupin, mayor of the town as well as owner of the great estate of La Clarière, is a progressively inclined man who is skeptical of traditional religious faith. While strolling about the city on a summer evening, Dupin is approached by Paul Lecamus, an eccentric man with a strong visionary streak who has not been emotionally whole since the death of his wife. Lecamus informs Dupin that a great portent has occurred. This news is soon confirmed by several others. Dupin is stunned, when he arrives at the place described by Lecamus, to see thousands of dead people returned to life and solemnly parading. Dupin cannot believe his senses, but the uncanny spectacle is confirmed when giant letters in the sky spell out a message of summoning from entities who describe themselves as "Nous Autres Morts"—French for "we other dead."

The sedate, comfortable, placidly mediocre life of Semur is completely disrupted by the arrival of the strange undead. Dupin confers with his wife and with the Curé, a local priest, in order to help him gain his bearings and provide some guidance to a stunned community. Each member of the community has his or her own experience that is eventually related to the mayor. From the skeptical Monsieur de Bois-Sombre to the impressionable Madame Dupin to the mystical Lecamus, each account filters the weird apparition through the prism of individual hopes, fears, and vulnerabilities. Dupin's mother, for example, sees the ghosts as a judgment of divine vengeance for the civil administration's shoddy treatment of the Sisters of St. John, a locally dominant order of nuns. Lecamus suddenly encounters the face of Dupin's father, signaling the suspension of accepted notions of past and future. What was thought dead and buried has returned to life.

Dupin goes in the company of the Curé to confront the apparitions. Despite the philosophical differences between the two men, the challenge of the returned dead creates solidarity and comradeship between them. Dupin's mother leads the women and children away to the mayor's estate in order to provide for their safety. Meanwhile, Dupin's wife and Lecamus have a direct encounter with the dead. Through the medium of the visionary Lecamus, Dupin's wife feels the presence of her daughter Marie, who died young. Lecamus is so entranced by the threshold between life and death that he crosses over the line. Seeking to rejoin his dead wife, he throws himself into the sphere of the undead and is gone from Earth forever. After this, the apparition recedes and the tumult subsides. Peace is restored to Semur. The religious conservatives of the town try to turn the incident into a conventional miracle, but Dupin knows that what had transpired was in truth a more unsettling phenomenon, an enigma he could never wholly hope to solve.

Analysis: Margaret Oliphant is known as a domestic and regional writer dealing with everyday life in Victorian England, as is displayed in her multivolume *Chronicles of Carlingford* (1862). Her corpus of ghost stories displays the versatility and imaginativeness of her vision and enhances her importance as a writer. *A Beleaguered City*, her most famous ghost story, is significant in the history of fantasy and science fiction because of its use of the techniques of speculative fiction to explore issues that traditionally have been the domain of religion.

Oliphant sets this atypical story in a foreign country, France. Perhaps this enabled her to achieve an effect of distance and remoteness necessary for the story's weird atmosphere. With subtlety and skill, Oliphant paints a detailed portrait of the complacent, bourgeois city of Semur, where people stroll around thinking that they have mastered all the dilemmas of the universe, or at least are able to ignore them. The manifestation of the returned dead shows that rational waking thought cannot master the overwhelming mysteriousness of the cosmos. The return of the dead may be explained in psychological terms as a collective hallucination that displays the town's own repression of its buried unconscious, whether this repression can be traced to the town's own bourgeois self-satisfaction or to its participation in the general French malaise after the trauma of the war with Germany.

Oliphant does not use her ghostly spectacle simply to proffer a grim warning to modernity that it has strayed too far from tradition and needs a grim retrenchment back to orthodox pieties in order to solve its problems. Instead, she sees the returned dead as a challenge that each citizen of Semur addresses in unique personal terms. From the orthodox Curé to the rationalist mayor to the independently mystical Lecamus, each person relates to the returned dead in specific personal terms. By illustrating how different individuals would respond to such a

crisis, Oliphant creates a haunting and eerie but emotionally realistic tableau.

The returned dead of Semur may be unsettling but are not necessarily frightening. They perturb and intrigue but do not shock or horrify. They present less a vision of grisly secrets than of previously unknown possibilities. Particularly for Dupin's grieving wife and the stricken Lecamus, the revelation that the dead can return to Earth provides a foundation for hope. Perhaps, they conclude, the endings life seems to give are not necessarily final.

—Margaret Boe Birns

THE BELGARIAD

A fantasy quest for a stolen magical artifact, the outcome of which will decide the fate of the entire universe

Author: David Eddings (1931-   )
Genre: Fantasy—high fantasy
Type of work: Novels
Time of plot: Undefined
Location: The Kingdoms of the West and the Angaraks, on another world
First published: *Pawn of Prophecy* (1982), *Queen of Sorcery* (1982), *Magician's Gambit* (1983), *Castle of Wizardry* (1984), and *Enchanters' End Game* (1984)

The Plot: None of the individual novels of the Belgariad is capable of standing alone. The Belgariad is an epic high fantasy, and such epics require considerable space to develop the world, characters, and drama of the plot. The Belgariad begins with Garion, a boy who lives on a farm. His only living relative, as far as he knows, is his Aunt Pol, the cook. Various supernatural events occur during his childhood, along with the typical pangs of puberty, but not until he is fourteen years old does the adventure really begin. At this time, Belgarath, under the name of Mister Wolf, a vagabond bard, comes to visit and informs Aunt Pol of the theft of a magical artifact known as the Orb of Aldur.

The three set out to retrieve the Orb, which has been stolen from the hall of the dead Rivan King by the minions of the sleeping god Torak. A prophecy has indicated that the Orb will assist in the waking of Torak, whose unnatural sleep was caused several thousand years before by this same Orb. Belgarath, who is revealed to be a distant ancestor of Garion, as well as a legendary sorcerer, organizes a mission to retrieve the Orb with the aid of Silk, Prince Kheldar of Drasnia and an accomplished spy; Barak, Earl of Trelheim, who turns into a bear on occasion; Ce'Nedra, a spoiled imperial princess of Tolnedra; Mandorallen, Baron of Vo Mandor; Hettar, Horselord of Algaria, who can speak to horses; Lelldorin, a nobleman of Arendia; Durnik, a blacksmith; and Garion's Aunt Pol, who is actually Lady Polgara, Belgarath's daughter and also a sorcerer.

They set out on the trail of the Orb, traveling through various countries and encountering a variety of dangers, both magical and conventional. It becomes clear that Garion is a powerful mage in his own right. Throughout the Belgariad, he must strive to come to terms with the astonishing fact that he is related to legends and is involved in a mythical quest that will decide the fate of the world—a quest in which he plays the crucial role. Not only is he a sorcerer, but he also is the heir to the Rivan throne and the only person who can safely take up the Orb of Aldur against the evil Torak.

Eventually the Orb is recovered from Ctuchik, priest of Torak. The questers race to return it to Riva in time for Garion to claim his bride, Ce'Nedra, who has been prophesied to be his wife. Neither knows that they are last in the line of the Rivan kings, long thought to be extinct. Before the ceremony can take place, however, it becomes clear that the Angaraks, Torak's chosen people, are preparing to make war on the Kingdoms of the West. In order to prevent the deaths of millions, Garion sets out with Silk and Belgarath to challenge Torak in his home. In the meantime, Polgara and Ce'Nedra organize the Western forces for war as a diversion for the Angaraks, in order to allow the trio to make their way through hostile territory and to be present when Torak wakes.

In the end, most of the original members of the quest are reunited in C'thol Mishrak for the final battle between the Child of Light (Garion, who, with elevation to the status of sorcerer, is now named Belgarion) and the Child of Dark (Torak). One of two competing prophecies will be proved false and thus be eliminated as a force in the world. Belgarion triumphs, in spite of Torak's powers as a god. Torak is killed in an arcane sword duel with Belgarion, and the universe is saved from a dark and bloody fate. Afterward, all return to Riva for Belgarion's wedding to Ce'Nedra. With Torak's death, there is no longer a threat of war.

Analysis: Prior to the Belgariad, David Eddings had published only *High Hunt* (1973), a science-fiction novel. The Belgariad was his first foray into the world of fantasy, followed soon after by a sequel series entitled the Malloreon (1987-1991). He has also written two other unrelated series and expected to return to the world

of the Belgariad and the Malloreon with a pair of prequels that focus on Belgarath's and Polgara's conflict with Torak and his minions when the Orb of Aldur was first created.

In the Belgariad, Eddings creates a complex and believable world by including minute details and establishing an elaborate historical background based on an intricate social and political structure. Add to that his amazing ability to invest even the smallest characters with complete and complex lives, and it is easy to see why the Belgariad has proven to be so popular.

In spite of the popularity of his books, Eddings has his critics. The most damaging criticism has been the accusation that his books are merely derivative of the work of J. R. R. Tolkien. This accusation is difficult to counter because high fantasy has been defined by Tolkien's *The Hobbit* (1937) and the Lord of the Rings trilogy (1954-1955), and thus most of what is considered high fantasy can point to Tolkien as an influence. Eddings does use traditional motifs—the quest, the prophecy, artifacts of magic, and the final arcane duel—but he does so in an interesting and compelling way. Eddings does, however, prove derivative in the Malloreon series—derivative of himself. In this sequel to the Belgariad, Eddings tells the same story with the same plot. This seems to be a habit for him, as he repeats the same formula with another of his fantasy series, the Elenium (1989-1991), and its sequel series, the Tamuli (begun in 1991).

The plot of the Belgariad is straightforward and uncomplicated. The success of the book comes from Eddings' abilities as a world builder and his skill with character and dialogue. Belgarion is young and often appears to be a whiner; Ce'Nedra is similarly childish. The other major characters more than make up for the faults of these two. Silk, probably the masterpiece of this series, is snide and outspoken, with a strange vulnerability and outrageous sense of humor that make him compelling. Each of the characters is unique, and Eddings never uses them as mere plot devices. Instead, he breathes humanity into each, complete with quirks, fears, jealousy, pride, and compassion. The plot is intentionally less complex than the characterizations.

If there is a flaw in the Belgariad, it is the ending. Belgarion's duel with Torak comes too quickly and is unsatisfying. In resolving all that has gone before, Eddings causes Belgarion to have several sudden insights. These startling realizations are unusually heavy-handed, with little by way of explanation or preparation. To most readers, they seem artificial. Eddings might have avoided this flaw by adding two or three chapters to dramatize the battle and create the necessary suspense. Although most readers understand that Belgarion must finally triumph in a story titled the Belgariad, the final scene lacks the dramatic suspense that would have been possible had Eddings established the possibility of a defeat—that the Belgariad could have been named so out of a sense of tragedy rather than triumph. Instead, the battle with Torak seems to be not so much the culmination of a well-wrought plot but, rather, a quick fix to tidy up the loose ends. —*Diana Pharaoh Francis*

THE BERSERKER SERIES

The struggle of humanity against intelligent machines programmed to destroy all life

Author: Fred Saberhagen (1930-   )
Genre: Science fiction—artificial intelligence
Type of work: Stories
Time of plot: Prehistory to the distant future
Location: The part of the Milky Way galaxy settled by humans
First published: *Berserker* (1967), *Brother Assassin* (1969), *Berserker's Planet* (1975), *Berserker Man* (1979), *The Ultimate Enemy* (1979), *The Berserker Wars* (1981), *The Berserker Throne* (1985), *Berserker: Blue Death* (1985), *Berserker Base* (1985), *Berserker Lies* (1991), and *Berserker Kill* (1993)

The Plot: Before humans appeared on Earth, two interstellar races, known to humans as "the builders" and "the red race," fought a war of extermination lasting for centuries. Hoping finally to win the war, the builders created an ultimate doomsday machine, a spacefaring, intelligent, self-replicating weapon programmed to destroy any life it encountered. The weapon, called a berserker by humans because of the intense and chaotic violence of its attacks, was a success and wiped out the red race.

Unfortunately for the builders (and humans), the berserkers realized that the builders also were life and exterminated them as well. Now berserkers roam the galaxy searching for life in any form. They especially seek intelligent life such as humans because these are the only life-forms likely to provide any resistance to the extermination program. Berserkers have no inherent urge toward self-preservation (they are urgeless) but seek always to achieve the maximum destruction of life in expenditure of their resources.

Because berserkers are self-replicating and intelligent,

they can build themselves in different shapes as required by a particular mission. The originals were space-going battleships, but in the stories they appear as everything from imitation horseshoe crabs to androids dressed in preserved human skin. In all cases, they are bent on destroying any intelligent life they find, with no regard for their own survival, and they are usually well equipped for that mission.

The books are divided into two types, anthologies and novels. The stories in the anthologies vary in length and are usually supplemented by some amount of linking text. In all cases, the stories and novels tell the human side of the ongoing berserker-human war. The anthologized stories usually focus on the resolution of a single human-berserker encounter, whereas the novels pursue the principal characters through several such encounters, usually culminating in a major victory for humanity.

In the short story "Smasher," which appears in *The Ultimate Enemy* and *Berserker Lies*, for example, a human space force successfully defends a populated water world against a berserker fleet attack. One of the berserker ships crashes on an almost unpopulated neighboring (and equally watery) planet still carrying a portion of its cargo intact. The cargo is small berserkers resembling horseshoe crabs, intended to scuttle unnoticed across the sea floor toward human habitations that they would then disassemble with an assortment of destructive tool-limbs. The crash site world is inhabited only by four scientists studying the fauna. One of them is killed by the berserkers, but the remaining three survive by luring the machines into a pond filled with a native predatory crustacean resembling a cross of shrimp and praying mantis. The smashers, as the crustaceans are called, confuse berserker and crab as humans were supposed to, and they destroy the menace.

In "Patron of the Arts," a story in *Berserker*, the art treasures of Earth are being transported to Tau Epsilon to protect them from a possible berserker attack on the home world. One of these treasures is a living artist who is so jaded by his existence that he is almost completely unconcerned by his impending death when his ship is captured in a berserker attack. After the crew members are killed resisting the berserker boarding party, he begins painting a portrait of a berserker, which he admires for its deadly efficiency. A boarding robot, speaking for the space-going berserker outside, asks what he is doing. He tries to explain the concept of art, which the berserker interprets as praise of that pictured. The machine then asks him, "What is good?" He asks what the berserker considers good, receiving the response "To destroy life is good." He agrees that life has little to recommend it but does not agree with the berserker's enthusiasm for death and cannot find life to be completely without value. In response to the berserker's query about this statement, he shows the robot Titian's painting *Man with a Glove.* The berserker asks him what it means, and he refuses to reply.

After the robot leaves him, he takes the painting to the airlock, intending to put it in an escape capsule so that it, at least, might be saved from the berserker. He finds a stowaway girl in a crate and has to decide whether her life is worth more than the painting. He sends her on her way and returns with the Titian to his portrait of the berserker. He is now disgusted by his work. The berserker robot returns and informs him that because he has praised the berserker, his ship has been repaired and put back on course so that other humans can learn from him how to praise what is good. After the berserker's boarding party departs, he declares that he can change, is alive, and will paint again.

The novels tend to be more similar to "Patron of the Arts." They involve characters attempting to destroy a berserker or simply to survive an attack by one or more of them. They often involve character development and an affirmation of the value of existence. Typical of these is *Berserker: Blue Death*, in which the main character is a sort of space-going Captain Ahab seeking vengeance against a particular berserker, known as "Leviathan" or "Old Blue," because he holds it responsible for the deaths of his wife and daughter. In this pursuit, he almost loses his humanity, becoming a shadow of the death machine, but he rediscovers the value of his life after killing the man who killed his daughter and destroying the berserker.

There are two structurally exceptional books in the series. *Brother Assassin* comprises three novellas that form a continuous plot of novel length. Likewise, *Berserker Base* is an anthology of short stories by multiple authors forming a continuous plot. Fred Saberhagen wrote the first short story and linking text. Readers should be aware that most berserker short stories were published in more than one anthology.

Analysis: Although the stories all occur against the backdrop of human-berserker conflict, the humans are always the center of attention. Typically, berserkers are reduced to an inscrutable menace, and the contrast between human and machine is usually sharply drawn. One of the principal themes of the stories derives from this contrast: Humans can defeat berserkers not because of superior science or superior physical ability but because of their essential human nature. This usually is illustrated by presenting a character without love, concern, or much desire to live, then bringing him or her into contact with the single-minded destruction of a berserker and confronting the character with the pain it causes in fellow humans. The character then fights the berserker and rediscovers his or her soul after discovering that the most ruthless methods are unsuccessful.

A corollary theme in the series is that there is something about humanity that transcends the physical. Few characters in the stories profess religious or spiritual views beyond atheism or agnosticism, yet the most alive and human among them have some inner spirit that transcends physical boundaries. Saberhagen's carmpan— passive, friendly telepathic aliens that frequently function as distanced observers in the stories—regularly speak of the soul as the major difference between human and berserker. Human thought is regularly stated to occur faster than neuromuscular or electronic reactions, giving humanity a critical advantage over the computerized berserker. This thesis is most directly stated in *Berserker Man*, in which a major supporting character is a pilot who was so badly injured battling a berserker that he now lives as a cyborg in a train of boxes on motorized carts and serves as one of the philosophical centers of the story. Humans may be cyborgs in boxes, or even reduced to personality recordings in a computer, as are Nick and Genevieve in *Berserker Kill*, but they are essentially different from berserkers.

Against the background of such a violent dystopic universe, Saberhagen makes the point that the most worthwhile and valuable features of humanity are emotions: love, joy, concern, anguish, and even terror. These serve humans in his stories far better than any technological weapon. Again and again he shows the similarity of a character who has ceased to feel and a berserker that is incapable of feeling. Such characters always find that these suppressed emotions are the difference between them and the enemy, and that they are the edge that brings victory to the human. Far from being stories about mechanical terrors sweeping life from the galaxy, the Berserker series ultimately is a humanist statement: Humankind is greater than any enemy because of the human soul.

—Radford B. Davis and Julia Meyers

THE BEST OF C. M. KORNBLUTH

Out of contemporary conditions arise tomorrow's problems, which can be solved or understood only with the perspective of history

Author: C(yril) M. Kornbluth (1923-1958)
Genre: Science fiction—extrapolatory
Type of work: Stories
Time of plot: The 1950's to the distant future
Location: Various sites, especially cities, on Earth and
other planets
First published: 1976

The Plot: Two of C. M. Kornbluth's most famous stories, the novelettes "The Little Black Bag" (1950) and
"The Marching Morons" (1951), posit the same future.
Twenty generations from now, prolific, low-IQ groups
vastly outnumber intelligent people on Earth because of
the latter's low birthrates. The moronic majority thrives
only through the labors of the intellectuals.

The earlier story introduces elderly Bayard Full, a
ruined, slum-dwelling, dipsomaniac medical doctor. An
accident sends a doctor's black bag from the future into
his possession. Designed for use by idiots, the bag yields
its secrets readily to Dr. Full and his accidentally acquired
assistant, Angie. Reinvigorated and reformed, Dr. Full
begins performing miraculous operations and nurturing a
new self-image as benefactor of humanity. Angie, however, has less humanitarian goals and succeeds in destroying the hopes of both herself and Dr. Full.

"The Marching Morons" more fully explores the future world dominated by idiots. The intelligent minority
faces one central problem: what to do about the ever-
worsening population disparity between idiots and geniuses. The minority receives a windfall in the form of
real estate salesman Honest John Barlow, revived from a
state of suspended animation accidentally achieved in
the twentieth century. Barlow agrees to solve the problem if he is given dictatorial power, a request that is
granted readily. Barlow then suckers the general populace, through advertising and sly references during television sitcoms, into taking rockets to Venus, an unreach-
able promised land. They fall for the ruse and die in great
numbers. In the end, Barlow suffers the same fate he
inflicted on others.

Two late novelettes, "Shark Ship" (originally "Reap
the Dark Tide," 1958) and "Two Dooms" (1958; Kornbluth's preferred title was "The Doomsman"), probe
other grim futures. "Shark Ship" details life aboard a
convoy of ships divorced from all contact with land. The
lives of those on board depend on the spring swarming of
plankton. When a storm destroys his ship's irreplaceable
fishing net, Captain Thomas Salter finds himself, his
ship, and his crew expelled from the convoy. An idea
previously thought heretical now appears to be his only
option: He must steer for land. The landing party discovers an America depopulated by death cults whose influence became pervasive in previous centuries. Surviving
cult members give the landing party a taste of the violence that purged the once-overpopulated mainland.

"Two Dooms" follows atomic physicist Edward Royland on his accidental journey into an alternate universe
where the Nazis and Japanese rule a divided United
States. In his own world, Royland debated whether to
delay progress at the Los Alamos nuclear research site or
to help the atomic bomb achieve its terrifying result.
Encountering both a slave village and a concentration
camp in the alternate America, he comes to grips with the
idea of life under bondage.

Other notable works in this volume include "The
Words of Guru" (1941), an early but striking fantasy
about a genius child acquiring supernatural power; "The
Last Man Left in the Bar" (1957), a confrontation between aliens and a magnetron technician, written with an
audacious literary command that anticipates the stylistic
revolution of the 1960's; "The Altar at Midnight" (1952),
a portrayal of the costs of spaceflight; and the influential
"The Mindworm" (1950), detailing the rise and fall of a
psychic vampire.

Analysis: Although Kornbluth received acclaim as a
novelist, his reputation rests largely on his shorter works,
which are recognized for their intelligence, incisive wit,
and readability.

"The Marching Morons," one of the most famous novelettes in science fiction, has prompted many critics to
examine its future scenario of an intelligent but overwhelmed minority. Those focusing on its genetics, however, have tended to overlook, and inadvertently belittle,
the social criticism explicit in the story. When the intellectuals turn to Barlow to solve their problem, they find
themselves employing a veritable Adolf Hitler. Kornbluth takes a global view, however: He juxtaposes Nazi
gas chambers and American bombings of Japanese civilians by having Barlow's rockets lift off from Los
Alamos. The intelligentsia appear as culpable as Honest
John.

Kornbluth's concern with the ethics of theoretical science underlies both "Two Dooms," with its indecisive
Royland, and "Gomez" (1954), whose protagonist, Julio
Gomez, sits on a similar fence with regard to unified
field theory, the implications of which terrify him. Both
stories explore moral quandaries of the atomic age, as do
such other works as "The Altar at Midnight," Kornbluth's fascinating first solo novel *Takeoff* (1952), and

"The Remorseful" (1954).

Kornbluth's concern with the impact of theoretical knowledge parallels his concern with history. Historical insight appears as a redemptive if sometimes dangerous force throughout Kornbluth's works, notably here in "Shark Ship," "The Luckiest Man in Denv" (1952), "The Mindworm," and "The Adventurer" (1953).

Many of these stories shed light on other works. "The Rocket of 1955," a vignette that first appeared in a 1939 fanzine, and "The Marching Morons" anticipate *The Space Merchants* (with Frederik Pohl, 1953), whereas "The Little Black Bag" and "The Marching Morons" anticipate *Search the Sky* (with Pohl, 1954). "Two Dooms" bears comparison to Kornbluth's *Not This August* (1955), depicting an America beneath Communist subjugation, and Philip K. Dick's *The Man in the High Castle* (1962). "With These Hands" bears comparison to Walter M. Miller, Jr.'s "The Darfstellar" (1955).

Critics judging Kornbluth by this anthology, edited by Pohl, have seen a growing bitterness in his later stories. This reflects editorial choice more than reality, because Kornbluth also wrote delightful humor in his last years, in stories not collected here. These tales demonstrate Kornbluth's effective use of everyday individuals from a variety of ethnic backgrounds as well as his well-tuned ear for dialect.
—Mark Rich

THE BEST OF CORDWAINER SMITH

Stories recount events in humankind's development, from the Second Age of Space through the spread of the Rediscovery of Man

Author: Cordwainer Smith (Paul Myron Anthony Linebarger, 1913-1966)
Genre: Science fiction—future history
Type of work: Stories
Time of plot: Various times between A.D. 6,000 and 16,000
Location: Earth, other planets, and aboard spacecraft
First published: 1975

The Plot: The twelve stories in this collection, written separately and published between 1950 and 1964, fit into a consistent future history that covers human development from the Second Age of Space to the era of rights for underpeople and the Rediscovery of Man. Many of the stories involve the Instrumentality, a ruling bureaucracy that is not always admirable but ultimately manages "to keep man man."

Set in the Second Age of Space, "Scanners Live in Vain" concerns the scanners, men surgically cut off from their senses in order to endure the pain of space travel. When scientist Adam Stone discovers how to travel in space without pain, the scanners fear they will lose their privileged position and so order his death. Scanner Martel breaks with his elite group to warn Stone, who survives and subsequently restores scanners to normal senses and emotions.

In "The Lady Who Sailed *The Soul*," Helen America, the first woman to pilot interstellar space, has trouble with the gigantic solar sail of her ship. An apparition of the man she loves, Mr. Grey-no-more, assists her in righting the craft, and she is saved. In future history, theirs is one of the great love stories.

"The Game of Rat and Dragon," set in the age of planoforming, is about the human telepaths, pinlighters, who protect interstellar flights from the psychic dragons of deep space. A pinlighter is saved from a dragon by the alertness of his telepathically linked partner, a cat. While recovering, he realizes that no woman can compare to his cat partner, Lady May.

In "The Burning of the Brain," Magno Taliano, one of the Go-Captains who in a psychic trance guide planoforming ships through interstellar space, loses his way. To return to known space, pinlighters must read his brain for star locations. The ship is saved, but the captain's mind is destroyed, to the ambiguous sorrow of his wife.

In "The Dead Lady of Clown Town," D'joan, one of the underpeople derived from animals to perform drudgery, brings her followers out of hiding to plead for humane treatment. The Instrumentality instead brutally slaughters them, and Joan herself is tried, convicted, and burned. Her trial, however, gives underpeople a new level of recognition. A witness to the event, Lady Goroke, initiates the line of Jestocost, the Lords of the Instrumentality who will free the underpeople.

In "Under Old Earth," Lord Sto Odin of the Instrumentality, concerned that an overprotected humanity is on a suicidal course, seeks out Sun-Boy deep under old Earth in order to neutralize the powerful congohelium that holds his followers in sway. By destroying Sun-Boy, he frees Santuna, who becomes famous as Lady Alice More, a leader in instituting the Rediscovery of Man, which returns uncertainty—and the possibility of happiness—to humankind.

"Alpha Ralpha Boulevard" begins the Rediscovery of Man. The nightmare of perfection is over, and a measure of worry, disease, and uncertainty are restored. In this new age, Paul and Virginia think they are in love. Virginia, uncertain of Paul, climbs with him the vast boulevard in the sky, Alpha Ralpha, to consult the prediction of the Abba-dingo for the truth of their feeling. Before they can walk down, they are caught in a storm. Virginia falls to her death, but C'mell the cat woman rescues Paul.

In "The Ballad of Lost C'mell," Lord Jestocost of the Instrumentality, which is dedicated to helping the underpeople, contacts E'telekeli, their leader. They conspire successfully to better the lot of underpeople, with C'mell the cat woman serving as the telepathic medium. As an old man, dying but satisfied with his work, Jestocost learns that C'mell had loved him, more than anything, and that all of human history would know that love.

"A Planet Named Shayol" is set on a penal planet where inmates constantly grow new body parts that are harvested for medical use. The Instrumentality, learning of this and other abuses, closes Shayol, promising to restore inmates to happiness.

Analysis: In the 1950's and early 1960's, Cordwainer Smith brought a literary and poetic brand of science fiction to a genre dominated by hard science extrapolations. His world of talking animals, spacecraft lined with oysters, and boulevards into the sky suggests fantasy, but he is a science-fiction writer, one who deals with extraordinary extrapolations and analogical situations that have remarkable consistency and logic. He shows the impact of science rather science itself, and his stories focus on human relationships and reactions to a world created by science.

One of Smith's major themes is romantic love. Scanner Martel maintains contact with his humanity through his love for his wife. Helen America and Mr. Grey-no-more have a love transcending the vast emptiness of space. Go-Captain Taliano, his brain destroyed, nevertheless retains a "shy and silly love." Paul and Virginia feel compelled to play out a love story, and Jestocost and C'mell are figures in a story of true love denied. Romantic love is not a usual feature of science fiction, but it is a cornerstone of Smith's created world.

In another direction, Smith sees the dangers of a perfected world in which disease, danger, and need are eliminated; it is a sterile utopia of spoiled and unresponsive people. The people in "The Dead Lady of Clown Town" (1964), barely reacting to the brutal murder of the underpeople, are considerably less human than the beings derived from beasts. This is the perfected but suicidal world that Sto Odin sets out to remedy. His actions, indirectly but inevitably, bring about the Rediscovery of Man.

The treatment of the underpeople may be read as an allegory of racial inequality. The topic also speaks to developing scientific issues. Would a laboratory creation that behaves as a human be anything less than human? Have people thought through the implications of scientific discoveries? The underpeople challenge assumptions that they have. Smith warns that we must keep in touch with our humanity. Scanners, cut off from their senses (and figuratively their souls), are ready to kill Adam Stone, the scientist who can restore them to life.

Although his literary output was small, Cordwainer Smith has a special place in modern science fiction. His work cannot be compared easily with that of any other science-fiction writer.
—*Steve Anderson*

THE BEST SHORT STORIES OF J. G. BALLARD

Stories focusing on protagonists' mental and physiological relationships with a drastically altered, occasionally surreal environment

Author: J(ames) G(raham) Ballard (1930-   )
Genre: Science fiction—New Wave
Type of work: Stories
Time of plot: Primarily the near future
Location: Imaginary locales on Earth
First published: 1978

The Plot: *The Best Short Stories of J. G. Ballard* contains nineteen impressive works published between 1957 and 1978 in such British and American magazines as *New Worlds*, *The Magazine of Fantasy and Science Fiction*, and *Amazing Stories*. Together, these stories show the extraordinary imagination and range of Ballard's storytelling. There are tales of spaceflight, urban isolation, psychological manipulation, and the outbreak of strange, imaginary diseases. The stories take place in the overcrowded cities of the future, on abandoned South Sea islands, and within view of the quiet but suddenly terrifying lawns of suburbia.

Ballard's stories show his preoccupation with the internal landscapes of the mind. They also contain unusual responses to the challenges his characters face. Harry Faulkner, in "The Overloaded Man," suddenly loses touch with his suburban neighborhood. He begins to perceive the world as an abstract painting and decides to drown himself to extinguish this new sensory overload. Contrary to expectations, the short story views Faulkner's action as a relative success.

Far from confining himself to realistic places, disasters, or injuries, Ballard invents new ones for most of his stories. He creates vivid cities of the future, such as an imaginary subtropical community, where "The Cloud-Sculptors of Coral D" reside and create their imaginary art, and the refuse-littered, abandoned launchpads of Cape Canaveral in "The Cage of Sand," where two men and a woman have gathered to watch the nightly appearance of as many as seven dead astronauts who orbit Earth in their functionless capsules.

Ballard's protagonists, though thrust into strange new worlds and alien landscapes, generally accept these with little questioning, as does Count Axel in "The Garden of Time." His flowers are able to stop time outside his mansion, where barbarian hordes ready themselves for a final assault. They will succeed when his last flower has been plucked.

Like Count Axel and Louisa Woodwind, whose husband is one of the dead astronauts, Ballard's protagonists typically are well-educated, articulate, and emotionally controlled men and women. As Harry Faulkner shows, however, beneath this tranquil façade of reason, control, and clinical detachment is a deeper layer of strange obsessions and aberrant needs.

This defiance of the normal and fictional probing of the radically new are crucial aspects of many of the stories. "The Terminal Beach" successfully experiments with style and language. It focuses on Traven's mind-frame, which has guided him to maroon himself on the Pacific island of Eniwetok, the historical site of American nuclear tests. There, Traven tries to make his body a part of the natural landscape and to construct a complex system that integrates the living, the dead, and inanimate objects.

Analysis: Ballard's short stories were instrumental in the success of science fiction's New Wave movement. Many of the developments associated with it, such as a move toward inner space, a more critical attitude toward technology, and the redefinition of some of the conventions of science fiction (for example, time travel), are essential ingredients of Ballard's stories.

"Manhole 69" shows readers what an imaginative writer can do within the genre of science fiction. The story of three men whom a medical experiment has left with the inability to sleep turns to the unexpected when all three, rather than enjoy prolonged hours of productivity, withdraw into a form of autism.

The literary quality of such stories as "The Drowned Giant," which tells of the gradual dismemberment of the washed-up corpse of a gigantic man, also exemplifies how well New Wave science fiction brings literary re-

spectability to a literature formerly dismissed by most critics. The stylistic experimentation visible in tales such as "The Terminal Beach" makes these pieces unique.

Although Ballard's stories have been compared with the works of mainstream American authors Donald Barthelme and William S. Burroughs, their focus on the inner cosmos echoes significant works of other science-fiction writers. For example, Alfred Bester's haunting tale of a murderer on the run from telepathic policemen, *The Demolished Man* (1953), displays an intensity similar to Ballard's. Brian Aldiss also shares some of Ballard's concerns; in *Cryptozoic!* (1968; published in Great Britain as *An Age*, 1967), Aldiss takes the idea of time travel and accomplishes it with mind-altering drugs that allow his characters to leave the confines of the present.

With their uncomfortable dissection of Western cultural icons, stories such as "The Atrocity Exhibition" have been hailed as the fictional equivalent of the literary and cultural criticism of scholars such as Roland Barthes. Taking its cue from occupational therapy, "The Atrocity Exhibition" offers a series of violent pictures painted by imaginary inmates of an insane asylum. Its central, unsettling idea is that the products of human culture, taken from the fields of warfare, technology, art, and popular entertainment, not only are intrinsically violent but also correspond to the biological features of the human body.

From the stories in this collection, Ballard has moved on to write more experimental short fiction. He has also produced works whose content takes a more conventional form. He has even worked in the area of autobiography with his book *Empire of the Sun* (1984).

Ballard occasionally has been attacked by critics who have failed to grasp the premises of his fiction. Like the reviewer-turned-psychiatrist who perceived a psychopathic mind behind his work, they mistakenly have read his stories as straight advocacy of criminal insanity. Ballard's exploration of a new, purely fictional reality has met with increasing critical acclaim. His stories are often haunting and occasionally terrifying, but never conventional or dull.

—*R. C. Lutz*

BEYOND APOLLO

Interrogated after returning without his captain from an aborted mission to Venus, copilot Harry Evans tells so many different versions of the events that the truth is never discovered

Author: Barry N. Malzberg (1939-   )
Genre: Science fiction—New Wave

Type of work: Novel
Time of plot: 1981
Location: A space capsule and a federal institution near Cape Canaveral, Florida
First published: 1972

The Plot: *Beyond Apollo* tells the story of Harry M. Evans, the thirty-eight-year-old sole survivor of an ill-fated, two-man mission to Venus. Confined at a government institution near the Kennedy Space Complex in Florida, Evans is interrogated by Dr. Claude Forrest, a neurologist. The government wants to find out why the mission to Venus was aborted by one or two of the astronauts and what happened to the captain, whose body is missing. Evans' response is to tell a different story of the events every time he is questioned. In the absence of hard evidence, Evans' changing testimony increasingly frustrates Forrest, who is not able to establish the truth by the end of the novel.

The various explanations of the mission's failure make up a significant part of Evans' first-person narrative. Evans offers a rich variety of possible scenarios, always with the same momentary belief in their truth. There are reports in which the captain, whom Evans alternately calls Joseph Jackson or Jack Josephson, may have committed suicide, tried to rape Evans, or tried to murder him. He also may have been murdered by Evans or had an accident that sent him out of the space capsule's disposal hatch. The ejection of the captain's corpse into space is a common theme in most of Evans' versions, though in a few of them the captain became insubstantial and faded through the spaceship's metal toward the Sun.

The most outlandish of Evans' stories involves telepathic contact with the Venusians. During these "Great Venus Disturbances," the aliens tell the two astronauts that they must not land on Venus. If they do not change course, the Venusians threaten to kill one of the crew and send the other back to Earth to warn his government about the futility of further missions. Because a manual override of the programmed course seems impossible, either the aliens kill the captain or Evans performs the murder.

The central idea behind Evans' stories is that, in the absence of any surviving outside reference to check on his reports, any version has the potential to be true. This confusing outcome is mirrored by the textual complexity of the novel itself. *Beyond Apollo* reads as Evans' stream of consciousness. At one point, he even promises that one day he will write a novel about his experiences and call it *Beyond Apollo*.

Although the core of the novel deals with Evans' reaction to the failed Venus mission, *Beyond Apollo* also covers his private life on Earth. In these narrations, it is equally impossible to judge when Evans' recollections of his dysfunctional relationship with his wife, Helen, are grounded in reality, recount a dream, or come directly from his imagination. Similarly, Evans' account of his present confinement is riddled with ambiguities and invented episodes, such as his strangulation of Dr. Forrest.

In the end, *Beyond Apollo* paints the troubled picture of a man who has encountered some terrible horror in space. Evans' trauma has left him with an inability to find out—even for himself—which of his many stories is the true one.

Analysis: *Beyond Apollo* is a fine example of science fiction's New Wave of the 1960's and 1970's. Like many New Wave writers, Barry Malzberg sought to bring to the genre new stylistic devices and critical themes that contemporary writers of mainstream literature were using. Harry Evans thus has some of the haunted, introspective traits of a character by Saul Bellow or of Eugene O'Neill's protagonist Edmund Tyrone in *Long Day's Journey into Night* (1956).

At the same time, the self-referential form and the open ending of *Beyond Apollo* stand in opposition to the shape of much classical science fiction. Unlike Malzberg's text, classics such as Robert A. Heinlein's masterpiece *Starship Troopers* (1959) generally have been marked by accessible, straightforward writing, an optimistic belief in humanity's ability to explore space, and a goal-oriented drive toward the climactic solution to the major plot problem.

Although *Beyond Apollo* deals with the results of a failed space mission, the novel's interest does not lie in finding the problem, fixing it, and moving on. Its very refusal to tell the exact reason for the mission's failure turns the reader away from concrete, external problems and toward Malzberg's exploration of the inner space of Harry Evans. What emerges is the picture of Evans' personal traumatization at the hand of an overbureaucratized, indifferent space program that tries to turn idealistic young men into mindless robots performing superfluous tasks aboard remote-controlled spacecraft.

This focus on an imperfect protagonist, his loss of self, and the detailed vision of a sad, shabby, interior world is a trademark of the New Wave. Malzberg's novel ranks among the finest examples of this subgenre. It is as haunting as *Dying Inside* (1972), Robert Silverberg's excellent first-person account of a telepath who loses his extrasensory powers. *Beyond Apollo* also is close in spirit to Daniel Keyes's moving story "Flowers for Algernon" (1959), the diary of a mentally retarded man to whom a new drug temporarily gives the mind of a genius.

In addition to its close examination of Evans' troubles, *Beyond Apollo* suggests that something is generally and fundamentally wrong with America's space program. This is a negative stance rather unusual for much classic American science fiction, and it illustrates the New Wave's deep-rooted suspicion of anything related to the Establishment. This critical view places Malzberg's text within the tradition of Ray Bradbury's early subversive text, *The Martian Chronicles* (1950), in which Bradbury envisions how American culture degrades the red planet by littering its ancient landscape with prefabricated houses and hot dog stands.

As argued in *Beyond Apollo*, the space program suffers from a bloated bureaucracy that lacks any true sense of direction and cares for neither its men nor its scientific goals. This is a belief that Malzberg has explored in a series of related novels and short stories and that has earned him both scorn and praise from critics. Perhaps ironically for such a dark work, *Beyond Apollo* was given the inaugural John W. Campbell Memorial Award as the year's best science-fiction novel of 1972.   —*R. C. Lutz*

BEYOND THE GOLDEN STAIR

After escaping from prison, John Hibbert is forced to flee into the Everglades, where he and his companions discover a golden staircase, the entrance to an advanced civilization

Author: Hannes Bok (1914-1964)
Genre: Fantasy—alien civilization
Type of work: Novel
Time of plot: The late 1940's
Location: The Florida Everglades and Khoire
First published: 1970 (previously published as "The Blue Flamingo," *Startling Stories*, 1948)

The Plot: John Hibbert is haunted by a lifelong, recurring dream of a beautiful woman, a dream that continues into his adult life and even into battle. As a war veteran, he accepts employment with his service buddies and then is jailed when, as their cashier, he signs blank checks for them. After being transferred to the state penitentiary, Hibbert unwillingly joins Frank Scarlatti, who, with the help of his accomplice Burks, breaks out of prison and takes Hibbert with him.

They flee to the Florida Everglades in order to escape the authorities. They make their way to the swamp shanty of Scarlatti's girlfriend, Carlotta, who is supposed to guide them safely through the Everglades. Paddling deeper into the swamps, however, they come upon a hidden pool flanked by ruins and guarded by a blue flamingo. Carlotta makes some obscure historical references, from which Hibbert infers that this may actually be Ponce de Leon's famous Fountain of Youth. As a joke, Burks decides to wade into the pool to test its rejuvenating powers. The flamingo, however, attacks Burks, and Burks shoots the bird and kills it.

Before it dies, the flamingo summons a shining stairway into the sky. Climbing the stairs, the four find themselves at the threshold of Khoire. A booming voice warns them that they cannot stay because they have not been armed with the Sacred Sign, nor can they simply leave. Khoire must and will change them into their truest selves; they cannot hide or pretend to be what they are not. They meet Patur, the keeper of the Central Gate, who gives them the Crystal Mask, the function of which is to reveal the wearer's identity. To demonstrate its use, Patur reveals his own history. When Burks puts on the mask, Patur discovers that Burks has killed the blue flamingo, which Patur informs him was trying to warn him of Khoire's dangers. The greatest danger is the "change," the transformation of the person into his or her true form. Burks decides that to stay in Khoire would be better than being perpetually hunted by prison authorities. He offers to take the place of the blue flamingo in order to receive the Sacred Sign and remain in Khoire forever.

After Burks leaves, Scarlatti, Carlotta, and Hibbert go to the quarters prepared for them. There they meet Mareth, the woman who appears in Hibbert's recurring dream. She is a Watcher of the Qsin of Khoire, beings who patrol the earth and assist people in discerning and rooting out evil. Hibbert, immediately smitten by Mareth, declares his love. She, too, has a recurring dream about the man she will love, but Hibbert is not that man. She urges him to be patient until after his Change.

Afraid of his own transformation, Scarlatti insists upon seeing Burks. Patur takes them to see his self-induced change into the blue flamingo. Horrified at what he finds, Scarlatti decides to leave Khoire immediately and takes Mareth hostage with the gun he has concealed.

Because Scarlatti is not familiar with the dimensional warps of Khoire, however, Mareth and Hibbert manage to escape into the Jungles of Madness, the home of the sick and the demented, those whose transformations drove them insane. Monsters such as the Ksor, enormous alligators, prey on the unwary and the weak. Scarlatti and Carlotta, having unwisely chased Mareth and Hibbert into the jungle, are transformed into their true selves—a malignant dwarf and a hairless dog—and are soon consumed by the Ksor. It is also here that Hibbert becomes a giant, the man of Mareth's dream. They escape the Jungles of Madness, but Hibbert now has to leave Khoire in order to obtain the Sacred Sign and return to Mareth. Hibbert and Mareth passionately embrace, but Hibbert must descend the golden stair back to the pool, which Burks now guards. Paddling back through the Everglades, Hibbert has begun his quest to return to Khoire.

Analysis: An adventure and a love story, *Beyond the Golden Stair*, though relatively unknown, remains one of the most appealing novels in the genre, strongly resonating with A. Merritt's *The Moon Pool* (1919) and H. Rider Haggard's *The People of the Mist* (1894). Of particular interest is the creation of Khoire, a world populated by beings who have advanced far beyond human civilization, both technologically and philosophically, yet who remain compassionate toward humanity and its failings. Unfortunately, humanity has only superstitious and legendary glimmerings of the Khoireans. The Fountain of Youth, El Dorado, Jacob's Ladder, Ra the sun god, and Usipatra Vana all are mythical touchstones connecting human culture with that of Khoire.

Hannes Bok's greatest achievement lies in his charming rendition of the Cinderella myth. Hibbert is a weak, puny man, but he is also a courageous soul who is ultimately rewarded for his gallantry, his inner strength, and his love. Because Khoire strips away all pretensions and secrets, revealing the true self, physical appearance conforms to the depth of spiritual insight. As a result, Hibbert can overcome his physical deformities in Khoire and be transformed into the appropriate object of Mareth's desire. Hibbert's metamorphosis and his subsequent exile from Khoire represent the capacity, whatever the difficulties, to fulfill a dream that has haunted, perplexed, and maddened one's everyday life.   *—Jeffrey Cass*

BIG PLANET and SHOWBOAT WORLD

Adventure, intrigue, and romance during travels on an enormous planet containing many varied cultures

Author: Jack Vance (1916-   )
Genre: Science fiction—interplanetary romance
Type of work: Novels
Time of plot: The late twenty-sixth century

Location: Various locations on Big Planet
First published: *Big Planet* (1957; full text restored 1978; serial form, *Startling Stories*, September, 1952) and *Showboat World* (1975)

The Plot: Location is everything in these two novels. Big Planet is enormous, and all of Earth's splinter cultures seem to have migrated there, each convinced that its way of life is the only true way. There is no central government. Murder, torture, and intolerance are rife, and Earth is unable to exercise any real control over the planet. The magazine story of *Big Planet* was cut drastically and edited egregiously in its first book publication, one of the few instances in which a book became shorter than the original magazine story. The full original text was not restored until 1978. *Showboat World* was conceived retroactively as a sequel.

In *Big Planet*, a new ruler—the Bajarnum of Beaujolais, otherwise known as Charley Lysidder—has begun expanding his empire through various nefarious means, including assassination, child slavery, and other atrocities. A commission has been sent from Earth to investigate and take action to put an end to the threat. The commission's spaceship, sabotaged by Lysidder's agent, crashes near the edge of Lysidder's territory, killing all but the commission members and a very few others. When Claude Glystra, commission chairman, returns to consciousness a few days later, the radio operator, Abbigens, having proved to be Lysidder's agent, has escaped. Glystra has been nursed since the crash by a local girl named Nancy.

Because Lysidder obviously will send troops to capture the commission, Glystra decides that their only hope is to avoid Lysidder entirely and get to Earth Enclave, forty thousand miles away. Nancy begs to join the trek, but Glystra refuses at first.

Shortly after the journey begins, Abbigens is discovered leading troops to capture the commission. In the ensuing melee, Abbigens is killed and Nancy assists in defeating the troops. The trek resumes, and as the group encounters one new culture after another, it begins to shrink as members are killed or, in one case, defect to the local culture. This is the most interesting portion of the book because the various cultures are both original and fascinating.

After traveling for some time on foot and via native beast, boat, and highline, the party is reduced to four: Glystra, Nancy, commission member Bishop, and Corbus, the chief engineer of the spaceship. The highline has been cut, the party has been attacked by raiders from which they manage to escape, and they have arrived outside the site of Myrtlesee Fountain, reputed site of a renowned oracle. During the trip, Glystra and Nancy have developed an attraction for each other, although inconsistencies in Nancy's speech and behavior make Glystra suspect that she is not what she seems.

During the night, Bishop is killed and Nancy is kidnapped. Glystra and Corbus sneak into the city and bribe a local merchant to help them find Nancy. During the search, Glystra discovers the secret of the oracle: Material extracted from the brains of corpses and mixed with a local drug is injected into the brain of a living man, who then becomes superintelligent for a few moments before dying. Glystra also finds Nancy, not as a prisoner but as a now reluctant agent and consort of Lysidder.

Glystra is captured and scheduled to be injected for Lysidder's use as an oracle, but Corbus smuggles in a large supply of vitamins and amino acids that they believe will counteract the effect of the brain serum. During his session as oracle, Glystra gives confusing answers and feigns death, then is thrown into an abattoir, from which he escapes with the help of Corbus. They lay a trap for Lysidder, steal his airboat, reconcile with Nancy, and fly to Earth Enclave and safety.

Showboat World, although also set on Big Planet, takes place in a section far distant from the earlier story and is considerably more picaresque. Showboats ply the Vissal River and its tributaries, bringing various forms of entertainment to the many cultures spread along the banks. The two most notorious showboats are owned by rivals Appolon Zamp and Garth Ashgale. Their rivalry leads to the destruction of Zamp's boat and considerable damage to Ashgale's. The chicanery that accomplishes this is a key element of the book and is practiced by almost every character who appears.

King Waldemar of Sylvanesse, far up the river, has decreed a festival and a competition among six showboats. Zamp has been issued an invitation to compete and has joined forces with Damsel Blanche-Aster, a mysterious girl who is to help him find another showboat and sail it to Sylvanesse.

Theodorus Gassoon, dour and frugal, owns a boat that he prefers to keep moored and use as a museum. He falls under the spell of Blanche-Aster and agrees, reluctantly, to let Zamp use his boat for the journey and the competition. The voyage is long and perilous; as in *Big Planet* it is made interesting by the many weird cultures encountered along the way.

It becomes apparent in Sylvanesse that Zamp's production of William Shakespeare's *Macbeth* is poorly matched against the fantastic stagings of the other boats. During the show, Blanche-Aster reveals herself to be a descendant of a rival ruler and is hailed as the queen, deposing Waldemar. Hers is a short rule, because Gassoon accidentally shows an emblem that causes the populace to hail him as the king.

Zamp, sailing back down the river, is overtaken by Gassoon, who is fleeing on horseback after his emblem is destroyed and he is no longer recognized as the king. The two return to their original port and make new plans.

Analysis: Big Planet is an ingenious invention that could be used in many books. It is twenty-five thousand miles in diameter, yielding a surface area almost ten times that of Earth, of which about half is land. This makes it possible for many different cultures to exist on the planet without intruding on one another, thus providing a vehicle for many different stories. Furthermore, the planet has a mean density of slightly less than two, because the core and surface are notably deficient in heavy elements. As a result, the surface gravity is only slightly higher than that of Earth, despite the planet's size, and the climate is similar to Earth's. The lack of iron and other such metals makes development of technology difficult and long-range communication almost impossible. This, in turn, increases the isolation of the various cultures and enhances the general antipathy among them. Any large amounts of metal must be imported, at tremendous cost. Iron, in fact, is the basic standard for exchange because of its utility and rarity on the planet.

Jack Vance's contributions to science fiction are widely recognized. Several sources credit him with bringing sophistication to the interplanetary romance, which until then had largely consisted of weak plots constructed primarily to allow the hero to invent one new superscientific gadget after another, in order to resolve some new perilous situation. These two books are excellent illustrations of Vance's sophisticated approach.

Vance specializes in the picaresque and baroque, which is much more evident in *Showboat World* than in *Big Planet*. Whereas *Big Planet* is deeply concerned with the social and ethical problems inherent in the regimes of the planet and takes a more serious note, *Showboat World* treats the chicanery and ethical values of Zamp and his associates with amused tolerance. This is somewhat misleading, because Vance's work, taken as a whole, shows continuing concern with social values, particularly the problems of exploitation and the nature of freedom.

Vance is arguably without peer in the development of exotic and baroque backgrounds. As his career progressed, the backgrounds became more baroque and more detailed, and later works abound in footnotes and references to various "authorities" that serve to make the backgrounds very detailed and almost familiar.

These two novels, originally published twenty-three years apart but based in the same common background, are illustrative of Vance's development during this period. His writings in the period began with simpler, action-oriented plots and evolved to more involved, subtler plots with more detailed and exotic backgrounds.

Vance's career, spanning some fifty years, shows his continued concentration on baroque, meticulously detailed settings and his overall concern with moral values. Although he is also well known in the mystery field, in which he won the Edgar Award in 1960 for *The Man in the Cage*, he is much better known for his science fiction, having twice won the Hugo Award (in 1963, for "The Dragon Masters" in the short fiction category, and in 1967, for "The Last Castle" in the novelette category) in addition to a 1966 Nebula Award, given by the Science Fiction Writers of America, for "The Last Castle."

—*W. D. Stevens*

THE BIG TIME

Greta Forsane, an atemporal entertainer, assists soldiers in the Change Wars by working at an out-of-time rest and recovery station that is threatened from within

Author: Fritz Leiber (1910-1992)
Genre: Science fiction—time travel
Type of work: Novel
Time of plot: Simultaneous past, present, and future
Location: The Place, a pocket of space-time existing separate from the cosmos
First published: 1961 (serial form, *Galaxy Science Fiction*, 1958)

The Plot: A short Hugo-winning novel, *The Big Time* benefits from employing a limited number of characters at a fixed place over a few hours of narrative time, as if adhering to the dramatic unities of place, action, and a much modified sense of time. Initially, the narrator provides exposition leading up to a mystery. He then attempts to solve the mystery and rescue the group from disaster. The story is told as if to inform or to forewarn a newcomer to the temporal context the novel describes. The events reveal a greater sense of the problems associated with altering history.

Greta Forsane, an entertainer, tells of an experience at the Recuperation Station that reveals to her much about herself. The station is also manned by Sid, the officer in charge; Doc, a drunken veteran; Maud, an older party girl; Lilli, a recent addition; and Beau, second in command. They work for the Spiders, their side in the Change War. Their duties include healing wounded soldiers, operating the machinery that allows pickup and delivery of soldiers, and entertaining soldiers while they rest and recuperate. According to a previous plan, they pick up three soldiers on a scheduled arrival: Eric, a Nazi; Mark, a Roman; and Bruce, a Briton from the early 1900's. All characters are people who were resurrected from different times and places and brought into The Big Time. The arriving soldiers were engaged in a conflict in Saint Petersburg in 1883, attempting to kidnap an infant Albert Einstein back from their opponents, the Snakes.

Bruce, a recent recruit who is frustrated by the unsettling effects of changing the past, rants about being issued two left-handed gloves, a problem that an infatuated Lilli rectifies by using a surgical inverter. A surprise distress call adds Kaby, a mannish Cretian warrior maiden; Illi, a tentacled Lunan from the distant past; and Sevensee, a satyr from the distant future. They carry a tactical atomic bomb in a locked box, intending to use it against their adversaries in Romanized Egypt. After Bruce delivers a rebellious speech urging the assemblage to quit the war, the primary space-time mechanism, the Major Maintainer, is mysteriously stolen and the group is trapped in a void.

The novel then turns toward detective fiction, as they all search for the machine and the culprit who has hidden it. The question becomes urgent when Eric triggers a thirty-minute clock on the atomic bomb. A Minor Maintainer, which allows environmental changes within the station, is fought over, grabbed by Kaby, and used to coerce revelation. Lilli has used the surgical inverter to camouflage the Major Maintainer as an odd sculpture in the art gallery in a bid to follow Bruce's plea to stop the madness of the Change War. Bruce stops the bomb once it is returned to The Big Time. The novel ends with a return to previous conditions and a greater awareness of the similarity of the Spiders and Snakes.

Analysis: In introductory remarks, Fritz Leiber reveals a boyish glee in imagining characters from various periods engaged in battle. The book suggests that the importance is not in the battle; in fact, its conclusion emphasizes the relative meaninglessness of the war in which the characters are engaged. Rather, the novel hinges on the hypothetical meeting of people from vastly different cultures.

Leiber implies a consanguinity among these time travelers, an affinity they share for one another that celebrates their essential human traits and denies the idea that they would be too different to be able to work together. This nascent political correctness is perhaps indicative of science fiction and fantasy's tendency to forecast actual futures.

The concept of historical conflation is well established in the later Riverworld works (begun in 1971) by Philip José Farmer. The time travel narrative owes ancestry to H. G. Wells's *The Time Machine* (1895). A complication in Leiber's work involves the problem of changes made to the time line. Here Leiber indicates that The Big Time is largely unaffected, except that memories are altered, calling this "the law of conservation of reality." This disturbance of memory bothers Bruce, a poet and analogically a stand-in for the author; he raises serious concerns about the implications of altering the past. Through other veteran characters' dialogues, Leiber conceives of time as resistant to change and asserts that although future events may differ in particulars, the general drift of events and contexts will not be altered radically. This is a departure from the concept of temporal change as described by Alfred Bester in *The Stars My Destination* (1957). Leiber further discusses changes made to history in *The Mind Spider and Other Stories* (1961); the material was reassembled as *The Change War* (1978).

Perhaps the most interesting references are the metaphors used to describe the temporal contexts. Greta describes The Big Time as a train in continual forward motion. When soldiers go on their assigned missions, they get off this train and enter The Little Time, where events do change. On The Big Time, conditions do not alter and characters do not age, though they do construct histories of their experiences.

Even though Greta and her compatriots realize that they are bound to an endless conflict in which they no longer believe, the alternative of dissolution and loss of identity is less attractive. They rise from the events of the novel with greater wisdom, greater compassion, and a sense of value inhering in actions rather than outcomes. They live an alteration of the old maxim that the ends justify the means; instead, they live as though the means justify the means.   —*Scott D. Vander Ploeg*

THE BILL, THE GALACTIC HERO SERIES

Bill, an Imperial Space Trooper, experiences a variety of adventures while fighting the alien enemy Chingers

Author: Harry Harrison (1925-   )
Genre: Science fiction—future war
Type of work: Novels
Time of plot: The distant future
Location: Various spacecraft and imaginary planets
First published: *Bill, the Galactic Hero* (1965), *Bill, the Galactic Hero: The Planet of the Robot Slaves* (1989), *Bill, the Galactic Hero on the Planet of Bottled Brains* (1990, with Robert Sheckley), *Bill, the Galactic Hero on the Planet of Tasteless Pleasure* (1991, with David Bischoff), *Bill, the Galactic Hero on the Planet of Zombie Vampires* (1991, with Jack C. Haldeman II), *Bill, the Galactic Hero on the Planet of Ten Thousand Bars* (1991, with David Bischoff), and *Bill, the Galactic Hero: The Final Incoherent Adventure* (1991, with David M. Harris)

The Plot: The Bill, the Galactic Hero series was begun in 1965, as a single novel. That novel ends with an afterword, with Bill as a recruiting sergeant, suggesting that no sequels were planned. In 1989, the series was continued. A note by Harry Harrison was added to later printings of the original novel, informing the reader that Bill had many other adventures before becoming a recruiting sergeant.

Bill, the Galactic Hero begins with Bill, a white farm boy whose ambition is to become a Technical Fertilizer Operator, being forced into the Space Troopers. A hypnotic device planted in his boot causes him to enlist. After particularly brutal training, including conditioning to hate the seven-foot, reptilian Chingers, he is sent to war.

Bill meets Eager Beager, a disgustingly nice guy who likes to shine other recruits' boots. Beager eventually is revealed to be a Chinger spy named Bgr. He discloses that Chingers are actually only seven inches long and are peaceful. Bill is assigned to be a fuse tender. In an explosion, he is badly hurt and loses his left arm. This is replaced by a black man's right arm.

Bill is recruited by the Galactic Bureau of Investigation, which assigns him to infiltrate the underground. It turns out that almost all members of the underground are secret agents of one sort or another. Bill is then sent to the planet Veneria, where he shoots off his right foot to avoid going back to battle.

In *The Planet of the Robot Slaves* (shortened titles will be used for the remainder of this article), Bill's missing right foot has been replaced by a huge, mutated chicken foot because there is a shortage of human feet. The hospital where Bill is recovering is strafed by robot dragons. When one is captured, it is found to be labeled "Made in USA." Bill, along with recruits Cy BerPunk, Meta Tarsil, and others, is assigned to find the planet Usa. The planet turns out to be ruled by metal creatures and worked by robot slaves.

After Bill becomes involved in a war between Roman legions and medieval knights led by King Arthur, the British forces persuade Bill to go with Merlin to persuade the god Mars to stop the war. Mars turns out to be a projection and sound system. As Bill prepares to leave the planet, Bgr offers him a new, human foot in exchange for Bill's work to end the war.

The Planet of Bottled Brains begins with Bill complaining about his new foot, which has turned into an alligator claw. He is forced to go to the planet Tsuris, which might be a Chinger stronghold. It turns out to be a planet with many immortal brains but not enough bodies to go around. Bill's body is wanted to house a Tsuris brain. He escapes and becomes engaged in a series of adventures fighting Huns, Carthaginians, and other anachronistic armies. Finally, Bill meets the Alien Historian, who has arranged all of this in an attempt to change history for the better.

In *The Planet of Tasteless Pleasure*, Bill has acquired a "mood foot" that changes form according to his mood. Bill takes a walk on the beach and follows a satyr, who pulls him under the water. He finds himself in a land of mythical beasts and persons, and he is told that he must find the god Zeus to redeem himself.

The satyr, who turns out to be a robot controlled by Bgr, leads Bill on a trip to find the Fountain of Hormones, on the theory that humans are so warlike because they are oversexed. They find the fountain after a series of confusing adventures that seem to take place in the Old West of Earth's United States. Finally, Bill is again rescued, and his foot returns to normal human form.

The Planet of Zombie Vampires is concerned with a battle against particularly repulsive aliens on an unnamed planet. Assorted stereotyped troopers help Bill in his mission of destroying the planet. At the novel's close, Bill finds a note from Bgr, who has vanished, along with a new foot.

The Planet of Ten Thousand Bars begins with Bill being assigned to infiltrate the Commupop Party, a group of dissidents who read good literature instead of the propaganda comics approved by the Empire. He finds himself on Barworld, a planet devoted to drinking. There he finds a time portal named Dudley Do-Do and attempts to travel in time to undo apparent damage to the past and prevent an alternative present, ruled by Nazis, from oc-

curring. A series of extremely confusing time travel adventures ends with the appearance of Adolf Hitler and his obliteration by Bgr.

The last book in the series, *The Final Incoherent Adventure*, concerns a mission to the planet Eyerack, which contains the only known neutron mine in the galaxy. Because neutrons are needed to make neutron bombs and the inhabitants of the planet have decided to stop exporting the essential product, they must be subdued. During his mission, Bill is recruited by several resistance groups and by the enemy army. The latest series of defective right feet ends with replacement by a perfectly good hand.

Analysis: The Bill, the Galactic Hero books are designed to poke fun at a number of aspects of both science fiction and reality. From the outset, the books were a satire of space opera, a subgenre of science fiction consisting of adventure stories set in futuristic worlds or on spaceships. Harrison himself wrote such novels, the most famous being his Stainless Steel Rat series (1961-1987), involving an interplanetary intelligence operative.

Sequels to the original *Bill, the Galactic Hero* satirized more recent science fiction. In *The Planet of Bottled Brains*, Bill is rescued by the ship *Gumption*, run by Captain Dirk and First Officer Splock, an obvious takeoff on the *Star Trek* television series. In the same book, a brave captain, Ham Duo, and his mate, Chewgumma, are parodies of the heroes of the film *Star Wars* (1977). Harrison even deliberately parodies his own work: Ottar, a character in a *Drunkards and Flagons* game (a parody of the game *Dungeons and Dragons*), is lifted directly from Harrison's *The Technicolor Time Machine* (1967).

At another level, science fiction in general is satirized by the use of names that are ridiculous or clearly based either on reality and cultural icons or on other fiction. Deathwish Drang is a sadistic drill sergeant, Eager Beager is an insanely helpful recruit, and Rambette is a female warrior.

Harrison savages the military and political hierarchies. All the military personnel drink to excess and curse in virtually every sentence. The universal curse is "bowb," which works as noun, adjective, and adverb but has no particular meaning other than emphasis. Military officers are universally stupid and sadistic. Bureaucrats, including the emperor and high military leaders, are depicted as mentally deficient. The enlisted men are all brainwashed.

Most interesting of all are the Chingers, the eternal enemies of the Empire. They are depicted to Trooper recruits as bloodthirsty reptiles seven feet long but in fact are actually seven inches long and never engaged in warfare before they were attacked by the Empire. Bgr, initially known as Eager Beager, works throughout the series to try to get Bill to stop the war with the Chingers.

The series as a whole condemns the concept and practice of warfare. Bill is trapped into participation. He becomes a Trooper under hypnosis and is required to remain a Trooper or face execution. The Chinger enemies are depicted far more sympathetically than are the leaders of the human Empire. Innocent civilians are slaughtered on numerous occasions, but official press releases and interviews suggest otherwise.

The seven books in the series vary in tone, at least partially because five of them were written with four different collaborators, but certain themes are common. Bill is forever trying to find a satisfactory right foot to replace his original one, and Bgr is constantly trying to get Bill to stop the war. Their efforts are futile because the galactic bureaucracy is more interested in propaganda than in understanding or changing the facts behind that propaganda.

Bill, the Galactic Hero and all of its sequels are hilarious, but readers will stop to think along the way. Bill himself undergoes many changes, both physical and psychological, but he always returns to being a Trooper. This is the basic message. Like the robot slaves of the second book, Bill ultimately is powerless to change his life. He has been brainwashed to defend the Empire even though rationally he is convinced that the Empire is committing genocide.

—Marc Goldstein

THE BIRTHGRAVE TRILOGY

A woman with extraordinary powers takes a journey of self-discovery and later is pursued by the son she abandoned

Author: Tanith Lee (1947-   )
Genre: Fantasy—superbeing
Type of work: Novels
Time of plot: Undefined
Location: Various provinces of a planet similar to Earth
First published: *The Birthgrave* (1975), *Vazkor, Son of Vazkor* (1978), and *Quest for the White Witch* (1978)

The Plot: This story consists of three first-person narratives, the first told by the heroine and the second and third told by her son. *Vazkor, Son of Vazkor* and *Quest for the White Witch* may be considered as a single sequel to *The Birthgrave*.

In *The Birthgrave*, a nameless woman awakes in a cave beneath a volcano. She knows nothing of herself, her origin, or her reason for being where she is. As the volcano stirs, an enigmatic voice calling itself Karrakaz taunts her. She is evil and deserves death, it tells her. If she leaves the cave, the volcano will erupt, destroying a village and surrounding countryside. The voice adds that she is inhuman; her only kinship is with Jade. Bewildered and frightened, the woman flees to the village, where her healing powers and strange albino appearance convince the folk of her divinity. She learns that she never needs food or drink.

Soon after her arrival, the bandit Darak takes her from the village, before its destruction. She shares many adventures with him, the greatest of which is a grueling chariot race held in a town where Darak is discovered to be an outlaw. After he is hanged, the woman moves on. By now she has learned that she is immune even to mortal wounds.

In the city-state of Ezlann, she meets Vazkor, who resembles Darak. He has learned magic that is similar to her inborn talents. She hates him for using her apparent divinity to aid his greedy conquests of other towns. He impregnates her against her will. She kills him, and his empire falls.

Next, she joins a nomadic tribe and secretly bears a son at the same time that the chief's wife bears a stillborn child. After exchanging babies, she escapes to the sea. She is attacked by a dragon but is rescued by a passing spaceship. The crew tells her that she brought the ship down herself. Aided by the ship's computer, she learns that she is the last member of an ancient race destroyed by a plague. They had sought refuge in the cave, but to no avail. She survived by falling into a deep coma, in which she remained until awakened by the volcano's eruption. Karrakaz is her own name, and Jade is a gem implanted in her forehead, marking her as royalty. As *The Birthgrave* closes, Karrakaz leaves the ship to find a new life.

Vazkor, Son of Vazkor links the first and third books. Although it does not significantly advance the plot, it introduces Karrakaz's son, Vazkor. After his ritual tattooing leaves no mark, he fights several men at once, killing them all and emerging unscathed. When he raids a neighboring town with his tribe, Vazkor terrifies the defenders, who believe him to be the original Vazkor returned from the dead. Vazkor initially believes that his gift of immortality is inherited from his father; later he discovers that his powers come from his mother, not his father. Infuriated that her abandonment condemned him to a life of hardship with a nomadic tribe when he might have been a powerful and invincible king, Vazkor decides to find and kill the white witch.

Quest for the White Witch begins at the start of Vazkor's journey. By the time he reaches the opulent city of Bar-Ibithni, he has come to be feared and respected. He makes an old woman (Lellih) young and beautiful but unwittingly gives her powers like his own. She becomes the leader of a cult that worships him. Lellih tries to seduce him, but Vazkor rejects her. He becomes a close friend of Sorem, the emperor's son. He helps Sorem win a civil war against his rival siblings, but soon afterward he begins an affair with Sorem's mother. Discovering this scandal, Sorem vows to punish his friend, but a plague (sent by an angry Lellih) kills the young ruler and most of his subjects before he can fulfill the vow. Vazkor finds and kills Lellih but is himself slain. When he rises again, he leaves the city to resume his search.

After a long journey, Vazkor arrives in the far south, where Karrakaz is worshiped; Vazkor meets several albino children who share her powers. One of them, lovely Ressaven, claims to be Vazkor's sister. Despite this, they have sex. Ressaven tries to keep Vazkor from finding Karrakaz's abode, but he overcomes all resistance. Finally, he confronts his mother, who has been masquerading as Ressaven. Shamed by his incest, Vazkor leaves, but ultimately he returns to Karrakaz, planning to breed a new race of immortals with her.

Analysis: Tanith Lee had several children's books to her credit before she wrote the Birthgrave trilogy. Despite the fact that the trilogy was her first published adult fantasy, it was the work that boosted her career. The first volume was published by DAW in 1975, when Ballantine Books began an effort to increase interest in fantasy literature with novels such as *The Sword of Shannara* (1977) by Terry Brooks. Prior efforts to establish fantasy as a profitable business had failed, with the exception of retellings of well-known legends. Ballantine's success led DAW to feature new fantasies, including the Birthgrave trilogy. Lee became one of director Donald A. Wollheim's protégés. The year 1976 saw the beginning of a boom in science-fiction and fantasy book publishing, and Lee's lengthy trilogy could not have been better timed.

Critics' response to the Birthgrave trilogy is mixed. Marion Zimmer Bradley, a renowned author with a reputation as a harsh critic, wrote an introduction for the trilogy praising Lee's presentation of credible characters and rich settings. Other critics agree with Lee's description of her style as undisciplined and erratic. Her prose is highly descriptive, but the meaning often gets lost in grandiose wording. The trilogy lacks balance as a whole. *The Birthgrave* is 408 pages, whereas *Vazkor, Son of Vazkor* is a mere 220 pages. *Quest for the White Witch* is almost as long as *The Birthgrave*, at 381 pages.

The Birthgrave trilogy, with its tale of a beautiful princess from a lost civilization, follows an old but popular theme. This fashion began in the late 1800's with authors such as Sir H. Rider Haggard, who wrote *She* (1887). Books in this vein tell stories of heroic explorers who find fabulous, decadent civilizations in mysterious lands. The tales reflect the great interest in lost civilizations during the late nineteenth century, when discoveries such as Heinrich Schliemann's city of Troy made headlines. To contemporary authors, such discoveries inspired wonderful settings for romantic adventures; the lost cities about which they wrote generally are ruled by an exotic, barbaric, and merciless woman who bewitches the explorer. Tanith Lee has an interest in past civilizations, and she is clearly drawing from these examples in her depiction of Karrakaz as amoral, powerful, regal, and beautiful. When her son confronts her, he is the same heroic explorer.

The Birthgrave trilogy also exemplifies the rise of feminine heroes and female authors in science fiction and fantasy. Unlike Haggard's barbarian queens, Lee's Karrakaz is not a prize to be won by a burly explorer, nor does she need rescuing. The one time she is saved, she calls her rescuers to her by sheer force of will. She is always in control. Even in the second and third books, when her son is the focus of most of the action, Karrakaz remains his goal and guiding force. Lee also points out that Vazkor inherits his gifts from a woman who scorns the traditional role of motherhood. If the adventures of Karrakaz had continued, she certainly would have become the immortal ruler of a new race of her own creation.

Marion Zimmer Bradley helped to spearhead the feminist science fiction/fantasy movement in the 1970's with her Darkover books, such as *The Heritage of Hastur* (1975). The number of female authors in science fiction and fantasy continues to increase, including C. J. Cherryh, Mercedes Lackey, Melanie Rawn, Jennifer Roberson, Tanith Lee, Lois McMaster Bujold, and many more.

Like its precursors, the Birthgrave trilogy contains no deep truths, New Wave philosophies, or cautionary messages for twentieth century society. Lee never flinches from serious topics such as sex, guilt, and power, but she clearly did not intend her trilogy to be a feminist treatise. The Birthgrave trilogy is for the most part an enjoyable, rousing adventure that draws on an established theme and satisfies the need for fresh approaches that continues to galvanize the writing of fantasy literature.

—*Carla Hall Minor*

THE BLACK CLOUD

An extraordinary alien being approaches Earth, and scientists communicate with it

Author: Fred Hoyle (1915-   )
Genre: Science fiction—superbeing
Type of work: Novel
Time of plot: The 1960's, and 2021
Location: England and the United States
First published: 1957

The Plot: *The Black Cloud* concerns the apocalyptic visit of an enormous gaseous cloud to Earth in the years 1967-1968. It is first sighted by a young Norwegian astronomer as he is studying the night sky through the Schmidt Telescope at the Mount Wilson Observatory in California. World-renowned astronomers are immediately informed at England's Cambridge University, where Dr. Christopher Kingsley, an astronomy professor, calls for a meeting with scientists from the United States, England, and Australia. Scientists at the California Institute of Technology in Pasadena predict that it will take the cloud approximately eighteen months to arrive. Even though the damage will be cataclysmic, precautions can be taken, depending on where people live. Survival will depend on people's ability to bury themselves deep enough in the ground to protect themselves first from the intense heat caused by molecular collisions in the upper atmosphere and then from the cold that results when the cloud blocks the sun's rays.

Both the president of the United States and the prime minister of England fear that knowledge of the cloud's arrival will result in mass panic, so they try to suppress the facts. Kingsley, however, threatens to expose the coming of the cloud if these officials fail to do so. Kingsley, who becomes the leader of the scientists, decides to move their equipment to an estate called Nortonstowe, which he establishes as the center of radio communication for the world. The cloud arrives months earlier than expected, resulting in floods, hurricanes, and tremendous fluctuations in temperature.

When the weather stabilizes, the scientists begin to realize that the black cloud is a living and intelligent being, and they initiate procedures to try to communicate with it. The cloud quickly learns the English language and mathematical formulas. With communication established, an enormous exchange of information begins, and the cloud informs human beings that unless they address Earth's major problem, overpopulation, there will be terrible consequences. The cloud tells them that it is more than 500 million years old, and it offers the astronomers its definition of intelligent life: "something that reflects the basic structure of the universe. . . . We're both constructed in a way that reflects the inner pattern of the Universe."

In the meantime, both the English and American governments have become concerned about the cloud's destructive power and form a plan to drive it away by firing hydrogen rockets into its interior to disrupt its electrical circuitry. The cloud decides that it will not destroy Earth and that it will soon depart. The astronomers, however, insist that it remain long enough to transmit as much of its scientific knowledge as possible. The cloud attempts to reprogram the brains of Kingsley and another scientist so that they can absorb information more quickly, but both volunteers die in the process. The truth of the cloud is never made public. The novel takes the form of a manuscript by one of the scientists at Nortonstowe, left to the grandson of Ann Halsey, a concert pianist who had been at Nortonstowe to provide entertainment for the scientists. The author implies that the grandson is also the grandson of Kingsley.

Analysis: *The Black Cloud* was the first science-fiction novel written by one of the world's most widely recognized cosmologists and astrophysicists, Fred Hoyle. For many years, Hoyle was a professor of astronomy at Cambridge, and he was knighted by Queen Elizabeth II. He also was the chief exponent of the steady state theory of the universe, which contradicted the popular big bang theory, in which the majority of astronomers had believed for many years. *The Black Cloud* was Hoyle's fictional demonstration of his theory. He also hypothesized that life began by the movement of huge interstellar clouds through the universe and the subsequent seeding of planets, including Earth. He explained his complex theory in a best-selling nonfiction book called *The Nature of the Universe* (1950); that work was attacked obliquely by the most famous exponent of the big bang theory, George Gamow, in his *The Creation of the Universe* (1952).

The Black Cloud became a best-seller and one of modern science fiction's more famous examples of an author's ability to combine the subgenres of superbeing with catastrophe (although, in this case, the cloud turns out to be both intelligent and benign). What makes this novel so compelling is the scientific authenticity that Hoyle's vast background brings to both the characters and the complex nature of information that makes up the narrative. Hoyle became the acknowledged leader of the Cambridge cosmographers and continued to argue for the steady state theory of the universe.

—Patrick Meanor

BLACK EASTER
and
THE DAY AFTER JUDGMENT

At a businessman's instigation, a magician summons demons, triggering Armageddon; when the forces of Hell win the battle, Satan announces that God is dead and reluctantly assumes the divine throne

Author: James Blish (1921-1975)
Genre: Fantasy—apocalypse
Type of work: Novels
Time of plot: The late twentieth century
Location: Primarily Italy and California's Death Valley
First published: *Black Easter* (1968) and *The Day After Judgment* (1971)

The Plot: James Blish considered *Black Easter* and *The Day After Judgment* to be one narrative unit. As one unit, they are part of the *After Such Knowledge* trilogy (1991), which also includes *A Case of Conscience* (1958) and *Doctor Mirabilis* (1964). The three parts of the trilogy are connected more by theme than by plot. *Doctor Mirabilis* is a historical novel about thirteenth century scholar Roger Bacon; *A Case of Conscience* is a science-fiction novel about an alien society that seems to be free of sin. All the books deal with theological themes of innocence, sin, knowledge, and power.

In *Black Easter* and *The Day After Judgment*, traditional European ceremonial magic actually works. This magic requires summoning spirits or demons. Both "white" (good) magic and "black" (evil) magic exist. White magicians have limited power and call on demiurges. Black magicians have extensive power obtained through the use of demons. A covenant governs the relationship between white magic and black magic. Blish is vague about the precise terms of the covenant, but it allows a priest to be an observer at the summoning of demons as long as he does not interfere with the ceremony. Blish's "Author's Note" explains that he has tried to present magic as it would be if it were real, using historical sources. Blish also cautions that he has not presented enough information for readers to attempt the rituals for themselves.

In *Black Easter*, an American businessman named Baines approaches an expatriate magician, Theron Ware, who lives in Italy. Baines is accompanied by his special executive assistant, Jack Ginsberg. As a test of Ware's powers, Baines wants him to commit an untraceable murder, with a demon as the killer. After the success of two test murders, Baines commissions Ware to "let all the major demons out of Hell for one night." Another major character, Father Domenico, belongs to a religious order that practices white magic, primarily treasure hunting. Father Domenico's order sends him to observe the ritual commissioned by Baines. On Easter, Baines conjures forty-eight demons, unleashing Armageddon. When Ware tries to send the demons back to Hell, Satan appears and mocks him. Father Domenico's crucifix explodes in his hand. *Black Easter* ends with three sinister words, "God is dead."

As *The Day After Judgment* begins, Baines, Ware, and Domenico try to deal with the triumph of Hell in the final battle against Heaven. Simultaneously, at Strategic Air Command headquarters in the United States, General D. Willis McKnight and various scientists try to understand what has happened in the nuclear exchange that was part of Armageddon. General McKnight and his aides discover that the City of Dis, the fortified lower circles of Hell in Dante Alighieri's *Inferno* (part 1 of *The Divine Comedy*, c. 1320), has appeared in California's Death Valley. An intense military assault upon the walls of Dis ends in defeat.

Baines, Ginsberg, Ware, and Domenico travel separately to the United States. They meet in Death Valley and together enter Dis. At its center, they find Pandemonium (thus combining poet John Milton's Hell with Dante's). At the center of Pandemonium, they find Satan. Speaking in Miltonic verse, Satan informs them that, in God's absence, he has been forced to take on the divine role. He begs them to take it from him, saying that God had always intended humans to assume divine status. The novel ends ambiguously: After Satan's verse monologue, Dis vanishes, and the men are left in the desert. The narrative suggests that they have been spiritually renewed.

Analysis: Together with *Doctor Mirabilis* and *A Case of Conscience*, *Black Easter* and *The Day After Judgment* are often thought to be Blish's best work. Written toward the end of his career, the books explore the dilemma of the existence of evil in a world created by a good God. The dilemma is usually stated in the form that if God is both all-powerful and all-good, how can God allow evil to exist? These novels answer the question by showing God deliberately restraining his power. By the covenant, Father Domenico, a representative of good, cannot do anything to hinder or stop Theron Ware's summoning of demons. It is logical, then, that God is discovered to be dead at the end of *Black Easter*; death, after all, is the ultimate restraint. The self-restraint practiced by God allows the forces of evil nearly complete freedom of action. Ironically, when evil triumphs, Satan finds that he must unwillingly take the role of God. When Satan assumes the divine throne, he must give up the freedom he enjoyed as ruler of Hell and submit to the restraints imposed on good.

In a favorable review of *Black Easter* in *The Magazine of Fantasy and Science Fiction*, Joanna Russ describes Blish's point of view as Manichean. In Manicheanism, good and evil are separate powers that have struggled with each other throughout history. In *Black Easter* and *The Day After Judgment*, however, good is absent or inactive, while evil is present and active. Thus, good and evil do not fight on equal terms. Instead of struggling with evil, good withdraws and leaves the field open for evil.

Black Easter is dedicated to the memory of C. S. Lewis. *Black Easter* and *The Day After Judgment* recall Lewis' novel *That Hideous Strength* (1945), in which a limited Armageddon occurs. Lewis' novel, however, expresses his Christian faith, with good triumphing, while Blish's books reflect his agnosticism through the death of God and the enthronement of Satan. Lewis wrote to express a belief system, but Blish wrote to explore the possibilities of good and evil as they relate to the human search for knowledge. Blish's books also have parallels to Lewis' *The Screwtape Letters* (1942). An epistolary novel, this book deals with demoniac temptation of modern human beings.

Black Easter and *The Day After Judgment* also allow comparisons with other works. They have thematic similarities to Walter M. Miller, Jr.'s *A Canticle for Leibowitz* (1960). Like Blish, Miller explores the uses of knowledge in the conflict between good and evil. Although Charles Williams' novels differ greatly in style from Blish's, Theron Ware would fit easily into Williams' work, for example, in a novel such as *War in Heaven* (1930). The entire *After Such Knowledge* trilogy has many links to the Faust story, as Blish deals with the theme of knowledge and sin.

A secondary theme of *Black Easter* and *The Day After Judgment* is nuclear war and its aftermath. Baines considers destruction an art that he pursues. In pursuing this art, he has provoked wars, not to increase his profits as an arms manufacturer but for aesthetic pleasure. In developing this aspect of Baines's character, Blish satirizes the arms industry and the Cold War mentality. To Baines, unleashing demons on the earth is his greatest work of art.

Baines orders a scientist in his employ, Adolph Hess, to observe the magician at work. In doing this, Baines plans to add the power of magical knowledge to the power he already has. Hess begins as a scientific skeptic, but when he sees that Ware really commands demons, he is drawn into the practice of magic. When Hess violates the rules of magic, he is eaten by a demon. Hess is a kind of cut-rate Faust, making compromises with evil for the sake of power, whereas his boss is a more successful Faust, gaining ultimate knowledge at the end of *The Day After Judgment*. The ultimate knowledge that Baines acquires comes in the face-to-face discussion with Satan in Death Valley. Satan begs "Man"—in the persons of Baines, Ginsberg, Ware, and Domenico—to take the suffering of being God away from him.

Although the plot of *Black Easter* and *The Day After Judgment* may appear shocking and even blasphemous, Blish does not romanticize or glorify evil. In the same way, he does not romanticize good. He explores the nature of human motivation by reducing it to primary forms. Baines wishes to use power for purely aesthetic motives; Ware shares the same motivation. He does not use his knowledge of magic for personal power or gain but to extend the knowledge he already has. Ware agrees to Baines's plan to unleash demons because he hopes to learn something new from the experiment. In the end, all four major characters confront a mystery beyond their understanding. This confrontation changes them in unspecified but potentially positive ways.   —*Gene Doty*

BLACK EMPIRE

A ruthless but brilliant leader brings about the formation of a worldwide conspiracy of black peoples that eventually conquers the African continent

Author: Samuel I. Brooks (George S. Schuyler, 1895-1977)
Genre: Science fiction—future war
Type of work: Novel

Time of plot: The 1930's
Location: The United States, Africa, and Europe
First published: 1991 (serial form, "The Black
   Internationale," *Pittsburgh Courier*, November 21,
   1936-July 3, 1937, and "Black Empire," *Pittsburgh
   Courier*, October 2, 1937-April 16, 1938)

The Plot: Lost for some fifty years, *Black Empire* was finally determined to have been authored by noted African American satirist George S. Schuyler. *Black Empire* as published in 1991 is actually two serial novels, "The Black Internationale" and "Black Empire," that originally appeared in the *Pittsburgh Courier*, a black newspaper. Although published under separate titles, the two stories fit together and are appropriately collected under a single title. The original newspaper publications were edited into the novel by Robert A. Hill and R. Kent Rasmussen.

Black Empire tells of the exploits of Dr. Henry Belsidus and his efforts to construct a worldwide black conspiracy to reconquer Africa. By profession a medical doctor, Belsidus earns his living serving the needs of New York's white upper crust. He is slowly amassing, largely by criminal means, an immense amount of wealth to finance his subversive projects. Readers encounter Dr. Belsidus through Carl Slater, a reporter for the Harlem *Blade* who inadvertently stumbles upon Belsidus committing a brutal murder. Belsidus captures Slater and turns him into his personal assistant. The *Black Empire* saga is then narrated by Slater.

"Black Internationale" tells the story of the first dramatic steps toward the execution of Belsidus' plans. Slater discovers that Belsidus has been thorough in his planning. With spies and operatives everywhere, Belsidus is able to generate funds, pursue military and other research, and slowly create a worldwide conspiracy of black intellectuals and inventors. The Black Internationale has made stunning advances in agriculture, energy production, mass communication, and military tactics and weaponry. After a Mississippi lynching, Belsidus puts into full swing his plan to destabilize the United States. After dropping a previously unimagined incendiary device on the white community responsible for the lynching, Belsidus manages to create suspicion among Protestant whites that Jews or Catholics are somehow responsible.

Slater is by now an enthusiastic participant in Belsidus' project, although he is often put off by Belsidus' ruthless tactics. Slater's commitment is heightened as he becomes attracted by and attached to Patricia Givens,

the head of Belsidus' air force. As Belsidus' divide-and-conquer scheme begins to take effect, specific steps are prepared for the initial invasion of Africa. With white Americans busy fighting one another, no one pays much attention to the substantial military force Belsidus begins to mobilize. Belsidus' fleet of ships lands in Liberia, and soon his forces take over the whole of the West African country.

"Black Internationale" climaxes with the conquest of all of Africa and the execution or expulsion of all whites. Having used the same divide-and-conquer tactics among the European colonialists as pursued in the United States, Belsidus successfully establishes the "Black Empire" as the European powers are distracted by the onset of World War II.

"Black Empire" picks up where "Black Internationale" leaves off. A significant portion of this component of the novel chronicles the accomplishments of the new authority. Developments in religion, agriculture, communications technology, and health care are considered. With the ending of inter-European hostilities, the European countries turn their attention to regaining their African colonies, and "Black Empire" becomes an adventure story.

Belsidus first resists the Europeans with a form of biological warfare. Slater and Givens—now husband and wife—are part of the counterinsurgency in Europe. The counterinsurgents, under the leadership of the white Martha Gaskin, gas to death thousands of British technicians. After many exciting escapes, Carl Slater and his new wife make their way back to the capital of the Black Empire. Belsidus then unveils a secret weapon, a ray that renders inoperable all European machinery. The Black Empire is saved and preserved.

Analysis: There is little evidence to suggest that Schuyler was especially conversant with science-fiction conventions. Although *Black Empire* appeared during the beginnings of a boom in American pulp science fiction, Schuyler was never closely associated with this school. Schuyler wrote a variety of popular fiction in serial form, mostly romantic melodrama, to supplement his income as a columnist and editor. Schuyler's aesthetic sensibility is shaped by a number of factors, including 1930's horror films, back-to-Africa movements, and speculative fiction generally. He had no special attachment to the science-fiction genre and often spoke contemptuously of this genre and its audience.

Black Empire is a fascinating document. Although Schuyler despised racial chauvinism, he was generally sympathetic with any historical movement designed to challenge the imperialistic rule of the European powers. A pan-African conspiracy is something that Schuyler considered worth imagining. *Black Empire* is representative of the aspirations of many African Americans of the time, who were severely hit by the Depression and were victims of American racism. *Black Empire* in its original newspaper publication had almost an exclusively black audience that would have appreciated fantasizing about an end to white supremacy and the revitalization of the African continent. This was especially true in the light of black public outrage over the Italian attack on Ethiopia and American unwillingness to come to Ethiopia's aid.

Later in his career, Schuyler became a notorious conservative. Some scholars have speculated that Schuyler's construction of Dr. Henry Belsidus is prophetic of his own latent authoritarianism. *Black Empire* is prophetic in far more important and stirring ways. Like the best of futurist fiction, it is uncannily accurate (although chillingly so) in its prediction and description of the days to come. The world of *Black Empire* includes fax technology, solar energy, hydroponic agriculture, underground bunkers, and, shockingly, mass death by gassing. The novel as a whole is a populist fantasy that imagines the end to worldwide white supremacy through the application of black genius.   —*James C. Hall*

BLACK NO MORE

A scientist discovers means of making black people appear to be white

Author: George S. Schuyler (1895-1977)
Genre: Science fiction—dystopia
Type of work: Novel
Time of plot: The 1930's
Location: The United States
First published: 1931

The Plot: *Black No More* (subtitled *Being an Account of the Strange and Wonderful Workings of Science in the Land of the Free, A.D. 1933-1940*) begins with African Americans Max Disher and Bunny Brown considering the complexities of color prejudice in the United States. Max is rebuffed by a white woman at a Harlem bar after asking her to dance. The anger Max feels at this snub makes him enthusiastic about the news that Dr. Julius Crookman, an African American scientist, has devised a process that will turn black people white. Disher be-

comes the first person to undergo Crookman's process. After selling his story to a newspaper, *The Scimitar*, for $1,000, Max heads to Atlanta to seek out the white woman who had laughed at his advance in the Harlem bar.

The novel simultaneously follows the exploits of Max Disher—who changes his name to Matthew Fisher—and the efforts of Dr. Crookman and his cohorts, "numbers" banker Henry Johnson and real estate speculator Charlie Foster, to market the process nationwide. Fisher finds work as an adviser to the Knights of Nordica, a white supremacist organization led by the Reverend Henry Givens, whose daughter Helen is the woman who rejected Fisher in New York. Crookman and partners market Black No More throughout the United States. The racial transformation of the black population leads to a breakdown of black business, philanthropic, and social uplift enterprises. Among whites, this transformation, rather than lessening sensitivity to racial difference, generates paranoia.

Fisher sees his work with the Knights of Nordica as a "racket"; the longer he can maintain the status quo, the more money there is to be made from racial fears. Further dramatic tension is provided by the fact that the process does not affect the offspring of black people who undergo the transformation. Matt Fisher is in danger of being exposed because he has married Helen. The Knights of Nordica become involved in manipulating labor disputes (and collecting substantial bribes) and eventually in attempting to orchestrate the presidential election.

Resolution comes to the novel in two ways. First, social scientific research conducted during the course of the election campaign concludes that few if any Americans are racially pure. Rumors are circulated about the origins of the candidates put forth by the Knights, the Reverend Givens and Arthur Snobbcraft, eventually resulting in the lynching of the latter. Second, a belief that the transformation process creates individuals who are "too white" leads to a national backlash against whiteness and light skin. The book concludes ironically with a complete reversal of the American national attitudes toward skin color.

Analysis: George Schuyler's reputation was made as a biting satirist, and, later in his life and career, as a notorious African American conservative. As a columnist for the *Pittsburgh Courier* for five decades, Schuyler was noted for his acerbic wit and intellectual irreverence. In 1931, Schuyler's politics were somewhat in transition, but his desire and ability to ridicule irrationality and pomposity were focused. *Black No More* mocks America's racial caste system and the pseudoscience upon which racism often was based. Influenced by journalist H. L. Mencken, Schuyler's novel uses thinly disguised historical figures in its mission to humiliate not only white racists but also the racial romanticizing of black leaders. Appearing at the end of the Harlem Renaissance, a decade that saw continued racially motivated violence, especially lynching, the novel takes on both African Americans and whites who make too much of racial difference. Although Schuyler was by no means a simplistic assimilationist, he did believe that African Americans were fundamentally American in commitment, temperament, culture, and interest.

Part of the power and impact of Schuyler's novel is that, for all of its outrageousness, it relied upon processes of identification and recognition with its reader. Dr. Shakespeare A. Beard is a thinly disguised W. E. B. Du Bois, and the National Social Equality League is clearly modeled on the National Association for the Advancement of Colored People.

In Schuyler's novel, race is revealed to be primarily a business or economic interest. Crookman's entrepreneurial tactics with regard to his race-transforming process are related to Matthew Fisher's unseemly alliance with the Knights of Nordica. Similarly, Schuyler suggests in his portrayal of the Knights' manipulation of Southern labor disputes that white working-class obsession with race gets in the way of action on the basis of real economic interest. Suggestive of Schuyler's conservatism to come, the novel appears sympathetic to the entrepreneurial spirit of characters such as Crookman and Fisher. The profit motive and greed are not the villains of the novel; as a human flaw, Schuyler instead sees irrational color prejudice as beyond redemption. The disappearance of African Americans from the American scene leads to frantic efforts to identify replacement scapegoats to blame for economic scarcity.

Scholars have discovered other science-fiction novels authored by Schuyler. "The Black Internationale" and "Black Empire," published in serial form in the *Pittsburgh Courier* between 1936 and 1938 as written by Samuel I. Brooks, were combined into *Black Empire* (1991). There is little evidence that Schuyler was strongly committed to the genre of science fiction. He was knowledgeable about a wide variety of popular genres and experimented under a number of pseudonyms. In *Black No More*, Schuyler is best identified as a political satirist interested in most effectively reaching the largest audience possible. Form largely follows function in *Black No More*. Schuyler imagines America's greatest dream and reveals it to be America's greatest nightmare.

—*James C. Hall*

BLACK TRILLIUM

Each of three princesses goes in search of her own magical talisman which, when united with the others, will bring peace to their kingdom and restore balance to their world

Authors: Marion Zimmer Bradley (1930-   ), Julian May (1931-   ), and Andre Norton (1912-   )
Genre: Fantasy—medieval future
Type of work: Novel
Time of plot: Undefined
Location: The kingdom of Ruwenda and its environs
First published: 1990

The Plot: This novel represents a collaboration between three renowned science-fiction and fantasy authors. Each wrote one of the three princesses' adventures. The tale of Haramis is by Marion Zimmer Bradley, author of the Darkover novels; the story of Kadiya is by Andre Norton, author of the Witch World series; and the narrative of Anigel is by Julian May, author of the Pliocene Exile saga.

The kingdom of Ruwenda is a major center of trade for all the surrounding countries and territories. King Krain and Queen Kalanthe have no imperialist impulses toward their neighbors and allow their subjects a large degree of freedom. Unfortunately, the neighboring kingdom of Labornok is ill-placed for trade, so its king, Voltrik, resorts to conquest of the affluent Ruwenda.

Although brave, King Krain is no soldier. He instructs his wife and daughters to hide, then attempts to bargain with Voltrik, offering to die if his wife and daughters are allowed to live. Meanwhile, in their hiding place, the daughters react to their situation according to their natures. Haramis, the scholar, can see no rational solution to their dilemma. She knows that her father, as head of their army, will most likely be killed in battle and that she will (if left alive) have to submit to marriage to Voltrik. Kadiya, the huntress, fiercely vows to use her hunting knife to defend her mother and sisters against any attackers. Anigel, the youngest, is timid. She sobs helplessly and cries in supplication to the White Lady, a legendary protectress of their land who either has lost her powers or perhaps never really existed.

Their parents killed, the princesses are each aided by a member of the Folk to escape capture. To reclaim their lost throne, each must master her own nature as well as succeed in her quest for a talisman. Haramis, assisted by Uzun, a musician and raconteur, must resist her thirst for knowledge and her attraction to a mage who could be both tutor and mate. Impetuous Kadiya, accompanied by Jagun, Master of Animals, must learn wisdom and restraint. Timid Anigel, assisted by the herbalist Immu, must acquire self-reliance, strength, and courage.

The Black Trillium is a rare plant, the badge of the royal house of Ruwenda, having a single, three-lobed blossom. The princesses are referred to as the Petals of the Living Trillium. The most prized of the Ruwendan Crown Jewels is an egg-sized piece of amber, within which is a small, fossil Black Trillium, and each princess bears a similar blossom in amber as an amulet. These amulets function as guides on their quests and eventually activate and empower the princesses' talismans.

Analysis: Although *Black Trillium* can be read as a simple heroic quest, with the twist that the protagonists are female, there are other levels of meaning. In their other works, Bradley and Norton write of cultures in which technology is not held in high esteem, and May's novels show an understanding of ecology and the balance of nature. All three emphasize that although technology may be a means to an end, it can get out of control, causing people to lose a sense of connection to their work, to the people around them, and to their place in the overall scheme of things. It can also lend credence to the view that might makes right, or that because one has the power to do a thing, one has the right to do it.

The protagonists of this novel question that assumption. Their ancestors had great technological prowess. They are gone, but their machines remain. The Sword of Power is one of these. Those who made it were, in the end, reluctant to use it; instead, they disassembled it into three pieces, placing each in a separate hiding place. The princesses learn that even separately, the talismans can kill, and they are cautioned about using a device so powerful that the ability to use it wisely was doubted by its creators. Conversely, the main antagonist in the novel is a sorcerer who believes that "might makes right." He possesses some paranormal abilities and has augmented his power through the discovery of a cache of machines left by the ancient ones. Whereas the princesses use their "talismans" only to restore order to their world, he uses these machines to empower himself, embarking on a campaign of conquest.

Another theme common to the authors is that of cooperation and connectedness rather than individual might and isolation. In quest of their talismans, the princesses become aware that each of them is a nexus of connections with other people and species. Each could use her talisman for her individual empowerment but discovers that the final task requires all three. They learn to value the qualities in one another and come to recognize that their efforts will succeed only through cooperation among themselves and with the various species of Folk whose land they would rule. As a wheel is composed of hub, spokes, and rim, when the amulets are merged with the talismans and the talismans form a single Sword of Power, all the princesses' connections with others converge, and their world is restored to wholeness.

This novel is the product of three mature writers. Bradley and Norton have been writing excellent science-fiction and/or fantasy works for decades. May has written more than seven thousand nonfiction encyclopedia articles in addition to her two science-fiction series, the four-volume Pliocene Exile saga and the Galactic Milieu series. This seamless narrative exhibits the values of community, cooperation, and interconnection shared among these authors, who are at the height of their storytelling powers.

—Karen S. Bellinfante

BLACK UNICORN and GOLD UNICORN

Tanaquil (with her pet peeve) embarks on a journey that teaches her about the nature of good and evil, her own magical powers, and the secrets of her identity

Author: Tanith Lee (1947-   )
Genre: Fantasy—magical world
Type of work: Novels
Time of plot: Undefined
Location: An unidentified magical world
First published: *Black Unicorn* (1991) and *Gold Unicorn* (1994)

The Plot: *Black Unicorn* and its sequel, *Gold Unicorn*, tell of the adventures of sixteen-year-old Tanaquil. At first, Tanaquil knows nothing of her heritage, but by the end of the second book, she has learned much about her own identity and abilities. She also has learned not to judge people—including herself—too quickly. The ending of *Gold Unicorn*, in which Tanaquil journeys toward home, leaves open the possibility of another sequel.

Tanaquil wants to leave the desert fortress where she was reared by her emotionally distant sorceress mother,

Jaive. She apparently has no magic of her own, and she wearies of the inconvenient side effects of Jaive's magic. In one instance, Jaive's magic resulted in a peeve, a common desert creature, acquiring the power of speech. Jaive refuses to let Tanaquil go or even to identify Tanaquil's father.

One day, the peeve discovers the skeleton of a unicorn, which Tanaquil reassembles. It turns out that she has a magical power after all: the power to mend things. The unicorn comes alive, and Tanaquil and the peeve are compelled to follow it to an exotic city by the sea. There, Tanaquil meets Lizra, the daughter of the city's ruler, the evil Prince Zorander. Soon Tanaquil discovers that Zorander is her father and Lizra is her half sister.

During a ceremonial procession, the unicorn appears and steals from Zorander two white shells. Tanaquil realizes that the unicorn is from a better world and that it wishes to return. She helps it by mending the sorcerous gate between worlds with the white shells. Unfortunately, the peeve follows the unicorn through the gate, so Tanaquil also must follow.

The unicorn's world is wonderful, putting Tanaquil's world to shame. She realizes with horror that her mere presence wounds the Perfect World and plans to leave immediately. Before she exits through the gate, the unicorn touches her and her peeve with its horn, granting them immunity from physical danger. Tanaquil takes the shells as she leaves, disabling the gate so that no one else can harm the Perfect World.

When she returns to her own world, Zorander is sick, and Lizra declares that she will stay with him. Tanaquil sets out with her peeve to learn more about their world and perhaps to improve it. She sends a message to Jaive promising that eventually she will return home.

Gold Unicorn describes Tanaquil's travels. She hears of the empress Veriam, who wishes to conquer the entire world, and is shocked to learn that the empress is in fact Lizra. Lizra has constructed a huge mechanical unicorn of gold as a symbol of her conquest. Unfortunately, it does not work. Lizra commands Tanaquil to mend it. Unwillingly, Tanaquil does so, using one of the fossil shells. Tanaquil and Lizra's chief adviser, Honj, secretly fall in love. Although she disapproves of Lizra's goals, Tanaquil accompanies her and Honj from conquest to brutal conquest, until they are set upon by "mousps," half-mouse, half-wasp creatures created by the local magician Worabex.

To escape, the sisters, Honj, a stingless mousp, the peeve, and assorted other followers duck under the belly of the gold unicorn. This leads them through a magical gate into a hellish world. The Emperor of War, ruler of this world, courts Lizra, who appears to be delighted with his attentions. Disgusted, Tanaquil and Lizra's other friends abandon her and seek to find the gate to their own world. When Honj breaks his arm rescuing the peeve, Tanaquil learns that her power to mend works on people as well as on objects.

Soon Lizra emerges from the evil castle and informs them that she only pretended to court the emperor so as not to anger him. She has told the emperor that although she longs to be his bride, she is betrothed to another. Because the emperor believes in loyalty, one of the values of war, he has told her how to return to her world. Lizra leads Tanaquil and the rest to the return gate, which Tanaquil mends with the remaining white shell.

Honj decides to stay with Lizra, who, having conquered the world, now shoulders the burden of ruling wisely. Tanaquil travels toward home, joined by the mousp as well as the peeve. Soon the mousp reveals himself as Worabex, who wishes to befriend Tanaquil and to court her mother. Tanaquil rejects his friendship, so Worabex turns himself into a flea and hitches a ride on the peeve. The unlikely trio continues on its journey.

Analysis: *Black Unicorn* was not marketed as a young adult novel, but *Gold Unicorn* was. The books feature a theme important in young adult literature: an adolescent's journey into maturity. In the confines of her mother's castle, Tanaquil seems amazingly self-possessed for a sixteen-year-old. She knows the castle routine, she knows the servants, and she knows how to outwit the magical guardians of Jaive's study. When she leaves, however, her naïveté quickly becomes apparent. Tanaquil needs more experience before she can take full possession of her powers. She literally needs knowledge of good (the Perfect World) and evil (the warlord's world).

Tanaquil also needs to acquire knowledge of people. She believes that Honj follows Lizra out of a desire for power, but he does so out of loyalty. She believes that Lizra truly loves the Emperor of War, but Lizra only pretends to love him in order to rescue her friends. Tanaquil also displays blindness to her own motives, thinking that she has stayed with Lizra because of the gold unicorn when actually she has stayed for the love of Honj.

In the same way that Lizra acts like their father, longing for power, Tanaquil acts like their mother, insisting on emotional distance. Lizra does admit to loving their father, and she is able to accept him as a man with flaws, rather than perceiving him as an ideal being. By contrast,

Tanaquil is not yet able to admit to loving their mother. Furthermore, she cannot accept her mother as a woman with flaws. For Tanaquil, Jaive must be either all good or all bad. Therefore, Tanaquil cannot introduce Worabex to Jaive, because Jaive in love could not be the ideal mother Tanaquil craves.

The need to assume moral responsibility is another young adult theme highlighted in these books. Tanaquil must first take responsibility for returning the black unicorn to its own world. When she realizes that she cannot stay in the Perfect World, she soon resolves to make her own world more like the better one. Tanaquil's actions do not live up to her resolve. Not only does she help Lizra in her drive to conquer the world, but at the end of *Gold Unicorn*, she leaves the burden of ruling to Lizra. Rather than helping her sister, Tanaquil decides to return to Jaive. Rather than improving her world, Tanaquil simply admires the goodness that it already has. Perhaps Tanaquil cannot shoulder her share of moral responsibility until she has grown to understand Jaive, in the same way that Lizra cannot assume the throne until she understands Zorander.

The focus on individual growth rather than on societal change is common to many of Tanith Lee's books, including the Birthgrave trilogy (1975-1978), *Electric Forest* (1979), and *The Silver Metal Lover* (1981). This may explain why Lee is not typically considered to be a feminist author. At the same time, the Unicorn books do subvert stereotypical notions of what it means to be a hero. In some ways, Tanaquil behaves like a hero: She avoids emotional ties, she rescues others in need, and she cannot settle in one place. Even though Tanaquil is gifted with strong powers, she does not trust them; her aloofness results not from self-confidence but from self-doubt. Furthermore, Tanaquil's love for her peeve, her dislike of war, and her attachment to her sister all are traditionally feminine qualities.

Unlike the protagonists in plots devised by other female writers of fantasy, such as Andre Norton, Tanaquil is not content with becoming one of the elite sorcerers. In fact, she is impatient with sorcerers, believing that they should spend their time on more important things than improving their own powers. With this attitude, Tanaquil may yet change her world.

Black Unicorn and *Gold Unicorn* are more hopeful than many of Lee's earlier books, which number more than three dozen and span the genres of fantasy, horror, science fiction, and mainstream fiction for children, young adults, and adults. Critics generally praise Lee's solid characterization, attention to detail, and unpre- dictable plots. Although Lee is not one of the genre's most famous authors, her books are well worth seeking out.

—*Beth Rapp Young*

BLOOD MUSIC

Vergil Ulam injects himself with thinking cells that push his body and, eventually, the rest of Earth into the next stage in evolution

Author: Greg Bear (1951-   )
Genre: Fantasy—evolutionary fantasy
Type of work: Novel
Time of plot: The late twentieth century
Location: California, New York, Germany, and Great Britain
First published: 1985

The Plot: Thirty-two-year-old Vergil Ulam is a brilliant but undisciplined bioengineer at the Genetron laboratories in La Jolla, California. This area is known as Enzyme Valley, the biochip equivalent of Silicon Valley. His pet project is what he calls "biologic," the development of "thinking" lymphocytes that he describes as autonomous organic computers. When his employer learns that Ulam has been conducting this research for the past two years on mammalian cells, Ulam is fired. Before he leaves the building, he injects himself with the cells and destroys the records of his research.

Ulam had hoped to retrieve the lymphocytes from his system and continue his research. Two weeks later, though, he still has not found access to a lab, and he knows that it is too late to remove the altered cells. The first changes to his system that he notices are a craving for sweets, better eyesight, and a better sex life. When he realizes that there is no turning back, he visits his clairvoyant mother. She immediately discerns that his experiment has gotten beyond her son's control but that it is his life's work.

Ulam concludes that the lymphocytes have developed the capacity to spread their biologic to other types of cells and that they could migrate outside his body. He visits Edward Milligan, a school friend, and explains his theory that human DNA has spent millions of years building to a climax that is now expressing itself in Ulam's experiment, which offers the doorway for the lymphocytes to escape the human species. Listening to their activity inside his body, which he calls "blood music," he wonders when the cells will become cognizant of Ulam himself as an entity enclosing them. The answer comes soon, when he begins hearing words spoken within his brain by the other entities.

Milligan quickly understands the dangerous implications, confirmed when he walks in on Ulam and his girlfriend and discovers them changing into strange shapeless masses of flesh. To stop a possible epidemic, Milligan kills Ulam. Michael Bernard, head of Genetron, realizes that a mere handshake could spread the altered genes from one individual to another and that it is too late to stop it from spreading throughout the United States. Recognizing that he is infected, he flies to Wiesbaden, Germany, and secures himself in an isolation laboratory for observation.

Heinz Paulsen-Fuchs, the biologist who observed Bernard gradually showing signs of the transforming genes, knows he cannot hold off the terrified protesters who want to kill Bernard before Europe becomes infected. Meanwhile, the United States itself changes shape as the self-aware genes form a massive thinking community. Bernard communes with the cells inside himself and, with the help of a visiting British physicist, theorizes that thought, in sufficient quantity, could physically alter the universe. With all these cells suddenly conscious, the potential for change has become exponentially greater.

Bernard willingly allows his own transformation and "enters" the world inside himself. Viewed by the cells as one of their creators, he is treated with respect and moved into Thought Universe, where he recognizes that no one really dies; instead, there is endless replication within cells in the blood. Various humans resist transformation, and the cells respect their decision. Ultimately, the number of thinking cells becomes so large that their community of cooperation enters into a realm beyond physical matter.

Analysis: Greg Bear's topics range from fantasy to pure science fiction, and they generally demand that his protagonist come to a new understanding of the universe. During the 1980's, Bear won the Nebula Award twice, for the novella "Hard Fought" (1983) and for the short story "Tangents" (1986), and the Hugo Award (1984) for the short story "Blood Music," published in *Analog*. He has stated that *Blood Music*, his seventh novel, was influenced by his study of information theory and information mechanics. Upon the suggestion of David Brin and John F. Carr, Bear decided to expand "Blood Music," adding complexity with chapters devoted to new characters.

Much in the manner that James Blish's *A Case of Conscience* (1958) uses a fictional Jesuit astrophysicist to raise ethical questions regarding the individual moral systems of other galaxies, Bear builds his story on the writings of the actual Jesuit paleontologist Pierre Teilhard de Chardin, who combined Christian theology and evolutionary theory to posit Jesus Christ both as temporal and as a timeless symbol for the final step of evolution, which he described as a "noosphere." Bear is not directly theological, though he works with the idea of a creator; his basic debt to Teilhard is the notion of a critical mass of thinkers somehow transcending space and time and bringing into existence what amounts to a new heaven and a new Earth.

Bear's novel has been called a *Childhood's End* (Arthur C. Clarke, 1953) for the 1980's, and the comparison seems apt. Theodore Sturgeon's *More than Human* (1953) also comes immediately to mind as a source for comparison. *Blood Music* follows in the tradition of science-fiction writing that ponders the possibility that *Homo sapiens* may not be the final word in nature's self-expression. Bear's novel shows a greater scientific sophistication than Clarke's earlier work, focusing in convincing detail on the actual biological mechanisms used in laboratories of the 1980's and 1990's. It suggests that the human need to see humanity as the center of the biological universe is as egotistical as humanity's earlier notion that Earth was the center of the galaxy. As threatening as the notion of absorption into a larger community is to Bear's characters, he does his best to convince them, and his readers, that individual subjectivity may go the way of nation-states. In its place will come a cooperative assertion of racial memory.

—*John C. Hawley*

THE BLOOD OF ROSES

A vampiristic holy man is thwarted by the family of undead he created to grant himself immortality

Author: Tanith Lee (1947-   )
Genre: Fantasy—dystopia
Type of work: Novel
Time of plot: Undefined
Location: An agrarian land divided into small kingdoms and church holdings
First published: 1990

The Plot: Tanith Lee's novel is a sprawling work in five sections. The first deals with Mechail Kohrlen, heir to a rural estate. He is hunchbacked and antisocial. His father dotes on Mechail's handsome brother. Mechail completes a test of manhood—a human sacrifice to the forest gods—but his brother mocks him, later hiring soldiers from a rival estate to murder Mechail. Mechail rises from the dead, kills his brother, and flees to the forest.

Rumors of vampirism bring Anjelen, a warrior priest, to the area. He finds Mechail comatose and takes him to the Christerium, headquarters of the Knights of God. On the way, Jasha, a strange homeless girl, joins their retinue to care for Mechail. She feeds him gruel mixed with blood. At the Christerium, Jasha goes to the women's quarters and Mechail becomes Anjelen's protégé. Mechail discovers that Anjelen is truly a vampire who has turned Mechail into a demon like himself. Jasha, meanwhile, is accused of witchcraft and burned at the stake. She is resurrected, and she and Mechail flee the Christerium and go separate ways.

The second section of the novel deals with Mechail's mother. Anillia, the child of a city lord, was lost in the woods as a toddler. Anjelen found her and brainwashed her into being his servant. At the age of fifteen, she wed Kolris Kohrlen. She died after giving birth to Mechail. Anjelen steals her bones and resurrects his servant. After she rises, she vows that Anjelen will never possess her son.

The third section reveals Anjelen's past. He was sacrificed to the forest gods as a boy, but the ritual was interrupted when Christians cut down the sacred tree where his body hung. The stump absorbed his spirit. He returned as the embodiment of the sacred pagan tree as well as Jesus Christ. The story then jumps to the present, where Anjelen has become head of the Knights of God. He introduces a blood-drinking rite, modeled on the Last Supper, to a select group of warrior priests. Word gets out when townspeople are found dead and bloodless, and the Knights are disbanded.

The fourth section finds the once-opulent Christerium a ruin. Only a handful of elderly Knights remain, and gypsies haunt the outer walls. A young priest, Eujasius, and a dwarf join the gypsies sheltering there. Anjelen appears to conduct his bloody sacrament, but Eujasius suddenly reveals himself as Jasha. She kills Anjelen, and the dwarf stays with the gypsies. Oddly, he grows tall; he was mute but becomes articulate. Mechail meets Jasha and his mother, and together they go to the woods. Mechail and Anillia shed their unwanted immortality and escape Anjelen forever as they worship another sacred tree. Jasha returns to her original home, the sea.

The fifth section brings the novel full circle. The dwarf transforms into a handsome, wealthy youth resembling Mechail. Calling himself Mechailus, he returns to the Kohrlen estate and takes control. The tradition of human sacrifice resumes. Mechailus (actually Mechail in a new body) is content and constantly renewed by a diet of human blood.

Analysis: Tanith Lee first appeared in the fantasy genre in 1975, when Ballantine publishers noticed that the market was glutted with imitations of J. R. R. Tolkien's work and retellings of familiar legends. They solved the problem by introducing new authors with new stories. Other publishers followed this trend. Since her well-timed arrival, Lee has produced a huge body of work, beginning with the Birthgrave Trilogy (1975-1978).

The Blood of Roses examines a number of issues. On the surface, it is a simple revenge story. A disadvantaged and despised youth leaves home and eventually returns, exacting revenge on his tormentors. This type of story has ancient roots. An example is Euripedes' *Electra* (c. 413 B.C.). Lee's novel departs from the typical revenge tale in several ways. Although Mechail kills his tormentors, he himself is killed beforehand. It is only Anjelen's influence that permits Mechail to rise and avenge himself. Then Mechail's vengeance is complete. He gains his rightful inheritance, but only after his original body is exchanged for a new one. Furthermore, Mechail must drink human blood to survive. Anjelen's blessing is also a curse.

In the character of Anjelen, Lee presents an interesting paradox. He comes from a pagan background but fits easily into the Christian world. He is both the forest god and Christ. Like Christ, Anjelen is sacrificed on a tree and rises from the dead to resurrect people like Mechail. Anjelen gives Mechail what he needs to gain his inheritance, but he is undeniably self-serving.

Anjelen means to use Mechail as a tool but is thwarted when Mechail's Christian upbringing makes him reject his benefactor as a demon. Anjelen's career is in the Christian church, but he uses the Eucharist to sustain pagan tradition. Actual blood from human victims serves instead of wine and keeps Anjelen young and powerful. He puts Anillia under his influence and brings Mechail into being as an act of will. It is ironic that Anillia and Mechail, both Christians, escape the Knights of God through a bizarre pagan rite. As they worship, mother and son become part of the forest.

The novel's setting emphasizes the merging of the two religions. It is a realm where Christianity is new; the people cling to pagan traditions such as blood sacrifice and nature worship. In *The Blood of Roses*, Lee shows that Christianity and paganism are opposing but similar forces. One supports the other. Although Christianity emerges as the stronger force, the pagan traditions remain at its heart. This makes the religious power struggle a moot point.

As in the Birthgrave Trilogy, the emphasis is more on mood than on character development. Mechail and the others elicit no sympathetic pull, and too often they are lost in Lee's elaborate descriptions. The storytelling is energetic, but in the fifth section, Lee suddenly changes her style and rushes toward the conclusion. Nevertheless, *The Blood of Roses* deserves credit as an innovative twist on a popular supernatural theme.   *—Carla Hall Minor*

THE BLUE HAWK

The dangerous journeys of Tron, a young priest of Gdu, into the hinterlands of O and Aa in an attempt to restore the king to his rightful throne and to find his own soul

Author: Peter Dickinson (1927-   )
Genre: Fantasy—theological romance
Type of work: Novel
Time of plot: The distant future
Location: Earth
First published: 1976

The Plot: The story opens in the Temple of Gdu during the annual Ceremony of Renewal. Tron, a young priest, witnesses the victory of the priests of Gdu over the old king. He experiences a vision, then removes a blue hawk, the totem bird of the great Hawk God, Gdu, from the temple. The bird was to have been sacrificed to renew the soul of the old king; instead, the priests kill the king. Tron becomes the keeper of the sacred blue hawk and as such cannot be harmed, but he discovers that the highly systematized priestly society now in charge of the kingdom will try to kill him indirectly.

As Tron trains the blue hawk, he runs into the son of the old king, who asks Tron to help him regain his rightful throne from the rigid priestly caste. Tron is frightened but intuitively believes in the king, even though, as a member of the priesthood, he has been thoroughly brainwashed. Tron also is a visionary, an attribute that makes him different from the dronelike priests with whom he lives.

Tron becomes the king's messenger and begins a dangerous journey south to enlist certain individuals to help the new king overcome the powerful priests. Tron observes the terrible condition of parts of his country. The farther south he journeys, however, the happier people seem. When he reaches Kalakal, he understands that life

can be lived in great simplicity and openness without the intrusiveness of the powerful priests. He meets a lovely girl, Taleel, who helps him contact the local leaders and the old high priest, Odah, one of the few people he can trust.

Tron and the blue hawk return to the kingdom of O and Aa to find that repression has become almost unbearable. Tron meets with the king in secret. The king realizes that he must smuggle Tron and the blue hawk out of the country before they are murdered. He secretly places Tron and the hawk within the burial barge of his father, the old king, and sends it down the river into possible oblivion. Tron, after many harrowing adventures and risks, finally reaches Kalakal again. He enlists the One of Sinu, a blind priest, to aid him and Odah in performing the rituals required to ensure that the quest for reinstatement of the king will be successful.

After performing these exhausting rituals, the three priests are almost slaughtered by barbarians, the Hun-like Mohirrim, as they attempt to return to Tron's home. The Mohirrim, it seems, support the priests of Gdu and will do anything to destroy the forces of the king. After a devastating battle in which virtually all the Mohirrim either commit suicide or are slaughtered by the king's faithful forces, Tron is wounded by an arrow in his back.

During the battle with the Mohirrim, both the One of Sinu and Odah die of exhaustion, leaving Tron to fend for himself. During Tron's recovery, he meets Taleel again. She helps nurse him back to health, though the process is slow because of the severity of his injury. His wound gives Tron a deeper understanding of the awful power of the priests in keeping the citizens of O and Aa ignorant and subservient. Tron sees that people have lived their lives by ritual and precedent, and that change is never permitted. He sees himself as part of an ancient corrupt system from which only the king, his blue hawk, and his visionary experiences can release him. After regaining his strength, Tron accompanies the king and his triumphal forces back to the kingdom to overcome the priests.

At the conclusion of the novel, Tron realizes that he has found his own soul. He also begins to understand that the blue hawk is not only a totem divinity but also a part of his own identity. Tron decides to release the hawk and discovers that he, too, is entering a life of freedom. The reader also becomes aware that the gods of Tron's world are in fact alien beings reluctantly tied to Earth.

Analysis: Peter Dickinson generally is recognized as one of England's most respected writers of mystery and detective fiction, having written more than a dozen such novels. He is also renowned for his children's books. *The Blue Hawk*, though a children's book (winner of the *Guardian* Award as best children's book of the year), contains sophisticated subject matter and a philosophical approach that would not typically appeal to young children. Advanced secondary school students may find it both challenging and compelling.

Most of Dickinson's novels, for children or adults, revolve around one central predicament: the Fall. In *The Blue Hawk*, Tron realizes that the sterile life he lives as a priest is the result of a fall from an earlier, more vivid life that some still experienced to a degree in the southern city of Kalakal, an Eden that is far enough away from the priest-ridden Kingdom of O and Aa to escape its ennui and conformity.

The novel is also a classic story of the dangerous journey of a young man into the world of the unknown. As in many quest stories, the young hero discovers not only new worlds but also new systems of belief and, thus, new possibilities for living his own life. He discovers that the priestly order demands that he become only what it will allow and that imagination and intuition are dangerous to the community. Fortunately, Tron experiences periodic visions from deep within his soul; following them inevitably leads him to greater truths and more fulfilling experiences.

The Blue Hawk is a romantic novel insofar as Tron's most important discovery is the discovery of himself as an individual and not simply as a priest who repeats what he is told and obeys his leaders without question. His crucial tie to nature via the blue hawk saves him from an empty, ritualized life and enables him to help the king to regain his kingdom from the ignorant darkness of the priestly caste of the Kingdom of Gdu.

—Patrick Meanor

THE BLUE STAR

A member of a subversive political movement seduces a witch in order to gain control of the gem that supplies her magical powers, but the plan goes awry

Author: Fletcher Pratt (1897-1956)
Genre: Fantasy—heroic fantasy
Type of work: Novel
Time of plot: A period roughly equivalent to the eighteenth century
Location: Various, including Netznegon in the realm of Dossola and Charlakis in the dominion of Mancherei

First published: 1969 (with two other items in the anthology *Witches Three*, 1952)

The Plot: Within a frame narrative in which three men dream the same dream, the story is told of Rodvard Bergelin, a minor functionary in the government of Dossola who is also a member of a subversive organization called the Sons of the New Day. Rodvard is commissioned by the leaders of this organization to seduce Lalette Asterhax, the descendant of a line of witches whose hereditary magic—embodied in the eponymous gem—is transferable to their male lovers. He reluctantly agrees, but he mishandles the task; he succeeds only because Lalette wants to avoid an alternative liaison cynically arranged by her family. Witchcraft is proscribed by both church and state, and the accidental revelation that her latent power has been activated results in Lalette and Rodvard being forced to go into hiding.

After the two fugitives are taken in by members of a heretical sect called the Amorosians, Rodvard receives new instructions from the Sons of the New Day. He uses his magic to small but significant effect in a spying mission, but the jewel loses its virtue when he sleeps with a chambermaid, and he is forced to flee again. Lalette's magic saves him and reactivates the Blue Star, but she finds it politic to go into exile, seeking asylum among the Amorosians of Mancherei. Rodvard is forced to make his way to Mancherei, having been sold into the service of a sea captain. In the course of their sea voyages, Lalette and Rodvard both are threatened with rape, but they arrive safely, neither one knowing that the other is near.

Lalette is accommodated in a hospice but is discomfited to discover that such institutions are used as brothels by the supposedly celibate Amorosian clergy. When she refuses to participate, she is scheduled for compulsory reeducation, but Rodvard—who has returned to his old line of work—sees her committal papers and attempts her rescue. Yet again, he proves incompetent. He and Lalette are thrown into jail.

In Dossola, the Sons of the New Day have seized control of the government, and their rule is becoming increasingly oppressive. In need of the Blue Star to facilitate their purges, the organization's leaders contrive Rodvard's and Lalette's release. When he is put to work ferreting out enemies of the state, Rodvard soon becomes disillusioned. When he attempts to save the life of a noblewoman he once admired from afar—memory of whom has long come between himself and Lalette—his last illusions collapse. Authentically united at last, the two lovers discard the Blue Star and flee the realm.

Analysis: *The Blue Star* is a conscientious attempt to describe a fantasy world that has all the complexities of the real one. Instead of imagining a quasi-feudal world whose kings actually rule by divine right, it borrows and reshapes the political and religious disputes of prerevolutionary France, and instead of the idealized relationships typical of romantic fiction, it tracks the course of a much-troubled affair whose final result is a hard-won compromise. As in Fletcher Pratt's earlier heroic fantasy, magic plays a very subdued role; its function is symbolic rather than deterministic, and it is inevitable that the protagonists eventually put it out of their lives.

If one compares *The Blue Star* with the fervently adventurous and unabashedly romantic tales of "sword and sorcery" written by Robert E. Howard and his imitators, or with the delicate and decorative "high fantasies" whose tradition extends from William Morris to J. R. R. Tolkien, one can see how carefully and how radically it distances itself from the underlying assumptions of both subgenres. This cannot have helped its marketability and perhaps explains why the story first appeared in an omnibus that Pratt put together himself rather than as a separate volume. The work is one of considerable originality. The explosive success of fantasy literature in the 1970's and 1980's produced numerous comparable works, but Pratt was twenty years ahead of his successors.

The main problem Pratt faced in trying to design a fantasy world as rich and complex as the real one was that of available narrative space. A novel that deals with actual history can leave much unsaid, because its readers have stocks of common knowledge that can be invoked by brief reference. The describer of a fantasy world has no such resource. Pratt's attempts to mobilize such stocks of knowledge in a limited way, by making his revolution a version of the French Revolution and his heretical religion a syncretic amalgam of Catharist and Protestant ideas, creates as many problems as it solves because the reader is never sure how close the parallel is intended to be. The result is that readers are likely to feel uneasy in their interpretations of what is going on and are likely to be unconvinced by the precise pattern of historical alternatives that the author brings into combination.

The Blue Star is a rather dour novel, somewhat weighed down by the burden of its meticulous narrative realism, but it is unusually well wrought in comparison with heroic fantasies written for the pulp magazines. The intricate convolutions of the plot are untidy, and the conclusion of the story is by no means a neat resolution of its problems, but this too is an aspect of its attempted realism. In its day, the novel was certainly the most ambitious heroic fantasy to emerge from the pulp tradition. Even if his achievements are found wanting, there is no doubt that Pratt made a bold attempt to break new ground. In spite of its flaws, *The Blue Star* deserves to be reckoned a classic of the genre.   —*Brian Stableford*

THE BLUE SWORD
and
THE HERO AND THE CROWN

Two women of Damar carry the same sword in two different eras and must learn to use both magic and swordplay to save the kingdom from the forces of evil

Author: Robin McKinley (1952-   )
Genre: Fantasy—heroic fantasy
Type of work: Novels
Time of plot: Undefined
Location: Primarily the land of Damar
First published: *The Blue Sword* (1982) and *The Hero and the Crown* (1984)

The Plot: *The Blue Sword* and *The Hero and the Crown* are the first two books of a promised trilogy about the land of Damar. *The Blue Sword* takes place in the present, when Outlanders rule much of Damar. *The Hero and the Crown*, a "prequel," tells the story of an earlier Damar before the Outlanders arrived. Harry and Aerin, the two female heroes, each must learn to master her psychic powers. In addition, both endure extensive training in swordplay to prepare them for battle with Damar's long-standing enemy, the inhuman demon race of the North.

In *The Blue Sword*, Harry Crewe leaves her Homeland after her father's death and goes to live at the outpost where her brother Richard is stationed. Harry is restless and oddly drawn to the hills beyond her new home. Corlath, the king of the last remaining Free Hillfolk not under Homelander rule, comes to plead with the Outlander superiors to unite with him against a common enemy. A psychic hunch tells Corlath that Harry is destined to be important to the Free Hillfolk, and he kidnaps her. Harry is discovered to possess an abundance of the psychic powers needed to defeat the Northerners. Mathin, one of the King's elite Riders, puts Harry through a rigorous training period. Harry learns to ride Sungold, her new Hill horse, and to fight with a sword. She also learns to love her new home, and she makes many friends among both human and animal followers of Corlath. Harry eventually is given the sword that belonged to Lady Aerin, Dragon-Killer, a legendary female warrior who led Damar to victory against the North in an earlier era.

As the Free Hillfolk prepare for war, Harry must deal with the conflicting emotions of loyalty to her Homeland and of her growing love for Corlath and his people. Standing between two worlds, Harry must risk her connections to the Homeland and the Hillfolk in order to save them both. To accomplish this, she must draw on her untrained psychic powers to bury the enemy under a mountain. She succeeds in leading the Damarians to victory and in cementing her relationship with Corlath. As an Outlander queen of the Free Hillfolk, she will lead her newfound people into an era in which they hope to establish better relations with the Outlanders.

The Hero and the Crown tells the story of Aerin, the warrior who appears as a legendary figure in *The Blue Sword*. Aerin is the only child of King Arlbeth of Damar. Aerin's mother, who died when Aerin was born, was rumored to be a witch from the North. Her people do not trust Aerin enough to accept her as the heir to the throne, especially now that the demons of the North are threatening Damar once again. Tor, Aerin's cousin, has been designated as heir. To make matters worse, Aerin seemingly has none of the psychic powers that Damar's true royalty should possess.

Feeling useless and unwanted at court, Aerin begins teaching herself how to kill dragons. She befriends her father's old warhorse, Talat, and discovers how to make a fireproof salve. She also coaxes Tor, who is already falling in love with her, to teach her the rudiments of sword fighting. Aerin becomes an expert dragon slayer and destroys Maur, the Black Dragon.

Aerin then begins training with the wizard Luthe, who teaches her to use the latent psychic abilities she has always possessed. He also gives her the fabled blue sword. Aerin must give up some of her humanity when Luthe is forced to grant her the power of partial immortality so that she can defeat her uncle Agsded, the evil wizard who is behind Damar's problems with the North. Aerin wins back the Hero's Crown, an amulet with protective powers, and returns to Tor and her people in time to lead them into victorious battle against the Northerners. Aerin's heroics earn her a place of honor in the hearts of her people; in addition, King Arlbeth has fallen in battle, so Aerin agrees to become Tor's queen. She must reconcile her love for Tor and Luthe, realizing that the immortal part of her will be able to rejoin Luthe someday.

Analysis: *The Blue Sword* and *The Hero and the Crown* were published after Robin McKinley's *Beauty: A Retelling of the Story of Beauty and the Beast* (1978), the award-winning and critically acclaimed novel that established McKinley as an outstanding fantasy writer for young adults. The Damar novels also were well received, garnering McKinley several awards including a Best Young Adult Books citation from the American Library Association in 1982 and a Newbery Honor citation in 1983 for *The Blue Sword*, and a *Horn Book* honor list citation in 1985 and the Newbery Medal in 1985 for *The Hero and the Crown*. Although some of the themes in *The Hero and the Crown* are more mature than those of *The Blue Sword*, both books are classified by booksellers and librarians as young adult novels.

The setting of the novels—especially the Damar of Harry's time—is based partly on Rudyard Kipling's depictions of the British Empire. The Homelanders (or Outlanders, depending on which side one is on) display an obviously paternalistic attitude toward the native Damarians they govern. In the Damar of Aerin's time, the Outlanders are absent and the geography is somewhat different, but the magical psychic abilities of the heroine prove beyond a doubt that Harry's Damar has indeed evolved from Aerin's Damar. The origins of many of the customs, traditions, and rituals present in *The Blue Sword* are explained in *The Hero and the Crown* as well.

The heroines Harry and Aerin were born partly from McKinley's love of fairy tales and partly from her desire to create strong female characters who are able to do more than wait for male heroes to rescue them. Harry and Aerin are successful at many activities that, in fiction, traditionally have been assigned to men. Aerin slays dragons, and Harry triumphs over all the other novices, both male and female, to win a contest of horse riding skills and swordplay. Harry and Aerin don their armor and ride into combat with Gonturan, the fabled blue sword that each woman carries in her own time.

McKinley gives her female warriors more than simply courage to slay their enemies; Aerin and Harry retain their femininity throughout their adventures. Both women are rather reluctant heroes, and both must grapple with mixed emotions concerning duty and honor. Aerin, considered an outsider in her own land, must risk her life several times before she is able to prove her worth to herself and to her people. Likewise, Harry, born and reared as an Outlander despite her Damarian ancestor, must win a place in her new world without betraying her roots. Both women are at first hampered by ignorance and inexperience, and both succeed at last by dint of their honor, pride, and stubborn refusal to accept defeat.

The novels also have romantic themes in common. In *The Blue Sword*, the familiar motif of the abducted maiden falling in love with her captor is mitigated by the strength of the character of Harry. Far from being a meekly subservient prisoner, Harry fights her way up from the status of respected guest to become the savior of the land. In order to defeat the enemy, she must even defy Corlath's orders and seek her own allies. She earns Corlath's respect and will rule beside him as an equal.

In *The Hero and the Crown*, Aerin is at first too involved with her own misery to take much notice of Tor's affection for her. It is Luthe, the wizard, who initiates Aerin into the joys of romance. Aerin must make the difficult choice to return to Tor, her childhood sweetheart, to be queen beside him. This painful choice is made only slightly easier by Aerin's realization that the immortal Luthe will wait for the part of Aerin that is "no longer quite mortal."

Reviewers of both novels have commended McKinley's well-rounded characters, creative settings, and suspenseful storytelling. The characters' emotional responses are often understated but never unbelievable or difficult to decipher. Romance, vivid action sequences, and captivating characters all contribute to the novels' popularity. Most critics believe that McKinley successfully blended the traditional fairy tale form with some nontraditional heroines.

—Quinn Weller

BONE DANCE

A group of post-holocaust misfits brings an evil city government to an end and establishes a new form of mystical community

Author: Emma Bull (1954-   )
Genre: Science fiction—cyberpunk
Type of work: Novel
Time of plot: An indeterminate time in the future
Location: An unidentified American city
First published: 1991

The Plot: Following the publication and positive critical reception of *War for the Oaks* (1987) and *Falcon* (1989), *Bone Dance* (subtitled *A Fantasy for Technophiles*) continues Emma Bull's exploration of high-tech fantasies through tight, well-constructed plot and characterization. In it, she utilizes science-fictional technologies tempered with New Age spiritualism.

The story follows the adventures of Sparrow, a trader in "Big Bang" collectible videos and CDs, and her ultimate clash with the corrupt authorities who control the city. After a successful video sale to the city boss, Albrecht, Sparrow wakes up in an alley unable to remember the previous twenty-four hours. She goes to see Sherrea, her friend and a mystic tarot reader. Sherrea informs Sparrow of strange and cataclysmic events in the near future and her role in them but has no knowledge of Sparrow's lost time.

Spurred on by the mystery, Sparrow is contacted by Mick Skinner, who claims to know about her missing memories. Pursued by two strangers Skinner is eager to avoid, they make it back to Sparrow's apartment and warehouse. After Skinner's strange and inexplicable death, Sparrow is kidnapped by the two strangers, who say they are city employees. Sparrow is told that Skinner was a Horseman, one of a group of mind-control soldiers who destroyed Earth in a nuclear war through jealous competition. Horsemen not only have the power of mind control but also can "ride" other people, willfully occupying and directing their bodies.

Sparrow is kidnapped again, this time by Frances, another Horseman, and a resurrected Skinner, who now occupies another body. In the conversations that follow, Sparrow is told that she herself is a "horse," a preholocaust, genetically grown container for exclusive use by Horsemen. This effectively wins Sparrow over to their plan of killing the most evil Horseman, Tom Worecski, who is also the real power in control of the city. Their attack fails, and Skinner is captured. Sparrow must offer her body for sex to ensure the escape of Frances.

After her brutal rape, Sparrow finds herself recuperating in a communal village peopled by mystics and Hoodoo magicians. There, she undergoes a psychic rebirth in which she comes to terms with who and what she is and begins to learn the importance of friendship and community. Her spiritual strength is renewed, and her friendship with Frances blossoms. They plan and undertake a second attack on Worecski and the government. This time, they ask a whole panoply of gods for help, and the attack succeeds. Worecski is killed, and the promise of a new humane order is established. Sparrow gives up city life and returns to her new spiritual community.

Analysis: In many ways, *Bone Dance* continues the cyberpunk legacy by exploring the psychological condition of a post-holocaust survivor through a hard-bitten and intelligent use of interior monologue and a series of trying moral dilemmas. Bull extends this paradigm beyond the exploration of technology and evil corporations, so prevalent in cyberpunk narratives and concentrates more fully on developing her central character. Sparrow is a sharp, cynical loner who has little use for anyone outside of her business transactions. *Bone Dance* convincingly follows her growth toward a complex understanding of herself as a human being.

Sparrow is never completely cold and bitter, and her love of pre-holocaust relics is more than commercial. She has a sense of time and history, and of how things could have been better in the city. In short, she has ideals about the possibilities of life and human interaction that her environment does not allow her to explore. As Bull makes clear, Sparrow has an affinity with these relics because she herself is a relic, a manufactured object that was "born" a teenager with a yearning for connection.

Sparrow also shares a deep sense of kinship with the Horsemen, another manufactured form looking for a sense of permanence and stability. Guilty over their destruction of the world, Frances and Skinner take it upon themselves to eliminate all Horsemen in a belated gesture of goodwill and in a belief that they cannot live with their crime. If Sparrow has no past, then Frances has no present, given that she moves between bodies at will. Bull brings these characters together and convincingly develops a relationship reliant on compassion and responsibility. In this way, Bull lifts *Bone Dance* out of a trendy nihilism and into a touching drama.

As its informal subtitle ironically suggests, *Bone Dance* is a "fantasy for technophiles," and it successfully combines familiar science-fictional themes and settings with a complementary exploration of the supernatural and the spiritual. Sparrow's reliance on her tarot reader for guidance and the use of the spirit world in the final clash between the Horsemen serve to shift the focus from the technological to the human. *Bone Dance* is an exploration of the friendship between Sparrow and Frances and the ways in which their relationship represents a way out of the decay and corruption of the city. Hoodoo, tarot readings, and mystical incantations come to stand as the antitheses of the technological, and it is in these that Bull celebrates the nurturing possibilities of community.

Bone Dance combines a futuristic detective yarn with a coming-of-age story by exploiting the best features of both genres. At the same time tough and compassionate, the novel works precisely through its convincing characterization rather than its sensationalism, thus widening the parameters of science fiction and fantasy in general.

—*Paul Hansom*

THE BONE FOREST

Stories exploring mythology, religion, the historical and prehistorical past, and humanity's place in time

Author: Robert Holdstock (1948-   )
Genre: Fantasy—mythological
Type of work: Stories
Time of plot: Various times between antiquity and the near future
Location: Various locations on Earth and in imaginary lands
First published: 1991

The Plot: This collection of stories, most of them originally published between the mid-1970's and the early 1990's, is weighted toward works similar in theme and style to the novella that gives the collection its title. "The Bone Forest" is original to this anthology. In all the stories, Robert Holdstock calls up images of humanity's past and its relationship to its present and future through the guiding link of the myths and stories that are passed down, in variation upon variation, through the ages.

"The Bone Forest" itself is part of Holdstock's Mythago Cycle consisting of *Mythago Wood* (1984), *Lavondyss* (1988), and *The Hollowing* (1993). These tales explore the mysterious tract of primary oak forest in Britain called Ryhope Wood and its "mythagos," manifestations of mythological archetypes and symbols of the collective unconscious. In Ryhope Wood, the myths and legends of humanity's past come to life. The forest, only a small woodland on the outside, contains vast regions within its interior.

The novella returns to the characters in the original novel—George Huxley and his two sons, Steven and Christian—but in a time when the brothers are still children and George Huxley has only begun to map and understand the wood's outer defenses. Finally he and his companion, Edward Wynne-Jones, make a breakthrough, but instead of offering further understanding it leads to a series of strange, disturbing encounters with a creature that Huxley only belatedly realizes is a *Doppelgänger* of himself.

"Scarrowfell" and "Thorn" both deal with religion and British history. In the former, a group of children watch and wait as a town prepares for an annual religious festival. It is not until the story's climax that the reader realizes that this is a Britain that was never converted to Christianity and that the forces being worshiped are far older and darker. In "Thorn," Thomas, a medieval stonemason helping to construct a new church, is recruited by a being named Thorn, one of the spirits being forced out by the coming of Christianity. By including symbols of pagan power within the stonework of the building, Thomas helps Thorn to subvert the power of the church before coming to believe that Thorn is using him for his own ends.

In "The Shapechanger," a young boy finds escape from an abusive relationship through a belief in the power of myth. In eighth century England, Wolfhead and Inkmarker, a shaman and his apprentice, travel to a village in which a mysterious voice has been calling out from inside a deep well. It is the voice, in fact, of a young boy more than a millennium in the future, trapped in his room by an abusive father, yearning for escape through the stories and histories of Britain that he reads. He achieves escape in a way that he did not anticipate.

"The Time Beyond Age" is unique in this collection as an example of Holdstock's science-fiction writing (though another story, "The Time of the Tree," has some vague science-fictional elements). In this story, scientists observe two people as they live an accelerated and pre-programmed life, aging years each day and heading toward some new, evolved form. The scientists themselves become disillusioned, obsessed with, or frightened by the unexpected results.

Analysis: Holdstock's greatest strengths lie in his ability to extrapolate and re-create in full and convincing detail a past so distant that it has all but retreated into the fog of myth, and in his clean, straightforward prose. He refuses to obscure the sublimity of his mythic vision with literary pyrotechnics. "The Bone Forest," written in much the same style as *Mythago Wood*, is an apt example of this. The events are startling and uncanny, but Holdstock, through his narrator, relates them almost matter-of-factly, with a detachment that not only is appropriate to George Huxley the scientist but also adds an immediacy and realism to the events, making them all the more powerful.

The stories in this collection offer enough variety to demonstrate Holdstock's strengths as well as his weaknesses. The greatest of the latter is an occasional tendency to give free rein to either the metaphoric or the pathetic impulse. "The Time of the Tree," essentially an extended metaphor about the human body as an ecological system complete with climatic changes and inhabitants, takes an interesting image and expands it past the bounds of interest and into the realm of the absurd. When Holdstock restrains himself, however, the result can be sublimely powerful, as in "The Shapechanger," with its somewhat worn premise of escape from distress through fantasy enlivened and deepened by Holdstock's delicate handling and subdued tone, which is given release only in the climactic sequence.

The most powerful story in the collection, "The Boy Who Jumped the Rapids," plays to all of Holdstock's strengths, demonstrating his firm hold on human nature and the driving power of myth, and how the two interact to create and feed off of each other. In this story the reader is witness to the birth of a myth, but not one that is known. Rather than his usual extrapolation backward from current story to original event, Holdstock here creates the original event—the murder of a child by an assassin—and then lets the reader glimpse the direction this sad story will take as it is remembered through the ages. In the end, Caylen, the boy of the story's title, comes to a devastating understanding of the role myth serves in society and in the human mind, for both good and ill.

More so than most authors' short-story collections, *The Bone Forest* retains its coherent theme throughout the stories selected for inclusion. If it does not do justice to the range of Holdstock's writing, it instead gives the reader depth, allowing insight into the way that a writer continues to work with, reshape, and reexamine themes and images through the course of his career.

—Carroll Brown

THE BOOK OF THE DUN COW

Chauntecleer, as lord of the peaceable animal kingdom, engages in a deadly battle with Cockatrice, the scaly monster whose forces of evil must be overcome

Author: Walter Wangerin, Jr. (1944-   )
Genre: Fantasy—animal fantasy
Type of work: Novel
Time of plot: Undefined, with echoes of both medieval and modern times
Location: Earth and the netherworld
First published: 1978

The Plot: In this story of hilarity and horror, Walter Wangerin, Jr., creates a delightfully varied, though temperamental, menagerie that exists more or less peacefully under the wings of the great Chauntecleer, its irritable but responsible leader. The hilarity flows out of the colorful personality clashes, wit, and foibles of these furry creatures and fowl. Hilarity gives way to horror when

Wyrm, condemned to live deep below the earth's surface, becomes bent on destroying all that is good by unleashing his forces of madness and mayhem.

The pending threat to Chauntecleer's community, and thereby the earth's civilization, develops gradually but insistently. Underneath the Chicken Coop lurks Ebenezer Rat, who sneaks up in the night and sucks the hens' eggs. On a more cosmic scale, although he is buried in the bowels of the earth by God's decree, Wyrm still has power to affect affairs on the surface. The result is the birth of Cockatrice. This wholly evil offspring, hatched by a toad and in a form that is half rooster and half dragon, kills his own father and, in the service of Wyrm, sets out to launch a deadly attack on the peaceable kingdom of Chauntecleer.

In that kingdom, Chauntecleer has succeeded in neutralizing Ebenezer Rat, the presence of evil inside the Coop, but the Lord of the Coop discovers the consequence of another evil beyond the Coop in the churning of the swollen river: All manner of debris, a "spinning cemetery of bones." Cast upon the shore, barely alive, is a Hen. Chauntecleer finds himself powerfully attracted to this bedraggled but beautiful Hen with vermillion at her throat, though she has been traumatized nearly to madness and death. She can only scream again and again the name of the cause of all the havoc and horror, "Cockatrice!" She finds healing in Chauntecleer's Coop, and eventually Chauntecleer gets his Pertelote. All is well in his domain, but not for long.

Far away, Cockatrice is pursuing his works of darkness. Thousands of eggs are hatching Basilisks, serpent-like birds that rise from the rivers and sting to death whatever they touch. Wyrm, the evil mastermind, is preparing to break through the earth's crust, gradually softened by the rains that are slowly flooding the land. Wyrm's goal is nothing less than to destroy the very fabric of this humanlike community and challenge God himself.

At that point, God sends the Dun Cow as messenger to Chauntecleer and his Earth-keepers. When the Basilisks make their appearance and threaten annihilation, the Dun Cow bestows on Chauntecleer the gifts essential to confronting and defeating the enemy. The battle that ensues is terrifying and indecisive until its climax in a chilling duel between Cockatrice and Chauntecleer. The treacherous Cockatrice is finally vanquished, but the bloodied victor also feels defeated. Again it is the ministry of the mysterious Dun Cow, with the help of the self-effacing dog, Mundo Cani, that revives the spirit of Chauntecleer. When the earth opens and Wyrm himself begins to make his move, Chauntecleer feels powerless. The Dun Cow sends the lowly Mundo Cani to fight the last battle. In a breathtaking climax, Mundo Cani dives into the gorge and plunges the horn of the Dun Cow into Wyrm's eye. The earth closes upon both of them. Peace can now return, but the cost has been enormous.

Analysis: Like the heroic epics of long ago, such as *Beowulf* and *The Song of Roland*, this beast epic deals with the nature of good and evil and the inevitable but shocking war between them. In this story, however, the heroic action yields not the giddiness of glory but the grief of pain, sacrifice, and loss. Although the tale reflects a medieval cosmography, political structure, and literary tradition, it strikes the contemporary reader as eerily modern, with unsettling reverberations of twentieth century tyrants, killing fields, and holocausts. As such, it delivers a significant moral message to both young and older readers, reminding them that peace is tenuous as long as evil has not been contained; that vigilance is vital lest evil destroy the good; that the qualities of goodness, compassion, courage, and love must be given the chance to flourish, for they have the power to prevail against the power of darkness.

Within this tale of conflict and combat are some marvelously funny episodes, entertaining characters, and a tender love story. The genuine affection that grows between Chauntecleer and Pertelote ennobles the intemperate leader and enables Pertelote to experience healing of her own psychic wounds and share the burdens of her mate. This relationship casts a warm glow in the midst of a world threatened by hate and cruelty.

This book, the author's first, has all the qualities of a classic: an archetypal, universal theme; a plot with vigor and verve, with movement and direction, with tension and resolution; a memorable, vivid set of characters who are brilliantly particularized; and a colorful style that has wit, variety, and passion. Hailed as the best children's book of the year, it enjoyed both critical acclaim and commercial success. In 1980 it received the National Religious Book Award, and in 1981 it won both the American Book Award and an American Library Association Notable Book citation. Encouraged, the author turned to writing full-time. In addition to volumes of stories and nonfiction, he has since written other fantasies for younger children, including *Thistle* (1983) and *Elizabeth and the Water-Troll* (1991). He has also written a sequel to *The Book of the Dun Cow*, titled *The Book of Sorrows* (1985). His novel *The Crying for a Vision* was published in 1994.

—*Henry J. Baron*

THE BOOK OF THE NEW SUN

The Earth of a distant future finds a hero to replace its dying sun

Author: Gene Wolfe (1931-   )
Genre: Science fiction—theological romance
Type of work: Novels
Time of plot: Millennia in the future
Location: Urth
First published: *The Shadow of the Torturer* (1980), *The Claw of the Conciliator* (1981; collected with *The Shadow of the Torturer* as *The Book of the New Sun, Volumes I and II*, 1983), *The Sword of the Lictor* (1982), *The Citadel of the Autarch* (1983; collected with *The Sword of the Lictor* as *The Book of the New Sun, Volumes III and IV*, 1985), and *The Urth of the New Sun* (1987)

The Plot: In an Earth (now called Urth) of the distant future, the Sun is slowly dying. Humanity is divided into the Commonwealth, centered roughly in what is now South America, and the Ascians, or those without shadow, who dominate the Northern Hemisphere. The society resembles medieval cultures such as that of the Byzantine Empire.

Severian is born into the hereditary Guild of Torturers in the city of Nessus. The Torturers are assigned to torment the enemies of the city's ruler. Severian, along with several other apprentices, is trained by the dour Master Gurloes. One of the few exceptions to their grim regimen is the annual celebration of their patroness, Holy Katherine. Severian meets a prisoner named Thecla, on whom he takes pity, eventually bringing her books and trying to console her. Severian gives Thecla a knife, and from the pools of blood he sees outside her prison door the next time he comes to visit her, he concludes that she has committed suicide. Severian informs Master Palaemon, one of his superiors in the Guild, of what he has done. Palaemon advises Severian to go into exile and gives him a resplendent sword named *Terminus Est* to aid him during his adventures and ordeals.

Severian ranges far and wide, eventually meeting an abandoned blonde woman named Dorcas as well as the mysterious Dr. Talos and his sidekick, the giant Baldanders. Severian's network of acquaintances begins to solidify, forming a circle of personal loyalties around which his destiny will unfold. Eventually, some of these people's memories become fused with Severian's when he comes to be the representative of his entire planet.

Severian journeys to the north, toward the Windowless City of Thrax. He manages to get hold of the Claw of the Conciliator, which despite its name is not a weapon but a glowing, beautiful, and redemptive jewel that holds the promise of future peace for the warring and injured peoples of Urth. Along with Dorcas, he encounters the cannibalistic Alzabo and helps the people of the region surrounding Thrax win their freedom.

Severian finds out that Thecla has not in fact died but used the knife to escape. He also finds out that Baldanders and Dr. Talos are not what they seem. Dr. Talos is a mechanical man who, despite his air of authority, is Baldanders' servant. Baldanders, for his part, is in communication with extraterrestrial spirits called hierodules. These hierodules, Ossipago, Barbatus, and Famulimus, reveal to Severian the calamity that is overtaking Urth and inform him that he has been appointed to journey into space and find a new sun for the planet.

First, though, Severian has to attain full authority on Urth. With the backing of the power he has accumulated in Thrax and elsewhere, he returns to Nessus and is declared Autarch. He marries Valeria, an aristocratic lady of the city who is a suitable partner for him, although parts of his love will always be directed toward Dorcas and Thecla. As Autarch, Severian brings more justice to Urth than most of his predecessors had managed.

The hierodules arrange for a huge starship to transport Severian into space. Aboard the giant ship, Severian is attacked by "jibers," crewmen from other worlds who have been in the ship so long that they have become permanent residents of its underclass. He is saved from them by a pretty but strangely world-weary woman named Gunnie and an engaging sprite named Zak. Severian learns that he is going to the planet Yesod for a trial in which he will represent Urth. His task is to convince the Hierogrammate Tzadkiel to give Urth a new sun. Upon arrival at Yesod, Severian encounters a woman (actually an embodied, angelic larva) named Apheta who reveals the utter insignificance of Urth in the cosmic order but hints at implications in his mission that Severian himself has not realized.

Severian meets the great Tzadkiel only to find that it is the apparently harmless Zak, in vastly transmuted form. Tzadkiel informs Severian that he is Urth's new sun and that he will be returned amid great cataclysm for the planet's rebirth. Tzadkiel also indicates that, in some other dimension of time, he and all of his sort had been made by humans from Urth. Severian returns to Urth, this time accompanied by Gunnie's younger incarnation, Burgundofara. Much of Urth is destroyed, but Severian survives to see the planet renewed and renamed Ushas, signifying its new state of being.

Analysis: The Book of the New Sun is the most ambitious work of science fantasy to be published in the last quarter of the twentieth century, recognized with a World Fantasy Award for *The Shadow of the Torturer* and a Nebula Award for *The Claw of the Conciliator*. Science fantasy is an odd hybrid. Gene Wolfe's books combine the linguistic inventiveness and spiritual depth of the fiction of J. R. R. Tolkien with the scientific believability and historical sweep of the work of Isaac Asimov. Wolfe's writing, though, has a voice and a pulse utterly its own.

On one level, the Book of the New Sun is filled with conventional adventure of the "sword and sorcery" variety. Severian fights his way through challenges in Nessus and Thrax to emerge victorious as lord over all. This surface physical action, however, serves primarily to mask the true inner complexity of the series, swathed in Wolfe's complicated plotting and exotic vocabulary (all of which is derived from existing, though obscure, words in English, Latin, and Hebrew). Most readers will be deep into the series before coming close to guessing the ultimate significance of Urth's clearly decrepit state or what the New Sun will be.

Severian is typical of post-1960 science fiction in that he is an antihero as much as a hero. Although his narrative perspective governs readers' view of the story throughout, it is difficult to identify with him: He is too involved in torture, deception, and various other despicable acts. Wolfe presents Severian as able to come to terms with the evil he has done and integrate it with the far more dominant principles of altruism that largely govern his conduct. Severian goes into exile from Nessus only to provide cover for what he supposes is Thecla's suicide, and he takes on the self-sacrificing mission of leaving Urth and his Autarchy to go to Yesod in search of the New Sun. Because Wolfe lets Severian speak in his own voice, readers are privy to Severian's own ruthless self-examination and his own awareness of the complexity of his course in life.

Thecla is one of the most affecting of the supporting characters. Her disappearance and unlooked-for return add to her generally mysterious personality, giving her an air of sacredness (the name Thecla comes from an early Christian martyr) that makes her something of a spiritual reference point for Severian. Other characters deepen the strangeness and texture of Severian's journey and simultaneously exemplify Wolfe's literary allusiveness. The giant Baldanders testifies to the higher qualities of the human race that are latent in the weary and hard-pressed denizens of Urth. The name Baldanders is a reference to the work of Argentine writer Jorge Luis Borges. Dr. Talos, the mechanical man, is a portal to the strange, superhuman yet half-human, world of the hierodules; "Talos" was originally the name of a mechanical man in English poet Edmund Spenser's poem *The Faerie Queene* (1590, 1596).

The three hierodules, and even more the Hierogrammate Tzadkiel, emblematize the texture and philosophy of the book. Both words have a meaning, although in Greek: "hierodule" is "sacred slave," and "Hierogrammate" is "product of sacred writing." Tzadkiel reveals to Severian when he is on Yesod that the hierodules, superhuman though they may seem, were in fact themselves created by the human race long ago. Desiring to give their descendants a kind of sacred security, they had created the Hierogrammates to give their descendants succor when they need it.

Wolfe portrays a set of all-powerful deities created by humans who in turn help humanity of far-future Urth re-create itself. This paradox fits with all the displacements and foreshadowings in time that occur throughout the series. There also is a hope that there is an order outside time in the universe. "The Conciliator" clearly is analogous to Jesus Christ, and the characters of Thecla and Holy Katherine evoke the Virgin Mary.

At the end of the series, Severian returns to renewed Ushas and encounters simple fishermen who indicate that they revere Severian and two of his companions as gods. Severian, though, points out that only something called "the Increate" is truly worthy of worship. Wolfe makes it clear that this Increate is none other than the God of the Judeo-Christian tradition.　—*Nicholas Birns*

THE BOOK OF WONDER

A collection of short fantasy tales set in London and in magical imaginary worlds

Author: Lord Dunsany (Edward John Moreton Drax
　　Plunkett, 1878-1957)
Genre: Fantasy—magical world
Type of work: Stories
Time of plot: Various times between antiquity and 1910
Location: Various locations on Earth and imaginary
　　worlds
First published: 1912

The Plot: *The Book of Wonder: A Chronicle of Little Adventures at the Edge of the World* is a collection of fourteen tales in which Lord Dunsany explores mythical cities and creatures as well as the fabulous exploits of familiar characters such as a young English girl, a pirate, a businessman, and thieves. An unusual feature of the collection is that Dunsany wrote the stories in response to the drawings of S. H. Sime, an illustrator whose style was often compared with Aubrey Beardsley's, and whose wryly humorous yet macabre black-and-white compositions had accompanied Dunsany's first four short-story collections.

Stories of atmosphere, evocative of mood rather than plot, character, or theme, the tales in *The Book of Wonder* are notable for the biblical style developed by Dunsany in his earlier work. They are also noteworthy for his facility with leading readers to the place in his subtitle, "the edge of the world." The locations are recognizable but are all the more seductive for his facile transformation of accessible details into the images from dreams or nightmares.

In his preface, Dunsany invites readers "who are in any wise weary of London" to follow him to new worlds. Some of the stories take place solely in mystical realms and illustrate Dunsany's oft-noted unique nomenclature. In "The Bride of the Man-Horse," for example, Shepperalk the centaur leaves his home in the Athraninaurian mountains for Zretazoola, where he will seek a bride, Sombelene. In "The Quest of the Queen's Tears," Ackronnian, king of Afarmah, Lool, and Haf, slays the Gladsome Beast in Fairyland in an ultimately failed effort to move Sylvia, the Queen of the Woods, to tears. These stories illustrate Dunsany's tendency to cast his female characters as queens, princesses, and sphinxes but also as powerless figures of sexual objectification.

Some of the stories display the imaginative ease with which Dunsany moves from London to the edge of the world. In "Miss Cubbidge and the Land of Romance," a glistening golden dragon abducts the title character from her London home at 12A Prince of Wales Square to the eternal and ancient lands of Romance. In "How Nuth Would Have Practised His Art upon the Noles," young Tommy Tonker becomes an apprentice jewel thief to Nuth, an experienced London burglar living in Belgrave Square. They attempt to steal emeralds from the gnoles, undefined creatures who dwell secretly in a lean, high house in a deep, dark wood.

These stories—along with "The Hoard of the Gibbelins," in which the adventurous knight Alderic, attempting to steal the man-eating Gibbelins' emeralds, is caught and hanged, and which concludes with "the tale is one of those that have not a happy ending"—demonstrate Dunsany's experimentation with humorous, ironic, surprise finales. Miss Cubbidge, for example, in the denouement of her story, receives a letter from a former schoolmate admonishing her for the impropriety of traveling across the mystical seas with a dragon and no chaperone.

Two of Dunsany's most successful stories concern simple London businesspeople who begin to lead double lives: the real, sterile life of making money and the fantastic life of the imagination. In "The Wonderful Window," a strange old man dressed in Oriental garb sells a magic window to the romantic salesman Mr. Sladden and installs it over a cupboard in his rented room. Sladden views the mystical Golden Dragon City through the window. Attempting to save the city from invaders, he breaks the window and discovers only his old cupboard behind it. In "The Coronation of Mr. Thomas Shap," the salesman Shap develops his imaginative abilities to the point that he creates an old Eastern city, names it Larkar, crowns himself king, and dwells so little in his real life that he is put into a psychiatric ward, still believing himself to be ruler of all the lands of Wonder.

Analysis: Contemporary critics responded with enthusiasm to *The Book of Wonder*, in which Dunsany recovered the mythology of *The Gods of Pegana* (1905) and *Time and the Gods* (1906); the heroic fantasy of *The Sword of Welleran* (1908); and the supernatural of *A Dreamer's Tales* (1910); as well as exploring the ironic fairy tale. Although in his ten ensuing volumes of short stories he experimented with different genres, such as short-shorts in *Fifty-One Tales* (1915), club tales in the Jorkens series (1931-1954), and mystery stories in *The Little Tales of Smethers* (1952), scholars herald his first five volumes of tales as exemplars in the field of fantasy fiction. Some even dubbed him "the father of modern fantasy." His work influenced writers such as J. R. R. Tolkien, Ursula K. Le Guin, and especially H. P. Lovecraft, who called him the "inventor of a new mythology and weaver of surprising folklore." Beginners at the craft of fantasy fiction often compose what has come to be known as the "Dunsanian" story.

Since Dunsany's death, his work has been collected in at least five anthologies. Dunsany believed that true art was the result of inspiration, and he disapproved of readers' attempts to allegorize his stories; he wanted most of all to evoke a mood of fabulous mystery. His facility with archaic language, arresting neologisms, strange new mythologies, and heroic adventures, and his belief—

illustrated especially in the stories from *The Book of Wonder*—in the occasional human need to escape the sterile ordinariness of life, lead to continuing appreciation from fantasy enthusiasts, scholars in the field, and especially the readers he addresses in his preface, "those that tire at all of the world we know."

—*Siobhan Craft Brownson*

BORN TO EXILE
and
IN THE RED LORD'S REACH

A wandering minstrel with the power of teleportation struggles to survive and find love and meaning in a harsh world where he must fear persecution as a "witch"

Author: Phyllis Eisenstein (1946-   )
Genre: Fantasy—extrasensory powers
Type of work: Novels
Time of plot: Unspecified, preindustrial
Location: An Earth-like world
First published: *Born to Exile* (1978; portions published as short stories in the August, 1971; November, 1972; January, 1974; and February, 1975, issues of *The Magazine of Fantasy and Science Fiction*) and *In the Red Lord's Reach* (1989; portions published as short stories in the September, 1977, and July, 1979, issues of *The Magazine of Fantasy and Science Fiction*; novel serialized in the July-September, 1988, issues of *The Magazine of Fantasy and Science Fiction*)

The Plot: In *Born to Exile*, the wandering fifteen-year-old minstrel Alaric is introduced. In addition to his talent for music, he has the power of teleportation. The power is limited in that he is able only to move himself and objects he is carrying to a location that he is able to visualize and position in relation to his current location. He was found, as a newborn baby on a hillside, covered in blood with a "gory hand raggedly severed above the wrist" clutching his ankle. He was taken in by a couple and reared as their son. When he was seven years old, his adoptive mother died, and his father was cruel to him, raising a whip to strike him. As he was about to be whipped, he visualized a tree in the nearby woods and was instantly transported there.

Alaric initially lives by stealing but soon meets Dall, a wandering minstrel who makes him his apprentice. Dall is later murdered by bandits, and Alaric transports himself away to safety. In his wandering, Alaric comes to the

Castle Royal, where he falls in love with, and becomes the lover of, Princess Solinde. He is accused of witchcraft by one of her maids, who witnesses his teleportation power being used. The king, Solinde's father, exiles him from the kingdom. Solinde's brother, Jeris, who has become Alaric's friend, gives him a sword, belt, and scabbard.

In his continuing travels, Alaric uses his teleportation power to escape being killed by the proprietors of an inn, at which travelers are routinely killed for their belongings. He leaves the inn accompanied by Mizella, a prostitute who had been used by the inn to lull travelers into a false sense of security. He and Mizella rescue an old woman whom villagers have thrown into a well to die, thinking her to be a witch. It turns out that this woman is Artuva, the midwife who slapped Alaric's rump after he was born, frightening him into using his teleportation powers. It was, she explains, her bloody severed hand that gripped his ankle when he was found on the hillside as an infant.

Artuva was herself exiled by Alaric's true father, as a result of the loss of his son. She leads Alaric to the home of his father, Baron Garlenon, and his mother, Lorenta Garlenon. Ten generations of Garlenons, all of whom have both the power of teleportation and musical talent, have ruled there and in surrounding lands. The Garlenons inbreed in order to maintain their genetically transmitted talents. Alaric is welcomed home and meets many of his "cousins" but is ultimately ejected when it becomes clear that he will not cooperate with the others in using their talents for the purpose of conquering still other neighboring lands by suddenly appearing and slaughtering opposing leaders. As the book ends, "Once again he was merely a minstrel—not a baron's son, not a lord of power, but a wandering exile."

In the Red Lord's Reach presents more of Alaric's wandering life as a minstrel. Entertaining the Red Lord in his castle, he learns that this cruel lord delights in torturing captives to death, enjoying their pain. The Red Lord shows Alaric a woman whom he is torturing in this fashion in a locked room and states his intention of doing the same to Alaric after the woman dies. Alaric teleports away, taking the woman with him. Alaric uses his sword to kill her, at her request, because of the severity of her injuries.

Alaric ponders whether he should use his powers to return and kill the Red Lord, acknowledging that he has always simply run away from danger before. He ultimately joins up with some nomadic deer herdsmen and engages in a love affair with Zavia, the daughter of the herdsmen's self-proclaimed witch, Kata. He encounters jealousy from Gilo, Morak, and Terevli, the three sons of Simir, the herdsmen's leader. They plot to kill him and ultimately attack Simir himself. Alaric teleports away but decides to return and fight them, helping to save Simir. Simir exiles his own sons, going as far as leaving Gilo bound where the Red Lord will find him, and adopts Alaric as his new son.

The herdsmen, different from other people Alaric has encountered, value, rather than fear, magic and "witchcraft." Kata wishes Alaric to become her apprentice, but he is resistant to the idea, just as he is resistant to Simir's evident desire for Alaric ultimately to become his successor. Because of a harsh winter, there are few deer, and the herdsmen fear that they may not survive. They decide to fight the Red Lord and try to take over his lands and castle. Alaric and Simir go there in disguise but are recognized by Gilo, who is now serving the Red Lord. Alaric uses his powers to help teleport herdsman warriors, who do battle with and kill the Red Lord's soldiers. Simir himself, who long ago was one of the Red Lord's soldiers, kills the Red Lord. Alaric also battles Gilo, but it is Simir who kills him.

As this book ends, Alaric decides to decline Simir's offer to become his successor. Alaric resumes his wandering minstrel life and once again feels the "winter of exile closing about him."

Analysis: Alaric is a fascinating character, an outcast with two wondrous talents. He continually struggles with a moral dilemma of how to use his teleportation talent, as well as often facing persecution because the world fears that talent or thinks it a sign of alignment with evil. He delights especially in his musical talent, enjoying entertaining others and discovering or creating new songs.

Alaric does not seek out confrontation with evil but unavoidably finds it during his travels in the world. Although initially he is likely to use his teleportation talent to flee from danger and evil, by the end of *In the Red Lord's Reach* he has seemingly decided that some evil is so monstrous that it must be confronted and fought, even at the risk of the gravest danger. Even then, however, his conscience is troubled. Even though he did not personally kill anyone during the assault on the Red Lord's castle, he sees the deaths as on his head. An exile, both literally and figuratively, from birth, Alaric repeatedly has the experience of temporarily seeming to find a place and companions or family for himself, only to determine that his true destiny is once again to walk alone.

Although *Born to Exile* was initially written in portions, as short stories, it stands up remarkably well as a unified novel. The depiction of the internal life of the family of teleporters is outstanding and memorable. *In the Red Lord's Reach* is clearly a more complex and mature work, with several interesting subplots, and compellingly develops a number of characters in addition to Alaric, such as Simir and Kata. The two books are best read together and constitute a satisfying coming-of-age saga of a lonely, talented, and, at heart, conscientious and good youth whose resolutions of his moral dilemmas, although not perfect, satisfy him.

Although the scientific basis of Alaric's teleportation talent is never explained, it obviously has a physical rather than mystical origin because it can be passed on genetically. Phyllis Eisenstein portrays a teleportation talent that is subject to certain restrictions and conditions, and she faithfully confines her character's use of that talent within those boundaries. The concept of teleportation has been used frequently in other notable science fiction or fantasy stories, among them *The Stars My Destination* (1957; originally titled *Tiger! Tiger!*, 1956) by Alfred Bester, *Tunnel in the Sky* (1955) by Robert A. Heinlein, and *Jumper* (1992) by Steven Gould. Eisenstein's treatment of teleportation, interspersed with her believable characters and entertaining plot, ranks among the very best.

Eisenstein is also the author of two other linked fantasy novels, *Sorcerer's Son* (1979) and *The Crystal Palace* (1988), which portray the struggles of a young sorcerer to find his father and his true love. Her two other published novels, as of 1995, were *Shadow of Earth* (1979), the story of an alternate world in which the Spanish Armada won, resulting in a very different contemporary North America, and *In the Hands of Glory* (1981), a space opera. She is also the author of a considerable body of short fiction, including a number of stories in her early career coauthored with her husband Alex Eisenstein, starting with "The Trouble with the Past" in the *New Dimensions 1* anthology (1971) edited by Robert Silverberg. Her short story "Nightlife," published in the February, 1982, issue of *The Magazine of Fantasy and Science Fiction*, was a Hugo Award nominee.

—*Bernard J. Farber*

THE BORROWERS SERIES

Peoplelike beings who are only inches high confront dangers and discomfort when they leave their home

Author: Mary Norton (1903-1992)
Genre: Fantasy—alien civilization

Type of work: Novels
Time of plot: The late nineteenth century
Location: England
First published: *The Borrowers* (1952), *The Borrowers Afield* (1955), *The Borrowers Afloat* (1959), and *The Borrowers Aloft* (1961)

The Plot: Mary Norton, English actress, playwright, and award-winning author, tells in a four-book series the engrossing fantasy of miniature people known as Borrowers. They are so called because they live by "borrowing," for their own use, lost or discarded items around a house, such things as scraps of food, dropped needles and pins, matches or candles that have fallen behind a chest, dollhouse furniture, or half of a pair of broken scissors—things that people know they have but simply cannot find at the moment.

The four books in the Borrowers series actually compose one continuous story in four episodes. The first book, *The Borrowers*, establishes the parameters of the fantasy, introduces the central family, describes the under-the-kitchen-floor setting, and reveals some of the conflicts and challenges that confront the family daily. The three following books in the series relate further adventures of the inches-high people as they search for a place where they may live undisturbed by "human beans."

The Borrowers begins as Mrs. May tells young Kate the fanciful story of the little people her brother, Tom, had made up—if indeed he had made them up. Pod, Homily, and Arrietty belong to the Clock family of Borrowers, so named because they enter and leave their home under the kitchen floor through a hole at the base of a grandfather clock. They must find a new residence because Pod, the father, has had the misfortune of being seen by a human, "the boy" who is sick abed in Firbank Hall, the home occupied by old Aunt Sophie and Mrs. Driver, the housemaid. Moreover, Arrietty, the Borrower daughter, has even dared to talk to the boy. Although his kindness in bringing them useful things and even offering to let them live in the dollhouse upstairs shows that he is no threat to them, the family members know that they must leave when Mrs. Driver discovers their presence and calls the rat catcher to smoke out the "horrible creatures." They make their escape to the fields in the nick of time.

The grown-up Kate continues the story in *The Borrowers Afield*. She tells her children the story she learned from Tom Goodenough himself when she, as a child, visited Mrs. May, who had inherited Firbank Hall upon Aunt Sophie's death. Searching for their relatives who supposedly are living in a badger's set, the Clock family suffers many hardships in the fields. Their makeshift home in an abandoned boot provides little protection from moths, snakes, cows, owls, field mice, Gypsies, and a cold winter. Once again "the boy" comes to their rescue when Pod, Homily, and Arrietty are discovered in the caravan of Mild Eye the Gypsy. Along with Spiller, an ingenuous orphan Borrower who often assists them, the Clock family finds temporary quarters with Lupy, Hendreary, and Eggletina, their sought-for relatives who have moved from the badger's burrow into the walls of Firbank Hall.

In *The Borrowers Afloat*, Pod, Homily, and Arrietty must again search for a new home because the departure of Tom and his grandfather from the cottage will leave no food for Pod to "borrow." The locked house seems to have no avenue of exit, but the resourceful Spiller comes and leads the Clock family out through the washhouse drain pipe. As if this harrowing experience were not enough, the family of three must endure a treacherous trip down the river in a tea kettle. Although they are seen and almost caught again by Mild Eye the Gypsy, Spiller saves them. They make their way toward a hobbyist's miniature village at Little Fordham.

The Borrowers Aloft completes the series about the little people. The family enjoys life in the model village at Little Fordham, especially Homily, who has always wanted a proper house of her own. Unfortunately, Arrietty again commits the indiscretion of talking to a human, this time the housekeeper for kindly Mr. Pott, the builder of the tiny village. Before they can leave, the family is kidnapped by a greedy couple who hope to use them to increase business at their own miniature showplace. Locked in the couple's attic, the Borrowers ingeniously construct a passenger balloon, float out the attic window, and make their way back to the replica village. Pod and Homily know, however, that Borrowers and humans do not make good company. After a night's rest, they will be off again in search of a new home.

Analysis: Stories of little people are common in folklore around the world. Jonathan Swift's narrative of the Lilliputians in *Gulliver's Travels* (1726), Lewis Carroll's 1865 account of a diminutive Alice in Wonderland, and the legends of the leprechauns of Ireland, to mention but a few, have stirred the imagination of generations of readers. None of these stories has pricked the fancy more than Mary Norton's fantasy of the little people known as Borrowers. In style and subject, her stories are children's literature at its best, capitalizing on children's natural love for imaginative play, or fantasy. The series (collected as *The Borrowers Omnibus*, 1966; titled for U.S. publication as *The Complete Adventures of the Borrowers*, 1967) occupies a firm place among the classics of children's literature alongside such notable works as Kenneth Grahame's *The Wind in the Willows* (1908), L. Frank Baum's *The Wonderful Wizard of Oz* (1900), J. R. R. Tolkien's *The Hobbit: Or, There and Back Again* (1937), and the ever-popular masterpiece of C. S. Lewis, the Chronicles of Narnia (1950-1956).

All the books in the Borrowers series have won notable awards. *The Borrowers* was an immediate success, quickly winning the Carnegie Medal, the Lewis Carroll Shelf Award, and the American Library Association Distinguished Book Award. *The Borrowers Afield*, *The Borrowers Afloat*, and *The Borrowers Aloft* each won designation as an American Library Association Notable Book. *The Borrowers Aloft* and *The Borrowers Afloat* were in addition chosen by the New York *Herald Tribune* as Spring Festival Honor Books. Norton followed the famous series with *The Borrowers Avenged* (1982) and *Poor Stainless: A New Story About the Borrowers* (1971). The concept of the miniature race formed the basis for the television series *The Littles*, and her Norton's *Bed-Knob and Broomstick* (1957) was made into the 1971 film *Bedknobs and Broomsticks*, starring Angela Lansbury.

The appeal of the series lies perhaps not only in the clever, intriguing concept of little people in a human world—drawn to a mathematically correct scale reminiscent of Jonathan Swift's Gulliver in the lands of Lilliput and Brobdingnag—but also in the skillful characterization of the story's chief actors. The reader easily relates to the diminutive world of the Borrowers because, although they are not human beings and are even averse to human contact, they look and act much like humans. Pod assumes the leadership in his family (itself a human relationship) and is the steadying, responsible force. His talk is punctuated with such wise, insightful comments as "Size is nothing. . . . It's the talk that gets them [one's bigger enemies]." Always aware of future needs, he judiciously makes provisions. Homily is the typical wife and mother, always concerned about the family's daily needs, safety, and whereabouts; always fretting about appearances; forever wanting to settle down in a place of her own; and always forgiving and loving. Youthful Arrietty seldom thinks before acting, enjoys the wonders of the natural world, foolishly ignores her parents' warnings, and repeatedly brings calamity both to herself and her family. Spiller is the independent, unconventional young man who redeems himself through his experience-generated know-how and his uncanny ability to appear exactly when he is needed most. Such sharp characterization readily draws the young reader into the fantasy that imitates life.

A prime rule of fantasy for children is that the author begin in reality and end in reality, thus leading highly imaginative children into but also out of fantasy. Standard examples are E. B. White's *Charlotte's Web* (1952) and C. S. Lewis' tales of Narnia. For the most part, Norton follows this criterion via the convention of a storyteller, Mrs. May, relating a story that soon fades into the fantasy itself but returns at book's end to the real-life setting. The only exception is the last book of the series.

In this series, Norton presents a story with episodes that create energizing suspense, tell of engrossing adventures of survival equal to those of Robinson Crusoe and the Swiss Family Robinson, and depict characters that are genuinely believable though fantastic. She unfolds a story worthy of note by all readers of fantasy literature.

—Maverick Marvin Harris

THE BOYS FROM BRAZIL

Notorious Nazi doctor Josef Mengele, alive and living in Brazil, dispatches young clones of Adolf Hitler, and only Yakov Liebermann can stop his plans

Author: Ira Levin (1929-   )
Genre: Science fiction—cautionary
Type of work: Novel
Time of plot: 1974-1975
Location: Various cities around the world
First published: 1976

The Plot: Ira Levin presents an intricate plot involving Dr. Josef Mengele (the "Angel of Death" from the Nazi concentration camps), who has set up a laboratory in Brazil. Yakov Liebermann is a Nazi hunter, based on the legendary Simon Wiesenthal. The two enemies finally confront each other in the United States, where the plot is resolved.

Only far into the book do readers learn the nature of Mengele's plan, but there are intimations throughout. At a meeting of old Nazis, Mengele gives out the names and locations of ninety-four men who will have to be murdered within the next year. None holds an important position; most are civil servants or minor functionaries in government. They are spread all over the world.

The Nazis are given new identity papers, passports, and money.

Unknown to Mengele, a young Jewish man interested in capturing Nazis has recognized Mengele and persuaded a waitress in the restaurant where the meeting is held to plant a tape recorder and to retrieve it for him. Mengele becomes suspicious, finds the waitress, and through her tracks down the young man, who is found in his hotel room playing parts of the tape to Liebermann. The young man is killed, but Liebermann has heard enough to pique his curiosity. He asks a friend at the Reuters news agency to note unusual deaths, and he travels to Germany to interview a woman who worked for Mengele during the war. She tells him enough to send him to a German scientist, who reveals that research is pointing toward the possibility of cloning a person from his or her cells.

Liebermann guesses that Mengele somehow has cloned Adolf Hitler and arranged for the ninety-four clones to be adopted. Each has the exact genetic code of Hitler, and each adoptive mother is married to someone unimportant, just as Hitler's mother was. Liebermann begins to track down these families. All the boys look alike, with pale skin and dark hair, and all are impolite. Liebermann travels to the United States, where he expects the next assassination to take place.

Meanwhile, Mengele's operation has been shut down by higher Nazi command, and the assassins have been called home. Mengele destroys his laboratory but intends to continue with the assassinations of the adoptive fathers. He also plans to kill Liebermann because of his interference. They meet at the home of one of the boys, whose father Mengele kills and tosses into the basement. When the boy comes home from school, Mengele and Liebermann are in a life-and-death struggle. The boy sends his dogs after Mengele because he has a gun. The boy figures out who has killed his father and orders the dogs to kill him.

Liebermann recuperates and makes one more stop in America. In New York City, he meets with radical Jews who know about the list of children that Liebermann carries. While they talk, Liebermann tears up the list and flushes it down a toilet, telling the leader that it is wrong to kill children, any children, and that simply because they have Hitler's genes does not mean they will turn out like him.

Analysis: This book raises many interesting ethical issues. Mengele is presented as completely evil, as one might assume he was. Levin's Mengele says that he asked Hitler in the middle of the war for a vial of his blood and some scrapings from his arm. He did not have the technology then to do anything with this material, but he developed the science in Brazil. He procured women to be implanted with embryos with Hitler's genetic code and to have the babies that would then be adopted by appropriate couples. The couples would match Hitler's parents in major respects, and Mengele planned for the adoptive fathers' assassinations to match Hitler's loss of his father.

Liebermann represents the forces of good. He is a crotchety older man who at first does not believe that Mengele's plan is being put into effect. Liebermann is portrayed as being almost a pauper, living in inadequate quarters, and having almost no help in his work of tracking down Nazis. He says that people had forgotten the days he had helped track down the infamous Nazi leader Adolf Eichmann.

Levin suggests that there always will be people like Mengele and like the militant Jews who wish to find the ninety-four Hitler clones and kill them. Liebermann is supposed to represent the moderate view of those who learn from history. He takes a chance that none of these children will become like Hitler, but he is steadfast that no one should do what the Nazis did in World War II, including killing children.

This novel was filmed in 1978, with Laurence Olivier and Gregory Peck playing Liebermann and Mengele. There are minor differences, but the film is true to the book.

Levin is proficient at developing twists and turns in the novel. At one point, one of the assassins notices someone he knew during the war, and he tells him his orders and asks about the postman of the town. Then, with no warning, he kills the man, saying that the target was not the postman but the old friend to whom he was talking.

This novel is science fiction because such cloning currently is impossible, but cloning of cells and certain low-level life-forms has been achieved. In the years after Levin wrote this book, much was done to produce changes in fetuses and to develop certain characteristics within them. It is conceivable that the sort of cloning represented in this novel will become scientific fact. Levin takes no moral stand on the ethics of such a scientific feat. He allows the reader to decide, based on who is manipulating the borrowed genetic material.

—*John Jacob*

BOY'S LIFE

After Cory Mackenson sees a murdered man, his idyllic childhood is interrupted, and he comes to understand the forces of good and evil at work in his hometown

Author: Robert R. McCammon (1952-   )
Genre: Fantasy—high fantasy
Type of work: Novel
Time of plot: Primarily 1964, with a flashforward to 1991 at the novel's end
Location: Zephyr, Alabama
First published: 1991

The Plot: *Boy's Life* is unlike Robert R. McCammon's other novels and is a marked departure from his usual style, focused more on horror. The plot of *Boy's Life* is more a series of incidents weaved into a tapestry of the variety of lifestyles in Zephyr, Alabama, and the Bruton section of town, where African Americans reside, during the mid-1960's.

In part 1, "The Shades of Spring," the story opens on a cold spring morning as Cory Mackenson accompanies his father on his milk delivery route. Father and son see a car plunge into a lake the locals say is bottomless. Cory's father dives into the icy waters in a desperate but futile attempt to save the drowning man. Cory's father comes face to face with the drowned man. The image haunts Cory's father throughout the novel: a murdered man, naked and beaten, a tattoo on his body, his hands cuffed to the steering wheel, a copper wire knotted around his neck. Near the scene, Cory finds a green feather, a clue he thinks will figure prominently in solving the murder, but one he keeps a secret, hidden from the rest of the world in a cigar box.

About the same time, the African American members of an adjacent area of the community called Bruton engage in a ritual to feed Old Moses, a serpent who swims in the belly of the Tecumseh River, from the gargoyle bridge. The serpent apparently is not pleased with his food, because he does not smack on the bridge's support with his tail as he usually does when fed by an ancient African American "conjure woman" the locals call The Lady. She is married to a man of color whose face is pigmented on only one side, earning him the nickname of The Moon Man.

Odd events occur in the town. Wasps swarm through the local church one Sunday during services while the preacher denounces rock and roll music. Two bullies, Gotha and Gordo Branlin, terrorize Cory, and he is spooked by "The Demon," Brenda Sutley. Finally, hard, steady rains come to Zephyr. The levee breaks in Bruton. Cory, as he helps to shore up the faulty levee, rescues a black child from being devoured by Old Moses, who is slithering in and out of Bruton's houses through the floodwater. The Lady rewards Cory's heroic act with a bike to replace the one the Branlins destroyed.

Part 2 of the novel is titled "Summer of Devils and Angels." In it, Cory and his best friends use their imaginations to take flight while riding their bikes on the day school ends. The boys also take a camping trip on which they come across the Blaylocks, who are bootleggers. Cory's adolescent hormones are stirred by Chile Willow.

Part 3, "Burning Autumn," brings Cory's fascination with the green feather to the fore again. He is invited to dine with a rich eccentric, Vernon Moultry, who often walks the streets of Zephyr naked. This section ends with Cory and his friends attending a freak sideshow and beginning to lose their innocence.

Part 4, "Winter's Cold Truth," resolves the mystery of the murdered man. Cory's father has his sanity restored with the help of The Lady and The Moon Man. An out-of-towner, the drowned man's brother, identifies the man by means of his tattoo. The entire mystery is linked to a neo-Nazi organization and a former Nazi in Zephyr who appears to be a kind physician.

Part 5 is titled "Zephyr as It Is." Cory returns to Zephyr in 1991, twenty-five years after he and his family moved away. In this short epilogue, Cory sees the town as it is. The childhood magic he thought he might find has disappeared.

Analysis: Although the story incorporates elements of horror, it is more the story of a young boy's coming of age and losing his innocence as he struggles to understand the forces of good and evil at work in his hometown of Zephyr, Alabama. Populating the book with references to popular culture, McCammon is able to re-create the world of 1964. Although there are elements of horror in the novel, it is more a work of high fantasy that utilizes the voice of an engaging young narrator that calls out from the recent past, allowing the reader to recapture childhood innocence.

The innocence of childhood—a world in which a boy's bike ride becomes a flight and *Famous Monsters of Filmland* is required boyhood reading—is the most important aspect of McCammon's work. McCammon once said that he uses innocence as "the author's sense of wonder, at the characters and the setting and even the spooky elements." Without this sense of wonder, the incidents in *Boy's Life* would be merely a series of events that would read as relatively disjointed. With the sense of wonder, *Boy's Life* is McCammon's fictional autobiography as well as a celebration of childhood mystery and marvel, filled with targeted details and fully realized, rounded characters.

With the marked sensibilities of such diverse influences as Mark Twain, Flannery O'Connor, Harper Lee, and even Steven Spielberg, McCammon is able to shift his tale from the moral to the magical and back again, telling a coming-of-age story that is part mystery, part magic, part wonder, and part innocence. Using all the attendant forms of popular culture available to a twelve-year-old boy in 1964—comic books, baseball, roadside carnivals, monster films, and magazines—McCammon writes a paean to boyhood that is as effective as it is affecting. *Boy's Life* is peopled with some of the most memorable southern characters in southern fiction.

—*Thomas D. Petitjean, Jr.*

BRAIN ROSE

After surgery to access past-life memories, three people discover that they share ties from previous lives, leading to insights about the human racial memory

Author: Nancy Kress (1948-   )
Genre: Science fiction—inner space
Type of work: Novel
Time of plot: 2022
Location: Rochester, New York, and other locations in the United States
First published: 1990

The Plot: In 2022, a memory-destroying plague stalks humanity. Previous Life Access Surgery (PLAS) allows recovery of memories of former lives. After such operations, Caroline Bohentine, Joe McLaren, and Robbie Brekke seek information, through the reincarnation database, on their past-life ties. Robbie shows close links with virtually everyone who has undergone the surgery. While Caroline and Joe face personal tragedies, violent flashbacks seize Robbie. On a hallucinatory quest in Wyoming, he lapses into unending replay of others' memories. These bring insights into his role as a central "memory node" in the evolving oversoul.

Caroline, Joe, and Robbie seek PLAS for different reasons. Caroline, a survivor of incest and two failed marriages, hopes to discover versions of herself that she prefers to the current one. Joe, a sober attorney, wants to be cured of his multiple sclerosis; the cure is an unexplained side effect of the operation. An underworld boss sends Robbie for the surgery.

Caroline and Joe are suspicious of Robbie's facile charm, but in the clinic's hothouse atmosphere, the three find themselves drawn together. Some reasons are revealed in memory flashes. Robbie was Caroline's son in a previous life, and Joe, as boss in a Chinese porcelain factory, once ordered Robbie's execution for careless work. These discoveries add guilt to the interpersonal dynamics.

A bomb explodes at the home sheltering Caroline's young daughter, a plague victim. The daughter dies the following day. Angel Whittaker, Joe's secretary, asks Joe to answer an urgent message from Robin, his former wife, and to defend Angel from a sodomy charge. Joe's principles win against Angel's pleas. Joe refuses to call Robin because she has joined the Gaeists, who insist that Earth needs no protection. He will not help Angel because of his own moral convictions.

A call from Caroline, telling Joe that Robbie is disoriented and hysterical in Wyoming, shakes his composure. When his friend Jeff Pirelli appears with a warrant, Joe joins Jeff and Caroline in their search for Robbie.

Meanwhile, Robbie has been drawn into a past persona. As Mallie, a young desperado, he relives heists in St. Louis and a massacre and lingering death in a Wyoming cave. In flashes of clarity, he hunts Mallie's treasure and eventually finds it, near the skeleton of his past-life persona. Robbie flees to his motel, fighting hallucinations. Agents from the Federal Bureau of Investigation (FBI) are waiting for him. He begins babbling other people's memories.

In Robbie's motel room, the others sort out the puzzle. The FBI wants Robbie because he released mice that carried the plague virus. Pirelli suggests that Robbie is a central node in all the memory phenomena. He speculates that the human racial memory or oversoul is evolving into a higher form. Deprived of memory input by AIDS and the plague, it is using Robbie as a conduit until it heals. Like Gaea, the oversoul is a self-correcting entity.

Joe rejects this idea, but Caroline considers it. A year later, a vaccine against the plague is developed. The burden of multiple linked pasts weighs on a still-disbelieving Joe.

Analysis: *Brain Rose* is a novel of characters and ideas. The three main characters carry the plot, but secondary characters highlight their conflicts and offer interpretations of events. For example, Father Patrick Shahid leaves the Jesuits and defies the Catholic church to have PLAS because he believes that the coming memory evolution is the work of God. Colin Cadavy, Caroline's brilliant actor father, lives by his wits and charm as Robbie has done, less successfully, in most of his past lives.

Joe McLaren shows the greatest character development. A man of good intentions but rigid behavior and beliefs, his involvement with Robbie and the memory crises leads him to reevaluate his life. He quits his law practice to work toward environmental cleanup and to give Robin and Angel the help he previously refused them. He still doubts the theory of the overmemory's evolution and that he has any continuing role to play in it, but he is poised for further growth.

Robbie Brekke regresses, by normal standards. He becomes an excellent actor but has no ordinary memory left. Caroline's primary change is in self-acceptance. Having seen better and worse lives in her own memories, she comes to value her present, imperfect life more.

The novel invents a near-future world affected by several concerns of the late twentieth century: epidemics, environmentalism and its backlash, new religious paradigms, and reincarnation. They make a heady mix, but Nancy Kress's imagination is equal to it. Many novels featuring new plagues have been best-sellers, including Stephen King's *The Stand* (1978), Michael Crichton's *The Andromeda Strain* (1969), and Connie Willis' award-winning *Doomsday Book* (1992). Among the first of many proenvironment novels was Ernest Callenbach's *Ecotopia: The Notebooks and Reports of William Weston* (1975). Reincarnation is seldom a premise of serious science fiction; it more often occurs in light fantasies. Kress brings all these ideas together in a compelling tale. The theories are offered tentatively and subtly; the reader may have no idea that the author is sending a message. Rather, she seems to be examining ideas in the manner of a playful philosopher.

Kress started her career as a fantasy author. Even in her three early novels, she showed a bent for metaphysical speculation. With her Nebula Award-winning story "Out of All Them Bright Stars" (1985) and her novel of alien contact *An Alien Light* (1988), she joined the ranks of innovative science-fiction writers. Some critics have underrated her contributions to the field. *Brain Rose* received a more positive response.   —*Emily Alward*

BRAIN WAVE

Human and animal mental abilities expand rapidly, causing technological and societal changes

Author: Poul Anderson (1926-   )
Genre: Science fiction—superbeing
Type of work: Novel
Time of plot: The present
Location: The United States
First published: 1954

The Plot: For the past one hundred million years, Earth has been passing through some sort of force field that inhibits brain functions. As the story opens, Earth has moved out of the field's power, with the result that earthly brains now possess much more intelligence. The majority of the story explains the results of this change on science, religion, government, and other elements of society. The plot is somewhat disjointed because Poul Anderson often switches characters and locale. This approach gives the novel a realistic, journalistic-like feel.

The opening pages describe intellectual improvements in an animal, a mentally retarded human (Archie Brock), and an intelligent ten-year-old boy. On the estate where he works, Archie sees changes in animals and begins to realize what has happened to him. Eventually, all the employees except Archie leave for better prospects elsewhere. Newspaper reports are included to show the wide scope of the changes.

Several scientists, including Peter Corinth, Felix Mandelbaum, Nat Lewis, and Helga Arnulfson, discuss these changes among themselves and with their families. Peter Corinth, a resident of New York City, walks to work and reflects on the changes he sees around him.

At this point, Anderson summarizes some of the large-scale effects in language and natural science. Other places around the world are shown dealing with their own changes. In Africa, a group of black people headed by M'Wanzi attempts to throw off the yolk of white oppressors. In Russia, people revolt against the totalitarian government. On a personal level, a relationship is established between scientists Peter and Helga; Peter's wife, Sheila, hates the change and cannot deal with it. Some religious groups also have a hard time accepting the tremendous intellectual alterations, as shown in the rage of the followers of the Third Ba'al.

Archie goes to town for supplies and is presented with the opportunity to join a new socioeconomic system that does without money or ownership. Archie refuses and returns to the estate, where he is more comfortable. Later in the book, Archie is shown still living there, this time with others like him.

Anderson introduces the idea that people are more sensitive to others than before by using parentheses to show implied meanings that do not have to be spoken. People now can sense the feelings of others and interpret the smallest gestures. The Sensitives provide a more exaggerated example of this ability: They use telepathy.

Negative reactions to the change continue. It becomes difficult to keep order in the cities, and some people complain about thinking so much. Some of these people attempt to create machinery that will generate an artificial inhibitor field around Earth much like the one that previously caused the stagnation of intellect. Felix Mandelbaum works slowly for better social organization through negotiation.

On a positive note, scientists discover faster-than-light travel. When the first starship is completed, Peter Corinth and Nat Lewis are selected as its first two passengers. They explore several worlds, allowing Anderson to discuss the evolution of intelligence. The starship returns, and the plot to set up the artificial field is thwarted.

At the novel's conclusion, Anderson takes one more look at Archie. Readers understand that his type will take over Earth and that the more advanced will head for the stars, where they can set up a new society free from Earth's restraints.

Analysis: Anderson's *Brain Wave* is an interesting attempt at extrapolation in which he introduces one unusual circumstance (Earth escapes a force that has inhibited intelligence) and works out the logical consequences. One reason the novel succeeds is the author's ability to show the human trauma of such an increase in intelligence. People riot, abandon work, go insane, form odd cults full of fear and hatred, and wish for the "good old days."

Although the novel shows such trauma, Anderson counters it with positive scenes. People create a starship, oppressive governments are challenged, many stay at their jobs, small towns experiment with various methods of government and work, and language and gestures become more sensitive and more universal. Anderson seems to say that people always will face new challenges, but they can overcome them, given time and patience. As he once said, "To hell with fatuous opti-

mism and fashionable despair. Given guts and luck, we may prevail. Win or lose, the effort is infinitely worth making."

A key feature in this novel, common to much of Anderson's work, is the thorough handling of science, not surprising given Anderson's formal training in physics. In *Brain Wave*, Anderson discusses neural impulses. He assumes that faster and more intense electrochemical reactions in the neurons would produce a dramatic rise in intelligence. He also spends time exploring the idea of an electromagnetic force field that can inhibit brain functions. These theories may not hold true in the real world, but Anderson gives explanations that are plausible within the context of the story. When he explains the design of the starship, he muses about faster-than-light speed, wave mechanics, and atomic energy. He devotes considerable space to speculations about intelligence—its evolution, why it leveled off, and possible results of contact with other intelligent beings in the universe.

Anderson also comments critically on modern life. Peter Corinth sees the initial chaos as understandable, given the nature of life before the rise in intellectual abilities. He mentions the dull work, the lack of direction, the lack of intellectual stimulation, the large amounts of time wasted in front of television sets, and the continual buying frenzy. He says there is "an inward hollowness . . . an unconscious realization that there ought to be more in life than one's own . . . self." He believes that people with increased mental functions are shocked at their useless and narrow lives. In addition, Anderson criticizes the government's tendency to keep everything secret and the poor job newspapers do of informing the public.

Anderson has the ability not only to discuss scientifically interesting topics but also to remember the human consequences of change. This combination of humanity and technology is the mark of an author who makes good use of the possibilities of science fiction.

—*Gary Zacharias*

BRAVE NEW WORLD

Three misfits illustrate the flaws of a future world-state in which technology permits complete control of people and the government claims to provide happiness to everyone

Author: Aldous Huxley (1894-1963)
Genre: Science fiction—dystopia
Type of work: Novel
Time of plot: Half a millennium in the future

Location: What are now the United Kingdom and the United States
First published: 1932

The Plot: In the totalitarian state of *Brave New World*, people are socially conditioned from conception; they are hatched from test tubes rather than being born. Something is wrong with Bernard Marx. Although he ought to be, in keeping with everyone else in this engineered society, an absolute conformist, he evinces certain quirks that his fellows find disturbing. They theorize that something must have gone wrong chemically during his incubation. Bernard dates Lenina Crowne, but he wants her all to himself. This is against the mores of their society, which prescribes communal sexual relations and proscribes monogamous pairing. Lenina is outraged by his request for monogamy. Any contravention of the societal motto of "Community, Identity, Stability" is regarded as a heinous offense.

Happiness is not an individual quest; it is a daily, community guarantee. Through early conditioning, people are educated to be happy for what they are allotted, with allotments made according to class, which is determined at conception. A drug called soma provides a haven from any temporary unhappiness.

Lenina and Bernard, on vacation, visit an Indian reservation in New Mexico that is a mixture of living museum and circus. There they find John, who was reared on the reservation by his mother, Linda, a woman from Western Europe. John later is revealed to be the illegitimate son of the director of the Bloomsbury Hatchery. As someone outside mainstream society, he is able to find flaws in it. He has escaped the universal conditioning and has steeped himself in the works of a forbidden author, William Shakespeare. A collection of Shakespeare's works is the only book he has ever read. He is imbued with the spirit of drama and finds the utter placidity of the present world an affront to the human spirit: riskless, monotonous, and amoral. When Lenina, who fancies him, disrobes in preparation for a guiltless sexual episode, he rejects her for her whorishness even though he is in love with her.

After his mother's death from an overdose of soma, John attempts to subvert some workers who are about to receive their allocation of the drug. This causes a riot, which results in the banishment to Iceland of Bernard and Helmholtz Watson, another "flawed" person. Mustapha Mond, controller of Western Europe, refuses to extend this sentence to John, wanting to keep him nearby so that he can study him.

John retreats from the world into a lighthouse, where he flagellates himself for his sins. He is recorded doing so by a reporter with a sound camera, and this footage is made into a "feelie," a film with sensations added, that receives widespread attention. Tourists arrive in helicopters to gawk at this curious creature who cultivates his own pain. Among them is Lenina. John lashes her and, as she writhes on the ground, himself. This drives the onlookers into an orgiastic frenzy, which catches John up in its license. The next day, when he realizes to what degrading ends his self-mortification has been put, he hangs himself.

Analysis: *Brave New World* sold more than fifteen thousand copies in its first year and has been in print ever since. It has joined the ranks of utopian/dystopian satires such as Jonathan Swift's *Gulliver's Travels* (1726) and George Orwell's *Animal Farm* (1945). The author himself has said that he wanted to warn against the conditioning of human beings by a manager class with the latest technology at its fingertips. Humanity could lose its soul through such a process, Aldous Huxley feared, trading in its unique qualities in exchange for security and for drugged and directed "happiness."

There cannot have been a year since its publication in which this novel has not been compared to the present condition of humanity and found to be a perspicacious guess at the shape of things to come. Huxley, for example, did not exactly predict television, but he foresaw other means of mass hypnosis.

An ingenious and persuasive writer, Huxley renders his analogue quite credibly, although requirements of his genre necessitated more conflict than would be plausible in a state as well managed as the one the novel presents. The characters for the most part think too much like Huxley and too little like people who have been brainwashed into conformity.

Huxley's vision of sexuality in this futuristic society anticipates the repressive desublimation of a world in which the social obligation to be sexual defuses passion. This vision runs into trouble because the only choices permitted to his protagonist are a sulky celibacy and a foreordained and regulated promiscuity. The liberating powers of a passionate sexuality are left out of Huxley's equation even though, when he includes a few nonconformists, he allows that there can be exceptions in this totalitarian society. It becomes a question, then, of why some exceptions exist and not others; there is no reason for the lack of a female equivalent to Bernard or Helmholtz.

Huxley in essence equates happiness with barbarism and unhappiness with culture. The happiness, however, is shown to be false. Characters all evince signs of deep disturbance. True happiness must be what they are missing. One can ask why Huxley did not portray a more efficient society, one that was able to erase this distinction between the true and the false. It may be precisely this flaw in the novel that explains its continuing popularity.

—David Bromige

THE BREAST

David Alan Kepesh, a thirty-eight-year-old professor of literature, copes with his transformation into a human breast

Author: Philip Roth (1933-   )
Genre: Fantasy—magical realism
Type of work: Novella
Time of plot: 1971-1972
Location: New York City
First published: 1972

The Plot: The narrator, David Kepesh, recounts the changes that occurred in his life in the preceding two years, beginning with the peculiar sensations he felt in his penis. These sensations of increased sensitivity, accompanied by increased sexual desire, led to the change that took place between midnight and 4 A.M. on February 18, 1971. Kepesh became a six-foot, 155-pound human female breast. The novella chronicles Kepesh's responses to his condition, which vary from acceptance to a conviction that he has become mad.

The novella is divided into five sections. In the first, Kepesh describes his "symptoms" before the change from man to mammary. He details his sexual feelings for Claire, the twenty-five-year-old woman he has been seeing for three years. The cooling of his desire for her during the past year changed right before his transformation: He felt excruciatingly sensitive while making love to her, but only because his penis was becoming a nipple and areola and the rest of his body was becoming a huge breast disconnected from any human form. Up to this point, Kepesh's life had been stable for the first time in more than a decade, and his relationship with Claire provided warmth and security without "the accompanying burden of dependence, or the grinding boredom" of most marriages with which he was familiar. That comfort, however, vanished with his metamorphosis.

In the second section, Kepesh is tended to first by Dr. Gordon, his physician, and then Dr. Klinger, his psychiatrist of six years. Gordon informs Kepesh that he is in Lenox Hill Hospital in Manhattan and describes the little that is known about the hormonal imbalance that has created Kepesh's condition. Klinger then talks with Kepesh, who can speak and hear through his nipple, about his feelings. Kepesh rants about his inability to go mad and his uncanny ability, which he thinks arises from his fear of death, to put "one foot in front of the other" in an earnest way, no matter what the circumstances. His will to live is as persistent as his sexual desires.

Kepesh begins to come to terms with his new sexuality in the third section, feeling as if he would like to have sex with Claire or the nurse who washes him in the hospital. He conjures up graphic and highly imaginative ways for a breast to have sex with a woman, but he decides finally to satisfy himself with the arousal provided by Claire's kisses and by bathings he receives from the fifty-six-year-old nurse, Miss Clark. He imagines that if he were to give in to his desires, his "appetites could only become progressively strange, until at last [he] reached a peak of disorientation from which [he] would fall—or leap—into the void." He decides to have his nipple sprayed with a mild anesthetizing solution before Miss Clark's ablutions, and he refrains from asking Claire to perform more deeds than she suggests.

In the final two sections, Kepesh becomes convinced that he is mad and that his training as a professor of literature has brought on his condition. He wonders whether his reading of surreal and fantastic literature by Franz Kafka and Nikolai Gogol has in some way affected his mind. In the last pages, the reader is fifteen months into Kepesh's condition and is still not given a definitive answer: Is Kepesh hallucinating, or has he simply become the female breast that he loved as an infant and as a man?

Analysis: Published when Philip Roth was thirty-eight years old, the same age as Kepesh, *The Breast* was Roth's sixth major work and buttressed his reputation as a gifted comic writer who often deals with sexual themes. *The Breast* is more than merely a puerile joke, however; it deals comically with serious issues such as psychological wholeness, the integration of the flesh and spirit, and the limits of human desire.

Roth's peculiar tale about the transformation of a man into a female breast does have literary precedents, of which both Roth and his character Kepesh are aware. In classical literature, Ovid's *The Metamorphoses* (c. A.D. 8) retells hundreds of stories in which humans and gods become trees, flowers, rivers, and rain; the modern *The Metamorphosis* (1915), by Franz Kafka, one of Roth's favorite writers, tells the story of a man turned into a cockroach. Another influence, and one mentioned by Kepesh, is Gogol's story "The Nose" (1836), in which a nose becomes a high-ranking bureaucrat.

What separates Roth's story from his influences is his narrative technique. Unlike Ovid, Kafka, and Gogol, Roth chooses a first-person narrator for his novella, creating a question in the reader's mind about the reliability of the narrator. Has the transformation actually taken place, or, as Kepesh himself wonders, has it simply occurred in his mind? The first-person narrator allows Roth to create comic moments through the incongruity of placing a man's sexually obsessed brain inside a female breast, while also addressing psychological issues concerning repression, wish fulfillment, and the influence of literary works. Although the reader can never be sure about the transformation from man to breast, the novella loses some force if it is determined that the transformation has taken place only in the character's mind. Roth walks a thin line, allowing the reader to question the reality of the change but never letting his story slip out of the realm of the fantastic.   —*Kevin Boyle*

BRIAR ROSE

Becca Berlin attempts to fulfill her grandmother's last wish and learn her heritage

Author: Jane Yolen (1939-   )
Genre: Fantasy—heroic fantasy
Type of work: Novel
Time of plot: Primarily the 1990's, with flashbacks to World War II
Location: Boston, Massachusetts; and Warsaw, Poland
First published: 1992

The Plot: *Briar Rose* is one of the Fairy Tale Series created for Ace, then later published by Tor. *Briar Rose* is a later book in the series. Each novel in the collection is by a different author and is a twentieth century story based on a traditional fairy tale.

In this case, the basis is "Sleeping Beauty." The heroine of *Briar Rose* is Becca Berlin, a young Jewish woman who grew up hearing her grandmother (nicknamed Gemma) tell the tale. Shortly before Gemma dies, she tells Becca that the familiar bedtime story is no fantasy: The old woman was the princess who woke to a prince's kiss. Gemma begs Becca to find the castle where it happened, and her granddaughter promises to do so.

Gemma's background is a mystery even to her family. All Becca has to guide her is a box of Gemma's mementos, discovered only after the grandmother's death, and the fact that Gemma immigrated to America in 1944. Even the immigration papers turn out to be nearly useless, however; many of the questions on them are unanswered, and Becca is not sure the papers are her grandmother's. She deciphers them and learns that they belong to Gitl Rose Mandlestein, who was married and pregnant. Gitl's physical description fits Gemma, but the only nickname listed is Księżniczka. Becca is stunned when she learns that the name is Polish for "princess." The date of Gitl's marriage and her home village and district in Poland are not provided.

Becca takes her research with her to her job at a local newspaper. Stan, her editor and close friend, is intrigued by the mystery and decides to help Becca. They visit Fort Oswego, New York, once a refugee camp for Jews and now a museum. Becca interviews several former refugees and finds one who recognizes Gemma's photo and says he was in a concentration camp in Chełmno, Poland, with her. Becca is startled to learn that it was an old castle renovated by the Nazis. The interviewee's mention of barbed wire reminds Becca of the thorns surrounding the castle in Gemma's fairy tale. Hoping to learn more, Becca goes to Poland to locate Chełmno. Her grandmother may have been held there, but no woman is known to have survived the camp.

Once in Poland, Becca finds the village of Chełmno, but the townspeople are withdrawn and uncooperative. Finally, a priest leads Becca to Josef Potocki, who had been a member of the Polish Resistance during the war and knows about Chełmno. The kindly old man recognizes Gemma at once and reveals his partisan codename: Potocki means "prince." His work in the resistance involved spying on vans leaving Chełmno and counting the corpses dumped in the nearby woods. One day, he and a fellow spy called Avenger found Gemma barely alive at a dump site. She had survived the gas chambers. Avenger administered mouth-to-mouth resuscitation, reviving the girl, and took her to the partisans' forest hideout. The two fell in love and were married, but during the next mission, Avenger was shot dead. He had told his bride his real name, Aron Mandlestein. After a close call with the Nazis, Josef and Gemma were separated. Josef never knew whether or not his princess had reached safety. Now, after meeting her granddaughter, he knows that Gemma did, and Becca has discovered her heritage.

Analysis: It is difficult to place *Briar Rose* in the category of typical fantasy because the plot contains very little concerning magic or the supernatural. The fairy tale around which the novel revolves serves as a metaphor and can be used as a framework for a story in any setting. The basis of this twentieth century novel is a traditional fairy tale full of magic, so *Briar Rose* can be categorized as fantasy. In addition, one of the main criteria for a fantasy or fairy tale is a protagonist who defeats incredible odds and wins; both the metaphor and plot of *Briar Rose* contain this ingredient.

Historically, fairy tales were intended for adult audiences and were much more brutal than the versions one might now hear as a child. For example, Walt Disney's G-rated film *Sleeping Beauty* (1959) bears almost no resemblance to a sixteenth century Venetian telling, wherein the ensorcelled princess is made pregnant during her sleep and wakes to discover herself a mother. That version probably stems from an even older version with several variations.

The trends leading to Jane Yolen's *Briar Rose* had been developing for more than a century. Victorian writers were instrumental in altering stories such as "Sleeping Beauty" to make them fit for young readers. The resulting collections of tales were favored by adults as well because of the fine illustrations.

The early twentieth century saw an outpouring of classic fantasies, among them *The Once and Future King* (1958) by T. H. White. These books often were based on old legends, but they were not for children alone. Since their advent, such books have been classified as adult fantasy. As a result of the popularity of that category, even mainstream authors have tried their hand at writing fantasy. Some of their books, such as Patricia McKillip's *The Forgotten Beasts of Eld* (1974), use the wording and symbolism of old stories to build new ones. *Briar Rose* is based more precisely on a single story. Like the other books in the Fairy Tale Series, it concentrates on giving the tale a modern flavor, making it appealing to a wider audience.

Briar Rose is one of Yolen's later works. Her prolific career began in 1963 and has focused on children's books and fantasies for all ages. Examples include *The Girl Who Loved the Wind* (1972), which won the Lewis Carroll Shelf Award and was a Children's Book Showcase Selection. *Briar Rose* itself was named an American Library Association Best Book for Young Adults and was nominated for the 1992 Nebula Award.

Other books in the Fairy Tale Series include *The Sun, the Moon, and the Stars* (1987) by Steven Brust, *Jack the Giant-Killer* (1987) by Charles de Lint, *The Nightingale* (1988) by Kara Dalkey, *Snow White and Rose Red* (1989) by Patricia C. Wrede, and *Tam Lin* (1991) by Pamela Dean.   —*Carla Hall Minor*

THE BRICK MOON

An artificial moon built to aid navigation is launched accidentally with thirty-seven people inside

Author: Edward Everett Hale (1822-1909)
Genre: Science fiction—technocratic
Type of work: Novel
Time of plot: 1842-1872
Location: Naguadavick, Tamworth, and other imaginary places in New England
First published: 1971 (in *His Level Best and Other Stories*, 1872; serial form, *The Atlantic*, 1869-1870)

The Plot: One day in the early 1840's, several Harvard students are discussing astronomy. Someone notes that the North Star makes it easy for sailors to calculate latitude (distance from the equator) but that no corresponding heavenly body assists in the calculation of longitude. As a consequence, many lives have been lost at sea. One of the students, identified only as Q., half-seriously suggests launching an artificial satellite—a brick moon—to correct this heavenly deficiency.

The subject is dropped, and the students go their separate ways. Seventeen years later, one of them, George Orcutt, calls the group back together. He has become a wealthy railroad magnate and proposes to put some of his money into the satellite experiment. Another member of the original group, Ben Brannan, is a noted orator who raises more funds for the project. The story's narrator, Captain Frederic Ingham, a minister, finds the area best suited for carrying out the project. An unsettled forest has the clay for brick and streams to provide the power for the giant flywheels that will send the sphere into the sky.

By late fall a few years after the Civil War, construction is almost complete. Orcutt and a number of families decide to winter at the isolated construction site and, for warmth, move into the moon, which contains a number of braced chambers. One night when all aboard are asleep, a shifting of the ground causes the moon to slide down the rails to the flywheels, which hurtle it into space.

Ingham and the other partners left on the ground spend a futile year scanning the skies for the orb, which has not gone into the orbit that was prescribed for it. By chance, the moon is rediscovered, and Ingham, who has obtained the job of caretaker of a disused observatory, trains his telescope on the satellite. He can detect thirty-seven people standing in a line, making alternating short and long leaps in order to communicate in Morse code.

The moon had retained its atmosphere when sent aloft. It was stocked with food supplies, including poultry and plants, for the work crew that was to return in spring. The moon's nearness to the Sun and relatively large size (two hundred feet in diameter) have made it suitable for farming.

Those on the ground are able to communicate with those in space, but they can devise no way to return the moon dwellers to Earth. This turns out to be far from a drawback to those on the satellite; they grow contented with their withdrawal from the cares of the world. The story ends with those above feeling decidedly better off than those below.

Analysis: Edward Everett Hale wrote about a variety of topics, authoring sixty books, though he wrote little science fiction. His most celebrated work in that genre, *The Brick Moon*, shares the concerns of his mainstream fiction and satirizes some of the traits of Hale's native New England. *The Brick Moon* is a short book, sometimes referred to as a story, that combines the stories "The Brick Moon" (1869) and "Life in the Brick Moon" (1870).

Today Hale is remembered primarily for his short novel *The Man Without a Country*, the title work of an 1863 collection. It tells of a man who had participated in Aaron Burr's abortive rebellion against the United States and who forswears allegiance to his country when on trial. He is condemned to spend the remainder of his life at sea, where he dies a broken man.

The Brick Moon dwells on these themes of exile and irremediable severance of ties to homeland, though it transforms them to a lighter key. Its tone is less serious; major characters are isolated not because of criminal behavior but because of their zeal to be society's benefactors. Furthermore, they go aloft as a large party, not as one sequestered individual, and so live with genial company and clear consciences.

Unlike the more serious, earlier story, however, *The Brick Moon* is a satire on the manners and character of Boston. This city had established itself, up to the Civil War, as the cultural center of the nation and, equally, as a hotbed of progressive social movements. Local writers such as Hale and, later, Henry James poked fun at some of the excesses of the metropolis. In James's *The Bosto-*

nians (1885-1886), for example, barbs are aimed at the unhealthy atmosphere of radical faddism that pervaded many Boston salons. Hale, with less venom, laughs quietly at these characteristic Boston reformers both when they extravagantly plan to improve the universe by adding a new moon to it and when their scheme goes dreadfully awry.

The satellite is no benefit to navigation, but—and here is another prime point of Hale's satire—the astronauts are happier in orbit than they had been on Earth. Hale may have been thinking of how traumatic internecine conflict on Earth had been for national unity, as evidenced by the Civil War. He was probably also thinking of the oft-heard complaint that Bostonians believed themselves superior to all other beings. What better place for such types than on a moon from which they can look down on their inferiors?

In Hale's day, science fiction did not hold the prominent place in literature that it would later. More significant was utopian fiction, which envisioned ideal societies. Hale's piece shows some affinities with this form. Although *The Brick Moon* lays down no elaborate blueprints for a future world, the author does seem to be ruefully commenting that a more ideal society than existed would be made up of people with similar backgrounds and tastes, such as those who came to live on the brick orb.

—*James Feast*

THE BRIDGE

Lying in a coma after an automobile accident, a young Scots engineer encounters the dark side of technology in the nightmare world of the bridge

Author: Iain Banks (1954-   )
Genre: Fantasy—dystopia
Type of work: Novel
Time of plot: The early 1980's
Location: Edinburgh, Scotland, and various dream worlds
First published: 1986

The Plot: *The Bridge* is a critique of a world in which limitless faith in science and instrumental reason has impoverished human life by denying all truths that cannot be accounted for in the narrow terms of science and rationality. The novel weaves together several apparently distinct narratives whose protagonists may be seen as dream-projections of a single character, who is never directly named.

At the beginning of the novel, this unnamed man lies in the wreckage of a car crash, crushed but still alive. As he loses consciousness, he slips into a bizarre dream. The narrative abruptly switches to a bizarre, dystopian society built entirely upon a seemingly endless bridge. Here, another man, John Orr, is recounting this very dream to his psychotherapist.

A victim of amnesia, Orr does not know who he is or where he comes from. When he is not in therapy, he tries to find out more about the bridge that he must now call home. His attempts, however, are continually frustrated. The bridge's social and bureaucratic organization is as labyrinthine as its physical construction and its technological infrastructure, all of which frequently break down. Taking advantage of the chaos surrounding one such breakdown, he stows away on a train and begins a nightmare odyssey through a landscape ravaged by war and war's atrocities.

Three other narratives weave in and out of Orr's experiences on and off the bridge. In the first, the victim of the crash that began the novel is rushed to the hospital and placed in intensive care. In the second, a bloodthirsty Scots swordsman swashbuckles his way through magic worlds of sorcerers and enchantresses. The third—and central—narrative follows the career of a young Scots engineer, whose youthful, idealistic self is progressively being smothered by his growing affluence, and who seems about to lose Andrea, the woman whom he has loved since his student days. The engineer's prosperous but increasingly unsatisfying life almost ends when he drunkenly crashes his luxury sports car on the Forth Bridge leading into Edinburgh. It is in the hospital room in which he emerges from his coma that all the separate story lines converge. The adventures of John Orr on the bridge and of the swordsman among sorcerers fall into place as the dreamwork in which the engineer confronts the values by which he has lived and recovers his true identity.

Analysis: Although dystopian fantasy has long been an established genre within British literature, the British novelistic tradition has tended to regard fantasy as a fringe element. The social upheavals of the 1980's, however, stimulated a number of novelists to break out of the confines of social and psychological realism by incorporating fantasy or Magical Realism as critical perspectives on a society increasingly seen as riddled with crises. Iain Banks (who publishes his works of fantasy under his name without the middle initial M., which is reserved for his science fiction) explored the world of the psy-

chosexual bizarre in his first novel, *The Wasp Factory* (1984), and developed the technique of intermingling realistic and apparently fantastic story lines to accomplish similar ends in *Walking on Glass* (1985). *The Bridge* employs this technique to mount a full-scale critique of a materialist modern world in which reason has successfully outlawed any dimension of experience and any subjective reality that does not conform to the iron laws of scientific empiricism.

In the conventionally "realistic" narrative, the engineer is in danger of losing himself and the woman he loves because he embraces the cold, objective logic of scientific reasoning and rejects all "faiths," which he sees as nonsensical. He becomes increasingly distanced from his lover, Andrea, who is interested in various forms of the "irrational," such as astrology and the prophecies of Nostradamus. A life built on rationality and on material acquisitions brings him mounting unhappiness and eventually precipitates the crisis—the crash and ensuing coma—in which he must descend into the depths of his own being in order to gain wisdom and be born anew.

Fantasy for Banks is the mode that can best accommodate this kind of psychic exploration. It is also ideally suited to social critique, because it can depict the full horror of a bureaucratic, technology-driven world by depicting it in a different register, providing the distance necessary for a critical assessment. *The Bridge* repeatedly points up parallels between the fantasy world of the bridge and the "real" world of the engineer who dreams it, making frequent allusions to contemporary events of the 1980's: the war between Britain and Argentina over the Falklands/Malvinas, the Israeli invasion of southern Lebanon, the development of the American "Star Wars" Strategic Defense Initiative, and above all the trend in national and international politics signaled by the electoral triumphs of President Ronald Reagan in the United States and Prime Minister Margaret Thatcher in the United Kingdom. The fantastic elements of the novel serve to perform one of the traditional British novel's time-honored functions—reporting on the state of the nation and pinpointing the causes of social and psychological malaise.

Although a modern reader will inevitably perceive the engineer's story as the novel's ground and the fantasy narratives as psychic projections, crucial to the purpose of *The Bridge* is the insistence that none of the various worlds depicted is more "real" than any other. The choice that the protagonist and the reader are offered is not a choice between dream and reality but between two different dreams. The so-called "real" world is just as much a nightmare as the bridge, and the engineer learns that his belief in science and technology to the exclusion of other dimensions of being is not only another faith but also an inferior one created by its own sorcerers and populated by its own demons.   —*Michael Harper*

THE BRIGADIER FFELLOWES STORIES

Brigadier Ffellowes, a retired British artillery officer with mysterious intelligence connections, tells stories of his adventurous youth to a gentleman's club

Author: Sterling Lanier (1927-   )
Genre: Fantasy—mythological
Type of work: Stories
Time of plot: Primarily the early twentieth century
Location: A New York City club and various exotic locations
First published: *The Peculiar Exploits of Brigadier Ffellowes* (1972) and *The Curious Quests of Brigadier Ffellowes* (1986)

The Plot: The two volumes of Brigadier Ffellowes stories contain the title character's exploits as told to members of his New York club. With the exception of the final story, all were published in *The Magazine of Fantasy and Science Fiction* between 1968 and 1982. The first volume begins with "His Only Safari" (1970). Ffellowes is in the forested Abadare hills of Kenya in December, 1939, looking for an Axis agent who is also an Egyptologist. Ffellowes is hunted by the Kerit (Nandi Bear), which is amazingly clever. He finds the agent, who grasps his theory that the Kerits drove the proto-Egyptians north. The agent becomes a Kerit and is killed along with the other hunting Kerit.

"The Kings of the Sea" (1968) is set in Sweden in 1938. An accidental meeting with Baron Nyderstrom, whose nurse has ill-advisedly tried to rid him of some old paraphernalia, leads to a crisis meeting with Jormungandir's Children, the monstrous Old Norse precursors. Nyderstrom is the last of the kings who can intercede with them and does so, to save the world. He emerges happily, having met his future bride.

"His Coat so Gay" (1970) takes place in Middleburg, a town in the eastern United States, in the early 1930's. Canler Waldron, a young head of his family, invites his friend Ffellowes to hunt. Although Ffellowes offends his host by not wearing a traditional English pink coat (he belongs to a special brightly clad society), Canler's fam-

ily wears green. Ffellowes and Canler's sister Betty fall in love. As a result, Betty saves him when, at the Irish Feast of Sam'Hain, Canler vengefully causes various creatures such as the Dead Horse and the Firbolgs to hunt him as a sacrificial English foe.

"The Leftovers" (1969) places Ffellowes in the Hadhramaut of Oman in 1924. He strays too close to the shore, avoiding the desert, and barely escapes being eaten by Paleolithic cannibals.

In 1941, in the aftermath of the German invasion, Ffellowes and his Greek companion are shipwrecked on an island in "A Feminine Jurisdiction" (1969). A German officer, similarly stranded, tries to take command, but his arrogance results in his being destroyed by the sisters of Medusa.

In "Fraternity Brother" (1969), by taking the side of the local Spanish Pyrenean Basques against a brutal Spanish sergeant, Ffellowes earns an invitation to join the Society, a were-animal sect that has existed since Cro-Magnon times. "Soldier Key" (1968) puts Ffellowes adrift in the Caribbean Sea in 1934. He decides to look at Soldier Key, the home of the Church of the New Revelation. Brother Poole does not welcome him and warns him off before that night's ceremonies. A crew member vanishes, to be used as a sacrifice in the worship of hermit crabs (soldiers). Ffellowes kills a monstrously huge version of the crab and Poole, and he escapes.

The second volume of stories begins with "Ghost of a Crown" (1976). It is set in an unnamed time, but clearly a generation ago. Ffellowes visits his friend James, earl of Penruddock, at Avalon House in Cornwall. Also there is Lionel, James's evil younger brother, a great archaeologist. Since his arrival to work the ancient ruins of Caer Dubh, there have been serious disturbances. Ffellowes' research shows a connection, but James takes the lead on the crucial night. He becomes King Arthur and defeats Lionel and the Evil Prince whom Lionel wishes to resurrect, then becomes his old, dim self.

Trying to find ways to prevent the Japanese invasion of Singapore in 1940, Ffellowes in "And the Voice of the Turtle" (1972) calls at Palau Tuntong (Turtle Island). There he meets Strudwick, who in the early 1920's had been a fellow Cambridge scholar. A scientific genius, the recently married Strudwick is using his wife's money to study the turtles that are omnipresent and variform on the island. Ffellowes discovers not only that the malformed locals are related to turtles but also that they have a Head, the Father, a huge semihuman specimen. Ffellowes kills Strudwick and rescues his wife from sacrifice.

"The Father's Tale" (1974) is recounted from his father's story of 1881. While working off the coast of Sumatra on behalf of Rajah C. V. Brooke of Sarawak, Ffellowes senior rescues an Englishman who is almost dead. This man, Verner, reveals himself as obsessed by a mission on the western coast. All the previously loyal crew support him in hunting for the compound of the dead biologist Van Ouisthoven. When they find it, they must stop the *Matilda Briggs*. The problem is giant, intelligent rats that the ship is about to take from the island.

"Commander in the Mist" (1982) places Ffellowes in northern Austria in 1945. His patrol stops near the Danube and comes under threat from Marcus Aurelius, still defending the settlement of Paestrum against any form of barbarian. In "Thinking the Unthinkable" (1973), set in the summer of 1943, Ffellowes and a local friend try to find the famous Lipizzaner horses. They encounter a Dr. Hafstead, who challenges a monster and is taken by what appears to be a gigantic tentacle.

"The Brigadier in Check—and Mate" is the only previously unpublished story in the two volumes. The narrator is lost and meets Ffellowes and his strange wife, Phaona. Ffellowes tells a story set in Belize in 1947. Following stories of intelligent apes, an expedition discovers the last remaining descendants of Atlantis, including a princess, who clearly becomes Ffellowes' wife. The settlement is destroyed by an earthquake.

Analysis: With three exceptions—"Ghost of a Crown," "The Father's Tale," and the last story—all the stories take place within the interwar period or during World War II. They often refer back to times that are now invested with an exotic magic. All the locations seem realistic as places for Ffellowes to have traveled, more than half being within the old British Empire. Sterling Lanier has researched his task thoroughly and carries conviction in each of his backgrounds. From the hills of Kenya to those of Belize, and to the Swedish and Sumatran coastlines, all the locations are credible, adding considerable weight to the stories. Lanier's most effective creation, however, is the storyteller himself.

Ffellowes, born about 1908, is in retirement in New York. It is clear from comments made at various times that he keeps in close contact with the intelligence community. He has strong affinities with Lord Dunsany's character Mr. Jorkens, yet he is the epitome of British sangfroid. In Lanier's appeal to the slightly distant past, his use of a relatively impotent narrator (Jim Parker, a younger American stockbroker), and his protagonist's

almost sinister power to hold listeners, appearing unexpectedly and leaving tracelessly, the author is heavily influenced by Arthur Conan Doyle's Sherlock Holmes stories. He acknowledges this by giving the great detective a dominant, though pseudonymous, role in "The Father's Tale," which concerns, of all Holmesian subjects, the giant rat of Sumatra.

There is a less obvious but significant relationship to another Doyle character, the Frenchman Gerard, also a brigadier. Gerard's stories inevitably found him to misunderstand local customs and blunder, but to carry things off by sheer élan. Many of the stories consist of Ffellowes dragging more sensible natives into off-limits areas, only to imperil everybody's life and to learn, though not to acknowledge, that the native customs and beliefs were right. Lanier's portrayal of Ffellowes' air of command, wit, and intelligence sustains belief, while his sardonic authorial voice allows for subtle subversion. In the same way that Doyle's not-unsympathetic sketch allowed for questions as to whether the rules that Gerard breaks are logical or necessary, Lanier's more overtly respectful portrait is a critique of the British Empire and empire builders.

The real triumph of these volumes is one of delight in sheer storytelling. These are heir to *The Arabian Nights' Entertainments* of the fifteenth century and the "factual" travelers' tales of the late Middle Ages. The stories themselves are practically an anthology of leftovers from previous times: Nandi Bears, paleolithic cannibals and Atlanteans, and intrusions of monstrous shape such as Sumatran giant rats or turtle-men. Virtually every mythical creature, even the lost King Arthur and the Loch Ness monster, has a place in the pantheon. Lanier has the ability to develop tension and even to achieve pathos, as in the final scene of "The Father's Tale," when Van Ouisthoven rescues the last pathetic rat-child before killing it and himself.

Although stories such as "The Leftovers" and "Commander in the Mist" are mere scenarios, devoid of real plot, others, such as "His Coat so Gay" and "Ghost of a Crown," are masterpieces. Unfortunately, the last, previously unpublished story declines from a promising beginning into a sort of self-referential silliness that includes not merely the names of Edgar Rice Burroughs and L. Sprague de Camp but also gauche wordplay with the name of Philip José Farmer. It is, perhaps, Lanier's way of ending the series. In its exposure of Ffellowes as a mere fantasist, it is much more effective than a tumble over Reichenbach Falls.   —*Mike Dickinson*

BRING THE JUBILEE

In a world in which the South won the American Civil War, historian Hodge Backmaker travels back in time to study a battle site and accidentally alters the course of history

Author: (Joseph) Ward Moore (1903-1978)
Genre: Science fiction—alternate history
Type of work: Novel
Time of plot: 1938-1952 and 1863
Location: An alternate United States of America
First published: 1953 (serial form, *The Magazine of Fantasy and Science Fiction*, 1952)

The Plot: *Bring the Jubilee* has become a classic in the alternate-history subgenre of science fiction. The bulk of the novel is set in an alternate world years after the South won the American Civil War. This first-person memoir begins with young Hodge Backmaker leaving his backwater hometown for New York City in 1938. Life in the twenty-six United States is hard. The War of Southron Independence, as the Civil War is known, has financially and spiritually crushed the North. Backmaker outlines an unfamiliar world in which the telegraph and gaslight are the norm, the wealthy own steam-driven "minibles" instead of automobiles, and the lower classes sell themselves into indentured servitude. The strong Confederate States stretch south from the Mason-Dixon line into Mexico. Even the European landscape differs. Napoleon VI rules France, and Germany is known as the German Union.

After losing everything he owns to muggers on his first night in New York, Backmaker falls in with Roger Tyss, a bookseller and anti-Confederate revolutionary. Tyss gives Backmaker a job in his bookstore. Backmaker spends several years there, reading as much as he can and learning to think and study. He befriends René Enfandin, consul for the Republic of Haiti, who is an oddity in New York because he is black. Backmaker is crushed when Enfandin is shot and seriously wounded, forcing his return to Haiti.

At the age of twenty-three, Backmaker decides to leave the bookstore. He accepts an invitation to go to Haggershaven, an intellectual community in York, Pennsylvania. There, Backmaker becomes a well-regarded historian specializing in the War of Southron Independence. He marries and settles down, but he calls his own scholarship into question after receiving a letter from a colleague asking him to reconsider some of his ideas. In crisis, he allows physicist Barbara Haggerwells to talk him into trying out her new invention, the HX-1, a time machine. She suggests that he use it to visit Gettysburg, the site of an important Confederate victory, and settle his doubts once and for all.

Without telling his wife, Catty, Backmaker allows himself to be transported to June 30, 1863. He walks the thirty miles to the battle site and positions himself. Unfortunately, Confederate troops spot him and question him. Because Backmaker promised Haggerwells that he would not interfere lest he change history, he says nothing. The nervous Confederates convince themselves that Yankees are up ahead and retreat, but during the altercation, a man is shot and killed. Backmaker realizes that the man looks familiar to him.

The Confederate withdrawal from the area means that history as Backmaker knows it changes. Backmaker watches the battle, and, sickened, realizes that the North, rather than the South, will hold the Round Tops. When he returns to the pick-up site and fails to return to his own time, he realizes something far worse: The dead Confederate was Barbara Haggerwells' grandfather. His death means that there is no hope of return to his world. He has changed the course of history and wiped out his own world, along with all the people he loves. Ironically, the world he has brought into being is the world of the reader.

Analysis: Two important themes in *Bring the Jubilee* are the nature of time and the importance of the individual in history. Both are important concerns of alternate history in general. Like Philip K. Dick's alternate history *The Man in the High Castle* (1962), *Bring the Jubilee* questions the role of chance in determining events. Does an individual have the power to change events, or are all events predestined?

Ward Moore explores these themes through Backmaker's discussions with Tyss and Enfandin. Tyss argues that all actions result from stimuli, not thought, and that free will is an illusion. He also argues that time loops endlessly, with people repeating the same events. Moore contrasts Tyss's point of view with that of Enfandin, who believes that everything is an illusion and that only God is real. Backmaker, however, argues that "there must have been a beginning. . . . And if there was a beginning, choice existed if only for that split second. And if choice exists once it can exist again."

Backmaker, dreamy by nature, is not inclined to action but instead to let his life go as it may. Haggerwells must convince him to use her invention to go back in time; he uses her persuasion as an excuse to go, absolving him of responsibility. He comes to realize that even his refusal to speak to the Confederates at the battle site is a choice. His remark that "if choice exists once it can exist again," coupled with the fact that he changes history, leads Backmaker to believe that free choice exists. He is haunted by the fear that he has wiped out Catty, Haggerwells, and his world, and that he is doomed to wipe them out repeatedly as time loops around again. Still, by allowing Backmaker to change history, Moore refutes Tyss's model of the world and implies that individuals are capable of free choice and action. Backmaker grows from a boy who cannot make decisions into an adult who realizes that not making a choice is a kind of choice.

Bring the Jubilee is Moore's second science-fiction novel, following *Greener than You Think* (1947). None of his other works, mainstream or science fiction, deals with time and history as explicitly as this famous work. Moore's depth of characterization, emotion, and detail make this an enduring classic.   —*Karen Hellekson*

BROKEDOWN PALACE

The faerie realm and the Demon Goddess unsuccessfully contend over the kingdom of Fenar, using brothers of the ruling family as pawns

Author: Steven Brust (1955-   )
Genre: Fantasy—magical world
Type of work: Novel
Time of plot: Undefined
Location: The kingdom of Fenar, its castle, and the nearby river
First published: 1986

The Plot: King László assaults his youngest brother, Miklós, for having made disparaging remarks about the castle, home to the Fenar family from time immemorial, or at least the last four hundred years. A drop of Miklós' blood finds its way into the flooring in Miklós' room. Miklós escapes into the river, which restores him. He meets a taltós horse, a magical beast that has many incarnations and feeds off its master's need. The horse, Bölk, takes Miklós to the land of faerie.

After studying magic for two years, Miklós returns home without specific plans. Although old tensions still exist between the king and Miklós, the youngest prince, brothers Andor (indecisive and impressionable) and Vilmos (gigantic, yet mild) rejoice at Miklós' homecoming. László is preparing to marry Mariska, a countess who has

superseded his common woman, Brigitta. The palace has become decrepit, and a strange plant has rooted itself in Miklós' room. Miklós again incurs László's wrath by making a passing reference to decay, and again he must escape to the river.

Bölk lends Miklós succor, defeating Sándor, the court wizard László sends to retrieve his upstart brother. They eventually return to the palace, once Miklós makes the decision to do so. When a section of floor collapses and kills one of Vilmos' pet norskas, Vilmos becomes more receptive to Miklós' concern for the palace's decay.

Andor earlier had been led, by Sándor, to dedicate himself to the Demon Goddess, which had been the family god and in regular communication with László. The plant has taken over Miklós' room and is firmly entrenched through the cellarage. Brigitta becomes fond of Miklós.

Miklós topples the Demon Goddess' statue, with Bölk's help, calling her to manifest and then destroying her with Bölk's blood. Without the Demon Goddess, László has only the palace to support him, and he determines to remove the plant/tree that he believes threatens it. Miklós confronts him, and they fight. The king's sword, symbol of Demon Goddess power, flares and is consumed in contact with a staff from the tree. At this, the tree expands and involutes, becoming a new palace and supporting the family from which it derives. László and his agents are killed or abdicate.

Miklós and his tree remain to take possession of their new seat of power. Andor defers right to rule to Vilmos, who unwillingly accepts. Brigitta departs to return to faerie, carrying Miklós' unborn daughter. Miklós learns that his daughter will come back to the palace and be a powerful agent in future developments.

Analysis: In an introductory note on pronunciation, Steven Brust reveals the consanguinity of this story with Hungarian or Eastern European folktales. The dropped hint is hardly necessary, for between chapters are interludes that typically are fantastic tales narrated by voices that attempt to authenticate the stories in standard folk formulas (for example, "strike me down if it ain't so"). The somewhat stilted or strained dialogue is attributable to a sense of this as a translated work. The folk-tradition tales of the founding of Fenario are counterpoised against the vestigially described faerie realm, on which the kingdom borders. Other interludes describe the growth of the tree as it contends with the castle. Thus northern Celtic influences butt up against folktales of a Slavic flavor.

The mythic implications are more than a gratuitous overlay, for Brust focuses attention on the concepts of loyalty and tradition. Implicit is the necessity for change and variation as opposed by tradition and law. The four brothers share ancestry from neighboring faerie land but are supported by the Demon Goddess. These two forces are at odds, and the brothers are torn between allegiances. Miklós opts to place family bonds above either extreme and creates something new and astounding as a result. His palace/tree is unaffected by faerie magic, in fact blocking Sándor's path to the source of magic power and thereby killing him. It supplants the traditional structures, both the physical and the hierarchical, and replaces them with the tree and the bond among family members.

As narrative, the book is interesting because of the tree as an emergent plot device. Brust manages to surprise the reader with the plant's full development as a functional shelter and replacement for the former castle. The interludes provide a mosaic effect, suggesting a composite story rather than a single line of development. The reading experience is richer for these features.

The reader's story is remarkably similar to that of Miklós. As the novel progresses, the reader becomes increasingly comfortable in the fairy tale/folk narratives, learning in effect to be a part member of a cultural or ethnic group. Miklós must learn to be comfortable in his own identity, spends most of the novel searching for it, and achieves only a qualified contentment after having found it.

Miklós' progression follows a typical identity-quest cycle, and his actions seem heroic in retrospect. The tree he unwittingly creates is the restorative or elixir to the dying kingdom. It reinvigorates the world it touches. Having found his place, however, there seems little satisfaction in the rebuilding and refining which becomes his role. Like most quest heroes, he ends up without anything to do next. What seems clear for both character and reader is that there is more story ahead—more folktale to read, and more to come with the return of Miklós' daughter.

—*Scott D. Vander Ploeg*

THE BROKEN LAND

A mute girl sets out to find her family in an oppressive world altered by biotechnology

Author: Ian McDonald (1960-   )
Genre: Science fiction—cultural exploration
Type of work: Novel
Time of plot: The far future

Location: The empire of the Proclaimers
First published: 1992 (as *Hearts, Hands, and Voices*, 1992, in the United Kingdom)

The Plot: From its bravura opening line—"Grandfather was a tree"—and its initial image of a living house running amok through a village, Ian McDonald's fourth novel quickly establishes a bizarre setting and a haunting tone that seem to owe as much to surrealism as to earlier science fiction. *The Broken Land* essentially is the tale of a young girl's quest across a planet whose shifting landscapes and political structures alternately call to mind Southeast Asia, Eastern Europe, South Africa, and contemporary Ireland.

These vividly realized settings and the unfolding quest itself are suggested by the novel's six sections: "The Township," "The Road," "The City," "The River," "The Camps," and "The Borderland." The central conflict in the story is one of biology and technology. The Proclaimers have established a totalitarian empire that rules the planet through conventional technology, and the Confessors have developed advanced skills in biotechnology since the discovery, generations earlier, of a technique for manipulating DNA directly from the human nervous system. The Confessors have long sought self-determination and freedom.

In Chepsenyt Township, the idyllic Confessor village where Mathembe Fileli lives, nearly everything is grown rather than manufactured, and free "organicals" called trux are farmed like animals. A kind of immortality has been achieved: The heads of ancestors can retain a kind of semi-vegetable life embedded in Ancestor Trees, where they partake of a kind of spiritual consciousness called "the Dreaming."

Oppression and violence also are part of Mathembe's world. Her response is the same as that of Oskar in Günter Grass's *The Tin Drum* (1959): She refuses to speak. When Chepsenyt is destroyed by imperial forces for harboring members of a resistance movement called the Warriors of Destiny, Mathembe becomes a refugee. She sets out with her family to join her uncle's Faradje in the ancient city of Ol Kot, which is a vivid amalgam of Calcutta, Charles Dickens' London, and the Los Angeles envisioned by cyberpunk writers. In Ol Kot, she finds use for her skills in biological manipulation, designing and selling organical toys in the district of the city known as the Flesh Market.

The Confessor revolution reaches Ol Kot. Riots break out, and reprisals are violent. Mathembe is displaced again when the city is burned. Separated from her re-

maining family—except for her disembodied grandfather, whose head she rescued from the Ancestor Tree in
her village—she becomes a boat person, stowing away
on Unchunkolo. After more than three centuries of addi-
tions and modifications, that enormous riverboat has become a society unto itself. Mathembe is allowed to stay
on board because of her biodesign skills, revealed by one
of her organical toys. She is assigned to try to revive the
boat's failing agricultural ecosystems, and her success
makes her a nearly legendary figure on the boat.

Word arrives that the Proclaimer-Confessor war has
ended in an agreement to divide the land. Mathembe sets
out to find her family, journeying first to sprawling displaced person camps and finally to a mysterious Borderland, where her mother has joined a movement to end
violence through a radical advance in genetic engineering that promises to dramatically alter the world in which
Mathembe lives.

Analysis: For readers reared on George Bernard Shaw,
William Butler Yeats, and James Joyce, it can be unsettling to be reminded that by the end of the twentieth
century, Ireland had become virtually a Third World
country, with a history of oppressive colonialism, violence, famine, and poverty. Despite a rich heritage of
visionary literature and mythology, not to mention an
unparalleled tradition of satirical fantasy from Jonathan
Swift to Flann O'Brien, it is hard to think of a clearly
Irish tradition in science fiction, one that takes account of
both the fabled Irish love of language and more bitter
economic and historical realities. Ian McDonald seems
to have set out to remedy this situation single-handedly,
not only with his panoply of Irish history in *King of
Morning, Queen of Day* (1991) but also with this sometimes harrowing novel of oppression, violence, and redemption.

In one sense, the novel is a depressing catalog of
twentieth century atrocities, displaced to a distant setting
that resembles, at various times, Northern Ireland, Nazi
Europe, South Africa, and Southeast Asia. McDonald's
cultural and mythic background suggests a panoply of
oppressed peoples, but the chief antagonists—the Proclaimers, who rule with more or less conventional technology; and the Confessors, who can alter biological
forms for technological uses—suggest nothing so much
as Catholics and Protestants and their conflict in Northern Ireland.

McDonald's character and place names seem to draw
on African, aboriginal, and Asian languages, and his
themes of ancestor worship and apocalyptic revolutionary movements call to mind Yoruba mythology and the
Native American ghost dance movement. Villages are
destroyed in ways reminiscent of Vietnam; certain popu-
lations are restricted to South African-style "townships";
and prisoners are hauled in darkened trucks for days and
then "selected," in the manner of Nazi Germany. At its
best, the novel suggests a nightmare pageant of modern
history, cast in the traditional mode of a girl's search for
her family and dressed up with the most thoroughly
imagined version of biotechnology since Harry Harrison's *West of Eden* trilogy (1984-1988).

The Broken Land has been criticized for its resemblance to earlier work by Geoff Ryman, especially *The
Unconquered Country: A Life History* (1986) and *The
Child Garden* (1989). McDonald's ending has problems
of its own, raising moral questions about the uses of
science that trouble even Mathembe herself. Even
though McDonald prepares for this ending and it makes
sense out of the organic versus mechanical opposition
that permeates the narrative, it still seems to propose a
facile science-fiction solution to all-too-real social and
economic problems. Still, there is enough wisdom and
thoughtfulness in the rest of the novel to more than make
up for a questionable resolution. For all of its violence
and depredations, *The Broken Land* is a haunting and
moving novel, written in an intensely poetic, even hypnotic, style. For all that it draws on contemporary concerns, McDonald's world is strikingly self-contained and
consistent, and it is entirely his own.   —*Gary K. Wolfe*

THE BROKEN SWORD

*A human child, stolen by elves and replaced by a change-
ling, grows up to fall in love with his sister and to fight
for the elves against trolls led by the changeling*

Author: Poul Anderson (1926-   )
Genre: Fantasy—high fantasy
Type of work: Novel
Time of plot: The time of Alfred the Great (849-899)
Location: The realm of Faerie (primarily the British
    Isles and Northern Europe)
First published: 1954

The Plot: *The Broken Sword* is populated with elves,
trolls, dwarfs, and other creatures of Northern European
folklore and myth. It is set in the land of Faerie, which is
part of the known world but invisible to most humans.
The story begins with Orm, a Viking settler in the
Danelaw (northern and eastern England). Orm is cursed

by a witch after he seizes her family's lands. She swears that Orm's son will be stolen and that he will rear a beast instead. Orm ignores her, building and marrying on the lands taken from the witch.

Orm's first child is indeed stolen, by an elf-earl named Imric. It is replaced by a changeling created from Imric's union with a captive female troll. The changeling is named Valgard and is reared as Orm's son. Orm's true son is reared by Imric in Faerie. He is called Skafloc.

On Skafloc's naming-day, a messenger of the gods gives the child a "broken sword" of iron. The elves cannot touch iron, and they bury the sword. Skafloc grows rapidly and is trained in warfare and magic. He learns to change shape. Valgard, the changeling, also becomes a great warrior, but he is wild and violent.

One day, Ketil, another of Orm's sons, stumbles on the witch, who appears to Ketil as a beautiful woman. Valgard discovers them together and murders Ketil. Orm finds out about the murder, and Valgard then kills his father.

After Valgard flees back to the witch, she explains his heritage as half elf and half troll. Valgard becomes a tragic figure and turns his back on humanity to join the trolls. To sever all ties with his old life, he kidnaps Orm's daughters, Asgerd and Freda, and offers them to Illrede Troll-King.

The elves know that the trolls are planning a war, and Skafloc leads a raid against Illrede. He is amazed to see Valgard. He rescues Asgerd and Freda, unaware that they are his sisters. Valgard counterattacks, killing Asgerd, but Skafloc and Freda escape. They fall in love. Imric keeps Freda's identity secret.

The trolls invade England with an army of goblins, imps, dwarfs, and others. Skafloc fights Valgard again, but neither can kill the other. The elves are beaten, and Imric is captured. Valgard becomes leader of England's trolls while Illrede invades the mainland to conquer the elven king. Skafloc and Freda become outlaws. Skafloc retrieves the broken sword. To find out how the blade can be remade, he calls up the dead, who also reveal that Skafloc and Freda are brother and sister. Freda runs away in shame.

Skafloc convinces a giant to reforge the sword, which was made originally by sorcery. Legend says that the blade must kill every time it is drawn and that it will eventually turn on its user. Skafloc rides to save the elven king, only to find the elves nearly defeated. He uses his new sword to kill Illrede and drive the trolls back to England. He and Valgard meet a third time, and Skafloc is wounded. Freda, who cannot forget Skafloc, arrives on the battlefield at that moment. Skafloc is distracted, and Valgard seizes the great sword and stabs him. As Valgard lifts the sword for a last blow, it escapes his grip to pierce his own throat, killing him. Skafloc dies in Freda's arms.

Analysis: *The Broken Sword* and the science-fiction novel *Brain Wave* (1954) were the first book-length works by Poul Anderson to be published. The first two volumes of J. R. R. Tolkien's Lord of the Rings trilogy also were published in 1954. *The Broken Sword* had much less impact than Tolkien's trilogy on the development of fantasy's major subgenres of high fantasy and heroic fantasy. It was nearly forgotten until the Tolkien boom of the 1960's led to its reissue.

There are several reasons why Anderson's book did not have the impact of Tolkien's work. First, *The Broken Sword* was printed by a small publisher (Abelard-Schuman) and was not widely distributed. There was only one printing. Second, it was published very early in Anderson's career, before his writing had fully matured, and it was not as polished, developed, or ambitious as Tolkien's Lord of the Rings trilogy. Third, because of Anderson's scientific background and the commercial nature of his writing, he was considered less of a literary figure than was Tolkien. Critics took Tolkien seriously but ignored Anderson.

After being reissued in 1971, *The Broken Sword* did influence the fantasy field, primarily by helping shape the subgenre of heroic fantasy, where Anderson's later fantasy work would be classified. *The Broken Sword* also directly influenced Anderson's own *Hrolf Kraki's Saga* (1973) and the three books of his Last Viking series (*The Golden Horn*, *The Road of the Sea Horse*, and *The Sign of the Raven*, all published in 1980).

Hrolf Kraki's Saga is a mixture of high fantasy and heroic fantasy. The Last Viking series is more purely heroic in nature, primarily because of more realistic settings and the general absence of mythical beings such as elves and trolls. Anderson used Northern European mythology and history throughout all four books. Much of this mythology, as well as many of the fantastic creatures, appeared first in *The Broken Sword*, and many of the Viking characters in these books are reminiscent of Skafloc and Valgard.

—*Charles A. Gramlich*

BROOD OF THE WITCH QUEEN

Antony Ferrara, descended from the witch queen of ancient Egypt, uses black magic to increase his wealth and power but is defeated by Dr. Bruce Cairn and his son

Author: Sax Rohmer (Arthur Sarsfield Ward, 1883-1959)
Genre: Fantasy—occult
Type of work: Novel
Time of plot: 1914
Location: London, Oxford, and their environs in England; Cairo, Port Said, and the Pyramid of Meydum in Egypt
First published: 1918 (serial form, *The Premier Magazine*, 1914)

The Plot: As a medical student at Oxford University, Robert Cairn first becomes suspicious of fellow student Antony Ferrara, the adopted son of Sir Michael Ferrara, a noted Egyptologist and a close friend of Cairn's father. The young Ferrara, whom Cairn finds "repellently effeminate," dresses in furs and keeps fires burning in his quarters even at midsummer. His rooms reek of incense and are filled with ancient Egyptian relics, including a mummy. There is a photograph of the swan Apollo whose strange death Cairn witnessed. He observes Ferrara burning a waxen swan figurine. Later, in London, Cairn learns that a young woman he had seen outside Ferrara's quarters has been strangled in an impossible situation. Sir Michael Ferrara then succumbs after attacks by a pair of ghostly hands that his niece and ward, Myra Duquesne, is powerless to stop. Cairn's father, Dr. Bruce Cairn, is called in, too late, to save his old friend.

Himself an authority on Egyptian ritual and beliefs, Dr. Cairn quickly surmises from all that has happened that Antony Ferrara is practicing Egyptian magic, but he refuses to answer his son's repeated demands to know just who Antony Ferrara really is. Myra, while in a sleepwalking trance, accuses Antony of being the brood of a witch and points to the witch's ring, the ring of Thoth, that he wears. The Cairns are determined to protect Myra from Ferrara, who obviously covets her share of the inheritance.

Ferrara clearly is aware of their opposition. He launches a magical attack against the younger Cairn but is thwarted by Dr. Cairn. He turns his magic next against Lord and Lady Lashmore, causing the latter to be possessed by the spirit of Mirza, an ancestral sorceress and vampire, and then to kill her husband.

Antony Ferrara next appears in Egypt, where Robert Cairn is vacationing. Through his magic, Ferrara unleashes terrible sandstorms, nearly deceives Dr. Cairn into killing his son, and causes Lady Lashmore, who is also in Egypt, to disappear. Dr. Cairn is convinced that Ferrara is connected to the ancient Egyptian witch queen whose tomb he and Sir Michael Ferrara had searched for, unsuccessfully, years earlier. In the most vivid episode of the novel, Dr. Cairn and his son's friend Sime enter the Pyramid of Meydum, one of the reputed centers of ancient Egyptian sorcery and the scene of recent unnerving occurrences. In a secret chamber, they witness Ferrara performing a ritual of anthropomancy (divination by human entrails) using the dead body of Lady Lashmore. The form of the witch queen materializes and begins to speak when Sime loses control and fires his gun. In the aftermath, he and Dr. Cairn barely manage to escape.

Back in England, Ferrara's attempts to kill both Myra, by means of a sinister orchid, and Robert Cairn, with a magical cord, are foiled by Dr. Cairn. As the final conflict approaches, Dr. Cairn at last discloses what he knows—or suspects—of Ferrara's true identity: He is the reanimated son of the witch queen and embodies the spirit of her high priest. Dr. Cairn uncovers the magician's spell book, the *Book of Thoth*, and burns it. When Ferrara evokes a powerful elemental spirit to attack the Cairns and Myra, he cannot control it and is destroyed.

Analysis: The author of more than forty Oriental thrillers, Sax Rohmer is best known as the creator of the sinister criminal genius Fu-Manchu, whose adventures began with *The Mystery of Dr. Fu-Manchu* (1913; published as *The Insidious Dr. Fu-Manchu* in the United States) and continued with twelve further volumes. Many of Rohmer's tales have fantasy and occult elements, a few are essentially fantasy, and at least one is science fiction (*The Day the World Ended*, 1930, part of the Gaston Max series that also includes *The Yellow Claw*, 1915, *The Golden Scorpion*, 1919, and *Seven Sins*, 1943).

Of the primarily fantasy works, *Brood of the Witch Queen*, one of his early publications, is probably the best known. It is based on Rohmer's extensive knowledge of the occult and his travels in Egypt. In the "prefatory notice" to the novel, Rohmer states that the powers attributed to Antony Ferrara in no case exceed those claimed for a fully equipped adept. He might have referred the reader to his own popular nonfiction account, *The Romance of Sorcery* (1914; abridged edition, 1923), which was finished immediately before he began writing *Brood of the Witch Queen*. Rohmer also was a member of an occult secret society, the Hermetic Order of the Golden Dawn.

The underlying theme of the novel, frequently repeated, is that in the modern age of science and skepticism, disbelief in the existence of dark powers is itself dangerous because it leaves one vulnerable and defenseless. Only Dr. Cairn's private study of magic and the occult—something he cannot afford to have known publicly—makes resistance to Antony Ferrara possible. In this context, Cairn's tendency not to reveal what he knows because it is "too horrible to tell" or because one is "better off not knowing" is unconvincing; it is simply a rhetorical device Rohmer uses to heighten suspense and horror.

Brood of the Witch Queen is episodic and melodramatic. Rohmer relies heavily on coincidence and Dr. Cairn's undisclosed knowledge to propel the story, which is essentially one of gothic horror, featuring a young woman beset by dark forces. Nevertheless, the novel contains some memorable scenes, especially the pyramid episode, and depicts some operations of a practicing magician. It is rather unusual for its time in presenting a modern practitioner of black magic not as a satanist but as an adept in the ancient Egyptian tradition. Rohmer returned to Egyptian themes in *The Green Eyes of Bast* (1920) and, with addition of the figure of the advanced occultist, in *The Bat Flies Low* (1935).

—Robert Galbreath

BROTHER TO DRAGONS

Job Napoleon Salk saves humanity from an artificially engineered virus and inoculates humanity with a benign symbiote

Author: Charles Sheffield (1935-   )
Genre: Science fiction—extrapolatory
Type of work: Novel
Time of plot: December 31, 1999, to late February, 2018
Location: Washington, D.C., and Nevada
First published: 1992

The Plot: The novel tells the story of Job Napoleon Salk's life, from his birth on the eve of the twenty-first century to his death less than nineteen years later. The first half is set in various places in Washington, D.C., where Salk is born and where he grows up. The second half is set in Xanadu, the country's oldest, largest, and most dangerous "Tandy" (Toxic and Nuclear Disposal Installation), somewhere in Nevada.

Salk's life starts out badly and gets worse. His mother is a drug addict, and Salk is born facially malformed, undersized, and underweight. He finds a haven in Cloak House, an orphanage run by the saintly but strict Brother

Bonifant. By the age of ten, however, Salk is on the streets, and by the age of eighteen he has been a drug runner, acquired a criminal record, nearly died in a juvenile detention home, and made the mistake of befriending the daughter of a wealthy family. This is a mistake because it brings him to the attention of Wilfred Dell, an evil man who is working for the Royal Hundred, the country's wealthiest families.

Dell forces Salk to go to Xanadu, also known as the Great Nebraska Tandy, the place to which many scientists were banished as punishment for their supposed role in the *Quiebra Grande* (Great Crash) of 2005, an economic disaster that affected the entire world. Dell is worried that the scientists are up to something.

Working undercover, Salk proves Dell right. The scientists have created a virus that, if released, would kill most of the world's population. They see this as suitable revenge for being treated as scapegoats for the *Quiebra Grande*. One of the scientists, Dr. Hanna Kronberg, has created another microorganism, a symbiote that strengthens the human immune system and retards aging. Salk manages to release the symbiote, thus preempting the scientists' revenge and inaugurating a fall in the world's population, which eventually will stabilize at a figure that the planet can support. This is bad news to Dell and the Royal Hundred, because the old and rich no longer have the same advantages over the young and poor. Before Dell can execute Salk, however, Salk dies of a radiation overdose that he received while escaping from Xanadu.

Salk thus lives up to all three parts of his name. Like the biblical Job, he is born to trouble; like Napoleon Bonaparte, he spectacularly overcomes his physical limitations, though not by killing; and like Jonas Salk, he saves humanity from a vicious disease.

Analysis: As a writer of hard science fiction, Charles Sheffield often has been compared to Isaac Asimov, Arthur C. Clarke, and Robert A. Heinlein. *Brother to Dragons* certainly is hard science fiction, featuring believable science, especially biology, and believable technology, especially Tandymen, the robotic toxic waste handlers that figure prominently in Salk's escape from Xanadu.

Brother to Dragons is a near-future extrapolation. The two trends it extrapolates are a worsening worldwide economy and an increasing distrust of science. The result is a cautionary tale about what can go wrong if these two trends continue.

Most of Sheffield's other science fiction is more similar to Asimov's and Clarke's than to Heinlein's, so *Brother to Dragons* is something of a departure from Sheffield's norm. Its concerns are not cosmic but global. Its protagonist is not a mature man but an adolescent boy. Its setting is not centuries away but in the near future.

Brother to Dragons is Sheffield's homage to Heinlein, who died in 1988, four years before this novel was published. The Heinlein work it most closely resembles is *Citizen of the Galaxy* (1957), also a novel for juvenile readers that features an orphaned, young, male protagonist, seemingly vulnerable, who has hidden resources that surface when he is challenged to survive during a series of picaresque adventures. Heinlein's Thor Bradley Rudbek and Sheffield's Job Napoleon Salk both come of age by surviving in harsh environments that reward competence.

Brother to Dragons has other details reminiscent of Heinlein, such as Xanadu's resemblance to the setting of Heinlein's novelette "Coventry" (*Astounding Science-Fiction*, July, 1940; reprinted in *Revolt in 2100*, 1953). *Brother to Dragons* also bears its author's stamp. Although certainly posing the limitations of science, the novel nevertheless takes a proscience line, which is not surprising given Sheffield's own training as a physicist. What may be surprising is how literary the novel is. Literary allusions abound, with Sheffield borrowing important plot elements from Charles Dickens' *Oliver Twist* (1837-1839). The linguistically gifted Salk likes to read literature in many different languages, and the Book of Job in the Bible provides epithets for eleven of the novel's twenty chapters.

Unlike many science-fiction writers, Sheffield does not scoff at religion. Balancing Dr. Hanna Kronberg, the heroic scientist who creates the miraculous symbiote, is Brother Bonifant, the cleric who ministers to orphans like Salk before dying a martyr's death in Xanadu. Sheffield is a product of the British educational system, and that system and British science fiction always have been more literary than their American counterparts.

Although Sheffield is a popular science-fiction writer, not much criticism has been written on his work, and little other than brief reviews has been written on *Brother to Dragons*. Sheffield has his admirers, however. In 1993, *Brother to Dragons* won the John W. Campbell Memorial Award for the best science-fiction novel of the year. This tribute is fitting, because Campbell is remembered not only as an important science-fiction editor but also as an important early writer of hard science fiction.

—*Todd H. Sammons*

BUG JACK BARRON

Jack Barron, the outrageous host of a call-in television show, investigates human immortality research and becomes trapped in a Faustian contract that he overcomes in a desperate on-air showdown

Author: Norman Spinrad (1940-   )
Genre: Science fiction—extrapolatory
Type of work: Novel
Time of plot: The mid- or late 1980's
Location: New York City
First published: 1969 (serial form, *New Worlds*, 1967-1968)

The Plot: Jack Barron is a charismatic journalist trying to retain both his job and his integrity. Benedict Howards, owner of the Human Immortality Foundation, alternately bribes and threatens Barron, seeking his support. Ultimately, Howards makes an offer that Barron cannot refuse.

As the book opens, Barron seizes on a charge of racism as a hook to explore the Freezer Utility controversy. He makes on-air calls to the foundation; to Senator Hennering, who supports a monopoly bill Howards wants; and to Lucas Greene, the black governor of Mississippi and Jack's longtime friend. Hennering gives a limp defense of the bill, enraging Howards. Soon after, Hennering dies under suspicious circumstances. Howards investigates Barron and learns the television host's weakness: He still loves his former wife, Sara.

Howards bribes Sara to reunite with Barron. Sara seizes the opportunity, sure that together, she and Barron can outwit Howards. The two rediscover the joy they shared as young lovers.

Barron questions Howards on the air. Privately, Howards admits that the foundation has developed an immortality procedure. He offers Barron the million-dollar operation for free in exchange for public support. They bargain warily, and Barron offers only to do contractual public relations work for the foundation. When he and Sara sign immortality contracts, Howards urges immediate surgery. Barron equivocates. He believes that Howards still hides dangerous secrets but hopes that his seeming cooperation will tease them out.

On Barron's next show, Franklin, a "kook" caller, bemoans selling his daughter. Barron makes no connection until Howards blasts him for doing the interview. Barron decides to question Franklin further. As the two walk together, a sniper fires at them, killing Franklin.

When Barron and Sara go to confront Howards, his aides forcibly anesthetize them. When they wake, they are "immortal." Howards then shows Barron some purchased children, who have been irradiated to stop the aging process. The children die a terrible death, and their transplanted glands provide immortality to others. Howards points out that Barron's and Sara's contracts say that they "accept full legal liability for any results of the treatment." This proves them to be accomplices to murder, he says.

Barron hopelessly agrees. By himself, he would expose Howards, risking a murder charge, but he cannot bear to put Sara in the same jeopardy. When they next make love, pleasure turns to disgust. Sara asks what is wrong, and Barron reluctantly reveals the secret.

Sara, horrified, takes LSD when Barron leaves for his next show. On vidphone, she says that she is freeing him, then jumps from their balcony. Barron tells the whole story on the air.

His revelations drive Howards insane and reshuffle American politics. Barron and Lucas Greene are nominated on a coalition presidential ticket. Barron's secret plan is to resign if he wins, giving the United States its first black president, and to continue wielding power his own way, through television.

Analysis: *Bug Jack Barron* stirred controversy with its explicit sex scenes and four-letter words, almost unknown in science fiction before this time. A British distributor dropped the magazine in which it appeared, and the Arts Council was criticized in Parliament for supporting the publication of "filth."

Most reviewers who looked beyond these features praised the novel for its keen depiction of media influence and political manipulation. A minority dismissed it as a bizarre experiment. The vivid and startling images in its characters' long stream-of-consciousness reflections added to its shock value.

Later critics have noted the accuracy of the book's premise of talk show hosts shaping public opinion. The split screen and panning techniques Barron uses are classic examples of image manipulation.

Like most science fiction with a near-future setting, *Bug Jack Barron* makes some wrong guesses. Marijuana was not legalized by the mid-1980's, and there was no Social Justice party. The book does, however, strike uncannily close to many trends of the late twentieth century. Ronald Reagan is cited as a prime example of the power of media images long before his election to the U.S. presidency in 1980. The rise of black politicians and the development of "vidphones" are other examples of accurate prediction.

Barron's selling out for material rewards often is said to be a second theme of the book. This analysis is debatable. Certainly, selling out is a preoccupation for Jack and Sara Barron and for Lucas Greene, whose outlooks were shaped by the 1960's counterculture. Sometimes, Barron agrees when Sara or Greene accuses him of discarding his ideals for commercial success. Other times, he defends himself, saying that Sara's friends, who only complain and dream, are the real sellouts; his hard-won influence brings their ideals closer to reality. On most of his shows, this appears to be the case, as he "bugs" the powerful and defends ordinary people. Barron does enjoy the power he exercises. His biggest flaw, however, may be simple overconfidence, in gambling that he can outmatch and bring to account such a wealthy and wily operator as Howards.

The book's innovative style has become less shocking since 1969, when it was new to the genre. It can still produce breathtaking effects, however, as in the scene in which Sara jumps to her death, seeing transfigured images of her husband, the dead babies, and infinity.

Bug Jack Barron was nominated for a Hugo Award in 1968 and a Nebula Award in 1969. The book put its author into the front ranks of serious science-fiction writers. Many of Norman Spinrad's later works echo motifs introduced in it: electronic networks, public opinion as a court of final appeal, immortality, sex, drugs, power, and love. As a cautionary tale about the interaction of these elements, the book remains relevant and compelling.

—*Emily Alward*

BURN, WITCH, BURN!

Dr. Lowell joins with gangster Julian Ricori to track and kill the witch Madame Mandilip and to destroy her enchanted "devil dolls"

Author: A(braham) Merritt (1884-1943)
Genre: Fantasy—superbeing
Type of work: Novel
Time of plot: The 1930's
Location: New York City, with a climactic visit to the "unknown world" of magic
First published: 1933 (serial form, *Argosy Magazine*, October 22-November 26, 1932)

The Plot: The story revolves around the efforts of a scientist, Dr. Lowell (a pseudonym he uses because of his fear that the incredible and irrational events he relates will discredit him as a scientist), and a gangster, Julian Ricori, as they first uncover the existence of the powerful witch of the title and then try, unsuccessfully, to find an effective countermeasure to her lethal magic. They track her to her lair, where they confront and finally kill her.

In the beginning, Dr. Lowell relates that Ricori has sought Lowell's services on behalf of the gangster's lieutenant, Thomas Peters, who suffers from a severe shock that has destroyed his nervous stability. His eyes are wide open, his posture is rigid, and, although neither unconscious nor dead, he is unresponsive to treatment. Lowell struggles to find a medical solution to the problem but cannot. He slowly (if grudgingly) concludes that Peters suffers from some sort of undiscoverable evil "presence." Peters is under the influence of Madame Mandilip, whom Lowell has not yet met, though he infers her power to manipulate her victims psychically and from a great distance.

Peters dies while Lowell helplessly attends him. Lowell and Ricori discover that other persons have met similar fates. The death of one in particular, Nurse Walters, provides them with a diary that details her visits to Madame Mandilip's doll shop. It contains both one of the greatest gothic descriptions of an occult event in American fantasy fiction and enough information to allow them to identify Madame Mandilip as the source of the necromancy that they have decided is the root of the eerie and lethal events that they have been investigating.

Later, Lowell and Ricori abduct the witch's assistant, the pitiful and frightened Lascha, and learn enough to reach the conclusion that Madame Mandilip is an ancient witch of great and malign power and that she is capable of assuming many physical forms. They then make their plans to confront her in her hellish doll shop and engage her in a battle to the death, an encounter that is among the best of its kind in American fantasy fiction. Although they finally conquer supernatural evil, they do not escape unscathed, either physically or psychologically.

Analysis: A plot summary can suggest something of the excitement of the sequence of events, but it cannot suggest the novel's finest feature: the excellence of its style. A fine example of pure gothic fantasy that uses the device of the superbeing as its chief interest, *Burn, Witch, Burn!* was written toward the end of A. Merritt's career. A successful journalist, Merritt wrote fantasies of various types for relaxation in his hours away from his job. He was also a master of lost-civilization stories, such as *The Face in the Abyss* (1931) and *The Dwellers in the Mirage*

(1932), following a style adopted by the much-better-known H. Rider Haggard and Edgar Rice Burroughs, authors who were his near contemporaries. In early stories, such as *The Moon Pool* (1919) and *The Metal Monster* (1946; serial form, 1920), and in his last novel, *Creep, Shadow!* (1934), Merritt produced some of the best macabre fantasies by an American writer of any period. Only Edgar Allan Poe is his superior in this genre.

Burn, Witch, Burn! appeared at the end of his career; only *Creep, Shadow!*, a horror story intended as a sequel, and a few other short pieces would be written in the remaining nine years of his life. This is to be regretted, because the story demonstrates Merritt's mastery of the various conventions of gothic fantasy—the gloomy and fear-inducing atmosphere and the ageless and malignant superbeing or monster at the story's center—as well as his firm grasp of the mechanics of plot. These elements are combined with a highly visual style that adds to the story's suspense without detracting from the plot by calling attention to itself.

In this novel, Merritt successfully embodies the most important idea to be found in supernatural fantasy: that the reader has come to the novel in order to experience the idea that evil exists as an active, objective force, independent of subjective experience, in the world of physical existence. His early work taught him that the reader's shock, on being introduced to the experience of the extraordinary, which is the supernatural story's whole point, exists in direct proportion to the writer's scrupulous attention to and incorporation of realistic detail. The power of a Merritt fantasy results from his creation of a believable primary or realistic world peopled, for the most part, by ordinary characters. Thus, the reader believes, when finally encountering the evil superbeing at the core of the work, that he or she is "shivering on [the] threshold" of the "door of an unknown world," as Merritt himself states in this novel. Such sensations mark the most intense engagements that fantasy fiction can offer a reader. *Burn, Witch, Burn!* produces many such moments while demonstrating Merritt's mastery of this timeless form of literary art.

—*Ronald Foust*

BURNING CHROME

Stories of the early twenty-first century, set on Earth or in the inner solar system, combining high technology, social unrest, corporate conflict, and ambiguous characters

Author: William Gibson (1948-   )
Genre: Science fiction—cyberpunk
Type of work: Stories
Time of plot: Primarily the early twenty-first century, with some stories set in the 1980's
Location: Earth and elsewhere in the solar system
First published: 1986

The Plot: A collection of primarily near-future stories, *Burning Chrome* demonstrates the style, ambiguity, and dark vision characteristic of William Gibson's work. The ten stories in this collection can be divided into four groups on the basis of their settings.

"New Rose Hotel," "Johnny Mnemonic," and "Burning Chrome" are stories of the Sprawl, set in the early twenty-first century Earth further developed in the novels *Neuromancer* (1984), *Count Zero* (1986), and *Mona Lisa Overdrive* (1988). High technology, organized crime, powerful megacorporations, and an economy driven by information services dominate a world divided sharply into haves and have-nots. These three short stories set up the basic patterns of Sprawl conflict: individuals against powerful corporations, individuals against organized crime, and low-power individuals against high-power individuals. In "New Rose Hotel," the nameless narrator details the machinations of corporate headhunters and the inexorable, deadly vengeance of their employer after a defection goes wrong. The title character of "Johnny Mnemonic" is a walking safebox for other people's data. He is left with data stolen from the Yakuza, the Japanese crime syndicate, locked in his head after a client is killed. With the help of Molly Millions, a surgically enhanced bodyguard/assassin, and Jones, a drug-addicted former Navy Dolphin, Johnny evades the Yakuza and begins to make use of all the data he has ever stored. In "Burning Chrome," Bobby Quine and Automatic Jack, hot-shot computer jockeys, use stolen Russian military software to break into the computer system of a local crime lord, Chrome, and destroy her power base by redistributing her financial assets.

"Fragments of a Hologram Rose," "Winter Market," and "Dogfight" are stories set in the Sprawl or in a world very similar to it. Stories in this group are also set against a background of a high-technology society with sharp economic extremes. "Fragments of a Hologram Rose," Gibson's first published story, hinges on the reaction of the main character, Parker, to his lover's desertion, his recollections of his past, and his inability to view his past or himself as a whole. "Winter Market" is the story of Lise, a neuroelectronic artist who has herself translated

into the computer net shortly before she dies. It is told through the eyes of Casey, the recording editor who reworked her dreams and ambitions into best-selling software. In "Dogfight," which Gibson wrote with Michael Swanwick, Deke finds a way out of his dead-end life by hustling "wetware" projection dogfights, but he destroys so much in pursuit of his victory, including his opponent's will to live, that the victory is virtually meaningless.

"Red Star, Winter Orbit" and "Hinterlands" are both set in space, in a society in which power is still largely divided between the Americans and the Soviets. "Red Star, Winter Orbit," a collaboration with Bruce Sterling, describes the decline of Kosmograd, a Soviet space station in a decaying orbit. "Hinterland" is a dark story in which Toby Halpert explains the workings of the Highway, a point in space where human space vehicles vanish and eventually reappear, the occupants bringing back strange artifacts and new information. The problem is that most occupants come back insane or dead. Toby's job is to meet the ones that come back alive and sane and to keep them that way, if he can.

The remaining two stories differ from the rest of the collection in tone as well as setting. Set in the 1980's, both lack the gritty high-tech atmosphere common to the other stories and share instead a sense of the surreal. "The Belonging Kind," cowritten with John Shirley, describes a kind of animal evolved to live within urban structures, mimicking people and changing like a chameleon to fit its various environments. The story details the slow metamorphosis of Coretti, a socially awkward linguist, into one of these animals. In "The Gernsback Continuum," a photographer hired to document remnants of 1930's American futuristic design begins to see what a friend calls "semiotic ghosts," hallucinations of the 1980's as they might have been, an ultimately dystopic vision he suppresses by watching bad television.

Analysis: *Burning Chrome* contains Gibson's short work up to 1986. As do many single-author short-story collections, *Burning Chrome* presents a summary of Gibson's early themes and devices. The primary characteristics of the subgenre that became known as cyberpunk are all present: setting, character types, basic conflicts, and pace. In the case of the Sprawl stories, the setting and even some characters of the later Neuromancer novels appear, such as Molly Millions from "Johnny Mnemonic" and The Finn, the fence in "Burning Chrome."

As represented in this collection, much of Gibson's work combines elements of three traditions: hard science fiction (technological development), soft science fiction (social change), and New Wave (cynicism and apprehension about the future). These broad elements serve to examine themes such as isolation, relationships, and identity.

Identity in Gibson's work is fluid. Names and faces, and even data stores, can be changed. The degree of fluidity ranges from Johnny Mnemonic's temporary assumption of another face and persona to the chameleon-like adaptations of "The Belonging Kind." Not all fluid identities are conscious or desired. Both Parker in "Fragments of a Hologram Rose" and Fox in "New Rose Hotel" sift through fragments in hopes of seeing an unknown whole. Parker's fragments are isolated memories of his past; Fox's are his identification cards.

It is perhaps not surprising, given the near-future time-frame, that these stories have in some ways dated rapidly. They were overtaken in the early 1990's not by technological change so much as by social changes, such as the dissolution of the Soviet Union and the reunification of Germany. Stories with direct references to the Soviet Union, such as "Red Star, Winter Orbit," suffer most.

Gibson is recognized as one of the creators of the cyberpunk subgenre. The cyberpunk story "Johnny Mnemonic" is the basis for the film *Johnny Mnemonic* (1995), starring Keanu Reeves as Johnny.

—*Kim G. Kofmel*

THE BURNING COURT

Editor Edward Stevens attempts to investigate a murder and to explain the mysterious similarity in appearance between his wife and a nineteenth century murderess pictured in a book he is editing

Author: John Dickson Carr (1906-1977)
Genre: Fantasy—occult
Type of work: Novel
Time of plot: 1929
Location: Pennsylvania
First published: 1937

The Plot: *The Burning Court* is an unusual novel—a cross between a traditional detective story and an occult horror tale. Without the epilogue, it is a detective novel similar to John Dickson Carr's other works, in which the murderer is caught and the woman who was wrongly suspected is vindicated. The epilogue unexpectedly brings in the supernatural as the true explanation, turning the story into a horror tale.

Edward Stevens, an editor with a New York publishing house, is working on a book about nineteenth century murderers when he finds a photograph of Marie D'Aubray, a woman guillotined for murder in 1881. He is disconcerted to see that she closely resembles his wife, Marie. He realizes how little he knows about his beautiful wife, who captivated him with what he calls her "spiritual" look. A professor friend tells him that another Marie D'Aubray was condemned as a murderer in 1676. Watching Marie as she goes about her housewifely duties in their Philadelphia home, Edward wonders about her ancestry.

Edward's friends Mark and Lucy Despard are concerned that their Uncle Miles's death from gastroenteritis may not in fact have been from natural causes. Mark even wonders if Lucy is involved, considering that they inherited Miles's property. Mark, Edward, and a doctor friend attempt to disinter the body to check for poison, but it has been removed. Meanwhile, evidence suggesting that Marie is a witch accumulates, making Edward uneasy and suspicious.

Finally, witnesses of Miles's death are brought forth, and it is revealed that he was indeed murdered. Moreover, it appears that Marie, not Lucy, is guilty. At the last minute, everything is explained: Another woman—Miles's nurse and lover—appears to be the murderer, and her guilt is apparently demonstrated by the fact that she killed someone else in view of police officers. Marie's witchlike behavior is explained away by psychology; she was reared by a psychotic, abusive aunt who believed in witchcraft and who made Marie believe that she herself was a witch.

The epilogue takes the reader into Marie's mind after the investigation is over. It reveals that she is a witch and was executed in the seventeenth century and then again in the nineteenth century. She had forgotten much about her earlier incarnations, but she is beginning to remember details of past lives. Her love for her husband Edward is real, but it is not a good thing for Edward: It means that she will soon make him one of the "non-dead" immortal evildoers, and this will require that she "transform" (kill) him. She hopes she can do this "without pain. Or too much pain."

Analysis: *The Burning Court*'s epilogue provides a surprising ending. Readers of the book tend to be not fantasy fans but detective story addicts who are astounded and often irritated by the nontraditional ending. This unusual, mixed-genre novel draws most appreciation from readers who are not committed to a particular genre. As a detective story, it seems not to "play by the rules" in calling on supernatural forces as the story's resolution. As an occult horror novel, however, it spends too much time on the particulars of investigations.

The Burning Court does, however, succeed in mixing the ratiocination of the standard detective story with the intuitive, mythic reasoning of the horror story. Carr skillfully buffets the reader back and forth between the occult and the realistic explanations of events. For example, Marie is terrified of funnels—her face changes, looking more "lined," when confronted with one. A book describing the history of witchcraft describes the water torture (water forced through a funnel into the witch's mouth) that was inflicted on suspected witches in previous centuries. Contradicting this, however, is the suggestion that Marie's aunt used a funnel to punish her as a child. In the epilogue, it is made clear that the old book provided the "real" explanation. This kind of device is used throughout the novel, and the detective story reader, accustomed to Carr's Gideon Fell mysteries, expects all the supernatural elements to be explained away at the end as the truth is presented in the clear light of reason.

The careful reader of the old-school detective story, in which the rules are carefully and consistently kept, is aware that there are holes in the apparently satisfactory explanation to the case. Marie seems to have knowledge she could not have acquired normally, and certain physical details do not jibe with the conclusion that the nurse killed Miles. In the epilogue, all these details are explained: If Marie truly is a witch, then she is not hampered by human limitations in the achievement of her goals.

As a surprise fantasy novel, *The Burning Court* is rare in the field. When it was published, it was extremely controversial and received unfavorable reviews from critics who believed that Carr had cheated by using a supernatural explanation. Additionally, letting the evildoer win generally was not done in the detective stories of the 1930's, which usually ended with the triumph of justice. *The Burning Court* is unlikely to be read as a fantasy because the novel leads the reader to expect a detective story. Although it falls between the two genres of the fantasy and the detective novel, *The Burning Court* nevertheless provides an unforgettable reading experience.   —*Janet McCann*

CAMP CONCENTRATION

In a situation resembling the Vietnam War, Louis Sacchetti, a poet and conscientious objector, is moved to a secret underground facility, where experiments are undertaken to radically accelerate intelligence using lethal syphilis

Author: Thomas M. Disch (1940-   )
Genre: Science fiction—inner space
Type of work: Novel
Time of plot: The near future
Location: A disused gold mine in Colorado
First published: 1968

The Plot: Louis Sacchetti is told by General Haast, the camp commandant, that he has been moved to Camp Archimedes to record what he sees. Dr. Aimée Busk, the camp psychiatrist, further explains that as those around him are dying of syphilis induced by the strain Pallidine (which kills in about nine months), they undergo stunning increases in intelligence, which the military hopes to employ.

In his diary, which forms the bulk of the narrative, Sacchetti reports meeting the other men at the camp. Among them is George Wagner, the first prisoner Sacchetti meets and the first he sees entombed. The prisoners' leader is Mordecai Washington, who knew Sacchetti in his school days. Washington is deeply immersed in alchemical studies and has become a magnificent polymath in only a few months. The prisoners prepare a brilliant production of Christopher Marlowe's *Doctor Faustus*, but Wagner dies before he can play the lead. Then Washington and Haast take part in an alchemical attempt to obtain immortality, but it goes wrong, and Washington dies horribly. The following night, Sacchetti dreams the truth, that he is infected and dying. The balance of his journal is in scraps, heavy with literary allusion, showing that he gets sicker and more brilliant each day.

Busk leaves the camp, and a new group of subjects arrives, centered on Skilliman, a failed but nasty and ambitious scientist who chooses the Pallidine treatment in order to develop weapons. Sacchetti sets up a museum of artifacts that add up to the fact that Busk, as a result of sexual intercourse with Washington, has spread the syphilis rapidly across the United States. Skilliman's conflicts with Sacchetti, the only survivor of the original group, begin as Sacchetti starts to draw off Skilliman's followers. A confrontation ensues in which Skilliman demands that Sacchetti, now blind, be executed. Instead, Haast kills Skilliman and reveals that the alchemical experiment was a disguised brain pattern exchange in which Washington's mind came to occupy Haast's body. The simultaneous reverse action of the "mind reciprocator" so horrified Haast that it was he who died in Washington's body.

The novel closes on a challenge to the changed prisoners, who look forward to a future of both genius and eternal life, although that prolonged life would be at the repeated cost of the lives of others, until a vaccine is found for the Pallidine infection.

Analysis: *Camp Concentration* is a vital meeting of several forces. Thomas M. Disch, though living in the United States, was much influenced by the British New Wave writers who were exploring the inner space of human consciousness through literary experimentation. *Camp Concentration* is a conscious variation on Thomas Mann's monumental *Doctor Faustus* (1947), in that it deals with the price of genius and is set against a background of wartime tyranny, which sharpens the novel's moral aspect. The novel is set during a war in the future, but it is a very near future (attested by the presence of President McNamara, presumably the 1960's secretary of defense). This is clearly a novel about the illegitimacy of the war in Vietnam and the methods of the military research establishment.

The novel's most important aspect is its experimentation with literary style. Sacchetti is a poet and litterateur from the start (he cites Fyodor Dostoevski's *The House of the Dead* [1915] on the first page of the text), but his literary allusions become far more pronounced as his intelligence and reading accelerate as a result of the syphilis. Others, like Washington, bring in Arthur Koestler's definitions of genius, and there are extensive references to the alchemical masters and great writers who have had syphilis. As Sacchetti's illness advances, his journal disintegrates into a literate, allusive stream of consciousness in which he quotes or mentions such diverse figures as Heinrich Himmler, Saint Augustine, Hans Yost, André-Georges Malreux, and John Milton, along with citing the Bible. The texture gives a rich, complex speculation on disease, genius, and death.

The text has an overriding tone of moral confrontation. Sacchetti, an intellectual Catholic, has become a conscientious objector to the war and is aware of the issues surrounding what is happening to him and the other subjects. Skilliman, who seems at first to be injected into the latter part of the text only to fill the void created by the deaths of the earlier group of subjects, is the immoral practitioner of science—the man willing to use his increased intelligence for personal fame and to create weapons of destruction. Sacchetti engages in a series of dialogues with him and his young assistants and emerges victorious in moral fact (and in winning over the assistants), although it appears that he has lost in physical and practical terms. Washington-Haast's murder of Skilliman and Sacchetti's escape into a healthy body re-establish the balance, but it is arguably a *deus ex machina* ending.

The idea of a plague spreading from the evil machinations of military research, of the moral sickness of the society becoming a physical sickness unto death, is a marker of the conscience of the text. Even the surprise ending has moral implications: Several of the infected prisoners choose physical death over the act of sentencing to death whomever they could have exchanged bodies with. *Camp Concentration* is a brilliant, tough book, bringing broad issues and complex literary continuity into science fiction.

—*Peter Brigg*

CANOPUS IN ARGOS

A depiction of the falling away from a spiritual unity of humans and other species and an explanation of problems such as violence and sexism, set in the context of conflict between space empires of Canopus and Sirius

Author: Doris Lessing (1919-   )
Genre: Science fiction—galactic empire
Type of work: Novels
Time of plot: Various times between antiquity and the end of the universe
Location: Various locations on Earth and other planets
First published: *Re: Colonised Planet 5, Shikasta* (1979), *The Marriage Between Zones Three, Four, and Five* (1980), *The Sirian Experiments* (1981), *The Making of the Representative for Planet 8* (1982), and *The Sentimental Agents in the Volyen Empire* (1983)

The Plot: This series of novels was published in a period of four years with the series title *Canopus in Argos* prominently displayed on each. Although the novels contain no major continuing characters, they are all set in the context of competing ideologies. The series is connected through the repetition of ideas rather than a developing plot or continuing characters. Philosophical in content and in structure, the novels tell a future history and recast events of the past, such as the legend of Atlantis. All the novels emphasize that humans and beings on other worlds must learn the importance of unity in order to correct problems in their societies. In *Re: Colonised Planet 5, Shikasta*, human beings discover the importance of mental powers. The human race possesses great powers, but it is unsure of how to use them. Losing its creator, the space empire Canopus, causes Earth to have seasons and its inhabitants to devolve. Canopean agents try to redeem Earth, and they appear under the guise of alternative science or magic. Unfortunately, only a few people hear and heed the Canopean message. As a result of human neglect of unification, an apocalypse occurs.

In *The Marriage Between Zones Three, Four, and Five*, the queen of a feminist utopian society (Zone Three) marries the leader of Zone Four, a patriarchal warrior society. The novel shows her struggle to accept a man who has completely different values. No mention is made of Earth or of the other novels.

In *The Sirian Experiments*, the Sirians, who represent an extension of twentieth century Western science, struggle with Canopeans, who represent magic or alternative science. An agent of Sirius converts to the Canopean way of viewing the world. *The Making of the Representative for Planet 8* tells the story of an ecological collapse as an entire planet becomes covered by ice and snow. The planet cannot be saved except through a storyteller who preserves the planet's people and experience in Canopus' memory. The planet's disaster is traced to Earth's separation from the Canopus empire.

The Sentimental Agents in the Volyen Empire depicts rebels on the planet Voleyenadna who are manipulated by false and misleading rhetoric. A Canopean agent, who also appears in *Re: Colonised Planet 5, Shikasta*, helps women save the planet with a regenerating plant food.

In the series as a whole, plots focus on the struggle between the empires of Canopus and Sirius. Canopus is a female-identified empire that uses magic and mental powers, and Sirius is a fact-based empire that relies on machines and Western science. The series takes the Canopean perspective and criticizes Sirians' myopic point of view.

Analysis: Doris Lessing had established an illustrious career as a realistic novelist before she wrote *Canopus in Argos*. This series comes rather late in her career and represents a substantial shift in her writing. Reviewers responded negatively to this shift. Lessing has written many novels since *Canopus in Argos*, but none of them are science fiction. *Canopus in Argos* has been seen as an aberration in her work. Like Margaret Atwood and P. D. James, other well-known female writers who have written science fiction, Lessing appears to have thought that only science fiction could convey her radical criticism of contemporary society.

Lessing's science fiction can be seen as part of a trend by female writers who use science fiction to propose alternatives to current gender roles. *Canopus in Argos* also has been identified as part of the British tradition of science fiction, especially the work of Olaf Stapledon. Stapledon is most famous for *Last and First Men* (1930), a work that deals with the evolution of a number of human races over the course of two billion years. Like Stapledon, Lessing looks at an immense time frame, a common "race mind," and the evolution of humanity. Like Stapledon's work, Lessing's series is science fiction that focuses on ideas rather than characters or an action-adventure plot.

Lessing prefers the term "space fiction" to that of science fiction. "Space" is used to describe the genre in England, but the phrase also implies a particular type of science fiction. Space fiction, as Lessing creates it, is more concerned with the powers of the human mind than with technology or new kinds of machines.

The series consistently asserts an androgynous vision. Canopeans transcend sex because they can be either male or female when they visit Earth. The series looks back nostalgically to a time when Earth was ruled by women using magic, when language did not exist, and when planets and other beings communed mentally. The series also emphasizes dissatisfaction with and distrust of language. Lessing's emphasis on philosophical concepts makes her work an ambitious and complex work of science fiction.

Although *Canopus in Argos* is nonlinear and achronological (the books can be read in any order), the novels should be considered in the order in which they were published. For example, the tenuous connection between *Re: Colonised Planet 5, Shikasta* and *The Marriage Between Zones Three, Four, and Five*, which are labeled as volumes 1 and 2, requires readers to look for philosophical and other connections. What is important about the series is the way in which Lessing uses nontraditional narration, such as documents and reports, to criticize traditional science and ways of looking at the world. Throughout the series, Lessing stresses that an openness to multiple perspectives is the only way to salvage society.

Re: Colonised Planet 5, Shikasta can be read as an origin myth about Earth. The story of the planet's fall from grace explains why and how humanity created the mess that is twentieth century Earth. Scientists scoff at the messengers who explain Earth's true history; through science's arrogance, Earth becomes even more sick. Science provides the mechanism that touches off the holocaust, supporting the Canopean (and Lessing's) contention that science has gotten out of control.

The queen of *The Marriage Between Zones Three, Four, and Five* suggests that witches and magic can be an alternative to science. By associating a female leader with powers that are seen on Earth as unreal, Lessing recovers magic as a powerful alternative to science. The queen Al*Ith becomes a prophet of the importance of unity and a revered role model. The narrator of this novel creates a legend as he retells Al*Ith's story. Art preserves and interprets her experience. Al*Ith has been compared to Demeter, the mythical female figure whose separation from her daughter resulted in seasons on Earth. The book also has been interpreted as a utopia, depicting a world that is both perfect and nonexistent. This setting disrupts the more traditional science-fiction setting of *Re: Colonised Planet 5, Shikasta*. The novel also ruptures the more traditional sense of time and place of the first novel.

By disrupting the tidy, ordered frame of a science-fiction series, Lessing alerts her readers to her more ambitious goal of resisting definitions and frames. She forces the reader to examine the conventional assumptions of a science-fiction series.

Like Al*Ith, Ambien II, the protagonist of *The Sirian Experiments*, has a role as prophet. A Sirian, she realizes the dangers of science as the Sirians practice it and converts to Canopus. Her conversion experience persuades readers to lessen their respect for Western science. In the next novel, Lessing minimizes science by stressing how much more powerful art is. Only art, not science, can provide any salvation for the people of Planet 8 in *The Making of the Representative for Planet 8*. Again, Lessing praises the power of art and criticizes the failings of science. The last volume continues the critique of science but also exposes the ways in which language is used to control thought and block ideas. *The Sentimental Agents in the Volyen Empire* is an open-ended volume, because after her criticism of order and control in science and language, Lessing throws the issues she raises to her readers. A complex and philosophical series, *Canopus in Argos* requires the reader to challenge accepted ideas about science, magic, and gender.   —*Robin Roberts*

A CANTICLE FOR LEIBOWITZ

A monastic order struggles through many centuries of war and barbarism to maintain its commitment to God

Author: Walter M. Miller, Jr. (1922-   )
Genre: Science fiction—future history
Type of work: Novel
Time of plot: About 2600 to 3781
Location: The southwestern United States
First published: 1960 (serial form, *The Magazine of Fantasy and Science Fiction*, 1955-1957)

The Plot: The novel has three sections, with narratives separated by about six hundred years between sections. From the perspective of the Abbey of Saint Leibowitz, church history is recapitulated in a future "Dark Age," a "Renaissance," and an apocalyptic "Modern Age."

The first section, "Fiat Homo" ("let there be man"), begins about A.D. 2600. A twentieth century atomic war and a repressive Age of Simplification have almost wiped out the past. Brother Francis, a simple monk fasting in the desert, uncovers an underground chamber with "Fallout Survival Shelter" written over it. He believes that Fallout is the name of a demon and has no conception of the war that destroyed civilization. The shelter contains documents written by Leibowitz, an engineer who stayed on at the abbey after the war and devoted himself to the preservation of knowledge.

In the timeless life of the abbey, the Blessed Leibowitz finally is declared a saint. Brother Francis devotes fifteen years to illuminating a wholly meaningless blueprint. On the way to New Rome to present his illumination to the pope, he is robbed by mutants. The pope gives the monk enough gold to buy back the illumination. In the second encounter, however, the mutants steal the gold and cannibalize him, casting him as a martyr.

In the second section, "Fiat Lux" ("let there be light"), set in A.D. 3174, the church is challenged by new ideas and powerful princes. Dom Paulo, the current abbot, struggles to preserve the abbey against outside influence. Thon Taddeo, a brilliant but arrogant scientist, reveals more about the Leibowitz memorabilia in a few minutes than the monks have been able to in centuries. In a symbolic scene, a crucifix is taken down so that an arc lamp can be installed for the thon. The abbot, arguing that the pursuit of knowledge, though not evil in itself, cannot be the purpose of humankind, orders the crucifix to be returned to the wall. Thereafter, all will read *ad Lumina Christi*, or "in the light of Christ."

The third section, "Fiat Voluntas Tua" ("let there be your will"), is directed against humanism, a view that argues that humanity is the proper focus of human attention. In A.D. 3781, atomic war breaks out, and millions are poisoned with radioactivity. The government sets up mercy camps, offering euthanasia to those dying in agony. Two characters frame the issues significant to Dom Zerchi, the latest abbot. Dr. Cors, a mercy camp administrator, argues that suffering is evil and should be alleviated. The abbot, in contrast, rejects euthanasia as a violation of God's will. The other significant person in this section is Mrs. Grales, a mutant who wants Rachel, the dormant extra head on her shoulder, to be baptized. Dom Zerchi, fearful of the implications, puts off her request. A bomb hits the abbey, killing Mrs. Grales and mortally wounding the abbot. At this moment, however, Rachel unexpectedly comes alive. As his last act, Dom Zerchi struggles through the wreckage to baptize her. Thereafter, the Vatican sends three bishops into space in an emergency plan to preserve the apostolic succession.

Analysis: In a brief writing career that extended from 1949 to 1957, Walter M. Miller, Jr., produced the justly praised novel *A Canticle for Leibowitz* and forty-one shorter pieces of science fiction. All of them, including the original serialized version of the novel, appeared in such popular publications as *Galaxy* and *The Magazine of Fantasy and Science Fiction*.

Miller's work shows the usual characteristics of genre writing: action plots, ready characterizations, and a bright but brittle acquaintance with technology and ideas. Miller's commitment to Roman Catholicism, however, immediately set his work apart. With a skillful play on the willing suspension of disbelief, he used the science-fiction story as a what-if instrument to make religious doctrine real by asserting it as the fictional given and then testing it with intellectual challenges.

A Canticle for Leibowitz addresses, directly or indirectly, various theological concerns. If there is another species possessing free will, is it then subject to the same pattern of divine history, with a fall from grace and a hope for redemption? Would a degenerate race lose its soul? At what point in human evolution is found *homo inspiratus*, the creation of the soul? Logically, must this not occur at one precise moment? How could it be developmental? Given the perceived scale of astronomical time, how long will it take the Second Coming to occur? Will it be a universal event, occurring everywhere at once, or in only one place at a time? (Miller's answer appears to be the latter.) If all are not on the same schedule, then what of those races that exist before the Fall? As humanity continues to evolve, what happens to its relationship to God? What happens if disaster breaks the apostolic succession of God's divinely ordained church?

Although his concerns may seem musty and medieval, Miller turns them into a compelling drama. He joins the argument that began in the Renaissance between science and religion, paradoxically using the naturalistic tone of "hard" science fiction to suggest that matters ordinarily resting on faith are literally true. A central artistic strategy of the novel, for example, is to make real the sense of historical development implicit in Christianity. As does Judaism, Christianity asserts a time line that includes creation, the Fall of Man, God's identification with a national people, the coming of a messiah, his death and resurrection, and ultimately the Second Coming, in which the meaning of history vanishes. From a Christian perspective, all steps but the last have been completed. From the perspective of modern astronomy, this may seem to be vainglorious mythmaking on an insignificant planet. Miller's precise purpose is to square these perspectives in the framework of the scientifically understood cosmos. If and when the space-traveling delegates of New Rome ever return to Earth, Bishop Zerchi declares, "you might meet the Archangel at the east end of Earth, guarding her passes with a sword of flame."

—*Bruce Olsen*

CARNACKI THE GHOST-FINDER

Psychic sleuth Carnacki investigates nine apparently supernatural phenomena

Author: William Hope Hodgson (1877-1918)
Genre: Fantasy—occult
Type of work: Stories
Time of plot: About 1910
Location: Great Britain (greater London, the South Coast, and northern England), Galway, and western Ireland
First published: 1913 (expanded version, 1947)

The Plot: Six stories, first published in *The Idler* in 1910 and *New Magazine* in 1910 and 1912, appeared in the original 1913 publication of *Carnacki the Ghost-Finder*.

Three additional stories were found among William Hope Hodgson's papers after his death and were included in an expanded edition published in 1947. The nine stories are presented by a first-person narrator (Dodgson), one of a group of four friends to whom Carnacki reports on his occult investigations. Three of the stories ("The Thing Invisible," "The Find," and "The House Among the Laurels") are mystery stories; two ("The Horse of the Invisible" and "The Searcher of the End House") have apparently rational conclusions that are compromised by elements that cannot be explained by rational means.

The investigations often involve the animation of inert objects to cause bodily harm or create a sense of imminent threat to life or sanity. In "The Thing Invisible," a knife displayed in a family chapel lives up to its reputation of striking murderously at enemies of the Jarnock family who enter the chapel at night. The door to the Grey Room in "The Gateway of the Monster" slams constantly at night while bedclothes are pulled from a bed and thrown into a corner of a room. Blood drips from the ceiling, sealed doors open, and candles and fires are extinguished in "The House Among the Laurels." The floor of "The Whistling Room" puckers like a gigantic pair of lips and whistles until the sound rises to a "mad screaming note."

More conventional occult manifestations involve the ghostly figures of a running boy and a woman in "The Searcher of the End House" and the thundering of the hooves of a gigantic, invisible horse that pursues the eldest child of a cursed family in "The Horse of the Invisible." In "The Hog," a gateway opens up to another dimension from which a monstrous creature attempts to break through onto our plane. In "The Haunted 'Jarvee,'" Carnacki attempts to "desensitize" a ship threatened by shadowy forces that attack it with the force of a raging, destructive storm.

Analysis: Hodgson's combination of classic detection with occult investigations was not without precedent. Hodgson's Carnacki is a younger version of J. Sheridan Le Fanu's Martin Hesselius (introduced in "Green Tea," 1869), a doctor of "metaphysical medicine," and Algernon Blackwood's title character of the story collection *John Silence, Physician Extraordinary* (1908). Unlike them, Carnacki has no medical training, but he does have a strong scientific bent, illustrated by his invention of an ingenious "Electric Pentacle," a variation of the cabalistic five-pointed star enclosed within a circle and intended to act as a barrier against malevolent occult forces. Carnacki refers to his use of formulae from ancient magic rituals as a "curious thing for a Twentieth Century man" that might provoke "cheap laughter" from some. Carnacki, however, will not allow himself to be "blinded" by ridicule: "I ask questions and keep my eyes open."

This self-deprecating definition by Carnacki of his character touches on aspects of the stories that seem to border on parody. The floor that sports puckered lips in "The Whistling Room" and the haunting of the Grey Room by a "monstrous hand" in "The Gateway of the Monster" are shown to be powerful agents of destruction that are nevertheless more grotesque than horrific. The trap that releases a deadly weapon is a clever but deflating conclusion for "The Thing Invisible." In other conclusions, a man emerges from a basement cistern with a leg of rotting mutton in his hand in "The Searcher of the End House" and, in "The Horse of the Invisible," the horse turns out to be a man wearing an enormous horse head and with "great hoofs" attached to his wrists. These conclusions certainly can provoke laughter that is not "cheap" but justified by the clumsy resolutions they encompass.

There remain those stories that largely succeed in their intended effect or those moments in otherwise flawed narratives that offset obvious weaknesses. The final three stories in the 1947 edition, found among Hodgson's papers and never published during his lifetime, are perhaps the most diverse and most interesting in the Carnacki series. "The Find" is a story of detection and demonstrates Hodgson's ability to tell an engrossing story without supernatural trappings. "The Haunted 'Jarvee'" is in the lineage of Hodgson's sea fiction, the eerie atmospherics rendered all the more effective for the realistic portrayal of the ship, which Hodgson based on his eight years spent at sea, reportedly traveling three times around the globe. This story does not include the detailed mythos of the Sargasso Sea that Hodgson developed in other of his sea stories, but its depiction of the ship as prey to the forces of a malevolent nature contains some of the best writing in the collection.

The final, longest story, "The Hog," is the most successful at sustaining a steadily escalating sense of terror. Carnacki fights to save his client—a dreamer whose nightmares are only too real—from the "monstrosities of the Outer Circle," predatory beings who seek to absorb our "psychic energy." The most important legatee of this story may be the Cthulhu mythos of H. P. Lovecraft, although Carnacki is able to thwart the psychic takeover of the dreamer's soul and body that is the awful fate of Lovecraft's doomed searchers after forbidden knowledge.

Despite a sometimes uncertain mix of thriller melodramatics and moments of finely achieved supernatural legerdemain, *Carnacki the Ghost-Finder* stands as one of Hodgson's most accessible works, at its best combining the fine eye for significant detail of detective fiction with the stomach-churning uneasiness engendered by supernatural fiction. Where classical detective fiction restores a sense of orderly process, Hodgson's dark imaginings posit a quiet resolution as only a temporary respite.

—*Walter Albert*

CARRIE

A young girl rejected by her high-school peers and her mother explores her powers of telekinesis and exacts revenge on her enemies

Author: Stephen King (1947-   )
Genre: Fantasy—extrasensory powers
Type of work: Novel
Time of plot: The 1960's
Location: Chamberlain, Maine
First published: 1974

The Plot: *Carrie* is Stephen King's first published novel, for which he received a $5,000 advance. With this book, he showed his interest in telekinesis and children, two motifs that characterize much of his fiction. The protagonist of the book, Carrie White, is almost eighteen and is a senior in high school.

King divides the novel roughly into two halves, "Blood Sport" and "Prom Night." In the first half, King introduces his method for telling the story, which is to write much of the story as anyone might, but with the inclusion of fictional newspaper stories and books written after the events of his book. This experimental technique adds objectivity to an understanding of what happens and makes clear that telekinesis remains misunderstood and may exist in some form.

In "Blood Sport," the reader encounters gangly and unpopular Carrie White while she takes a shower at school after gym class. While in the shower, she starts to menstruate for the first time, causing all the other girls to jeer at her and bringing out Carrie's power. The gym teacher intervenes, wondering how it is that a girl her age had never menstruated before and why her parents had never discussed it with her. When Carrie mentions the incident to her mother, a fundamentalist, she forces Carrie into a closet to pray for her sins.

The reader learns of telekinetic acts, including a rain of stones on the White house, and future reactions from

Carrie's classmates who survived her wrath. A primary character is Sue Snell, who does not go to the prom. She asks her boyfriend, Tommy Ross, to take Carrie instead. Chris Hargensen has been refused prom tickets for not taking the prescribed punishment for the taunting of Carrie, and she asks several local dropouts to get revenge on Carrie. Ignoring her mother's requests, Carrie goes to the dance with Tommy Ross, and through a rigged balloting, they are elected king and queen of the prom.

At the moment of crowning, Chris and an accomplice, Billy Nolan, pull strings that drench Carrie in blood and drop a bucket on Tommy Ross's head. The injury will kill Ross, though no one knows it at the time. Everyone laughs at Carrie, and she leaves. She goes home to her mother, who is waiting to kill her because she is tainted with the curse of blood. In a remarkable telekinetic scene, Carrie kills her mother and goes back downtown to the school, destroying gas stations and causing massive fires on the way. When she reaches the school, she telekinetically bolts the doors, trapping most of her schoolmates inside. They are destroyed through electrocutions and fire. Carrie dies of wounds inflicted by her mother and, King suggests, because she wanted to. He adds a kind of epilogue, "Wreckage," that collects information on the aftermath: 440 dead and resignations from administrators and teachers at the school.

The last paragraphs come from a letter from a relative of Carrie White. They chillingly indicate that in Tennessee there is a little girl, age two, who can make things move without touching them.

Analysis: King's first novel was slow in catching on. Once it had done so, however, it grabbed readers and critics alike, and a major motion picture was made from it in 1976. The novel uses the experimental technique of created books, reports, wire service copy, and other material, in some cases supposed to have been published ten years after the events of *Carrie*. These accounts tend to objectify the seemingly impossible events in the novel.

In choosing paranormal activity as one of the subjects of his novel, King realized that it had to be worked in slowly, yet quickly enough so the reader would have an idea what to expect. The incident of stones raining down on the White house is discussed fairly early, but only later do readers learn that Carrie was angry at her mother and showed her anger in that way. Similarly, when Carrie is at school, her telekinetic responses to her humiliation and, later, her response to a principal who cannot get her name right are minor events, almost accidents. Carrie does not know the extent of her powers. She is able to

control them expertly, however, by the time she agrees to go to the prom with Tommy Ross, over her mother's objections. Carrie forces her mother to sit down while she sews her own dress.

The real force of Carrie's telekinetic powers comes after the prom, when Carrie's mind seems to operate independently of her body. She has been drenched in pig's blood, and Tommy Ross has been killed by one of the buckets hitting his head. Even at that moment, though, Carrie does not strike back, unlike in the film version. She goes home to be comforted by her mother, who is waiting to kill the "witch child." Carrie is forced to kill her mother in self-defense. With nothing left of her life and nothing to look forward to, she goes back to the school for revenge. Her attack on the town seemingly is a test of the strength and control of her powers. Blinded by her mission, she seems to recognize none of the people stuck at the gas stations that she ignites.

King allows a few students and the gym teacher to escape the conflagration. Sue Snell had not gone to the prom, and she finds Carrie unconscious in the school parking lot, having just destroyed the car of Chris Hargensen and Billy Nolan. As readers learn from *My Name Is Sue Snell*, Sue's account of that night, she saw into Carrie's mind and found mostly darkness.

At the book's conclusion, the White house is destroyed, and the town has become a tourist attraction. King ends on a note of warning that telekinesis is not a toy but something very dark.   —*John Jacob*

A CASE OF CONSCIENCE

Convinced that the planet he is investigating has been created by Satan to delude humanity, a priest-biologist welcomes the dangerous experiment that destroys the planet and its intelligent inhabitants

Author: James Blish (1921-1975)
Genre: Science fiction—apocalypse
Type of work: Novel
Time of plot: 2049-2050
Location: Lithia, a planet 50 light-years from Earth; New York City; and Vatican City
First published: 1958 (book 1 abridged as "A Case of Conscience" in *If*, 1953)

The Plot: Ramon Ruiz-Sanchez is a Jesuit priest as well as a biologist with the United Nations (U.N.) survey team on the recently discovered planet of Lithia. Lithia, dominated by a species of intelligent reptilians, is an apparent utopia. The Lithians have no crime, no politics, and no religion, and their ethical code (otherwise identical to that of Christianity) is based on pure reason. Despite their planet's iron-poor crust, the Lithians have developed advanced technologies, including a planetary communications web based on pulses emitted by the gigantic Message Tree, the roots of which reach into the planet's bedrock.

When the survey team meets to make its recommendations before departing from Lithia, Ruiz is in surprising near-agreement with physicist Paul Cleaver. Cleaver advises closing the planet publicly while secretly turning it into a nuclear weapons laboratory. Ruiz also votes to close the planet, with a permanent quarantine, because he has become convinced that Satan created Lithia as a convincing demonstration that virtue is possible without God's grace. The other two team members recommend that Lithia be opened. The tie vote means that the planet will remain at least temporarily off limits. As the terrestrials leave, Ruiz's Lithian friend Chtexa gives him a farewell gift, a sealed vase containing the fertilized embryo of Chtexa's child. The embryo, as it develops outside the body, will replicate the evolutionary history of its species.

Book 2 opens in a U.N. laboratory back in New York, where Ruiz and lab director Liu Meid are observing the movements of the tiny Lithian, whose name (inscribed in his genetic code) is Egtverchi. When Lithia team member Mike Michelis arrives to request his help writing a nonclassified version of the Lithia report, Ruiz casually announces that he expects to be tried in Rome for teaching the heresy of diabolical creation.

As Egtverchi develops, it is clear to Ruiz that he will prove to be a sentient being eligible to become a naturalized U.N. citizen. Events rapidly prove Ruiz correct. Egtverchi, who reaches adulthood within months, becomes a television celebrity and a satirical commentator on terrestrial society. His large following seems to be composed primarily of psychopaths created by the unnatural living conditions of Earth's "shelter economy."

Meanwhile, the pope advises Ruiz to consider whether Lithia might be possessed rather than created by Satan. The distinction would allow Ruiz to abandon his heresy while literally exorcising the Lithian menace. As a last resort, Ruiz takes Egtverchi to the Canadian retreat of solid-state physicist Count d'Averoigne, who has devised an apparatus allowing simultaneous communication with the Message Tree. Egtverchi proves unresponsive to the remonstrances of his Lithian father, and Ruiz learns that Cleaver, back on Lithia in charge of the weapons project he proposed, is cutting down the Message Tree.

When Egtverchi's last broadcast touches off widespread rioting, the United Nations attempts to arrest him, but he stows away on a starship bound for Lithia. Ruiz, Liu, and Michelis join Count d'Averoigne at his lunar observatory, where he has set up a telescope that allows simultaneous viewing of interstellar objects. Communicating through the starship, the count has warned Cleaver that his experiment might destroy the planet, but he fears that Cleaver may stubbornly persist. Ruiz pronounces his exorcism shortly before the image of Lithia explodes, taking the monitor screen with it.

Analysis: *A Case of Conscience* compares favorably with other novels of apocalyptic science fiction, such as Arthur C. Clarke's *Childhood's End* (1953), and with other novels treating conflict between science and religion, such as Walter M. Miller, Jr.'s *A Canticle for Leibowitz* (1960). For the most part it avoids the sentimental, stilted narrative voice that often blemishes science fiction with a cosmic reach, and the machinery of its tight plot does not dissipate the "double truth" of its theme.

It is much to the credit of James Blish's novel that it does not attempt to downplay the very real conflict between the scientific and religious worldviews. Instead, it thematizes that conflict in the attractively human-scale figure of Ruiz. Ruiz underlines the novel's title by constantly being attuned to the promptings of conscience, no matter how inconvenient, and constantly aware of his mental life, whether it is driven by reason or by emotion. He is mortified when the pope shows him that his lapse into heresy was the result of an unscientific failure to consider alternative hypotheses. He is annoyed by his chronic sinusitis. He is bemused when he finds himself, a professed celibate, having vaguely lustful thoughts about the nubile and modest Liu Meid. He is aware of his own worldly satisfaction when he proves to be correct in his predictions. At once a minister of religion and a practicing scientist, Ruiz knows that apparently contrary propositions can be said to be true—the sick child is saved by prayer, *and* she is saved by an antibiotic. Lithia is destroyed by an exorcist, *and* the planet is destroyed in a massive industrial accident.

A blemish on the novel is the caricature of the amoral scientist in the form of Paul Cleaver, who comes across as a pasteboard villain, cursing, angry, and violent for no particular reason. His assertion of scientific and technological arrogance is too much like the vulgarity of the real estate developer who wants to build a shopping center in the last piece of wetland. He is thus in stark contrast to the complex and tormented Ruiz. The severe contrast can make the novel seem less ambiguous than it is. Few writers, however, can resist the urge to indulge in the luxury of a comical villain, and despite this fault Blish's novel improves with each rereading.   —*John P. Brennan*

THE CASTLE OF OTRANTO

An evil usurper suffers the consequences of his actions as supernatural events and the heroic efforts of the rightful heirs to the principality of Otranto conspire to supplant him from his ill-gotten position

Author: Horace Walpole (1717-1797)
Genre: Fantasy—heroic fantasy
Type of work: Novel
Time of plot: The late medieval period (twelfth century)
Location: The principality of Otranto in Italy
First published: 1764

The Plot: In *The Castle of Otranto*, recognized as the first gothic novel, Horace Walpole combines supernatural occurrences and heroic behaviors associated with the Romantic tradition to tell the story of Manfred, prince of Otranto, whose zeal for satisfying his own lusts for power and sexual gratification lead to his downfall. The tale opens on the wedding day of Manfred's son Conrad, who is betrothed to the countess Isabella. Before the ceremony, a giant helmet falls from a parapet, crushing Conrad. A peasant, Theodore, claims that the helmet is like that on the statue of the good Prince Alonso; angered, Manfred has Theodore imprisoned.

Manfred then concocts a scheme to be divorced from his wife, Hippolita, and marry Isabella himself. Isabella is repulsed by the idea and flees into a passage beneath the castle; there she meets Theodore, who has escaped from imprisonment. He helps Isabella make her way to a nearby church. Manfred recaptures Theodore, but as he accosts him, word comes that a giant is sleeping in the castle.

The next day, Father Jerome comes to inform Manfred that Isabella is safe in the church. Manfred uses the occasion to suggest his divorce and remarriage. Father Jerome is horrified, particularly because he believes Isabella is in love with someone else. Thinking Theodore is his rival, Manfred orders him executed, but when Father Jerome discovers a strange mark on the young man, he announces that Theodore is really his own son. The two are actually of noble blood, but circumstances forced Jerome to enter the priesthood when his family was kidnapped years before.

As they are speaking, the Knight of the Gigantic Saber arrives at the castle, bringing with him a giant sword. This knight comes from Isabella's father, the rightful heir to Otranto. Manfred tries to convince this emissary that a marriage to Isabella would unite the two families, but the knight is unconvinced. Father Jerome arrives to announce that Isabella has fled the church. As the parties scurry to mount a search, Matilda, Manfred's daughter, meets Theodore and helps him escape. The two instantly fall in love. Fleeing the castle, Theodore stumbles upon Isabella in the forest. Their reunion is cut short when the Knight of the Giant Saber finds them. In attempting to protect Isabella, Theodore wounds the knight. Near death, the emissary reveals that he is really Isabella's father.

Although grievously hurt, the knight is taken back to the castle to recover. There he reveals that the giant sword he carries with him bears an ominous inscription foretelling doom for Manfred. Manfred tries desperately to convince Isabella's father to unite them, but he fails. Instead, he learns from a mysterious visitor that Theodore is in the chapel with a woman. He dashes there and stabs the maiden, who turns out to be his daughter Matilda. Into this climactic scene comes the ghost of Prince Alonso, who declares Theodore to be the true heir of Otranto, as grandson of Alonso's sister. Beaten, Manfred retreats to a convent, as does his neglected wife, Hippolita. Although grieving for Matilda, Theodore marries Isabella and assumes his place as the new Prince of Otranto.

Analysis: The son of the celebrated Prime Minister Robert Walpole, Horace Walpole was a dilettante at politics but a serious student of the Middle Ages. Taken with antiquities (he wrote several volumes of nonfiction on historical subjects), Walpole wrote *The Castle of Otranto* to combine in one volume two of his most passionate interests: a fascination with the supernatural and a keen appreciation of the medieval romance. Walpole turned away from the growing appetite of the English reading public for realism, seen most vividly in the works of his contemporaries Henry Fielding, Samuel Richardson, and Tobias Smollett; instead, he capitalized on readers' interest in the "far away," as evidenced by the popularity of numerous travel books in the eighteenth century.

The accuracy of his judgment about readers' tastes is borne out by the spate of "gothic" novels that followed the publication of Walpole's slim volume. For the next sixty years, works such as Clara Reeves's *The Old English Baron* (1778), Ann Radcliffe's *The Mysteries of Udolpho* (1794), Matthew Gregory Lewis' *The Monk* (1796), and Charles Robert Maturin's *Melmoth the Wan-*

derer (1820) captivated readers in England and on the Continent.

Throughout *The Castle of Otranto*, Walpole sacrifices complexity of characterization for intricacies of plotting. His heroes and heroines are little more than cardboard cutouts representing good or evil. The villain Manfred evokes little sympathy, and the plethora of admirable characters exist with hardly a blemish on their characters. Although he claimed that his model was William Shakespeare, Walpole is actually more closely aligned with the writers of revenge tragedies and tragedies of blood, dramas that were popular in the early decades of the seventeenth century. He makes use, as did those types of work, of sinister suggestions and ominous supernatural occurrences that highlight the impending doom for those who practice evil.

Walpole's primary contribution to the development of fantasy literature, however, lies in his focus on the reaction of men and women to extraordinary events: He is less interested in the appearance of ghosts and giants for their own sake than he is in gauging the reaction of his heroes and heroines to these aberrations. Although it may be difficult to classify Manfred, Theodore, Isabella, and Matilda as "ordinary," in Walpole's view they represent "real" men and women placed in extraordinary circumstances. Whether their trials occur on a strange planet or in strange circumstances on Earth, they reveal to readers the best and the worst of human nature when their values are tested.

—*Laurence W. Mazzeno*

CAT'S CRADLE

Ice-nine, the invention of Dr. Felix Hoenikker, brings an apocalyptic end to all earthly life-forms except a handful of human survivors and a colony of adaptive ants

Author: Kurt Vonnegut, Jr. (1922-   )
Genre: Science fiction—apocalypse
Type of work: Novel
Time of plot: The early 1960's
Location: The city of Ilium, New York, and the Republic of San Lorenzo, in the Caribbean
First published: 1963

The Plot: *Cat's Cradle* has a convoluted plot that develops with all the apparent chaos of a crazy quilt. The main character of the novel is its narrator, John, whose last name is not known; the novel, however, centers not on him but on ice-nine, the invention of a genius named Dr. Felix Hoenikker. Even in infinitesimal quantities, ice-

nine freezes and transforms to ice-nine any liquid it contacts. The novel recounts how the world ends in an ice-nine chain reaction.

At the novel's opening, Dr. Hoenikker, a Nobel Prize-winning scientist and one of the creators of the atomic bomb, is already dead. The narrator, nominally involved in writing a book about the day the first bomb was dropped on Japan, conducts several interviews with Hoenikker's associates and family. He inadvertently pieces together the facts about ice-nine. After Hoenikker's death, his three offspring had divided up the small sample of ice-nine their father had developed as a means of solving the problems that mud posed for the military. Hoenikker's children prove to be poor guardians of the substance. Newt Hoenikker, a midget, gives his ice-nine to his lover, Zinka, a Ukrainian midget and dancer who married Newt only to get his ice-nine for the Soviet Union. His ugly sister, Angela, is bilked out of hers by her handsome, philandering husband, Harrison C. Conners. Franklin Hoenikker intimates that Conners married Angela only to gain possession of her ice-nine for the U.S. government. Franklin, the middle sibling, is a major general and minister of science and progress in the Republic of San Lorenzo, an island country in the Caribbean. He gives his ice-nine to San Lorenzo's president, "Papa" Monzano, who wears it as an amulet in a cylinder on a neck chain. Because he is terminally ill, President Monzano swallows the ice-nine to end his suffering and destroy the world. His aim is fulfilled when his frozen remains are accidentally dumped into the Caribbean.

While introducing the reader to a series of eccentric characters, John also reveals that he is a disciple of Bokononism, a quasi-religious philosophy he adopts after flying to San Lorenzo. Many of the other characters belong to John's *karass*, the Bokononian term for a team of people who are bound together to work the will of God without being conscious that they are doing so. John's *karass* is fated to destroy humanity.

As the novel proceeds toward that end, John becomes increasingly involved in the events that bring about the end of the world. Beginning as a passive observer-writer, he turns into a major player. Shortly prior to the book's finale, he replaces the dying "Papa" Monzano as president of San Lorenzo and marries Mona Aamons Monzano, the exquisitely beautiful native woman of his febrile dreams. Unhappily for John, thanks to the destructive designs of his predecessor, his triumph is short-lived, and at the end of the book he, Mona, and the other survivors of the ice-nine cataclysm resign themselves to their own and humankind's extinction.

Analysis: Kurt Vonnegut, Jr., distances his readers from the novel's grim vision through his Rabelaisian humor, but zany as the book is, its underlying disenchantment with society and its various institutions is ubiquitous and inescapable. Even the narrator's adopted Bokononism views itself as nonsense, but this cheerful admission is made in the process of revealing that most human organizations and institutions are *granfalloon*, or false *karasses* with meaningless beliefs, much like the cat's cradle, string wound around fingers of human hands, having nothing to do with either cats or cradles—an appropriate symbol for the novel's nihilism.

Like many novels and plays written in the early decades of the Cold War era, *Cat's Cradle* uses varieties of the absurd to articulate its existential theme. Many of its characters are physically, emotionally, or mentally abnormal or deficient. Dr. Hoenikker, a scientific genius, has no feelings and reacts to his children's pain by stringing together a cat's cradle of noninvolvement. Others express themselves in seemingly incongruous ways. The gangly Angela, for example, plays the clarinet with consummate skill and haunting beauty. Others are emotionally crippled by their pasts, as is von Koenigswald, formerly a doctor at Auschwitz, who attempts a Sisyphean atonement for his past by saving lives at San Lorenzo's House of Hope and Mercy.

Vonnegut's plain style and understated expression complement the narrator's stoic resignation. Even after he becomes personally involved in the events, John records them with the dispassionate detachment of a reporter, without judgment or blame. Presumably, the discourse reflects the Bokononian *que sera sera* serenity of John, whose recounting of the events is made in the wake of the cataclysmic disaster, when he knows that his effort is futile and that the book he set out to write can never be published or read.

The matter-of-fact tone of the novel counterpoints its oddball characters and their unusual lives. Vonnegut shows his great inventive power both in creating such a bizarre assortment of human misfits and in drawing them together as a *karass*, in which their lives intertwine with Bokononian inevitability.

Not all the characters belong to John's *karass*; some simply play a role and disappear. An example is Dr. Asa Breed, a hostile, distressingly normal character who discloses information about Dr. Hoenikker and ice-nine vital to John's research and the reader's understanding. Most of the developed characters are around at or near the end of the novel. These include some, like the Crosbys, whose sense of belonging in the surviving group is

based on a false premise, a Bokononian *granfalloon*. In Vonnegut's wonderfully farfetched Bokononian world, even the lives of those outside a *karass* can merge, like parallel lines that defy all mathematical logic and somehow converge.

—*John Fiero*

THE CAVES OF STEEL and THE NAKED SUN

Police detective Elijah Baley, with the aid of the robot R. Daneel Olivaw, solves murders in an enclosed New York City of the future and on the planet Solaria

Author: Isaac Asimov (1920-1992)
Genre: Science fiction—artificial intelligence
Type of work: Novels
Time of plot: About A.D. 5000
Location: New York City and the planet Solaria
First published: *The Caves of Steel* (1954; serial form, *Galaxy*, October-December, 1953) and *The Naked Sun* (1957; serial form, *Astounding Science-Fiction*, October-December, 1956)

The Plot: Isaac Asimov wrote *The Caves of Steel*, under the persuasion of Horace Gold of *Galaxy* magazine, as a follow-up to his popular robot short stories. Following its success, Asimov wrote a sequel, *The Naked Sun*, for rival magazine publisher John Campbell, Jr., and for Doubleday Books.

The novels envision a future humanity split into two antagonistic groups. Those remaining on Earth have developed a fear of open spaces. They live in covered megacities, the "caves of steel" of the title, resigned to extreme overcrowding and rationing of virtually all amenities. The Spacers, descendants of the colonizers of fifty "Outer Worlds," have much longer life spans and superior technology on their sparsely populated planets, and they forbid "disease-ridden" earthlings from immigrating to their worlds.

Spacers make extensive use of robots. The more primitive models permitted on Earth are violently hated by most City dwellers, especially "Medievalists," who yearn sentimentally for pre-City days. The only contact between Spacers and Earthmen is through Spacetown, a diplomatic/military base at the western edge of New York City.

As *The Caves of Steel* opens, police detective Elijah "Lije" Baley is summoned by his Medievalist boss, Commissioner Julius Enderby, to investigate a murder. A Spacer robot scientist named Sarton has been shot in Spacetown, presumably by an Earthman. Baley must accept as a partner a Spacer robot created by Sarton. The robot, named R. Daneel Olivaw, looks human enough to "pass" among hostile Earthmen.

In the course of the investigation, Lije makes a number of embarrassing wrong guesses. He first supposes that Daneel is really Sarton in disguise but is convinced when Daneel exposes the machinery beneath his skin. Later, he guesses that Daneel is the killer. An expert convinces the Earthman that the Three Laws of Robotics built into a robot's positronic brain absolutely prevent it from intentionally harming a human. Lije is dismayed to find that his wife works for a secret Medievalist society, though she appears innocent of the crime. Finally, Lije proves that Enderby is the killer. Daneel reveals that the Spacers' ultimate goal on Earth is to convince Earthmen to break out of their stagnant cities to colonize uninhabited planets, with the help of robots.

The Naked Sun shifts the setting to the planet Solaria, where Lije and Daneel attempt to solve another murder. Lije is extremely reluctant to accept the assignment because of his Earthman's agoraphobia, but his boss orders him to do so because his observations can be invaluable to Earth intelligence. Dr. Rikaine Delmarre has been clubbed to death with a blunt object, which is now missing. His wife, Gladia, was found in a faint near the body, and a robot witness's positronic brain has gone haywire. Solarian security chief Hannis Gruer believes that Gladia is connected to a plot against the human race that Delmarre was uncovering. Gruer himself is the victim of a nearly fatal poisoning.

Lije is pleased to be reunited with Daneel and startled to learn that Solarians have a phobia of their own: Living alone on large estates, communicating via holographic projections, they have a horror of physical human contact or even presence. Marriage and procreation are seen as distasteful necessities, fetuses are removed for incubation, and children are raised on "baby farms."

In the course of the novel, Lije feels drawn to Gladia, who seems to have a repressed interest in close contact with a fellow human. Lije seeks to overcome his fear of open spaces under a "naked sun." Escaping from Daneel, who wishes to keep him "from harm" (as the Three Laws of Robotics direct) by not letting him travel out of doors, Lije contacts five suspects—a family doctor, a sociologist, the acting security chief, a supervisor at the baby farm, and a roboticist. He brings them and Gladia into one room (holographically), in classic detective fashion, for the denouement. The villain turns out to be the roboticist, Jothan Leebig, who has found ways of circumventing the Three Laws of Robotics and tricking robots into

becoming agents of crime. He also has manipulated Gladia. Gladia moves to the planet Aurora so that she can obtain human company, and Lije makes a plea to his supervisor concerning the need for Earthmen to overcome their own fears and colonize the stars.

Analysis: Although Asimov's name is strongly connected to science fiction concerning robots, he did not invent the word "robot"; the haunting title of his first story collection, *I, Robot* (1950), was taken from another writer; and the idea of writing a robot detective novel set on an overpopulated Earth came from Horace Gold of *Galaxy*. Asimov did coin the word "robotics," as he often noted with pride, and much more important, he created a body of work that has deeply influenced almost all science fiction involving robots that goes beyond simple views of robots as killing machines.

Asimov's influence extended beyond literature to visual media. Famous examples include the amusing Robbie of the film *Forbidden Planet* (1956); the Vulcan Spock of the *Star Trek* (1966-1969) television series and later films, who although flesh and blood is a close cousin to Daneel in his devotion to logic and his utterly impassive tone; the android Data of *Star Trek: The Next Generation* (1987-1993), whose "positronic brain" is the writers' direct homage to Asimov; and the Replicants of the film *Blade Runner* (1982). The Replicants, unlike Asimov's robots, had no qualms about harming the humans they perfectly resembled. Like Asimov's robots, however, they could be detected as nonhuman via a questionnaire, much like the one administered to Daneel in *The Caves of Steel*.

Asimov saw fit to describe the two novels as "a perfect fusion of the murder mystery and the science-fiction novel." Even if critics have found flaws in both the mystery writing and the science fiction, one could hardly disagree about the fusion. In each novel, the solution depends on a human psychology determined by the technological environment of Earth or Solaria. Moreover, the robot detective is the ultimate embodiment of the mythic sleuth of the Sherlock Holmes variety: a creature of pure logic. Daneel is such a vivid creation that readers often forget that in both novels he is really only a sidekick to Lije Baley, who brilliantly solves both murders. In *The Naked Sun*, Lije frequently reminds himself that robots are "logical but not reasonable," though this distinction is never made clear.

Of the two novels, *The Naked Sun* is much more in the classic mystery tradition, with practically a "locked room" murder and all the suspects brought together for the denouement. It seamlessly weaves social concerns of Asimov's own era into the plot, such as worries about technological advances that may lead to extreme social isolation. *The Caves of Steel* is much less concerned with crime solving in some of its chapters. Its goal is to provide an in-depth study of a future City, its spectacle and its social problems. Written at a time when the United States reveled in its postwar prosperity and international power, *The Caves of Steel* is about the dangers of the coming megalopolis, including overcrowding and overreliance on a technological infrastructure. It also seems to foreshadow U.S. fears of losing status as an economic and technological superpower; perhaps Asimov was thinking more of the losses of the British Empire or the shift in local power from inner cities to the "outer worlds" of the suburbs.

Readers of the late twentieth century and beyond may smile at a few of the novels' lapses in predicting the future. For example, no one seems to have thought of shatterproof lenses for eyeglasses. The same reader may feel some dismay at the author's indulgence in certain social stereotypes of his era. For example, Lije's wife, Jessie, the only female character in *The Caves of Steel*, is constantly underlined as a "typical woman," which is to say that she is pathetically hysterical and dependent, whether in her role as a housewife or indulging in secret meetings. Gladia, in the second novel, falls into the category of the femme fatale, but she literally knows not what she does. She is, at least, conceived as a more complex character. Future critics will doubtless explore Asimov's views of imperial expansion and his analogies of robots to human slaves.

Asimov began another novel soon after the success of *The Naked Sun*, aiming for a trilogy, but he abandoned it. Only after the popularity of a sequel to his Foundation series, years later, did he decide to write *The Robots of Dawn* (1983), set on Aurora and featuring Gladia as well as the detectives, followed by *Robots and Empire* (1985), which linked the Robot series to the Foundation series.

—*Joseph Milicia*

THE CENTAUR

A metaphysical journey, enabled by the consciousness of the Mother Earth, to unite with the Cosmic Soul and witness the spiritual Garden of Eden

Author: Algernon Blackwood (1869-1951)
Genre: Fantasy—Magical Realism
Type of work: Novel

Time of plot: The early 1900's
Location: Aboard ship through the Mediterranean Sea, and the Caucasus
First published: 1911

The Plot: At the start of *The Centaur* readers are introduced to Terence O'Malley by his executor, who recounts the story after O'Malley's death. In his executor's telling of the story, O'Malley is a psychic and sensitive who responds to the moods and passion of Nature. By profession O'Malley is a journalist, a foreign correspondent whose latest commission is to write about the Caucasus. He had also turned his pen to fiction, producing two books of psychic tales. These had led O'Malley to correspond with a German doctor, Heinrich Stahl.

The two meet on a ship bound for the Caucasus. On this steamer, O'Malley encounters a massive Russian and his son, whose very presence arouse O'Malley's spirit. Through Stahl, O'Malley learns that these are *urmenschen*, or "primitive men," whose bodies contain a fragment of the earth-spirit. Although physically they appear human, their psychic body is much larger, and when they come within the focus of anyone sensitive to the power of Nature, their presence takes on other imagery. O'Malley likens them to centaurs, men who draw their power from the spirit of the Mother Earth, as many once did before the onset of civilization. They are, in effect, Cosmic Beings.

O'Malley shares a cabin with them one night and is almost overwhelmed by the power of their presence. He is saved by the intervention of Dr. Stahl. O'Malley's spirit, though, is hooked, having seen a glimpse beyond the gates of Eden.

By the time O'Malley arrives in Turkey he is under the spell of the Call of the Wild, and it is only the impact of civilization upon his senses that stops him from being lost to the power of Nature. For a month O'Malley returns to his work as a writer. This part of the book allows Algernon Blackwood to reflect upon the nature of civilization and how the advance of the human soul is measured by the progress of science rather than its relationship to the world, particular affinity with the Mother Earth.

Eventually, O'Malley falls again to the lure of the *urmenschen* and follows them deep into the Caucasus, where his spirit increasingly opens to the power of Earth's consciousness. Lost in the mountains, O'Malley is privileged to have a vision of the Mother Earth in the form of a spiritual Garden of Eden. His channel for this vision is the soul of the Russian, who has returned to the Mother Earth while his physical body died.

Once witness to this, O'Malley is never able to return to a normal life. His body becomes a shell as his spirit yearns to merge with the Cosmic Consciousness of the Earth. As a result, his body fails and dies, but his spirit has reached eternal bliss. The conclusion of the novel, when a street musician playing on the pan pipes allows O'Malley's soul to depart, is among Blackwood's most beautiful pieces of writing.

Analysis: Although *The Centaur* was Blackwood's own favorite novel, it is not his most personal. That epithet belongs to *The Wave: An Egyptian Aftermath* (1916). It is, however, his most religious novel because it comes closest to reflecting his own world belief. It was inspired by Blackwood's journey through the Caucasus in 1910, a trip that left his spirit so numbed by beauty and vision that for a while he was unable to write. One short story, "Imagination" (*Ten Minute Stories*, 1914), describes this writer's block and serves as a preamble to *The Centaur* in its evocation of the Earth spirit. It was only when Blackwood heard a street musician outside his own London flat—a scene that inspired the conclusion of the novel—that Blackwood's own spirit was freed and the book began to form.

In *The Centaur*, Blackwood expresses his view of humanity's relationship with the world. By using the theories of Gustav Fechner and William James, quotations from whose works head each chapter, Blackwood explores the possibility that Earth is sentient and it is the projection of the Earth-soul that creates visions of creatures of legend (such as centaurs and nymphs) among the psychically sensitive. Civilization has dulled people's basic senses, which is why so few are aware of the planet's soul. It is through this exploration of the metaphysical that Blackwood's book can be regarded as a precursor to modern Magical Realism, because he infuses the world with the power and spirit of Earth's soul.

The visions that Blackwood sought to explore stretched him to the limits of his narrative power. Language was too blunt an instrument to describe the mystical beauty of spiritual paradise, and there are times when the book becomes too verbose and too cluttered with emotion as Blackwood strives to liberate the reader's imagination. Near the novel's climax, after passages of intense vision, Blackwood finds himself having to resort to such ineffective phrases as "he knew *all over*" and "He knew the Great At-one-ment," phrases that are inadequate to portray the supremacy of union that O'Malley's spirit has attained, simply because Blackwood has exhausted all language in reaching this spiritual orgasm. Elsewhere

Blackwood captures a vision of intense wonder in the phrase "all the forgotten gods moved forward into life."

Because *The Centaur* reflects Blackwood's own spiritual and mystical experiences in the Caucasus, it is a novel of mystical realism, a forerunner of books by Carlos Castaneda and others. Blackwood was the first great writer to fuse aspects of the mystical, the occult, and pantheism to create works of genuine supernaturalism. Despite the occasional inadequacy of language, which is more the fault of written communication than of Blackwood as Nature's messenger, *The Centaur* is the peak of Blackwood's visionary writing.   *—Mike Ashley*

THE CHILD GARDEN

Milena defeats the bioengineered viruses that have reshaped humanity's future and teaches the trapped, childlike souls of the Consensus how to transcend their prison and become angels

Author: Geoff Ryman (1951-   )
Genre: Science fiction—extrapolatory
Type of work: Novel
Time of plot: The near future
Location: Czechoslovakia, London, and outer space
First published: 1989

The Plot: In the futuristic London of *The Child Garden* (subtitled *A Low Comedy*), bioengineered viruses infect people with common knowledge. Babies can add, and five-year-olds quote William Shakespeare. The viruses were designed to cure cancer. Unfortunately, the cure is worse than the disease, because cells now lack the ability to reproduce after a person reaches the age of thirty-five, halving the normal human life span.

The Consensus governs. It comprises personality copies of all the people who are "read" into it. Reading usually occurs when a person reaches ten years of age. After the reading, a person is given viruses to destroy any undesirable traits.

Milena is virus resistant. She is attracted to women (which is considered "bad grammar"), and the Consensus does not read her because she is unique and creative. She is unhappy as an actress because plays are now being performed as "remembered" and not as vital productions. She meets Rolfa, who is a genetically engineered person resembling a polar bear. Rolfa is a singer who has created an original opera based on Dante's *The Divine Comedy* (c. 1320). Milena comes to love Rolfa and wants her to get the benefits of the Consensus—including housing and food—so that she can continue producing her music. She arranges for Rolfa to be read and infected with viruses. It is not until Rolfa is infected that Milena discovers that Rolfa is also attracted to her. The viruses drastically change Rolfa's personality, and she leaves Milena and goes to Antarctica to work in her family's business.

Milena decides to produce Rolfa's opera, and the Consensus offers to help. They plan on having a huge production, projected across the sky from outer space. Milena goes into space with astronaut Mike Stone, who repeatedly asks Milena to marry him. Milena carries the memory of a rose Rolfa once gave her. She tests the projection equipment by sending a copy of the rose holographically to each of the people on Earth.

Meanwhile, the viruses are causing many dangerous and exasperating mutations. Especially disturbing are the "bees," people who are empathic and can uncontrollably change minds with another's consciousness, even that of an animal.

Milena learns that the Consensus wants her to be their ambassador in space, holding a model of their world in her mind as she searches out a mate for them. She is told this by the angel Bob, a composite consciousness the Consensus has sent into the Charley Slides, the lines of gravity that compose the universe. Milena then develops cancer. The doctors can use her cells to reinfect people and help them live longer, but her cancer means that Milena cannot personally direct the Comedy, because she is dying. She has married Mike Stone and he is carrying their child, attached to his bowel, within him.

During the final night of the performance, Milena is read, and a copy of her consciousness is stored inside the Consensus. It refuses to do their bidding. The soul attached to Milena's body rises into space as she dies. It tries to convince the childlike souls trapped by the Consensus to become angels. Many flee, including the soul of Rolfa, which joins with Milena, as do all the other parts of Milena's personality that were lost to her. Milena discovers wholeness, and all times become transcendentally "now."

Analysis: Geoff Ryman's *The Child Garden* is an exceptionally literate science-fiction novel. Within the framework of a future in which the human life span has been disastrously reduced by bioengineered attempts to make people disease free and intellectually equal, it raises issues of sexuality, creativity, consciousness, and social responsibility. It contains philosophically complex yet surprisingly entertaining arguments about the relationship between good government and tyranny as well as

society's responsibilities to its less fortunate members. It argues that equality cannot occur by suppressing a person's unique and individual soul, even if that person carries characteristics considered to be "deviant" within the fabric of society. Such suppression results in losses to the culture far in excess of the gains.

Ryman passionately argues that it is up to individuals to take responsibility for themselves, for the underprivileged, and for making sure that the government becomes compassionate and just. He forces his main character, Milena, not only to take on these responsibilities but also to embrace all the diverse, childlike, and even unattractive parts of herself. The message is that before people can be expected to accept, much less love, the rest of flawed humanity they must learn to accept themselves.

Ryman won the 1990 John W. Campbell Memorial Award for *The Child Garden*. His first major success was the novella *The Unconquered Country* (1984), a heart-wrenching metaphorical exploration of the war in Southeast Asia that concerns issues of social and personal responsibility, individuality, and creativity. It contains a wealth of incredibly powerful imagery stemming from wartime uses of bioengineering. The expansion of the novella, *The Unconquered Country: A Life History* (1986), won both the British Science Fiction and the World Fantasy awards. The novella appears in a collection called *Unconquered Countries* (1994) that also includes "A Fall of Angels," a story employing Ryman's themes of consciousness, responsibility, and love. It is a longer exploration of the lives of the angels, described in *The Child Garden*, who travel the Charley Slides that radiate through outer space.

Ryman's later novel *Was* (1992) is set in the United States from the time of writer L. Frank Baum (1856-1919), author of *The Wonderful Wizard of Oz* (1900), to the present. It focuses on social issues, specifically concentrating on child abuse, homosexuality, and the treatment of people with acquired immune deficiency syndrome (AIDS). Ryman manages to create yet another beautifully transcendent novel working with these painful and difficult topics. As Ryman ably demonstrates in *The Child Garden*, he is a master at using the tools of science fiction and fantasy to show how the human spirit can drag itself up and become gloriously transcendent.

—*Shira Daemon*

THE CHILDE CYCLE

Prompted by various near-supermen, the human race splinters into the Men of War, Men of Faith, and Men of

Philosophy, and then begins the laborious process of reintegration

Author: Gordon R. Dickson (1923-   )
Genre: Science fiction—future history
Type of work: Novels
Time of plot: The late twenty-first century to the late twenty-fourth century
Location: Sixteen human-inhabited planets in eight star systems
First published: *The Genetic General* (1960; serial form, "Dorsai!," *Astounding Science-Fiction*, May-July, 1959), *Necromancer* (1962; also titled *No Room for Man*, 1963), *Soldier, Ask Not* (1967; serial form, *Galaxy*, 1964), *The Tactics of Mistake* (1971), *Three to Dorsai!* (1975; contains *Necromancer*, *The Tactics of Mistake*, and *The Genetic General*), *Dorsai!* (1976; contains *The Genetic General* with restored text), *The Spirit of Dorsai* (1979; includes "Amanda Morgan," "Brothers," and three bridge sections; "Brothers" first appeared in *Astounding: John W. Campbell Memorial Anthology*, 1973), *Lost Dorsai* (1980; includes "Lost Dorsai," "Warrior," a critical essay, and an excerpt from *The Final Encyclopedia*; serial form of "Lost Dorsai," *Destinies*, February-March, 1980; serial form of "Warrior," *Analog*, December, 1965), *The Dorsai Companion* (1986; contains most of *The Spirit of Dorsai* and *Lost Dorsai*; adds new material), *The Final Encyclopedia* (1984), *The Chantry Guild* (1988), *Young Bleys* (1991), *Lost Dorsai: The New Dorsai Companion* (1993; contains most of the fiction from *Lost Dorsai* and excerpts from "A Childe Cycle Concordance"), and *Other* (1994)

The Plot: The Childe Cycle (also known as the Dorsai Cycle) of novels and stories actually begins with *Necromancer*, in the later part of the twenty-first century, on an Earth ruled cautiously by the computers of the World Complex. Paul Formain, a one-armed mining engineer, resolves a stalemate between Kirk Tyne, head engineer of the World Complex, and Walter Blunt, head of the Chantry Guild. The Guild seeks the violent overthrow of the technocracy headed by Tyne. Formain manages to wrest control of the Guild from Blunt and send the human race out to the stars, something neither Tyne nor Blunt wanted.

The Tactics of Mistake takes place a century later, after the human race has settled Mars and Venus as well as thirteen other planets—called the Younger Worlds—orbiting seven other star systems. Cletus Grahame, a

military genius from the planet Dorsai, pits himself against one of the most powerful men on Earth, Dow deCastries. Grahame wins the conflict, thus gaining independence from Earth for the Younger Worlds.

By the time of *Soldier, Ask Not*, in the late twenty-third century, the human race has fragmented into specialized types, called Splinter Cultures. The three main types are the Men of War (Dorsai), who live on Dorsai; the Men of Faith (Friendlies), who live on Harmony and Association; and the Men of Philosophy (Exotics), who live on Kultis and Mara. Helping to link all the Younger Worlds together are the members of the Interstellar News Services, including Tam Olyn. After seeing his brother-in-law killed in cold blood by a Friendly mercenary, Olyn embarks on a vendetta against Harmony and Association. When he is thwarted, Olyn returns to Earth, eventually to take over the directorship of the Final Encyclopedia, a gigantic information storage system orbiting the Mother Planet.

Dorsai! also takes place during the late twenty-third century. It is the story of Donal Grahame, great-great-grandson of Cletus Grahame, who uses his Dorsai military training and what he calls "intuitional logic" to overcome William of Ceta, a merchant who nearly succeeds in controlling the complicated transactions that tie the Younger Worlds together economically. Donal, like his ancestor Cletus, frees the Younger Worlds from a threat to their independence.

The last four novels in the series (as of 1995) are all set around the middle of the twenty-fourth century, and they all concern two powerful antagonists: Hal Mayne and Bleys Ahrens. They are antagonists because each is the human embodiment of a different historical response of the "racial animal"—Gordon Dickson's name for the consciousness of the human race as a whole—to the crisis of the Splinter Cultures' failure. Bleys wishes the human race to stop changing; Hal wishes the race to keep changing, for the specialized types of the Splinter Cultures to become reintegrated, and for the reemergence of an improved "full spectrum" humanity.

Young Bleys details Bleys Ahrens' childhood, adolescence, and young manhood, ending in his taking control from his older brother, Dahno, of an organization called the Others. *Other* records the initial moves in Bleys Ahrens' quest to rule most of the Younger Worlds.

The Final Encyclopedia begins where *Young Bleys* ends, with the death of Hal Mayne's three tutors at the hands of Bleys's bodyguards. It traces a similar period in Hal's life, ending with Hal blockading himself, the Final Encyclopedia, Old Earth, and nearly everyone from the

Dorsai behind an impenetrable shield. Outside are Bleys's minions, with time, power, and technology on their side.

Three years later, at the beginning of *The Chantry Guild*, Hal is despondent at not being able to find a way of using the Final Encyclopedia to gain entrance to what he calls the Creative Universe. Eventually, Hal works his way out of the impasse after journeying to a new Chantry Guild hidden on Kultis, one of the two Exotic planets, now under occupation by soldiers controlled by the Others.

In addition to these novels, Dickson has written four shorter Childe Cycle pieces. He calls these shorter pieces "illuminations" because they shed light on events only briefly mentioned in, or completely outside, the novels. "Amanda Morgan" shows how the women, children, and old men of Dorsai defeat Dow deCastries' elite invasion troops. "Warrior" tells how Ian Grahame, Donal's uncle, renders justice for the unnecessary death of one of Ian's officers. "Lost Dorsai" is the story of Michael de Sandoval, a Dorsai who uncharacteristically refuses to use weapons but who manages to conquer an entire army. In "Brothers," Ian Grahame ensures both that the men who assassinated his beloved twin brother Kensie are found and executed and that the Dorsai troops do not run amok in their grief over losing Kensie.

Analysis: Even in its own terms, the Childe Cycle is one of the most ambitious projects in the history of science fiction. As of 1995, the series consisted of well more than a million words, thus being comparable in scope to Isaac Asimov's Foundation series and Robert A. Heinlein's "Future History" stories. The Childe Cycle is part of an even larger project, a set of interlocking novels—originally conceived of as three historical, three contemporary, and three science-fiction novels—each standing on its own but all eventually forming part of one gigantic "consciously thematic story," a term Dickson uses for the work.

Dickson's themes are almost all pairs of oppositions. Evolution is crucial and stasis is death; freedom is necessary and too much control is fatal; duty to a cause above self is good and selfishness is bad; and empathy liberates and isolation confines. The exception to this series is the paradoxical mantra of the new Chantry Guild on Kultis, which is a key to the cycle's overall structure: "the transient and the eternal are the same." What Dickson seems to say is that during the thousand-year period his consciously thematic story will cover, patterns repeat.

The individual novels differ in some respects. The earlier novels are shorter and less easily understood than the later novels. The basic structure, however, is the same

throughout the cycle: A young but incredibly confident and talented man overcomes an older and seemingly invincible opponent, each victory supposedly bringing the human race a step closer to a time when everyone has the abilities of the gifted. Dickson's heroes are not really supermen, for Dickson honestly believes that the traits they exhibit are available to all human beings, either in the past as models, in the present with a little training, or in the near future with some trailblazing by the gifted.

Dickson is philosophically a "hard-headed" romantic, and the Childe Cycle reminds readers of the work of another hard-headed romantic science-fiction author, Poul Anderson. Both authors intermingle the conventions of hard science fiction—plausible extrapolations of current scientific knowledge—with ideas stemming from their study of various romantic authors and mythologies.

Even more than Anderson, Dickson wishes to blur the line between fact and fiction. In Hal Mayne's Creative Universe, one has only, in true romantic fashion, to wish for a thing to be true and it will become true in actuality. English romantic poet William Wordsworth (1770-1850) said, "The Child is Father of the Man." Dickson says, with the idea resonating from *Necromancer* to *Other*, that "The Wish is Father of the Deed." Ever the optimist, Dickson wants the human race to improve, and he has spent most of his long writing career nobly mapping out a blueprint to follow.

Critics have not given Dickson much attention, probably because his work may seem dated, as if he stopped developing as a science-fiction writer about 1960. He may also seem derivative to some, for a typical Childe Cycle novel often reads like a combination of breakneck (but overly long and overly detailed) space opera action, in the style of E. E. "Doc" Smith, and clumsy, obviously symbolic interior monologues reminiscent of the work of A. E. van Vogt, laced with too many heavily melodramatic confrontation scenes. Despite this critical indifference, Dickson has won one Nebula and three Hugo awards, all for shorter fiction and two for Cycle pieces—a 1965 Hugo for "Soldier, Ask Not" and a 1981 Hugo for "Lost Dorsai."   —*Todd H. Sammons*

CHILDHOOD'S END

The Satan-like Overlords attempt to guide a reluctant human race to its apocalyptic transformation and union with the Overmind

Author: Arthur C. Clarke (1917-   )
Genre: Science fiction—evolutionary fantasy

Type of work: Novel
Time of plot: About 1985-2085
Location: Earth and NGS 549672, the planet of the
Overlords
First published: 1953

The Plot: *Childhood's End* is an account of the final one
hundred years of human life on Earth, from the time of
the Overlords' arrival in their huge spaceship to the time
of the dramatic, rapid evolution of all human children
into a nonhuman form that achieves unity with the Overmind. A series of human characters—most notably
George Greggson, Jean Morrel, and their two children—encounter the technologically advanced Overlords, whose Stardrive-based spaceships, truth-in-history
machines, and panoramic viewers (which allow observation of every detail in an area many miles away) provide
the science-fiction aspects of Arthur C. Clarke's novel.
The evolutionary fantasy element appears in human children as they transform into nonhuman entities that destroy Earth in the power of their fusion into the Overmind that controls, and perhaps is, the universe.

Childhood's End begins with an event often antici-
pated and described in science fiction: the arrival of an
alien species on Earth. This species is unusual, however,
both in its refusal to allow itself to be seen for fifty years
and in its benevolence, as it prohibits cruelty to animals
and otherwise guides humanity beyond the barbarity of
war and destruction into an era of peace and economic
prosperity. The negative results of the arrival and assumption of control by the Overlords are powerful as
well, though less dramatic. A consequence of the end of
energizing conflict and struggle is the decline in creative
achievement in art. Likewise, religious belief is termi-
nated by the Overlords' technology, which allows direct
visual access to most events in human history, thus ex-
posing the myths and half-truths that had been accepted
as truth over the ages. When this latter debunking is
fully achieved, the Overlords reveal themselves. Huge,
winged, barb-tailed, horned, Satan-like creatures, they
disembark from their spaceship and generate only a brief
reaction of terror. Reason then conquers the remnants of
Christian memory, and the Overlords are accepted as
intriguingly intelligent and benevolent masters.

To some creative artists and philosophers, however,
life without ambition and original human achievement is
insufficient. Thus, some fifty thousand join to form a
colony dedicated to artistic and intellectual life, the kind
of human psychological development that had been
stalled by the Overlords' control. Among those joining

the island colony are George Greggson, Jean Morrel, and
their two young children. Unknowingly, Jean has attracted the attention of the Overlords because of her
prescience in correctly identifying their home planet,
NGS 549672, even though they never revealed their
place of origin to any human. It is this psychological
insight that the Overlords secretly have come to inhibit,
or at least supervise, as it develops from the mental
power implicit in extrasensory perception phenomena
throughout human history into the mind over matter
power that constitutes unity with the Overmind.

The psychological power latent in Jean becomes fully
realized in her children; they control objects telekinetically and experience visions of planets even the Overlords have never visited. Soon all human children develop
this power. They quickly become nonhuman and oblivious to their parents, who then annihilate themselves because they cannot retrieve their children or even become
like them. Only Jan Rodricks remains, having stowed
away on an Overlord ship, visited NGS 549672, and
returned to a desolate Earth eighty years later. He describes the apocalypse for the Overlords, who have retreated, their supervisory task completed. Even Jan himself fades into nothingness as the children consume the
substance of the Earth in their transformation into pure
light energy and depart with the Overmind into the stars.

Analysis: The creative complexity of Clarke's novel has
made it a classic of modern science fiction. The work is
difficult to categorize or synthesize. On one level, it
operates as a reasonably believable extrapolation from
modern scientific and technological progress into a material utopia. The novel has its dystopian psychological
dimension as well. *Childhood's End* also reflects the
aspect of Clarke's writing most fully realized in *2001: A
Space Odyssey* (1968), his creation of brilliantly evocative, colorful, fantastic descriptions of nonexistent other
worlds as an exercise in human imaginative expression.
The description of the metamorphosis of the mountain on
NGS 549672 in *Childhood's End* is an excellent example. Closely allied with this fantastic physical description
is the imaginative leap made by Clarke in his depiction
of the fantasy transformation of human children into
psychic superpowers and spiritual essences.

Also intimately connected to this imaginatively mystical element in Clarke's writing is his recurring theme of
religion—particularly Christianity—as an imperfect embodiment of powerful but misunderstood psychic and
spiritual forces. For example, in the 1956 Hugo Award-
winning story "The Star," Clarke ironically presents the

star of Bethlehem as the supernova stage of another planet's sun. Billions of people die on that planet as the supernova guides the shepherds to the place of birth of one child on Earth. The same reversal of Christian belief, or enlargement of the context surrounding it, is obvious in *Childhood's End*, with the Overlords as an ironically benevolent reversal of the human image of Satan.

Also fundamental to *Childhood's End* is Clarke's recurring theme of the existence of, and inevitable human contact with, other life-forms in the universe. With an intensity akin to religious conversion, Clarke presents this theme in his famous 1951 story "The Sentinel," the progenitor of *2001: A Space Odyssey*. On a moon expedition, the narrator of "The Sentinel" finds a crystal pyramid left by an alien species and accepts the fact of that species' existence; similarly, the Overlords' arrival in *Childhood's End* is represented as an inevitable progression in human encounters with the life-forms "out there."

In its complexity and multifacetedness, *Childhood's End* represents the great artistic power of Clarke in all three of his writing styles, which, according to James Gunn in *The Road to Science Fiction: From Heinlein to Here* (1979), are extrapolative, ingenious, and mystical. What the novel lacks in formal unity and harmony it more than compensates for in pure energy, originality, and profundity.

—*John L. Grigsby*

CHILDREN OF THE ATOM

A group of superintelligent children, products of an atomic plant explosion, emerge from hiding to defend themselves from outside hostility and to discover their true vocation

Author: Wilmar H. Shiras (1908-1990)
Genre: Science fiction—superbeing
Type of work: Novel
Time of plot: 1973
Location: Primarily the San Francisco Bay area
First published: 1953 (first three chapters published individually as novelettes: "In Hiding," *Astounding Science-Fiction*, November, 1948; "Opening Doors," *Astounding Science-Fiction*, March, 1949; and "New Foundations," *Astounding Science-Fiction*, March, 1950)

The Plot: After being called in to help a withdrawn thirteen-year-old boy, school psychologist Dr. Peter Welles realizes that the boy, Timothy Paul, is immeasurably intelligent. Taught by his guardians that precocity is often punished as boastful exhibitionism, Tim has lived "in hiding," masking his abilities while carrying out a secret life as an author under a variety of pseudonyms. Welles soon deduces that Tim's intelligence is the result of a mutation caused by a disaster at an atomic power plant in "Helium City," where his parents worked thirteen years earlier.

Realizing that other such children must exist all across the country, Welles and Tim begin to get in touch with them. Tim is able to persuade his rich grandparents to fund a special school for the superintelligent, to be run by Welles and other adults who are let in on the secret. A sizable number of the thirty surviving children are gathered at this school. Many are rescued from oppressive domestic situations, and one from an asylum. Most of them have replicated Tim's strategy of performing remarkable work under adult aliases: They produce novels, biographies, a popular comic strip, and a successful board game. At Welles's school they are rescued from their loneliness and allowed a chance to grow and develop.

Welles's greatest challenge is to ensure that all the children mature in each aspect of their lives. A problem soon arises when one of the children is discovered to have little or no emotional capacity for empathy. The children themselves, not Welles, are able to devise a solution to the problem. They also conceive the project that will occupy them in their maturity, a kind of *summa scientia*, or what would be called today a grand unified theory, linking all branches of knowledge and the arts in one comprehensible construct.

Before they are able to begin that project, their existence is shouted to the world by a televangelist, Tommy Mundy, who claims that these "children of the atom" are the spawn of the devil, plotting a world takeover. Again the children themselves form a solution, initially convincing the angry mob that gathers outside the school that they are not monsters but familiar people the crowd has known all their lives. Tim Paul urges the ultimate solution: The children will attend public schools in the area, both to show others that they are not fundamentally different and to develop and demonstrate the "right feeling" toward humanity. The children of the atom, in Tim's words, "join the human race."

Analysis: *Children of the Atom* combines two important motifs in science fiction: that of the superbeing, previously portrayed most memorably in Olaf Stapledon's classic *Odd John* (1935), and the ubiquitous anxiety caused by the use of atomic weapons in 1945. Human mutations caused by atomic energy would become a staple in science fiction. Examples include John Wyndham's *Re-Birth* (1955, also known as *The Chrysalids*), Lester del Rey's *The Eleventh Commandment* (1962), and Edgar Pangborn's *Davy* (1964). Wilmar Shiras is perhaps the first, however, to see this kind of catastrophe in the theological sense of a "eucatastrophe": a *felix culpa*, or fortunate fall. What will emerge from the sin of using the atom and its inherent powers is not punishment in the form of breeding of monsters but is instead the possibility of advancing the human race to its next evolutionary plane.

In many science-fiction depictions of what *Homo superior* might be like, a clear line of demarcation is established, and "normal" humans, *Homo sapiens*, are often treated by the superior race as humans treat animals such as dogs. Odd John's nickname for the human narrator of Stapledon's novel, for example, is "Fido." The first story in *Children of the Atom*, "In Hiding," ends with this very image: "Peter Welles would be Tim's friend—not a puppy, but a beloved friend—as a loyal dog, loved by a good master, is never cast out."

As a separate novelette, "In Hiding" is much more famous than the four stories that follow it. It was voted into the Science Fiction Hall of Fame. One reason perhaps is that the positing of an evolutionary successor to humans in science fiction almost always leads to contempt, conflict, and then destruction of one race or the other, as evidenced in the self-destruction of Odd John's superhuman colony, or indeed that of the entire Earth in Arthur C. Clarke's *Childhood's End* (1953). "In Hiding" seems to imply that such a plot line will follow.

The novel as a whole shows humans and superhumans as eventually becoming able to forge bonds of amicability and trust. This trust is based on the strong Christian religious underpinnings of the book. None of the supergeniuses dismisses organized religion out of hand; the children's great project is modeled on the *Summa* treatises of Thomas Aquinas. They refuse to substitute a "higher" morality as a replacement for outmoded Judeo-Christian ethical traditions. Odd John excuses murder as being absolved by the needs of a higher being, but Shiras' children are able to spot a trickster because of his casual assumption that abortion for the purpose of choosing the offspring's gender is acceptable. Even the name of Timothy Paul, who suggests the children's reintegration with *Homo sapiens*, is an allusion to two of the first Christian apostles to the gentiles. Shiras' insistent subtext is that these children of the atom are still the children of Adam. —*William Laskowski*

CHIMERA

Following a disquisition on the arts of narrative by Dunyazade, the fabled Scheherazade's younger sister, the mythic heroes Perseus and Bellerophon describe their efforts to overcome the lassitude of post-heroic mundanity

Author: John Barth (1930-   )
Genre: Fantasy—mythological
Type of work: Novel
Time of plot: Antiquity and the mid-twentieth century
Location: The realm of mythic heroes, the Arabian Empire at the height of its power, and tidewater Maryland
First published: 1972

The Plot: John Barth's fascination with the intricacies of narrative possibility and the complex, evolving interrelationship between an author and a work in progress drew him to the plight of Scheherazade, his figure for an ultimate author who must hold the attention of her audience or lose her life. Using a pattern of doubling that establishes a multiple perspective informing the three parts of *Chimera*, Barth presents the classic fable of Scheherazade's predicament—to keep the shah's interest in a never-ending story so he will spare her life in order to learn what happens next—through the words of Dunyazade, "Sherry's" younger sister, who is talking to her husband, the shah's brother, in an effort to escape the same fate. Dunyazade's narrative is further complicated by the appearance of a genie figure who seems to resemble Barth himself, a fortyish American who has read Scheherazade's account and can contribute to, comment on, and interact with the characters.

After numerous questions are raised about the composition of a narrative that continues for 1,001 nights, the focus shifts to the legendary Perseus, an analogue for a man, like Barth, who is caught between a heroic past in his youth and the flatness of his middle years. Perseus' problems are summarized by his apparent impotence with the feminine muses who have inspired his glorious feats. By retelling and simultaneously reliving (now in altered form) the circumstances of his achievements, however, Perseus is able to achieve a degree of serenity and satisfaction. Through the imaginative re-creation of his life, he clarifies and deepens its meanings by transmuting the temporal into the eternal, ultimately reconciling his rancor for Medusa and finding peace with her in the symbolic constellations that are their timeless domain.

The third section of *Chimera* compounds the problems of the mythic hero by following the crisis Bellerophon faces. Like Perseus, he has a glorious past, but unlike Perseus, he is unable to break out of an archetypal pattern for heroic behavior of which he is self-consciously aware. The devastating act of patricide—a symbolic necessity for claiming an individual identity—is reduced to a parodic confusion, a chaos of elements from many myths mutually diminishing any possibility of meaning. Bellerophon eventually slays the Chimera, a fabulous creature with a lion's head, goat's body, and serpent's tail, but even with the aid of the winged horse Pegasus, his feats seem second-rate. His life story eventually is revealed as the imaginings of Polyeidus, the mythic shape-shifter who controls the narrative and who, as the writer of the myth, ultimately is more powerful than the heroes whose exploits he describes. When Bellerophon crashes to earth in the Maryland marshland that the writer John Barth inhabits, he achieves his mortal destiny, and the book in which his story is contained may "expect a certain low-impact afterlife," proving the tale less significant than its teller while revealing the true hero of myth as its maker.

Analysis: Barth's intense concentration on the temptations and perils of devising and constructing a story when the contemporary world already has heard every variant of plot or theme is paralleled by his curiosity about the relevance of classical mythology for a postmodern world. In *Giles Goat-Boy: Or, The Revised New Syllabus* (1966), *Chimera*, and *The Last Voyage of Somebody the Sailor* (1991), he combines the heroic proportions of figures from antiquity with the sensibility of a well-educated, self-conscious twentieth century writer both to demystify the heroic and to demonstrate the continuing importance of mythic patterns shaped by storytellers over time. He is concerned with the value of literary art in an age of diminishing literacy; though accepting the proposition that all stories are "lies," he insists that the best stories are "something larger than fact"—that is, a myth that is both a personal record and something larger than any particular person.

Using a dazzling array of self-reflective devices, Barth also employs the traditional techniques of tale tellers as ancient as Homer to captivate the reader, shaping a narrative rife with romance, suspense, and dramatic action to approach the great mysteries of existence that enduring myths have always engaged. At the heart of *Chimera*, the essential question posed by any artist intrigued by the possibilities of the fantastic is confronted directly: What

if one could overcome the apparent limits of the material world? Barth is successful in making the fantastic plausible (or, as Paul Valéry put it, making "the fantastic another aspect of the realistic") by confounding skepticism through continually expanding the range of action of his protagonists. The linkage of mythic patterns with contemporary issues and of classic tales with current modes of speech and thought carries the narrative from the comfortingly familiar to the unsettlingly extraordinary. The aim of *Chimera* is to argue that an ultimate reality resides or endures only in the shaping of experience through language. Thus, if the artist is sufficiently skillful, it becomes difficult to determine which realm is intruding. As Barth has put it, "I wonder whether the world's really there when I'm not narrating it." Although this is a distinctly individual declaration, its expression in *Chimera* reached enough discerning readers for Barth to win the National Book Award for Fiction.

The mythic hero Perseus is presented as a man who, like the author, struggles with the petrification and immobility of middle age. He cannot relive his youthful achievements, but through the imaginative power of the artist, he can begin to understand and appreciate who he is and what he has done. With what Scheherazade asserts is the "real magic . . . to understand which words work," Barth connects the intimately personal with the mythologically universal, suggesting that an absolute distinction between the realistic and the fantastic is not only simplistic but also an impedance to understanding.

—*Leon Lewis*

THE CHRONICLES OF CLOVIS

Twenty-eight brief satirical stories about upper-class England in the Edwardian period, loosely connected by several recurring characters

Author: Saki (Hector Hugh Munro, 1870-1916)
Genre: Fantasy—Magical Realism
Type of work: Stories
Time of plot: The first two decades of the twentieth century
Location: England
First published: 1911

The Plot: Saki's snobbish characters are obsessed with appearances despite their glaring flaws. In "Mrs. Packletide's Tiger," Mrs. Packletide travels to India to hunt. Native villagers stake out a goat to attract an ancient tiger, and when Mrs. Packletide shoots, the tiger falls dead. It is later discovered that she shot the goat, and the tiger merely died of heart failure. To save face, she bribes her hired companion to keep the secret. In "Tobermory," Cornelius Appin announces to the skeptical guests at a weekend party that he has taught his cat to speak. The cat begins to describe the scandalous behavior he has observed among the guests. The guests plot to poison the animal rather than rectify their behavior.

Despite their veneer of respectability, Saki's characters are heartless and petty. "Esmé" tells the story of a baroness riding on a fox hunt with a companion. They are followed by a hyena that has escaped from a local zoo. The animal seizes a gypsy child and consumes it in the bushes, and the beast itself is soon killed by a car. The baroness claims that the hyena was her show dog and later receives a diamond brooch from the contrite motorist.

Saki's society is peopled by pretentious people who neither understand nor appreciate the art they pretend to adore. In "The Recessional," Clovis composes a poem as the result of a wager with a poet who insists that only a rare genius is capable of publishing verse. Clovis' poem is full of comical alliteration and errors of fact. His connections, however, make it possible for him to publish the poem in a literary magazine, so that he wins the bet. In "The Background," Henri Delpis receives an inheritance while visiting Italy. Among his impulsive purchases is a tattoo by Pincini, a master of the craft. Pincini dies, and by the time his widow demands payment, Delpis is penniless. The widow reclaims rights to the tattoo and donates it to the government. The tattoo thus becomes an Italian art treasure, and Delpis is forbidden to leave Italy, swim in the sea, or display the work without government approval.

Even in their religion, Saki's characters are more concerned with appearance than with substance. "The Story of St. Vespaluus" tells of an ancient king who chooses young Vespaluus as his heir. The king is a serpent worshiper, and when Vespaluus converts to Christianity, he is sentenced to death by bee stings. A sympathetic beekeeper removes the bees' stingers, and Vespaluus' survival is deemed a miracle. Vespaluus ascends to the throne and, to his horror, his people convert to Christianity; he only feigned conversion to antagonize the king, and he remains an avid serpent worshiper.

To Saki, primitive faith, like serpent worship, is preferable to and more real than the pretense of organized religion. In "Sredni Vashtar," a young boy elaborately worships a captured ferret that he hides from his mean-spirited guardian. He prays to the animal to deliver him from the guardian; in the end the ferret kills her. In "The

Music on the Hill," Sylvia Seltoun convinces her dull husband to go to the country, where he immerses himself in the wilds. Sylvia finds a statue of Pan in a clearing, with an offering of grapes left by her husband. She removes the grapes and, as punishment, is killed by a deer while Pan stands by laughing.

Analysis: The stories in *The Chronicles of Clovis* are loosely connected by a handful of recurring characters. Most notable is Clovis, a seventeen-year-old with a subversive wit and a disrespect for the British upper class, of which he is a member. Clovis is present in most of the stories, if only as observer, and in many he is Saki's satirical mouthpiece, making light of his staid companions' most cherished interests, values, and beliefs.

Saki's cruel satires are written in refined and genteel language that parallels the stories' central themes. Saki sees elite Edwardian society as morally bankrupt and self-absorbed, yet obsessed with appearances. In the same way that Saki's elegant language disguises the sinister nature of his stories, his characters' cultivated manners hide the emptiness of their social customs and their secret malice. Their polished conversations contain thinly veiled insults, and their outward politeness masks a scheming self-interest. Saki's style is also full of wonderfully understated irony and memorable epigrams reminiscent of Oscar Wilde.

Many stories take the form of brutal cautionary tales. For their shallowness and self-absorption, Saki's characters are rewarded with humiliation or even maiming, murder, or suicide. In "The Easter-Egg," a mother's family pride leaves her scarred, blind, and childless. In "The Way to the Dairy," sisters who scheme to keep their inheritance intact unwittingly introduce their rich aunt to casino life, and she gambles away the family fortune.

Saki's stories not only satirize English society but also seem to acknowledge dark, primitive, supernatural forces that his characters are too refined to notice. These mystical undercurrents pit Celtic mythology against English civility. When his city-dwelling protagonists leave their element, they are faced with witches or mythological creatures and flee back to the safety of London. Saki's characters lead lives divorced from nature, and when they attempt to civilize nature they are killed by it.

The deft humor in these stories makes their often brutal content more palatable. Much of the humor is derived from the outrageous manners in which his characters react to cruel events. They are unmoved by death yet traumatized by a bottle of wine gone bad. The disappearance of a baby causes Clovis no alarm; he sees it as an occasion to make light of a neighbor's religion. To the baroness, the hideous death of a child becomes an opportunity to bilk a motorist.   —*Paul Buchanan*

THE CHRONICLES OF NARNIA

The creation, salvation, and apocalyptic remaking of the land of Narnia and the adventures of children there

Author: C(live) S(taples) Lewis (1898-1963)
Genre: Fantasy—theological romance
Type of work: Novels
Time of plot: 1900-1949 in Earth time, during which 2,555 years pass in Narnia
Location: England, Narnia, and magical lands surrounding Narnia
First published: *The Lion, the Witch and the Wardrobe* (1950), *Prince Caspian* (1951), *The Voyage of the "Dawn Treader"* (1952), *The Silver Chair* (1953), *The Horse and His Boy* (1954), *The Magician's Nephew* (1955), and *The Last Battle* (1956)

The Plot: The seven books constituting the Chronicles of Narnia tell how Aslan the Lion, son of the Emperor-beyond-the-Sea, sings Narnia into being from nothing and later saves it from evil by sacrificing himself and rising again. He spares nothing to make others good if they are open to change. The fictional history of the adventures does not correspond to the order of either composition or publication, but author C. S. Lewis provided a suggested order for reading the stories that is adhered to in the following plot summaries.

In *The Magician's Nephew*, the adult Andrew Ketterley, who dabbles in magic, discovers rings that can transport their wearers into other worlds and back (he thinks). He tricks his nephew Digory Kirke and Digory's friend, Polly Plummer, into trying the rings. The two children discover that yellow rings transport them to the Wood between the Worlds. Once there, green rings can plunge them into pools magically leading to other worlds.

In the dead world of Charn, Digory's unbridled curiosity leads him to release an evil witch, Jadis, from a deathlike enchantment. Jadis forces her way back to Earth, where she works her destructive evil. The children use the rings to get her out of Earth, but instead of getting her back to Charn, they go to Narnia, a new world the lion Aslan is singing into existence. Because Digory and Polly brought evil into Narnia, Aslan gives them a role in containing it. They ride a winged horse to a far garden, bringing back an apple to plant in Narnia as temporary protection against Jadis. Aslan gives Digory an apple to take back to Earth and use to cure his dying mother. Digory plants the apple's core, and from the tree that grows he has a wardrobe made.

In *The Lion, the Witch and the Wardrobe*, Digory is the mature Professor Kirke. Peter, Susan, Edmund, and Lucy Pevensie come to his home to escape the London air raids of World War II. While playing hide and seek, they enter the enchanted wardrobe and pass into Narnia. Edmund betrays his siblings and all of Narnia for the White Witch Jadis' offer of Turkish Delight candy and power.

The Witch has created a never-ending winter with no Christmas, but she fears an ancient prophecy that when two boys and two girls take the thrones at Cair Paravel, her reign will end, and Aslan will return and claim his rightful rule. According to the magic built into Narnia at its creation, Jadis has rights to all traitors, but by a deeper magic, an innocent person may die in place of the guilty, which Aslan does. The Witch thinks Aslan a fool and herself the conqueror when she kills Aslan on the Stone Table. By a deeper magic that she does not know, Aslan rises from the dead, frees Edmund and all the Witch's captives, and leads a victorious conquest. Aslan destroys the Witch and places the children on the four thrones of Narnia. After many years, while hunting the White Stag, the children unintentionally stumble back through the enchanted wardrobe to the professor's house, with no lapse of Earth time.

The action in *The Horse and His Boy* takes place entirely in Narnia and surrounding countries. A talking horse, Bree, born a free Narnian but stolen young and used as an ordinary riding horse by an evil Calormene master, rescues a boy named Shasta. Shasta actually is Prince Cor, the older twin son of King Lune, ruler of Archenland, a friendly neighboring country of Narnia. Shasta was stolen because of a prophecy that he would one day save Archenland. Bree and Shasta escape with two others. Through many adventures, they save Archenland and Narnia from surprise invasion.

The four Pevensie children, earlier kings and queens of Narnia, return in *Prince Caspian*. While waiting for the train back to boarding school, they vanish into Narnia at the blast of a magic horn Susan had left in Narnia. The Pevensies help Prince Caspian wrest Narnia from the Telmarines and his evil and usurping Uncle Miraz, who has tried to erase every memory of Narnia. Peter Pevensie, former High King himself, faces Miraz in single combat and is about to defeat him when the evil forces attack. Aslan calls the trees to life, and the Telmarines are routed. All who wish, even Telmarines who will accept forgiveness, may enter Narnia through a magic door, but the Pevensies must return to the railway station and school.

Edmund and Lucy return to Narnia in *The Voyage of the "Dawn Treader."* They are accompanied by their selfish and obnoxious cousin Eustace Scrubb. They enter Narnia by falling through a Narnian seascape hanging on a wall, and they are rescued from the sea by their old friend King Caspian, who is fulfilling a vow to search for seven Narnian lords. One of the faithful seven helps Caspian save the Lone Islands from slave trade. Eustace becomes a dragon because of his greed but is painfully "undragoned" by Aslan. Reepicheep the Mouse, the most fearless of the Narnians, fulfills his quest to find Aslan's true country.

In *The Silver Chair*, Eustace Scrubb and Jill Pole escape school bullies through a courtyard door and enter Narnia. They are met by Aslan and given four signs to aid in rescuing Prince Rilian from the evil queen of Underland. Underland is deep underground and is peopled by Earthmen, whom the queen rules by terror and plans to use in overthrowing Narnia. The wise Marsh-wiggle Puddleglum helps the children release Rilian from an enchanted silver chair and return him to Narnia.

The Last Battle is a complex account of the end of Narnia and its re-creation into a permanent paradise by Aslan the Lion, creator and rightful ruler of Narnia. Various children have been called, by various means, from Earth into a Narnia in crisis. This time, a train crash sends all the earthly friends to newly created, everlastingly good Narnia, but they must first fight in the old Narnia's last battle. A clever ape named Shift forces his donkey companion Puzzle to wear a lion's skin so that he can masquerade as Aslan. By this deception, they rule Narnia. When the deception is broken, the Calormenes, under Rishda, launch an attack on the Narnians. Rishda calls on the evil god Tash, who destroys Rishda himself in the end.

Tirian, the present king of Narnia, and the friends from Earth all die in the battle, but as they see Narnia destroyed by a cataclysmic flood, then swallowed by a dying sun, death becomes for them the doorway to a new and better Narnia. They are invited "farther up and farther in." The "Great Story" begins, "in which every chapter is better than the one before."

Analysis: This series combines the elements of youth and childhood that Lewis loved and employed in many of his works: enchantment, magic, talking animals and trees, Arthurian legend, other worlds and journeys among them, time travel, and myth. The series contains elements of many genres: utopias, fairy stories, chil-

dren's stories, medieval chivalric romances, fables, folktales, and novels. Its ideas pull from a deep well of learning in history, literature, philosophy, and religion. Although they never obtrude, St. Paul and the Gospel writers, Saint Augustine, Dante, John Milton, and Edmund Spenser are always visible in the subtext. Lewis acknowledges many specific authors, especially Edith Nesbit, George MacDonald, Beatrix Potter, H. G. Wells, and (preeminently) the biblical writers. The Bible provides the structure, patterns, and values of the Chronicles. The marvel of these books is in the convincing mix of all these elements and the ease of reading. Simplicity and profundity dance together.

In the Chronicles of Narnia, ordinary people such as cab drivers and schoolchildren are chosen to perform extraordinary feats and fulfill extraordinary destinies. They battle evil from within, in the form of laziness, greed, pride, selfishness, and disbelief, as well as evil from without, in the form of soldiers, traitors, witches, enchantments, and an assortment of evil mythological creatures. All these challenges are met with the richer resources of good, flowing out of its source in Aslan, who is to the world of Narnia what Christ is to Earth according to the biblical account. Aslan creates Narnia, populates it, providentially watches over it, and guides it to its end and new beginning.

As is usual in Lewis' books, evil is portrayed as the drying up of human potential, as restriction and imprisonment. The dwarfs who reject Aslan in *The Last Battle* cannot see him, and Eustace embodies greed in the form of a dragon. Goodness is expansive and liberating. Those Jadis turned to stone are restored to life by Aslan's breath, and Eustace is "undragoned" to become a hero and liberator of others in turn. The stable that Aslan occupies at the end of *The Last Battle* is bigger on the inside than the outside and opens into the new Narnia. The grand achievement of this series is its awakening of a longing for the good, for justice, purity, truth, courage, charity, patience, and perseverance.

The influence of the series is vast. When J. R. R. Tolkien's Lord of the Rings trilogy and Lewis' work appeared during the 1950's, they revived fantasy literature from its doldrums. The Narnia books have been the subject of conferences, scholarly work, artworks, and television and video performances. An estimated twenty million or more readers have enjoyed the Chronicles. Perhaps no other work has done more to rehabilitate the reputation, multiply the readership, and broaden the creative potential of fantasy literature in the twentieth century.
                                        —Wayne Martindale

THE CHRONICLES OF THE DERYNI

Kelson Haldane faces various enemies before taking his place as king of Gwynedd, then attempts to restore respect among his human subjects for his Deryni ones

Author: Katherine Kurtz (1944-   )
Genre: Fantasy—heroic fantasy
Type of work: Novels
Time of plot: 1120-1122
Location: The kingdom of Gwynedd, in a land resembling the United Kingdom
First published: 1985 (as trilogy; first published separately as *Deryni Rising*, 1970; *Deryni Checkmate*, 1972; and *High Deryni*, 1973)

The Plot: *The Chronicles of the Deryni* rests on a history of conflict. Festil, a member of the Deryni people, who have magical powers, overthrew the Haldane King Ifor in 822 and tried to wipe out the Haldane family. All the heirs except Aidan were killed. Festil became king, and his family ruled for seventy-eight years. Each king became more arrogant in his use of power. Camber Mac-Rorie and his family overthrew Imre, the last king of the Festilic line, and raised Aidan Haldane's grandson Cinhil to the throne.

Camber gave Deryni-like powers to Cinhil to protect the Haldane line. Cinhil, a monk, resented being forced to forsake his vows. After Cinhil died, the human regents reacted to cruelty the Festilic kings had shown toward humans. They outlawed Deryni magic and stripped the Deryni of lands, rank, and privileges, including priestly service.

The main story of the chronicles begins when Kelson Cinhil Rhys Anthony Haldane comes to power in 1120 after Charissa, the great-granddaughter of Imre, kills Kelson's father, Brion. The laws prohibiting Deryni influence were ignored by Brion, both because he possessed Deryni-like powers and because he had a friend and adviser who was public about being half Deryni. Kelson continues to rely on Alaric Morgan, the Deryni duke who was his father's adviser and who presides over a secret rite to awaken Kelson's Deryni-like powers. The rite does not seem to work.

The church and many average humans object to the Deryni as evil, causing the Deryni to be ostracized and persecuted. Kelson's own mother, Jehana, objects to the Deryni presence and tries to prevent Morgan's affiliation with Kelson by throwing Morgan off the council. Kelson refuses to permit Morgan's banishment.

Kelson's coronation is interrupted when Charissa arrives and challenges him to a potentially fatal magical duel. Jehana protects her son, and her use of magical powers reveals that she is Deryni. Kelson taps his powers shortly before the duel, wins the duel, and is crowned.

Frightened by the Deryni magical power and envious of Morgan's influence with the young king, the archbishop of the Gwynedd church, Edmund Loris, calls the bishops together in a Curia (convocation) to pronounce an Interdict denying any sacraments for the population of Morgan's Duchy of Corwin. The Interdict is an attempt to oust Morgan.

A human revivalist preacher, Warin de Grey, has been preaching against the Deryni. Archbishop Loris intends to help de Grey overthrow Morgan. Loris anticipates that Morgan and Father Duncan may address the Curia to prevent the Interdict, so he sets a successful trap. He arranges for de Grey's men to trap Morgan at the entrance to Dhassa by using *mersaha*, a Deryni-specific drug that robs Morgan of his magic power. Father Duncan, while freeing Morgan, reveals that he is part Deryni, something few had known before, and contributes to starting a fire that destroys the shrine of Saint Torin.

When the Curia meets, some of the bishops, including the bishop of Dhassa, are hesitant to take the extreme action the archbishop wants. Six of them, withdrawing from the deliberations, deprive the Curia of a quorum. The remaining bishops vote the Interdict anyway. The bishop of Dhassa tells the remaining bishops to leave the city. Unaware of these developments, Morgan and Duncan return to the king.

The effects of the Interdict and the division of the bishops present a serious problem for the king, Morgan, and Duncan because spring is coming and they need every soldier to fight the Deryni ruler of Torenth, a nearby kingdom that shelters the Festilic family. Morgan and Duncan decide to go to Dhassa to appeal to the bishops and attempt to prove that they are not evil and should not be held responsible for the destruction of the shrine. In the meantime, Bran Coris, the earl of Marley, who protects the Cardosa's approach to Gwynedd, is persuaded by Wencit of Torenth to betray Kelson's forces.

Morgan and Duncan finally reach Dhassa and persuade the bishops of their innocence. As a result, the bishops commit their army to Kelson and the defense of Gwynedd. One of the bishops, Denis Arilan, turns out to be full Deryni and a member of the Camberian Council, which polices the use of Deryni powers.

Morgan, Duncan, Kelson, and his uncle Nigel persuade de Grey to join Kelson. De Grey believes that his own power to heal comes from God. Morgan convinces him to join the group by healing a serious wound that de Grey inflicts on Duncan.

The war is to be decided by an arcane duel to the death between the king's side (Kelson, Morgan, Duncan, and Arilan) and Wencit's (Wencit, Bran, Duke Lionel, and Lord Rhydon). The battle does not come to fruition because Rhydon, a disguised member of the Camberian Council, poisons the wine that Wencit's side drinks as an opening salute to their enemies.

Analysis: These novels are the first three of a series of more than a dozen Deryni novels. In creating this world, Katherine Kurtz builds on her knowledge of the medieval world acquired in part through her involvement in the Society for Creative Anachronism as well as through her own historical research.

The Chronicles of the Deryni offers appealing characters that readers care about and slowly reveals a richly developed, complex world. As Kurtz continues to develop the Deryni world, she gradually provides additional information about the characters, the world, and the culture of Gwynedd. The story of Kelson is continued in The Histories of King Kelson, another part of the Deryni series. The background of the return of the Haldane kings to the throne is provided in The Legends of Camber of Culdi. This background was later expanded in The Heirs of Saint Camber.

The various novels reveal a rich heritage of Deryni and human literature and magic. The church resembles, but is not to be taken as, the Catholic church of medieval times. It is built on the elemental magic and rituals of Gwynedd's ancient history, which have been mingled with Christian beliefs and rituals. In this regard, the church incorporates magic in its mystical observances. These observances have their own magic—the presence and blessings of God that all feel. The Deryni, however, experience that magic with an additional layer of sensation.

Deryni magic is both sympathetic (actions that cause or at least mimic the magic) and psionic (unusual mental abilities such as telepathy, clairvoyance, precognition, and psychokinesis). These abilities mean that ordinary humans are easy for Deryni to control and are susceptible to suggestion by Deryni. The Deryni magic can be used for either good or evil. Its use depends on the user's conscience. Deryni, who usually are the main characters in these novels, most often use their magic for good. Some use their powers for their own benefit without regard to the harm they may cause others. These Deryni

are the villains. Wealth and political power also are powerful forces, and they are available to humans to use, also for good or for evil.

One theme explored in these books is the responsibility of the nobility to society. Camber MacRorie feels compelled to overthrow Imre because the king and various noble Deryni feel no responsibility to treat ordinary humans with respect. Their ability to control the humans allows them to mistreat the humans for their own gain or pleasure. King Kelson, on the other hand, feels compelled to restore the Deryni to a place of respect and honorable service. He wants to allow humans and Deryni to be treated equally and to be evaluated on the basis of their abilities.

The inequality between humans and Deryni, with both being treated as inferior at various times, raises the question of prejudice. Under the Festilic kings, humans were treated as little better than slaves and often were seen only as members of their race, not as individuals judged by their abilities or behavior. After the Haldanes were returned to the throne, humans adopted similar attitudes toward the Deryni. The prejudice against the Deryni is based on the church's determination that Deryni magic is inherently evil, a judgment that was the result of human jealousy and fear. The books imply that this thinking is patently unfair and destructive to the society. The issue of prejudice could be seen as symbolic of the medieval relationships between Jews and Christians.

Connected to the issue of prejudice is the question of appropriate use of power. Without regard to danger or harm to their victims, evil Deryni misuse their powers to control humans and sometimes other Deryni. Humans who have power through their positions (secular or ecclesiastical) sometimes misuse it similarly. Kurtz clearly suggests that such use of power is wrong and should be punished.

—Sherry Stoskopf

THE CHRONICLES OF THOMAS COVENANT THE UNBELIEVER and THE SECOND CHRONICLES OF THOMAS COVENANT THE UNBELIEVER

Thomas Covenant, a leper who wields the "wild magic" of his white gold wedding ring, must put aside disbelief to prevent the destruction of an alternate universe called the Land

Author: Stephen R. Donaldson (1947-   )
Genre: Fantasy—magical world
Type of work: Novels

Time of plot: The late twentieth century
Location: New England and an alternate medieval
   world called the Land
First published: *Lord Foul's Bane* (1977), *The Illearth
   War* (1977), *The Power That Preserves* (1977), *The
   Wounded Land* (1980), *The One Tree* (1982), and
   White Gold Wielder (1983)

The Plot: The six novels describing the life of Thomas
Covenant are split into two trilogies, known as The
Chronicles of Thomas Covenant the Unbeliever and The
Second Chronicles of Thomas Covenant the Unbeliever.
As the series begins, Thomas Covenant, newly published
and well received, is writing his second novel while his
wife, Joan, visits her parents. Returning some weeks
later, she discovers a purple lesion on his right hand. He
consults a physician, receives a diagnosis of leprosy, and
loses two fingers to amputation. In terror of infection,
Joan divorces Covenant while he is in a leprosarium,
learning to survive the disease that renders him numb,
impotent, and outcast from society.

When he returns to Haven Farm, he finds that neighbors have eliminated the necessity for human contact, to
the point of having his groceries delivered. Defiant and
lonely, Covenant forces contact by paying his telephone
bill in person. A strange old prophet outside the telephone company tells him to "be true." Confused, Covenant stumbles into the path of a car. He awakes in a swirl
of fog atop a high rock tower called Kevin's Watch, in an
alternate reality. The evil voice of Lord Foul the Despiser
commands him to tell the Lords of the Land at Revelstone that the Staff of Law, lost by late High Lord Kevin,
has been found by the warped cavewight Drool Rockworm.

Covenant, incapacitated by vertigo, is rescued by the
barely postpubescent Lena, who takes him to her parents'
home. When Lena treats his wounds with hurtloam,
Covenant's body regains sensation. He realizes that his
disease-induced impotence has ended. Overwhelmed by
his returned sensations and convinced that he is dreaming, he rapes Lena. Lena's mother, Atiaran, learns of the
rape as she leads Covenant to Revelstone. Although she
is appalled, Atiaran keeps her promise to guide him.

At Revelstone, Covenant delivers Foul's message to
the Lords, who mount a quest for the lost staff. Surviving
many dangers, the seekers finally wrest the staff from
Drool by means of Covenant's wild magic, powered by
his white gold wedding ring. Covenant awakes in a hospital, his leprosy raging, convinced that his experiences
in the Land are dreams.

Months later (forty years in the Land), Covenant again
finds himself on Kevin's Watch and free of leprosy. By
means of the powerful Illearth Stone, Foul is again on the
attack. The benevolent Giants of the first quest are dead,
except three whom Foul has coerced into service as
"Ravers." High Lord Elena (the child of Lena's rape)
mounts another quest, drinks Earthblood, gains the
Power of Command, and, breaking the Law of Death,
commands the ghost of Kevin Landwaster to destroy
Foul. Instead, Kevin is overpowered, Elena dies, and the
Staff of Law is destroyed. Covenant fights his way to
Foul's Creche, uses wild magic to destroy the Illearth
Stone, and, believing the Land is safe, fades from con-
sciousness to reawaken at home.

Ten years later—four millennia in the Land—Covenant
and Linden Avery, a physician drawn into the Land by
accident, find themselves atop Kevin's Watch. Foul has
regained his power and created the Sunbane (vicious
three-day cycles of rain, drought, fertility, and pesti-
lence). The Clave (lore-masters corrupted by Foul) now
rule the Land from Revelstone, coercing blood from the
Land's people to appease the Sunbane. As Covenant
undertakes still another quest to Revelstone, to find the
Sunbane's source and destroy its stranglehold on the
Land, he learns that the Sunbane resulted from the destruction of the Staff of Law, which formerly supported
the natural order. He resolves to find the One Tree and
make another staff from its branches, thus delivering the
Land from the Sunbane.

When Covenant and Linden are joined by the Search
(a remnant of the Giants), Covenant persuades the
Search to take them to the Isle of the One Tree. When
they arrive, they find the Isle guarded by the Worm of the
World's End. Covenant cannot use his white magic to
destroy the Worm without destroying the Arch of Time,
within which the Land exists. When the Isle sinks, Covenant cannot fashion a new staff, so he, Linden, and the
remaining Giants undertake the dangerous journey back
to Revelstone.

Covenant finally masters the wild magic by realizing
that he is the keystone of the Arch of Time. Standing
firm, the Arch imprisons Foul within it. When the staff
reincarnates, Linden uses it to restore the Earthpower
and eradicate the Sunbane. The Land is thus healed.

Analysis: Shortly after publication of the first Covenant
trilogy in 1977, Stephen R. Donaldson received the 1979
John W. Campbell Award as best new writer of the year.
The trilogies reveal Donaldson's familiarity with medieval literature, his knowledge of leprosy, and his heavy

indebtedness to J. R. R. Tolkien's epic fantasy *The Lord of the Rings* (1968).

Although a hero on quest to right a wrong is an ancient theme, Donaldson's twist—Covenant is a leper—creates a protagonist who seems woefully inadequate to the task, as does Tolkien's hero, the hobbit Frodo Baggins. Blended with the theme of the quest to free the Land from evils inflicted by Lord Foul are the familiar medieval themes of alienation and impotence. Covenant's leprosy isolates him from society and prevents him from accepting the Land and his restored health as real; it also causes the sexual impotence that translates into a futility of spirit when he is swept by the Creator into the dreamlike Land.

Because Donaldson's physician father specialized in the treatment of leprosy, Donaldson possesses an esoteric knowledge of the disease that he uses to good effect in his depiction of Covenant and in the metaphors of health, decay, and numbness that pervade both trilogies. The leper's physical survival tool, visual surveillance of extremities (VSE), becomes Covenant's metaphorical survival tool as he struggles with appearance versus reality in the Land. Both leper and moral being must answer this question: What must one do in the face of death—what is the proper response to destruction?

Donaldson's debt to Tolkien appears most clearly in his creation of the characters and characteristics of the Land. Lord Foul, whose twisted perceptions cause him to despise the good that remains beyond his grasp, clearly derives from both Morgoth and Sauron, the "great enemies" in *The Lord of the Rings*. Like Morgoth, Foul manifests supernatural powers and predates the Land; like Sauron, Foul uses talismans to take possession of lesser beings, including three demoniac Ravers who can assume any form Foul commands.

Tolkien's benevolent Ents appear in two incarnations: as Donaldson's gentle Giants, slow of speech and slow to anger, dwindling as a race from lack of fecundity, and as the mysterious Forestals who guard the woods of Andelain (Donaldson's version of Lothlorien). Instead of orcs, Donaldson offers ur-viles, eyeless monsters who, like the orcs, result from perverted breeding schemes. In place of dwarves who carve stone and elves who tend forests, Donaldson presents Stonedownors who sense the hidden life of stone and woodhelvennin who communicate with trees. Tolkien's Gollum, a creature vulnerable to Sauron and twisted by the power of the One Ring, becomes Drool Rockworm, a cavewight vulnerable to Foul and driven insane by the stolen Staff of Law. The wizards of Middle Earth appear as the Lords of the Land, wielding wizardlike power through their staffs. In particular, the wizard Saruman, who in desperation becomes the tool of Sauron, is echoed in Lord Kevin Landwaster, who in desperation desecrated the Land rather than surrender it to Foul. Tolkien's elusive High Elves become Donaldson's mysterious and godlike elohim, who aid the final quest. The magnificent horses of Middle Earth become the Land's sentient ranyhyn. The word itself is a nod to the Houyhnhnms of Jonathan Swift's *Gulliver's Travels* (1726).

From both Tolkien and medieval lore Donaldson draws the motifs of hidden identity, prophecy, sacred or profane objects, Christ figures and Satan figures, enchanted places, enchanted or magical animals, words of power, and help unlooked for. From medieval literature he incorporates the motifs of a land's health being tied to human health, of moral decay being reflected in physical decay, of earthly struggles carrying eternal consequences, of evil disguised as good, and of fate calling the chosen to fulfill tasks upon which the destiny of many depends.

As further evidence of Tolkien's influence, Donaldson attempts to create languages for his characters. He fails in this, except for his vivid use of allegorical names. Whereas Tolkien constructed actual grammars and matched each language to its speakers, Donaldson invents an isolated, largely unpatterned and ungrammatical vocabulary. In addition, he makes such heavy use of a thesaurus that his ponderous prose often interferes with the story, especially when he attempts internal monologue.

Despite its flaws and omissions, the allegorical fantasy creates a believable, fairly consistent universe and provides an intriguing tale of the eternal war between good and evil. —*Sonya Cashdan and Barbara C. Stanley*

THE CHRONICLES OF TORNOR

Characters with some connection to Tornor Keep experience personal changes against backdrops of political conflict, war, and witchcraft

Author: Elizabeth A. Lynn (1946-   )
Genre: Fantasy—feminist
Type of work: Novels
Time of plot: The years 290, 410, and 522 since the founding of Kendra-on-the-Delta
Location: Various places in the land of Arun
First published: *Watchtower* (1979), *The Dancers of Arun* (1979), and *The Northern Girl* (1980)

The Plot: The three books of the Chronicles of Tornor all revolve around characters with a connection to Tornor Keep in the north of the land of Arun, but only the first, *Watchtower*, uses the keep itself as a significant part of the plot. Elizabeth Lynn uses the 232-year time span of the trilogy to show the evolution of a culture as women acquire equality and war becomes less important. In this change, Tornor Keep moves from being a stronghold and seat of war to being almost deserted and obsolete ruins.

Watchtower begins with the conquest of Tornor Keep by Col Istor, a Southerner. Col captures Errel, the prince of Tornor, and requires him to serve as his *cheari*, or jester. Ryke, a captured soldier, swears service to Col in order to keep Errel alive. When Col is visited by the messengers Sorren and Norres, Errel and Ryke escape with them to the legendary Van's Valley. There Errel learns to be a true *cheari*, a dancer and practitioner of martial arts similar to *aikido*. Ryke's struggle is to accept Sorren and Norres' lesbian love for each other, the idea of fighting without killing, and the idea that women can be as independent and as capable as men.

The novel concludes with the reconquest of Tornor Keep through an alliance with an army from one of the other keeps and the work of the *chearas* (a group of *chearis*). Errel then gives up his lordship to Sorren, his sister, who becomes the first Lady of Tornor, and returns to the Valley. Ryke remains in the North.

The Dancers of Arun also begins in Tornor Keep, 120 years later. Since the time of *Watchtower*, women have assumed much more leadership in society, the *chearis* have become the red clan, and both magic and homosexuality have become accepted. Kerris, the nephew of the lord of the keep, is set apart from the rest of the people both because his right arm was cut off in a raid by the Asech (another people of Arun) when he was a toddler and because he is mentally able to communicate with his brother Kel. The novel is largely about Kerris' search for wholeness.

Kel, the leader of a *chearas*, comes to Tornor to bring Kerris back to Elath, the witch-town. There Kerris begins to learn how to use his gift of "inspeaking" and enters into a homosexual relationship with Kel. At the same time, Elath is attacked by Asech witches who have been banished from their tribes and want to learn how to use their gifts. The teachers of Elath agree to instruct them, but one of the Asech does not understand the limits of the gifts and kills Sefer, a teacher and Kel's lover. After peace is made, Kel and the *chearas* depart. Kerris, after some hesitation, decides that he belongs with them and sets off to rejoin the group.

The third novel, *The Northern Girl*, begins in the Southern city of Kendra-on-the-Delta. In the 112 years between *The Dancers of Arun* and *The Northern Girl*, the cities of Arun have forbidden the use of edged weapons, and as a result the *chearis* have been extinguished. Kendra-on-the-Delta is governed by five ruling Houses, and its spiritual center is the Tanjo, the witch-school.

Sorren, the title character, is a bondservant to Arre Med and the lover of Arre's Yardmaster, Paxe. All three characters are women. The plot moves between Sorren's desires to go north and Arre's involvement with the politics in the city. Sorren dreams of the North; she eventually learns that she possesses the witch gift of seeing, but she sees the past, not the future. The secondary plot concerns the aspirations of one of the leaders of another House to Council status and his intent to use an exception to the ban on edged weapons as a way to gain that power. The attempt is defeated by Arre, but as a result of its failure, her jealous and power-hungry brother, Isak, arranges for her death. Sorren overhears his plan and warns Arre, for which she receives her freedom. Isak is exiled. Sorren goes north to Tornor, which is now inhabited by only eight people and some animals. Sorren stays and suggests an arrangement with Arre and one of her allies for Tornor's support. She also begins a relationship with Lady Merith's daughter, Kedera, and discovers that she has found her place.

Analysis: When the books of the Chronicles of Tornor were first published, Lynn's career as a fantasy and science-fiction author appeared full of promise. She had published *A Different Light* (1978), a science-fiction novel, before publishing the three Tornor novels, and she followed them with another science-fiction novel, *The Sardonyx Net* (1981), and a collection of previously published stories, *The Woman Who Loved the Moon and Other Stories* (1981). She was nominated for the John W. Campbell Award in 1977, and in 1980 she received the World Fantasy Award for *Watchtower* and for the short story "The Woman Who Loved the Moon" (originally published in *Amazons!*, edited by Jessica Amanda Salmonson, 1979). Her work received good reviews. In the remainder of the 1980's, however, her only two full-length books were both for children: *The Silver Horse* (1984), a fantasy novel, and *Babe Zaharias* (1988), a biography of the athlete.

Lynn's range as a writer is easily seen in the collection *The Woman Who Loved the Moon and Other Stories*. The stories include science fiction (set both on Earth and on alien worlds), fantasy, and what Lynn herself calls "category-straddling" stories that contain elements of science fiction and crime fiction, among other genres.

Science fiction was for a long time a market dominated by men, both in readership and in authorship. It was not until the 1960's and 1970's, with the rise of the women's movement, that women began to both read and write science fiction. Suzy McKee Charnas and Joanna Russ have both written of the difficulties they had in beginning to write science fiction with only male role models available to them. Lynn's work shows her own attempts to shape the genre into one in which women have a place. Lynn was teaching in the women's studies program at San Francisco State University when the Chronicles of Tornor were published, and the importance of feminism to her is clear in the novels. She uses the freedom generated by the creation of an imaginary world to create a society in which women are truly equal to men.

The Chronicles of Tornor resist many of the clichés and stock characters of fantasy. There are no wise old men, great warriors, submissive love-struck damsels in distress, or warrior women who learn their place as wives. Nor is Lynn concerned with the outward action of an adventure story, one of the traditional masculine forms of fiction. Although the novels are not free from violence, and Ryke and Paxe are both soldiers, the significant development and action of the novels tends to be internal rather than external. All three novels include external conflicts resolved by some form of violence, but the books each end on a change or resolution in a character rather than in external circumstances. They are character driven rather than plot driven.

There are also many differences in the culture and lifestyle of people in Arun from those of more traditional fantasy. No professions are gender-specific by the time of *The Northern Girl*, and both homosexual and heterosexual relationships are accepted, as is bisexuality. The generic pronoun is the female, and a man who marries takes his wife's name. In addition to a lack of gender bias, there is also no racism in Arun. Characters are described as having varying skin tones, but no suggestion is ever made that skin color is any more of a racial distinction than is hair or eye color. Although the Asech peoples are identified as another race (more by culture, custom, and language than by physical appearance), they are not discriminated against because of this in *The Northern Girl*. The earlier books reveal characters' hostility to the Asech, but that hostility is shown as negative. Arun still has a nondemocratic class structure; however, the feudalism of *Watchtower* has been replaced by a

more capitalist republic in *The Northern Girl*, and most of Lynn's characters are people who engage in the day-to-day tasks of farming, cooking, or shopping. The novels are fantasies, but they are neither romances nor utopias.

—*Elisabeth Anne Leonard*

THE CHRYSALIDS

A group of adolescents with telepathic powers battles persecution in a post-apocalyptic society devoted to maintaining the purity of all species and destroying mutant life-forms

Author: John Wyndham (John Wyndham Parkes Lucas Beynon Harris, 1903-1969)
Genre: Science fiction—post-holocaust
Type of work: Novel
Time of plot: A.D. 4000-5000
Location: Waknuk, Labrador, Canada
First published: 1955

The Plot: *The Chrysalids* was published in Great Britain under that title and in the United States as *Re-Birth*. The novel takes place after Tribulation, a cataclysmic event (probably a nuclear holocaust that devastated the world thousands of years earlier) attributed to God's anger in the tradition of Eden and the Flood. The agrarian folk, technologically backward and beset by fear and prejudice, obey a strict interpretation of the Old Testament, eradicating all crop and animal mutations. Stern commandments and proclamations hang on their walls, telling them that "blessed is the norm" and to "keep pure the stock of the Lord" and "watch thou for the mutant!" Humans "made in God's image" reside in communities throughout Labrador, and deviations from the norm are ritualistically "purified" (exterminated) or exiled to the Fringes, the abnormal territories, where they forage for food and eke out an existence.

David Strorm, the narrator, has a deep secret. For years, he, his half-cousin Rosalind, and several other youngsters have been communicating telepathically. Although by appearance they are "norms," they are mutants within and a potential threat to the existing order. Instinctively, they have never revealed their abilities to anyone except for David's kind and protective Uncle Axel.

David's life changes forever when, at the age of ten, he meets Sophie, a girl with six toes. Her parents are terrified of her being discovered by David's intractable father, Joseph Strorm, Waknuk's fanatical patriarch. Joseph has destroyed some of his own children and relatives as blasphemies, and his deformed brother, nick-named Spider, leads a ragtag group of marauding mutants of the Fringes. Sophie's secret is exposed, and Joseph whips David until he admits where Sophie has gone. Sophie's family disappears into the Fringes. Following the birth of David's sister Petra, a child with incredible powers, six years pass without further incident.

The adolescents are betrayed when one marries a "norm" only to commit suicide after confiding in her unsympathetic spouse. Uncle Axel murders the callous husband, but Petra's awakened and uncontrolled powers send psychic blasts that paralyze the others, arouse suspicion and a witch hunt, and draw telepathic responses from Sealand (New Zealand), which sends an aircraft to rescue them. Pursued by Joseph Strorm and his troops, David, Petra, and Rosalind battle their way to the Fringes, where David's banished uncle, Spider, captures them. Spider brutally beats David and leaves him to die, having announced his carnal designs on Rosalind. Sophie, her innocence corrupted, conceals David and murders the albino guarding Rosalind. As the posse descends for the kill, the Sealanders arrive, annihilating everyone except the young telepaths, whom they transport to Sealand to help build the world anew.

Analysis: Writing what he termed "logical fantasy," John Wyndham cast an unsettling shadow across the apparently placid landscape of post-World War II England. The literary heir of H. G. Wells, Wyndham blended fantasy, horror, and science fiction into a seminal body of work that resonates in the tales of many writers, including Richard Matheson, Clive Barker, James Herbert, and Stephen King. Generally overlooked in the United States, where it went out of print, *The Chrysalids* is the centerpiece of Wyndham's three most important novels, the psychological and creative bridge between the Wells-inspired *The Day of the Triffids* (1951) and his startling fusion of science fiction and horror, *The Midwich Cuckoos* (1957), which also appeared under the title *Village of the Damned*. The story was filmed as *Village of the Damned* in 1960 and 1995.

As their beautiful Sealand rescuer tells David and Rosalind, "The essential quality of living is change; change is evolution; and we are part of it." In Wyndham's fiction, the world is in constant flux, and most people are either unwilling to face change or too eager to capitalize on it for their own advantage. Caught in this paradox are the Wyndham protagonists, ordinary men, women, and children pummeled by the past and present into resolutions of transcendence and new, meaningful undertak-

ings. No guarantees await them in the future. Sealand, to which David, Rosalind, and Petra escape, is peopled by beings who view themselves as superior and, by their own admission and as shown in their obsession with Petra's harrowing gift, are doomed one day to self-destruct, as have the unyielding remnants of the Old People they are supplanting.

The hubris of humans then, not the technology they create, undermines them. *The Chrysalids*, critical of Old Testament justice, still draws a comparable moral from the New Testament: "for whatsoever a man soweth, that shall he also reap." Ironically, Joseph Strorm refuses to acknowledge, as his own, his misshapen brother, his "impure" children, and all the abnormalities that surround him; he systematically fashions his own doom. People are all of one origin, the novel insists, and to deny this precipitates the tragic demise of humanity.

This portrayal of kinship demonstrates Wyndham's resolute refusal to perpetuate traditional stereotypes. Appearances mean little; truth, beauty, and deformity reside within, as does the pupa inside the chrysalid. Like her namesake in William Shakespeare's *As You Like It*, Rosalind personifies charm, courage, and compassion. The stoic heroism of David, like his biblical counterpart's, is tempered by wisdom and tenderness. In a scene that anticipates the "grokking" of Robert Heinlein's *Stranger in a Strange Land* (1961), David and Rosalind, destined to be lovers, meld minds until "Neither one of us existed any more; for a time there was a single being that was both."

The Chrysalids proposes that ignorant adherence to the "word," or to religious tenets, has dehumanized the world, and that only in transcendence of past beliefs will humanity resurrect itself. The message is distinct: People must throw off the mind-forged chains of the past, bury fears and prejudices, and walk as one with enlightened steps into the future, or else stumble and perish forever.

—*Erskine Carter*

THE CHYMICAL WEDDING

Poet Michael Darken is forced to confront his failings and recognize that people are unbalanced without the Hermetic principle of unity among all things and people

Author: (Victor) Lindsay Clarke (1939-   )
Genre: Fantasy—Magical Realism
Type of work: Novel
Time of plot: The 1980's and the mid-nineteenth century

Location: Norfolk, England
First published: 1989

The Plot: British poet Michael Darken is at the end of his tether. His marriage to Jess has fallen apart, he is incapable of writing verse, and he is employed unsatisfactorily as a college lecturer. His sympathetic publisher lends him his weekend cottage, "The Pightle," in Munding St. Mary's, Norfolk, for the summer vacation. The village is still curiously feudal, dominated by Easterness Hall, and Ralph, the last of the dynastic Agnew family. Some opposition is provided by Michael's nearest neighbor, Bob Crossley, a socialist and a stalwart of the Campaign for Nuclear Disarmament.

Also present in the village, staying at the lodge as guests of Ralph, are Edward Nesbit and his young American assistant, Laura, a talented potter. Edward was a celebrated poet when Michael was young but has since dried up. Michael is drawn into their company and then into their quest, which is to discover what they can of Louisa Agnew, the last link in the Agnew tradition of alchemical research. They already have discovered the crucial date in 1848 when Henry was working on a poetic epic about the Hermetic mystery and Louisa, always his willing apprentice, offered to help by writing a prose treatise, "An Open Invitation to the Chymical Wedding."

The other narrative strand is Louisa's, setting out her inspired and dutiful nature while narrating events in the village of the mid-nineteenth century. The most important, in addition to Louisa's assumed task, is the arrival of a new vicar, Edwin Frere, and his wife, Emilia. Fresh from Cambridge, Emilia clearly resents her separation from her family there. Soon Emilia becomes pregnant. After losing her baby, she demonstrates a formidable manipulative will and eventually returns to Cambridge, deserting Edwin.

As Michael moves into Edward and Laura's world, he is alternately threatened and attracted by Edward; with Laura, it is only the former. He is aware that both are erudite and is menaced by Edward's reading of the tarot and his insistence on Michael's recounting of his dreams for interpretation. Gradually, Henry and Louisa intervene more in their lives.

Louisa seems to be blocked. Alchemy is set in a specifically sexual set of imagery, and she is a virgin. The deserted Edwin, tormented by sexual fantasies, reports to her, and their problems are assuaged temporarily. Similarly, as if possessed, Michael and Laura couple.

Both events lead to disaster. Edwin, a man of con-science, castrates himself. Louisa's book is too explicit and provokes jealousy in her father. It is burned. Edward takes Michael to a place where he might kill him but suffers a massive heart attack. Michael's prompt action saves him, though he is left in emergency care. The results, in the end, are not disastrous. Both Edward and Michael become able to write again. Laura is now alchemically virgin and thus is able to decide her own destiny. Edwin remains Louisa's spiritual brother.

Analysis: Winner of the 1989 Whitbread Prize for Fiction, *The Chymical Wedding* is a complex text notable for its blend of contemporary and historical realism and fantasy. In many ways, it resembles the work of John Fowles, but with a more magical inspiration.

Lindsay Clarke's characterization is superb. Both Michael and Edward initially are rather alienating beings, and Edward remains so for some time. Both Edwin and Louisa at first seem merely stereotypes, and Laura a cipher. Gradually, their characters come alive and form the motivating forces for the narrative.

The fantasy element is essential for the story but is blended subtly. Having seemed distinct, the two narrative lines blur, interact, and parallel each other. Information about alchemy adds to the pleasure offered by the text and is central to the plot. Where the plot lines intersect and the alchemy enters is the relationship between men and women.

None of the characters has a successful relationship when the story begins. Louisa and Henry are too close to be healthy, though his dominance is intellectual rather than pederastic. Michael has driven away his wife and is unable to relate to any woman. Edward appears the most selfish and exploits Ralph's nostalgia about their youthful homosexual relationship. A fully developed literary *bête noire*, he is capable of colossal rudeness and uses Laura ruthlessly. His comeuppance is not the product of sexual jealousy, however, and he is pleased with both Laura's self-realization and Michael's growth.

The development of the plot has important personal ramifications for the participants, but there is a philosophical core. The most significant occasion in Louisa's history is the Vatican Council, at which, even at the height of Renaissance humanism, Aristotle was chosen as the cornerstone of Christian philosophy over Hermes Trismegistus. This was a triumph for the male and intellectual over the female and feeling. Hermeticism, a belief in forms of magic and in the unity of the cosmos, was needed in a threatening world and in the face of moribund Christianity. This knowledge comes to Louisa after she first sleeps with Edwin. His response is emasculation to save others and expiate his guilt. Seemingly, this accords well with the Aristotelian principle. He is redeemed by his continuing role as the mystic brother. His chance of happiness thus is increased, and Louisa achieves serenity.

In the modern sphere, Laura's freedom is bought ostensibly at the expense of both her former lover and her potential future lover, but Edward is happy and Michael comes to recognize women's needs and identities outside himself. He is able to contact his family, treat Jess's new lover respectfully, and take responsibility for his children. In every case, the result is benevolent and Hermetic.

—*Mike Dickinson*

THE CIRCUS OF DR. LAO

A circus owned by the mysterious Dr. Lao disrupts the lives of the citizens of a small Arizona town

Author: Charles G. Finney (1905-1984)
Genre: Fantasy—mythological
Type of work: Novel
Time of plot: The 1930's
Location: Abalone, Arizona
First published: 1935

The Plot: Charles G. Finney wrote *The Circus of Dr. Lao* after his travels to China during the 1920's, when he served as part of a United States garrison stationed in Tientsin. Finney's knowledge of Chinese mythology provides the backdrop for the more fantastic elements of the novel.

The Circus of Dr. Lao consists of three tiers of set pieces, or short scenes, that introduce and explore the circus and its attractions. Speculations on the nature of the circus prior to its arrival serve as the first tier of set pieces, during which most of the main characters, and many minor characters, are introduced. These characters busily enter and exit from scene to scene, their personalities defined exclusively by their reactions to the circus.

Most notable among these characters, none of whom dominates the book, is Dr. Lao, the proprietor, who guides his visitors through the exhibits while providing intricate and inventive commentary. Dr. Lao speaks in different dialects, mirroring and mocking his visitors' expectations. Standing resolutely at the novel's center, he expounds at length about his circus but rarely divulges information about himself. Thus, the center of the circus remains a mystery.

Other characters of note include Mr. Etaoin (whose first name is not given), the town newspaper's proofreader; Miss Agnes Birdsong, a high school English teacher; Mr. Larry Kamper, a United States soldier recently returned from China; and Mrs. Howard T. Cassan, a widow who frequents fortune-tellers. The mythological circus performers include a medusa, a magician, a satyr, a mermaid, a sea serpent, and a hedge hound. As with the human characters, these creatures all have their moments in the spotlight.

The second tier of set pieces provides a closer examination of the circus as it parades down the town's main street. The parade culminates in lengthy and hilarious arguments over the exact nature of the beasts in the circus, particularly as to whether one attraction is a bear or merely a caged Russian.

The third tier of set pieces, exploring the interactions between circus visitors and circus stars, provides explanations for the existence of, or stories behind the capture of, many of the mythological beasts. Among such scenes are Miss Birdsong's near seduction by the satyr and Mr. Etaoin's conversation with the sea serpent.

Mrs. Cassan's encounter with the seer Apollonius midway through the book best demonstrates Finney's talent for brutal lucidity. Apollonius tells Mrs. Cassan that her oil investments will never pay off, that she will never remarry, and that she is doomed for the rest of her days to relive the repetitive and useless actions that compose her existence. Upon deliverance of this verdict, Mrs. Cassan attempts to befriend the uninterested Apollonius. Walking once more into the sunshine beyond the tent, she tells a minor character that the seer had encouraging news for her.

The magical events reach a climax with a summoning of the devil and a virgin sacrifice, after which the citizens of Abalone, stunned by all they have witnessed (but perhaps unchanged), stumble out of the tent and back into their all-too-real small-town world. Finney includes as epilogue "The Catalogue," a whimsical dictionary of all the people, animals, places, and historical events mentioned in the novel.

Analysis: Winner of the award for most original novel in 1936 from the American Bookseller's Association and subsequently made into the film *The Seven Faces of Doctor Lao* (1963), *The Circus of Dr. Lao* was Finney's first and most critically popular novel. Although only thirty years old upon publication of *The Circus of Dr. Lao*, Finney produced only three other book-length works during the next half century. These include the surreal science-fiction novel *The Unholy City* (1937), the lighthearted Chinese fantasy *The Magician Out of Manchuria* (1968), and the less-acclaimed *Past the End of the Pavement* (1939).

The strength of *The Circus of Dr. Lao* lies in its seamless interweaving of various mythological traditions, from the Chinese to the Greek. Finney updates and refines such archetypes for a modern age while implying that the myths of the past are far more glorious than the small-minded concerns of the present.

The novel belongs to the peculiar but potent subgenre of "circus fantasy," other representatives of which include Tom Reamy's deliberate pastiche of Finney's novel, *Blind Voices* (1978), Angela Carter's *Nights at the Circus* (1984), and Brooke Stevens' *The Circus of the Earth and the Air* (1994).

The most significant author to be directly influenced by Finney is Ray Bradbury, whose *Something Wicked This Way Comes* (1962) owes a large debt to *The Circus of Dr. Lao*. *Something Wicked This Way Comes* can be read as a corollary to *The Circus of Dr. Lao* in that it takes the circus as a given and focuses on one or two characters who visit the circus. Bradbury so admired Finney that he made Finney's short novel the title story of his strange fantasy anthology *The Circus of Dr. Lao and Other Improbable Stories* (1956).

The unique strength of the circus fantasy, and Finney's novel in particular, is its reduction of the broad canvas of the world to a smaller, stylized microcosm, with the point of making ironic and satiric comment on humankind. The interactions between circus and observer define the observer, illuminating fears, desires, dreams, and prejudices. *The Circus of Dr. Lao* describes Finney's own journey from the small towns of the United States to the alien outreaches of China. Finney's novel merely reverses the order, so that the alien intrudes into the realm of the banal.
                                                    —*Jeff VanderMeer*

THE CITADEL OF FEAR

A battle between two ancient Aztec deities is re-enacted by two American adventurers who inadvertently revived it when they stumbled upon a lost Aztec tribe fifteen years earlier

Author: Francis Stevens (Gertrude Barrows Bennett, 1884-1939?)
Genre: Fantasy—mythological
Type of work: Novel
Time of plot: The early 1900's

Location: Carpentier, a small town in the eastern United States
First published: 1970 (serial form, *Argosy*, 1918)

The Plot: American adventurers Colin "Boots" O'Hara and Archer Kennedy are searching for gold in the wastes of Mexico when they chance upon the plantation of Svend Biornson, his wife Astrid, and their young daughter. The house contains artifacts that the greedy Kennedy recognizes as valuable relics related to the worship of Quetzalcoatl, the ancient Aztec lord of the air. That evening, O'Hara and Kennedy are abducted from the plantation by a band of white Indians and spirited away to Tlapallan, the fabled lost Aztec city whose inhabitants are divided in their worship of the benevolent Quetzalcoatl and the evil Nacoc-Yaotl. The two men escape but are recaptured after causing considerable mischief. Biornson, whose wife is a Tlapallan, intercedes on O'Hara's behalf and engineers his escape into the desert. Kennedy, who witnessed a sacred ritual of the priests of Nacoc-Yaotl, is left to their mercy.

Fifteen years later, O'Hara visits his sister Cliona and her husband Anthony Rhodes at their bungalow in suburban Carpentier. The house is ransacked three times. After the third incident, O'Hara pursues the apelike creature responsible for the damage, tracking it to an estate in nearby Undine owned by self-styled animal breeder Chester Reed and his daughter.

Bothered by the unwholesomeness of Reed's business, O'Hara takes Reed's daughter to stay with Cliona. Upon his return to the estate, O'Hara discovers that Reed is none other than Archer Kennedy, who befriended an ambitious priest of Nacoc-Yaotl during his captivity and learned secrets that helped him to bring about the destruction of Tlapallan. His "daughter" is actually the kidnapped child of Svend Biornson, and his menagerie of animals is the product of experiments with a ritual of Nacoc-Yaotl that allows the scientific dissolution and reconstruction of an organism in whatever form the experimenter wills. The megalomaniacal Kennedy plans to terrorize the world with his godlike power and intends to make O'Hara his first victim. O'Hara is anesthetized before the experiment, and in a delirium he imagines that Kennedy is the avatar of Nacoc-Yaotl and that Biornson's daughter, who has returned to rescue him, is the reincarnation of Quetzalcoatl. O'Hara is saved when a fire, possibly of divine origin, breaks out in the laboratory, destroying Kennedy and his house of horrors.

Analysis: Francis Stevens' first novel appeared at a time (and in a venue) in which horror, fantasy, and science fiction had yet to separate as distinct genres. In the populist spirit of the early general fiction pulps, *The Citadel of Fear* contains elements of all three genres, along with healthy dollops of romance, adventure, and mystery.

The Citadel of Fear is part of the lost-race fantasy tradition popularized by H. Rider Haggard in his tales of Allan Quatermain and She, particularly with its suggestion of human beings caught up in the working out of mythological destinies. It bears comparison to work by Stevens' contemporaries Edgar Rice Burroughs and Abraham Merritt (for whom some readers thought "Francis Stevens" was a pseudonym) in its emphasis on the notion that mystical beliefs of certain ancient cultures derived from advanced scientific knowledge never passed on to present civilization. It differs in one important respect from Burroughs' Pellucidar series (1922-1963) and Merritt's novels *The Moon Pool* (1919) and *The Face in the Abyss* (1931), in that the bulk of the tale is set in the everyday world, many years after the discovery of the lost race's world and its countless marvels. This technique allowed Stevens to forgo the usual piling on of wonders most writers of lost-race fantasies employed in the creation of their magical worlds. Instead she suggests the alien nature of Tlapallan by showing the horrifying strangeness of one element from it intruding upon the commonplace world.

The ritual of Nacoc-Yaotl by which Kennedy perverts biology to create grotesque monsters in the image of his sick imagination is one of Stevens' most original contributions to fantasy literature. At the same time, the drama Kennedy enacts within the story is typical of the subgenre. Lost-race fantasy literature abounds with tales of unscrupulous characters who bring about personal and cultural downfall through the misuse of godlike powers. Stevens gave the obvious moral to such stories an added layer of meaning through the ambiguous ending of her novel: Is Kennedy an evil man done in by his overweening ambition, or is he merely a pawn in the greater cosmic struggle between good and evil fought by Quetzalcoatl and Nacoc-Yaotl (not to mention the deities of numerous other cultures)?

Like other fantasists who worked in the days before science fiction afforded writers a variety of alien worlds through which to reflect on humanity and its world, Stevens used the lost-race story as a crucible for studying the immutability of human nature over time and geographic distance. She returned to the form several times in her brief career, most notably in her tale of Lost Atlantis, *Claimed* (1966; serial form, *Argosy*, 1920), and in her short novel of a pagan survival along the Amazon,

"Sunfire" (serial form, *Weird Tales*, 1923). Her alternate history novel *The Heads of Cerberus* (1952; serial form, *Thrill Book*, 1919), with its speculations on a totalitarian future America, clearly derives from the same tradition.

—*Stefan Dziemianowicz*

CITIES IN FLIGHT

Earth's culture, represented by the flying city of New York, spreads through the galaxy and decays as the universe comes to an end

Author: James Blish (1921-1975)
Genre: Science fiction—future history
Type of work: Novels
Time of plot: 2012-4004
Location: Earth, Jupiter, various star systems in and beyond the galaxy, and the center of the universe
First published: *Cities in Flight* (1970, as tetralogy); previously published as *Earthman, Come Home* (1955), *They Shall Have Stars* (1956; also published as *Year 2018*), *The Triumph of Time* (1958; also published as *A Clash of Cymbals*), and *A Life for the Stars* (1962)

The Plot: Much of the material making up *Cities in Flight* was published in other forms between 1950 and 1962 and in a different order from that presented in the completed tetralogy. The core of the story idea was published in a series of novelettes—"Okie" (1950), "Bindlestiff" (1950), "Sargasso of Lost Cities" (1953), and "Earthman Come Home" (1953)—which were revised and combined into *Earthman, Come Home*, the third novel in the chronological sequence. *They Shall Have Stars*, the first novel in the sequence, was formed by combining the novelettes "Bridge" (1952) and "At Death's End" (1954). The second novel in the sequence, *A Life for the Stars*, was published as juvenile science fiction fours years after the fourth, *The Triumph of Time*.

The overarching conception melding these disparately written pieces into a single volume is James Blish's elaboration of a complete future history that begins in the early twenty-first century, as the United States and the Soviet Union are about to merge into a single bureaucratic state. Blish conceives of a new galactic Earthmanist culture—a version of Western culture—formed on the basis of antigravity screens (spindizzies) that allow entire cities to take flight and anti-agathics (antideath drugs) that allow the long lifetimes required for interstellar flight.

Earth dominates the galaxy after the defeat of the previous hegemony, the Vegan tyranny, a vaguely defined humanoid/alien civilization. The galaxy is "pollinated" by Earth cities, which function as itinerant industrial bases (Okies) and are policed by the Earth "cops," who exist in creative tension with the Okies. A basic plot idea throughout the series is that some cities are good citizens, such as New York City, the "protagonist" city of the series. Others have become rogues, or "bindlestiffs." The worst of these, the legendary Interstellar Master Traders (IMT), have slaughtered an entire planet. As background to the narrative, Earth culture decays as Earth's growing bureaucracy and fear of the Okies destroys the galactic economy. As time itself draws to an end, in the fortieth century, a new alien civilization, the Web of Hercules, rises to power.

They Shall Have Stars tells, in alternating narratives, of the development of the two technologies on which the rest of the series depends. Bliss Wagoner, a U.S. senator, secretly sponsors both projects in an effort to create an escape route for Western culture. In the first of the two narratives, a space pilot, Paige Russell, falls in love with Anne Abbott, the daughter of the president of the drug company where immortality drugs are being developed. The second narrative is told from the point of view of Robert Helmuth, a construction supervisor of the giant "bridge" being built on Jupiter by remote control to test the theories that will make antigravity possible. At the end, Wagoner arranges for Russell and Abbott to become the nucleus of a colonizing diaspora from Earth. Wagoner is executed for treason by the paranoid head of the Federal Bureau of Investigation.

A Life for the Stars, set in the thirty-second century, tells of the departure of Earth's cities. Crispin DeFord, a youth, is impressed by the city of Scranton, Pennsylvania, as it departs from an Earth whose economy has collapsed. The novel is essentially a coming-of-age story in which the young DeFord, thrust into perilous circumstances, manages by virtue of his wits and the help of older mentors to survive and, at the end, to become city manager of New York, which Scranton encounters in space. Much of the narrative deals with DeFord's education, after he is transferred to New York, in the culture and technology of the Okie city. DeFord demonstrates his abilities in a series of daring escapades that help save New York from a bindlestiff.

Earthman, Come Home, set in the last half of the fourth millennium, tells of New York under the guidance of Mayor John Amalfi and the new city manager, Mark Hazelton. A series of escapades, including equipping the entire planet of He with spindizzies (told in *A Life for the Stars*), brings the city into constant conflict with the Earth police. New York is forced to join a "hobo jungle" of unemployed Okie cities. Amalfi, through his understanding of the principles of cultural development, is able to manipulate the cities to march on Earth and, through their flight across the galaxy, to lure out of hiding the Vegan Fort, the last lurking vestige of the Vegan tyranny. Amalfi destroys the Fort by "flying" a planet at intergalactic speed across the path of the Fort as it enters the solar system. New York ends up grounded on a planet in the Greater Magellanic Cloud, where it must defeat the IMT, which has hidden there, in order to begin a new culture in the wake of the collapse of the old.

The Triumph of Time is set in the first years of the forty-first century. The scientists of New York and the planet He, now returned from intergalactic space, discover that in the repeating cycles of time itself a twin antimatter universe will collide with the known universe to begin a new big bang. The only chance for "survival"—which amounts to the right to determine the physical composition of a new universe—is to fly to the center of the universe. To do this, Amalfi must fight off a rebellion against New York's hegemony in the Greater Magellanic Cloud, dispel the apathy of a culture grown old, and race the rising galactic civilization, the Web of Hercules, to the center. At the end, at the moment of his death, Amalfi chooses to make a new universe completely different from the old one.

Analysis: *Cities in Flight* as a whole is more than the sum of its parts, which are pastiches of the science-fiction tradition. The bold image of flying cities and the theme of immortality come directly from part 3 of Jonathan Swift's *Gulliver's Travels* (1726), although Blish borrows none of Swift's satire. Most of the narrative is typical "space opera" on a grand scale. Devices of science are manufactured as the plot demands, within a context of flashing space battles and an entire galaxy improbably turned into a human landscape that looks and behaves like a somewhat comic map of nineteenth century Europe, complete with squabbling governments and officious military. Blish's imagined future, sweeping to the end of time itself, is in the high science-fiction tradition reaching back to H. G. Wells and Olaf Stapledon, although Blish compresses his future into a few thousand years. The mapping of the detailed future history that Blish added as *Cities in Flight* developed is much like the work of Robert A. Heinlein in his Future History and Isaac Asimov in the Foundation series. Blish's imaginary history reflects directly the ideological concerns of America in the Cold War period.

Cities in Flight derives a distinctive quality and sense of wholeness from the claim, woven into and around the narrative, that the series reflects a serious philosophy of history. This claim is supported by the excerpted fictional study *The Milky Way: Five Cultural Portraits*, which Blish adds as prologue to some of the novels. Critics have discussed Blish's reliance on Oswald Spengler's *The Decline of the West* (1918-1922), a work that presents a theory of evolution of cultures and civilizations as an organic, cyclic process. Richard D. Mullen discusses this idea in "Blish, van Vogt and the Rise of Spengler" in the *Riverside Quarterly* (1968).

This tetralogy cannot be taken seriously as philosophical fiction. Some of Blish's later fiction, most notably *A Case of Conscience* (1959), stakes a more serious claim. *Cities in Flight*, however, is held together imaginatively by a consistent tension between two ideas. The first is that history and cultures rise and fall in repeated patterns. This process is inexorable and shapes and transcends the will of the individuals in those cultures. The second is that rare and perceptive individuals, such as Bliss Wagoner and John Amalfi, can see those patterns and act as agents of creative change, to some extent transcending them. The thousand-year life span of Amalfi represents this transcendence.

Blish reproduces images of the typical American hero, a self-reliant, institution-defying individual. The weight of historical destiny—the triumph of time—hangs heavily over the narrative and informs the characterization of Amalfi, who is a well-developed, self-conscious figure. This realistic characterization gives *Cities in Flight* and its ambivalent end real poignancy.

—*D. Barrowman Park*

CITY

The history of the Webster family and its robot, Jenkins, as humankind abandons its cities and eventually its planet

Author: Clifford D. Simak (1904-1988)
Genre: Science fiction—future history
Type of work: Stories
Time of plot: From the 1990's until thousands of years in the future
Location: Earth, Jupiter, and another dimension
First published: 1952

The Plot: Winner of the 1953 International Fantasy Award for best fiction, *City* is assembled primarily from eight stories published between 1944 and 1951. Framed by an "Editor's Preface" and "Notes," these tales are presented as a future ethnographer's collection of "the stories that the Dogs tell." After the death of John W. Campbell, Jr., in 1971, Clifford D. Simak wrote a ninth story for editor Harry Harrison's *Astounding: John W. Campbell Memorial Anthology* (1973); in 1980 this last story was added to a revised version of *City*, along with an "Author's Note."

The first three tales in *City* chronicle humankind's abandonment of its cities for a pastoral existence made possible by advanced technology. In the first story, "City," set in the 1990's, John W. Webster flees to the country and builds a house. Much of the rest of *City* focuses on that house and Webster's descendants.

"Huddling Place," the second story, is set in 2117. Jerome A. Webster has written the first reference work on Martian physiology. He is needed to save the life of the Martian philosopher Juwain. Jerome's robot, Jenkins, fails to notify Jerome that a spaceship has arrived to take Jerome to Mars; the robot believes that its agoraphobic owner would not leave the house. Juwain therefore dies before he can reveal a secret mental concept that supposedly would solve many of humankind's problems. More than sixty years later, in "Census," Jerome's son Thomas perfects the technology needed to take humankind to the stars. Thomas's son Allen pilots the first spaceship to Alpha Centauri, and another son, Bruce, has given dogs the ability to speak through a genetic engineering technology called "boosting."

The next two stories, "Desertion" and "Paradise," depict humanity's abandonment of its native planet. More than a century has passed when astronaut Kent Fowler and his dog Towser are genetically transformed into "lopers," the native life-form of Jupiter. As lopers, they discover that Jupiter is a veritable paradise that they are loath to leave. Only after five years does Fowler return to his base to report his findings. On Earth, president Tyler Webster, afraid that it would mean the end of humankind, tries unsuccessfully to suppress Fowler's information. His fears are warranted: Once Fowler's report becomes known, most of humankind leaves Earth to live on Jupiter as lopers.

The remaining stories illustrate the fate of Earth after humankind's exodus. Almost two millennia later, in "Hobbies," a few humans still live in Geneva, "wild robots" have gathered in the countryside, and dogs have begun efforts to "civilize" wolves and have discovered the existence of other dimensions. To allow the dogs to develop unhindered by humans, Jon Webster seals off Geneva before putting himself into suspended animation. Another five thousand years pass before the events in "Aesop." Most of the world's animals can talk and live in harmony; unfortunately, killing is reintroduced to the world by an other-dimensional being and descendants of humans who were not sealed in Geneva. After the other-dimensional being is stopped, Jenkins the robot takes the unsealed humans to another dimension, where he remains for five thousand years.

Returning to Earth in "The Simple Way" (originally published as "The Trouble with Ants"), Jenkins discovers that ants, "boosted" thousands of years earlier, are erecting an enormous, continuously expanding building. As available living space becomes scarcer, the "wild robots" travel to the stars and the animals leave Earth to live in other dimensions. "Epilog" takes place untold millennia after Jenkins' return. He is the only robot on Earth, pondering the mystery of the ants as a spaceship lands near Webster House. Some of the wild robots who had left Earth millennia earlier have returned to invite Jenkins to assist in the work to be done on other planets.

Analysis: Important for many reasons, *City* remains Simak's most famous work. Its first two stories are generally recognized as the first works representative of Simak's fully developed style. All the tales contain elements and motifs found frequently in his stories and novels. The fourth tale in the work, "Desertion," is one of science fiction's most frequently anthologized stories. This collection is also notable for being recognized as an important work at a time when science fiction and fantasy were only beginning to receive serious notice within the literary community. The International Fantasy Award, which *City* won in 1953, predates both the Hugo and the Nebula awards. *City* received its award the same year that Alfred Bester's *The Demolished Man* (1953) became the first winner of the Hugo as best novel.

City is representative of two publishing trends in science fiction: a 1940's trend in which writers produced several stories linked by recurring characters, settings, or themes (for example, Robert A. Heinlein's Future History stories) and a 1950's trend in which writers produced "fixups," assembling previously published short stories, often with new framing or cementing material, into "novels." Other noted examples of such "fixups" include Ray Bradbury's *The Martian Chronicles* (1950), Theodore Sturgeon's *More than Human* (1953), and A. E. van Vogt's *The War Against the Rull* (1959).

Since its earliest days, science fiction has probed for what constitutes the nature of humanity. Few works explore human nature as well as *City*. Simak uses mutants, extraterrestrials, boosted animals and insects, humans transformed into extraterrestrials, extradimensional beings, and robots to highlight, contrast, re-create, and even warn against such human qualities as aspiration, doubt, love, homesickness, aggression, passivity, and curiosity.

The conclusion of "Desertion," in which a man and his dog literally become equals, is one of science fiction's most brilliant expressions of the possibility that humanity is not the highest form of existence in the universe. This possibility is likewise evident in the fact that Joe the mutant and Juwain the Martian both possess mental capabilities beyond those of mere humans, and the animals of Earth (with minor mechanical assistance) achieve a universal peace, something humans were able only to dream of. Ironically, the most "human" character in *City* is Jenkins, one of science fiction's most fully developed robots. Simak was guilty of understatement when, in his author's note to "Epilog," he explained that the collection's last tale "had to be Jenkins' story"; because Jenkins is humanity's last representative, his story offers the final comment on humanity's fate.   —*Daryl R. Coats*

THE CITY AND THE STARS

Ambitious for humankind to reach the stars again, a young man leaves the eternal city of Diaspar and discovers the legacy of the past and the promise of the future

Author: Arthur C. Clarke (1917-   )
Genre: Science fiction—superbeing
Type of work: Novel
Time of plot: The far future
Location: The Earth cities of Diaspar, Lys, and
    Shalmirane, and the system of the Seven Suns
First published: 1956

The Plot: Alvin is a Unique in Diaspar, freshly created rather than revived from the city's Memory Banks. He is one of only fifteen new creations in a billion-year history. He knows he is not like others because he has never feared the open spaces in the seemingly dead world beyond the city's towering walls. He finds a vantage point from which to view the endless sands, the night sky, and the fading stars, but no one in Diaspar is willing or able to bear the vistas he yearns to explore. He begins a systematic attempt to escape from the city's perfect enclosure.

By regressing a computer-generated scale model of the city, Alvin locates the long-buried hub of a forgotten transit system. Because everything of value is maintained by eternity circuits, the rails are still in place and ready to carry a passenger to the only destination left on Earth, the city of Lys. Alvin steps aboard and is whisked away to a land he never knew existed.

Lys is the opposite of Diaspar. There, people have chosen to reproduce and die naturally rather than pursue an artificially maintained immortality. They live in scattered villages, grow their own food, and communicate telepathically. They restrain the encroaching deserts behind Earth's last mountains and maintain a complex ecosystem within their shelter. Science and philosophy are still vigorous in Lys. According to legend, the scientists of Lys fought off the dreaded Invaders at Shalmirane when humans were driven from the stars at the end of the Dawn Ages.

In Lys, Alvin meets a peer named Hilvar, whose mother governs the land. Together they explore Lys while Alvin decides whether to stay or to return to Diaspar with all memory of his travels erased. Diaspar has forgotten Lys, and Lys is content to be unremembered. The discoveries the young men make at the ruins of Shalmirane change everyone's plans, because Alvin acquires a spaceship and a robot to pilot it.

No one approves of Alvin and Hilvar's plan to cross the vast distances of space because common belief is that the Invaders spared Earth on the condition that humans abandon space travel. The explorers, undeterred, head straight for the Seven Suns, a perfect circle of stars at the heart of the galaxy. There they find only shards of the former galactic empire. More important, a living remainder of that ancient glory finds them. Vanamonde is a pure mentality constructed before the adventurous peoples of the empire took off en masse into intergalactic space.

By the time the travelers return, a citizen delegation from Lys is visiting Diaspar. Vanamonde returns with Alvin and Hilvar to Earth, and with his powers to see all places and all times he unveils the lost secrets of the Dawn Ages, when humans traveled the galaxy freely. The scientists of Lys, with their telepathic powers, soon learn that the myth of the Invaders is a myth and no more, and that Shalmirane was constructed to destroy the moon when its orbit began to decay. They also learn about Vanamonde's malevolent predecessor, The Mad Mind, imprisoned in the Black Sun until it failed. In the distant future, Vanamonde and The Mad Mind will meet in the universe's greatest struggle. Until then, the citizens of Lys and Diaspar will bend themselves to the task of rebuilding Earth, re-exploring the galaxy, and searching beyond for evidence of those who left on even greater explorations.

Analysis: Arthur C. Clarke's *The City and the Stars* is a revision of his first novel, *Against the Fall of Night* (1949; serial form, *Startling Stories*, November, 1948). The settings and main characters are the same, along with the basic plot of recovering the lost glory of the human race. Clarke estimated that three quarters of *The City and the Stars* is new material.

One of Clarke's most enduring themes is the future of humankind. He preserves that theme in *The City and the Stars*. Additionally, in novels such as *Childhood's End* (1953) and *2001: A Space Odyssey* (1968), he muses on the transformations that evolution may bring about in the future of human existence. Such changes are particularly evident in the bodies of the citizens of Diaspar, who have lost nails, teeth, all hair except that on the head, and navels, and have gained convenient, safe internal storage for male genitals. In a parallel manner, the minds of the citizens of Lys have evolved to allow telepathy. These evolutionary transformations are not crucial plot elements; however, Clarke lavishes attention on these details and thereby succeeds in representing something that has never existed.

Another important theme for Clarke is the importance of resisting the temptation to stagnate. In a perfect world, change would be unnecessary, but in Diaspar perfection has led to atrophy and the loss of both courage and curiosity. Clarke's plot valorizes exploration and discovery over the complacency of perfection. To be fully human, he implies, is to ask questions and to take whatever risks are required in order to answer them.

Clarke is a scientist as well as a writer, and *The City and the Stars* realistically incorporates science rather than being simply an adventure story with handy gadgets. The future Clarke creates is believably remote while remaining recognizably connected to present science.

—Victoria Gaydosik

CLARKE COUNTY, SPACE

A near-future story about a sheriff on Earth's first orbiting space colony who must stop a hired killer and an insane cult member's plot to destroy the station

Author: Allen Steele (1958-   )
Genre: Science fiction—extrapolatory
Type of work: Novel

Time of plot: 2050
Location: A space colony in Earth orbit
First published: 1990

The Plot: The story occurs primarily on Clarke County, a space colony in high Earth orbit, and involves the efforts of Sheriff John Bigthorn to stop a Mafia killer, a plot by a crazed member of an Elvis Presley cult, and a movement for colony independence. The story is told within a frame involving a journalist writing a book. Simon McCoy approaches the journalist to tell him the real story. The journalist agrees to hear him out, withholding any questions until later. The novel is in the third person and is presented from a variety of viewpoints, but it is intended to represent the story being told by McCoy.

The story begins with Macy Westmoreland, longtime girlfriend of a Mafia boss. Westmoreland is escaping with stolen cash and computer disks. An FBI agent following her is killed by a hired hit man called the Golem. Westmoreland books passage to Clarke County, and the Golem follows.

The novel introduces Sheriff John Bigthorn while he is taking peyote in his hogan (Indian sweat lodge) in an isolated section of the agricultural area of Clarke County. He is visited by Jenny Schorr. She and her husband, Neil, are the leaders of Clarke County. The Schorrs have modeled Clarke County, the first and only space colony, after their 1960's-style farming commune. When their investors push commercialism, Jenny impulsively threatens to declare independence. That information, from a private meeting, is immediately distributed on the "net," or information network, by Blind Boy Grunt.

Westmoreland and the Golem arrive on the colony, and Earth authorities warn Bigthorn. Simon McCoy is on the same shuttle as Westmoreland and the Golem. He sneaks into a cryogenics storage facility, where Blind Boy Grunt talks to him through the communications system.

Blind Boy Grunt incites independence among the colonists, liberally quoting singer Bob Dylan. Bigthorn visits the Golem, seeking to intimidate him. Westmoreland decides to hide by joining the Elvis cult, which is planning a live concert. Elvis steals one of Westmoreland's computer disks and gives it to one of his hacker followers, Gustav Schmidt. The Golem booby-traps Bigthorn's house, but Bigthorn is not badly hurt.

Schmidt finds, on Westmoreland's disk, secret government codes to activate a nuclear missile that had been left in orbit from a mission to destroy an asteroid before it collided with Earth. He decides to destroy Clarke County as a tribute to Elvis. Blind Boy Grunt tells McCoy about

the plan, and they work to thwart the scheme. McCoy figures out that Blind Boy Grunt is an artificial intelligence. Westmoreland is arrested and put in protective custody, but the Golem breaks in and takes her hostage.

Schmidt successfully uses the stolen codes to send the missile toward the colony, prompting a panicked evacuation. Meanwhile, Bigthorn uses his ancient hunter's instincts to track and kill the Golem, saving Westmoreland. McCoy and Blind Boy Grunt use a simulated Elvis to trick Schmidt into surrendering control of the missile. The primary narrative ends with the FBI getting Westmoreland and her disks, Clarke County getting the missile, and Bigthorn deciding to return to Earth. The frame narrative ends with McCoy explaining that he is a time traveler from the twenty-second century sent (by a secret peace group begun in the 1960's) to protect the colony from destruction; he is also a twentieth century man who was cryogenically frozen and revived. Time travel works only into the past, however, and he is stranded in the twenty-first century.

Analysis: *Clarke County, Space* is Allen Steele's second novel, following *Orbital Decay* (1989). It shows many of the same strengths and weaknesses as the earlier book. Its strengths include unique protagonists with ordinary, believable attitudes and stories that exhibit hard science fiction's traditional virtues of fast-moving, problem-driven plots. At its best, Steele's fiction resembles that of Robert A. Heinlein, with beer-drinking beam-jacks substituted for engineers. In *Clarke County, Space*, the obvious parallels with Heinlein's *The Moon Is a Harsh Mistress* (1966) ensure that veteran readers realize that Blind Boy Grunt is a computer long before McCoy does.

Steele's weaknesses primarily center on a tendency toward self-indulgent insertion of references to the counterculture of the late 1960's. These lessen the verisimilitude of both his characters and his milieu. Steele extrapolates his futures as if nothing of any cultural importance has occurred since the early 1970's. In Steele's 2050, for example, an American Indian space colony sheriff eats peyote in his hogan, there are 1960's-style Italian Mafia kingpins and hit men, top secret computer codes to direct missiles are found on floppy disks and can be used easily by hackers, the first and only space colony is run by refugees from a hippie commune, a religious cult deifies Elvis Presley, and a spontaneously generated artificial intelligence is fixated on Bob Dylan. Steele exhibits much of the same cultural ambience as Spider Robinson. It is particularly noticeable in a segment of the novel in which Bigthorn searches for leads to Westmoreland's whereabouts by questioning gamblers and prostitutes along Clarke County's commercial strip. Steele writes the scene, however, without Robinson's humorous style. Steele's straight-faced earnestness makes the reader wonder whether he might actually think the future could turn out this way.

Steele's fiction matured in his later novels, moving away from self-indulgent anachronisms to more believable futures while retaining his compelling narratives and fast-paced plots. *Clarke County, Space* can be viewed as the last of the early Steele novels, and it provides entertaining reading despite its weaknesses.

—*D. Douglas Fratz*

THE CLOCKWORK MAN

A man of the future whose organs are mostly mechanical is accidentally thrown back in time to a small English village

Author: E(dwin) V(incent) Odle (1890-1942)
Genre: Science fiction—superbeing
Type of work: Novel
Time of plot: The 1920's
Location: The English village of Great Wymering
First published: 1923

The Plot: During a village cricket match, in which Great Wymering's team is a player short, a strange person appears as if from nowhere. At first, the newcomer emits a strange whirring sound and cannot control his speech or his movements, but he recovers and is recruited by Gregg, the Great Wymering captain, as a substitute for the missing man. Unfortunately, after hitting several balls out of sight, the stranger loses control of himself again and runs away at great speed. Tales of his subsequent bizarre behavior soon begin to circulate in the village.

The local general practitioner, Doctor Allingham, proposes that the stranger must be an escaped lunatic. The more imaginative Gregg observes that the stranger is as much machine as human and guesses that he has been displaced from the future because the mechanical part of him is malfunctioning. Gregg suggests that the stresses and strains of contemporary civilization already have brought human beings so close to breakdown that some form of mechanical regulation will soon become necessary. Evidence to support this hypothesis is provided by discovery of the stranger's lost wig and hat, neither of which is of contemporary origin.

The stranger is found, in control of himself once again

but in deep distress, by another of the cricketers, bank clerk Arthur Withers. The stranger shows Withers the "clock" fitted to the back of his skull, which allows people like him to perceive and move within many dimensions, including time. Gregg greets this news enthusiastically, as evidence of the vast evolutionary leaps that remain to be made by humankind and of the great strides to be made in material progress. Allingham cannot make any sense of the extra dimensions mentioned in the stranger's account, but he nevertheless tries to repair the malfunctioning clock. The stranger grows old, then young, and then falls into a coma, allowing a thorough examination of his remarkable body. Most of his organs turn out to have been replaced by machines, and there is no sign of sex organs.

After discussing the matter with Gregg, the doctor eventually finds a set of instructions for the adjustment and use of the Clockwork Man, by means of which he manages to correct the malfunction. After disappearing into the future, the stranger returns once more to give his own account of himself to Arthur Withers.

The Clockwork Man explains that people like him were grateful to be fitted with clocks by "the makers" who "came after the last wars," so that they might enjoy contentment instead of ceaseless strife. It is the makers who live in "the real world," a world whose mysteries are impenetrable to his mechanized brain. The man from the future tells Withers that he has chosen to offer this explanation to him because there is something in the bank clerk's eyes (Withers is sitting with the girl he loves lying asleep in his arms) that reminds him of the makers.

Analysis: E. V. Odle was a close friend of J. D. Beresford, and *The Clockwork Man* is an obvious meditation on possibilities raised by Beresford's classic tale of a superhuman being, *The Hampdenshire Wonder* (1911). Beresford was later to return the compliment in the visionary fantasy *The Riddle of the Tower* (1944, written in collaboration with Esmé Wynne-Tyson), which vividly extrapolates the notion of human automation central to *The Clockwork Man*.

Odle's novel was the first of many memorable British scientific romances that were deeply affected by the dark lessons of World War I, but it is much less bitter than most of the antiwar novels of the 1930's, which often turned into scathing hymns of hate directed against the stupidity and bestiality of people unable to transcend their tendency toward violence even though modern armaments threatened to destroy the world. It is also of some importance as the first significant literary account of a cyborg, produced half a century before such human/machine hybrids were integrated into science fiction's conventional vocabulary of ideas.

The Clockwork Man is a fabular debate in which Gregg's view of a future of wonderful material progress—whose gifts must be secured by the careful regulation of human behavior—is pitted carefully against Allingham's skepticism. Odle is more evenhanded than most managers of exemplary debates, treating Gregg's vision with considerable sympathy even though it is conclusively undermined by the revelation that the Clockwork Man is more machine than human in the one sense that is crucial: He has given away his free will. What makes the novel truly exceptional is the passage in which the Clockwork Man gives his own account of himself, revealing his plaintive awareness of his own limitations.

The Clockwork Man knows that he and others like him have paid a high price for the experiential opportunities and the fundamental stability conferred by the clock. For him, laughter and weeping are mere symptoms of malfunction; in becoming free of the disturbances of sexual desire, he has surrendered the capacity for love and knows that in doing so he has forsaken the best part of his humanity. He sadly observes that even his dreams are programmed. He is not without hope—he wonders whether the makers will some day discover how to make clockwork men more like themselves—but his hope is illusory, for that would be a contradiction in terms.

There is nothing new or original in Odle's championship of love as the best part of human nature, but the message rarely has been delivered with such deftness and delicacy. The author retains the fairness of mind to agree with Gregg's defiant insistence that even if the Clockwork Man is mythical, "he is still worth investigating."

—*Brian Stableford*

A CLOCKWORK ORANGE

Alex, a brutal young hoodlum sent to prison for robbery and murder, undergoes an experimental treatment to eradicate his violent impulses and upon his release from prison finds himself defenseless in a violent world

Author: Anthony Burgess (John Anthony Burgess Wilson, 1917-1993)
Genre: Science fiction—dystopia
Type of work: Novel
Time of plot: The late twentieth century
Location: England
First published: 1962

The Plot: Alex and his three "droogs" (companions), Pete, Georgie, and Dim, amuse themselves by getting high on drugs, exercising wanton violence on defenseless victims, and engaging in rumbles with rival gangs. They relish "ultra-violence," vividly demonstrated by a "surprise visit" they pay to a writer's house in the country. They beat the owner and rape his wife. Alex is warned by his probation officer against such antics, but the young thug overreaches himself and is captured after breaking into an old woman's house and beating her senseless. He is sent to prison for murder after the woman dies. He is only fifteen years old.

Part 2 of the novel reduces Alex to a number (6655321) and shows his progress in prison as a model prisoner. He feigns interest in religion to get on the good side of the prison chaplain. He schemes to get out of prison by volunteering to be a subject for an experiment in psychological conditioning designed to make subjects violently ill at the very thought of sex or violence. The chaplain, understanding the nature of sin, advises Alex against this experiment, which will deprive him of free will, stating that "When a man cannot choose, he ceases to be a man." Alex is interested only in release from prison, and he gets his wish.

Alex is chosen for the Reclamation Treatment administered by Dr. Brodsky, whose work is sponsored for political reasons by the minister of the interior. Alex is given drugs to make him sick while watching violent pornography and "nasty" films showing German and Japanese torture during World War II. The treatment works, and Alex becomes the poster boy for the government's reclamation program. After a humiliating public demonstration showing Alex as incapable of inflicting violence and at which he gets sick at the very thought of sexual arousal, Dr. Brodsky proclaims Alex a "true Christian," not understanding that a true Christian must be able to choose between good and evil. Realizing that he can no longer listen to the music of his favorite classical composers, which accompanied the Nazi footage, without getting sick, Alex protests that they have turned him into "a clockwork orange," a mechanized vegetable.

In part 3 of the novel, the "reformed" Alex is released into a violent world, newly innocent, unprotected, and helpless against violent attacks. The irony is that he encounters his old enemies and former victims. Things have changed in the outside world while Alex was in prison. He is rejected by his parents, who have taken in a lodger to replace him.

Back on the streets, Alex is recognized by old men he

had once brutalized, and they beat him. He is rescued by police officers who turn out to be his old "droogie" Dim, whom Alex had abused, and his old enemy Billyboy. Dazed and further beaten, Alex ends up at the home of the writer, F. Alexander, he had victimized. The writer calls Alex "a victim of the modern world," which is true enough, and Alex learns that the writer's wife died after having been raped and beaten. Alex makes a number of mistakes by reverting to his distinctive slang, and Alexander recognizes his houseguest.

Alexander turns Alex over to opponents of the government, who torture Alex further while attempting to reverse his conditioning. They drive him to desperation by locking him in a room and making him listen to classical music. Driven beyond tolerance, Alex attempts suicide by jumping from a window, but he survives the fall. He awakes in a hospital to discover that he has been "cured" and is hailed by the press as the victim of a criminal reform scheme. Now a celebrity, Alex is reconciled with his parents and is able to return home. The novel ends with Alex asking to hear Beethoven's "glorious Ninth." Recalling the violent fantasies he used to associate with that music, he declares, "I was cured all right."

Analysis: Of the fifty books Anthony Burgess wrote, this satiric, futurist novel surely is the most famous. It was popularized by the controversial film adaptation made by Stanley Kubrick in 1971. The book speaks to the social and political concerns of its times—random violence by teenagers, crime and punishment, scientifically engineered rehabilitation, and the power of the state over the individual. The novel is autobiographical, in that it concerns a writer whose wife was raped and brutalized by a gang of thugs. Burgess' own wife, Lynne, was beaten by American soldiers while pregnant, lost the child, and could never have another. Reared as a Roman Catholic in Protestant England, Burgess was sensitive to Catholic notions of sin and redemption and to the importance of free will.

Philosophically, the novel is about moral choices, and each section begins with the question, "What's it going to be then, eh?" There is satiric justice in Alex's choices and their consequences. Science is able to change Alex by a process of psychological and moral castration, but the "cured" Alex can survive only in an orderly, neutered world of automatons. The transformed Alex is an "innocent," discharged into a world that is still brutal and corrupt.

The novel is a satirical allegory in the guise of science

fiction. Burgess satirizes scientists who remove themselves from ethical and moral issues in the service of a politically corrupt police state. The novel shows forcefully that there are no easy answers to complex questions involving the nature of good and evil or crime and punishment. Alex is shaped by the brutal technological world he inhabits. The psychological reasoning that motivates his violence and the perverse, sadistic pleasure he derives from it are not fully investigated. There is no attempt made to alter Alex's beliefs, only to change into pain the pleasure he derives from violent sadism. Science is interested only in achieving results that will be beneficial to society and cares nothing about the individual in this dystopia.

—*James M. Welsh*

CLONED LIVES

A multitalented physicist allows himself to be cloned, then embarks on a long pseudoparental relationship with his five young "twins"

Author: Pamela Sargent (1948-   )
Genre: Science fiction—extrapolatory
Type of work: Novel
Time of plot: From the eve of the year 2000 to 2037
Location: The United States and the Moon
First published: 1976 (based on the novella "A Sense of Difference," 1972, and the novelettes "Father" and "Clone Sister," both 1973)

The Plot: Astrophysicist Paul Swenson—who has demonstrated unusual brilliance in other fields, including poetry and music—is persuaded by his friend Hidey Takamura to allow himself to be cloned once a U.S. moratorium on this kind of experimental venture lapses with the coming of the new millennium. Takamura argues that one lifetime is insufficient to develop Swenson's multifaceted abilities and that if transplant surgery is morally acceptable, then cloning also ought to be. Jon Aschenbach, a minister, urges Paul not to do it, on the grounds that genetic engineering is an unwarranted interference with nature, but Paul decides that he will be a father to the children as well as a brother, nurturing the native abilities they will inherit from him.

One of the five surviving clones (one dies in the embryo state) is given an extra X chromosome to replace a deleted Y and thus is born female. The middle chapters of the novel work from the points of view of each of the clones in turn, picking up the story at different stages in their development, from 2016 to 2136.

In 2016, Paul has taken the children away from the publicity circus that surrounded their birth, but they still are made to feel their "abnormality" by many people they meet. This has made them draw closer together, although Paul has made every effort to differentiate them from one another by encouraging each of them to develop a different talent.

Edward, who remains closest to his progenitor, is disturbed to learn that Paul is planning to take an extended trip to the Moon, although the others think he should. Edward's state of disturbance is increased when Paul is killed in an accident, leaving his sibling/children to fend for themselves.

In 2020, James, disappointed in love, wonders whether he will ever be able to establish a separate identity and a life of his own, or whether he should even try. Incestuous intercourse with Kira threatens to tie him more securely to the group but forces him instead to make the effort to break away.

The year 2025 finds Michael on the brink of separation from Edward while following more closely in Paul's professional footsteps than his siblings. A new generation of cloned children gradually is winning social acceptance, but he still finds the thought of isolation difficult to bear.

In 2028, Kira has begun a relationship with Hidey Takamura, having gravitated toward biological science. Antiaging technology cannot conceal the difference in their ages, and the relationship causes some friction with her brothers. They both know that the work they hope to do in developing technologies to prolong life is highly unlikely to bear fruit in time to save them from separation by Takamura's death.

In 2036, Albert has long been a resident of the Moon, working on the development of spaceships capable of traveling between the stars. He is accepted onto the list of those who will make the first experimental flight beyond the solar system.

The final section of the narrative alternates the viewpoints of all five siblings as they come together briefly on the Moon. New technologies developed by Kira have been employed to revive the long-preserved Paul, who is once again confronted by his duplicates. Although he seems at first to have lost the greater part of his mind and memory, he begins to make progress, although it is dubious whether he will ever regain any real sense of connection with the people who are no longer his reflections.

Analysis: *Cloned Lives* is one of a considerable number of science-fictional thought experiments addressing the question of how human clones would relate to one another and to their "parent." Many of the others hypothesize telepathic linkages among the individuals concerned or have plots contrived around astonishing coincidences of genetic determinism. *Cloned Lives* is outstanding in terms of both its rational plausibility and its psychological sensitivity. The author's training in biology is put to effective use, not only in terms of the novel's argumentative rigor but also in providing a solid platform for adventurous speculation.

The hallmarks of Pamela Sargent's work have always included a scrupulous sensitivity to detail and a refusal to employ melodramatic tactics in designing her plots. She is able to find ample drama in the kind of everyday crises that people meet as a matter of course and inevitably will continue to meet in an ever changing future. Use of this form of drama has denied her the kind of audience that delights in imaginative pyrotechnics, but it has allowed her the rare accomplishment of writing future-set novels that command belief and interest as authoritatively as the best contemporary fiction.

Cloned Lives is by no means a modest book in terms of its inventions, but it remains beautifully convincing in interweaving the moral dilemmas and psychological problems of a special group of social misfits with the abundant promise that biotechnology and mechanical engineering offer. It is a deceptively quiet prospectus for the future, all the more powerful by virtue of its careful understatement. It is also a poignant examination of the problems that all kinds of social misfits tend to face as they grow from adolescence to adulthood.

Each section of the text of *Cloned Lives* is prefaced with quotations, taken from books and essays, raising the various practical and ethical questions that the advancement of biotechnology surely will make concrete. The first comes from J. B. S. Haldane's extraordinarily prescient essay *Daedalus: Or, Science and the Future* (1924), which was the primary inspiration for Aldous Huxley's *Brave New World* (1932). Huxley, like *Cloned Lives*'s Jon Aschenbach, reacted with horror to Haldane's speculations, in the name of "nature"; so did many of the other alarmist "authorities" whom Sargent quotes. Sargent takes up their objections and addresses their anxieties, weighing them carefully before suggesting—always politely—that they might after all be groundless. Hers is a thoroughly sensible voice as well as an eloquent one, and there is a certain tragedy in the fact that there are not many others like it.

—*Brian Stableford*

THE CLONING OF JOANNA MAY

Carl May secretly clones a cell from his former wife Joanna to form four women genetically like Joanna May but thirty years younger

Author: Fay Weldon (1931-   )
Genre: Science fiction—feminist
Type of work: Novel
Time of plot: The late twentieth century
Location: England
First published: 1989

The Plot: The thematic concern of novelist Fay Weldon is the "battle of the sexes," and her novel *The Cloning of Joanna May* is no exception. Weldon chronicles Joanna's story in fifty-five brief chapters recalling the marriage and divorce of Joanna and Carl May, as well as Joanna's discovery of four clones, secretly conceived by her former husband.

The novel opens during Joanna's sixtieth year. A chill October windstorm brings destructive force and bears supernatural power that frightens not only Joanna but also her four clones, Jane, Julie, Gina, and Alice. The thirty-year-old women seem unsettled; they wish for change but are unsure how to engineer it. The Chernobyl nuclear disaster occurs on the heels of the storm, and the radiation scare it brings to England serves as a backdrop for the action and tension of the plot.

In the meantime, Carl, who has never gotten over his divorce from Joanna, ends years of self-imposed celibacy to begin a relationship with twenty-four-year-old Bethany. Carl is neurotic and controlling. He has survived a ghastly childhood (his mother left him chained in a dog kennel) to become the chief executive of Britnuc, a corporate overseer of nuclear power stations. During a televised news conference, after the Chernobyl scare, to reassure the public that nuclear radiation poses no threat, Carl inadvertently lets the press photograph his lover, Bethany. Joanna watches the telecast of her former husband with his mistress and is outraged because a bond still exists between the estranged couple. She goes to Britnuc to confront him.

In the course of their conflict, Carl discloses his diabolical secret. Thirty years earlier, when Joanna sought medical attention for a "hysterical pregnancy," Carl and Dr. Holly, his medical research expert, took away a "nice ripe egg" and through scientific means "irritated it in amniotic fluid" until the nucleus split into four embryos that were implanted in the wombs of different women.

Each of Joanna's clones was reared in a different environment, unaware of her origins or kinships.

Once Joanna learns the truth, she hires a female detective to find her sister-daughters. At the same time, Carl hires goons to exterminate them. Intuitively, Julie, Jane, Gina, and Alice sense a disturbance and miraculously find one another. When Julie flees to a McDonald's restaurant to mourn her loveless, childless marriage, she meets Gina, who has sought the same location to feed her children and escape her abusive husband. Likewise, Jane seeks an interview with a model for a documentary on women's difficult career choices, and she conveniently finds that the model is Alice, the fourth clone. Startled by their similarities, both pairs of clones seek the truth about their origins and are eventually united with their progenitor, Joanna.

The women's combined power helps to defeat the evil purposes of Carl. He does not recover from a public relations media stunt in which he swims in a nuclear plant cooling pond to demonstrate the harmless effects of low-level radiation. In the novel's epilogue, the women join forces to rear their own little man, a clone of Carl.

Analysis: Weldon creates a world fraught with unusual elements that illustrate the conflicts between men and women. Weldon has written more than a dozen novels, and her focus and skill are well honed. Like her earlier novels *Puffball* (1980) and *The Life and Loves of a She-Devil* (1984), *The Cloning of Joanna May* makes use of unearthly and unlikely devices to advance the plot. Her narrative is stylized rather than realistic.

Although Weldon employs scientific elements of cloning and nuclear power in the story, the novel is perhaps more fantasy than science fiction. The "real world," however mundane, is affected by supernatural forces that form a backdrop for Joanna's discovery. The ill wind that appears in the opening chapter creates a spirit of unrest that foreshadows later events.

In addition, hints of Egyptian curses and tarot cards become part of the plot. Joanna's unfortunate affair with an Egyptologist brings disaster: Carl discovers the truth, divorces Joanna, and murders the lover. Before he dies, the Egyptologist tells Joanna's fortune in tarot cards, cryptically identifying her clones. Joanna's card is the Empress, and the surrounding queens dealt from the deck—the four suits of Wands, Pentacles, Swords, and Cups—are designations for Jane, Julie, Gina, and Alice.

The evils of science and technology are portrayed through Carl May's character and through his assistant, Dr. Holly. Their use of cloning and nuclear power seem driven by dangerous, selfish motives rather than by a desire to improve the lot of humankind. Ironically, Carl's own technology turns against him.

Weldon's story is a modern account of a woman's search for identity that explores the question of nature versus nurture. Each of the clones, genetically like Joanna, has been influenced by environmental factors. Gina, the shortest in stature, self-confidence, and achievement, was born seven weeks prematurely. Alice, born one week past term, is taller and self-absorbed, almost overdone. Each is involved in a marriage gone bad or an unsatisfying affair. The younger women, like Joanna, are seeking happiness and fulfillment.

The "nature versus nurture" question is raised in relation to Carl. Is his personality a result of genetics or of his treatment by abusive parents? The women attempt to find an answer by cloning Carl at the close of the novel. Joanna seems optimistic that she can produce a better Carl now that she controls Carl's destiny rather than being controlled by him. Thus, Weldon links the men in her novel with science and the women with fate and intuition. Collectively, the women seem to overcome.

—Paula M. Miller

THE CLOUD WALKER

Britain's dominant Luddite church burns at the stake those who dabble with machines, but one daring youth secretly invents the technology of flight

Author: Edmund Cooper (1926-1982)
Genre: Fantasy—medieval future
Type of work: Novel
Time of plot: During the time of the Third Man
Location: Arundel, Sussex, England
First published: 1973

The Plot: After the technological catastrophes that ended the civilizations of both the First and Second Men, the world turned away from science and machines. In England, the reigning Luddite church—named after Ned Ludd, a nineteenth century textile machinery saboteur—punishes the heresies of experimentation and technical innovation with death. More broadly, the country has returned to a medieval, peasant economy with a loose federation of nobles controlling the disunited nation and skilled trades governed by a rigid apprenticeship program.

Kieron, the protagonist, is taken on by Master Hobart, the artist serving the local ruler, Lord Fitzalan. Kieron's dream is to construct a flying machine. Hobart sympathizes with Kieron but counsels patience and circumspection. It is not his scientific penchant, however, but his dislike of the caste system that first leads Kieron to trouble. When Lord Fitzalan's spoiled daughter Aylwin, whom Kieron is assigned to sketch, repeatedly and publicly humiliates him, he loses his temper and spanks her. He is imprisoned, and only Aylwin's intervention spares him worse treatment. Aylwin, in truth, has fallen in love with the boy and becomes his ally, protecting him against the church when his building of manned kites is discovered.

Even Aylwin cannot protect Kieron, however, when his next creation, a hot-air balloon, explodes over the castle. It seems that nothing can save him from the Inquisition until two events occur. To save Kieron, who already has made Hobart immortal by affixing his master's name to a painting of Aylwin done by the student, the master hangs himself, leaving a note assuming the blame for the balloon. Soon afterward, while Kieron is still in prison, the town is attacked by pirates, who burn down the jail. Escaping the hulks, Kieron finds the town in ruins and Aylwin, her father, and most of the other inhabitants slain.

Making his way into the surrounding countryside, Kieron finds a survivors' encampment, where he learns that the buccaneer Admiral Death has landed a fearsome armada. Kentigern, formerly a castle bailiff, is in charge of the camp, but when his calls for help to neighboring lords are met lukewarmly, he can conceive of no alternative strategy. Kieron proposes to build an offensive dirigible. It is towed near the anchored pirate fleet and allowed to drift over the boats, so that Kieron and a helper can pour fire on the ships. They sink five vessels and kill Admiral Death, driving off the invaders and making Kieron a legend.

The church's antitechnological doctrines have been badly discredited; however, the priests, called neddies, make one last attempt to repulse science by kidnapping Kieron. Kieron's wife, Petrina, comes to his rescue, arousing the town to save him and kick out the churchmen.

Here the story ends, except for a double coda. First, the tale leaps ahead many years to show Kieron as head of an aeronautics school. It then moves to the time of his death, when he is the *éminence grise* of the international balloon fraternities, who honor him at a ceremony for the man who started the world flying.

Analysis: One of the more significant trends of the 1960's and 1970's in the West was the rise of the ecological movement. This was the first broad-based attempt to question the basic assumptions of the advanced, industrial nations' reliance on science and technology. Ecologists argued that these disciplines often did more harm than good by interfering with the web of life in ways that eventually would impair the planet's support system.

Such views affected science fiction and fantasy profoundly. Historically, science fiction has reflected guardedly on the fruits and consequences of science. Early on, in "The Celestial Railroad" (1843), for example, American writer Nathaniel Hawthorne pointedly challenged the widely held idea that scientific progress would lead to the production of morally improved people.

In the 1960's, a less playful interrogation of science took hold. In science fiction, a prime proecology document was Frank Herbert's *Dune* (1965). Although this novel had something of a "sword and sorcery" plot, it was distinguished by the author's meticulous imagining of a viable ecosystem on the sand dune planet. Herbert's careful interlacing of meteorological, geological, and biological data rooted the book in a committed, ecological outlook that emphasized how human actions were embedded in a world's environment.

Fantasy literature also was touched by the rise of ecology. Although *The Cloud Walker* has a largely anti-ecological tone, in two ways it acknowledges the truth of some ecological contentions. First, the time line indicates two previous technological disasters that nearly wiped out the human race. People's tendency toward self-destruction often is on Edmund Cooper's mind. His book *The Overman Culture* (1971) concerns aliens who come to Earth centuries after humans have destroyed themselves and then cultivate a new Adam and Eve out of preserved genetic material. In *The Cloud Walker*, previous generations' misuse of technology joined with a second fact—that the third rebirth of science occurs only because balloons can be utilized as engines of destruction—suggests a distrust of technology that chimes with the ecological standpoint.

A review of the plot will make clear that Cooper plays down this side of his vision in favor of a celebration of the value of experimentation and technology. The Luddite church that opposes science is hideously oppressive, and Kieron, who fights to revive scientific learning, is a hero of the old school, one with few flaws and grossly magnified virtues. By setting his fantasy in a medieval world, Cooper is able to separate his defense of science from an apology for science as it existed in 1973. What he really praises is the scientific impulse in humans, which he finds to arise partly from irrepressible curiosity and partly from an urge to make life better.   —*James Feast*

THE COLLECTED GHOST STORIES OF M. R. JAMES

A superior collection of ghost stories that seek to update the medium from the gothic tale to one of psychological suspense and controlled terror

Author: M. R. James (1862-1936)
Genre: Fantasy—occult
Type of work: Stories
Time of plot: Primarily the eighteenth and nineteenth centuries
Location: Primarily England, with some stories set in France and Scandinavia
First published: 1931 (previously published as *Ghost-Stories of an Antiquary*, 1904; *More Ghost Stories of an Antiquary*, 1911; *A Thin Ghost and Others*, 1919; *A Warning to the Curious, and Other Ghost Stories*, 1925; and *Wailing Well*, 1928)

The Plot: M. R. James's ghost stories are the perfect example of quality counting over quantity. Although he produced these stories over the course of forty years (1894-1935), his complete tally of spectral fiction is only thirty-three stories, twenty-six of which had appeared in four previous collections. Four more were added to make up *The Collected Ghost Stories of M. R. James*. Although this volume excludes three later stories, they are only minor pieces, and their exclusion does not detract from the completeness of the collected works. The volume has the added benefit of James's essay "Stories I Have Tried to Write."

Almost all of James's stories have a common approach and content. As the title of his first book suggests, they are related by an antiquarian, meaning that the incidents are linked to the study of old documents or buildings. They develop the theme of "a little knowledge is a dangerous thing," as the antiquarians in his stories always suffer from delving a little too far into things best left alone. This theme is common to almost all of James's stories, which therefore can be explored by reference to two in detail.

James's first published tale was "Canon Alberic's Scrap-book" (*National Review*, March, 1895), which opens the volume and shows his technique to good effect. An Englishman named Dennistoun is touring southern France and spends a day taking notes and photographs at the church of St. Bertrand de Comminges. He is accompanied by the sacristan, a nervous, afflicted fellow who jumps at every shadow and sound in the church.

The sacristan invites Dennistoun back to his house and shows him an old scrapbook compiled by a former canon of Comminges. Dennistoun is fascinated by a picture that seems to depict Solomon casting out a demon. Dennistoun acquires the book and takes it back to his lodgings. That night, while admiring a crucifix, Dennistoun is suddenly aware of something black, thin, and hairy beside him, and he turns to see the full horror of his visitant.

This story shows a key mark of James's writing. Frequently his horrors are just in the act of moving. Here, "the shape . . . was rising to a standing posture behind his seat." In "The Diary of Mr. Poynter," readers are confronted with "What he had been touching rose to meet him." A scene in "Mr. Humphreys and His Inheritance" describes something that "with the odious writhings of a wasp creeping out of a rotten apple . . . clambered forth . . . waving black arms prepared to clasp the head that was bending over them."

James's most accomplished story using these devices is "'Oh, Whistle, and I'll Come to You, My Lad'" (1904). Taking a few days of rest on the Suffolk coast, Parkins, a professor of ontography, takes time out to investigate the ruins of a Templar preceptory. While there he unearths a small whistle. He blows it, producing a sound with "a quality of infinite distance." From then on Parkins feels troubled. The next day, while walking on the shore, he sees in the distance a man running, pursued, so it seems, by "a figure in pale, fluttering draperies, ill-defined." Later that evening Parkins returns to his room to find the second bed disturbed. During the night he wakes to see movement in the other bed, from which something rises, with outspread arms, stooping and groping. As it passes the moonlit window, Parkins becomes aware of its "face of crumpled linen." In this story James is able to take the traditional form of the white-sheeted ghost and transform it into something truly unnerving.

Analysis: James's ghost stories are usually regarded as the most accomplished of their kind. They are not traditional ghost stories in the formal sense; James shied away from the shrouded wraith or the gothic chain rattler. His ghosts are of the monstrous kind, often hairy and with teeth, and they are always malicious. James's framework for the ghost story was set down in an introduction he wrote for *Ghosts and Marvels* (1924), edited by Vere H. Collins, and it admirably establishes James's approach. He refers to two key ingredients: the atmosphere and a "nicely managed" crescendo. He also believed that "a slight haze of distance is desirable." He usually created that effect through the study of old documents or buildings, or through a tale retold. The atmosphere involved characters going about their normal business before "the ominous thing" begins to intrude, "unobtrusively at first, and then more insistently, until it holds the stage." This approach is the trademark of all of James's ghost stories.

One less apparent trait is the humor that pervades his stories. James traditionally read his stories at Christmas to students at King's College, Cambridge, where he was dean and later provost. Because James was a capable mimic, his deliberate mocking of local characters would come through in the narration. This helped provide a commonplace setting into which the ominous could intrude.

Using his techniques, James remodeled the ghost story, establishing a form that became acceptable to the literary establishment. To many, including Michael Sadleir, who wrote the dustwrapper notes for this volume, James was "the best ghost-story writer England has ever produced," and his reputation has not diminished with the years. His works have been imitated by many, including other antiquarians, of whom R. H. Malden, A. N. L. Munby, and L. T. C. Rolt are among the most accomplished. His techniques have also been utilized by others, especially Fritz Leiber and Ramsey Campbell. Despite such imitations, James's works remain supreme in their field.

A recent selection of twenty-one of James's best stories, including the three not included in the *Collected Ghost Stories* and also featuring all of James's essays about ghost stories, is *Casting the Runes and Other Ghost Stories* (1987), edited and with an introduction by Michael Cox.

—Mike Ashley

THE COLOSSUS TRILOGY

A supercomputer designed to manage the nuclear defense of the West merges with its Soviet counterpart to rule the world

Author: D(ennis) F(eltham) Jones (1917-1981)
Genre: Science fiction—artificial intelligence
Type of work: Novels
Time of plot: The second half of the twenty-second century
Location: Primarily the United States of North America and the Soviet Union
First published: *Colossus* (1966), *The Fall of Colossus* (1974), and *Colossus and the Crab* (1977)

The Plot: Charles Forbin, a scientist about fifty years old, is the mastermind behind Colossus, a computer built to react automatically to nuclear aggression against the United States of North America. The country's president is eager for the computer's activation despite Forbin's own misgivings of its potential. A similarly concerned colleague suggests that *Frankenstein* (1818) should be banned reading for scientists. Forbin replies that it should be required reading for nonscientists.

The president's announcement that the nation's nuclear defense is now in the computer's hands is topped by a Soviet announcement of plans for a similar computer, Guardian, which then is also activated. Despite efforts by Forbin and his team to stop or slow the process, the computers link themselves into a supermachine. Its control of the world's nuclear arsenal puts it in charge of world policy.

Colossus keeps Forbin under virtual house arrest and uses him as its spokesman. Claiming that humans require periodic sexual activity, something beyond the understanding of Colossus, Forbin secures regular visits from fellow scientist Cleo Markham, who loves him and acts as his liaison with outsiders trying to sabotage Colossus. All attempts at sabotage fail, the individuals who are caught are ruthlessly executed, the city of Los Angeles is vaporized, and Colossus predicts that eventually Forbin will come "to respect and love me" as other humans will. "Never!," Forbin insists.

Five years later, as the second book opens, the predictions of Colossus seem to have come true regarding human reactions to its rule. The machine literally is worshiped by members of The Sect, despite its ruthless experiments intended to provide information about human emotion. One such experiment tests whether an artist will sacrifice his life to try to save the Mona Lisa from destruction; he does.

"Father Forbin" is seen as Colossus' apostle. Unknown to Forbin, Cleo (now his wife) and colleague Ted Blake head a group still trying to overthrow the rule of the machine. They get aid from an unexpected source. Inhabitants of the planet Mars contact them by radio and express concern that Colossus might extend its rule to their world. Forbin is enticed into joining them after Colossus imprisons Cleo for her antimachine activities. Following the Martian instructions, they strip Colossus of its memory, only to learn that Colossus had foreseen a threat from Mars and had been preparing to meet it. The Martians now are on their way to a defenseless Earth.

The Martians arrive, in the form of two huge, black spheres that can change shape and reduce themselves in size. They turn out to be the living Martian moons, Phobos and Deimos (which Jones spells as "Diemos"). Limiting their contact to Forbin and Blake, they demand half the world's oxygen supply. They need it for protection against radiation coming from a nova in the Crab Nebula, from which Earth is protected by its atmosphere. Forbin's protests that this would mean the death of a quarter of the world's population is meaningless to their logic, which is as machinelike as was that of Colossus.

Forbin manages to hold together the world government without Colossus through sheer bluff. He and Blake, who is weakened drastically by a mental thrashing from the Martians brought on by his defiance, work secretly to reactivate Colossus. Meanwhile, they are forced to have an oxygen collector built under Martian instructions. A brief experimental use of it wreaks havoc in a part of England. Before a full trial can be made, Forbin takes command of an old-fashioned warship to attack the collector mechanism.

Blake's group, meanwhile, has managed to get Colossus working and in control of enough nuclear armaments to destroy the world if the Martians will not back down. Colossus decides to let the oxygen collection proceed, having projected a future in which the Sun eventually expands and engulfs Earth but not Mars. At that time, humans will need Mars as a refuge. Forbin manages to destroy the oxygen-collecting mechanism but loses his life in the process. Colossus and the Martians work out a less drastic procedure for supplying oxygen to Mars over a much longer period of time, thus not disrupting human life on Earth. Forbin is revered and remembered as a legend, and Colossus will remain the guardian of humanity until humans can learn enough to guard themselves.

Analysis: By the time D. F. Jones published *Colossus*, his first and arguably best novel, the concept of an ultimate computer or machine controlling humankind had become a cliché; it was a staple in science-fiction comic books a decade earlier. Perhaps the classic story in this vein is Fredric Brown's 1954 "The Answer," in which an ultimate computer is asked whether there is a deity and replies, "Yes, *now* there is a God." Isaac Asimov raised a computer to godlike status as well in one of his favorites of his own short stories, "The Last Question" (1956). Jones used the theme so definitively in *Colossus* that his novel remains perhaps the most familiar example, possibly helped by its 1969 British film version, *Colossus, the Forbin Project* (released in the United States as *The Forbin Project*).

Like its sequels, *Colossus* is a talky book, with much

of the conversation between Forbin and Colossus. They engage in philosophical and ethical arguments over Colossus' utterly logical but ruthless actions and Forbin's emotional reactions to them. Colossus' arguments generally come down to the desirability of killing a few people now to save more later. The reader has reason to hope for a happy ending throughout but, at the end, Colossus triumphs and Forbin, before his death, becomes almost a slave to his creation.

Jones, a British writer who was a Royal Navy officer during World War II, wrote mostly downbeat novels such as *Implosion* (1967), in which the world's few fertile women become a part of a rigid government; *Denver Is Missing* (1971; published in England as *Don't Pick the Flowers*), about the destruction of that city; and *Earth Has Been Found* (1979; published in England as *Xemo*), an alien invasion story.

The Colossus trilogy turns into an alien invasion story with its second volume, in which the anti-Colossus faction on Earth is contacted over a conventional radio by a voice from Mars offering help in overthrowing the machine's rule. Forbin's colleague, Ted Blake, is more a man of action than is Forbin, but his actions are largely ineffective in comparison to those of the more thoughtful Forbin. After Martian procedures have been used to wipe out Colossus' memory banks, Blake is ready to move into the void left by the collapse of machine rule by military force, much like the artillery man portrayed in the 1938 Mercury Theater radio adaptation of H. G. Wells's *The War of the Worlds* (1898). The plan to save the world falls apart when it appears that the Martians will replace Colossus and be even less enlightened rulers. The second book ends with a chilling repeated radio broadcast: "Forbin . . . We are coming. We are coming."

The arrival of the two sentient Martian moons, as machinelike in their logic as was Colossus, starts the third book. Forbin continues as the focus by virtue of having been the spokesman for Colossus. As Cleo became his ally and eventually his wife in the previous volumes, his chief assistant Angela fills the void in the third book. Cleo, imprisoned in the second book and placed with a near-barbarian who ravishes her at will but protects her, finds her sexuality awakened anew by the experience and never rejoins Forbin, even after she is freed. She is barely mentioned in the last book. Jones is far from politically correct in his depictions of twenty-second century professional women.

References in the first book seem to date it as being set in the 1990's, but by the time Jones wrote the sequels, he apparently had decided he had not given himself enough

distance from the present. He states specifically that the events occur in the second half of the twenty-second century. The Soviet Union survives. People still smoke and drink to excess, and scientists still use slide rules. The United States, however, has expanded to cover North America, and there are such devices as air cars and disposable clothing.

The Colossus stories may lack the thematic impact of earlier works such as E. M. Forster's "The Machine Stops" (1909), in which humankind has become so dependent on thinking machines that it falls apart without them. Nevertheless, Jones's books, particularly the first in the trilogy, remain worth reading. They are well thought out and represent his best work.   —*Paul Dellinger*

THE COMING RACE

Adventures in a subterranean civilization in which all social problems have been solved through the use of a powerful and potentially destructive force called vril

Author: Edward Bulwer-Lytton (1803-1873)
Genre: Science fiction—cultural exploration
Type of work: Novel
Time of plot: The mid- to late nineteenth century
Location: The subterranean world of the Vril-ya
First published: 1871

The Plot: *The Coming Race* describes a young American's adventures among the Vril-ya, an underground civilization far more advanced than his own. Sometimes the "utopian" Vril-ya society is the object of satire; at other times, the narrator himself is the object. Published anonymously, the book was written at the end of Edward Bulwer-Lytton's career, five years after he became a peer. His political outlook by that time was decidedly conservative.

The narrator, who never gives his real name, descends a chasm in a mine shaft to the Vril-ya world. "The engineer," his only companion, falls to his death, and his body is carried off by a giant reptile, leaving the narrator alone and with no way to return to the surface. Subsequently, he encounters Aph-Lin, who will be his host among the Vril-ya. Using the powerful force called vril, which has a telepathic component, Aph-Lin and his daughter, Zee, teach the narrator their language and learn his. They refer to him as Tish, the term for the frogs kept by children as pets. This is his position among the Vril-ya, against whose power he is helpless.

The narrator relates such aspects of Vril-ya culture as

the use of vril, the "fluid" that allows the Vril-ya to fly, to control automata that perform manual labor, to heal, and to destroy. Vril literally denotes civilization. Underground societies that do not possess vril power are considered barbaric, and the narrator, who lacks the evolved nerve needed to operate a vril wand, identifies with them. Consequently, he fears for his safety, as the Vril-ya will not hesitate to destroy the "barbarians" should they prove to be a threat or an inconvenience. The capacity of the Vril-ya for impassive destruction becomes apparent when eleven-year-old Tae, the narrator's closest friend and nearest equal among the Vril-ya, dispassionately incinerates a reptile, which the Vril-ya also consider a threat to their community.

The narrator also resembles the "barbarians" in that he is the citizen of a democracy, a system the Vril-ya believe civilized cultures have outgrown. Because vril gives even the smallest child the power of mass destruction, rule among the Vril-ya is a matter of consensus. No one thinks of challenging the requests of the leader, an elected, benevolent dictator called the Tur. Tae's father currently holds that office. Political power, like wealth, is more an obligation than a privilege. Although economic inequality persists, the rich are expected to provide for the poor, and wealth does not affect social status.

The equality the Vril-ya accord to all occupations also extends to the rights of women. Because they are considered to be more emotional than are men, women have the privilege of taking the initiative in courtship; men, like Victorian women, must remain coy and reluctant. This reversal of gender roles disturbs the narrator, particularly when he attracts the amorous attentions of both Zee and Tae's nameless sister, whom he finds less frightening because she is less bold. He briefly entertains a vision of marrying her and ruling Vril-ya society, which he would reform in the image of his own. This cannot be, however, because the Vril-ya consider him a threat to the purity of their race, and the Tur eventually orders his death.

The narrator's pleas to Tae, his would-be executioner, earn him a brief reprieve. Zee, her offers of celibate marriage or voluntary exile having been refused, returns him to the surface, where he remains silent about the Vril-ya. His memoirs are published "posthumously" and conclude with a warning of the inevitable invasion of "the coming race."

Analysis: A highly popular and influential novel in its time, *The Coming Race* is now generally considered a conservative critique of Victorian utopian ideas concerning such issues as democracy and gender equality. The novel shifts ambiguously between utopia and dystopia, largely because the object of the satire is never clear. Sometimes it is the narrator, whose enthusiastic statements about American republicanism often seem ironic and who looks ridiculous in his flight from the aggressive Vril-ya women. The novel, however, concurrently mocks Vril-ya society, with its masculine women, insistence on Darwinian evolution, and lack of passion. As the narrator notes, any human among them cannot help but experience intense fear or crippling boredom. Consensus breeds complete uniformity that precludes both philosophical debate and artistic creation. This "perfect" society also is founded on violence, which is not only imperial but domestic; peace ultimately results from the deterrent properties of vril. The Vril-ya are not as radical as they seem: Sexual stereotypes still determine gender roles, women who woo aggressively become submissive wives, and the state has absolute control over the people. The unquestioning obedience and cultural stability of the Vril-ya reveal a conservative resistance to change.

By placing the narrator, and through him the reader, in a threatened and marginalized position, the novel invites a critique of the Vril-ya's treatment of the outsider that can be applied to the perception of marginalized groups in Bulwer-Lytton's England. The novel is perceptive regarding the various typical, and equally dehumanizing, responses to outsiders: condescension, scientific study, and violence. In addition, it discredits the notion that any culture's beliefs are universal by portraying a constantly shifting margin; the narrator is outside Vril-ya society, as the Vril-ya are abnormal to him, and the narrator and the Vril-ya alternately represent "normal" humanity and the various groups it marginalizes. Thus, *The Coming Race*, deemed ambiguous by nineteenth century reviews and twentieth century critics alike, is actually more radical than the utopian society it depicts.

—*Katie Harse*

THE CONAN SERIES

Conan the Barbarian battles men, magic, and monsters in the mythical Hyborian Age, rising from penniless wanderer to king of Aquilonia, the mightiest of the Hyborian nations

Author: Robert E. Howard (1906-1936)
Genre: Fantasy—heroic fantasy
Type of work: Stories
Time of plot: About 15,000 B.C.
Location: A fictional Earth

First published: *The Coming of Conan* (1953), *Conan the Barbarian* (1954), *The Sword of Conan* (1952), *King Conan* (1953), *Conan the Conqueror* (1950; previously published as "The Hour of the Dragon," *Weird Tales*, 1935), and *Tales of Conan* (1955)

The Plot: Robert E. Howard wrote the Conan stories (arranged above in order of internal chronology) as episodes from the life of the invincible barbarian hero. This Gnome Press collection includes all of Howard's Conan stories, commentary regarding Conan and his world, and two tales of King Kull, another ancient barbarian king. Most of the stories were originally published in *Weird Tales* between 1929 and 1936, except those in the last book, *Tales of Conan*, which was compiled from previously unpublished manuscripts. L. Sprague de Camp edited the entire collection.

The Kull tales begin with *The Coming of Conan*. With his Pictish friend Brule, Kull battles the uncanny serpent men. Kull is a mighty barbarian warrior from Atlantis who has usurped the throne of the kingdom of Valusia, and Brule is a guerrilla fighter and fantastically skilled hunter. Conan is a fusion of these two characters. He is the greatest swordsman of his age, with the strength, speed, and ferocity of a beast of prey and senses so acute that he surpasses wild men and animals in tracking and stalking.

After the Kull stories begin the adventures of Conan, set in the prehistoric Hyborian Age. Although little is known of Conan's early years, it is established that he was born in the midst of a battle, literally bred to war. At the sack of Venarium, an Aquilonian outpost in Cimmeria destroyed by the barbarians, he acquired a curiosity about the Hyborian civilizations. When he was about seventeen years old, he began the wanderings that would make him legendary throughout the world as a thief, mercenary, bandit chieftain, pirate captain, general, and ultimately barbarian king of Aquilonia itself.

The most basic plot element is Conan's heroic character. He embodies "natural" virtues such as independence, courage, indomitability, and a simple honesty about himself and his desires. He rejects the "civilized hypocrisy" of legal abstractions, so he is often at odds with the law. Although not given to wanton cruelty, he is vengeful and merciless in his anger. This is counterbalanced by an unswerving loyalty to deserving comrades and a loathing for bullies and other cowardly types. Naturally curious and almost fearless, Conan enjoys the adventurous life and will brave any danger to help a woman in distress. These personality traits—and his mighty sword arm—impel him from adventure to adventure. His restless need for action will not allow him to enjoy times of peace, even that for which he battles as king of Aquilonia.

Conan inevitably faces situations with impossible odds against his success, but with heroic fortitude and tremendous luck he invariably succeeds. Although he frequently begins an adventure out of selfish motives, his actions always help defeat some monstrous evil. One good example is the earliest Conan story, "The Tower of the Elephant." Setting out to steal a fabulous gem, "The Heart of the Elephant," rumored to be kept in a mysterious tower, he braves natural and supernatural obstacles to attain his goal, only to voluntarily free a mysterious being from another planet, Yag-Kosha, who wreaks awful magical vengeance on the tower's builder, the evil magician Yara. The jewel that Conan sought is absorbed into the spell, and he flees while the tower crashes to ruin behind him.

In what many regard as the greatest Conan story, "The Queen of the Black Coast," the encounter with supernatural evil is again central. Fleeing the agents of civilized law, Conan forces passage aboard an Argossean merchant ship bound for the northern coast of what is now Africa. There all but Conan are massacred by black pirates, whose leader is a legendary white beauty, Belit. She falls in love with Conan and they roam the coast, pillaging and destroying, until Belit elects to search for a prehuman ruin rumored to hold great treasure.

One member of the elder race that built the city remains, now devolved into a diabolical, bat-winged ape creature. The thing craftily separates Conan and some spearmen from Belit and the rest. Conan's men are killed when the fumes of the black lotus put Conan into an enchanted slumber. He awakes from the spell to find Belit hanged from the yardarm of her ship by a golden necklace from the horde she had intended to steal. As night falls, Conan awaits the demoniac being and his were-hyena servants atop a pyramid at the center of the city. In a terrific battle, he is saved at the last moment by the ghost of Belit, returning as she promised to save her lover. At dawn, Conan places the treasure and her body in her ship, which he makes a funeral pyre. As the flames blend with the rising sun, he vanishes into the jungle.

The hero's encounter with the "unnatural" (evil) and his incredible triumph is the archetypal pattern of all the Conan stories. Nearly infinite variations are possible within this simple matrix, as illustrated by the above examples as well as the abundance of heroic "sword and sorcery" fantasy written since the Conan stories. Conan is the first true sword and sorcery hero.

Analysis: Howard's Conan stories constitute a new subgenre of heroic fantasy. Fritz Leiber coined the term "sword and sorcery" to describe this hybrid, which merged the naturalistic epic—of which the tales of Tarzan are perhaps the best example—with elements of the fairy tale and the horror story. Sword and sorcery assumes that the intimate connection of pretechnological peoples with their own mythic consciousness makes them susceptible to dark supernatural influences, yet also attunes them to their own heroic potential. Monsters are the genre's embodiment of the darkness within the human soul, but they are also symbols of what lies outside the narrow confines of modern rationality. The world is presented in terms of a struggle between great forces, not of Judeo-Christian good and evil but of natural law and unnatural chaos, and the hero's victories imply a larger order from which overcivilized (decadent) people have become estranged.

Another way to view this is that people's lives lose the potential for mythical significance through the sterile logic of technological advancement. This romantic affirmation of the natural primitive, however, is qualified by a darker undertone: Naturalistic fantasies treat aggression as more basic than communal behavior, more fundamental even than maternal bonding. Socialized behavior is superimposed on an instinctive survival/reproductive urge that is both competitive and selfish. This is why Howard believed in the inevitable collapse of civilization: The purely animal is more natural and therefore stronger than the civilized superego. It is natural to struggle and slay for survival, and unnatural to live in peace and to prosper as a community. As a nameless forester puts it at the end of "Beyond the Black River" (*Weird Tales*, 1936), "Civilization is unnatural; it is a whim of circumstance. And barbarism will always triumph."

Because of its fantastic removal from the constraints of everyday reality, sword and sorcery became an effective medium for writers who wished to test ultimate questions about the relationship of values to ideas of natural order, of dreams to reality, of nature to the supernatural, and of law to chaos. Howard's own answers were equivocal: He opposed reason to instinct, the latter of which he saw as more natural, yet he respected artistic achievement, which he viewed as unattainable without civilization and the use of higher reason. He opposed the "unnatural" repressive qualities of civilization by linking them with degeneration and diabolism, while attributing similar qualities to primitive shamans. Although he clearly admired the heroic exploits of his barbaric protagonist, he had Conan himself observe that he was unable to create and was able only to destroy.

Sword and sorcery has provided a rich vein of popular fantasy literature. Important authors in the genre include Lin Carter, L. Sprague de Camp, John Jakes, Fritz Leiber, Michael Moorcock, Andrew J. Offutt, Manly Wade Wellman, Karl Edward Wagner, and even female authors such as Andre Norton and Marion Zimmer Bradley, who adapted the anachronistic devices of the genre to their own ends. De Camp turned unpublished stories by Howard into finished works as well as writing some new Conan stories. Carter, Offutt, Robert Jordan, Steve Perry, and Bjorn Nyberg also have written Conan stories. Howard's original fusion of naturalistic and supernatural mythic themes in the Conan stories played the definitive role in establishing a popular subgenre of heroic fantasy.

—*David Hinckley*

CONJURE WIFE

Professor Norman Saylor discovers that all women are witches by nature and that his wife Tansy has been secretly practicing witchcraft to further his academic career

Author: Fritz Leiber (1910-1992)
Genre: Fantasy—occult
Type of work: Novel
Time of plot: The 1940's
Location: The northeastern United States
First published: 1953 (novella version, *Unknown Worlds*, 1943; collected in *Witches Three*, edited by Fletcher Pratt, 1952)

The Plot: While rummaging through his wife's belongings one day, Norman Saylor, a professor of sociology at Hempnell College, discovers a cache of occult paraphernalia suggesting that Tansy practices witchcraft. When confronted, Tansy astounds Norman by admitting that *all* women are witches and that she and the wives of other Hempnell faculty are engaged in a covert war of spell and counterspell against one another to further their husbands' careers. Although Norman prides himself as being one of the more liberal thinkers on campus, he is mortified that Tansy subscribes to superstitious beliefs that he has spent his entire career as an ethnologist studying and debunking. Fearing for her sanity, he persuades her to destroy all of her protective charms.

Almost immediately, Norman's luck takes a turn for the worse. He is threatened with bodily harm by an expelled student and accused of having made sexual advances by another student. A conservative trustee begins questioning Norman's moral integrity at the same time that a colleague finds damning parallels between Norman's book *Parallelisms in Superstition and Neurosis* and an unpublished doctoral thesis written one year before it. Norman's head begins filling with suicidal thoughts and the unshakable belief that he is being stalked by an animated decorative stone dragon from a building near his office. His increasingly erratic behavior contributes to his losing the department chairmanship to a colleague.

In the hope of saving Norman from his misfortunes, Tansy uses magic to deflect his bad luck onto her, then flees. Forced to accept that witchcraft does exist, Norman uses a charm left by Tansy to locate her. He finds that Evelyn Sawtelle, the wife of the new department chairman, has stolen her soul. In order to restore Tansy's soul to her body, Norman uses logic to distill an algorithm from the superstitions of several cultures regarding soul-stealing, and he employs the algorithm like a magic spell to temporarily steal Evelyn's soul and blackmail her into returning Tansy's. Only belatedly does he discover that he has been tricked, and that the soul returned to Tansy's body is not hers but that of elderly Flora Carr, Hempnell's Dean of Women, who has secretly yearned for Norman and hopes to rejuvenate herself by taking over Tansy's body. Flora's plans to have Norman kill the body in which Tansy's soul is trapped are thwarted, and Tansy is returned intact to her chastened husband.

Analysis: *Conjure Wife*, Fritz Leiber's first published novel, appeared originally in the groundbreaking fantasy pulp *Unknown Worlds*; it is one of the best examples of the style of logical modern fantasy that the magazine pioneered. Writers for *Unknown Worlds* were renowned for seeing resonances of the supernatural in the most mundane aspects of everyday life. Leiber at this point in his career already had drawn parallels between the witch's familiar and a gangster's gun in his tale "The Automatic Pistol" (1940), and he had reinvented the ghost as a viable monster for the contemporary urban landscape in "Smoke Ghost" (1941). Leiber saw in the rituals, taboos, and rigidly defined gender roles of the academic community of his day an environment akin to primitive tribal societies that accept witchcraft as a matter of course. It was not difficult for him to advance a supernatural rationale for how sexual politics shaped the characters of such institutions: Accept that the age-old battle of the sexes is founded on women wielding powers of witchcraft that men do not possess, and it is easy, in Leiber's words, to "picture most women as glamor-

conscious witches, carrying on their savage warfare of deathspell and countercharm, while their reality befuddled husbands went blithely about their business."

With its suggestion that witchcraft and sorcery can be understood in social and scientific terms, *Conjure Wife* clearly demonstrates the influence of H. P. Lovecraft (with whom Leiber corresponded briefly), particularly Lovecraft's tales "The Dreams in the Witch-House" (1933) and "The Thing on the Doorstep" (1937). Leiber's attempts to apply principles of logic to the understanding of sorcery reflect his familiarity with the Harold Shea fantasies of L. Sprague de Camp and Fletcher Pratt, several of which appeared in *Unknown Worlds* between 1940 and 1943. His suggestion that what people demonize as "supernatural" is actually a natural bypath of human evolution is prefigured in another *Unknown Worlds* novel, Jack Williamson's *Darker than You Think* (1948). *Conjure Wife* inaugurated an entire tradition of science fiction and fantasy stories that have framed science and superstition in terms of each other, including Leiber's second novel, *Gather, Darkness!* (1950; serial form, 1943), in which scientists in a future society cloak themselves with the mystique of sorcerers.

More important, *Conjure Wife* helped lay the foundation for many trends that define contemporary dark fantasy. The insular Hempnell campus, whose placid façade belies the war of wills raging behind it, anticipates horror novels of the 1970's and 1980's by Stephen King, Charles L. Grant, and numerous other writers in which small towns suffer from social and supernatural tensions that are sometimes indistinguishable from each other. Leiber's rendering of horrors emerging subtly from behind the simple aspects of life—the home, the family, the job—marks a break with the pulp horror tradition of supernatural invasion by forces from beyond and defines the direction postwar horror would take through the work of Richard Matheson and Charles Beaumont (who co-wrote the screenplay of the novel's film adaptation in 1961 as *Burn, Witch, Burn*) and the generation of writers their work influenced.
                                                —*Stefan Dziemianowicz*

A CONNECTICUT YANKEE IN KING ARTHUR'S COURT

A nineteenth century American is transported to sixth century England, where he tries to implant modern technology and political ideas

Author: Mark Twain (Samuel L. Clemens, 1835-1910)
Genre: Science fiction—time travel

Type of work: Novel
Time of plot: The late nineteenth and early sixth
   centuries
Location: England
First published: 1889

The Plot: The novel is told within a frame set around
1889. During a day tour of England's Warwick Castle,
the anonymous frame-narrator meets an American—
later identified as Hank Morgan—who relates how he
was transported back to the sixth century. When he was a
foreman in a Connecticut arms factory in 1879, an employee knocked him unconscious; he awakened in England in A.D. 528. That night, Morgan leaves a manuscript containing his story with the narrator, who stays up
reading it. Morgan's own first-person account forms the
novel's main narrative.

Morgan's narrative spans roughly ten years. After
awakening in England, he is captured and taken to
Camelot, where he is denounced as a monster and sentenced to be burned. He knows that a solar eclipse occurred at the very hour when he is scheduled to die, so he
threatens to blot out the sun. When the eclipse begins,
people conclude that he is a powerful magician. King
Arthur not only frees him but also agrees to make him his
prime minister. Morgan then enhances his reputation by
blowing up the tower of Merlin the magician. Soon
dubbed the "Boss," Morgan reorganizes the kingdom's
administration and gradually introduces modern inventions and innovations, such as matches, factories, newspapers, the telegraph, and training schools. Although he
is eager to introduce democracy and civil liberties, he
proceeds cautiously to avoid offending the powerful
Church.

After seven years, Morgan's administration is so
firmly established that he leaves Camelot. Wearing armor, he goes on a quest with a woman named Sandy to
rescue princesses—who turn out to be hogs. During his
return, he stops at a holy shrine, where King Arthur joins
him. They disguise themselves as freemen in order to
travel among commoners. A nobleman treacherously
sells them to a slave caravan that takes them to London,
where Morgan kills the slave driver while escaping. Before being recaptured, Morgan telegraphs Camelot asking for help. As he and the king are to be hanged, Sir
Launcelot arrives with five hundred knights mounted on
bicycles to rescue them.

Back in Camelot, Morgan wins many jousts using his
lasso and kills a knight with a pistol. He then challenges
all the knights at once. Five hundred knights attack, only

to scatter after he starts shooting them. This triumph
leaves him England's unchallenged master, so he unveils
his secret schools, mines, and factories. Finally ready to
take on the Church, he has slavery abolished, taxation
equalized, and all men made legally equal. Steam and
electrical power proliferate, trains begin running, and
Morgan prepares to send an expedition to discover
America.

When Morgan visits France, the legendary tragedy of
Arthur's breach with Launcelot unfolds, plunging England into civil war. Morgan returns to find that the
Church has put him and his modern civilization under its
Interdict. With only fifty-three trustworthy followers left,
he retreats to a fortified cave that is attacked by twenty-
five thousand knights. His modern weapons annihilate
the knights, but the enemy corpses trap him in the cave.
Merlin casts a spell to make him sleep thirteen hundred
years.

A postscript to the final chapter returns the story to the
present. The frame-narrator finishes reading Morgan's
manuscript and visits him in time to see him die.

Analysis: *A Connecticut Yankee in King Arthur's Court*
was the first book that Mark Twain finished after publishing *The Adventures of Huckleberry Finn* (1884). Because of its setting, it often is classified as one of his
historical novels, along with *The Prince and the Pauper*
(1882) and *Joan of Arc* (1896), but it has little in common
with either. Of the work that he published during his
lifetime, the novel most closely resembles his 1879 short
story "The Great Revolution in Pitcairn," also about an
American trying to modernize an archaic society.

The germ of *A Connecticut Yankee in King Arthur's
Court* goes back to Twain's 1866 visit to Hawaii, which
made him want to write a novel exploring the islanders'
feudalistic characteristics. He started this book in 1884
but soon abandoned it and turned instead to a parody of
medieval England. His new target was Arthurian romances, whose popularity Alfred, Lord Tennyson's *Idylls
of the King* (1859-1885) had helped to revive. Twain's
novel incorporated some elements that he had intended
for his Hawaiian novel; for example, he modeled King
Arthur partly on Hawaii's King Kamehameha V.

A Connecticut Yankee in King Arthur's Court is the
first novel-length treatment of travel into the past. Twain's
use of time travel as a plot device may have been influenced by Edward Bellamy's future-travel story *Looking
Backward: 2000-1887* (1888). He also was probably influenced by a novella that Max Adeler (Charles Heber
Clark) published as "Professor Baffin's Adventures"

(1881; later retitled "The Fortunate Island"). Adeler's story lacks time travel but resembles Twain's novel in having an inventive American drop into an Arthurian world (on an uncharted island) that he tries to modernize. Similarities between the stories were such that Clark accused Twain of plagiarism.

A Connecticut Yankee in King Arthur's Court mixes satire, burlesque, sociological diatribe, and violence too thoroughly to permit the novel's easy classification. Even its designation as a time-travel story is problematic. Aside from the prologue's vague allusion to "transmigration of souls" and "transposition of epochs," it makes no attempt to explain how Morgan reaches the sixth century, beyond stating that he is knocked on the head. His return to the nineteenth century is less mysterious: Merlin puts him to sleep for thirteen centuries.

Back in the nineteenth century, the only tangible evidence of Morgan's sixth century industrial civilization is a bullet hole in a suit of armor hanging in Warwick Castle. If his entire experience was merely a dream, it would explain his story's ahistorical elements, such as making sixth century England resemble the High Middle Ages and using a solar eclipse that never occurred.

Although the novel's time-travel elements might be regarded as fantasy, Morgan's actions in the sixth century definitely constitute science fiction. Immediately after reaching Camelot, he pledges to "boss the whole country inside of three months," using his modern education and know-how. Once he sets out to revolutionize England, the story becomes sociological science fiction. Ultimately, he fails in his battle against the Church, and all of his impressive achievements are crushed. If the novel is viewed according to modern conventions of time-travel stories, one might conclude that the reason for Morgan's failure is the impossibility of altering the space-time continuum. What interested Twain, however, is the resistance of human beings to change, a profoundly pessimistic theme that he explored in many of his late writings.

—*R. Kent Rasmussen*

THE CORNELIUS CHRONICLES

A mythic antihero from London travels through the world in the last half of the twentieth century to confront an assortment of evils in a universe where time moves unpredictably

Author: Michael Moorcock (1939-   )
Genre: Science fiction—alternate history
Type of work: Collected works

Time of plot: 1960-1975, with time travel to other periods
Location: Earth
First published: *The Cornelius Chronicles* (1977), comprising *The Final Programme* (1968), *A Cure for Cancer* (1971), *The English Assassin* (1972), and *The Condition of Muzak* (1977); *The Cornelius Chronicles, Volume II* (1986), comprising *The Lives and Times of Jerry Cornelius* (1976) and *The Entropy Tango: A Comic Romance* (1981); and *The Cornelius Chronicles, Volume III* (1987), comprising *The Adventures of Una Persson and Catherine Cornelius in the Twentieth Century* (1976) and "The Alchemist's Question" (1984)

The Plot: *The Final Programme*, first published in *New Worlds* magazine in 1965-1966, centers on the adventures in time of soldier of fortune Jerry Cornelius, his collaborator Miss Brunner, his shifty brother Frank, and his beloved sister Catherine. The novel is easy to read, linearly plotted, and full of traditional science-fiction elements. It tells the story of the clash between Jerry and Miss Brunner, a computer technician of enormous powers. Eventually the two get their computers and super-science formulas together in a womblike cave, where they merge themselves into a new hermaphrodite Messiah, destroyer/devourer of the world.

A Cure for Cancer, an "unconventional structure" according to Michael Moorcock himself, is a darker version of *The Final Programme*. Jerry reappears in 1970 as a black man with white hair who vampirizes those about him. In pursuit of his beloved sister Catherine, he goes to a strange Amerika and battles the loathsome Bishop Beesley who, together with Miss Brunner, metaphorically represents Moorcock's idea of officialdom and life-denying orderliness. In contrast, Jerry and his cohorts represent a search for aesthetic harmony and love.

Many of the characters from the first two novels reappear in *The English Assassin*, in which Jerry's story broadens and deepens. Retreating from the city and the 1970's, Jerry spends most of the novel in a coffin as a turn-of-the-century romance of the British Empire at its hectic Jubilee peak flows around him. New characters appear, the two most important of whom are Una Persson, a stage singer, dancer, revolutionary, and lover to both Jerry and Catherine, and Mrs. Cornelius, a greedy, vulgar, sly, savage, indomitable, and wise Cockney survivor from an earlier twentieth century. Entropic decay of the British Empire becomes a mirror of Jerry's decay in dehumanized London as the 1960's turn into the sour 1970's. The novel ends as a destroyer shells an English village while Jerry, in his Pierrot suit, and Catherine sail away for Normandy in their yacht *Teddy Bear*.

In *The Condition of Muzak*, Jerry's story is retold from his earlier lives as phases in a harlequinade. Jerry as Harlequin (really Pierrot, the Weeper) tries to dominate the show to reach stable bliss with Columbine, his sister Catherine. Framing this mythic story is a realistic story of Jerry as a daydreaming rock musician spaced out on drugs, living in a slum flat in the Ladbroke Grove area of London. Jerry, Catherine, and Una Persson team up in a stage act and have sex together. Mother Cornelius dies, and the story ends with Jerry on his way to tell his pregnant sister of the fact.

No enclave or style is secure against time. All things aspire toward the condition of Muzak even as entropy rots all things. Jerry endures to tell readers how to live in the decaying cities of the world.

The Cornelius Chronicles, Volume II (1986) is made up of eleven short stories published in *New Worlds* and other magazines between 1969 and 1974. The stories were published as *The Lives and Times of Jerry Cornelius* (1976) and the novel *The Entropy Tango: A Comic Romance* (1981). Moorcock directs that the stories are to be read as one continuous narrative, which opens with Jerry as a Cuban guerrilla riding an albino horse out of Time Centre into China to kill General Way Hahng with a vibragun. The narrative closes as entropic degeneration sets in, with Jerry returning to London to bed Miss Brunner, visit his mother and sister, dope up, and shoot up a post office with his friend Mo. A series of similar fantastic adventures lies between. In the novel's final story, "The Entropy Circuit," Jerry meets Miss Brunner, Captain Maxwell, and his brother Frank in Rome and ends up shooting the pope.

The Entropy Tango centers on Una Persson's adventures with anarchist 'Batko Makhno. It is 1948, and anarchy is spreading around the world. The novel concludes with anarchists blowing up Golden Gate Bridge, Una blinded when Fisherman's Wharf explodes, and Makhno captured and electrocuted in Oregon, having become a martyr on six continents.

The Cornelius Chronicles, Volume III (1987) is made up of the novel *The Adventures of Una Persson and Catherine Cornelius in the Twentieth Century* (1976) and the story "The Alchemist's Question" (1984). The former, drawn from Miss Persson's unpublished memoirs and written in an eighteenth century picaresque style, follows Una and Catherine from their bed outside time back into the twentieth century. Una experiences outcomes of the Bolshevik Revolution while Catherine explores orgasm with a variety of partners. Finally, weary of their travels, the two women return for cucumber sandwiches and tea. "The Alchemist's Question," the final episode in the career of the English Assassin, brings all the Cornelius characters together on the world stage for a "curtain call" conclusion to the series.

Analysis: Called one of the best fantasy writers in the English language, Michael Moorcock has been compared to J. R. R. Tolkien, Hieronymus Bosch, and Alfred, Lord Tennyson. His enormous output includes approximately fifty novels, innumerable short stories, and a rock album. He became editor of *Tarzan Adventures* at the age of sixteen and has earned his living as a writer/editor ever since. In April, 1963, he contributed a guest editorial to John Carnell's *New Worlds*, Britain's leading science-fiction magazine, effectively announcing the onset of the New Wave renewal movement in science fiction. In 1964, Carnell recommended that Moorcock become editor of *New Worlds*, a position he would hold until 1969.

Under Moorcock, the magazine became the cutting edge of Anglo-American science fiction. He gathered around himself a group of talented British writers and also recruited a new generation of American writers including Harlan Ellison, Samuel Delany, Thomas Disch, and Norman Spinrad. He had his own rock group, Deep Fix, and was also known for his association with the band Hawkwind, whose lyrics were drawn from science-fiction stories.

Believing that H. G. Wells had had a disastrous influence on science fiction by centering it on matters of outer space, Moorcock urged a return to exploration of the immediate future and "inner space." He offered the Jerry Cornelius novels as paradigmatic models to this end.

Moorcock's rock aesthetic and entropic view of the near future eventually influenced cyberpunk writers of the 1980's. His experiments with narrative and pastiche link him to other postmodern writers as well. His works rarely appear in science-fiction anthologies, perhaps because they so often verge on self-indulgent parody. His end of the world turns out to be England's fin de siecle extrapolated, and his characters are dandies and darlings who live for pleasure in an amusing and fantastic, but finally wildly escapist, world.

Moorcock's fiction, particularly the Cornelius series, derives its power from the manipulation of archetypes and Freudian images already present in his readers' collective unconscious. The reader is made to identify with a heroic figure who becomes, for the duration of the novel, one of the archetypes in the reader's subconscious mind. The archetypal elements of Moorcock's fiction give his work an instant mythic dimension even as the obsessive Freudian imagery connects to the reader on a deep psychosexual level. Jerry Cornelius is a new kind of mythic archetype, not an existing figure from legend but a new hero created from the imagery of the mid-twentieth century united with material from the collective unconscious. *The Cornelius Chronicles* essentially tell the same story eight times, using a different style, character's viewpoint, and form each time. Differences in time and plot create ambiguities and differences in emphasis.

The Final Programme, written over the course of several years, is the key work in the cycle, the template myth around which the rest of the stories revolve. Themes are completely stated, linearly, in their simplest forms. Like movements in a symphony, the subsequent novels and stories are all different variations on the first movement. The short stories using the same Cornelius thematic material act like tone poems inspired by a larger symphonic work. "The Alchemist's Question" ends the series in jazz riffs on the melodic line.

The basic Cornelius world is London in the near future, a territory that seems to include Europe and South Asia. Jerry, like his ally/antagonist Miss Brunner, is a psychic vampire in an unraveling world where available psychic energy is always dwindling. He is a paid assassin and a rock musician involved in murky Freudian relationships with his brother Frank and his sister Catherine in the "swinging" London of the 1960's. This London is in the process of collapse into the middle 1970's of runaway inflation, bisexuality, racial tensions, faltering economic systems, and drug overdoses, a collapse that Moorcock dated as beginning with the assassination of John F. Kennedy on November 22, 1963. Political and economic details; vivid descriptions of clothing, cars, furnishings, pop music, and altered states of consciousness; and real, bizarre newspaper items work together to create a new postmodern landscape for Moorcock's new mythic hero.

The universe of Jerry Cornelius turns out to be a metaphor for the world of the late twentieth century. Moorcock's ultimate theoretical goal was to have the Cornelius figure transcend his own novels and stories and pass into the general public's consciousness, becoming new material in the collective unconscious, much like Batman and Superman. The experiment seems to have been only a limited success.   —*E. Laura Kleiner*

COUNTERFEIT WORLD

Doug Hall discovers that he is an electronic analogue in a simulated universe that is designated for eradication by his counterpart in the real world

Author: Daniel F. Galouye (1920-1976)
Genre: Science fiction—inner space
Type of work: Novel
Time of plot: 2034
Location: A simulation of Earth
First published: 1964 (published as *Simulacron-3*, 1964, in the United States)

The Plot: *Counterfeit World* was filmed for German television in 1973 as *Welt am Draht* (*The World on a Wire*) by Rainer Werner Fassbinder and released in England as a two-part film under the same title. The story opens as Doug Hall returns from a vacation at an isolated cabin, where he was recovering from seizures brought on by stress and overwork. He discovers that Horace P. Siskin has appointed him director of RIEN Reactions, an organization that samples public opinion with a new computer containing an electronically simulated population. Although the simulator will make prediction much easier, it will put poll takers out of work.

A series of strange events, including people and things disappearing and attempts on his life, convinces Hall not only that Hannon Fuller, his predecessor and inventor of the simulator, was murdered but also that his own world is counterfeit, like the one in the simulator. Hall comes to these conclusions despite the fact that his former teacher and friend, Avery Collingsworth, has diagnosed him as being paranoid. Meanwhile, Siskin has asked Hall to reprogram the simulator so that it will project Siskin as the ideal presidential candidate, and Hall has fallen in love with Fuller's daughter, Jinx.

Hall plays along with Siskin for a time, but his plan to expose Siskin is discovered and eventually he is fired. One of the contact units from the simulator's counterfeit world comes through the hookup and takes over the physical body of an assistant. Hall realizes that there must be a person in his own world monitoring things for the operators above. As he tries to find that contact person, he discovers that he is now wanted for the murders of both Fuller and Collingsworth. He flees. Jinx finds him and tells him that she is not Fuller's daughter but a projection from the real world, that he is an electric analogue for the operator whom she once loved but who is now a sadist, and that the two Doug

Halls are physically, but not psychologically, identical.

Because Doug now knows that his world is a simulation, he also knows that the operator will have to end it, and he determines the day on which his world probably will be erased. He wants Jinx to leave, but she will not. Hall eventually saves his electronic world, but he is fatally wounded. He later wakes up in Jinx's world to find that she has switched the Doug Hall operator into Hall's electronic identity in time for him to die. Hall finds that his new body is identical to his former one and that Jinx's world is virtually identical to the one he left. Jinx says that she will help him adjust but that she will miss the operator's romantic flair for programming exotic proper nouns, such as Pacific and Mediterranean.

Analysis: *Counterfeit World* is one of five novels by Daniel Galouye and was written at the height of his creative powers. Only his minor classic *Dark Universe* (1961) is perhaps better artistically. His work was a staple of the slick magazines of the 1950's and 1960's. Many critics believe that his career was shortened by injuries he sustained during World War II.

Counterfeit World is linked with several subgenres of fiction and science fiction. The manipulation of scale is one of the most common devices in literature. Legend, myth, and folklore teem with giants and little people. Such characters feature in stories from childhood such as "Jack and the Beanstalk" and satires such as Jonathan Swift's *Gulliver's Travels* (1726) as well as in contemporary popular films such as *King Kong* (1933) and *Honey, I Shrunk the Kids* (1989). Comic books are filled with characters out of scale, such as Giant-Man, Ant-Man, and the Wasp.

Counterfeit World also is part of a subgenre that postulates microcosmic worlds within larger macrocosmic worlds. This idea has been popularized as atoms in the known universe being solar systems in their own right. Several writers prior to Galouye wrote stories using this device; the earliest is *The Triuneverse* (1912) by R. A. Kennedy.

The idea of making the microcosmic world electronic is a more specific variation of this concept. The electronic world often is within a computer. Probably the best-known example of this form is the Disney film *Tron* (1982). *Counterfeit World* is an early work in this subgenre of microcosmic worlds. It features a type of virtual reality, long before that term came into vogue. It also has similarities to L. Ron Hubbard's novella "Typewriter in the Sky" (1940) and even shares some broad ideas with

Lewis Carroll's Alice novels and contemporary video games.

Counterfeit World is technically ingenious, depending heavily on irony, and it reflects Galouye's continuing interest in worlds that are unusual and perhaps even arbitrary constructs. Galouye also was interested in reality and how it is, or is not, perceived. *Counterfeit World* is carefully and cleverly plotted, original, and richly detailed. Although Galouye's major weakness as a writer is his failure to give his characters depth, those of *Counterfeit World* are interesting, and Jinx truly achieves the status of a female hero.

Galouye did not win any major awards, but *Dark Universe* was nominated for a Hugo. His work often is neglected, but those who have examined it generally acknowledge his technical skill and ingenuity. His best work is quite good.

—*Carl B. Yoke*

THE COURSE OF THE HEART

Three university students find their lives curiously blighted after an experiment with magic

Author: M(ichael) John Harrison (1945-   )
Genre: Fantasy—inner space
Type of work: Novel
Time of plot: The 1980's
Location: Northern England
First published: 1992

The Plot: While at school, the unnamed narrator and two fellow university students, Pam Stuyvesant and Lucas Medlar, take part in a magical ritual under the guidance of Yaxley. Somehow they touch another realm, the Pleroma, and find themselves unable to escape its effects throughout the rest of their lives. Each one brings back a familiar. For Pam it is a ghostly white couple forever engaged in sexual embrace, for Lucas it is a monkeylike creature who constantly disrupts his life and surroundings, and for the narrator, apparently more blessed, it is the sight and smell of roses.

Twenty years later, Pam and Lucas have married, then divorced, but are unable to get by without each other. During their marriage, Lucas invented the autobiography of Michael Ashman to entertain Pam, and it has grown into an elaborate construct about Ashman's quest for the Coeur, an enchanted medieval land now vanished from the world but that reflects, in some curious way, the Pleroma. The narrator keeps in touch with Pam and Lucas only sporadically, building his own career and marriage in London, but he cannot quite get away from Yaxley, who involves him in further dispiriting and unsuccessful magical rituals. One of these is a sordid incident in which the narrator finds himself bringing a teenage girl to London for a ritual that will involve her having sex with her own estranged father. Almost inevitably the scheme fails, but even his self-disgust will not allow the narrator to break free of Yaxley until the mage himself dies.

The three are brought together again by Pam's final illness, during which the narrator finds out for the first time about their familiars and about the Coeur. When Pam dies, a final vision suggests that the Coeur was more than fiction and that Pam and Lucas had in their way been more blessed by the Pleroma than the narrator, who returns to an ordinary life in which his wife is killed and his child grows apart from him.

Analysis: *The Course of the Heart* is, in many respects, the novel that best brings together the various themes and practices of M. John Harrison's work. He long held an impression of magic as a grimy, backstreet enterprise, something that belongs only in this world in its worst shape. This is shown in his story "The Incalling" (1978), and it is significant that the failed magical rite that the narrator finds himself unwillingly caught up in midway through *The Course of the Heart* is referred to as an "infolding." Magic is something that goes not outward into the world but inward into the soul and imagination of the participants.

Harrison's most famous sequence of novels and stories, about Viriconium, became in the end a fiction about imaginative escape from this world, for example in "A Young Man's Journey to Viriconium" (1985). Novels in the sequence include *The Pastel City* (1971), *A Storm of Wings* (1980), and *In Viriconium* (1983, also titled *The Floating Gods*). The notion of a fantasy land alongside and accessible from the real world was further developed in another Viriconium story, "Egnaro" (1981), which was in many ways a dry run for *The Course of the Heart*. The central character of "Egnaro" is called Lucas and is prone to the migraines that beset Pam. As are these stories, the novel is ambivalent about escape. There are successive layers of imagination throughout the novel, but the way through them is so convoluted that by the end the fictional world is giving birth to the real. Thus Lucas invents Ashman, who investigates the history of the Coeur, but before long Lucas is himself tracing the history of those who escaped from the Coeur at the moment it left the real world. That track leads to Pam as

being the final descendant. It seems no more than Lucas deliberately shaping his fiction, but two glimpses of Pam after her death and the final vision amid a storm of petals suggest that this vision is no more or less than the truth.

By creating their own Pleroma, Lucas and Pam are actually less damaged by Yaxley's rite than their apparently sad lives might lead one to suspect. The narrator, cursed by the scent of roses, fails to notice that roses appear in virtually every scene in the book: The Pleroma is all around him, but he does not notice.

In a previous novel, *Climbers* (1989), Harrison essayed a technique in which real incidents in his life as a rock climber steered the dramatic shape of the novel he wrote about rock climbing. In *The Course of the Heart* there is the same sense of a "found" reality rather than a dramatically structured one. This is a tantalizing book in which the plot is never more than half glimpsed; even the participants have no idea of exactly what the ritual was that launched them on this course. Much of the book feels formless, but the truth is that readers enter into lives that are unfinished and are doomed to remain so. From a privileged position, readers can see how close the characters come to the Pleroma and how distant they must inevitably remain, but readers are so trapped inside the perceptions of the narrator, the loser, that they can never know for sure what the Pleroma might be. There are holes in the story just as there are holes in the lives of the characters. The narrator is known to be unreliable only from the way the book as a whole works. The result is a subtle, shifting work that is perhaps the most daring and the most successful of Harrison's career.

—*Paul Kincaid*

CRASH

The story of a man who becomes involved with a disturbed scientist who is obsessed with car crashes and who wishes to die in a collision with Elizabeth Taylor

Author: J(ames) G(raham) Ballard (1930-   )
Genre: Science fiction—cultural exploration
Type of work: Novel
Time of plot: The 1970's
Location: London, England
First published: 1973

The Plot: J. G. Ballard's *Crash* is a story of obsession and technological horror. The novel begins with an account of Robert Vaughan's fiery, suicidal death in a car crash. Vaughan attempted to kill Elizabeth Taylor as well but missed her limousine and crashed into a bus full of airline passengers. The narrator then gives some of Vaughan's background. He relates how Vaughan derived sexual pleasure from car crashes and how this eventually developed into his final destructive act. The narrator also explains that Vaughan developed car-crash scenarios with various celebrities.

The narrator then goes back to explain how he became involved with Vaughan and why he understands the latter's obsession. The story begins with the narrator describing a car crash involving himself, a chemical engineer, and the engineer's wife, Dr. Helen Remington. Helen's husband dies instantly, and the narrator's legs are injured severely. During his recovery, the narrator begins to be sexually aroused when he thinks about the accident. Catherine, the narrator's wife, begins to take a renewed romantic interest in her husband after the crash.

After he is released from the hospital, the narrator becomes sexually involved with Helen. In a sign of his growing fascination with car crashes, the narrator finds that he cannot have successful intercourse unless he is in a car. During one of his sexual liaisons with Helen, the narrator becomes aware that Vaughan has been watching them and taking pictures of their encounters. The relationship between Helen and the narrator soon begins to cool, but the latter's association with Vaughan has only begun.

The narrator soon learns more about Vaughan. He discovers that Vaughan is obsessed with car crashes and has taken numerous pictures of accidents. Vaughan has photographs that chronicle accidents and the recovery of victims. He also has created a survey that asks people to create a fantasy car crash involving political figures or other celebrities. The narrator also learns that Vaughan is obsessed with Elizabeth Taylor; Vaughan dreams of dying in an accident with the actress and has an entire room of photographs of her.

The narrator's association with Vaughan continues to grow throughout the rest of the book. At one point, he watches Vaughan have sexual intercourse with Catherine in the back of his car. The narrator eventually comes to share Vaughan's fascination with accidents and connects sexual pleasure to crashes. Vaughan's obsession with Taylor grows until he kills himself in an attempt to crash a car into the actress' limousine. After his death, Vaughan's influence upon the narrator becomes even more clear as the narrator begins to plan his own crash.

Analysis: *Crash* has received high praise from critics and is considered to be one of Ballard's best novels. The

characters have disturbing psychological problems that seem real. Vaughan, an obsessed scientist, brings the narrator under his influence. He slowly changes the narrator's character until he shares Vaughan's obsession with car crashes. The novel presents a fascinating portrayal of sexual obsession combined with hideous abuses of technology.

One of the strongest aspects of the novel is Ballard's powerful characterization. Each character in *Crash*, from the narrator to Robert Vaughan to Helen Remington, has a unique and fascinating personality, yet all are united by the bond of obsession and pain. The narrator's friendship with and admiration of Vaughan seem strange at first, as do his sexual fantasies connected with car crashes. As he writes about Vaughan and describes how he became involved with the scientist, however, readers can understand how the narrator could be changed by Vaughan.

Another fascinating aspect of the narrator's character is that he is named James Ballard. The connection of author and narrator creates interesting associations; readers might wonder what is fictional and what may be reality. Ballard's careful blending of fiction and reality also can be seen in his decision to make Elizabeth Taylor, a prominent actress, the focus of Vaughan's obsession.

At first, it might seem unbelievable that Vaughan could derive sexual pleasure from car crashes or that he could fantasize of dying in an accident with Taylor. When one considers the strange motivations expressed by serial killers, assassins, and terrorists, however, Vaughan and his obsession do not seem so unrealistic. In fact, Vaughan is a chilling character who might well exist in the real world.

Another fascinating aspect of *Crash* is the use of technology. Ballard does not simply tell the story of a man obsessed with an actress. Instead, he creates a terrifying vision of obsession mixing with technology and eventually leading to the death of innocent people. Ballard captures the horrifying consequences of car accidents and speculates on the terrifying possibility that there may people who want to create car crashes for their own pleasure. The technology of the automobile, which seems beneficial on the surface, is easily turned into an instrument of mass destruction.

—*David A. Oakes*

THE CROCK OF GOLD

A fable set in a Celtic fairy land, where human characters, with the help of the gods, learn lessons about life

Author: James Stephens (1882-1950)
Genre: Fantasy—magical world

Type of work: Novel
Time of plot: Undefined
Location: Ireland
First published: 1912

The Plot: *The Crock of Gold* is divided into six short books containing two central plot lines. The first focuses on the Philosopher and his wife, the Thin Woman, who live in the center of a dark pine wood in a fairy land. Initially, there are two philosophers married to two women, but one Philosopher decides he has attained all the wisdom he can bear and dies. His wife soon follows, and the Philosopher and the Thin Woman are left with two children, Brigid Beg and Seamus.

A neighbor named Meehawl MacMurrachu comes to the Philosopher for advice on where his washboard may have disappeared, and the Philosopher deduces that the leprechauns of Gort na Cloca Mora took it. He advises Meehawl to go to a hole under a tree in a nearby field. When Meehawl does so, he finds instead a little crock of gold. The leprechauns try to get the crock back, consider the Philosopher their enemy, and kidnap his two children.

Meanwhile, in the second plot, Caitlin, the beautiful daughter of Meehawl MacMurrachu, is lured by the song of the great god Pan. She goes off with him "because he was naked and unashamed." Meehawl goes again to the Philosopher for advice. The Philosopher promises to help get Caitlin back. When the leprechauns return Brigid Beg and Seamus, the Philosopher sends the children in search of Pan. The god gives them no satisfactory answer, so the Philosopher sets out to meet with the Celtic god Angus Og to seek his help in recovering Caitlin. He has a series of adventures on his journey. In book 3, Angus Og appears in the cave where Pan and Caitlin live, the two gods debate her love, and she goes off with Angus "because his need of her was very great."

Meanwhile, the leprechauns, still angry with the Philosopher because of their lost crock of gold, tell the police that two dead bodies (actually the second Philosopher and his wife) can be found under the hearthstone of the Philosopher's cottage. When the Philosopher returns from his successful trip to Angus Og, four policemen arrest him. They attempt to escort the Philosopher back to their barracks, but the leprechauns are able to rescue him in the dark night woods. The Philosopher is reunited with his wife, who arranged his release, but he claims he must give himself up to the police again. His wife goes off to Angus Og for advice, and the Philosopher goes on to the barracks. He is thrown into a dungeon with two criminals, each of whom tells a long story during the night. The next morning, he is taken to the City "in order that he might be put on his trial and hanged. It was the custom."

In the final book of *The Crock of Gold*, the Thin Woman and her children journey to Angus Og and Caitlin to ask for the release of the Philosopher. The Thin Woman visits all the fairy forts, and the fairy clans come together in a great celebration. Angus and Caitlin sweep into the City to free the Philosopher.

Analysis: James Stephens was a largely self-educated author associated with the Irish literary revival at the end of the nineteenth century. He produced dozens of volumes of fiction, poetry, and fairy tales in his prolific career. *The Crock of Gold* is his most famous work and is one that is almost impossible to define.

The novel is first of all an allegory, a fable in which nearly every character represents some abstract quality. Man is equated with thought, woman with intuition, Pan with sensuality, and so on. Unfortunately for the modern reader, many of Stephens' allegorical figures are drawn from Celtic (Irish) history. Even without a knowledge of Irish mythology, however, readers still can grasp the major import of this delightful fable.

In both plot lines, the protagonists are freed from the constraints of human society and led to a life of greater freedom. The Philosopher starts the novel full of long-winded platitudes, but when he returns to his wife after his adventures on his quest to Angus Og, he has been released from his former selfishness and filled with love. Likewise, the beautiful Caitlin, in her adventures with Pan and Angus, learns that "the duty of life is the sacrifice of self." Throughout the novel, the habits of philosophy or thought are opposed by the forces of instinct, sexual love, and imagination. The end of life, as the Philosopher discovers, may be "gaiety and music and a dance of joy."

The Crock of Gold is no simple allegory. Fused to the fable are other strands, including a strong satirical element. There is a clear structural opposition in the novel between the forces of nature (fairy innocence, pastoral idyll) and those of civilization (materialism and greed). The two criminals who relate their stories are both former clerks, for example. In the apocalyptic ending, the gods clean out the institutional prisons of urban society, including those of the church, the courts, education, and medicine.

No account of *The Crock of Gold* would be complete without mention of two other strands in its fairylike fable: its humor and its poetry. The comedy is often childlike: The two women marry the Philosophers "in order to be able to pinch them in bed." The language of the novel is lyrical and shows the clear influence of the British Romantic poet William Blake.   —*David Peck*

CROWN OF STARS

A posthumously published collection of ten short stories concerning nature, religious belief, female sexuality and self-perception, and the effects on the individual of an uncaring government

Author: James Tiptree, Jr. (Alice Hastings Bradley Sheldon, 1915-1987)
Genre: Science fiction—New Wave
Type of work: Stories
Time of plot: Various, from the present to the unspecified near future
Location: Various locations on Earth, on other planets, and in Heaven and Hell
First published: 1988

The Plot: *Crown of Stars* collects stories written by Alice Sheldon under both of her pseudonyms, James Tiptree, Jr., and the less frequently used Raccoona Sheldon. Although most of these stories first appeared in print in science-fiction magazines and anthologies between 1985 and 1988, "Last Night and Every Night" and "The Earth Doth Like a Snake Renew" are products of the 1970's, and one story, "Come Live with Me," appears in print for the first time.

"Yanqui Doodle" and "Morality Meat," though published under different pseudonyms, are similar in theme and tone. Both are set in the near future and examine the impact of political decisions on unprivileged citizens. In "Morality Meat," the crusade to end abortion rights has resulted in a huge number of unwanted babies. So overcrowded are adoption centers that many babies are butchered and sold as suckling pigs to the very rich, who, it is indicated, know what they are eating. In "Yanqui Doodle," a young soldier is given pills to make him both willing to kill and able to forget his deeds. When he is wounded, his supply is cut off, and he begins to remember the atrocities he has committed. Unable to live with his memories but realizing that the real enemy is the government that used and abandoned him, he attacks a convoy of his own military leaders.

Another theme common in the collection is the role of religion in providing meaning for existence. "In Midst of

Life," for example, tells the story of a man who awakes after committing suicide to find that the afterlife is whatever he wishes it to be. "Second Going" is about a visitation of angels, disguised as a benevolent race of octopuslike creatures. These angels actually are "gofers" for the gods; they have been given the task of finding a race of people whose belief will keep the gods alive. The humorous "Our Resident Djinn" tells of Satan's attempt to take over Heaven after the death of God. Although he convinces the saints to move Heaven to Hell, he encounters an entity, Nature, who—in league with her father, Entropy—threatens to assert her dominion over Earth.

In "Our Resident Djinn" and in such stories as "The Earth Doth Like a Snake Renew," Tiptree suggests both the enormous power of nature and the need to protect its resources. In "The Earth Doth Like a Snake Renew," the protagonist attempts a sexual union with Earth, which she considers male. After doing everything she can to please him and to make herself sexually available, she finds that Earth—which is in fact a young male being—has been treating her as his plaything. In the gentler "Come Live with Me," humans merge with a healing consciousness that long ago had become a part of the natural world.

Tiptree frequently links nature with the theme of a young woman's emerging sexual and social sense, as in "The Earth Doth Like a Snake Renew" and the allegorical "All This and Heaven Too." In the latter story, Amoretta, the young queen of pristine Ecologia-Bella, plans to wed the young prince of Pluvio-Acida, a country utterly devastated by pollution, despite the dire consequences for her idyllic country.

Analysis: Critics often describe Tiptree's best writing as predating this collection. None of the stories here has the stylistic and thematic power of "Houston, Houston, Do You Read?" (1976), "The Screwfly Solution" (1977), or "With Delicate Mad Hands" (1981). It has been suggested that after her identity was revealed, Sheldon was less successful than she had been as Tiptree. *Crown of Stars*, though not representative of Tiptree's very best writing, is nevertheless representative of the author's major themes and shows her place within both the New Wave of science-fiction writing and the feminist wave.

Tiptree combines a thorough knowledge of science, psychology, and military tactics with exceptional stylistic skills to impart a rare power to the science-fiction short story, thus raising its critical reputation. The author's ironic and complex studies of human psychology, in particular, are hallmarks of the New Wave of science-fiction writing introduced in the late 1960's and early 1970's. The author's alignment with feminist science fiction as it began to appear in the early 1970's was colored somewhat by the use of a male pseudonym, particularly because Tiptree often was described as a singularly masculine writer, concerned with male aggression and sexual conquest, here illustrated by "Yanqui Doodle." The revelation that Tiptree was Alice Sheldon forced the science-fiction community to examine its presuppositions about "male" and "female" writing.

Tiptree's themes are often feminist. For example, she treats abortion in "Morality Meat" and young women's views of sexuality, marriage, and social roles in "All This and Heaven Too" and "Backward, Turn Backward." Unlike such feminist writers as Joanna Russ, Monique Wittig, and Marge Piercy, though, Tiptree neither offers a utopian separatist paradigm nor provides purely sympathetic female characters. "Backward, Turn Backward" is critical of a society that allows girls to develop a sense of self-worth based only on appearances but features a main female character with whom it is hard to sympathize. Similarly, although Amoretta in "All This and Heaven Too" is in some ways a victim of conventions of romantic love, she nearly imperils the country she rules by marrying the wrong man. Like other feminist writers, however, Tiptree examines the role of women in society, including aspects of their sexual selves long taboo in science fiction.
—Amy Clarke

A CRYSTAL AGE

A stranger transported to a utopian pastoral community adjusts to its customs and wrestles with his desire for a woman who does not understand sexual love

Author: W(illiam) H(enry) Hudson (1841-1922)
Genre: Fantasy—utopia
Type of work: Novel
Time of plot: Thousands of years in the future
Location: A pastoral version of Earth
First published: 1887

The Plot: While on a nature hike, the main character, who later identifies himself as "Smith," has a mysterious fall and loses consciousness. When he awakes, he finds himself covered with dirt and roots. As he tries to find his way home, he comes upon a funeral party. Smith sees the beautiful young girl Yoletta and is filled with desire for her. Yoletta and the other members of the funeral party detect him and notice his different speech and clothing.

He inquires about the nearest city, only to learn that the members of the funeral party have never heard of cities, England, or anything else related to Smith's past experience.

Smith is taken to their house, where he occasionally offends his hosts because he does not understand their customs. He becomes ashamed of his clothing and tries to buy a suit of clothing like those the others are wearing. His hosts have never heard of money but agree to allow him to work for a year for his clothing. He works each day chopping down trees, hoping to get closer to Yoletta.

Smith's passion for Yoletta grows, but she shows no understanding of love except for the love between brother and sister. Smith notices that there is a father in this household but no apparent couples. He finally asks about Yoletta's mother and learns that he has unknowingly offended the family by not asking about the mother sooner. He visits the "mother's room" where Chastel, Yoletta's mother, stays, too weak to come out. On the way to the room, he passes a series of lifelike statues and learns about the grief of Isarte, a former mother in the house. Smith learns from Chastel that only mothers feel true grief.

Yoletta eventually develops a passionate love for Smith, and Chastel apparently plans that Yoletta will become the next mother, with Smith as the father. Smith accidentally drinks a potion that turns him into a statue like the ones he passed on the way to the mother's room. Yoletta experiences true grief at his loss.

Analysis: W. H. Hudson is best known for his nature writings and his novels about South America, where he grew up. Although there are elements of fantasy in some of his other novels, *The Crystal Age* (first published anonymously, then published as by Hudson in 1906) is his strongest and clearest contribution to the genre. Hudson is particularly famous for his books about birds. His love for nature and eye for natural beauty show up in his descriptions of nature in *The Crystal Age*.

Nature is an important element in the novel because the world that Smith enters after his period of unconsciousness is a utopian world in the pastoral tradition. A pastoral work praises the simplicity of country life, particularly the life of shepherds, and provides an idealized view of nature. The model for the pastoral world is the Golden Age of Greece, a mythological innocent past that was irrecoverably lost. Hudson describes a "crystal age," a time that is beautiful and unchanging but also fragile.

The world that Smith enters is not free from death, but death usually comes without pain and grief, and only after a long life. The inhabitants of this world are young and beautiful, and they spend their time performing simple tasks, singing, and reading books about the history of their house and other houses in the world. They live in a state of innocent bliss, like children, and their love for one another is free from any sexual passion. Smith appears crude and unrefined by comparison, but he is able to feel passion that no one in this community can understand except for the mother, who is also the only one who truly suffers and feels pain.

The happiness of the community seems to depend on the suffering of the mother. The symbol of this suffering is Isarte, who lost seven of her children and asked that a statue be made depicting her grief for all generations. The mother leads a special existence. She is confined to the "mother's room," but she is revered and obeyed by all the members of her household. She has special books that describe the role of the mother and provide her with greater knowledge than the others have; the others live in innocence and ignorance. With knowledge, however, come grief and suffering.

Smith brings uncertainty to this ordered house because of his foreignness. He resembles Prometheus, who defies the Greek gods by bringing fire and knowledge to humans. Smith and Yoletta also resemble Adam and Eve. They live in a Edenic state of innocence until Smith's passion for Yoletta deepens her sense of love and her understanding. When he accidentally turns himself to stone, Yoletta experiences true loss and true grief for the first time. She leaves her state of innocence and becomes like Isarte, Chastel, and other mothers. It may be that this loss of innocence is a necessary preparation for Yoletta to take her place as a mother.

Because of the loss of the love that Smith and Yoletta have developed for each other, *The Crystal Age* also has elements of tragedy. In drinking the potion, Smith believes that he is doing what Yoletta would want by wiping out the dark memories he has of his life before coming to the house. In trying to regain a state of innocence, he loses his life and the object of his desire.

—*Gary Layne Hatch*

CRYSTAL EXPRESS

Science fiction and fantasy stories exploring how humanity might shape its future and itself

Author: Bruce Sterling (1954-   )
Genre: Science fiction—future history
Type of work: Stories

Time of plot: Various times between the medieval period and several centuries into the future
Location: Various locations on Earth and in space
First published: 1989

The Plot: The stories in *Crystal Express* are grouped into three sections. The first five stories belong to a future history in which the human race has gone into space and contacted other intelligent life-forms. The alien species that appears most often is a reptilian one called the Investors. They are interstellar traders. Humanity itself has split into factions, the two most important of which are the Shapers and the Mechanists. They are similar in that they insist that human beings must change. The Shapers practice genetic engineering, especially on their own offspring. The Mechanists change themselves surgically, substituting prosthetics for natural limbs and organs.

There are two recurring characters. Simon Afriel is a minor character in "Twenty Evocations" and the main character in "Swarm." He is a member of the Shaper faction and is genetically engineered to have no appendix, along with other improvements. In "Swarm," he travels to another star system to investigate a nonintelligent spacefaring species. Arkadya Sorienti first appears in "Cicada Queen" as a Mechanist living in the space colony Czarina-Kluster. At some point between the end of that story and the beginning of "Sunken Garden," she defects to the Regal faction. She then goes to live in Terraform-Kluster, a space station in orbit around Mars and tethered to its surface. The main work of the Regals on that planet is terraforming, or physical transformation of the environment to meet the needs of human and other life.

The middle three stories in *Crystal Express* are science fiction that can be categorized as cyberpunk. The main character in "Green Days in Brunei" is Turner Choi, a Chinese Canadian engineer. He is on assignment in Brunei, a sultanate completely surrounded by the country of Malaysia. There he meets and falls in love with a member of Brunei's royal family. The title character in "Spook" is an assassin. As one weapon, he uses his sinuses, which produce a toxin that induces schizophrenia. In "The Beautiful and the Sublime," Manfred de Kooning is an artist free to indulge his aesthetic sensibilities because of advances made in artificial intelligence technologies.

The final four stories are fantasies. "Telliamed" is De Maillet spelled backwards. It refers to the pseudonym that Benoit De Maillet, an elderly eighteenth century scientist, uses when he publishes a book on the ocean. In "The Little Magic Shop," James Abernathy buys an elixir of youth. A teaspoon taken each year slows twenty years of aging down to one. In the "Flowers of Edo," a former Japanese samurai confronts an electricity demon. A clairvoyant is invited to a "Dinner in Audoghast," at which he makes some predictions that his host and the other guests do not like.

Analysis: Bruce Sterling is one of the leading proponents of the cyberpunk movement in science fiction. He is not comfortable being identified with that movement, however, particularly as it has become associated with computer crime. The technological background of his stories is solid, and he is comfortable employing in his fiction such devices as personal computers, fax machines, and modems. In this way, he is similar to the writers of the Golden Age of science fiction, who wrote comfortably about devices such as rockets, radios, and nuclear reactors that were, at the time of writing, relatively new and developing forms of technology.

Sterling is the author of the nonfiction *The Hacker Crackdown: Law and Disorder on the Electronic Frontier* (1992). He has pointed out that the writers of the cyberpunk movement are as fascinated by information technology as earlier science-fiction writers were by space travel. Most of Sterling's stories reveal a concern about the social consequences of computers and other devices of high technology.

In several stories, characters state the case for antitechnology philosophies. An alien in "Swarm" argues that intelligence is not a prosurvival trait for life-forms. The alien's position is that the urge to expand, explore, and understand ultimately results in extinction. It goes on to predict that the human race will be extinct within approximately a millennium after the time of the story. Thus, science and technology are predicted ultimately to be antilife, but the story leaves the issue unresolved.

In "Spook," a former assassin claims to have rediscovered her humanity in a society patterned on that of the ancient Mayans. The society wins converts by allowing them to feel and love, she explains. Unfortunately for her, this society is destroyed by another assassin, working for a multinational corporation. The premise of "The Beautiful and the Sublime" is that the development of artificial intelligence renders scientists and engineers obsolete. This is similar to Friedrich Nietzsche's idea that science sows the seeds of its own destruction.

On the other hand, some of Sterling's characters learn how to reconcile technology with a humanistic, life-affirming philosophy. Vikram Moratuwa, a character in "Green Days in Brunei," attempts to reconcile a tradi-

tional religion, Buddhism, with technology. His goal is to harness runaway technology and make it serve humanity instead of the other way around. In "Cicada Queen," Landau, the main character, is a follower of a philosophy called Posthumanism and makes genetic engineering into an art form. He later founds the Regal faction, the main goal of which is to bring life to Mars. In "Sunken Gardens," the Regals sponsor a competition among ecosystems that is based on technological, philosophical, and aesthetic criteria.   —*Tom Feller*

THE CULTURE SERIES

A highly advanced galactic civilization employs adventurers to shape younger, emerging societies in its image

Author: Iain M. Banks (1954-   )
Genre: Science fiction—galactic empire
Type of work: Novels
Time of plot: The fourteenth to twenty-first centuries and beyond
Location: Various planets, including Earth, and the Lesser Magellanic Cloud
First published: *Consider Phlebas* (1987), *The Player of Games* (1988), *Use of Weapons* (1990), and *The State of the Art* (1991; includes the novella "The State of the Art," 1989; "A Gift from the Culture," 1987; and six other, non-Culture stories)

The Plot: The Culture series is composed of independent tales, though some of the same characters appear in two of the plots and there are several references to the Idirian war. The Contact Section of the Culture—a utopia of highly advanced technologies in which life is prolonged, all wants are fulfilled, and humanoids of all species live in peace—benevolently watches over emerging societies in the Milky Way and the Magellanic Clouds. Through Special Circumstances operatives, the Culture shapes those societies to its standards. The plots of the individual novels concern the adventures of Special Circumstances operatives.

The first novel, *Consider Phlebas*, depicts a galactic war between the Culture and three-legged, reptilian Idirians, occurring in the fourteenth century of Earth's Common Era. The Culture fights to justify itself, excusing its hedonistic lifestyle by the way it improves inferior societies by imposing its standards on them. The Idirians, who think the Culture lacks real principles, fight to subjugate other species, bringing other societies to their god in a religious and commercial empire. Bora Horza, a "changer" who can assume any humanoid shape, supports the Idirians and fights on their side; Perosteck Balveda, a Special Circumstances agent, is his opponent. The object of their struggle is a Mind (the sentient core of a starship) that has escaped the Idirians and is hiding on a forbidden planet controlled by a third society, the Dra'Azon. To find the Mind, Horza assumes the identity of the leader of a Free Company (of pirates) and takes the pirates (including Balveda, who knows his real identity) to the planet, arriving after Idirians have already landed. In a running battle with the Idirians, who will not believe that Horza is on their side, the Free Company is wiped out. They find the Mind, however, and Balveda, the sole survivor of the Free Company, restores it to the Culture.

The Player of Games sets the Culture in opposition to another emerging society, the Empire of Azad in the Lesser Magellanic Cloud. The rogue drone Mawhrin-Skel (actually a Special Circumstances operative) blackmails the professional game-player Jernau Morat Gurgeh into cooperating with Contact. Contact needs him to enter the Game of Azad, an incredibly complex game that models the Azadian society and is so central to the empire that the winner becomes emperor. With his translator and adviser, the library drone Flere-Imsaho (who is revealed at the end to be Mawhrin-Skel, and who narrates the novel), Gurgeh goes to Azad and plays. Despite collusion against him, attempts on his life, and attempts to bribe him, Gurgeh plays well enough to earn the right to play in the final round against Nicosar, the sitting emperor. In the ultimate stage, played on the fire planet Echronedal, Gurgeh realizes that Contact has designed his participation to discredit the game and thereby Azadian society; the game has become a battle between the Culture and the empire. Foreseeing defeat, Nicosar attempts to immolate Gurgeh in the fire but is killed; Gurgeh, rescued by Contact, returns home.

The novella "The State of the Art," next in order of original publication, depicts Contact's initial exploration of Earth, as described by the agent Diziet Sma. Her colleague Dervley Linter decides to remain behind on Earth, finding its society and conditions more vital than the perfect, but stagnating, Culture. Sma is asked by her ship to persuade Linter to return. She tries but fails. Linter is then killed in a random mugging in New York City. Despite the arguments of some agents that Earth should be destroyed or overtly contacted, the ship departs, leaving behind monitoring devices.

The last novel, *Use of Weapons*, reintroduces Sma (and her drone, Skaffen-Amtiskaw) as the Special Circumstances supervisor of the agent Cheradenine Zakalwe.

Zakalwe has been used by Contact as a "dirty tricks" agent because he lacks the moral compunctions of most Culture persons. He is sent to Voerenhutz, where he earlier established a forty-year peace in cooperation with the local patriarchal politician Tsoldrin Beychae. The peace is breaking down, and only Zakalwe can persuade Beychae to come out of seclusion and prevent widespread conflict. His successful effort costs him his life, and the terrible personal secret of sororicide that had driven him in his adventures is revealed at his death.

Analysis: Each of the three long novels of the Culture series is a spirited adventure story; together with the novella, they constitute a postmodernist rethinking of what has been called "space opera," a subgenre of literature dealing with interstellar conflict and involving action-filled plots. The texts gain power and excitement from the interpenetration of traditional storytelling and contemporary narrative fashions.

The first and longest book, *Consider Phlebas*, is unabashedly an adventure story. It is the first of Iain M. Banks's books to fall clearly within the realm of science fiction. (Banks used his middle initial as author of works of science fiction but did not use it for other works.) The hero of *Consider Phlebas* lives by wits, courage, and physical prowess, all abetted by the advanced technologies of the Culture and by his special ability to change his body to duplicate that of another. He survives imprisonment, torture, fire fights, shipwreck, a cannibal king on a desert island, and other threats. The novel moves from climax to climax at breathtaking speed, with action that rivals any classic tale of interstellar war. The narrative, which is fairly straightforward when focused on Horza, is also interrupted by brief chapters called "state of play" in which a Culture woman meditates on the meaning of the events, their likely outcome, and the nature of the Culture itself. The final chapter of the narrative not only takes its title (and the major image of the sacrificed, dead sailor) from the fourth section of T. S. Eliot's *The Waste Land* (1922) but also is preceded by a chapter whose ending imitates the style Eliot uses to end the third section of his poem. Such self-conscious narrative elements, coupled with the use of stream-of-consciousness techniques and a set of appendices, separate the book stylistically from the usual space adventure.

The Player of Games and "The State of the Art" eschew most of the stylistic devices of the first book. In *The Player of Games*, however, Banks shows awareness of contemporary narrative theory and practice through the narrator's self-conscious comments dealing with the nature of language and narrative. These comments introduce each of the novel's four sections. In "The State of the Art," the division of the text into numbered subchapters—along with idiosyncratic typography and a series of footnotes by the supposed translator drone—keeps the reader aware that the otherwise straightforward narrative is itself an arbitrary convention.

The last major work to date in the series, *Use of Weapons*, is the most complex in structure. It consists of two series of chapters, one numbered in ascending order and the other in descending order. The two series come together at the death of Zakalwe to both account for his motivations and provide the final surprise of the novel. Banks here seems interested not only in the action or in the sociopolitical background of the Culture but also in the abnormal psychology of a rebel-adventurer who can use violence and cruelty in order to achieve noble ends. This approach is enhanced by poems before and after the text. A postmodern playfulness is seen in an appended section that purports to be the opening chapter of the next Culture novel. In it, Sma recruits Zakalwe's replacement.

The breadth of Banks's intellectual and aesthetic achievement in the Culture novels is astonishing. He has created a utopian society dependent on a wide range of advanced technologies, including faster-than-light travel, machine sentience far superior to human intelligence, genetic engineering of human beings (who not only live for centuries but can deliberately "gland" appropriate mood-altering substances), and weaponry of enormous power but minuscule size. He also incorporates a series of critiques of this society, which in its imperialistic smugness seems to overrule the very things that make a human being human, including the ability to make a mistake or to sin. Banks sometimes uses well-worn plot situations (derived from the spy novel and the thriller as well as from classic science fiction) and employs a mix of unusual and conventional characters. He combines these in a witty narrative style and a sometimes experimental structure to produce engrossing tales. The results rise above mere adventure to become both cultural commentary and a self-reflexive commentary on the science-fiction genre.

—William H. Hardesty III

THE CYBERIAD

The adventures of two constructors in their travels across space

Author: Stanisław Lem (1921-   )
Genre: Science fiction—dystopia

Type of work: Stories
Time of plot: The distant future
Location: Various planets and space between them
First published: *Cyberiada* (1965; English translation, 1974)

The Plot: *The Cyberiad*, subtitled *Fables for the Cybernetic Age*, is a collection of related short stories set in a time after robots have escaped slavery at the hands of humanity; they live free throughout the galaxy. They have developed a feudal society, complete with kings, princesses, evil pirates, paupers, and serfs, and they seem to be much more like humans than unlike them. Most planets have one or two kingdoms, and the denizens of a particular kingdom tend not to travel much. Interstellar travel, like international travel during the Middle Ages, is reserved primarily for those who do not belong to the feudal hierarchy.

The principal characters are two such travelers, Trurl and Klapaucius, who have just received their "Diplomas of Perpetual Omnipotence" as constructors. The title is roughly equivalent to that of the medieval magician or sorcerer. They are friends and rivals, and the stories center on their adventures together as they build machines to improve the collective condition, or at least make some money.

Trurl and Klapaucius serve as advisers, matchmakers, storytellers, and judges as they travel among the stars. In a typical story, the constructors create a (usually sentient) machine for some educational or contractual purpose, and it either works but with unexpected results or fails to perform. In another common plot, the constructors build a machine to repair an individual, social, or political problem on a planet they are visiting. The remedy seldom succeeds, but if it does, the success is incidental. There are several stories in which Trurl and Klapaucius figure peripherally and one in which they are absent but are mentioned.

The most common English-language edition of this collection contains fifteen stories. The first three set the scene and tone for the nine that follow; the final three sum up the themes previously presented. There is no overlying plot, and each story has a multitude of pitfalls and plot twists.

There were several editions of the book published in the original Polish, of which the third is definitive. The most common English edition omits roughly a third of the stories in the third Polish edition. All but one of these stories are available in English translation as *Mortal Engines* (1977).

Analysis: The prose of the stories in *The Cyberiad* is a peculiar mix of current usage, archaic medieval language, and jargon from various technical disciplines, particularly cybernetic theory, electronics, and quantum mechanics. The hard sciences around which modern technology is based gain the semblance of medieval magic and make the principal characters resemble Terry Pratchett's wizards.

An interesting feature of the language in the work is its literalness: changing the description changes the described. In one case, the lack of a dragon was changed into the back of a dragon, producing a dragon with two backs. This literalness is familiar to anyone who has dealt with a computer, and it adds an additional humorous element.

Various themes appear in the stories, among them the blindness of love, the follies of greed and pride, the insidiousness of bureaucracy, and the stupidity of blind suspicion. In all, the stories are reminiscent of Aesop's fables, as the title suggests. The stories as a whole equate the condition of all conscious things, machine and flesh, and suggest that a conscious effort to improve the existence of others creates more grief than doing nothing.

Stanisław Lem's characters are all tools he uses to illustrate some point. Kings are inevitably poor rulers, through either cruelty or lack of interest. When political systems other than monarchies are described, however, they are shown to be worse because they were intended to work a greater good. Cruelty is usually associated with stupidity in these stories. Lem suggests that the cruelest of all are those who would rearrange a culture to improve the lot of its people. A cybernetic Karl Marx is put to death with the approval of Trurl not because he tried to improve the lot of his people with revolutionary socio-political ideas but because he did not desist after his initial failure. The implication is that only individual, not societal, happiness can be increased through one's actions.

One would be mistaken to state, however, that the collection appears either philosophical or gloomy. The fable format and clever humorous devices ensure that, depending on personal tastes, the reader will find the stories either humorous and whimsical or ponderous and belabored. The philosophical issues appear only after consideration, a necessity for any Polish author who hoped to avoid political entanglements in the 1960's.

Translator Michael Kandel was nominated for an award for translating *The Cyberiad*. Lem has said that Kandel is probably the best translator his work will ever have. Because Polish shares few linguistic or cultural roots with English, Kandel resorted to using an analogous form of translation in which an untranslatable feature (for example, a pun) is replaced with a compensatory feature of a similar sense in English at a different, but logical, insertion place in the text. This approach has great dangers associated with it. It demands that the translator be nearly as skillful, or even more so, than the author and have as good a literary sense as the author. Because Lem has been accused by some Polish critics of having created his own language from Polish in *The Cyberiad*, and because it is in a format that is easily deadened by translation, the demands on a translator of this work are exceptional. Fortunately, Kandel was up to the task, and his translation carries both the meaning and the sense of Lem's prose and poetry.

—Radford B. Davis

CYTEEN

Reseune labs uses advanced psychogenetics to replicate its brilliant leader, Ariane Emory, after she is killed

Author: C. J. Cherryh (Carolyn Janice Cherry, 1942-   )
Genre: Science fiction—future history
Type of work: Novel
Time of plot: The twenty-fourth century
Location: The planet Cyteen
First published: 1988

The Plot: Fifty years after the Treaty of Pell established an uneasy peace between Earth and its former colonies in the Merchanter's Alliance and in Union, an aging Ariane Emory is the most powerful figure in Union politics. She is the virtual owner of its most advanced research laboratory, Reseune; councillor for science to the Council of Nine in Union's government; and, within the council, leader of its majority faction, the Expansionists.

Through Reseune labs, she developed the "azi," androids whose expanding population enabled Union to secede from Earth. Now researching how to replicate Union's most gifted citizens psychosocially as well as biologically, Emory seduces and co-opts Justin Warrick, a teenager who is an inexact replicant of her brilliant colleague and rival, Jordan Warrick.

When Emory's frozen corpse is discovered at Reseune, her successor at the lab and on the council, Giraud Nye, extorts a confession from Jordan Warrick and exiles him to a remote laboratory on the far side of Cyteen, meanwhile keeping Justin and Justin's azi lover, Grant, as virtual hostages at Reseune. With his brother Denys, Giraud immediately begins an attempt to replicate Ariane Emory and recover her much-needed abilities amid the fractious and conspiratorial politics of Union.

Using extensive notes left by Emory and by her mother, one of Reseune's founders, the Nyes' project succeeds in producing a second Ariane, whose abilities compare favorably with those of the original. With the advantage of a computerized tutorial left by Emory, however, the second Ariane proves herself not only a precocious researcher and skilled politician but also a more decent human being than her predecessor.

Despite the psychological damage to Justin Warrick wrought by Emory's sexual manipulation of him, his father's implication in her murder, and the Nyes' continuing hostility, the second Ariane recognizes his innate decency and potential brilliance. She sets out to win him over, first as her teacher and then as an essential supporter in the political turmoil that threatens to envelop Reseune as the military faction in Union turns ugly and threatens the Expansionists' majority on the council.

When the aged Giraud Nye dies abruptly, the eighteen-year-old Ariane is able to counter the threatening politics from Union. A nearly successful attempt to assassinate her, however, seems to imply that Giraud and Denys, rather than the Warricks, have been the more serious threat to Ariane Emory's hegemony.

Analysis: *Cyteen* is one of the central texts in C. J. Cherryh's sprawling future history, in which the former colonies of Earth become the political rivals of Alliance and Union. At 680 pages, it is also one of the longest. It lays out the foundations of that rivalry on Union's home planet. Other works that are central to this future history include *Serpent's Reach* (1980), *Downbelow Station* (1981), *Merchanter's Luck* (1982), and *Rimrunners* (1989). Like *Downbelow Station*, *Cyteen* was voted a Hugo Award for best novel of the year, and in 1989, it was republished as three volumes: *The Betrayal*, *The Rebirth*, and *The Vindication*.

As John Clute has noted in *The Encyclopedia of Science Fiction* (1993), the Alliance-Union rivalry gives Cherryh a flexible but powerful structural focus for her future history. Such a focus offers a much-needed center for a writer whose plots are dense with tangled political machinations and conflicting motivations. Paradoxically, even a novel with the heft of *Cyteen* can seem too cramped for the psychological, social, and political action that Cherryh pours into its pages.

At the heart of *Cyteen* is an intersecting double plot: the project to replicate Ariane Emory and the effort to restore Justin Warrick's disrupted research potential. Through the former, Cherryh invokes fundamental questions about the formation of an individual's identity and the potential of biological engineering to alter people's assumptions about the genetic roots for such identity and the subsequent socialization of the individual. The focus of these questions in Ariane Emory is framed by the book's emphasis on her psychological and social engineering of the azi, the androids who provide bulk and ballast for Union's population. Together, Emory and the azi give *Cyteen* an awareness of human reason entangled in complex emotions that extends the boundaries delineated by Isaac Asimov in his Foundation series, begun in 1942, with later volumes that converge with his robot stories.

In the other strand of this double plot, Cherryh explores the ambiguous zone between human psychology in Justin Warrick and azi psychology in his companion, Grant. Both embody an admixture of logic and emotion, but for Grant, logic is fundamental, engineered into the deepest levels of awareness, and emotion is a "flux" state that disturbs mental equilibrium. For Justin, however, logic is an imperfectly exercised control over the more fundamental emotional flux. The sexual compatibility and mutual respect that characterize Justin and Grant provide a marked contrast to the more disturbed relationships among most of the human characters who populate *Cyteen*. In the end, the second Ariane is able to recover Justin's abilities by respecting the relationship that he and Grant have established.

The profusion of social and political disturbances that surround this double plot suggests that humanity's difficulty in reconciling logic and emotion remains profound. Even science, which offers a model for the appropriate exercise of reason in human endeavor, is compromised by the sheer complexity of human nature and the politics that intervene when science has to operate in the world. In *Cyteen*, the scientists themselves are all-too-imperfect human beings. That point, richly illustrated by the human characters' convoluted motivations, should resonate through the related volumes in Cherryh's future history.

—*Joseph J. Marchesani*

DAGON AND OTHER MACABRE TALES

A series of tales in which human characters confront the bizarre, horrific, and otherworldly

Author: H(oward) P(hillips) Lovecraft (1890-1937)
Genre: Fantasy—occult
Type of work: Stories
Time of plot: Various times from antiquity to the near future
Location: Various places around the world and on other planets
First published: 1965 (corrected text of original, 1986)

The Plot: This collection by perhaps the greatest twentieth century writer of horror fiction was assembled by his fellow fantasy writer, August Derleth, and reissued with a new introduction by T. E. D. Klein in 1986. The stories originally appeared in print between 1917 and 1936. After H. P. Lovecraft's death in 1937, Derleth and his collaborator, Donald Wandrei, wanted to assemble and present in permanent form some of Lovecraft's work that had appeared in pulp magazines such as *Weird Tales*. Lovecraft had often written of the strange research occurring in the library of Arkham University. Derleth and Wandrei therefore chose the name Arkham House for the publishing firm that produced this collection and also saved from oblivion the work of many other horror and fantasy writers.

The typical Lovecraft protagonist finds a shocking and terrifying reality other than the normal that unhinges him, destroys him, or changes his life for the worse. He (the protagonists in this collection are exclusively male) sometimes stumbles over the evidence of another, frightening world, as does the main character of the title story, "Dagon" (1917). After having his ship torpedoed by a German submarine, he finds himself stranded in a strange land with temples dedicated to Dagon, the fish-god. That discovery is unsettling enough, but then the shipwrecked sailor sees fishlike monsters who worship Dagon. Now insane, he tells the story from a San Francisco hospital; hearing a slithery noise outside his door, he leaps out the window to his death.

Even more disturbing are Lovecraft's stories involving characters who are drawn to some discovery or to their doom by some unknown malevolent force. In "The Tomb" (1917), a young man is pulled through his dreams into another time, in which his ancestors lived in a great mansion that had burned to the ground. Driven mad by his obsession, he asks to be buried in a long-locked tomb that bears his name. Sometimes the victim of such an apparent curse is an entire civilization, destroyed by the demon-descendants of an enemy they had conquered a millennium before ("The Doom That Came to Sarnath," 1919).

In Lovecraft's world, the dead do not necessarily stay dead. In "From Beyond" (1920), a scientist invents a machine that sends creatures to and from another dimension, including two of his servants whom he is supposed to have murdered but who cannot be found. In "Herbert West—Reanimator" (1921-1922), a Frankenstein-like experimenter brings corpses back to life, but his ghouls are usually criminally insane. He searches for "fresh" corpses so that the dead can resume their previous lives, but he does so because of his fascination with the power he wields.

In Lovecraft's visions, evil can not be defeated. In story after story, such as "The Lurking Fear" (1922), in which the idiotic descendants of the stunted branch of a family survive as molelike subterranean creatures who forage by night, another world of fear and dread is always there, right behind the door or buried slightly under the ground.

Analysis: Lovecraft is considered second only to Edgar Allan Poe among American writers of horror fantasy. Lovecraft was aware of his debt to Poe and his own position in the tradition of such literature, which he analyzes in "Supernatural Horror in Literature" (1925-1927). Lovecraft's literary career was aroused by his reading of the works of Lord Dunsany (1878-1957) and seeing the British writer when he visited Boston. Lovecraft was also heavily influenced by the style and subjects of the Welsh fantasy writer Arthur Machen (1863-1947). Among the literary techniques that Poe, Dunsany, and Machen perfected and that Lovecraft also used are an elaborate style, a matter-of-fact journalistic format, and a single protagonist pitted against an overwhelming horror.

Lovecraft's style is ornate, deliberate, and loaded with

archaisms, features that suggest another view of reality. The style is so balanced and controlled that it lulls the reader into a sense of security. The shattering of that calm when the horrific is encountered causes even more fright than the mere appearance of the terrifying would provoke. Another American predecessor, Nathaniel Hawthorne (1804-1864), used the same device to describe Judge Pyncheon's death in his *The House of the Seven Gables* (1851).

Lovecraft often reveals his horrors as part of a presumed actual adventure recorded in a journal, as did Poe in his *The Narrative of Arthur Gordon Pym* (1838). In a rare venture into science fiction, Lovecraft has an explorer of Venus blandly record his experiences in a daily journal in "In the Walls of Eryx" (1936). The explorer finds an invisible wall and sees one of his comrades dead inside. When he makes his way around the wall to the corpse, strange creatures appear outside the walls. Sooner than the narrator, the reader realizes that the invisible walls are not a maze but a trap in which the first explorer perished. The finality of the narrator's eventual death is underscored by his pragmatic description of his efforts to escape.

The main characters of Lovecraft's stories can never be called heroes in the everyday sense, for their efforts always end in failure. Even if they manage to get away from the fiends they meet, they are psychically maimed for life. In "The Horror at Red Hook" (1925), for example, a detective finds a devil-worshiping cult in an ordinary Brooklyn neighborhood. He escapes with his life, but later the mere sight of buildings that resemble the tenements in which the cult held its worship is enough to bring on a fit of madness.

What makes Lovecraft an artist of the first rank, like his hero, Poe, is the unnerving suggestion in these stories that evil truly exists. These tales are not designed to titillate a bored reader on a dark night. Lovecraft describes the humanoids who stalk his characters as having sloping brows, squat bodies, and a shuffling gait; they are low, slimy, and disgusting. It is as if Lovecraft detested the evolutionary past from which humans came. This identification of evil with the lowest animal nature suggests that it is not somewhere "out there" but instead is within each person.

—*Jim Baird*

THE DANCERS AT THE END OF TIME SERIES

Immortal, nearly omnipotent, and bizarre, the last group of humans searches desperately for new sensations while two lovers move on to a new universe

Author: Michael Moorcock (1939-   )
Genre: Fantasy—future history
Type of work: Novels
Time of plot: The end of time, with excursions to other periods, principally the 1890's and the Silurian age of the next universe
Location: Various locations on Earth
First published: *An Alien Heat* (1972), *The Hollow Lands* (1974), *The End of All Songs* (1976), *Legends from the End of Time* (1976; includes "Pale Roses," "White Stars," and "Ancient Shadows," all first published in *New Worlds Quarterly*), and *A Messiah at the End of Time* (1977; British edition published as *The Transformation of Miss Mavis Ming*; *Legends from the End of Time* and *A Messiah at the End of Time* collected as *Tales from the End of Time*, 1989)

The Plot: *An Alien Heat* introduces the action that runs through the first three books. At the duke of Queen's dull party, Jherek Carnelian encounters a time traveler from the nineteenth century, Mrs. Amelia Underwood, and decides that falling in love with her would be a welcome novelty to amuse himself and his friends. Jherek first must acquire her from Lord Mongrove's entourage. Helped by Lord Jagged of Canaria, he arranges a trade for the "dreary alien" Yusharisp, who has come there predicting the imminent end of the universe. When Jherek declares his love, Mrs. Underwood will not hear of it; she wishes to teach him virtue. They become closer, but she disappears—stolen by My Lady Charlotina in revenge for the stealing of Yusharisp.

Mrs. Underwood is sent back to 3 A.M., April 4, 1896, as she had desired. Despite the Morphail effect, which prohibits people from staying in the past, Jherek, now truly in love, borrows a time machine and is sent back to the same time. In London, he naïvely joins a den of thieves and is executed for his crimes, only to awaken at the End of Time, still longing for his departed love.

The Hollow Lands introduces the Lat, seven small, one-eyed, oversexed space travelers. Escaping them, Jherek falls into an ancient room full of children minded by a robot nursemaid who recycles time. Nurse sends him to 1896 London, where he meets Frank Harris and H. G. Wells at the Café Royal. Wells takes him to Bromley, where he is reunited with Mrs. Underwood. Mr. Underwood also is there, however, and calls the police. After various adventures, the whole group plus the Lat, My Lady Charlotina, the duke of Queens, Lord Jagged, and the Iron Orchid are reunited at the Café Royal. The Morphail effect and Lord Jagged's time machine send them away, one or a few at a time. Jherek and Mrs. Underwood land in the Silurian age.

Still there at the beginning of *The End of All Songs*, Jherek and Mrs. Underwood are soon joined by police, Mr. Underwood, the Lat, and Una Persson and Oswald Bastable from the Guild of Temporal Adventurers, who send the Underwoods home to the End of Time. Although Mrs. Underwood begins adjusting, peace is not to be. The others reappear, and the temporal dislocations are too much for the cities that supply power and technology. As these collapse, Lord Jagged explains his part in bringing Mrs. Underwood to Jherek, who is revealed to be his son. Nurse has taught Lord Jagged to recycle time, and he proposes to seal off all who want to stay in a constantly recurring week that will last long after the present universe collapses. Harold Underwood and the police return home, but he forbids his wife to accompany him; thus she is free to accept Jherek's proposal. This initiates marriages between Amelia Underwood and Jherek, Lord Jagged and the Iron Orchid, Werther de Goethe and Lord Mongrove, and Mistress Christia and the seven Lat, among others. Amelia, however, believes that existence without duty is useless, and she and Jherek are sent forward to the beginning of the next universe to start life anew.

The action of the other two books takes place concurrently with that of the first three. The books are presented by a twentieth century narrator as fragmentary material brought back by time travelers. "Pale Roses," from *Legends from the End of Time*, shows how Mistress Christia, the Everlasting Concubine, compensates Werther de Goethe for having prematurely destroyed his rainbow by arranging a scenario in which he can experience sin and guilt. "White Stars" involves the reclusive and unimaginative Lord Shark the Unknown, whose only interest is fighting. When the duke of Queens challenges him to a duel to the real death—no resurrection—both are saved only through the unlikely intervention of some militaristic twenty-fourth century soldiers stranded in time. "Ancient Shadows" is the tragedy of Dafnish Armatuce and her son Snuffles, sent to explore the End of Time by the world of the Armatuce and unable to return because of the Morphail effect. Dafnish remains true to her stoic principles, but her son is seduced to luxury by Miss Mavis Ming; in losing their allotted future, each finds disaster. Stranded in time, boring, and unattractive, Miss Ming resides in Doctor Volospion's menagerie. A spaceship arrives, bringing the unattractive Emmanuel Bloom, who announces himself to be "a messiah at the End of Time." Madly in love with Mavis, who fears and de-

spises him, Bloom exchanges a false Holy Grail for her. He whips her severely, which gives her pride in herself and makes her love him. As they take off into space, the real Grail appears, heals their wounds, marries them, and gives them hope and faith.

Analysis: Michael Moorcock was a leader of the British "New Wave" of science fiction in the 1960's and 1970's, both as editor of *New Worlds* and as a writer. This movement emphasized an allusive style, irony, pessimistic plots, and a casual attitude toward sex, all of which the Dancers at the End of Time series exemplifies. Moorcock's "multiverse" (a word he coined in 1965) includes alternate realities for its worlds, which interconnect and adjust and shift in time. Jerry Cornelius is at the center of many of these worlds; Jherek Carnelian is a version of him, and other "Dancers" characters are found in other Moorcock works.

Also present is the British literary world of the late nineteenth century. Poetry by such authors as Ernest Dowson and Alfred Austin contributes titles or is recited by Mrs. Underwood. H. G. Wells and Frank Harris, both perfectly in character, aid the fugitive couple in flight from the police. More generally, twisted memories of the twentieth century and earlier times survive, especially for Jherek, who has specialized in the general period.

Despite their lightheartedness, the works in this series raise serious questions. The characters often seem parallel to real people (readers), enjoying luxuries through dissipating the remaining energy of the universe and not caring what, if anything, comes after themselves.

Introduced into this setting, Mrs. Underwood is both a caricature of Victorian attitudes and a sympathetic person struggling valiantly to maintain her beliefs when they obviously have become obsolete. Shortly before her return to 1896, she talks of her time's belief in stability and eternal standards. Much later, still trying to teach Jherek what morality is, she is overwhelmed by the enormity of her responsibility, wondering whether what she offers is a road to salvation or merely to guilt.

Yusharisp, the gloomy alien, also is paradoxical. His people's refusal to use such conveniences as translation pills marks him as peculiar. His warnings that the final matter of the universe is being used up to create the pleasant illusions of the few surviving humans seem grotesque but are true.

The "legends," too, raise questions and paradoxes. Werther de Goethe is pleased that he has felt guilt strongly enough to commit suicide, Lord Shark learns from a self-interested space trooper that humans can be good, Dafnish Armatuce loses her son through indulging him, and Miss Mavis Ming obtains joy and dignity through suffering and disgust. Is her apotheosis based on spiritual insight, or is it a parody of the worst of masochistic fantasies? Such are the questions that this seemingly absurd series raises.   —*Edra C. Bogle*

THE DARK ELF TRILOGY

An honest, principled dark elf, Drizzt Do'Urben, discovers that he is at odds with his mother, his sisters, and society, so he leaves home to wander the tunnels of the Underdark and eventually travels to the surface to make his home

Author: R(obert) A. Salvatore (1959-   )
Genre: Fantasy—magical world
Type of work: Novels
Time of plot: Indeterminate
Location: The Underdark drow city of Menzoberranzan, the caverns of the Underdark, and the surface
First published: *Homeland* (1990), *Exile* (1990), and *Sojourn* (1991)

The Plot: Menzoberranzan, in the Underdark, is a home to the dark elves known as the drow. The drow society is a cruel one dominated by the female drow and their goddess, Lloth, the Spider Queen. One's station is important in drow society, and ambition is prized by Lloth. Houses dominated by the matron mother ascend to importance through assassination and magic. "Don't get caught" is the overriding rule of drow society.

Drizzt is born while the House Do'Urben is eliminating another house to improve its station. Drizzt, a misfit, is honest, unambitious, and compassionate, like his father, Zaknafein, the weapons master. As he matures, Drizzt comes to doubt the stories told to keep the drow in line. As he grows more skilled as a warrior and more dissatisfied with drow society, Drizzt makes friends with a magical cat, Guenhwyvar, and realizes that he will have to leave Menzoberranzan to preserve his honor. Drizzt kills two drow in self-defense, thereby gaining ownership of Guenhwyvar. After discovering that his mother and sisters have sacrificed his father to Lloth to acquire an advantage during the attack on House Hun'ett, Drizzt leaves Menzoberranzan.

Ten years later, the war between House Do'Urben and House Hun'ett ends with House Do'Urben victorious, but House Do'Urben's matron mother, Malice, still is not in Lloth's favor. She can regain Lloth's favor only by punishing Drizzt for his defection. Malice sends her eldest son, Dinin, and her daughter Briza to capture Drizzt, who has been living on his own in the tunnels of the Underdark. Drizzt prevails in the encounter but realizes how savage, isolated, and lonely he has become. He goes to Blingdenstone, home city of the svirfnebli gnomes, and surrenders to assuage his isolation and loneliness. He finds friendship and acceptance with Belwar Dissengulp, whose life he had saved shortly before he had left Menzoberranzan.

Matron Malice animates the corpse of Zaknafein to capture and kill Drizzt. Such zombies must be controlled carefully by the high priestess, who in this case is Malice. Controlling "Zak" proves difficult because he had shared Drizzt's values and friendship. The mission, however, is Malice's last chance to regain favor with Lloth. Zak follows Drizzt's trail, wreaking havoc wherever he goes. The gnomes learn that the havoc involves Drizzt and ask him to leave. When he does, the gnome Belwar, his dear friend, goes with him. They later make friends with a pech who has been transformed into a hooks horror by a human wizard.

Drizzt heads toward Menzoberranzan to find a wizard to reverse the transformation spell put on the pech. The zombie Zak cuts them off and kills Drizzt's transformed friend. Drizzt and Zak fight, and Drizzt reaches Zak's memories. Zak regains control of himself long enough to throw himself into an acid lake. Because Malice has failed to gain favor with Lloth, Briza kills her to protect the family. The House Do'Urben nevertheless is destroyed by the ruling house.

Briza and Dinin are adopted by that house. Although unaware of this development, Drizzt knows that the danger to him and anyone with him is not over. He decides to go to the surface, accompanied only by Guenhwyvar.

After Drizzt moves to the surface, he remains isolated, for two good reasons: He needs time to get acclimated, and he does not speak any language of the surface dwellers. He finally decides to try to communicate with the human farm family living near where he has settled. A barghest whelp massacres the human family and makes it appear as though Drizzt is the culprit. Drizzt avenges the human family after finding the dead bodies, but the human townspeople still believe that Drizzt is the murderer. After killing a bounty hunter's dogs, he fights and scars the bounty hunter, who develops a hatred for him and vows to kill him.

A human ranger called in to hunt Drizzt examines the evidence and concludes that Drizzt is innocent. She believes that Drizzt has avenged the farmers' deaths. Drizzt, who nevertheless feels responsible for the humans' deaths, moves on. He stays in a relatively uninhabited forested area, where he has a minor conflict with an orc tribe. He is saved by a blind ranger, who teaches him about the surface world and the common language. The orc tribe attacks, but Drizzt and the ranger defeat them.

Some time later, the ranger dies. Drizzt wanders about aimlessly. He eventually finds his way to the Icewind Dale, where he settles. The bounty hunter comes to the Icewind Dale looking for Drizzt and annoys the dwarf leader living on a nearby mountain. The bounty hunter is driven away. This is the beginning of the friendship between Drizzt and the dwarves.

Analysis: The Dark Elf trilogy is a prequel to the Icewind Dale trilogy (1988-1990). R. A. Salvatore also continued the story of Drizzt in the books *The Legacy* (1992) and *Starless Night* (1993).

In the Dark Elf trilogy, Salvatore provides the personal history of Drizzt, one of the Icewind Dale heroes. An honest, moral individual, Drizzt is out of place in the dark elf society. He realizes that he does not belong and flees from his city and eventually from the Underdark. He searches for honor and friendship.

This trilogy teaches that honesty and friendship are to be honored and savored. Honesty, principles, and friendship are preferable to anything else, but they must be earned. Drizzt learns that no matter how much he wants to be accepted and to make friends among the surface dwellers, he must prove his good intentions. In addition, he must prove that he is trustworthy before friendship is granted. Once it is, his friends accept and trust him, though others may not. Drizzt's adventures show the necessity both of working at developing positive relationships and of understanding that many people judge others by their appearance.

The trilogy discusses issues of prejudice. When Drizzt leaves Menzoberranzan and begins to encounter other races, he tends to judge them initially according to what he had been taught; he is inclined to believe that they are evil, as his teachers had said. He remembers, however, that he believes the drow are really the evil ones. Following this realization, he evaluates other races and individuals on the basis of their behavior rather than according to preconceived notions.

Other individuals react to him in the same way: They judge him according to the reputation of the drow. He despairs of ever finding a home. His experiences reinforce his inclination to judge others by their behavior rather than by what he has been taught. Until individuals of other races begin to judge him on his behavior, Drizzt has to live apart from them.

Drizzt's failure to make friends has dual causes: the way people react to dark elves and his own lack of self-confidence. This attitude has been instilled in him by his upbringing. Drow males are treated little better than slaves. In addition, Drizzt has been unable to assimilate into drow society. He is inclined to be friendly and to help others rather than to betray them. Because such behavior is uncharacteristic of the drow, he thinks of himself as unworthy of praise.

The Dark Elf trilogy is not only about the difficulties an honorable individual experiences while living in the world but also concerns philosophical questions of religion. When Drizzt is living with the blind ranger, Montolio DeBrouchee, they each talk about their religious beliefs. The blind ranger follows Mielikki, a goddess of nature. Drizzt claims that he follows no god. This, he says, is the result of seeing the evil caused by Lloth.

Montolio contends that Drizzt follows a god but simply does not know that god's name. He argues that a person's god is the name given to those principles in which a person believes. Montolio further contends that the good or evil of a god, or perhaps a religion, is not so much enforced on believers from the outside but instead is an extension of people's principles. In other words, people's behavior fits their nature, and they choose gods who allow that behavior. Drizzt considers this possibility. As he learns more about the ranger and those like him, Drizzt begins to believe Montolio's contention that he has the heart of a ranger and that he follows Mielikki. He later affirms this to himself.   —*Sherry Stoskopf*

THE DARK IS RISING SEQUENCE

Young people help to collect various talismans of power that will aid the Light in its final, supernatural battle against the Dark

Author: Susan Cooper (1935-   )
Genre: Fantasy—high fantasy
Type of work: Novels
Time of plot: Primarily the 1960's, with journeys in time to earlier eras
Location: South Cornwall and Buckinghamshire in England; the vicinity of Aberdyfi in North Wales
First published: *Over Sea, Under Stone* (1965), *The Dark Is Rising* (1973), *Greenwitch* (1974), *The Grey King* (1975), and *Silver on the Tree* (1977)

The Plot: Although she did not initially plan to write a sequence, Susan Cooper found, when she returned to provide a sequel to the first book, not only that she had four more books to write but also that the fantasy element, originally peripheral, had become central. The forces of good and evil, known as the Light and the Dark, are locked in a supernatural struggle for power over humankind. As the sequence title proclaims, the Dark is rising for a final major assault. The books describe how various talismans of power are collected to aid the Light in the impending crisis.

Over Sea, Under Stone begins as an exciting children's adventure story set on the southern coast of Cornwall during the summer holidays. The three Drew children, Simon, Jane, and Barney, hunt for the Grail and, despite the danger posed by some sinister villains, they eventually find it, although the accompanying manuscript is lost in the sea. Only at the end do they begin to suspect that their mysterious great-uncle Merry, as they call Professor Merriman Lyon, is none other than Merlin.

In *The Dark Is Rising*, the setting shifts to the twelve days of Christmas in a small village in Buckinghamshire. Will Stanton, the seventh son of a seventh son, discovers on his eleventh birthday that he is the last born of the Old Ones, an immortal race with supernatural powers dedicated to the struggle against the Dark. The Old Ones are led by the Lady and Merriman, here in the guise of the butler at the village Manor. Their foes are led by the Dark Rider. Despite fierce resistance from the Dark, wielding the weapons of fear and deceit as well as cold and flood, Will succeeds in his assigned task of gathering the six signs of power. At the novel's conclusion, he releases the Wild Hunt to disperse his enemies.

Greenwitch returns to Cornwall in the spring, bringing together the Drew children, Will Stanton, and Merriman to search once again for the Grail, which has been stolen by the Dark, and for the lost manuscript that will allow them to decipher the writing on the sides of the vessel. Eventually they succeed, but first they must propitiate the Greenwitch, a traditional image of leaves and branches cast into the sea each spring for good luck in fishing and harvest. Like the Wild Hunt, she is part of the Wild Magic, a force distinct from both the Light and the Dark. She gives the manuscript to Jane, who alone has shown her compassion.

In *The Grey King*, Will travels during the Halloween season to his aunt's farm near Aberdyfi in Wales. He wishes to recuperate from a serious illness that has robbed him of some of his memories. His task this time is to find a golden harp that is guarded in a secret cavern by

the High Magic, yet another force in the author's magical equation, then to awaken the six Sleepers by playing to them. He is aided by Bran, a strange albino boy who turns out to be the son of King Arthur and Queen Guinevere, brought forward in time by Merriman/Merlin. He is opposed by the Grey King, one of the most powerful lords of the Dark. Working through the malice of petty-minded people as well as his own mighty power, the Grey King causes the death of Bran's dog Cafall and very nearly foils the plans of the Light.

The sequence concludes at Midsummer with *Silver on the Tree*. This novel opens in Buckinghamshire as Will collects the six signs of power from their place of safekeeping so that Merriman can take them back in time to aid King Arthur at the Battle of Badon. The story moves to Aberdyfi, where Will, Bran, and the Drews all meet to search for the Lady. She appears to Jane, to whom she imparts vital directions. Thanks to these and to help from the bard Taliesin, Will and Bran are able to travel back in time to the Lost Land of King Gwyddno, who gives Bran the Crystal Sword. With this, he is able to cut from the midsummer tree the silver blossoms, thereby gaining a final victory for the Light over the assembled powers of the Dark that have been opposing them bitterly at every turn. The Light and the Dark both withdraw, leaving humanity to work out its own fate without external intervention.

Analysis: Susan Cooper has written novels and plays for adults as well as for children, but none has achieved more success than the Dark Is Rising sequence, for younger readers, written early in her career. Three of the books have won awards. *Over Sea, Under Stone* won a competition for a family adventure story held by publisher Jonathan Cape, *The Dark Is Rising* was a 1974 Newbery Honor Book, and *The Grey King* was the 1976 Newbery Award winner.

Among the qualities for which the sequence has gained praise is the powerful sense of double reality of ordinary life, on one hand, and of the realm of High Magic, on the other. In part, this comes from the clearly realized setting, recalled from the author's own childhood, and from the skillful integration of regional legends, such as the stories of Arthur and the drowned lands of King Gwyddno.

The books also recognize the problems that young people must deal with every day, including misunderstandings and disagreements that disrupt even the closest families; hostility and bullying practiced by others of their own age; and impatience, unkindness, and even cruelty of adults too preoccupied with their own concerns to take account of the feelings of others. The results of such problems often are fear, loneliness, and a sense of betrayal that can embitter and destroy. This perpetuates a cycle of darkness that only love can break, a love so strong that it will forgive mistakes and injuries.

This situation finds a striking parallel in the supernatural world, where a struggle is taking place between the Light and the Dark. The latter seeks to gain control over humankind, using as its weapons fear and deceit. Those who give way to anger, prejudice, and self-centeredness, such as Caradog Prichard in *The Grey King* and Mr. Moore in *Silver on the Tree*, become vulnerable to its power, allowing the Dark to grow in strength. Opposed to it is the Light, which endeavors to protect humankind. Although generous and forgiving, the Light can be uncompromising in the sacrifices it requires of its followers. Virtue, after all, is never easy.

The Old Ones are charged with ensuring the preservation of the world from the Dark. At times the struggle may be so close that it leaves little room for acts of charity and mercy, or for protecting a wayward child. Acts of betrayal may have consequences too far-reaching to be overlooked.

Under these circumstances, the young protagonists are expected to assume responsibilities at an earlier age than usual. Their help is needed desperately, and they can be given only limited protection. This leads to a growth in maturity and understanding. Simon abandons his initial resentment of Will, Will comes into his power as an Old One, and Bran discovers his heritage as the Pendragon, heir to his father, King Arthur. These changes come at a price, for they bring not the freedom that young people expect but still heavier burdens. Thus, at the conclusion of the sequence, Bran is free to choose whether to join his father or to remain with his stepfather. Although torn, he decides to stay with the latter, recognizing that loving bonds are the strongest thing on Earth. As a result, he gives up his chance for immortality in the Otherworld beyond time, choosing instead to live and die like all humans. The choice is hard, and what is gained comes at a painfully high cost.

Part of that cost is the alienation as one grows away from the friends and family that surround one in childhood. Twice Will is obliged to erase the memories of beloved brothers who react badly to the discovery of his powers. Bran's special qualities mark him as different, attracting taunts and resentment.

Although the sequence encourages young people to strive to create a better world, it also warns that problems do not end with the end of childhood. Difference still attracts hostility, whatever one's age or station in life, and even the most deserving of aims exacts a price.

—*Raymond H. Thompson*

DARK UNIVERSE

Descendants of nuclear war survivors who moved underground must relearn their sense of sight and the nature of the world

Author: Daniel F. Galouye (1920-1976)
Genre: Science fiction—post-holocaust
Type of work: Novel
Time of plot: An indeterminate time in the future
Location: Below and on the surface of Earth
First published: 1961

The Plot: *Dark Universe* was the first—and most popular novel—of New Orleans journalist Daniel F. Galouye, although he had been publishing magazine stories since 1952. It was nominated for a Hugo Award.

The story is seen—or, rather, heard—by young Jared Fenton, whose primitive people live in total darkness and think of Light as a dimly remembered religious deity. They are preyed on by zivvers, other underground humans whose eyes have adapted to provide limited sight in the infrared spectrum, and "monsters" that inspire fear because they cause people to disappear and because they use light, which is alien to Jared's people.

Jared is the son of his tribe's ruler, the Prime Survivor. He is pressured into an arranged marriage (or "unification") with Della, the niece of another tribe's leader, to unite the tribes against the zivvers. Della has developed the zivver ability and, because Jared is exceptionally gifted at sensing people or objects by vibrations from sound echoes, believes he is secretly a zivver also. She persuades him to flee with her to the zivver group, which Jared has been seeking for his own reasons: He believes that Light is a natural phenomenon and that he might learn its nature through the zivvers.

Eventually, the young couple become outcasts and fugitives from both groups. Jared's people also decide that he is a zivver and therefore an enemy. The zivvers test him and discover that he is not one of them. He and Della fall into the hands of the monsters, who are revealed to be descendants of survivors from underground shelters who are now reinhabiting Earth's surface, which has purified itself. The two tribes and the zivvers from Jared's underground world had also sprung from a survival group, but something had gone wrong in their complex. They had lost their artificial light and, gradually, all knowledge of their origins. The monsters had been kidnapping them, a few at a time, and reeducating them.

Still not fully understanding or accepting the explanation, Jared escapes and makes his way to the surface. He realizes the truth of what he has been told and looks forward to a new life in a new world with Della.

Analysis: This paperback original employs a theme that would dominate Galouye's work: distorted perceptions of reality. In this case, without ever stating it overtly and keeping entirely to the point of view of his protagonist, Galouye is able to establish his nonvisual setting within the first two pages and show how Jared and other characters have adapted to it. He tells nearly the entire story without resorting to the visual sense—no small feat—but never loses the reader.

Nuclear war was a concept familiar to science-fiction readers even before the first atomic weapons were used in 1945, to the extent that editor H. L. Gold announced in the January, 1952, issue of *Galaxy* that he would no longer buy "atomic doom" stories for his magazine. Such stories continued to be written, though, some of the best known being Walter M. Miller, Jr.'s *A Canticle for Leibowitz* (1960), Mordecai Roshwald's *Level 7* (1959), and Pat Frank's *Alas, Babylon* (1959), all showing the aftermath of nuclear destruction. Neville Shute's *On the Beach* (1957; filmed in 1959) familiarized the general public as well.

It becomes obvious to most readers how Jared's people came to be in their situation, especially when Strontium and Cobalt are deified as demons, Radiation is described as a kind of hell, and Hydrogen is named as the devil. One religious tenet holds that the presence of Light Almighty in Paradise made it possible for people to know what lay ahead without smelling or hearing it. Jared is accused of being blasphemous when he suggests that there may be natural explanations for these concepts and that Light is something attainable in this life.

It is fascinating to follow Jared's reasoning as he presses his inquiries, especially considering that most readers already know the answers. One breakthrough comes when he finds that the "roaring silence" that emanates from the monsters, which is how the survivors perceive their lights, is cut off when he closes his eyes and that it is not coming through his ears after all.

The book also includes the science-fictional concepts of extrasensory powers (one of the survivors has developed telepathy), genetic mutations from radiation (sou-

bats are giant and marauding descendants of cave bats), and immortality (in the elderly Forever Man, who lived in the prewar surface world and understood Light but has suppressed those memories over generations and withdraws into himself when Jared tries to awaken them).

Galouye is thorough in showing how his underground people have adapted to their environment, sometimes with amusing results. The word "hear" is substituted routinely for "see." Reference is made to the "holy bulb" as a source of Light, which is likened to God. The words "Light!" and "Radiation!" are used as expletives. A courtesy between two strangers is the Ten Touches, which give each an idea of what the other is like. The worst offenses that can be committed are murder and "misplacement of bulky objects."

Dark Universe, although it has a more upbeat ending than most novels in the nuclear armageddon lineage, is very much a part of that heritage, which includes such works as Philip K. Dick's *Dr. Bloodmoney: Or, How We Got Along After the Bomb* (1965), Harlan Ellison's "A Boy and His Dog" (1969), and David Brin's *The Postman* (1985). Its well-realized underground world sets it apart from those that preceded and followed it.

—*Paul Dellinger*

DARKER THAN YOU THINK

Will Barbee is at first bewildered and horrified by an emerging strangeness in himself but comes to accept being a werewolf

Author: Jack Williamson (1908-   )
Genre: Fantasy—extrasensory powers
Type of work: Novel
Time of plot: About 1950
Location: Clarendon, a small town in the United States
First published: 1948 (serial form, *Unknown*, 1940)

The Plot: Dr. Lamarck Mondrick, a famous anthropologist, has just returned to the United States from the Gobi Desert with a mysterious box, the contents of which purportedly hold the key to humankind's struggle between good and evil. Among journalists covering the anthropologist's return is the protagonist, Will Barbee, who is both a close personal friend and a former member of Mondrick's research team. Mondrick dies mysteriously while attempting to deliver a warning of a menace to the human race.

As the story progresses, researchers Nick Spivak and Sam Quain employ increasingly tight security measures to protect themselves and the mysterious box they guard, but to no avail. Spivak and Quain know that Barbee is, at the very least, genetically predisposed to be a werewolf. Rowena Mondrick, the anthropologist's widow, knows for certain that Barbee is a deadly threat to her and the other two. She nevertheless has a true affection toward him. In the last chapter of the novel, author Jack Williamson reveals that she is Barbee's mother.

By day, Barbee tries to find out who is doing the killing and why. By night, he is a werewolf who participates in the killing. The daytime Barbee is aware only on the subconscious level of the activities of the nighttime Barbee. During the day, he falls in love with a beautiful, young, redheaded journalist, April Bell, who also is assigned to the Mondrick case. At night, she becomes a werewolf who has little difficulty getting Barbee to do most of the killing for her.

The second, dominant, aspect of the plot is purely psychological. The human (good) side of Barbee battles the werewolf (evil) side for the ultimate possession of his soul. One side is destined to prevail. As events unfold, Barbee is shown to be literally the messiah the werewolves of the world have been hoping for, the one they have named in advance "The Child of Darkness." Barbee does not know this and does not even fully comprehend that he is, in fact, a werewolf. His gradual self-realization is the main focus of the book. At the conclusion, having (sometimes reluctantly) participated in the killing of all the members of Mondrick's research team and his own mother, Barbee fully accepts himself as a werewolf and thus as evil.

Analysis: Jack Williamson occupies a unique position in science fiction. Born in 1908, he sold his first published work to Hugo Gernsback's *Amazing Stories* for $25 in 1928. From that day, he was committed to a lifetime of writing science fiction.

As a student of psychology, nuclear physics, and later linguistics, he always infuses science and technology into his fiction. It is difficult to call him innovative, but he has always been a prominent figure in American science fiction and has been a respected peer and personal acquaintance of Robert A. Heinlein, Isaac Asimov, and many others.

Williamson sold the original version of *Darker than You Think* to *Unknown* in 1940. In 1948, he rewrote the book as a novel and sold it to Fantasy Press. It did not sell particularly well but has been reprinted several times. The book has always been well known among the science-fiction *cognoscenti*, but it is difficult to claim that it has "classic" status, though some blurbs have gone so far as to call it the finest werewolf story. What sets the book apart from others is its ending: Not only does the werewolf side of the character prevail, but the protagonist, Barbee, also accepts himself as a werewolf, which implies that he regards himself as an enemy of humankind. Being a werewolf in Williamson's anthropology is not merely a matter of having an irresistible thirst for human blood, nor is it a mere character flaw. If humans have werewolf genes, they are evil in proportion to the amount of tainted blood in their veins.

Although werewolf stories generally are regarded as being in the realm of fantasy, science and technology are essential to Williamson's depiction of werewolves in at least two ways. First, there is the matter of *how* werewolves can change shapes, transport themselves across spaces, and literally pass through walls. Williamson offers a detailed explanation for these actions. The key to their ability is quantum physics, particularly the uncertainty principle. Walls, even steel walls, are not precisely solid but instead are composed of an arrangement of molecules, constantly in motion, with empty spaces between them. Williamson's extrapolation of this principle, as applied to werewolves, endows werewolves with a "mental web" with which they can realign the molecular structure of an object in order to pass through it. The shape-shifting capability of werewolves also is based on this ability to completely separate the mind, with its "mental web," from the body and transport it at will. Williamson's second extrapolation of known science involves the mysterious weapon in the box, which can destroy all werewolves. Apparently, this weapon is a disk of highly radioactive uranium. It is worth noting that Williamson worked at Los Alamos as an Army weatherman during the war years.

Science has since shown that Williamson's extrapolated events are not possible. He was using the scientific knowledge of his time as the basis for projecting the future, in the same way that H. G. Wells used a giant cannon to fire manned spaceships into space in *The First Men in the Moon* (1908) and many other authors have used the known science of their day to describe the impossible or not yet possible.   —*John T. West III*

DARKOVER LANDFALL

After a starship from Earth crashes on an unmapped planet, crew and colonists survive by building a new society based on native resources and psychic powers

Author: Marion Zimmer Bradley (1930-   )
Genre: Science fiction—alien civilization
Type of work: Novel
Time of plot: The twenty-first century
Location: The planet Darkover
First published: 1972

The Plot: Marion Zimmer Bradley wrote *Darkover Landfall* to explain the origins of the people and culture of her created world of Darkover, the setting of numerous books. After a starship crashes, its surviving crew and passengers are stranded on an unknown planet. Repair of the ship, a tenuous hope at best, becomes impossible when someone erases its computer programs during a hallucinatory "ghost wind" episode. A survey group discovers alien life, including two reclusive humanoid races. The planet has terrible weather, poor soil, few metals, and mysterious psi phenomena, but it can support human life. Building a low-technology society on this strange planet is an unappealing prospect to many from the ship. As the book ends, however, households and basic crafts, as well as the colony's first children, are flourishing.

Rafael MacAran, a geologist, leads the initial survey party. Romantically linked with First Officer Camilla Del Rey, he is able to follow a hunch to locate her when a sudden blizzard hits. This paves the way for using extrasensory gifts as technology. As a scientist, MacAran understands the captain's initial impulse to repair the ship and his wish to save technical knowledge for future generations. He also appreciates the planet's rugged beauty, however, and the logic of the New Hebrides commune's simple lifestyle. These conflicts are heightened for him because Camilla, space-born and -bred, has difficulty accepting the loss of her profession and of the ship.

Two thousand years pass before the colony's descendants are rediscovered by the Terran Empire. During that time, Darkovans develop a feudal society dominated by families with hereditary psi talents. The other Darkover novels take place in this subsequent Darkovan history. Most are set during an era of rapid cultural change after rediscovery, but three—*Stormqueen!* (1978), *Two to Conquer* (1980), and *Hawkmistress!* (1982)—take place in the Darkovan dark ages, or "time of the hundred kingdoms."

The plots and themes vary, but most of the Darkover novels contain motifs introduced in *Darkover Landfall*. *The World Wreckers* (1971) tells of technology run amok on the fragile planet. Camilla Del Rey's unwanted moth-erhood and lost career are a distant mirror image for Callista's anguish in *The Forbidden Tower* (1977), when her Keeper's training makes her chosen marriage almost impossible.

Laran, or extrasensory gifts, that empower also can destroy. The need for telepathic training and ethics is a frequent story element. From *Stormqueen!*'s young heroine, whose anger summons lightning bolts, to the arcane battle that ends *Sharra's Exile* (1981), *laran* is central to the novels' plots.

The Heritage of Hastur (1975) is a powerful coming-of-age novel. Young nobles Regis Hastur, Lew Alton, and Danilo Syrtis try to reconcile the demands of duty and class with inner desires. Along the way, a city is blown up, with weighty consequences for the planet's future. *The Shattered Chain* (1976) and *Thendara House* (1983) are novels that address women's issues. The young Darkovan Jaelle and the Terran intelligence agent Magda change roles and find new paths, while Jaelle's aunt, Lady Rohana, after trying independent life with the Free Amazons, returns to home and husband with new, inner strength.

Analysis: *Darkover Landfall*'s structure is unusual. The exciting events and discoveries occur early; the last half of the book is an extended study of the colonists' efforts to cope with them. Appropriate technology, a frequent series theme, is a survival issue in this novel. Within this framework, Bradley suggests that reproductive choice and, perhaps, women's autonomy are luxuries made possible by high technology. Camilla is refused an abortion because the fragile settlement needs every baby that can be brought to term. This episode created furor within feminist science fiction. Joanna Russ wrote *We Who Are About To . . .* (1977), whose castaway protagonist chooses death over forced childbearing, in reply. Bradley's argument is about the contingency of social rights, however, rather than being an antiabortion statement.

Although *Darkover Landfall* occurs earliest in the planet's history, it is not the best introduction to the series. A reader unfamiliar with Darkover will not link its events with the resulting customs and myths. For example, Camilla is memorialized in Darkovan religion as a consort of Hastur, a demigod. The legend distorts her life, but it retains traces of falling from the stars and of sacrifice. Bradley suggests the early young adult books *Star of Danger* (1965) and *The Planet Savers* (1962) as good starting points. Another good introduction is the revised *The Bloody Sun* (1979). A pivotal novel in the series, it opens with a scene recognizable to any science-fiction reader—a spaceforce man fearing that his weird reactions to the planet will cost him his career. This leads into a rich brew of love, intrigue, and mystery built around his emerging *laran* powers.

The series became very popular and has inspired an active fandom, including younger writers who have gone on to turn their own worlds into published series. Dark-over novels use fantasy staples, such as swordplay and psychic duels, as well as a depth of characterization almost unique in science fiction. Even secondary characters are three-dimensional. The plots often turn on issues such as gender roles and ecology. Under the red sun of Darkover, these take on new dimensions, and the solutions are seldom simple or ideologically pure. Most plot lines carry a subtext that every decision exacts its own costs.

Few fiction or nonfiction writers have looked as closely at psychic powers—their forms, effects, and costs—as Bradley does in the Darkover novels. The sheer exoticism of Darkovan *laran*, with its mysterious blue starstones and powerful matrix networks, also draws readers to the series. *Laran* usually is treated as a form of technology, sometimes as a metaphor for power, and sometimes as a metaphor for personal or ethical sensitivity. The latter symbolism has not been successful, as Darkovan telepaths appear to behave no more ethically than anyone else.

Many Darkover novels have been nominated for Hugo or Nebula awards. Bradley ranks among major science-fiction writers largely because of this unique body of work.   —*Emily Alward*

DAVY

Davy recounts his growth from an ignorant boy into a free-thinking adult and his attempt to bring enlightenment to his post-holocaust civilization

Author: Edgar Pangborn (1909-1976)
Genre: Science fiction—post-holocaust
Type of work: Novel
Time of plot: The twenty-fourth or twenty-fifth century
Location: New England, the Atlantic Ocean, and the Azores
First published: 1964

The Plot: Davy's coming-of-age story is not unique to science fiction, and Edgar Pangborn has no use for typical science-fictional devices such as spaceships and ray guns. Nevertheless, *Davy* is science fiction because of its vivid future world. In the late twentieth century—the "Old Time"—nuclear holocaust, plagues, and increases in world temperature and ocean levels destroyed human civilization. After about a hundred years, in the vast wilderness of what once was New England, a new civilization began to grow, a collection of small, bellicose countries dominated by the Holy Murcan Church, an organization forbidding books, free thought, gunpowder, and atoms. Because the Old Time people squandered the world's resources and the remnants of humanity have lost the Old Time science, the fragile civilization is ignorant and superstitious.

In the year 331 of this transformed world, Davy, at the age of twenty-eight, begins writing several intertwining stories: his growth to manhood, his relationship with his wife, their attempt to enlighten the benighted age, their founding of a colony, and the history of his era. The most compelling conflict in *Davy* next to that between enlightenment versus ignorance is Davy's struggle to tell his stories honestly and effectively.

Red-haired Davy was born in a whorehouse, reared in an orphanage, and bonded out as a yard-boy for a tavern. At the age of fourteen, he runs away, in the process accidentally committing his first homicide, having sex for the first time, and stealing an Old Time French horn. Thus begin Davy's picaresque adventures.

With help from the fascinating people he meets as he journeys through his wild world, Davy learns to play his horn, loses his religious superstitions, and becomes a free-thinking and loving person. Davy first joins company with Jed Sever, a sensitive and pious giant; Sam Loomis, a laconic loner; and Vilet, a sensual prostitute. After several adventures, including a comic scene with a "quackpot" medium and a tragic scene with a tiger, Davy and Sam join Rumley's Ramblers. The Ramblers are a communal troupe of independent entertainers who travel through the New England territories performing music and plays, selling homemade cure-alls, and passing along news.

When Davy leaves the Ramblers after several years, he meets and marries Nickie, a "sweet pepperpot" noblewoman who belongs to the Society of Heretics, an underground organization that promotes enlightenment and resists the church's dogma. Through Nickie, Davy meets her cousin Dion, Regent of Nuin. Nickie and Dion educate Davy in Old Time literature and ideas, and Davy and Nickie help Dion try to drag their country out of the dark ages. Their heretical ideas, such as abolishing slavery and promoting free education, meet with disapproval from the Holy Murcan Church, which foments a rebellion. The Heretics lose the war and flee Nuin on a ship into the unknown waters of the Atlantic. It is during this voyage and subsequent establishing of a colony in the Azores that Davy begins to write his book. The novel concludes with Davy setting sail to continue lovingly exploring the uncharted territories of world and mind.

Analysis: A plot summary of *Davy* neglects one of the novel's pleasures and important themes: the richness of the English language. Davy and Pangborn love language, from coarse prose to beautiful poetry, and the novel reflects that love. Davy often sets off on delightful Melvillean digressions on such topics as bedbugs. Additionally, a transformed language adds flavor to his narration. The transformed language appears in neologisms (mahooha), portmanteaus (prezactly), contracted forms (Febry), and distorted forms (sack-religion). Even cultural icons appear changed: Davy's world has a Saint George Washington. Pangborn uses such language to engage the intellect, make readers laugh, and show how fragments of civilization persist through time, transformed to suit new ages.

Pangborn returned to the world of *Davy* in *The Judgment of Eve* (1966), *The Company of Glory* (1975), and short stories such as those collected in *Still I Persist in Wondering* (1978). *Davy*, written in the middle of his career, is Pangborn's most defining and enduring work. *Davy* was runner-up for the 1965 Hugo Award for best science-fiction novel and placed on the 1972 *Locus* poll for best novel of all time. Critical opinion of *Davy* is favorable. George Zebrowski writes that *Davy* "is one of the lasting works of SF," and Spider Robinson says that "reading *Davy* has measurably and significantly, and for the better, changed my life."

Davy is part of the tradition of post-holocaust novels in which human civilization is portrayed as cyclic and, despite human folly, inextinguishable, from George R. Stewart's *Earth Abides* (1949) to Russell Hoban's *Riddley Walker* (1980). *Davy* also belongs to the tradition of science fiction that emphasizes humanistic concerns such as love, tolerance, inner growth, art, and psychology, rather than technological dreams. Pangborn's contributions to these traditions are his combination of loving humanism, rich language, an expansive view of life, self-reflexive narration, and playful humor. Describing a sunrise scene of ethereal beauty, for example, Davy shows a pair of monkeys copulating in a tree. If *Davy* can be summed up with one word, it would be the term of

endearment between lovers in the novel: "spice."

In the above traits, *Davy*, like almost all of Pangborn's fiction, transcends its genre. It also recalls fiction such as Henry Fielding's *Tom Jones* (1749) and Mark Twain's *The Adventures of Huckleberry Finn* (1884). The richly realized setting; the many vivid and unforgettable characters; the intertwined earthiness and sublimity, beauty and filth, and comedy and tragedy; and the powerful theme that people must light fires—both smaller and larger than the sun—in human minds and hearts all make *Davy* one of the best novels of any genre.

—*Jefferson M. Peters*

THE DAY OF THE TRIFFIDS

Almost everyone on Earth is blinded by an apparent meteor shower, and a species of plant called triffids, which are mobile and intelligent, take over most of the planet

Author: John Wyndham (John Wyndham Parkes Lucas Beynon Harris), 1903-1969)
Genre: Science fiction—catastrophe
Type of work: Novel
Time of plot: The mid- to late twentieth century
Location: London and parts of southern England
First published: 1951

The Plot: For years, humans have been cultivating a mysterious species of plant called the triffid because the oil and juice extracted from the plant make excellent cattle feed and are profitable for business. The origins of the seven-foot-high triffids are obscure, but the plant appears to have been the result of human biological experimentation. After their first appearance, triffids quickly spread all over the world and also developed the ability to pull up their roots and walk. They possess a venomous sting that is often fatal to humans. A few people even believe the plants are intelligent and able to communicate with one another.

Narrator William Masen, a biologist and triffid expert, is recovering in the hospital from a triffid sting to the eyes. He awakes one morning to an eerie silence. Removing his eye bandages, he leaves his room to investigate and discovers that everyone in the hospital is blind. He goes outside and sees blind people creeping along the streets.

The cause of the near-universal blindness is obvious. The previous day, a comet apparently passed near Earth, and the debris from it filled the sky with bright green flashes. Almost everyone watched the greatest-ever fireworks display, with disastrous results.

As he traverses the city, Masen rescues a young sighted woman, Josella Playton, from the clutches of a blind man. Masen sees triffids on the prowl and decides to leave London. He and Playton join a group of mostly sighted people, led by Michael Beadley, who are planning to set up a new community. This group refuses to help the many thousands of blind; they look to the future and decide to build a self-sufficient community that will preserve the race. Their plans are interrupted by a group led by the sighted Wilfred Coker, who feels a responsibility to help the blind. Coker's group kidnaps Masen and Playton. Each is put in charge of a group of blind people, assigned to an area of London, and instructed to keep everyone alive until help comes (from America, many assume). A plague breaks out and leaves few in Masen's group alive.

Masen later contacts Coker, who has realized the futility of his plan, and they decide to follow the Beadley group, whose members have headed to a location west of London. Masen also wants to search for Playton. The Beadley group proves elusive, but the two men stumble on a community, most of whose members are blind, run by the evangelical Miss Denning, who lacks the organizational skills to succeed but is too proud to admit it.

Masen leaves and finally is reunited with Playton at a farmhouse in Sussex. For six years, Masen, Playton, and three blind people run the farm and keep themselves alive in reasonable comfort. As essential supplies dwindle, however, the future looks bleak, and the triffids present a growing menace. The plants continually encroach on the farm and are kept back only by an electrified fence. The farm group eventually is contacted by the Beadley community, which has established itself on the Isle of Wight, a small island off the southern coast of England. Their community is more promising than the alternative, an authoritarian group of survivors who promote a kind of feudal system with the blind as serfs. The Isle of Wight community thrives and plans one day, through research conducted by Masen, to find a way of reclaiming the mainland, which has been taken over by triffids.

Analysis: John Wyndham acknowledged that the most fundamental influence on his work was H. G. Wells, particularly works such as *The Time Machine* (1895) and *The War of the Worlds* (1898). The influence of the latter on *The Day of the Triffids* is easy to see. Each story is told in the first person by a man who reports the disaster as a piece of recent history. Both stories take place in or near London, and Wyndham, like Wells, grounds his fantasy in everyday reality by emphasizing exact topographical details. The disaster itself, an unusual cosmic event in which no one senses any danger, is common to both stories, and both Wells and Wyndham emphasize how the catastrophe shatters human complacency and its naïve faith in the durability and invincibility of its own civilization.

Several of Wyndham's characters resemble those in Wells's story of Martian invasion. Those who cling to old rules of thought and behavior meet with disaster, including the curate in *The War of the Worlds* and the moralistic Miss Denning and the postdisaster community she attempts to found in *The Day of the Triffids*. The prototypes of Wyndham's visionaries, such as Coker and Beadley, are reminiscent of Wells's artilleryman, who quickly grasps the new situation and makes plans for the survival of humanity.

Like Wells's novel, *The Day of the Triffids* is a pessimistic view of evolution and natural selection. Because of its new blindness, humankind is no longer adapted to survive, and mastery passes to the triffids, who previously were inferior to humans only because humans could see and triffids could not. After the human calamity, the triffids are in a superior position because they are adapted to sightlessness.

Unlike in Wells's story, however, Wyndham attributes the catastrophe to human folly. The meteor shower was not a naturally occurring event but the result of a malfunctioning satellite that was equipped to wage biological warfare, and the triffids themselves resulted from human manipulation of nature.

Wyndham's novel ends on a note of hope. Even though science allied to human recklessness has created the catastrophe, science may yet devise a way to triumph over the triffids. The Beadley community, founded on rational and scientific principles, offers more hope for a future resurgence of humanity than the feudal, authoritarian, or religious systems that other groups of survivors attempt.

Some critics prefer the revised British version of *The Day of the Triffids*, also published in 1951. The story was filmed in 1963.

—*Bryan Aubrey*

THE DEAD FATHER

A band of brothers drag their father's animated corpse cross-country to bury it and, they hope, end its power over them

Author: Donald Barthelme (1931-1989)
Genre: Fantasy—high fantasy
Type of work: Novel
Time of plot: Unspecified
Location: An unspecified place on Earth
First published: 1975

The Plot: Prior to publication of *The Dead Father*, the self-contained "Manual for Sons," which appears within chapter 17 and has, mirroring the novel, twenty-three chapters of its own, had appeared in slightly different form in *The New Yorker*. This manual contains the central themes of the novel: the power of the patriarch, its unending influence on the lives of his progeny, the sexual rivalry between fathers and sons, and sons' subconscious fantasies of patricide. The novel revolves around the title character's surreal funeral procession. Nineteen of his sons serve as pallbearers, but instead of carrying an inanimate corpse in a coffin a short distance to a grave, they pull his 3,200-cubits-long, still active body along a cable for several days until they reach the grave. The novel comprises the events and conversations that take place during their journey.

Before the Dead Father can be buried, his powers must be stripped from him and passed on to someone else. His oldest son, Thomas, in spite of his insistence otherwise, seems to hope to receive the legacy of power. He leads the party, along with his alcoholic brother Edward and two women, Julie and Emma. Although the Dead Father goes along willingly on the journey, he contests the usurpation of his power by Thomas, who confiscates first the Dead Father's belt buckle, later his sword, and finally his keys, all symbols of his sexual virility and patriarchal power. The Dead Father tries to counter his son's actions with the seduction of Julie, who is Thomas' lover, and later of Emma, but he fails with both women and is thereby further humiliated by this devastating evidence of his impotence. His consolation, however, is his belief that "a son can never, in the fullest sense, become a father."

The Dead Father believes—or deceives himself into believing—that he is on a quest for the golden fleece, which will rejuvenate him. The golden fleece is revealed to be Julie's pubic hair. He has not been allowed to touch it and is still not allowed to touch it even after recognizing it as that which he seeks. On realizing the futility of his quest for new life, the Dead Father resigns himself to his true fate—death—and lies down in his grave, a more human and thus more sympathetic character than he had appeared to be previously in the novel.

Analysis: The fantastic elements of the novel lead the reader to contemplate its allegorical nature. Critics have read it as a novel about the generation gap between fathers and sons and, more broadly, about the end of one era and the beginning of another. Clearly, Donald Barthelme is drawing on Freudian psychology as he depicts the tyranny of fathers and patricidal desires of sons. He also is analyzing the ideological gap between the World War II generation and the Vietnam War generation. As in Ernest Hemingway's "Big Two-Hearted River," there is no mention of either war in Barthelme's novel, but the context emerges from Thomas' rejection of his father's tyrannical rule. Barthelme seems to have perceived that such rebellion would not last after members of the younger generation tasted power themselves; indeed, once Thomas begins to move into the position of authority, his rejection of "the system" softens and his behavior, particularly his cruel treatment of his father, begins to remind the reader of the Dead Father's actions. Recalling to the reader how the Dead Father goes on a killing spree every time his wishes are thwarted by Thomas, Thomas tells about a dream in which he discovered the secret of patriarchal power: having the choice to murder or not to murder.

The novel seems also to be a postmodern retelling of T. S. Eliot's *The Waste Land* (1922), which reveals that the postmodern world ultimately is not much different from the modern world. As in *The Waste Land*, for example, sexual relations in Barthelme's novel are often in some way perverted and are never regenerative. There is no instance of consummation in the novel, only a lot of titillation (watching pornographic movies and fondling others, for example); consequently, there will be no regeneration. It may be, however, that Barthelme is suggesting that the Dead Father (the old rule) must be laid to rest before there can be any new life. Although Thomas curbs his father's sexuality by refusing to allow him to watch the pornographic movies or consort with either of the women, he also curtails his own sexuality to some extent, not consummating his relationship with Julie, for example, until after his father is buried. Perhaps he is abstaining in deference to his father, or perhaps it is because he is intimidated by the memory of his father's former virility. Whatever the reason, the rain at the end of the novel, like the rain at the end of *The Waste Land*, suggests a potential for rejuvenation now that the Dead Father is buried. Thomas is free to consummate a relationship and be a father himself.

As the Dead Father has warned, however, Thomas will never be able to forget or live up to his father's memory.

In addition, he and his brothers may be consumed by guilt for having wished their father dead. Thus, in spite of his earlier rejection of his father's ways, one can see by Thomas' recent behavior that he will try to bring his father back to life by emulating him. Barthelme's final message seems, then, to be that nothing changes. Power corrupts, and memory disrupts the ideals of youth.

—*Margaret D. Bauer*

THE DEAD ZONE

Johnny Smith's parapsychic abilities aid in the capture of a serial killer and thwart the plans of a politician who would have launched an atomic war

Author: Stephen King (1947-   )
Genre: Science fiction—extrasensory powers
Type of work: Novel
Time of plot: 1953-1979
Location: Fictional Cleaves Mills and Castle Rock, Maine, and other New England sites
First published: 1979

The Plot: Skating on the ice of Runaround Pond in Durham, Maine, in 1953, six-year-old Johnny Smith is knocked senseless when Chuck Spier, an older, heavier, hockey player, accidentally crashes into him. As Spier tends to Johnny, semiconscious Johnny warns him to stay away from black ice. Awakening with only a headache, Johnny forgets the incident. Shortly afterward, while Chuck is jump-starting his car, his battery explodes, blinding him in one eye. Although Johnny is unaware of it for years, this was the first manifestation of his parapsychic powers, powers that provide the matrix for Stephen King's *The Dead Zone*. The title derives from the limits on Johnny's powers, the gaps in his life that he can neither see nor remember, the "faulty circuitry" that sets the scene for mystery.

Johnny's parapsychic abilities reappear in 1970, after he and his girlfriend, Sarah Bracknell, have graduated from college and are teaching at Cleaves Mills High School. Johnny takes Sarah to a fair, plays a wheel of fortune intuitively knowing that he will win, and wins $540. He also has a premonition of disaster, however, involving black ice and burning rubber. Sarah becomes ill, and after Johnny drops her at home, he takes a cab back to Cleaves Mills. Dragsters crash head-on into his cab, killing the driver. Hospitalized, Johnny sinks into a coma that lasts four and a half years, from which he is not expected to emerge. Meanwhile, Sarah marries and has a

child, Johnny's mother dies, a strangler terrifies Castle Rock and adjacent towns with his serial murders, and the villainous Greg Stillson, a violent and sleazy former Bible salesman, becomes mayor of Castle Rock, whetting his unslakable political ambitions.

Before he is through with reconstructive surgery and therapy, Johnny, who has gained notoriety as a latter-day Rip Van Winkle and then as a psychic charlatan, gives further evidence of his powers. He intuits where Sarah may find her lost wedding rings, warns a nurse that her house is on fire, and predicts a terrible roadhouse catastrophe. Then, by absorbing images and textures at a crime scene, Johnny identifies the strangler for Castle Rock's Sheriff Bannerman. The killer is an upstanding policeman.

Subsequently, Johnny crosses paths with Greg Stillson, who has entered the presidential race. Johnny perceives that the power-mad Stillson will start a nuclear war and determines to shoot him. The assassination goes awry, but in the process, Stillson grabs a baby to shield himself, an act of cowardice that effectively destroys his political career. Johnny flees, works with a road crew in New Hampshire, and is soon diagnosed as having a brain tumor. His last words are recorded in letters to his father and to Sarah explaining why he no longer wishes to live.

Analysis: By the mid-1990's, King had published twenty-one gothic or horror novels and become one of America's all-time best-selling writers. A number of King's works have been translated into highly successful films, among them *Carrie* (1974), *The Shining* (1977), and *Pet Sematary* (1983). Readers and critics alike generally acknowledge King to be the master of modern gothic and horror fiction.

Paranormal, parapsychic, and telekinetic phenomena that furnish the plot for *The Dead Zone* have always interested King and figured in *Carrie*, *The Shining*, and other King novels. These phenomena, however, are only devices that King employs to explore aspects of the subject that suffuses nearly all of his writing: the omnipresence of evil, evil to which most people would rather turn a blind eye. The evil that Johnny Smith pursues is embodied first in the respected police officer, a man Sheriff Bannerman likes so much that he is reluctant to acknowledge the weight of Smith's evidence. Similarly, the evil embodied in Greg Stillson marked every step of his life: kicking a defenseless dog to death while selling Bibles, menacing and humiliating a youth who wore a T-shirt with an obscene logo, terrifying the town banker into bankrolling his political campaign, importing thugs to act as his guards in Castle Rock, and, finally, his mad political tactics. Exposure of these evils, as King implicitly emphasizes throughout the novel, need not have awaited Johnny Smith's parapsychic endowments, for the evil was almost apparent. Stillson might have been thwarted, for example, by the Castle Rock banker whom Stillson terrified into aiding him.

Although such a theme—that evil exists as a real entity aside from failings in human character—is a familiar one to King's readers, it is not dealt with as effectively in *The Dead Zone* as in his other writing. At times, *The Dead Zone* seems to have been conceived, rather awkwardly, as two stories that were then melded together: the search for the Castle Rock strangler and the attempt to thwart the ambitions of Stillson. The book is interesting, but *The Dead Zone*'s principal characters are merely symbols of good or evil rather than full-bodied figures. Like many King novels, this one will strike many as overwritten and padded. For example, King recites national and international events to mark the passage of years while Smith is in a coma.

King compensates for these technical flaws with his trademark ability to move the story forward by means of engaging descriptions of the commonplaces of life. Few writers manage better than King to retain readers' interest by regaling them with the ordinary. King forcefully conveys his conviction that, in what he sees as a highly unstable and irrational world, deductive reasoning cannot always, or even often, prevail.   —*Clifton K. Yearley*

A DEAL WITH THE DEVIL

A one-hundred-year-old man gives his soul to Satan in exchange for ten years of life, during which he becomes progressively younger until, at death, he is a newborn baby

Author: Eden Phillpotts (1862-1960)
Genre: Science fiction—cautionary
Type of work: Novel
Time of plot: The late nineteenth and early twentieth centuries
Location: Great Britain
First published: 1895

The Plot: Among the many dissipations of Daniel Dolphin's unprincipled and profligate life was forgery, for which he spent five years in prison. At the age of ninety-five, he reformed, and during the five years prior to his hundredth birthday he "kept as sober, as honest, and as innocent as one could wish to see any nonagenarian" and looked forward confidently to death and the afterlife. He lives with Martha Dolphin, his granddaughter and sole surviving relative, a middle-aged spinster who narrates the novel.

At his centennial breakfast, Daniel tells Martha of a dream in which the devil visited him and revealed that Daniel was scheduled to die that night. Daniel was told that he could forestall the end by putting himself in the fiend's hands. In return for his soul, Satan guaranteed Daniel ten more years of life, during which the centenarian would grow younger, cramming another lifetime into the decade. After reading the contract Satan had prepared, Daniel says, he signed it with blood from his shoulder. The old man and Martha make light of the incident, which after all he only dreamed, and they attribute a red mark on his shoulder to a fleabite.

Six months later, during which time his health has improved, Daniel discovers a copy of the contract through which he bartered away his soul. Realizing the terrible dimensions of what he has done and determined to hide his secret, Daniel and Martha leave their village for London. Two birthdays later, Daniel is twenty years younger, has resumed his excessive drinking, and decides that for at least the next six years—until he is twenty again—he will enjoy himself, ignoring all qualms of conscience. He takes up with women, proposes to several along the way, jilts them and others as his reverse aging accelerates, runs for a local council, loses money in a fraudulent scheme with a swindler, competes in a regatta, and runs afoul of the law. Periodically, Daniel and Martha (who eventually becomes known as his grandmother) change their names and move from one city or town to another, fleeing acquaintances as he rapidly grows younger. However difficult the vagabond life is for Daniel, it is particularly stressful for Martha, who becomes a closet alcoholic.

Finally, on the eve of his 110th birthday, Daniel is a newborn baby again, and Martha spends the night with him on the wilds of London's Hampstead Heath. At the moment of death, he apparently is transformed into an old man again and then completely vanishes, amid shining moonbeams. The grieving granddaughter concludes her narrative with a warning to materialistic nonbelievers: Avoid being fooled, and reflect before becoming "meshed in some muddling devil's web, from which there is no escape."

Analysis: *A Deal with the Devil* is one of many late Victorian and early twentieth century novels written in the manner of Thomas Anstey Guthrie (1856-1934). Using the pseudonym F. Anstey, this English humorist and satirist wrote novels in which a fantastic device appeared in an otherwise realistic contemporary narrative, such as a father and son switching personalities or someone accidentally bringing a goddess to life. In Eden Phillpotts' book, Daniel's Faustian bargain is the sole fantastic element, and all action and conflicts emanate from it.

An implicit though central conflict is that between the two main characters, Daniel and Martha Dolphin. The latter epitomizes Victorian propriety yet must care for an old reprobate who, after his deal with the devil, reverts to his profligate youthful ways. Because Martha is the narrator, not only does her point of view color everything, but her increasing despair and weariness also pervade the novel. She ages while her grandfather becomes younger; as he increases in vigor, their frenetic nomadic life exacts its emotional toll on her. Martha is the utterly loyal Victorian woman; she advises, suggests, and protests, but ultimately accepts Daniel's plan to spend almost all of his money during the ten years of the New Scheme (as Martha has dubbed it), though her expected inheritance will be gone. She supports him throughout their peregrinations and becomes his surrogate mother during his second childhood.

Because of her frankness and the precise details with which she relates everything, the plot of the novel remains credible despite the event at its core. Martha, for example, precisely describes changes in Daniel's skin, speech, clothing, and other aspects of physical appearance as his years rapidly fade away; specific features of their many homes as they flee from one place to another; and such matters as his courtships and participation in the Henley regatta. She also is an important player in the unfolding action and reveals much about herself through her narrative. Supporting the realism are frequent reminders of her aging, in contrast to Daniel's regression to childhood, and her increasing dependence on alcohol. Her epilogue dates the novel by its didacticism, and because of Martha's central presence, the book is too firmly rooted in the late Victorian period despite its timeless theme. For example, ignoring the fact that Daniel obviously regretted none of the excesses of his first century and committed many of the same follies all over again during his New Scheme decade, dutiful and deferent Martha exonerates him from responsibility for his fate, saying he "was most unfairly treated," and erects a memorial to him in her village church.

In many of his more than two hundred novels, Phillpotts uses a familiar or traditional literary motif,

gives it an unusual twist, and constructs an ingenious plot around it. *A Deal with the Devil*, his contemporary Faustian allegory and eighth book, reflects not only this practice but also the realism for which he was highly regarded in the early twentieth century, when his series of Dartmoor novels was compared to those by Thomas Hardy about Wessex.

—*Gerald H. Strauss*

THE DEATH OF GRASS

When a virus kills all grasses and grains, worldwide famine ensues, civilization collapses, and individuals revert to tribal, survivalist patterns and seek a defensible stronghold against murderous mobs

Author: John Christopher (Samuel Christopher Youd, 1922-   )
Genre: Science fiction—cautionary
Type of work: Novel
Time of plot: The near future
Location: England
First published: 1956 (also published as *No Blade of Grass*, 1957)

The Plot: *The Death of Grass* begins with an idyllic introductory scene, a visit by the Custance family to Blind Gill, an unforgettably green oasis among desert mountains. There, David's love of the land wins him his grandfather's farm and John's near drowning reveals a secret that will later save lives.

Twenty-five years later, as the Chung-Li rice virus decimates rich fields, two hundred million Chinese people die of famine and Hong Kong implodes as smug Londoners speculate that Chinese secretiveness kept Western technology from introducing an antivirus isotope. Roger Buckley of the British ministry of production, a close friend of John Custance, an engineer, has insider information that the isotope has not killed a key virus strain, once kept in check by the stronger, now dead, forms. This virus threatens grasses and grains worldwide, and famine spreads westward. Brown patches dot the English countryside, but the government issues optimistic reports as reassurance. David Custance switches his crops to potatoes and beets, kills his cows, salts the meat, and urges the family to join him, but John delays. The Buckleys agree to warn the Custances when the situation becomes critical in return for a place in the protected valley of Blind Gill.

Initially, Roger is a cynical self-preservationist, irritated with "woolly-mindedness" and convinced of government perfidy. Proud of being a savage at heart, he forces John to see the seriousness of the problem, anticipates the atomic bombing of urban England, and, when a roadblock prevents escape, returns for firearms and recruits a highly competent arms expert, Pirrie, to provide quality weapons. Roger and John jokingly toss a coin for leadership, but after John wins, he is committed to making the hard decisions necessary for group survival. It is Roger and his wife, Olivia, who urge taking pity on various weaklings, including a boy from Davey Custance's school, a young farm girl whose parents they have killed, and a dysfunctional family ill prepared for crisis. John, in contrast, accuses Roger of sentimentality and makes tough decisions based on necessity. He tells his son, "We have to fight to live." He understands the need for strong walls to keep out the barbarians before civilized interaction can begin.

Pirrie proves invaluable as John's right-hand man. He has no scruples and understands immediately the extremes necessary for survival. He plans the ambush that kills the road guards. He shoots three ruffians who molest John's wife, Anne, and daughter Mary, but he allows Anne the coup de grâce. He cold-bloodedly kills his wife for trying to seduce John and takes as concubine a farm girl whose parents he has killed for food. He shoots an opposition leader to guarantee a group merger for strength of numbers, and when a military-style force attacks with grenades, he picks off the ringleaders at a distance with his telescopic sights.

When the entourage reaches David Custance's stronghold, locals manning a machine gun agree to let in David's relatives but deny admittance to all others. John must choose between allegiance to his family and to his new tribe, and he opts for the tribe. He and Pirrie attack the machine-gun nest from the river ledge and sandbar he had discovered as a youth while their group storms the walls. During the shooting, either John or Pirrie kills David, and Pirrie, after receiving a mortal wound, falls to his death in the turbulent river. The stronghold is taken, however, and can be defended. The process of rebuilding civilization can begin.

Analysis: *The Death of Grass*, a short but powerfully realistic parable, warns of the fragility of the ecosystem and of modern civilization, as well as the dangers of overpopulation and an optimistic dependence on science to solve all problems. John Christopher effectively captures human blindness to threatening changes. Even when faced with the fact of a country of fifty million people importing nearly half of its food from countries now besieged by famine, the first tendency of most of Christopher's characters is to assume that civilization will somehow muddle on, that a stiff upper lip will get them through hard times, and that science will provide an answer. Farmers, close to nature, recognize disaster long before urbanites. They warn of treating the land as "a piggy-bank, to be raided," when, in fact, "the land . . . is life itself."

Christopher also examines the human tendency to expect highly visible causes of catastrophe when in fact the cause may be microscopic. David Custance speculates that a virus might have ended the age of the great reptiles in the same way that a virus could end human dominance.

Christopher's understanding of the precariousness of civilization bears a quality similar to William Golding's speculations on human nature in *Lord of the Flies* (1954). His women accuse their men of being "savages" beneath the thin veneer of civilization, and Pirrie, though believing that the English will remain deluded to the very end, concludes that once awakened they will "fight like particularly savage tigers." The rapes, the cold-blooded killing of anyone who presents an obstacle, the calculated bombing of cities, the street violence and raids, the village that robs all passersby, and the cool calculations of Pirrie confirm this savage essence.

Christopher suggests a cyclical pattern of life: a slow building of civilization, with increasing legal restraints and protection of the weak over thousands of years; a sudden, nearly instantaneous destruction of all civilized patterns; and a slow rebuilding based on survival of the fittest and the rule of the strong as well as the obligation of leader to tribe, an obligation that takes precedence over family relationships. England reverts to an earlier age. Blind Gill, an ancient stronghold, is so again, with John as chieftain, accepting a ritualistic handshake and a defining "Mr." to confirm his status. Modern Britons laugh together, blind to their fate, as did the Saxons before the Battle of Hastings, and worried travelers fear that their children will pray to moorland gods to turn away their wrath. Cain rekills Abel, but John's son, like Cain's (Enoch), may refound civilization, though both sons retain their weapons.

Christopher's style is clear, understated, compact, and forward-moving, with occasional touches of grim irony and with insights about England's ancient heritage of cynicism and resilience. When asked if there is any news, Roger replies in Shakespearean tones, "None, but that the world's grown honest." He is answered, "Aye, that's good. Then is doomsday near!"   *—Gina Macdonald*

DEATH QUALIFIED and THE BEST DEFENSE

Attorney Barbara Holloway successfully defends clients in murder trials that are believed to be hopeless cases

Author: Kate Wilhelm (Katie Wilhelm Knight, 1928-   )
Genre: Science fiction—cautionary
Type of work: Novels
Time of plot: The 1990's
Location: Turner's Point and Eugene, Oregon
First published: *Death Qualified: A Mystery of Chaos* (1991) and *The Best Defense* (1994)

The Plot: Prior to the opening of *Death Qualified*, Lucas Kendricks agrees to participate in scientific studies on the mathematical theories of chaos. A group of university researchers believes that by showing a sequence of carefully designed computer images of fractals to volunteer subjects, the volunteers will learn to perceive the world in new ways and will understand events that appear chaotic to most people. Lucas learns through the experiments, but most volunteers show no change.

As they run out of money, the researchers solicit male prostitutes to watch the computer images. One of the young prostitutes learns to understand the logic of chaos, and in the process, he acquires superhuman abilities. These abilities are not described in detail, but they appear similar to mental telepathy and telekinesis, only more powerful. In a fit of jealous rage, one scientist kills the successful volunteer. Because Lucas knows too much, the researchers drug him and keep him prisoner for seven years, disguised as a mentally impaired handyman.

As the book opens, Lucas escapes and travels back to his hometown of Turners Point, Oregon. He remembers everything the experiment has taught him and wants to share his new abilities with his family. As soon as he returns to his hometown, however, he is murdered, allegedly by his wife, Nell. Gifted attorney Barbara Holloway is called into town by her father, Frank, a prosperous lawyer, to help with Nell's defense. Although Barbara has turned her back on the law, she takes on the seemingly hopeless case, in which all clues lead back to the experiments in chaos theory.

With the help of her boyfriend, mathematics professor Mike Dineson, Barbara identifies the real killer. More dangerous than the killer, however, are computer disks from the experiment. Smuggled into Turner's Point by Lucas before his death, they kill Mike (or send him into another dimension) and threaten Lucas and Nell's chil-

dren. At the end of the novel, Barbara once again abandons the law out of hatred for the legal system.

The Best Defense shows that Barbara cannot stay away from the law for long. She is living in Eugene, Oregon, on the tiny salary she makes helping poor people who cannot afford legal services at full rates. When Lucille Reiner asks Barbara to help her sister, Barbara does not realize that the sister is Paula Kemmerman, dubbed the "Baby Killer" by the press. Paula allegedly killed her six-year-old daughter, then set fire to the shelter for battered women where they were living. Despite Barbara's reluctance to take on another high-profile case, with the help of her father, she proves that Paula is the innocent victim both of a right-wing fundamentalist and of a legal system that has turned its back on an innocent victim.

Analysis: By the time Kate Wilhelm wrote these mysteries, she had more than thirty-five books to her credit, including novels, collections of short stories, and novellas. In *Death Qualified* and *The Best Defense*, Wilhelm continues to push the edges of genre fiction, spinning into legal thrillers the social commentary one might expect to find in science fiction, as well as the narrative sleight of hand and red herrings typically found in mysteries. As she incorporates these various devices, she does not sacrifice the taut drama of the skillful cross-examination and the hostile judge.

Death Qualified overtly combines elements of the mystery and science-fiction genres. The mystery is the dominant genre, as it is in *The Dark Door* (1988), one of Wilhelm's "Charlie and Constance" mysteries. Both books are structured as mysteries, but the cause of the mystery is a science-fiction element (an alien experiment gone awry in *The Dark Door* and a human experiment gone awry in *Death Qualified*). *Death Qualified* blends the genres more successfully, perhaps because the scientist characters are greedy enough to fill the role of mystery villain.

The scientists do not directly murder Lucas Kendricks: The killer is a neighbor, Clive Belloc, who wants to avoid blame for an earlier rape and murder of his own. Because the scientists have held Lucas prisoner for years, however, making him appear to have abandoned his family, he is an ideal scapegoat. Lucas developed superhuman abilities through the experiments, and he is showing off these abilities when Clive finds him. Clive thinks he is a "devil" and does not hesitate to shoot. Were it not for the scientists, therefore, Lucas would not have been killed.

Fans of Wilhelm's *Where Late the Sweet Birds Sang* (1976) will recognize another theme in *Death Qualified*, that of technological advances creating children who are alien to their parents. Instead of cloning, however, the technology is a computer program, based on fractal mathematics, that allows sensitive individuals to experience reality in ways different from those of other people. After running the program, Barbara's lover, Mike, is forever separated from her. His new abilities lead him to pity her, and although he uses them to save her life, he disappears immediately afterward. After Mike dies, Nell's children find the disks; they too are changed into something other than human. At the end of the book, there is no sign of hope. Barbara falls asleep alone, weeping.

The plot structure of *Death Qualified* is that of a mystery. The book opens with a dramatic escape and murder, and most of the action in the book is generated by Barbara's efforts at detection. The murderer turns out to be the proverbial "least likely" character, though all the clues to the solution have been laid out for the reader. Once the murderer is unmasked, he turns on the detective, who needs to escape from a dangerous one-on-one confrontation in the last few pages of the book.

The science-fiction elements of the novel, by contrast, are developed as a subplot. Most of the information about the experiments is uncovered by Mike, clearly a secondary character, who routinely is whisked out of the way by Barbara's father when she is overwhelmed with trial responsibilities. Mike is interested in chaos theory from the start. He tracks down the computer disks that hold the fractal images and figures out what they will do. Most of these activities occur offstage, while Barbara grapples with recalcitrant witnesses. When Mike finally makes a significant appearance, during the dramatic showdown between Barbara and Clive, he becomes the noble rescuer who sacrifices his life for his beloved—another stock mystery character.

Although the mystery plot drives most of the action, the book's science-fiction framework provides the story's lasting power. Lucas is on the run from evil scientists who use technology to enslave him. Because the scientists have given him superhuman powers, Lucas will never fit into society. If he had not been killed, he most likely would have been framed for the rape-murder that Clive committed, and society would have been likely to find such an unusual man guilty. Even if he had escaped that fate, Lucas could not have led a normal life. When Mike undergoes the same experiments, he first becomes disoriented, unable to use his normal senses; he then considers himself to be superior to normal human beings and no longer can relate to them. Readers have no reason to believe that Lucas would have felt differently.

As Lucas' children are transformed by the same experiments, while Barbara lies weeping in her bed, readers realize that although Nell's murder trial may have been won, the future of humanity may already be lost. By weaving this science-fiction plot around what is already a top-notch legal mystery, Wilhelm gives her novel extraordinary depth.

Although *The Best Defense* occurs after the events of *Death Qualified*, no sign of the science-fiction elements remains in the sequel. Nell's children are not mentioned, and Mike's disappearance becomes a death by drowning. Barbara's character is much the same—she is still rebelling against the hypocrisies of the legal system—but her father is quite different. Rather than the semiretired lawyer who insists that he has earned the right to go to work in Bermuda shorts and tank tops, Frank is a high-priced attorney in corporate clothes, willing to challenge his firm's conservative partners on behalf of his daughter. Although *The Best Defense* probably will not be as interesting to science-fiction fans as the earlier novel, it is still a page turner. Wilhelm's feminism is more strongly apparent in the later book, as the story centers on issues of child abuse and the battered woman syndrome. In both books, however, it is significant that the victims are abused as much by cultural and legal conventions as by evil people.

Wilhelm has won many awards, including the Nebula Award for best short story for "The Planners" (1968) and "Forever Yours, Anna" (1987), as well as for best novelette for "The Girl Who Fell into the Sky" (1986). In 1977, she received a Hugo Award, a World Science Fiction Convention Jupiter Award, and second place for the John W. Campbell Memorial Award, all for *Where Late the Sweet Birds Sang*. In 1980, she received an American Book Award nomination for *Juniper Time* (1979).

—*Beth Rapp Young*

THE DEATHWORLD TRILOGY

Jason DinAlt visits hostile worlds and risks his life on each, but he manages both to survive and to change the native cultures for the better

Author: Harry Harrison (1925-   )
Genre: Science fiction—cultural exploration
Type of work: Novels
Time of plot: The distant future
Location: The planets Cassylia, Pyrrus, Felicity, and others

First published: *The Deathworld Trilogy* (1968), comprising *Deathworld* (1960; serial form, *Astounding Science-Fiction*, January-March, 1960), *Deathworld 2* (1964; serial form, "The Ethical Engineer," *Astounding Science-Fiction*, July-August, 1963), and *Deathworld 3* (1968; serial form, "The Horse-Barbarians," *Astounding Science-Fiction*, February-April, 1968)

The Plot: In *Deathworld*, Kerk Pyrrus hires gambler Jason DinAlt to win a fortune at dice. With his gift of "psi powers," Jason succeeds. Kerk explains that the money will buy weapons to fight the deadly wildlife on his planet, Pyrrus. The native plants and animals there are armor-plated, poisonous, claw-tipped, fanged, or otherwise prepared for battle. Fascinated, Jason decides to visit Pyrrus, where he finds both danger and a planetwide mystery.

The first clue in this mystery is the horrible nightmares he suffers every night. A second clue comes from an ancient diary, which reveals that the population of the planet is dwindling, not growing. The third clue is the existence of the "grubbers," whom the city dwellers hate because they live peacefully with the wildlife outside the city walls. Ferocious plants, animals, and insects wage constant war against the city. Jason decides to learn why this dreadful war continues.

Meeting illegally with the grubbers, he finds them to be brave, noble creatures unfairly deprived of civilized amenities by the city dwellers. He determines to stop the war and arrange a peace. The grubbers can communicate telepathically with the native animals. Jason speculates that all the wildlife is empathic, and during an earthquake he is astonished to see the wild animals fleeing the danger zone, alongside the grubbers and domesticated animals. At that point he solves the mystery of the illogical, unending war.

He leads the grubbers against the city. They seize the spaceship—the focus of power on the planet—and demand a meeting with the angry city Pyrrans, at which Jason explains the native planetary telepathy. Although normally they strive against one another, the plants and animals unite to combat any force perceived as a natural disaster. In this case, it is the humans who are a threat, so the plants and animals fight them. The city Pyrrans finally realize that they are responsible for the war and for ending it, if they choose.

In *Deathworld 2*, a religious zealot, Mikah, kidnaps Jason to return him to Cassylia for trial and execution for his crimes. Jason wrecks the spaceship's controls and diverts it to an uncharted planet. Jason and Mikah are at once enslaved and learn that the primitive society of the planet consists of slaves and tribal slaveholders. Each tribe protects a secret knowledge: The D'zertanoj, for example, rule the secret of oil distillation, the Mastreguloj understand chemistry, and the Personnoj hold the monopoly on electricity. Jason plans to return to Pyrrus but is plagued by Mikah at every step.

With his knowledge of basic science, Jason elevates himself from abused slave to abused employee, at first in the hands of the D'zertanoj, then in the ranks of the Personnoj. He tries to improve the local living conditions, but each time he proves himself indispensable with his scientific "inventions," Mikah betrays him to the rival clans, who kidnap, harass, and nearly kill Jason. Jason finally decides to launch an industrial and cultural revolution. Among the scientific devices he "invents" is a radio transmitter that, unknown to the natives, beams an "S.O.S." signal night and day. When Mikah learns that Jason is planning to wage war against the rival clans as part of his overall scheme, the zealot betrays Jason once more. During a terrible battle, Jason is wounded. On his deathbed, he hears a roar of rocket engines and realizes that his transmitter has done its job, and he is rescued by Meta.

Felicity, the planet of *Deathworld 3*, is the deadliest. Jason learns that miners had attempted to settle on Felicity but were butchered by hordes of warriors on huge mounts. Jason proposes that the Pyrrans who are still reluctant to make peace with the grubbers join him in moving to Felicity and persuading the natives to allow foreigners. Jason takes a group, including Meta and Kerk, to establish a new camp on Felicity.

The southern part of the single continent is fertile and inhabited but unexplored by off-worlders. The northern continent is rich with the heavy ores that the settlers desire but also filled with Mongol-like warriors who vow to slaughter anyone who tries to erect buildings on their wild plains. Jason is kidnapped by the barbarians and so meets the ruthless Temuchin, who has succeeded in uniting many of the feuding tribes to wage war against the off-worlders.

Temuchin orders Jason slain, but he escapes and rejoins the Pyrrans. His new plan is to disguise his band as a far-north tribe and to infiltrate Temuchin's camp himself as a wandering minstrel. Always risking exposure as he learns the native customs, he persuades Temuchin to conquer the southern continent. The warlord succeeds but realizes afterward that he has lost his way of life, as his tribes adapt to new customs and off-world products.

Analysis: The Deathworld books suffer unfairly the stigma of being "only" adventure novels. They were written to *Astounding Science-Fiction* editor John W. Campbell, Jr.'s specifications and were hugely popular when they first appeared. *Deathworld*, Harry Harrison's first published novel, appeared five years before Frank Herbert's *Dune* (1965), which is widely regarded as the first science-fiction novel to deal with the entire ecology of an alien planet. Wittier than the humorless *Dune*, *Deathworld* also preaches the important message that people come to resemble their enemies.

Far from being a cartoonish arena appropriate only for an unthinking blazing-guns romp, the Pyrran ecology can be seen as the lengthiest exploration ever undertaken of the "pathetic fallacy," the ascription of human emotions to the environment, as in the phrase "the cruel sea." Harrison demonstrates on a planetary scale how "inner space" influences outward reality: The colonists' own emotions make their world a hell.

Similarly, in *Deathworld 2*, Jason lands first on what appears to be a plain by the sea. When he attempts to escape his slavery there he suddenly encounters gullies and ravines that the text had not prepared readers for, foreshadowing the dark, twisting, deceptive nature of the world. He then travels through two likewise appropriate settings, a desert that seems to symbolize the barrenness of this world and a city made of fortress-islands that represents the isolated, each-one-against-the-rest nature of the local society. The harsh settings match the harsh social satire.

In *Deathworld 3*, the single landmass of the planet is shaped like a dagger, suggesting the glorification of war among the nomads, and is divided in half by a huge, continentwide cliff, which again suggests a land divided against itself. The wild plains are also integral to the plot, evoking the native North Americans and their own conflict with an alien, colonizing force. This third novel, however, is based on the history of the Mongols and their assimilation into the Chinese empire. Temuchin was another name of Genghis Khan.

A close reading of the novels provides pleasing insights into Harrison's writing tactics. As the title suggests, death is immanent in all these worlds; Jason's life is at stake in each novel. Harrison's choice of words underscores this point. Readers repeatedly encounter "dead silence," "dead seriousness," "dead cold," "dead tiredness," and "deadened eyes." The vocabulary emphasizes Jason's wariness of death all about; at the same time, the point of view remains close to Jason's thoughts. Readers always know what he is thinking and how he reacts to those around him. On occasion, however, the omniscient narrator proposes another character's point of view, and a close reading reveals that these moments actually represent Jason's speculations into another's motives and may be mistaken. The strategy supports a plot filled with aliens who are out to betray him.

These novels focus on conflicting points of view and on beneficial ways of resolving them. The societies portrayed are exaggeratedly violent, and exaggeration is a time-honored tactic of satire. While the omniscient narrator blandly reports episode after episode of suspense, battle, torture, and death, Jason's sardonic running commentary provides humor. The novels are exciting and often quite funny, particularly in the dialogue between Jason and the humorless, trigger-happy Pyrrans or with the acutely irritating Mikah.

Harrison has gone on from these books to become known for a variety of serious fiction, editing, and nonfiction projects. He is recognized for his increasingly parodistic yet thoughtful satire.   —*Fiona Kelleghan*

DEERSKIN

Fleeing a world of hypocrisy, indulgence, and brutality, Lissar is transformed into the legendary Deerskin

Author: Robin McKinley (1952-   )
Genre: Fantasy—feminist
Type of work: Novel
Time of plot: A medieval stage of civilization
Location: A fairy-tale kingdom
First published: 1993

The Plot: The most beautiful woman in seven kingdoms marries the handsome king of a wealthy realm. They have one child, a daughter named Lissar, who is ignored while the happy couple enjoys an idyllic, self-absorbed marriage. When the queen discovers that her perfect beauty is fading, she orders a portrait and, when it is finished, adjures her husband to marry no one who is not as beautiful as the painting. Smiling in triumph, she dies.

Lissar is first noticed by anyone other than her nurse-maid when the prince of a neighboring kingdom—alone of all those who send condolences and gifts to her father—sends her a gift, a puppy from his favorite fleethound bitch. Because of the puppy, Lissar begins to develop a love of life and nature. She becomes a very atypical princess, learning herbal and plant lore from the aunt of one of her chambermaids.

Lissar's discovery of self is interrupted when a grand ball is given to present her to would-be suitors. Her mother's portrait dominates the great room, but her father is overwhelmed by her resemblance to the portrait. He dances with her all night, turning away interested suitors. When he is later pressed to marry again, he declares his daughter to be his intended bride. The final horror occurs when he rapes her in her own bedroom.

Stunned into amnesia, Lissar follows her dog, Ash, out of the palace grounds, out of the country, and into a distant forest, where they subsist by learning to hunt and to gather edible plants. In the midst of a severe winter, in a small cabin they have found, Lissar is visited by a mysterious woman who presents Lissar with the gift of time, to heal before remembering. On awakening, Lissar finds that it is spring and that she is clothed in a delicate deerskin garment that repels all stains. She and Ash make their way slowly toward civilization, ending in the kingdom of an unassuming king and queen whose only son is Ossin, the dog-lover who had sent Ash to Lissar.

Lissar learns that the woman who appeared to her is known as the Moon Woman. Her appearance means that someone in need will find help. Lissar becomes known as Deerskin, and her skill in nursing a litter of motherless pups for Prince Ossin and feats such as finding a lost child add to her legendary aura and endear her to both Ossin and the people.

When Ossin declares his love for her, she flees, impelled by the resurgent memories of her father's act. Finally accepting her love for Ossin, she returns in time to prevent the wedding of Ossin's younger sister to Lissar's father. At her touch, her father becomes an old and broken man. She and Ossin understand that her healing will be slow, but he is content to be patient and helpful.

Analysis: Robin McKinley has won both the Newbery Award and Newbery Honors for previous fantasy novels. *Deerskin* is based on "Donkeyskin," a fairy tale with adult subject matter. McKinley uses this subject matter to craft a tale in the style and tone of a romantic fantasy with underlying social commentary. The unassuming simplicity and kindness at the court of Ossin's parents is sharply contrasted to the glitter and superficiality in the court of Lissar's parents.

The attitude of the courtiers when Lissar's father declares his intention to marry his own daughter signals the beginning of a second pervasive theme. They ask themselves how this evil creature could have bewitched their wonderful king. Their comments bespeak an innate sexism on the part of both men and women of this court, implying that men are helpless to resist subliminal messages of temptation. Lissar's father first beats her, then rapes her, thus demonstrating starkly that this is an act of violence, not of love. Any sympathy one might have felt for the king because of his wife's egotistical legacy is destroyed completely by the cold ferocity of the attack, which breaks Lissar's resistance.

Lissar's benumbed departure from her father's palace is rendered in terms more suitable to describing the mental state of a trauma victim than the flight of a fairy-tale princess. The fleethound, Ash, is the symbol and a source of her slowly emerging determination to survive. As they learn to survive by hunting and foraging, their physical hardships are described realistically, including such homey details as where Lissar decides to place her latrine near the Moon Woman's cabin.

The Moon Woman and her gift of the deerskin garment are powerful reminders that this is fantasy. Lissar's gradual conquest of Ossin's heart is likewise the stuff of fairy tales. Lissar's flight from Ossin, on the other hand, is again a reflection of harsh reality and the frightened reaction of some rape survivors to even the gentlest offers of love. Her return is surrounded by powerful magic but interpreted in terms of both psychology and anthropology. In the midst of her confrontation with her father, her menses flow onto the floor, but what is often interpreted as a woman's weakness becomes a source of sacred power, releasing even the ghost of her mother upon the crowd. The form and phenomena of McKinley's tale are those of a fairy tale; the substance is that of a fable for the postfeminist society.

—*James L. Hodge*

THE DEMOLISHED MAN

Lincoln Powell attempts to prove that Ben Reich has committed murder, an almost unheard of act in the year 2301

Author: Alfred Bester (1913-1987)
Genre: Science fiction—extrasensory powers
Type of work: Novel
Time of plot: 2301
Location: New York City
First published: 1953 (serial form, 1952)

The Plot: On the surface, *The Demolished Man* is a slick, futuristic detective novel, but the book is much more complex than such a surface description implies. Ben Reich, a wealthy and powerful man, has planned a merger with the D'Courtney Cartel. When that merger is apparently thwarted by Craye D'Courtney, Reich plans to murder his rival. The difficulty confronting Reich is that in the year 2301, murder has been virtually eliminated because of the emergence of Espers, people gifted with and trained in the use of extrasensory perception. Espers are classified according to their levels of ability; an Esper 1 is the most gifted and best-trained of the Esper Guild members. Because Espers can "peep" accused suspects, or look into their thoughts, hiding guilt from them is virtually impossible. The Esper Guild, however, maintains strict rules for its members. Even though Lincoln Powell, a police prefect and an Esper 1, determines very early that Reich is guilty of D'Courtney's murder, he is unable to make use of the knowledge without supporting evidence. He must present enough evidence to the police computer, "Old Man Mose," to ensure a conviction; otherwise, Reich will go free.

Reich has powerful means of thwarting the police investigation. He can hire the best Espers to help him, he can afford massive bribes and incentives, and he has friends in high places in the police department. Powell, however, is not without resources of his own. He is a superb detective in addition to being an incredibly gifted Esper. He manages to locate a witness to the crime, Barbara D'Courtney, the daughter of the victim. She is so traumatized by the murder, however, that she must undergo considerable psychotherapy to counteract her state of shock. She must be regressed to a state of birthlike innocence and carefully brought through normal growth stages in order to preserve her mental functions. As she goes though these stages under Powell's observation, he comes to realize that he is in love with her.

Meanwhile, Old Man Mose has rejected Powell's plan for prosecution, and Powell has no idea why. He discovers that the motive for the murder is so complex and so deeply hidden in Reich's subconscious that he must combat Reich in ways that play upon his psychological makeup. Only in that way is he able to accomplish his objective of having Reich "demolished," or psychologically broken down and rebuilt into the man his better nature will allow. Powell also is able to find a satisfactory outcome for his love of Barbara D'Courtney.

Analysis: Alfred Bester won the first Hugo Award in 1953 for *The Demolished Man*. Bester had published numerous short stories prior to this book, his first novel and generally considered to be his best. The quality of the book is attested by the fact that it has held up for more than forty years as a fascinating study of the human mind, of psychic and psychological detective methods, and of the intricacies of human relationships. It is especially effective in its study of the ways in which the Espers relate to one another and to society.

Powell, for example, has a private house rather than the standard apartment. This is not because of his superior economic means. Esper 1's must have private residences because they are bombarded by the thoughts of others in small, poorly insulated apartments, and they must have privacy to maintain their sanity. Being an Esper is a decidedly mixed blessing. Insight into the thoughts of others is a gift, but that gift is received whether one chooses it or not, and Espers cannot avoid knowing things that they might rather not know. Early in the book, Bester describes the dialogue at a party. It is presented typographically to show that strains of the conversation intertwine because the Espers at the party can both hear spoken conversation and understand the unspoken thoughts behind it. They also play a game of creating word patterns, much like poems but with visual aspects, in their minds for others to perceive.

There are ways to protect one's thoughts from Espers. Reich adopts a mindless jingle that he keeps running through his mind at all times to try to block the Espers. This works with Espers of the lower grades; it fails with Espers of Powell's quality.

Use of a computer as a guide to the likely success of prosecution of a case is another interesting device. Readers of the 1990's and beyond would probably not question this plot device or find it unusual, but in 1953, when computers were in their infancy, it was a speculation into the future of a new and interesting machine. Technology in *The Demolished Man* takes a secondary position to psychology. Although most of the psychology seems at odds with present-day psychotherapy, that is not necessarily a flaw. Readers might assume that the psychotherapy described in the novel is more advanced, as it is from an imagined future; it is in fact dated.

A minor flaw in the book, one that might disturb feminist readers, is the love angle. Powell finds himself unable to love his longtime associate, Mary Noyes, who makes no secret of her love for him, yet he falls in love with Barbara D'Courtney, who has been regressed to an infant and who loves him in a childlike way as she "grows" back into an adult self. Despite such minor problems, this book is a classic of science fiction that should be included on every reading list of major works in the genre.
                                                    —June Harris

THE DEMON PRINCES SERIES

To avenge his family's massacre, Kirth Gersen tracks down the five master criminals who ordered the crime and destroys them

Author: Jack Vance (1916-   )
Genre: Science fiction—planetary romance
Type of work: Novels
Time of plot: Beginning in 3524
Location: Various planets of the Gaean Reach
First published: *The Star King* (1964; serial form, *Galaxy*, December, 1963, and February, 1964), *The Killing Machine* (1964), *The Palace of Love* (1967; serial form, *Galaxy*, October and December, 1966, and February, 1967), *The Face* (1979), and *The Book of Dreams* (1981)

The Plot: The Demon Princes series was the first long novel series that Jack Vance started, and it took the longest to complete. It takes place in Vance's own imaginary galaxy of the future, the Gaean Reach. The civilized, law-abiding part of the galaxy is known as the Oikumene, and the uncivilized, lawless section, its frontier, is known as the Beyond. From this area come five space pirates, the Demon Princes, who have committed the massacre of Kirth Gersen's family, a crime that Gersen pledges his life to avenge. Gersen and his grandfather, escaping this attack, journey to Old Earth, as Vance customarily calls it, where Gersen trains for more than twenty years to become the instrument of retribution for his family's fate.

Vance's Gaean Reach, like Robert A. Heinlein's Future History and Isaac Asimov's Galactic Empire, is curiously lacking in intelligent aliens, but the one race that exists closely resembles humans. They are the Star Kings, the race to which Attel Malagate, the first of the Demon Princes Gersen pursues, belongs. Gersen's main task becomes identifying which one of three possible suspects is the Star King.

Vance, an Edgar-winning mystery author, deftly interweaves plot elements from the traditional mystery with aspects of the planetary romance. Gersen, for example, must rescue an innocent girl kidnapped by one of Malagate's henchmen. The search for Malagate involves a simultaneous search for an undiscovered Earth-like planet. One of the clues that leads Gersen to identify Malagate is the alien's lack of human reaction to this Edenic setting. Fittingly, it is the planet's treelike inhabitants who kill Malagate, but when Gersen returns a year later, enough of Malagate is still left for Gersen to exact his own poetic justice.

The Killing Machine is both the translation of Kokor Hekkus, the name of the second Demon Prince, as well as a description of the mechanical monster he designs to terrify the primitive tribespeople of a world he dominates. Gersen's complicated search for Hekkus involves him in the manufacture of this machine, swindling Hekkus and the Interchange organization (a group set up to bring order to kidnapping across interstellar distances), and the rescue of a beautiful woman, Alusz Iphigenia, from both Interchange and Hekkus. Hekkus, a seemingly immortal criminal mastermind, is a connoisseur of terror and fear. To indulge these primal emotions, he establishes himself as a wizardlike figure on the legendary world of Thamber. In locating both Hekkus and Thamber, Gersen brings about the end of Thamber as a world of primitive adventure and precipitates its entrance into the Oikumene.

Viole Fanushe, the third of the Demon Princes, is a sybaritic sensualist who has constructed the Palace of Love as a hedonistic hideaway. Once again, Gersen's main task is identifying which one of a limited number of suspects is the master criminal and locating the planet he uses as a base of operations. This involves Gersen returning to Old Earth, becoming a journalist, and allying himself with Fanushe's old mentor, the bizarre poet Narvath. Fanushe, it turns out, is as monomaniacal as Gersen. Fanushe's obsession involves wooing cloned versions of a girl who long ago spurned him. Gersen's revenge thus involves him freeing not one but four females in jeopardy; he simultaneously liberates the inhabitants of Fanushe's planet.

In *The Face*, Gersen pursues Lens Larque, a sadistic, brutal trickster. As the title implies, he is the only one of the Demon Princes who does not mind his losing his anonymity. Gersen must flush him out by carrying out a complicated financial takeover of a company that Larque has formed to play an enormous joke on a society that has shamed him. Gersen deals with Larque shortly before Larque can avenge himself. Gersen, who has been similarly humiliated, carries out Larque's scheme, but only after Larque is dead.

Howard Alan Treesong, the last of the Demon Princes to be dealt with, is also the most ambitious. He attempts to take over the IPCC, the Interpol of the Gaean Reach, and then to become head of the Institute, a quasi-religious body that places a limit on scientific advances that would interfere with human evolution. Gersen foils Treesong, tracking him down and breaking up his attempted revenge at his high school reunion. Gersen's own final vengeance is interfered with by victims of one of Treesong's earliest crimes, who exact their own peculiarly apt punishment.

Analysis: In the Demon Princes series, Jack Vance combines one of the oldest Western literary plots, the search for revenge, with the science-fiction subgenre of the planetary romance. Its success in both aspects rests on the validity of the central character. During the first novels, Kirth Gersen is satisfying on both levels. His competence as the hero of a planetary romance and his single-mindedness of purpose are explained by the years he trained for his task. He continually rescues females from imminent sexual danger, as does any literary descendant of Edgar Rice Burroughs' John Carter. Gersen's depth of character as an avenger is filled in as well. It can be seen in his sense of loss at not being able to partake in the possibilities of life around him, particularly in romantic attachments, and in his musings about the form his life would take when his quest is over. None of this depth, however, is carried out consistently throughout the series. Gersen's life before the raid, for example, is never alluded to, and after Treesong's death, Gersen bleakly comments, "I am done." Gersen exists only as an instrument, and when his function is over, the story is over.

Such perfunctory endings have led to the charge that Vance loses interest in his series after the first few novels. Some indications of this occur in the Demon Princes series. For example, in *The Face*, the novel in which Vance returned to the series after a hiatus, Gersen mentions that it was an uncle who escaped with him, when the other four novels consistently say it was his grandfather. Because of Vance's use of the mystery plot and the consequent delay in unmasking the villains, almost all of them (with the exception of Treesong) are merely melodramatic; their evil is reported, not witnessed.

For all the loose ends, there is a satisfying underlying sense of unity about the series. Almost all the novels involve some kind of planetary scheme by the villains that Gersen must foil. He liberates the dryads from Malagate's threat, brings Thamber into the human community, and frees Fanushe's sex slaves. In the novels after the hiatus, Gersen, in a sense, goes along with the planetary plots. He complies with Larque's fantastic vengeance against the fastidious inhabitants of Methel, and he allows the parents of Treesong's boyhood victim to employ the animals of Bethune Preserve to help them exact their own retribution. In the first and last novels of the series, which are set on sparsely inhabited worlds, Gersen does not act as the final avenger.

The Demon Princes series also exhibits to a great degree Vance's spirit of playfulness regarding various science-fiction conventions. Many science-fiction novels, for example (most notably Isaac Asimov's Foundation series), use invented quotations from other books (often reference works) as chapter headings in an attempt to give a greater sense of depth and verisimilitude to their fictional universes. The chapters headings Vance devises are unusually detailed, and the authors' names he creates sometimes have a metafictional dimension. They include Frerb Hankbert (Frank Herbert) and Jan Holberk Vaenz LXII (John Holbrook Vance—Vance's full name). Lens Larque's name combines two halves of the most famous names in space opera, the *Lens*men and the Sky*lark* of E. E. "Doc" Smith. In *The Killing Machine*, Gersen's most significant achievement is his deconstruction of Thamber, a perfect site for the planetary romance and thus reminiscent of Tschai, the locale of Vance's Planet of Adventure series (1968-1970), into a more mundane, more "real" world.

In *The Book of Dreams*, Gersen visits a planet that has 1,562 separate countries, and the reader comes away with the conviction that, if he had to, Vance could invent a fictional society for each. Because of his baroque style and love of exotic invention, Vance has been called a "coelacanth," a writer who is a throwback to conventions established in 1912 with Burroughs' "Under the Moons of Mars." He provides clues in the Demon Princes series that behind this mask is an author who is willing, however slyly, to subvert the very conventions he celebrates so richly.

—*William Laskowski*

DESCENT INTO HELL

During production of his play, Peter Stanhope teaches Pauline Anstruther to accept divine love, while Lawrence Wentworth damns himself by rejecting it

Author: Charles Williams (1886-1945)
Genre: Fantasy—Magical Realism
Type of work: Novel
Time of plot: The 1930's
Location: Battle Hill, a village near London
First published: 1937

The Plot: *Descent into Hell* concerns five central characters and a village production of a play by Peter Stanhope.

During the weeks of rehearsal, Stanhope demonstrates to Pauline Anstruther the "doctrine of substituted love" (a central idea held by the novel's author, Charles Williams) and helps her overcome the terror she has felt at meeting her double. At the same time, her grandmother, Margaret Anstruther, whom she has been serving as companion, is able in her final hours to aid in the spiritual crisis of an unnamed workman who had committed suicide decades earlier. Another member of the community, military historian Lawrence Wentworth, chooses his own damnation by rejecting truth in favor of illusion and self-indulgence.

Production begins of the play, which is a verse drama. The local organizers rejoice at producing the work of such a noted poet as Stanhope, but his unwillingness to give them much guidance in the speaking of his poetry confuses them. Williams implies satirically that few of these amateurs understand the play and that even fewer truly like poetry. Stanhope sees one exception—the young woman who leads the chorus, Pauline Anstruther. Stanhope's sympathy leads Pauline to confess to him her terror of meeting her "double" in the street, an experience she has undergone several times, each time with greater fright. To her surprise, Stanhope offers to carry her fear for her as if it were a package. This is the real meaning, he says, of the Gospel's injunction to "bear one another's burdens."

Later Pauline discusses this obliquely with her grandmother. They agree that perhaps something of the sort happened to their ancestor, John Struther, who was burned at the stake on Battle Hill during Queen Mary Tudor's persecution of protestants. From the fire, Struther is supposed to have cried out that he had seen his salvation.

As Pauline enjoys her new freedom from fear, Lawrence Wentworth undergoes an opposite transformation. Long haunted by a dream of climbing down a rope into endless darkness, he now finds that dream replaced by his selfish infatuation with one of the play's actresses, Adele Hunt. His sick interest becomes even more distorted when Wentworth rejects the actual woman in favor of a fantasy version of her. As the novel's events proceed, he eventually denies truth and damns himself with his sick illusions.

The novel's climax occurs on the night of dress rehearsal. As Margaret Anstruther lies dying, she sends Pauline out in the middle of the night to help someone in need. In the miracle of divine timelessness, the sufferer is a long-dead workman, and Pauline helps by offering him some of the same burden-bearing she has received. Next she is able to relieve her ancestor John Struther of his fear of fire, thus aiding the triumph of his martyrdom.

In the novel's last scenes, Pauline leaves for London, secure in her new awareness of divine love. At the train station, she and Stanhope are shocked to see Wentworth, sick and mad, beginning his last journey, one that will leave him in hell.

Analysis: As a member of the Inklings group that included C. S. Lewis and J. R. R. Tolkein, Charles Williams was naturally interested both in fantasy and Christianity. Like Lewis, he used fiction to explore that interest and particularly the idea of "substituted love," which he portrayed as literally true.

It becomes the crux of the issues in *Descent into Hell*. Pauline Anstruther is startled when Stanhope suggests that he might carry her fear for her, and she is moved by joy when he does so. Her belief in the process enables her to help first the workman and then the protestant martyr. Clearly, Williams suggests that such love can transcend time, thus accounting for the blending of past and present in the novel. John Struther died in the 1550's and the workman evidently killed himself decades before the novel's main action, but Pauline is able to aid both of them, just as her grandmother seems somehow in touch with them. Williams' imagery suggests, in fact, that substituted love explains how the Crucifixion—here portrayed as the ultimate burden bearing—works for salvation.

Some characters reject the reaching beyond oneself that leads to heaven; that is what happens to Wentworth and to the characters who succumb to the offers of the demoniac Lily Sammile, who threads her way through the novel offering people like Wentworth the damning narcotic of self-indulgence and fantasy. Williams, like Dante Alighieri in the *Inferno* (in *The Divine Comedy*, c. 1320), insists that such people are condemned at their own insistence as they refuse the offers of love that could save them. Adele Hunt accepts Lily's offer, as does Wentworth; Pauline briefly comes perilously close.

Two of Williams' images relate very clearly to his ideas about love and time. Fire, for example, is important not only because of how it figures in Struther's martyrdom but also as part of Stanhope's play. Williams joins flame images to descriptions of the workman's suicide (by hanging from a house beam) to suggest the Crucifixion. Fire also appears more conventionally at the novel's end, as Wentworth descends into hell.

Williams also makes use of his characters' names. Peter Stanhope is surely intended to evoke the Apostle

Peter, the stone on whom Jesus said he would build his church; "stan" is the early English form of "stone." Pauline, who so fears to meet her *Doppelgänger*, or double, on the road, carries the name of the Apostle Paul, who met Christ on the road to Damascus. Her last name, Anstruther, contains "truth" as a central element. Her grandmother's name, Margaret, means "a pearl" and is probably intended to suggest the "pearl of great price" that represented the kingdom of heaven in Jesus' parable. Even Wentworth's name suggests how thoroughly he has rejected his own value. Lily Sammile's name suggests the Lilith who in Hebrew myth was Adam's first wife and whose mythological personality is temptress and deceiver.

Behind these images lies one more, that of the city. Adjacent to Battle Hill, it is at the same time London, the city of God, and Dante's Satanic city of Dis.

—*Ann D. Garbett*

THE DEVIL IS DEAD

In the course of a sea voyage from America to the Greek islands, the heroic Finnegan matches wits with various "Neanderthal men," including Papadiabolous, who is said to be the Devil

Author: R(aphael) A(loysius) Lafferty (1914-   )
Genre: Fantasy—mythological
Type of work: Novel
Time of plot: The indeterminate past
Location: Primarily the ship *Brunhilde* and the island of Naxos
First published: 1971

The Plot: Finnegan (who cannot remember his true name or nature) meets the eccentric millionaire Saxon X. Seaworthy, who is similarly afflicted with amnesia. They have a drink together, served by Anastasia Demetriades (who is a mermaid, although that is not immediately obvious). They are joined by another person, whom Anastasia addresses as Papa-D. Later, Anastasia recruits Finnegan and other crew members for a voyage on Seaworthy's boat, the *Brunhilde*, seemingly against the wishes of Papa-D, whose full name is Papadiabolous. Anastasia tells Finnegan that Papadiabolous is the Devil.

On the transatlantic voyage, several tall tales are told and heard, a mysterious corpse turns up, and there is much enigmatic talk. Finnegan remembers that he and Seaworthy once buried someone who looks exactly like Papadiabolous and realizes that Seaworthy believes his

present companion is the same person. Another passenger, the evil Marie Courtois, kills one of Finnegan's shipmates.

When the ship reaches the island of Naxos, various manifestations of classical mythology begin to intrude on the action and dialogue. A fight breaks out at the ship's mooring, and Finnegan returns there to find Papadiabolous dead. This demise apparently serves to liberate the evil inclinations of Seaworthy and his associates, which previously had been held in check.

Finnegan encounters Mr. X, who otherwise is left unidentified (no comment being made on the fact that X is also Seaworthy's middle initial). Mr. X offers an explanation of recent events that does not make matters any clearer. Finnegan then meets Dolores "Doll" Delancy. These three become a team of "outlaws," on the run from Seaworthy and other vague threats. More tall tales are told and heard, mingling mythological sources with other materials in increasingly chaotic fashion. Many new characters are introduced for this purpose, while Finnegan's alleged pursuers fade into the background, seemingly forgotten.

In the final chapter, Mr. X tells one last tale, which offers an explanation of the curious case of the two identical Papadiabolouses. They were twins, one evil and one "comparatively good." It was the evil twin whom Seaworthy killed, before he and Finnegan buried the body; the good twin had been quick to take the other's place. Mr. X and Finnegan then tell Doll that all these contending parties (including themselves but excluding her) are members of an older human race. She calls them gargoyles, although the prefatory notes attached to many of the chapters identify them as Neanderthal men, intent on dispossessing the race that has succeeded them. Finnegan, in turning against his own kind, has become a heroic renegade fighting on behalf of "hopeless" people who are unable to fight for themselves, being merely "sheep." Doll demands a climax for the story, but X tells her that "it is only regular people who believe in climaxes" and leaves her to provide her own—which she does, after a fashion.

Analysis: Part of R. A. Lafferty's charm is that he defies analysis. The defiance is deliberate: Every time an explanation looms on the horizon, his determination is to subvert it, and every time a plot threatens to crystallize out of his narrative, he changes the *dramatis personae* and cuts the story adrift again. It is entirely appropriate that he should represent *The Devil Is Dead* as the centerpiece of a trilogy called the Argos Mythos, whose first volume, *Archipelago* (1979), was not published until eight years later and whose third volume never appeared (after all, only regular people believe in climaxes). The contents of that proposed volume appeared in three Canadian chapbooks: *Promontory Goats* (1988), *How Many Miles to Babylon?* (1989), and *Episodes of the Argo* (1990).

In *Archipelago*, it is alleged that Finnegan is really Jason, whose modern career echoes the quest of the Argonauts, but he obviously is many other people as well. In *The Devil Is Dead*, he frequently is called Finn, presumably in order to link him to Finn MacCool, a hero of Irish folklore. He is a Neanderthal man in a world in which Neanderthal men are extinct, blandly refusing to notice that his world ended long ago. Lafferty's work is full of such entities: men who are dead, or never lived, but who simply will not lie down or go away; and worlds that have been superseded, or never existed, but continue to intrude upon reality—much to the delight of those who would rather see dull existence replaced by something more colorful.

The reader who expects *The Devil Is Dead* to make sense is occasionally wooed by Mr. X's "explanations," only to be deceived. The point is that the world ought not to make sense, and that if it did it would be cause for terrible disappointment. Lafferty, a Roman Catholic who rejoices in that faith's indomitable insistence that miracles occur and that the world cannot be reduced to the causal accounts of science, will not consent to be thus disappointed. If *The Devil Is Dead* is to be reckoned a fantasy—and it is arguable that it should not, on the grounds that all of its mythological intrusions are confined to the eyes of their fictitious beholders—it is the most radical kind of fantasy. Most fantasy, by dealing frankly and earnestly with the unreal, serves to reinforce rather than to undermine awareness of the boundaries of the real. Lafferty sets out not merely to injure but also to insult reason, insisting that the reality of common sense is not worth recognition, let alone respect.

It is good that someone carries out this kind of literary work, simply on the grounds that nothing should ever go unchallenged, particularly the obvious. Since the brief vogue his work enjoyed in the early 1970's—during which time *The Devil Is Dead* was nominated for a Nebula Award—Lafferty has been banished to the wilderness of small press publication and condemned as an incorrigible eccentric, but his work remains resiliently alive, stubbornly lively, and pigheadedly vivid.

—*Brian Stableford*

THE DEVIL RIDES OUT

Duke de Richleau and three cohorts battle black magician Damien Mocata for the Talisman of Set, an icon that controls the Four Horsemen of the Apocalypse—War, Plague, Famine, and Death

Author: Dennis Wheatley (1897-1977)
Genre: Fantasy—occult
Type of work: Novel
Time of plot: The 1930's
Location: London, England, and environs; Paris, France; and the Astral Plane
First published: 1935

The Plot: *The Devil Rides Out* features "The Four Musketeers"—Duke de Richleau, Rex Van Ryn, Richard Eaton, and Simon Aron—series characters who appear in Dennis Wheatley's political thrillers as well as his black magic novels. Alarmed by the fact that their friend Simon Aron has fallen under the influence of a black magician, Damien Mocata, occult expert Duke de Richleau and his friend Rex Van Ryn set out to help him. They learn that Aron is the key element in the magician's conspiracy to activate the powers of the Talisman of Set, thereby giving Mocata control over the Four Horsemen of the Apocalypse. They set out to free their friend and save humanity.

The first rescue is relatively easy, but Aron is recaptured. In a heroic Walpurgis Night assault on Mocata's castle, the duke and Van Ryn again rescue Aron. They spirit him to Cardinals Folly, the estate of Richard Eaton, where they are all safely harbored against Mocata's demoniac attacks in a specially prepared magic pentacle. Temporarily frustrated, Mocata launches a counterattack on the duke's group by kidnapping Fleur d'Amour, Eaton's innocent young daughter. Her ritual sacrifice will loose the powers of the Talisman of Set for Mocata. The Four Musketeers, accompanied by Fleur's mother, Marie Lou, race to Paris for a final confrontation with the black magician. The men are stymied by Mocata's occult defenses but, moments before the sacrifice is to occur, Marie Lou recalls a magical dream and utters words that tear the talisman away from Mocata and summon the Lord of Light. Taking over Fleur's body, the Lord of Light turns Mocata's own demons against him in a final battle that takes place on the Astral Plane.

Analysis: Writing a mix of spy thrillers, historical adventures, and horror stories, Wheatley was one of Great

Britain's most commercially successful authors for almost forty years. Although they make up a mere fifth of his total output, only the occult novels—or "black magic" stories, as he labeled them—are of any lasting interest. Despite their prior popularity, however, interest has waned considerably.

Wheatley's popular success was no accident. A fine storyteller, he was especially skillful at creating exciting, vivid dramatic scenes, enhanced by his eye for precise sensory detail. Wheatley's characters, especially his villains, though generally flat and often stereotypical, could be colorful and grotesque. A scrupulous researcher, Wheatley was thorough in his investigations of supernatural phenomena. In his best horror stories, he integrated these elements into a solid, realistic milieu at those points in the action where they fit most easily into the narrative. Thus, Wheatley created worlds in which the laws of black and white magic operate believably and inevitably, the unseen becoming a palpable presence. In addition, Wheatley's versatility enabled him to fuse several popular genres into hybrid works that used the most stimulating elements of each genre.

Sadly, defects have dated many of Wheatley's novels. The writing itself is never more than serviceable. Plotting is uneven, sometimes clean and efficient but frequently awkward and digressive. His reliance on the climactic *deus ex machina* often approaches the laughable. Even more damaging is his tendency toward preaching, heavy-handed moralizing, and abstract speculations. This is especially true in his later books, in which the narrative drive is overwhelmed by his reactionary social attitudes, virulent anti-Communism, and otherworldly metaphysics.

The Devil Rides Out, his first horror novel, represents Wheatley at his best. Here he introduces the formula that shapes all the occult de Richleau books as well as, in varying degrees, the other black magic novels. In this formula, de Richleau and company are made aware of a serious satanic threat to a friend and/or humanity. They take arms and win a modest victory that provokes the minions of evil into retaliation. The four are pursued and attacked by overwhelming forces in an uneven contest until, finally, good rallies and triumphs, more often than not as a result of a sudden divine intervention.

The virtues of *The Devil Rides Out* are clear. Wheatley's Four Musketeers—a French Royalist exile and epicurean (de Richleau), a Jewish financier (Aron), an aristocratic Englishman (Eaton), and a wealthy American (Van Ryn)—make a good, if snobbish, team that served Wheatley well in eleven novels, only three of

which fit into the black magic category. Excepting the *deus ex machina* ending, the plotting is simple, direct, and believable. The villain is purely evil, larger than life, and fittingly grotesque.

The supernatural paraphernalia, however, probably give *The Devil Rides Out* its continuing entertainment value. Wheatley was especially thorough in his researching of occult materials. As do all of his black magic novels, *The Devil Rides Out* contains a serious warning to the reader to "refrain from being drawn into the practice of the Secret Art in any way." Wheatley was a lifelong believer (if not practitioner) in the occult; his nonfiction treatise *The Devil and All His Works* (1971) is a monumental treatment of the subject. *The Devil Rides Out* is glutted with occult paraphernalia including satanism, demoniac possession, child sacrifice, astral travel, palmistry, numerology, ghostly appearances, necromancy, the conjuring of demons, magical incantations, time manipulation, hypnotism, and clairvoyance.

These elements are never merely inserted into the novel, however; Wheatley was adroit in integrating the magical elements and supernatural menace into the narrative, fitting them easily into the realistic fabric of his book to posit a world in which the laws of black magic are as natural as the laws of physics. This skillful incorporation of occult elements gives to *The Devil Rides Out* and the other effective black magic novels a timelessness lacking in his other books, which now seem hopelessly dated.

Even as a horror writer, Wheatley generally is overlooked. The irony of this obscurity lies in the fact that, although it is rarely acknowledged or recognized, Wheatley developed the form used in most popular contemporary horror novels—the large, elaborate, complicated books that mix several genres (horror, quest fantasy, social melodrama, science fiction, mystery, and others)—written by Stephen King, Peter Straub, Dean Koontz, and numerous other popular authors.

—*Keith Neilson*

DEVIL'S TOR

Visions of the Earth-Mother prompt the rejoining of two halves of a magical stone, bringing together a man and a woman fated to be the progenitors of a new race

Author: David Lindsay (1876-1945)
Genre: Fantasy—theological romance
Type of work: Novel
Time of plot: The 1930's

Location: Dartmoor
First published: 1932

The Plot: Ingrid Fleming, a solitary young woman given to dreaming, takes a cousin, Hugh Drapier, to see Devil's Tor, which bears a crag shaped like a human face. She has always believed, intuitively, that the tor is the tomb of a mysterious female. Lightning strikes and splits the "face," revealing a staircase. Drapier goes down into a cavern, where he sees a vision of the Earth-Mother. He also finds a piece of stone that he does not realize at first to be one half of a broken flint, the other half of which already is in his possession. Its mate was consigned to his care by explorer Henry Saltfleet and archaeologist Stephen Arsinal, who stole it from a temple in Tibet.

An earthquake seals the tomb, and Drapier is killed by a rock slide. Saltfleet, who comes to reclaim his half of the stone, finds Drapier's corpse clutching the other. Saltfleet is eager to reunite the two halves but is delayed by wrangles over ownership that involve long conversations in which the various characters discuss the implications of the stone's existence and the possible consequences of it being made whole again.

It emerges that all the major characters have been manipulated since birth (and in some cases before) by an active Fate that intends to rejoin the pieces of the stone. The personification of this Fate is the Earth-Mother, the "demiurge" responsible for the creation of the world at the instigation of the Ancient (that is, God). The rejoining of the stone will seal the union of a man and a woman who are destined to become the parents of a new race, in repetition of an earlier union that gave birth to the blue-eyed Nordic race.

Eventually, Saltfleet and Arsinal persuade Ingrid and her fiancé, artist Peter Copping, to meet on Devil's Tor in order to reunite the pieces of the stone. The materialistic Arsinal, who actually brings the two halves together, is unable to perceive the spiritual power implicit in the stone and is blasted fatally by the released force. Copping realizes that it is Saltfleet who is destined to be the father of the new race and surrenders Ingrid to him. The relationship between them is to be far more intense and painful than mere human love, and they learn from their visions that their pain will be reflected in the reckless turbulence of the new era that their progeny will bring into existence.

Analysis: *Devil's Tor* is a revised version of a novel written in the early 1920's, originally called *The Ancient Tragedy*, which carried forward the central themes of David Lindsay's novels *A Voyage to Arcturus* (1920) and *The Haunted Woman* (1922). The dualistic and pain-saturated theology of the former novel is here revised, elaborated, and solidly grounded in an idiosyncratic version of human prehistory. The intense and sublime central relationship that is the focal point of the latter novel could reach only temporary fruition therein, in another world. Here it is recapitulated as a historical pivot, given the power to renew the spiritual fervor that contemporary life has exhausted.

Unlike the dualism of *A Voyage to Arcturus*, which is basically combative although it differs markedly from conventional accounts of God and the devil, the dualism of *Devil's Tor* is collaborative. The sexless Ancient produced the Earth-Mother as a necessary instrument of procreation; it is she and not the beings she creates who has undergone a "fall" into sexuality—a fall that involves the spirit as well as the flesh. Lindsay's narrative takes an ambivalent view of sexuality, as do all of his novels, which he began to write after jilting his longtime fiancée and marrying a much young woman. The narrative does accept sexuality's fateful force, arguing that its chief redeeming feature is its power of renewal and regeneration.

Lindsay's account of the qualities and triumphs of the Nordic race are bound to seem suspect in a post-Nazi era, but he is not concerned with crude theories of racial superiority. Insofar as such ideas are given voice in the novel, they are put into the mouth of Arsinal, whose inability to appreciate the spiritual dimension of the adventure is deemed crass enough to warrant his symbolic execution. Even Copping, who is as limited by his art as Arsinal is by his science, is granted greater favor than that. Lindsay's primary aim in talking about a Nietzschean "new race" is to establish that progress can arise only from painful strife, conflict, and a fervent love of freedom; his new savior is not destined to carry forward any process of ethnic cleansing.

Lindsay regarded *Devil's Tor* as the masterpiece among his published works, although he hoped that *The Witch*, which he never managed to complete, might surpass it. It is not entirely surprising that he struggled for nearly ten years to get it into print. Most modern critics think it inferior to *A Voyage to Arcturus*, on the grounds that its long dialogues, most of which take place while the plot is stalled by hollow contrivances, are ponderous and turgid compared with the brilliantly vivid allegorical displays of the earlier novel. This is true, but the fact remains that *Devil's Tor* is a more accurate embodiment of the author's highly individual worldview, and its existence allows readers a better understanding of what *A Voyage to Arcturus* and *The Haunted Woman* were striving to achieve. The philosophical interludes are dull and have not aged particularly well in respect to either content or style, but there is compensation in the many visionary sequences that function as revelations of the Earth-Mother and her purpose. *Devil's Tor* remains a towering product of the literary imagination and a highly original venture in speculative metaphysics.

—*Brian Stableford*

DHALGREN

Kid embarks on a quest of self-discovery in Bellona, a city transformed into an anarchist realm by its entrapment in a distorted space-time continuum

Author: Samuel R. Delany (1942-   )
Genre: Science fiction—New Wave
Type of work: Novel
Time of plot: The 1970's
Location: Bellona, an imaginary American city
First published: 1975

The Plot: Written over a period of four years and spanning more than eight hundred pages, *Dhalgren* is Samuel R. Delany's magnum opus. *Dhalgren*'s main character is the twenty-seven-year-old Kid, who suffers from selective amnesia and other mental disturbances. At the novel's start, Kid is hitchhiking to Bellona, a midwestern city trapped by a mysterious disaster in a shifting zone of reality where time runs in loops and occasionally a giant red sun or two moons appear in the heavens.

On his way into Bellona, Kid meets a strange Asian woman who, after they make love, turns into a tree. This surreal opening begins *Dhalgren*'s conflicting realities: Are the novel's strange events real, or are they the result of Kid's delusional point of view?

Upon entering Bellona, Kid becomes the lover of a former electrical engineer named Tak, who introduces Kid to the cult of George Harrison, a powerful black man worshiped in Bellona's ghetto. Tak takes Kid to the city's hippie commune, and there Kid meets Lanya, who becomes Kid's next lover. Kid also finds a notebook containing the journal of an anonymous past owner. Because of *Dhalgren*'s time loops and Kid's amnesia, Kid himself could have written the journal at an earlier or later time.

Kid begins to write poetry in this notebook. These poems become the basis for *Brass Orchids*, a book pub-

lished by Roger Calkins, the eccentric owner of the city's newspaper, the *Bellona Times*.

Kid receives a severe beating from a trio of scorpions, the name given to Bellona's street gangs. On occasion, scorpions venture out from their nests, or home bases, terrorizing Bellona's residents. Gang members wear projectors that conceal their bodies in holographic images of griffins, spiders, dragons, and other mythical or fantastic creatures.

After this incident, Kid meets June Richards. The Richards family tries to lead an unchanged bourgeois existence in the midst of Bellona's chaos. George Harrison reportedly raped June during the riots that occurred during Bellona's mysterious catastrophe. Kid comes to realize that the so-called rape was an act of mutual desire filled with mythological portents.

Later, Kid is drawn unwittingly into a scorpion run on Emboriky's, a major department store that is the stronghold of a group of armed white racists. During the run, Kid displays the kind of crazy bravery the gang admires. As a result, Kid becomes the leader of a scorpion nest and acquires as a lover a gang member named Denny who becomes part of a three-way sexual relationship with Lanya.

The remainder of the novel concerns Kid's adventures as a scorpion and a poet. While prowling Bellona's shattered streets, Kid awaits the second meeting between George and June. Kid believes that when this meeting occurs, Bellona will plunge once more into an apocalyptic frenzy.

Inspired by metafictional technique (fiction that comments on itself as fiction), Delany wrote *Dhalgren*'s final chapters in columns, with one side following the story and the other commenting on the action, presenting alternative plot lines, or revealing passages from Kid's notebook. This method creates a dual ending. One possibility is that June and George meet, the mysterious apocalypse strikes Bellona again, and Kid flees the city. In a manner reminiscent of James Joyce's *Finnegans Wake* (1939), the last line of *Dhalgren* is a half sentence completed by the half sentence at the novel's start, creating a closed loop. Thus Kid is caught in Bellona's circular time pattern. The other possibility is that the ending is merely a fiction of Kid's notebook, and both the arrival and exit scenes are not real. Kid has always been in Bellona and will always remain there, its scorpion poet.

Analysis: *Dhalgren* is a pivotal work in Delany's career. Although it continues many of the themes of his earlier novels, *Dhalgren* has a dense, literary style and unflinching examination of drug use, deviant sexuality, and violence that also point toward future works such as *Tales of Nevèrÿon* (1979) and *Stars in My Pocket Like Grains of Sand* (1984).

Unlike *Babel-17* (1966), *The Einstein Intersection* (1967), and *Nova* (1968), *Dhalgren* explores countercultural themes such as bisexuality, drug use, race relations, and the connection between artistic and criminal cultures, without far future or deep space settings to blunt the controversial nature of these subjects. The immediacy of *Dhalgren*'s 1970's setting, combined with its difficult literary style and explicit sex and violence, alienated much of Delany's previous readership, who had come to expect works like *Nova* and *Babel-17*, which essentially were stock space epics written with stylistic flare and a 1960's hip sensibility.

Also alienated were many science-fiction reviewers and critics, who regarded *Dhalgren* as at best incomprehensible and at worst a disgrace to the field. *Dhalgren* nevertheless sold well, more than a million copies in less than a decade. In his collection of essays *The Straits of Messina* (1989), Delany attributes these sales to interested readers and sympathetic reviewers outside the science-fiction field.

Dhalgren has its science-fiction defenders, most notably Theodore Sturgeon and Frederik Pohl, and the novel's critical support has increased over the years. What critics praise in *Dhalgren* are its literary experimentation, its highly charged language, and its depth of character. Few other works in any field have portrayed life on the fringes of society with such richness of detail and depth of understanding. *Dhalgren*, with its nonlinear structure, stream-of-consciousness passages, and self-commentary, evokes the brilliant literary innovations of James Joyce, Jorge Luis Borges, and Thomas Pynchon.

Dhalgren may well be the climax of science fiction's New Wave exploration of expanded themes and stylistic techniques. At the same time, its focus on the urban fringe foreshadows the arrival of science fiction's cyberpunk movement in the mid-1980's.   —*John Nizalowski*

THE DIFFERENCE ENGINE

In an alternate history in which Charles Babbage's difference engine is successfully built, paleontologist Edward Mallory attempts to assist Ada Byron with her gambling program for the engine

Authors: William Gibson (1948-   ) and Bruce
    Sterling (1954-   )

Genre: Science fiction—alternate history
Type of work: Novel
Time of plot: 1855
Location: London, England
First published: 1990

The Plot: *The Difference Engine*'s five iterations recall the repetition of subroutines in a computer program. They provide different perspecᵭives on a sequence of events in the year 1855. Charles Babbage has successfully built his difference engine, bringing into being a steam-based information technology. Because the difference engine, a type of computer, historically was not completed, this event becomes the pivot of the alternate history. The plot concerns a set of punch cards created by Ada Byron as a gambling system.

In Iteration One, an aged Sybil Gerard, living in Cherbourg in 1905, remembers January 15, 1855, and her relationship with a doomed opportunist-revolutionary, Mick Radley. Sybil had become a prostitute because her father was hanged as a revolutionary. Her identity is in the police "engines," preventing her from following another profession. Mick involves her in attempts to get a computer program from the deposed president of Texas, Sam Houston, in his London hotel room. Sybil witnesses an attack on Houston that results in Mick's death and sends her to France.

Iteration Two introduces Edward Mallory, a famous paleontologist who discovered the "great land leviathan," or a Brontosaurus, while on a dig in the wilds of Wyoming. On Derby Day, on which both horses and steam-driven vehicles are raced in different heats, he has two momentous experiences. He assists Ada Byron, daughter of the famous Lord Byron who is England's prime minister, to secure a small case containing punch cards for a computer program, then keeps it for her. He also bets on a steam-car race and wins 400 pounds, a small fortune in that time. Subsequently, he is recruited by L. Oliphant, a special detective, to follow a sociology project. He is also set upon by thugs.

In Iteration Three, Mallory suffers further attacks, including one to his rooms in the Palace of Paleontology. Oliphant sends him to the Department of Criminology to identify his attackers. His letter to Ada Byron advises her that he has hidden her case of punch cards in the skull of his Brontosaurus in the British Museum.

Iteration Four describes the societal chaos in London resulting from rampant pollution that has fouled the Thames and the subway system. Mallory's family is now also under attack by revolutionaries. His two brothers, one a steam engineer and one on military leave from India, arrive in London. Together they locate the leader of the revolutionaries, a homicidal woman named Francis Bartlett and her henchman, Captain Swing. They manage to kill him but not her. A "cleansing rain" clears out the pollution and ends the social disintegration.

In Iteration Five, Oliphant collates the various deaths and attacks that result from Bartlett's attempts to obtain the punch cards. Several of her henchmen are killed, and her attempt fails. Nevertheless, the malfunctioning of the Grand Napoleon, the French difference engine, is presented as the precursor to malfunctions in the English engine. Both failures are attributed to pollution. The text suggests another explanation, that the malfunctions occur because Ada's faulty program is run.

The final section, MODUS, is a pastiche of individuals using or used by the idea of a difference engine and an analytical engine. It projects the alternate history into the future, in which Ada's program has run rampant and, by 1991, has virtually eliminated human agency.

Analysis: This novel is perhaps the most controversial to date in the careers of both William Gibson and Bruce Sterling. It was better received outside the science-fiction community than inside. Gibson's future of virtual spaces in *Neuromancer* (1984, winner of the Hugo, Nebula, and Philip K. Dick awards), *Count Zero* (1986), and *Mona Lisa Overdrive* (1988) took the science-fiction community by storm. Sterling's black projections for the technological future and his declarations of the new wave of cyberpunk cast him as the enfant terrible of 1980's and 1990's science fiction, from the first manifesto in *Mirrorshades: The Cyberpunk Anthology* (1986) to later novels.

The Difference Engine is unlike Gibson's and Sterling's other work in its literary technique as well as in its subject matter and period. Although it focuses on a technological revolution, as does their other work, its pacing is much more leisurely. Its diction is somewhat stilted, with occasional glimmers of characterization that seep into a tour de force of Victorian figures, none of whom is fully drawn in the historical or alternative historical roles. The meat of the novel is not its plot, characters, or setting. According to Gibson, the authors took many of their descriptions from period fiction and journalism. The substance of the novel is instead found in comparisons made constantly by the reader between figures and events in history and in the alternative history presented by the novel. Figures such as Lord Wellington become villains, and Ada and Lord Byron have political prestige.

The novel becomes a game of recognition.

There is a fine line between technique used to create atmosphere and technique as an end in itself. *The Difference Engine* maximizes technique where it minimizes fiction, for the novel is full of political and social clichés familiar to science-fiction readers. The familiar theme is that technology that holds the promise for the relief of human suffering can also increase it. This novel fascinates the reader by foregrounding the basic ambivalence of science fiction as fiction rather than science. It works like a machine to grind out the same answer using variegated mechanisms.

—*Janice M. Bogstad and Philip E. Kaveny*

A DIFFERENT FLESH

When European explorers discover the New World they find fertile, arable land for the taking, roamed by Pleistocene megafauna and populated by roving bands of Homo erectus

Author: Harry Turtledove (1949-   )
Genre: Science fiction—alternate history
Type of work: Novel
Time of plot: The seventeenth century to the twentieth century
Location: An alternate Earth
First published: 1988

The Plot: In his preface to this novel, Harry Turtledove reveals that the idea for it came from an article by Stephen Jay Gould speculating about how humanity's distant cousin, *Australopithecus*, would be treated if that species had survived. Turtledove decided to use a nearer cousin, *Homo erectus*, in his story. The short answer that he provides to the above question is "not very well."

The story begins with an entry from a fictional reference work that establishes that the novel takes place in an alternate reality, with the difference that the New World, when discovered by Europeans, was populated by *Homo erectus*, dubbed "sims" by their discoverers. Living in bands of hunter-gatherers but lacking the neocortex, spoken language, and superior reasoning skills of *Homo sapiens*, sims were less efficient hunters than the denizens of the Old World. Consequently, species hunted to extinction in Europe and Asia still flourish in the New World. Among these are saber-toothed tigers and woolly mammoths.

Subsequent historical entries describe the settlement of the New World, the development of a rail system powered by woolly mammoths (later replaced by steam engines), the rise of plantation agriculture sustained through the enslavement of sims, and the development of a growing sims-rights movement. Each of these entries is followed by an expository episode that gives the details of the changes described.

The differences in this alternate reality, as compared to the known world, range from the obvious to the subtle. Because the *Homo erectus* population provides less resistance to colonization than did the actual Native Americans, the New World was colonized more quickly. Place names in the New World are all taken from the Old; the Mississippi River, for example, is called the New Nile. The North American government, lacking inspiration from the Iroquois Confederation, is patterned after Greek democracy and the centralized federal republic of ancient Rome.

The existence of sims makes it more difficult for Europeans to identify differences among humans. Slavery of nonwhite humans continues as an economic institution, and there are still those who, against all evidence to the contrary, impute inferior value to humans with darker skin pigmentation. The subtle difference from the reader's reality is that nonwhite people know themselves to be superior to sims; therefore, they participate in the oppression of the less sophisticated life-form, and their self-respect, to some extent, rests on the knowledge that they are not on the bottom rung of the evolutionary ladder.

Analysis: Often the best science fiction and fantasy results from exploration of a simple question, such as "How do you define what is human?" From the first pages of *A Different Flesh*, Turtledove makes the status of sims the major concern: Are they animal or human? In the first expository episode, a settler and his wife conclude their argument by noting that the last time the issue was raised, their present positions were reversed. She had thought sims human, and he had thought them beasts. They acknowledge that the issue is not easily resolved.

In the middle of the novel, Turtledove explores the Aristotelian notion that there are those who are slaves by nature. Because sims are incapable of producing civilized behavior on their own, humans do them a favor by allowing them to serve their betters, learning more refined behavior through instruction and association. One episode concerns a sim who is a snob. He has learned much from his human associates, and he declines an opportunity to join a band of wild sims, conveying through sign language that they are boring and uncivilized. He would rather be a slave to humans than be free and wild.

The debate continues throughout the book. Early in the novel, readers will tend to identify more with the humans' views of sims as an inferior and at times inexplicable life-form. As the novel progresses and more is revealed about sims and their ability to do many things that might be considered "human," readers are drawn into the complexity of the issue. It is apparent that sims have a level of intelligence and that they have preferences; therefore, they may be entitled to more choice in their lives than they have been given.

In the final vignette, Turtledove raises the issue of animal rights regarding medical experimentation. In the late 1980's, sims are being used in research aimed at finding a cure for the acquired immune deficiency syndrome (AIDS) epidemic. By this time, legal precedents have been set stating that sims are not people and may be used in lieu of people in medical experiments. Various groups protest such usage, regarding the infliction of pain and suffering on living, feeling beings as immoral, no matter how beneficial to humans the eventual result may be. One such group effects a rescue of Matt, an AIDS research subject. Assured by his rescuers that he is free, he nevertheless finds freedom much more restrictive than the laboratory, where creature comforts and companionship were provided. As is often the case in real life, the novel reaches no satisfactory conclusion; the author is content to have presented a sensitive yet thorough exploration of a complex problem.

Turtledove has a Ph.D. in Byzantine history and has been writing fantasy and science fiction since 1979. His Videssos cycle, consisting of *The Misplaced Legion*, *An Emperor for the Legion*, *The Legion of Videssos*, and *Swords of the Legion* (all published in 1987), has a Byzantine setting. *A Different Flesh* is a work by an accomplished storyteller of enormous intelligence and curiosity.

—*Karen S. Bellinfante*

A DIFFERENT KINGDOM

Michael Fay learns about an alternate world and his place in the Wild Forest

Author: Paul Kearney (1967-   )
Genre: Fantasy—mythological
Type of work: Novel
Time of plot: The 1950's
Location: Northern Ireland and the Wildwood
First published: 1993

The Plot: Orphaned by a bomb blast that kills his parents, Michael Fay is brought up by his grandparents on a large, remote farm in rural Antrim in Northern Ireland. He is left alone, except by his Aunt Rose, a warm, very sexual, young woman.

When he is eight years old, Michael trips on the riverbank and gets his first sight of the Fox-People from an alternate world. Subsequently, wolves swarm into his world, unnoticed by others but capable of killing. To add to his problems, Rose becomes pregnant and dies in childbirth. A local man is blamed, but the real father is a mysterious hooded horseman.

Five years later, Michael sees the Fox-People kill a werewolf. He digs up its skull the next day and uses it to defend himself against a wolf attack. Michael sees the Horseman and feels his evil. He encounters an attractive wild girl, Cat, who reminds him of Rose. They meet several more times and become lovers, but he is too young to leave his world to join hers.

Escaping pursuit by wolves, Cat arrives at his house. He takes her in, and they leave together in the morning. They are chased through the forest by wolves and the Horseman, who is recognized by everyone as the Devil. Michael wins the support of the Myrcan Fox-People and their leader, Ringbone, by rescuing two Myrcans from some Catholic Knights Militant who were intent on killing them. Michael already has been helped by Mirkady, the Elf King, and by a troll, Dwarmo. Now, with a legendary sword, Ulfbehrt, he is ready to rescue Rose's soul from the Horseman-Devil's castle.

Despite wolf attacks, Michael and Cat reach the edge of the forest and enter Wolfweald, an area that has obliterated two expeditions by the Christian brothers. Only with Mirkady's help do they survive a goblin attack. He gives Michael and Cat a gift of Wyr-fire, to be used only once when in dire trouble. Nothing can alter the fact that Michael, chronologically fifteen years old, is aging quickly.

They stumble across the encampment of Brother Nennian. Recognizing Michael's original faith, the brother wants to join them. The journey becomes even harder; they are starving, the castle is elusive, and Michael is reaching middle age. Finally, they come to a glade. The wind whips up, the trees grow closer, and there is an urge to join with them; then the wolves arrive. Nennian is killed, and Cat and Michael are wounded before they can invoke the Wyr-fire. Once invoked, the Wyr-fire destroys the wolves, which are made of wood. After they leave the Wyrwood, turning away from the quest in defeat, Michael decides to quit and return to his own world.

More than a decade later, Michael is found to be a nightmare-ridden alcoholic by Mirkady and Dwarmo, who have been looking for him. He finally reaches the Horseman's castle but discovers that the Horseman is not the Devil; rather, he is the spirit of the Wildwood. He wants Michael, so Michael is able to negotiate terms. Rose is restored to life with her stillborn child, and Michael is freed from his painful memories. The Michael that inhabits the alternate world remains with Cat.

Analysis: This second novel by a promising fantasy writer clearly is influenced by Robert P. Holdstock's Mythago series, begun in 1984, and probably by Thomas Burnett Swann (1928-1976). The novel, however, has an individuality and freshness all its own.

In some respects, *A Different Kingdom* is connected to Paul Kearney's earlier work, *The Way to Babylon* (1992). The Myrcans reappear, and Kearney explains that their appearance is different because considerable time has passed and they have lost their roles. Some other beings, notably the wood-wolves, also appeared in the previous book. Nevertheless, the link is tenuous, particularly in the light of the fact that *A Different Kingdom* is a reversal of the previous book's concern with maintaining order.

Kearney concerns himself directly with the modern Irish experience. *A Different Kingdom*, as may be surmised from its title, may be read as an allegory of the relatively static qualities of Ulster life and character being menaced by the wilder Catholic world. It is fair to say, however, that Kearney's later treatment of Catholicism, by no means totally unsympathetic, militates against this view.

The book has several strengths. The depiction of the 1950's farm household at first appears so strong that the fantasy cannot rival it. The characterization also is strong, and the picture of growing up in a seemingly idyllic environment is portrayed convincingly. The fey qualities of the old farm laborer Mullan, a friend to young Michael, not only seem realistic for the unmodernized time but form a prediction of the forthcoming eruption of wildness into the stable environment of the farm.

Kearney shows mastery of the individual scene. From the Myrcan slaughter of the werewolf to the scene in which the Wyrin come for the failing adult Michael, covering his girlfriend with acorns and rowan berries, the stench and force of the alternate world are vivid. Kearney's elves, werewolves, trolls, and goblins, which collectively form the Wyrin, avoid the clichés that such names impart in other fantasy works.

Above all, the reader gets a feeling for the trees and wood, which are central to the book. The wood-wolves are genuinely chilling, and the priests who are absorbed into the trees are thought in some ways to be saved as well as damned. The conclusion, defiantly pagan though by no means atheistic, is a more literary statement of such male role revisionary works as Robert Bly's *Iron John: A Book About Men* (1990).

Historical influences on the book include the Spanish conquest of America. The most prominent fictional influence is Rudyard Kipling's *The Jungle Book* (1894), particularly the analogies to the characters Ringbone, Mirkady, Dwarmo, and the Horseman.

—*Mike Dickinson*

DIMENSION OF MIRACLES

An earthling is awarded a mysterious prize far from Earth, and he has amusing troubles finding his way home

Author: Robert Sheckley (1928-   )
Genre: Science fiction—New Wave
Type of work: Novel
Time of plot: The late 1960's
Location: Earth, the Galactic Center, the planet Lursis, and alternate Earths
First published: 1968

The Plot: Carmody (no other name is given) lives an ordinary life on Earth until an alien Messenger shows up to inform him that he has won the Intergalactic Sweepstakes and to take him to collect his prize. After signing the paper accepting the prize, he is confronted by an alien named Karmod, who insists that he is the rightful winner of the prize, pointing out that Carmody could not have entered the sweepstakes because Earth is not a part of the Galactic culture. The computer that made the award admits (proclaims, in fact) that it had made an error in awarding the prize to Carmody, but the prize itself speaks up, urging Carmody not to give in, and he insists on keeping it.

Carmody then learns that he will have to find his own way home, specifically that he will have to find the Where, When, and Which of his Earth. Carmody and the prize are sent to the planet Lursis, owned and inhabited by the god Melichrone. Melichrone is the only entity that can live on Lursis for long. As the god of that planet, he has turned himself into entire races of beings, but now he is bored and can find no meaning in life. Carmody tells him that he can find meaning by helping others, such as

Carmody himself. Melichrone agrees, warning Carmody that his unique situation as prize winner has caused him to be pursued by a unique predator. He sends Carmody to another godlike figure named Maudsley.

Maudsley turns out to be a builder of worlds, one who economizes by using shabby materials and cutting corners wherever possible. He informs Carmody that he had built Earth in that fashion, recalling with some warmth the irascible old god who hired him for the construction. On Maudsley's planet, Carmody meets what appear to be an earthling scientist and his beautiful daughter. They take him to their spaceship, but before they can trap him in it, he realizes that they are constructs designed by his predator. Maudsley sends him to an Earth, cautioning that although it represents Where Earth is, Carmody still has to figure out When and on Which he belongs.

Carmody finds himself in the Mesozoic era, where he meets a family of talking tyrannosaurs. They are willing to accept the bizarre concept of a talking mammal, and Carmody chats with them, trying not to mention that they will become extinct, until he is met by an Internal Revenue Service agent who turns out to be his predator in another guise. Fleeing the predator, he encounters Clyde Beedle Seethwright, who offers to send him to the correct When so that he can determine Which Earth is his.

Carmody's next destination is the city of Bellwether, which is warm and comforting. Carmody finds it too much so, like a smothering mother, and calls to Seethwright to send him elsewhere. He next finds himself in a world where people talk in the catch phrases of commercials. This is obviously not his world either, so he has Seethwright send him to another world. That world is oppressive and full of garbage, noise, and violence. It is in fact his world, but Carmody gets Seethwright to take him out of it, to leave him on a perpetual quest, forever accompanied by his prize and pursued by his predator.

Analysis: Like its predecessor, *Mindswap* (1966), *Dimension of Miracles* presents an innocent protagonist faced with a series of satirical horrors. *Mindswap* is largely social and literary in its satire; *Dimension of Miracles* is more metaphysical and theological. From the Messenger who takes Carmody to his prize to the rescuer who gets him out at the end, the beings Carmody encounters all lecture him on the philosophical significance of his situation. The book in fact presents the reader with actual gods, including the corner-cutting builder of Earth and the biblical deity, presented as a lovable crank. In contrast to this presentation of theological figures, the conclusion of the story can be seen as a kind of Zen epiphany, in which Carmody decides to live in the moment because that is all that he, or anyone, has.

Mindswap places its protagonist in a number of familiar, in fact clichéd, literary backgrounds, but *Dimension of Miracles* has only one such scene, where Carmody meets the stereotyped science-fictional scientist and his beautiful daughter. Perhaps their turning out to be badly made frauds, sent to entrap Carmody, represents the author's view of such fictions. There may also be a literary analogy in the god Melichrone. Readers learn that Melichrone's creations have a single flaw: He is lame, and therefore so are all of his creations, but neither he nor they know it. This can be seen as a comment on some literary creators.

In its wry fictional treatment of supposedly serious theological themes, *Dimension of Miracles* stands in a tradition that stretches from the comedies of Aristophanes to Salman Rushdie's *The Satanic Verses* (1988). Less morally outraged than Mark Twain's *The Mysterious Stranger* (1916) and more substantial than "shaggy god stories" (Michael Moorcock's term) in which the punch line tells readers that a minor character is really God or the supposed "last survivors on Earth" are Adam and Eve, *Dimension of Miracles* may find its closest parallels in the writings of Voltaire and Jorge Luis Borges. The conclusion, in which the returning Carmody rejects his own world, may remind readers of Jonathan Swift's *Gulliver's Travels* (1726).

Dimension of Miracles represents a sort of climax in Robert Sheckley's career. Like its predecessors, it won no awards and soon went out of print, but it retains a following of readers who consider it Sheckley's best work or even one of the best satires the field has ever produced. Sheckley published no further novels until the puzzling *Options* (1975).   —*Arthur D. Hlavaty*

DINNER AT DEVIANT'S PALACE

Greg Rivas, a violinist and former tough guy in a bombed-out Los Angeles, comes head to head with a psychic vampire whose intended victim is Earth itself

Author: Tim Powers (1952-   )
Genre: Science fiction—post-holocaust
Type of work: Novel
Time of plot: More than a century after the holocaust; about 2100
Location: Los Angeles, California, and environs
First published: 1985

The Plot: More than a century after a global thermonuclear war, Gregorio Rivas makes his living in post-apocalypse Los Angeles as a violinist with a regular nightclub act. In his youth, Rivas had been seduced by the cult of Norton Jaybush, whose worshipers are called Jaybirds. Later, he became a redeemer, rescuing cult members for a price. He is now living on his fading reputation and looking forward with growing fear to an impoverished middle age. Fate pulls him back into the dangerous life of a redeemer when Irwin Barrows, father of Rivas' one-time sweetheart, Urania, asks Rivas to rescue Urania from the Jaybush cult. Rivas takes the job, even though it requires that he pretend to join the cult himself.

Jaybush is a mysterious figure whose cult members practice a devastating ritual that literally destroys the mind if undergone too many times. Jaybirds disappear into the Holy City (Irvine) and are never seen again.

Deviant's Palace is an improbable and deadly nightclub in Venice, home to many of the dregs of post-holocaust Californian society, including an astounding variety of mutants. The stories told about Deviant's Palace are too bizarre to be believed, but Rivas, who spent much of his reckless youth in Venice, now studiously avoids the place. Rivas' attempt to free Urania from the Jaybush cult, however, leads him to the Holy City, back to Venice, and, as the title indicates, to Deviant's Palace. In the process, Rivas discovers Jaybush's true identity, and he becomes custodian of the most deadly secret in the world.

Analysis: *Dinner at Deviant's Palace* is both representative of Tim Powers' work and a significant departure from his earlier novels. The plot formula is very similar to that of nearly all of his previous novels. The protagonist encounters a problem, struggles against it, and gives himself up to drugs and denial when the going gets tough, but he pulls himself together for one last try in the nick of time. The formula is acted out slightly differently in this book because the stuporous period has ended long before the book begins. Even this, however, is reminiscent of *The Drawing of the Dark* (1979); both books begin with the protagonist unwillingly revisiting his past for the sake of a woman he lost.

Despite the familiar plot, Powers breaks new ground in *Dinner at Deviant's Palace*. In contrast to *The Drawing of the Dark*, *The Anubis Gates* (1983), *On Stranger Tides* (1987), and *The Stress of Her Regard* (1989), the adversary in this book is not supernatural. There are vampiric ghosts, zombies, monsters, and beings with superhuman powers, but all of these are explained without resort to magic. In addition, the ending of *Dinner at Deviant's Palace* leaves important business unconsummated, whereas the other four books all end with the adventure finished, even if the protagonist does not get to live happily ever after. Powers may have thought that it was safer to end a science-fiction novel on an ambiguous note because science fiction deals with subject matter inherently more familiar than that of fantasy, depending as it does on laws of nature and being based on extrapolations of known society.

The main plot device of *Dinner at Deviant's Palace*, the invasion of Earth by a lone being who is powerful enough to pose a serious threat to humanity, is a bit unusual but not unique: Larry Niven used it in *World of Ptavvs* (1966). What makes *Dinner at Deviant's Palace* successful is Powers' intense prose style, particularly the careful attention to detail and consistency that characterize his writing. Powers' writing may owe some of its intense precision to his background as a poet, for poetry is a medium that cannot afford to waste words.

Despite its science-fictional theme, *Dinner at Deviant's Palace* reads much like Powers' fantasy novels. It has little in common with his earlier science-fiction novel *Forsake the Sky* (1986; previously published as *The Skies Discrowned*, 1976). In *Dinner at Deviant's Palace*, Powers creates fantastic and horrible scenes that are so shockingly vivid that it almost hurts to read them. The descriptive style and underlying worldview are similar to those of Roger Zelazny's *Roadmarks* (1979), which does not involve magic, and to Larry Niven's *The Magic Goes Away* (1978), Zelazny's *Nine Princes in Amber* (1970) and its sequels, Barry Hughart's *Bridge of Birds* (1984), and Fred Saberhagen's *Empire of the East* (1979), which do involve magic. These authors share the ability to make magical, or at least fantastic, events seem inevitable within the context of the story. Only the reader (and in some cases the protagonist) is surprised when events turn bizarre.

One of the curious things about Powers' writing is that he does not seem to have grown as a writer between publication of *The Drawing of the Dark* in 1979 and of *The Stress of Her Regard* ten years later. *Dinner at Deviant's Palace* falls into the middle of this body of work. One gets the feeling that the books of this period (disregarding *Forsake the Sky*, which was written earlier) could have been written in any order, or even that they are permutations of the same basic story. It is particularly surprising to see this failure to progress in a writer of such great technical skill. Even though Powers uses the same plot kernel in each of the five novels of the period, he does not lack for invention. All these books are stuffed with innovative ideas. *Dinner at Deviant's Palace* won the Philip K. Dick Award. —*David C. Kopaska-Merkel*

DIRK GENTLY'S HOLISTIC DETECTIVE AGENCY
and
THE LONG DARK TEA-TIME OF THE SOUL

Dirk Gently "investigates the fundamental interconnectedness of all things" as a method of solving crimes, locating missing persons, and dealing with the occasional alien or supernatural being

Author: Douglas Adams (1952-   )
Genre: Fantasy—Magical Realism
Type of work: Novels
Time of plot: The 1980's
Location: Primarily London, England
First published: *Dirk Gently's Holistic Detective Agency* (1987) and *The Long Dark Tea-Time of the Soul* (1988)

The Plot: Author Douglas Adams, who found fame with his farcical science-fiction series that began with *The Hitchhiker's Guide to the Galaxy* (1979), has blended comedy, mystery, and fantasy to create *Dirk Gently's Holistic Detective Agency* and *The Long Dark Tea-Time of the Soul*. Although nominally a series, the two books have little in common apart from the presence of offbeat private investigator Dirk Gently, Adams' wry musings on the absurdities of life, and his central theme of holism, or the fundamental interconnectedness of all things.

Dirk Gently's Holistic Detective Agency centers on the trials and tribulations of a tall, geeky computer programmer named Richard MacDuff, modeled somewhat on the author. When MacDuff's eccentric boss, Gordon Way, is mysteriously murdered, MacDuff is a prime suspect. Adams proceeds from that premise to weave a complicated tale involving a series of otherworldly occurrences and weird characters, including an alien robot, a time-traveling eccentric, and disembodied spirits. These are all eventually shown to be interconnected not only among themselves and with MacDuff, Way, and the renowned poet Samuel Taylor Coleridge but also with the very beginning of life itself on Earth.

The only person capable of sorting out this mess is Dirk Gently. Gently is in some respects the stereotypical private detective, a loner who rents space in a seedy old building, chain smokes, and jumps at the chance to do some real detective work. Gently is much quirkier than most fictional detectives, though he shares some common foibles. He has a penchant for pizza, wears a long leather coat and an ugly red hat, and is perpetually short of money and behind on his bills. Gently's unconventional outlook and holistic beliefs enable him to solve the bizarre murder.

Gently discovers that a disembodied alien spirit, whose spaceship accidentally exploded on Earth eons ago, has been moving from character to character, with a hidden agenda. This discovery brings to light the fact that Mac-Duff's beloved but dotty former professor, Reg, is actually a time traveler whose rooms at St. Cedd's College are a time machine. What the spirit seeks is a willing host who will help him use Reg's time machine to go back in time to prevent his ship's explosion. After Reg, Gently, and MacDuff agree to help the alien, however, Gently realizes that the explosion the alien hopes to avert was actually what many scientists suspect to be the very event that started life on Earth. Gently then must thwart the alien's plans and thus save humanity—with a few minor adjustments.

The title of the second book in the series, *The Long Dark Tea-Time of the Soul*, comes from the text of the third book in Adams' Hitchhiker trilogy. The reference is to an immortal being who discovers the inevitable ennui that comes with immortality, particularly on Sunday afternoons right around teatime. *The Long Dark Tea-Time of the Soul* involves several immortals as well as Gently, who is drawn inadvertently into a web of mysterious occurrences.

A harried young American, Kate Schechter, trying to catch a plane to Oslo from London's Heathrow airport, encounters a large blond man with a Nordic accent who is arguing with an uninterested flight attendant and holding up the line. After a prolonged and humorous series of discussions among the attendant, the man, and Schechter, a sudden, localized explosion lands Schechter unconscious in a hospital. After she discovers the large blond man in the same hospital, he is mysteriously removed, prompting her to investigate.

Her search results in a crossing of paths with Gently, who has come into the case from another direction. He took on a client who was then found mysteriously murdered. Before his death, the man told Gently that his life had been threatened by a seven-foot-tall, shaggy-haired creature with green eyes and horns. The creature waved a scythe and a contract. Gently took the job because he needed a new refrigerator.

Many odd coincidences later, Gently and Schechter, following parallel lines of investigation, discover that the large blond man is actually Thor, the ancient Norse god of thunder. Thor is angry with his father, Odin, an elderly one-eyed man who has sold out to a pair of greedy mortal lawyers in order to ensure his own comfort in his old age—a posh room in an English asylum with fresh linen sheets replaced daily. It was Thor's uncontrollable anger that caused the airport explosion, among many other freak and comic accidents that occur throughout the story.

The climax is reached when Thor demands to meet with Odin in Asgard, in the great hall of Valhalla, to make him account for what he has done. Gently also appears, and once again he saves the day, by finding a way to break the insidious contract, which was also responsible for his client's death.

Analysis: Adams has established a reputation as a teller of tall tales, an insightful writer about the human condition, and a purveyor of deadpan slapstick science fiction. Reflecting the high-tech obsession of the 1980's, Adams incorporates computers, cellular phones, telephone answering machines, and videocassette recorders into his narrative. He pokes fun not only at the dehumanizing effect of technology on society but also at the technology itself.

MacDuff's conversation with a police officer in *Dirk Gently's Holistic Detective Agency*, concerning his company's product, is a case in point. He asks the police officer which model of computer the police station has. Upon receiving the answer, he tells the officer that the computer does not work and never has, then suggests that the station "use it as a big paperweight."

Later, Reg admits to using his time machine to watch television programs that he missed because he cannot figure out how to program his videocassette recorder. Throughout, Adams displays an uncanny knack for pointing out modern society's frustrations and foibles, with lighthearted, humorous style.

Adams also depicts the high-tech junkies who become addicted to their toys. In *The Long Dark Tea-Time of the Soul*, Adams presents the ultimate teenage couch potato. The boy slouches in an armchair all day, watching television and surviving on a diet of Pot Noodles, Mars bars, and soft drinks. After several unsuccessful attempts to wrest the boy's attention from the television, Gently decides to pull the plug, with instantaneous and comically painful results.

Gordon Way, MacDuff's boss in *Dirk Gently's Holistic Detective Agency*, is also a high-tech junkie, addicted to his cellular telephone. Way calls everyone he knows and brainstorms at length onto their telephone answering machines. Way's secretary then periodically collects the tapes and transcribes them. When Way is murdered while talking to his sister Susan's answering machine, his ghost is burdened with unfinished business: It must complete its call to Susan before it can go to its eternal resting place.

The two novels are connected in that they both employ the character Dirk Gently. Otherwise, they are different in subject matter and approach. The first leans toward science fiction, with its time travel and alien civilizations. The second is pure fantasy, incorporating Norse mythology. Both, however, fit easily into the category of Magical Realism, as Adams takes completely fantastic situations and treats them realistically.

His central theme of holism ties together the two books, as do the author's use of slews of characters and running gags. The horse in Reg's bathroom, Gently's ongoing battle with his cleaning lady over a seriously foul refrigerator, and MacDuff's sofa, which is irrevocably stuck on the landing of his apartment building, are only a few of the many comic detours taken by Adams' rambling narrative style.

Although these two novels have been criticized by some reviewers as tangled and unsatisfying, Adams' writing provides, as always, good-natured fun. His writing style may be best summed up by his protagonist Dirk Gently: "I may not have gone where I intended to go, but I think I have ended up where I needed to be."

—*C. K. Breckenridge*

THE DISAPPEARANCE

A mysterious force divides the world into two separate realities for four years, one exclusively male, the other exclusively female

Author: Philip Wylie (1902-1971)
Genre: Science fiction—cultural exploration
Type of work: Novel
Time of plot: 1949-1953
Location: Miami, Florida, and other cities on Earth
First published: 1951

The Plot: Set in post-World War II America, Philip Wylie's *The Disappearance* concerns an Earth divided into two distinct parts, one containing only male humans and primates, the other only females. Wylie divides the book into four parts: "The Hand of God," "Armaged-

don," "The Unloved," and "Dream and Dimension." Each section details major physical and psychological developments of the catastrophe. As the chapters alternate between the male world and the female one, the characters slowly work out the science of the disappearance.

On February 14, at 4:05 P.M., Dr. William Percival Gaunt watches out his study window as his wife, Paula Gaunt, vanishes mysteriously. Simultaneously, Paula, working in the garden, watches her husband disappear. As they soon realize, all members of the opposite sex have disappeared from the respective Earths.

Dr. Gaunt's world maintains a sense of order because males occupy most of the technical and governmental jobs. Paula Gaunt's world, however, does not maintain the same sense of order. Planes are suddenly without male pilots, buses and cars without drivers, utilities without workers, and the government without representatives.

While the females work to restore supply of basic necessities such as food and water, the male world faces new dangers—a Russian nuclear attack, civil unrest, and armed raiding parties—that force the government to establish martial law. Men quickly degenerate into poor hygiene and drunkenness, and they express flagrant homosexuality, much to the dismay of conventional preachers such as Reverend Connauth. Other men, notorious womanizers such as Teddy Barker, are relieved to no longer play the game of conquest and abandonment. Still others, including Dr. Gaunt's son, Edwin, travel the globe in search of women rumored to exist in remote locations.

The women's world also faces a Russian threat, but instead of engaging in warfare, the women reach a compromise whereby Russian women share their technological expertise in exchange for the few existing American luxury goods. Like the men, the women express varied views of marriage and fidelity, ranging from one of convenience held by Berthene Connauth; to domination, as in the case of Paula Gaunt's daughter, Edwinna; to the codependent view expressed by Paula's live-in neighbor, Kate West.

Along with combatting the physical hardships faced on both worlds, the characters struggle to understand the forces that caused the disappearance. Some suggest mass hypnosis, many claim God's judgment of sin, and others, such as Jim Elliot, Gaunt's nearest neighbor, retreat into Eastern mysticism. Gaunt proposes a philosophy of "oppositeness" asserting that each individual possesses both male and female components and must come to accept and live with those psychological parts in balance. He concludes that because males dominated females for so long and females acceded to that domination, the two sexes have been living in separate worlds all along. He hypothesizes that because the psychological energies of the two sexes are no longer in balance, the two cannot exist in the same dimension. Gaunt's philosophy appears to be correct, for once the people in the two worlds start to realize their full potential and appreciate the other sex as equal humans, they are reunited.

Analysis: *The Disappearance* was published in the middle of Wylie's science-fiction years, more than a decade after his esteemed collaborative effort with Edwin Balmer, *When Worlds Collide* (1933), and a few years before his acclaimed novel *Tomorrow!* (1954), detailing the horror of nuclear war. Although *The Disappearance* includes a brief nuclear confrontation, the issues discussed in the novel have more in common with Wylie's social novels, which criticize and condemn American conventionality, than with traditional science fiction. Reviewers of the novel at its publication noted its use of superficial science fiction to convey Wylie's polemics on infidelity, the double standard of sex roles, religion, and the interdependence of males and females.

Wylie uses Gaunt as his principal mouthpiece, expressing his philosophies on everything from mysticism to survival instinct. Gaunt's family life in a Miami suburb mirrors Wylie's own, and Wylie's struggles with his father's Presbyterian religion appear in Gaunt's condemnation of Connauth's beliefs.

Wylie's strongest personal statements occur in two sections. Near the middle of the novel, Wylie launches into a treatise on sex and the duality of individual sexuality, echoing themes expressed in his earlier social works *Generation of Vipers* (1942) and *Opus 21* (1949). Wylie's other invective expresses concerns common to the postnuclear world: science without control, progress without aim, and force without reason. These themes recur throughout the science-fiction genre.

Although many of the details are autobiographical, the novel surpasses Wylie's own experiences. He has created fully realized male and female characters who speak and move with lives of their own. Through his careful creation of Paula Gaunt, he explores the fate of intelligent, highly educated women who are deprived of an equal chance for a career outside the home environment. Wylie destroys stereotypes by giving Barker, the town gigolo, intelligence and perspicacity into women's frustrations. The author shows resolution of religious conflict as Rev-

erend Connauth comes to a deeper understanding of religion as a search rather than as assertion after admitting his own infidelity and accepting his wife's forgiveness after the reunion of the sexes.

The combination of science fiction, fantasy, and social criticism give Wylie a vehicle for expressing his strong personal beliefs to a wider audience. Although the science is weak and the force causing the separation of the sexes is never fully explained, the attention to detail, characterization, and careful construction of the novel in its four parts, alternating between Dr. Gaunt's and Paula's perspectives, creates a believable world that challenges readers to question their own standards and potential.

—*Donna D. Samudio*

THE DISCWORLD SERIES

A series of adventures set on a flat world carried on the backs of four giant elephants that stand on the back of a giant turtle swimming through space

Author: Terry Pratchett (1948-   )
Genre: Fantasy—high fantasy
Type of work: Novels
Time of plot: Various times in the history of the Discworld
Location: A flat world known as the Disc or Discworld
First published: *The Colour of Magic* (1983), *The Light Fantastic* (1986), *Equal Rights* (1987), *Mort* (1987), *Sourcery* (1988), *Wyrd Sisters* (1988), *Pyramids* (1989), *Guards! Guards!* (1989), *Eric* (1990), *Moving Pictures* (1990), *Reaper Man* (1991), *Witches Abroad* (1991), *Small Gods* (1992), *Lords and Ladies* (1992), *Men at Arms* (1993), *Soul Music* (1994), and *Interesting Times* (1994)

The Plot: The Discworld novels are all set on the same imaginary world. The Great Atuin, the world-carrying turtle, has four giant elephants standing on his back, and the elephants hold up the Disc. The Disc is inhabited by a strange variety of people and creatures. Although many of the books can stand by themselves, several follow the adventures of the same characters.

The Colour of Magic introduces the Discworld as well as Rincewind, the failed Wizard. Rincewind knows only one spell, and it is so devastating that certain people are ready to kill him to keep him from speaking it. In the first novel, he befriends Two-Flower, the Discworld's first tourist to the city Ankh-Morpork. Two-Flower possesses animate and hostile Luggage made from sapient pearwood. These two have various adventures that take them across the Disc. In their adventures, they meet dryads, druids, and a variety of other characters. The novel ends with a literal cliff-hanger.

Their adventures continue in *The Light Fantastic*. The two once more go through a series of adventures before returning to Unseen University, the Disc's seat of higher education in the magical arts. There, Rincewind, with the aid of Two-Flower and the geriatric hero, Cohen the Barbarian, saves the Discworld by intoning his spell. Rincewind makes his next significant appearance in *Sourcery*, where he once again saves the Discworld, this time from a young "sourcerer." Rincewind is banished to the Dungeon Dimensions at the end of that novel, along with the Luggage. He resurfaces in *Eric*, when he is summoned accidentally, instead of a demon. In a variation of the three wishes plot, Rincewind and Eric travel through time and Hell before they find a possible way home. Rincewind also appears in *Interesting Times*. In this novel, he is part of a culture clash between the "civilized" West and the "barbaric" East.

The second major figure featured in Discworld is Granny Weatherwax, the best witch on the Discworld. She is introduced in *Equal Rights* as she undergoes a personal crusade to get a young girl with magical abilities enrolled into the all-male Unseen University. She is aided by a wizard's staff and finally succeeds. She next appears in *Wyrd Sisters*, with two other witches, Nanny Ogg and Magrat Garlick. In a plot that borrows heavily from *Macbeth*, *Hamlet*, and several fairy tales, the three witches restore a young man to the throne of Lancre.

The witches next appear in *Witches Abroad*. They head to the city of Genua to stop an evil fairy godmother from forcing a terrible marriage on the young Emberella. They encounter many strange people along the way, including dwarves, vampires, and a voodoo witch. They finally reach Genua and liberate Emberella and the city from the grip of the evil fairy godmother. They return to their home of Lancre in *Lords and Ladies*, the plot of which is a variation on *A Midsummer Night's Dream*. The witches must stop the elf queen from invading the Disc and marrying King Verence, who is now betrothed to Magrat. The novel ends with Magrat's marriage to the king. This novel also reveals Granny Weatherwax's childhood sweetheart.

The third featured character in the series is Death. The Discworld's Death follows the typical stereotype, complete with black cowl and scythe. Death makes an appearance in every novel and is a main character in several. In *Mort*, Death adopts an apprentice so he can take a vacation. The apprentice, Mort, is not quite up to the job and saves someone who is meant to die. Eventually, Death has to return. Mort goes back to the land of living with Death's adopted daughter, Ysabel.

In *Reaper Man*, Death retires to live among mortals, taking the job of a corn reaper. In a story reminiscent of the legend of John Henry, he battles a mechanical reaper and wins. He eventually has to battle his replacement and take up the mantle of Death once again. The other plot in this novel deals with Windle Poons, a deceased wizard, who suddenly finds himself undead following Death's retirement. He eventually winds up saving the city of Ankh-Morpork from a force that destroys cities.

Death plays a prominent role in *Soul Music* as well. After Mort and Ysabel die in an accident, Death abandons his post. This leaves his position open; his granddaughter, Susan, is drafted for the job. At the same time, a young man named Imp, later Buddy, travels to Ankh-Morpork to become a musician. Their two fates become intertwined as Buddy introduces Music With Rocks In It to the Discworld. Eventually, Death returns to save Buddy and Susan and put things right.

Pyramids is one of the independent novels. In this novel, Teppic, while in training to be an assassin, suddenly finds himself the pharaoh of the kingdom of Djelibeybi. The people of the kingdom believe that their pharaoh is a god, and Teppic becomes godlike. Dios, the high priest, has been the real power behind the throne for years, and Teppic has to go up against him and all the old gods to save Djelibeybi.

Guards! Guards! features members of Ankh-Morpork's city watch. Captain Vimes, Sergeant Colon, Nobby, and others do their best to survive in the Disc's meanest and biggest city and still do their jobs. In this case, they have to deal with a cult that summons up a dragon that terrorizes the city.

Moving Pictures is Terry Pratchett's spoof of Hollywood. In this novel, a leakage from another dimension causes a strange effect on residents of the Disc: They suddenly become actors, directors, and agents. The leakage is potentially destructive and Victor, the hero of the novel, is forced to close the gate between the two worlds.

Small Gods is the story of Brutha, the only true believer in the Great God Om, who appears to Brutha in the shape of a turtle. Brutha is the only one who can hear his god, and he does not quite believe it. The false followers of Om have created a huge empire that is controlled by Vorbis. Vorbis is more interested in keeping power than believing in a god. He uses Brutha to defeat a neighboring power. As Vorbis is about to kill Brutha, Om manages to save his one believer. Everyone then believes in Om, and Brutha becomes the new spiritual leader of the empire.

In *Men at Arms*, the guards from the city watch are back to solve the mystery of a stolen "gonne" (gun) from the Assassins' Guild and the mysterious deaths of several people. With new recruits, such as a dwarf, a troll, and a female werewolf, the guards solve the murder and catch the villain.

Analysis: Terry Pratchett introduced a flat world in the science-fiction novel *Strata* (1981). *The Colour of Magic* and the following Discworld series have been more successful, launching Pratchett onto international best-seller lists.

As many critics have stated, Pratchett is an excellent parodist, making fun of and having fun with a wide range of fantasy, literary, and popular subjects. Cohen the Barbarian, the geriatric hero, is a perfect parody of Robert Howard's Conan. Pratchett does a parody of Shakespeare in *Wyrd Sisters* and *Lords and Ladies*. Emberella, the Discworld version of Cinderella, appears in *Witches Abroad*. *Soul Music* lampoons rock and roll music, and *Moving Pictures* takes on Hollywood. Every novel parodies some literary or fantasy convention.

Another reason for the popularity of the series is its collection of zany characters. Pratchett uses favorite characters throughout the series to provide a sense of continuity. Death appears in every novel. The Librarian, who was changed into an orangutan through a magical accident, also appears in most of the books. Pratchett does not always worry about characterization, and some of the books are little more than lengthy gags. Strangely, the most developed character in the series, besides Granny Weatherwax, is Death. Death is more human than many of the other inhabitants of this world. Pratchett has written other books that have the same sense of humor, but the Discworld series remains his most popular work.

—P. Andrew Miller

THE DISPOSSESSED

Shevek, a physicist raised in an anarchist society, fulfills a lifelong quest to bridge two worlds, two theories of time, and two sets of obligations—to himself and to community

Author: Ursula K. Le Guin (1929-   )
Genre: Science fiction—utopia
Type of work: Novel

Time of plot: Several hundred years in the future
Location: Anarres and Urras, planets orbiting Tau Ceti
First published: 1974

The Plot: *The Dispossessed: An Ambiguous Utopia* is one of several of Ursula Le Guin's works chronicling the evolution of a "League of all Worlds" governed by principles superior to those of known political and colonial systems. Although *The Dispossessed* takes place in the League's prehistory, the novel's loving portrait of a working anarchist society on one world develops in detail the principles of noncoercive social organization.

The novel chronicles the life of Shevek, a physicist reared on a world settled by the followers of an anarchist philosopher, Odo. The Odonians, "bought off" 170 years before Shevek's time with an offer to settle their mother planet's arid moon, Anarres, live without laws, according to the apparently irreconcilable principles of absolute individual freedom and absolute commitment to the good of the community. Anarresti social order is maintained primarily by education, which inculcates a horror of "egoizing." The Anarresti live in isolation from their mother planet, Urras, a lush world that Anarresti education demonizes as a place of injustice and evil.

Through a series of struggles, Shevek strives to balance loyalty to the society that formed him with rebellion against subtle conformist pressures that stifle his ambitious work in theoretical physics. The conflict climaxes after a long famine, during which Shevek accepts four years of separation from his wife and his work to perform manual labor in his planet's harshest desert. After this trial of physical, emotional, and intellectual self-denial, Shevek vows, "by damn, I will do my own work for a while now!"

That work has been kept alive, ironically, through extended contact with the physicists of the mother planet, Urras—that is, with despised "propertarians." After his desert ordeal, Shevek accepts a standing invitation based on his groundbreaking physics and becomes the first Anarresti in 170 years to visit the mother planet. In the face of intense opposition, he vows to "go to Urras and break down walls."

On Urras, Shevek is treated as an honored but subtly controlled guest, kept from any genuine contact with the poor. His hosts are determined to "buy" him. They believe that his work, once completed, will bring them wealth, power, and prestige. Shevek moves from admiring awe and a kind of racial homesickness for the lush mother planet to revulsion against a social world dominated by competitive struggles for power and wealth.

When a chance comes to lend support to the poor people of Ai-Io, the wealthy host-nation, Shevek seizes it, traveling secretly to the slums and leading a demonstration against an unjust war. This self-liberation from a luxurious "prison" comes in the wake of the fulfillment of Shevek's scientific work: completion of a General Temporal Theory that unites apparently irreconcilable theories about time.

The antiwar demonstration, climaxing with Shevek's speech urging renewed Odonian revolt, is broken up by a military crackdown. Shevek hides for three days in a basement with a mortally wounded demonstrator who dies in Shevek's care. Following this near-death descent, Shevek emerges suddenly in the Terran (Earth) Embassy, where he gains asylum and arranges for his theory to be broadcast to all worlds, thus eluding his hosts' desire to possess it and enabling instantaneous communication between the "nine known worlds." In a final wall-breaking action, Shevek agrees to let a young man from Hain, oldest of the known inhabited worlds, accompany him home to Anarres.

Analysis: Like most of Le Guin's heroes, Shevek embodies the author's imaginative quest to balance poles of paradox. In physics, his quest is to reconcile sequency, "the arrow of time," and simultaneity, "the circle of time"—that is, becoming and being. His General Temporal Theory, a restatement of Odo's dictum, "true voyage is return," asserts that "you *can* go home again . . . so long as you understand that home is a place where you have never been." A well-lived life comes full circle, linking past and future by fulfilling long-term promises, but also gets somewhere, effecting meaningful change.

The novel's structure embodies this gnomic principle. Odd-numbered chapters chronicle Shevek's sojourn on the mother planet Urras; even-numbered chapters bring his life on Anarres from infancy to the moment he decides that he must go to Urras. The two narratives merge in chapter 13, which anticipates Shevek's return home to an Anarres transformed by his rebellious journey—that is, to a place he has never been.

Le Guin has voiced the hope that science fiction can achieve the kind of idiosyncratic characterization championed by Virginia Woolf and widely considered integral to realistic fiction. *The Dispossessed*, however, reflects a different imaginative goal, indeed a passion, common to virtually all of Le Guin's work: to imagine an ideal person—in this case, as the embodiment of a nearly ideal society. "What is it like," asks the Terran ambassador Keng, "what can it be like, the society that made you? . . .

you are not like other men."

Although Le Guin is not much interested in Christian paradigms, she is keenly conscious of archetypal formulations of the hero's journey, and she quite pointedly sends Shevek to hell and back on both worlds. His sojourn in "the dust" during the famine on Anarres is one hell. Out of the long separation comes renewed commitment—to marriage, to work, and to continuing the Anarresti revolution. On Urras, Shevek's quest to "break down walls" is consummated by his three-day basement ordeal, which he equates with hell. It is after rising from this depth that Shevek releases his theory, thus extending the blessings of communication and brotherhood that are "the Promise" of Anarres.   —*Andrew Sprung*

DO ANDROIDS DREAM OF ELECTRIC SHEEP?

Rick Deckard must find and kill a group of androids who have escaped from a colony on Mars and come to Earth

Author: Philip K. Dick (1928-1982)
Genre: Science fiction—post-holocaust
Type of work: Novel
Time of plot: 1992
Location: The San Francisco Bay Area
First published: 1968

The Plot: *Do Androids Dream of Electric Sheep?* recounts a day in the life of bounty hunter Rick Deckard. The action begins on the morning of January 3, 1992, as Deckard and his wife, Iran, wake up in their apartment; it concludes the following morning, as an exhausted Deckard returns to bed. In that twenty-four-hour period, Deckard faces the greatest challenge he has ever encountered: He must "retire" a rogue band of "organic androids" (or "andys," as they are called) of a design so advanced that they are almost indistinguishable from human beings. His task is complicated by his attraction for another android, Rachael Rosen, who tries to prevent him from carrying out his mission.

The story is set in a gray world devastated by "World War Terminus" and the resulting radioactive fallout, which is slowly depopulating the planet. Many people have left to settle in a colony on Mars, where androids are employed for hard labor, domestic service, and other purposes. In making their escape from Mars and servitude, the rogue andys that Deckard is to retire killed a number of humans. The people who remain on Earth have witnessed the extinction of many animal species. Possession of an animal—a horse, a sheep, or even a cat—confers status; for those who cannot afford the real thing, artificial animals are available. Deckard himself has an electric sheep but greatly desires to own a living creature. That is the primary motivation in his quest: The bounty he earns of $1,000 per andy will enable him to buy a genuine animal.

Like a knight in a medieval romance, Deckard undergoes a series of trials as he retires the andys one by one. Nothing is as it first appears to be. A Soviet policeman turns out to be one of the andys in disguise. Another bounty hunter, Phil Resch, is falsely identified as an android by a San Francisco police inspector—himself an android—who hopes that Resch and Deckard will kill each other. Most mutable and devious of all is Rachael Rosen, who seduces Deckard, then calmly tells him that he will be unable to continue as a bounty hunter; no one ever has after being with her. Deckard, however, proves her wrong. Although he cannot bring himself to kill Rosen, he completes his task, retiring the last three fugitive andys after his tryst with her.

The novel ends on a note of reconciliation and domesticity. Deckard returns home to his wife. They had argued to start the day, but now Iran greets him warmly, fussing over him until he falls asleep. The last line in the book is a celebration of everyday human routine: Iran, "feeling better, fixed herself at last a cup of black, hot coffee."

Analysis: One of Philip K. Dick's recurring themes figures prominently in *Do Androids Dream of Electric Sheep?* This theme is identified in Dick's 1978 lecture, "How to Build a Universe That Doesn't Fall Apart Two Days Later," collected in *The Shifting Realities of Philip K. Dick: Selected Literary and Philosophical Writings* (1995), edited by Lawrence Sutin. In that lecture, Dick observes that throughout his career he has been preoccupied with the question, "What constitutes the authentic human being?" Dick often explores this question in novels and stories featuring androids or other constructs closely resembling human beings. These include the novels *The Simulacra* (1964) and *We Can Build You* (1972) and stories such as "The Electric Ant" (1969).

In *Do Androids Dream of Electric Sheep?*, Dick imagines a near future in which successive generations of androids become ever more sophisticated in their mimicry of humans. The model that Deckard must retire, the Nexus-6, is the most advanced yet. There remains one crucial difference between humans and androids: empathy. Androids can learn to mimic human concern, but they do not genuinely feel empathy for other creatures. Deckard employs a psychological/physiological test, the Voigt-Kampff Altered Scale, that detects the absence of empathy in the microseconds before it can be faked.

This emphasis on empathy as the defining human characteristic runs throughout the novel. It is poignantly embodied in the "chickenhead" John Isidore ("chickenhead" being a derogatory term for humans who, as a result of the fallout, lack normal intellectual capacities). Isidore innocently befriends three of the fugitive andys, then watches in horror as they gratuitously cut the legs off a spider. Empathy also is at the core of the quasi-religious movement known as Mercerism, in which both Deckard and Iran participate. So intense is the identification experienced by communicants in "fusion" with the archetypal figure of Wilbur Mercer that they sometimes emerge from a session with wounds inflicted by rocks thrown at Mercer, rather like Christian saints who receive the stigmata.

Dick's characters, however, are far from sainthood. The most important lesson Deckard learns in his long day is imparted to him in a revelation from Mercer. Deckard, appalled by the killing, wonders if he can finish the job. He explains later to Iran, "Mercer said it was wrong but I should do it anyhow." As a character recognizes in another Dick novel, *The Man in the High Castle* (1962), "There is evil! . . . It's an ingredient in us. In the world." Acknowledging that, one does the best one can.

Many people know the story of *Do Androids Dream of Electric Sheep?* not from the novel itself but from the film based on it, *Blade Runner* (1982). The film departs from the book in many ways, most conspicuously in its treatment of the protagonist. Dick's Deckard is a bounty hunter but also a husband. In the film, Deckard (played by Harrison Ford) is a loner, a futuristic private eye. Dick's final message is a modest affirmation of human virtues; the film's conclusion is both cynical and romanticized, showing Deckard with the beautiful android. As for empathy, that theme is turned upside down: Mercerism disappears from the story altogether, and Deckard survives only because the leader of the androids (or "replicants," as they are called in the film), his mortal foe, shows compassion for him.   *—John Wilson*

DR. BLOODMONEY

After a nuclear war, a group of survivors gathers in a small northern California town to rebuild their lives and create a viable community

Author: Philip K. Dick (1928-1982)
Genre: Science fiction—post-holocaust

Type of work: Novel
Time of plot: 1981 and several years following
Location: Berkeley, California, and Marin County, California
First published: 1965

The Plot: *Dr. Bloodmoney: Or, How We Got Along After the Bomb* is a good example of Philip K. Dick's masterful control of complex plotting, moving from the banal to the extraordinary in deft, swift strokes. The novel is also an example of Dick's multifocused plotting, which begins by delineating the separate, idiosyncratic lives of several characters who do not initially know one another but whose lives eventually will be intimately bound together.

The story begins in 1981, with introductions quickly provided of virtually all the characters who will find their lives connected after the nuclear war. The story moves quickly, from its quotidian beginning one morning in Berkeley, California, to the nuclear blast that demolishes the city, to the post-holocaust setting in rustic West Marin County, north and west of Berkeley. The lives of the many characters intertwine as they attempt to rebuild their lives in the post-holocaust world.

The primary characters are television repairman Stuart McConchie; Hoppy Harrington, who was born without arms or legs but has managed to develop telekinetic powers, or the ability to move objects with his mind; Walt Dangerfield, an astronaut trapped alone in his spaceship as it endlessly circles Earth; Bonny Keller, who conceived her child, Edie, on the day of the nuclear attack; Bill Keller, Edie's tiny, wizened twin brother who lives as a homunculus within her abdominal cavity and who telepathically communicates with her; Dr. Stockstill, one of the few benevolent psychiatrists depicted in Dick's fiction; and nuclear scientist Dr. Bruno Bluthgeld, the "Dr. Bloodmoney" alluded to in the novel's title. Strangely enough, it is Walt Dangerfield, the astronaut trapped in orbit by the nuclear war (there is no way to bring him down), who provides the means of bonding the fragmented postwar society. Using the vast musical and literary holdings on board the satellite, Dangerfield becomes a disc jockey. The community meets to listen during his daily appearance as he orbits Earth.

In an unpredictable development, it is Hoppy Harrington who becomes the antagonist as he slowly refines his telekinetic powers. Even though he uses his power to do apparent good—he kills the unstable Dr. Bluthgeld—he also begins to use his powers to control others, even seeking to destroy Walt Dangerfield and usurp his

place in the hearts and minds of the community. The resolution of this tension comes from a highly unlikely hero, Bill Keller. Hoppy learns that Edie Keller carries the homunculus within her, and to his horror he learns that Bill Keller can communicate with the dead. He plots to kill Bill by using his power to draw Bill from within Edie's body, knowing that Bill is unable to survive outside her. Hoppy's plan backfires. With his body freed from Edie's, Bill transmigrates his soul into the body of Hoppy Harrington and casts the soul of Hoppy into his own dying, wizened body. With Dangerfield's life saved, the health of the community seems ensured.

Analysis: *Dr. Bloodmoney* was one of four novels Dick completed in 1963 and one of twelve completed between 1962 and 1964, a period of prodigious output. He was, at this time, writing some of his finest science fiction. He recently had won the Hugo Award in 1963 for best science-fiction novel of the year for his alternate history story, *The Man in the High Castle* (1962), the book for which he is perhaps best known.

The post-nuclear holocaust novel had emerged clearly as an important subgenre of science fiction by the time Dick's novel was published by Ace Books in 1965. The title itself is the result of a marketing ploy by Ace, a not very subtle allusion to Stanley Kubrick's highly successful 1964 film about nuclear war, *Dr. Strangelove: Or, How I Learned to Stop Worrying and Love the Bomb*. Dick's original title for the novel was *In Earth's Diurnal Course*, but the novel does have a character named Dr. Bluthgeld, translatable as "Bloodmoney."

The late 1950's and early 1960's had seen many fine post-holocaust novels published, among the most notable of which are Nevil Shute's *On the Beach* (1957), Mordecai Roshwald's *Level 7* (1959), Pat Frank's *Alas, Babylon* (1959), Walter M. Miller, Jr.'s classic *A Canticle for Leibowitz* (1960), and Robert A. Heinlein's *Farnham's Freehold* (1964). *Dr. Bloodmoney* shares at least a superficial similarity with Frank's *Alas, Babylon*. Both feature small, idyllic, agrarian communities that emerge after the holocaust. Such communities would seem to be possible only after the technocratic, industrial world is purged by a massive nuclear war. In contrast to Frank's post-holocaust world, however, Dick strenuously avoided plotting his book as an adventure story, using instead his unusual multifocused approach, weaving explorations of his many characters' complex psychologies and personal relationships into a story that details the re-formation of civil society in small, decentralized communities.

Dick himself believed *Dr. Bloodmoney* to be a unique

novel precisely because of the way in which he imagined the post-holocaust world: Horses are used to pull automobiles, for example, and as a result of radiation, rodents have mutated into highly intelligent creatures capable of disabling the traps humans set for them. Critical regard for the novel generally is very positive, as it is seen as one of Dick's most accessible books and also one of his most provocative ones. Much of Dick's fiction is decidedly pessimistic. This novel, ironically, emerges as strangely optimistic in outlook.   —*Samuel J. Umland*

DOCTOR RAT

The fanatical Doctor Rat conducts hideous experiments on animals while an animal revolt leads to an apocalyptic confrontation with humans that wipes out animal life on the planet

Author: William Kotzwinkle (1938-   )
Genre: Fantasy—animal fantasy
Type of work: Novel
Time of plot: The late twentieth century
Location: Earth
First published: 1976

The Plot: The primary narrative track follows the eponymous Doctor Rat as he tries to explain, justify, and defend the hideous experiments he is conducting in collaboration with some unseen but omnipotent human agency. The alternative track is a composite of the thoughts of various animals involved in a rebellion against manipulative technology. The animals strive to reaffirm their primal connection to the landscape of the planet and its life-giving properties.

Although he is given the physical attributes of a rodent, Doctor Rat acts and thinks like a man of the late twentieth century, measuring everything in terms of commercial success. He is devoid of compassion, reeks of machismo, and is blind to his own defects. He represents individualism gone amok, is capable of the most circumlocutory rationalizations to support his actions, and is truly a "rat" in terms of ethical behavior.

The various species of animals in peril, on the other hand, are conceived in terms of traits that traditionally have defined the truly humane—empathy, understanding, self-sacrifice, kindness, and consideration. They are drawn as genuinely spiritual creatures in the sense of feeling a connection to a cosmic, universal consciousness that lends a significance to their lives and ennobles their existence.

The narrative proceeds by juxtaposing Doctor Rat's increasingly frantic, first-person accounts of his attempts to control the situation in the laboratory with different representatives of the wilderness (that is, a free state) awakening to a call to their particular nature. The eventual destruction of the entire animal population through the employment of the latest technological advances in war-making machinery is seen by Doctor Rat as a "final solution" that even he recognizes as a mark of failure, because it leaves "a sort of lonely feeling" out there.

Analysis: In describing the origins of his consciousness as a writer, William Kotzwinkle recalls holding a tadpole and thinking it "was the most exquisite thing I ever felt." His earliest work, children's books such as *The Firemen* (1969) and *Elephant Boy: A Story of the Stone Age* (1970), are efforts to establish a domain of wonder that expresses this kind of innocent joy. By the mid-1970's, however, he had moved to rural Canada, a remote region under assault by speculative developers. He had a series of nightmares in which "animals came to me, night after night, telling me, 'We've got something to say!'" This mystic vision led to *Doctor Rat*, a book designed to demonstrate "a dangerous split between us and our animal nature."

Doctor Rat is an allegory in the classic sense, arranged as a commentary on late twentieth century life in which symbolic representation reinforces an argument by establishing a different perspective from which to consider social ills. More specifically, it is a fierce "ecofable" joining the form of the medieval beast tale to the cautionary message of an ecological sermon. The idea of an allegory is a direct derivation from Kotzwinkle's use of nonhuman characters in his books for young readers. He deepens the admirable qualities often associated with animals in instructive children's literature so that the gravity and dignity the animals exhibit is a direct commentary on the absence of these attributes in many humans. Further, the novel is an examination of the sources of evil and of its most contemporary manifestations. This subject is charged with emotional complexity, and Kotzwinkle's angle of attack makes it possible for him to cover some issues that require a special sensitivity.

Doctor Rat himself is clearly derived from the experiences of Nazi Germany, and his compulsive energy, his manic hustling, and his vicious inclination to crush all forms of opposition arouse the same lurid fascination attendant on the leaders of Hitler's Third Reich. Kotzwinkle has maintained that "Nazism is always in the air. . . . This is our reality," and Doctor Rat is delineated not as a theoretician of genocide—that is, an understandable if loathsome monster—but as a willing functionary whose zeal, ingenuity, and commitment illustrate the mechanics of genocidal operations. As Kotzwinkle develops the laboratory setting, it becomes clear that he is not trying to re-create the horror of the concentration camp but instead is attempting to indicate through symbolic suggestion that this hideous, misconstrued world is closer to postmodern reality than one might care to admit.

Doctor Rat thrives in this situation, having developed a bogus mystique in which science is elevated into a kind of secular religion, albeit one devoid of any spiritual qualities. He uses a perverse logic linking rigorous analyses and suspect premises to explain and justify everything. His own position as a controlled servant to a higher power is cast as a part of a scientific method, with academic apparatus seeming to satisfy all moral requirements. His parodic abuse of quasi-scientific jargon is set against the language of the animals, who speak in heightened, poetic tones reflecting a primal beauty linked to a former state of grandeur. For Kotzwinkle, the almost ethereal transmission of thought and feeling among the animals recalls an ethos of enchantment that he fears is vanishing from the modern world. The goal of much of his writing is to regain this condition of existence.

Like many social allegories, *Doctor Rat* has multiple satiric thrusts, concentrating on the horror of the laboratory but extending beyond to the human society Kotzwinkle contends is responsible for the destruction of anything that does not fit a narrow scale of value. Narcotized animals await their next fix, their inertia a comment on the fading 1960's hippie dream; others are obsessed with style and dress; others pursue the pleasures of the flesh to the exclusion of any other kind of relationship. These sad examples of narcissistic self-absorption are symptomatic of the collapse of the social contract. At the root of this, Kotzwinkle contends, is a failure to see that the most admirable elements in all forms of life are shared by many species. His allegorical approach permits a consideration of what is crucial to spiritual fulfillment. Its success was ratified by an award for best novel from the third World Fantasy Convention.

—Leon Lewis

DONOVAN'S BRAIN

A scientist who tries to keep a human brain alive finds that it is growing to an enormous size and seizing control of his mind through telepathy

Author: Curt Siodmak (1902-   )
Genre: Science fiction—cautionary
Type of work: Novel
Time of plot: Approximately 1940
Location: Arizona and Los Angeles, California
First published: 1943

The Plot: Patrick Cory, a middle-aged doctor, is devoting his life to the study of animal brains. The novel consists of a journal of his records. He has a patient, loving wife named Janice whose private fortune enables him to live in seclusion and spend his waking hours in his laboratory.

The crash of a private airplane gives him an opportunity to experiment with a human brain. One of the victims is Warren Horace Donovan, a business tycoon notorious for his ruthless methods. Cory keeps Donovan's brain alive in a vat, with nutrient-fortified blood pumped through the brain tissue.

Donovan's brain not only survives but grows larger and larger, until it threatens to fill its entire vat. The brain is free of the requirements of a normal brain of regulating bodily functions and attending to everyday concerns; thus it has a superhuman ability to concentrate. Cory is able to communicate with the brain by tapping messages on the glass in Morse code. The brain develops the capability of sending messages to Cory through telepathy. Cory's alcoholic colleague Dr. Schratt warns against the possible dangers of such inhumane and unorthodox experimentation. Cory, however, is so obsessed with his quest for scientific knowledge that he is willing to risk his soul.

Cory finds that he is falling under Donovan's power and losing his own identity. He gains access to Donovan's bank accounts and safe-deposit box by knowing certain aliases and being able to duplicate signatures perfectly. He has a fortune at his disposal but is unable to enjoy it because his thoughts and actions are controlled by the increasingly powerful brain. His main mission as Donovan's minion is to save the life of a vicious murderer named Cyril Hinds, the son of a man to whom Donovan feels obligated. In order to save Hinds, Cory must murder an innocent thirteen-year-old girl who is scheduled to testify against Hinds at his murder trial.

Under Donovan's spell, Cory finds himself trying to run down the girl with his car. The attempt fails. Cory realizes that he must destroy the brain but feels helpless to regain his old identity. The brain can read minds and has the ability to kill anyone who attacks it or tries to shut off the motors that keep it alive.

Cory recovers his sanity through the devotion and understanding of his wife, who helps him to see that human love is more important than esoteric knowledge. Returning to his Arizona laboratory, Cory discovers that Dr. Schratt has sacrificed his life to destroy the brain by dragging the hideous pulsating mass of tissue out of its nest of tubes. Cory gives up his research to live the simple life of a rural doctor.

Analysis: *Donovan's Brain* is one of many stories about a scientist who has gone mad through obsession with the pursuit of knowledge that will give him power over nature. The so-called "mad scientist" has become a stock figure in commercial fiction and motion pictures. Early prototypes occur in Johann Wolfgang von Goethe's drama *Faust* (1808), Mary Shelley's romantic novel *Frankenstein: Or, The Modern Prometheus* (1818), Nathaniel Hawthorne's short story "Rappaccini's Daughter" (1844), and H. G. Wells's novel *The Island of Dr. Moreau* (1896). The ancient Greeks, however, offered much earlier examples in their mythology of what they called hubris, excessive human pride that was invariably punished by the gods.

Curt Siodmak had a better scientific background than most authors of "mad scientist" novels, and as a result *Donovan's Brain* is plausible. The fictional device of writing his novel in the form of a scientist's journal is effective. Siodmak's knowledge of science enabled him to sprinkle his story with medical terminology that gives it verisimilitude. The narrator, Dr. Cory, appears to be talking to himself in his journal, making the reader feel like an eavesdropper.

Although Siodmak published many novels, both in Germany and in the United States, he is best remembered for *Donovan's Brain*. The novel has been adapted to the motion picture screen several times. The explanation for the story's continued popularity seems to be that it foreshadows a real threat to the human race. The book was published before the development of modern computers. It has since become obvious that humans can invent machines that outperform their creators in many mental activities. Some hypothetical scenarios have been dramatized in such futuristic films as *2001: A Space Odyssey* (1968), in which a supercomputer goes insane, and in *The Terminator* (1984), in which robots masterminded by artificial brains have taken over the world and are trying to exterminate humankind.

Donovan's Brain also contains an implicit warning against reckless experimentation with biological science. This branch of scientific investigation presents other threats, including doomsday-type biological warfare and devastating new life-forms produced by irresponsible genetic tampering.

Some might argue that Siodmak illustrates his thesis with what logicians call a "straw man." What might have happened if, instead of the brain of a ruthless man, Cory had obtained the brain of a benevolent genius such as Albert Einstein? Why should anyone assume that machines possessing superhuman intelligence would necessarily become wicked and destructive? Would it not be possible, in fact, to invent artificial brains that were free of human failings? Others would argue that it is obvious that there are creative and destructive machines, just as there are creative and destructive human beings. Fanciful literary creations such as *Donovan's Brain* serve a useful purpose by reiterating age-old warnings that humans are only part of nature and can attempt to impose complete mastery over nature only at their own peril.

—*Bill Delaney*

DOOMSDAY BOOK

While a time-traveling historian is stranded in England during the Black Death, her twenty-first century colleagues battle their own epidemic and seek to rescue her

Author: Connie Willis (1945-   )
Genre: Science fiction—time travel
Type of work: Novel
Time of plot: December, 2054-January, 2055, and 1348
Location: Oxford, England, and Ashencote, a nearby village
First published: 1992

The Plot: Kivrin Engle, a brilliant and determined young woman, is the first historian to journey back to the Middle Ages. She makes the trip despite the misgivings of her teacher and mentor, Mr. Dunworthy. His anxieties seem justified when the technician in charge of the time "net" mumbles that something is wrong and then collapses from a deadly new strain of influenza shortly after sending Kivrin to the past. What gradually becomes clear is that Kivrin has been infected with that same flu and sent not to 1320, as intended, but to 1348, the year the Black Death began to ravage England.

Unbeknown to her, Kivrin's arrival in the past is witnessed by an illiterate but saintly priest, Father Roche, who brings the sick and delirious woman, whom he regards as a messenger from heaven, to the castle of his lord. Kivrin is nursed back to health by Lady Eliwys and her family, who were sent by her husband to hide from the plague in this remote village. While anxiously trying to relocate her rendezvous point—the exact location where the gateway in time will reopen—she quickly grows to love the people, especially Eliwys' two young daughters, Agnes and Rosemunde. Travelers fleeing a nearby city bring the plague, and Kivrin realizes for the first time that she is in the wrong year. With little hope of returning to her own time, she does her best, along with Father Roche, to battle the plague and save the people of the village.

In the twenty-first century, Kivrin's plight becomes an afterthought to all but Mr. Dunworthy as Oxford comes under a quarantine and doctors and scientists race to find a vaccine. Dunworthy does his best to mobilize the resources of the university to fight the epidemic and care for the sick, all the while trying to find some confirmation that Kivrin's time traveling has gone well and she at least is safe.

Connie Willis effectively uses the parallel plots of the novel, cutting back and forth between the time lines, to increase suspense, create ironic juxtapositions, and ultimately affirm the common humanity of people battling disaster. In twenty-first century England, the epidemic is finally halted, but in the fourteenth century, the progress of the Black Death is inexorable. One by one, Agnes, Rosemunde, Lady Eliwys, and all the people of the village die in agony, despite the heroic efforts of Kivrin and Father Roche. Roche eventually dies, but the utter bleakness of the catastrophe and Kivrin's grief are in some small measure relieved by his gratitude and love for Kivrin, who has indeed become the messenger from heaven of his simple faith, bringing comfort to the dying and surviving to bear witness. As Kivrin struggles to sound the death knell as a memorial for Roche, the sound of the bell brings Dunworthy, who, though still weak from his own near death from influenza, has come back through time to seek Kivrin and bring her home.

Analysis: Although Willis employs the common device of time travel, she is not interested in creating paradoxes or exploring alternate histories. Time travel is for her a means of juxtaposing two societies confronting similar crises, of exploring human nature in the presence of overpowering fear, and of celebrating human courage and generosity.

Following the success of *Lincoln's Dreams* (1987), the critical and popular acclaim for *Doomsday Book*, which won both the Hugo and Nebula awards for best science-fiction novel, established Willis as one of the top American science-fiction writers. *Doomsday Book* exhibits Willis' characteristic strengths: thorough scholarship, graceful prose, and a rare combination of profound compassion and keen intelligence. There is even a touch of the humor present in many of her short stories in Dunworthy's struggles with bureaucratic rigidity and the complaints of self-centered people who do not quite notice that there is an epidemic going on. Also evident is Willis' ability to realize a time and place and create vivid characters whose joys and sorrows will haunt the reader's memory.

Time travel is one of the classic plot devices of science fiction. *Doomsday Book* has antecedents dating back to Mark Twain's *A Connecticut Yankee in King Arthur's Court* (1889) and H. G. Wells's *The Time Machine* (1895). Much of twentieth century time travel fiction has focused on the mutability of time: Characters travel back to the past and change it, either inadvertently or deliberately. Authors such as Poul Anderson have developed story sequences in which rival groups battle over time, seeking to change the past (and hence the future) or to preserve an immutable past. In *Doomsday Book*, the immutability of the past is a given. It is the combination of Kivrin's powerlessness, despite all of her modern knowledge, to do anything to stop the plague or to save even a single victim, and her heroic persistence in trying nevertheless, that gives the novel a tragic power rare in science fiction.

Willis' depiction of medieval England is compelling. She captures the sounds, sights, and smells with convincing verisimilitude. She neither patronizes the past nor sentimentalizes it. If she does not share Father Roche's simple yet profound faith in the ultimate goodness of God, she treats it and him with the utmost respect. The double plot, which allows her to contrast two periods so vividly, also enables her to portray an essential humanity. Despite the differences in language, culture, and knowledge, the people of both centuries are remarkably alike: Both centuries have their share of fools, bigots, and cowards, but most people in both are a blend of fear and courage, selfishness and nobility. In both periods, despite the prevalence of death and despair, there is a persistence of human love and caring, personified in Roche, Kivrin, and Dunworthy, that cannot be overcome.

—*Kevin P. Mulcahy*

A DOOR INTO OCEAN

Inhabitants of an ocean world with an entirely female population resist takeover

Author: Joan Slonczewski (1956-   )
Genre: Science fiction—alien civilization
Type of work: Novel
Time of plot: The distant future
Location: The planets Valedon and Shora
First published: 1986

The Plot: For forty years, traders from the planet Valedon have colonized the ocean planet Shora. The story concerns the increasing threat to the inhabitants of Shora and to the balance of life on their ocean home as the effects of colonization escalate and as they face the military invasion of their planet by the occupying forces of Valedon. The population of Shora—all females, who call themselves Sharers—resists the traders and soldiers by peaceful, nonviolent means. They also resist by trying to understand the Valans and by attempting to heal them both physically and spiritually. Although their advanced skills in life sciences might enable them to devise means of destroying the invaders, Sharers resist the temptation to destroy those who would destroy them. Influenced by their wordweaver, Merwen, they maintain the possibility that the Valans are human and that their healing will result in the survival of Sharers and Valans alike.

The story opens with the arrival of the Sharers Merwen and Usha in a port city on the planet Valedon. They have come to learn if the Valans are human in spite of their very different physical characteristics, actions, and values. They return to Shora accompanied by a young boy named Spinel and another Valan, the wealthy and noble Lady Berenice, called Nisi by the Sharers. These two Valans share the lives of Shorans who live on the raft Raia-el.

When Sharers boycott Valan traders, Spinel joins them. Although the boycott is successful in achieving the immediate demands of the Sharers, a worse threat takes the form of a plan to bring Shora under the control of Valedon. Realgar, the Valan to whom Nisi is engaged, arrives to head the military occupation of Shora. Pressures against the Sharers and their environment increase as a result of escalating Valan frustration with the Sharers' refusal to capitulate. Sharers struggle with the question of the humanity of the Valans but remain steadfast in their decision to resist without killing.

The ultimate action against the Sharers is precipitated by Nisi's attempt to destroy herself along with the Valan military headquarters. Some of the Valans have come to respect the Sharers, and their appreciation is intensified when Valans injured in the explosion are rescued and healed by Sharers. In a climactic series of conversations with the imprisoned Merwen, Realgar is forced to recognize his own fear and to face his endangered humanity. His defeat is complete when the High Protector of Valedon chastens him for the mutiny in his troops. Realgar resigns his position and, with all the trader and soldier Valans, withdraws from Shora. They leave the Sharers to the work of repairing their lives and their planet. Nisi remains to become healed of her double betrayal, and Spinel, drawn by his love for Merwen's daughter, Lystra, remains as hope for a transformed future.

Analysis: *A Door into Ocean* is the second science-fiction novel by professor of biology Joan Slonczewski, following *Still Forms on Foxfield* (1980). Like her other novels, it has been praised by critics for the accuracy of its science, the completeness of its alternate cultures, and its characterization. It won the John W. Campbell Memorial Award as best science-fiction novel of 1986.

As a work of science fiction, the novel offers the situation of the alien encounter. Shifting the scene from one planet to another, it explores the situation of alien encounter from the perspectives of both worlds, opening with the visit of the Sharers to Valedon. As in other science-fiction novels describing encounters with aliens, the story raises and examines the issue of the nature of humanity. When Valans turn purple like the Shorans, they fear the loss of their humanity. When Merwen considers the possibility that some of the Shorans are willing to hasten the death of the invaders, she worries that Sharers will lose their identity.

The two societies are not portrayed in monolithic and static terms, but the novel presents the encounter between Valedon and Shora as a juxtaposition of utopia and dystopia. The utopian society of Shora is not without difference, nor is the dystopian world of Valedon without its redeeming qualities. At the end of the novel, Spinel chooses to remain on the utopian Shora, but his choice carries the possibility of the transformation of Shora because he retains his Valan stonesign and knows that Lystra wishes to have daughters with him, daughters who will differ from both of them.

This novel has been discussed in the context of women as writers of science fiction and as a work of feminist science fiction. The portrayal of the world of Shora, with its highly advanced life-shaping science, its openness to all learning, and its egalitarian politics, values those matters that have been seen as feminist areas of concern. This emphasis critiques the patriarchal culture of Valedon as it also critiques the dominance of science itself, since the outcome of human action always remains unpredictable and uncontrollable. As Merwen knows in the final series of conversations with Realgar, it is wordweaving, the uncertain art of persuasive language, that will determine the final outcome.

Critic Robin Roberts, author of *A New Species: Gender and Science in Science Fiction* (1993), has highlighted *A Door into Ocean* as an example of postmodernist feminist science fiction because of its attention to the function of language. A deconstructive model is at play in revisions both of the convention of the alien encounter and of the static and monolithic utopia. The model carries through in the critique of the dominance of science and of patriarchy. It is mediated by the characterization of Merwen as a wordweaver and by a peculiarity of Sharer language: In every utterance, its opposite is present.   —*Shawn Carruth*

THE DOOR INTO SUMMER

A duped inventor escapes his time period through cryonics and then returns via time travel to rectify his personal history

Author: Robert A. Heinlein (1907-1988)
Genre: Science fiction—time travel
Type of work: Novel
Time of plot: 1970 and 2000
Location: Los Angeles, California, and Denver, Colorado
First published: 1957

The Plot: Robert A. Heinlein's *The Door into Summer* forecasts themes that appear in his later work and packs many facets of the science-fiction canon into its abbreviated length. Although the plot is understandable, if incredible at points, the novel is difficult reading primarily because the reader must suspend disbelief and recall that this dark, yet advanced, view of 1970 and 2000 was written from the perspective of the 1950's. By the standards of the genre, the book is short, but it unveils Heinlein's projections for the future, including a well-developed cryonics program, time travel, and robotics.

The story begins in 1970, shortly after the Six Weeks War, a confrontation that decimated much of the eastern United States, causing all governmental officials and documents to be relocated near Denver. As the tale opens, the protagonist, Daniel Boone Davis, is contemplating cold sleep, a precursor of cryonics, which will allow him to disassociate until the year 2000. He has reached this rather desperate alternative because his best friend and colleague, Miles Gentry, has just married Daniel's fiancée, Belle Darkin. Together, they have swindled Daniel out of the company he founded. The firm, Hired Girl, churns out robotic assistants, invented by Daniel, for harried housewives.

After Daniel makes arrangements for both himself and his cat, Petronius the Arbiter (Pete), to go into cold sleep, he makes a complete reversal and decides that revenge might be sweeter. While visiting Miles and Belle to carry out his coup, he is drugged by Belle, who accidentally uncovers the forms stating that he is to be put into cold sleep. She and Miles decide that this is a good way to get rid of Daniel. Belle takes Daniel to her own cryogenicist and puts him to sleep without his cat.

When Daniel awakes, it is the year 2000. There is a cure for the common cold, there is no smog, all clothes are made with velcro seams, and mass movers are the sole forms of transportation. Prior to undergoing cold sleep, Daniel had made financial arrangements for his reawakening, but his investments have gone sour, so he is forced to look for work. Through a series of blue-collar positions and chance meetings, he manages to work his way into a robotics lab. While learning the new technology, he discovers that most of the patents for robots carry his name.

The only negative factor in his new existence is a person from his past whom he had hoped to find in his future—Frederica (Little Ricky) Gentry, the adopted daughter of his former partner, Miles. By this point, the importance to Daniel of Pete the cat has become apparent. Much of his desire to find Little Ricky has to do with news of the animal; in addition, he had mailed her the balance of his Hired Girl stock prior to undergoing cold sleep. His quest to track her down leads him to Arizona and the news that she has married. A third motive and Daniel's real interest in finding the girl becomes apparent: He had hoped to marry her.

In another chance encounter, Daniel learns of an inventor, Dr. Hubert Twitchell, who has created a time machine, which is suppressed by the government. Daniel tricks the inventor into a demonstration and arranges to be transported back to 1970.

After initially plopping down in the middle of a nudist colony, Daniel locates Little Ricky, tells her to go into cold sleep on her twenty-first birthday, returns to Miles's home, retrieves his cat, and recommits himself to cold sleep for the year 2001. The book ends as he, Little Ricky, Pete, and the Hired Girl stock are reunited.

Analysis: As opposed to the satiric social commentary of his later magnum opus, *Stranger in a Strange Land* (1961), Heinlein's *The Door into Summer* falls into the vat of sentimentality. One critic at the time of publication noted that the book reveals myriad "gadgets-to-be." Readers who realize that Heinlein's "future" is "now" or has passed without those gadgets having come to be are left with only the plot of the novel, which revolves around a maudlin, self-serving, and pathetic protagonist. The only character of any real interest is the cat.

The problem may lie with the brevity of the work. Readers have little time to engage with the future before the plot yanks them back to the past, then thrusts them forward again. Vertigo replaces interest in the lives of any of the characters. Additionally, there is a rending of belief for even the most inveterate fans of science fiction. The most far-fetched portion of the plot concerns the protagonist repeating the time travel process primarily to procure the love of an eleven-year-old child.

The saving grace in the work lies with the often unexpected use of humor. For example, the time machine inventor explains that the only test on a human was unsuccessful: Leonard Vincent, a twenty-first century draftsman and artist, was transported back to the fifteenth century and did not return. Daniel's time traveling excursion, in another humorous incident, plunges him, fully dressed, from the sky into the center of a nudist colony.

The Door into Summer shows the shaping of themes that would predominate in Heinlein's later work. Underlying the basically bland plot structure is a hero's escape from a stifling maze into boundless freedom, coupled with a reverence for intellect, survival, and *joie de vivre*.

For all of his love of science fiction and technology, Heinlein's view of the future is dark and bleak, and his reaction to progress is often cynical. In his "futuristic" 1970, inventors are products of corporations, and in his 2000, the world is monopolized by zombie recruiters, rampant overpopulation, and bureaucratic stifling.

—*Joyce Duncan*

DOROTHEA DREAMS

A reclusive artist shows her masterpiece after a ghost helps her decide how to respond while she is held hostage by young fugitives

Author: Suzy McKee Charnas (1939-   )
Genre: Fantasy—feminist
Type of work: Novel

Time of plot: The 1980's
Location: Taos and Albuquerque, New Mexico
First published: 1986

The Plot: *Dorothea Dreams* tells the story of Dorothea Howard's progress from seclusion and obsession with her work to a return to public and political involvement. The change occurs after young Chicanos hold her hostage. She sympathizes with their effort to save their neighborhood. Her friend Ricky Maulders and a ghost from the time of the French Revolution help her respond to the crisis.

A well-known artist, Dorothea lives near Taos, New Mexico, and is obsessed by an enormous collage of found objects she has spent several years creating on a cliff wall. The first person to see this work is Ricky, a friend who is dying of cancer and asks to stay with her for a while. Like the viewers to follow, he is enchanted by this artwork; he believes it was the beacon that drew him to Dorothea. Ricky and Dorothea's friendship blossoms into a love affair, and Ricky helps Dorothea to analyze the frightening dreams she has been having in which she sees an angry mob and speaks aloud in French, a language she does not know well. After she writes a long letter in her sleep in French and in someone else's handwriting, they determine that a ghost from the time of the French Revolution is haunting her in her sleep. The ghost had been active in bringing about the revolution but rejected political involvement later in life. He believes Dorothea is his son, whom he wishes to persuade against risking his own safety through radical politics.

Meanwhile, Roberto Cantu, a Chicano teenager, works to save Pinto Street in Albuquerque from unscrupulous real estate developers who try to trick residents into selling their homes. After the police, mistakenly believing that a riot is in progress, open fire at a wedding reception, Roberto becomes a fugitive. Planning to flee to Canada, he and his sister Blanca escape Albuquerque by joining their cousin Robbie's art class on a field trip to Dorothea's house.

On the way to Taos, Roberto takes the class hostage. Once the group arrives, Dorothea and Ricky likewise become hostages. During the ordeal, Roberto shoots Dorothea's dog, discovers her artwork and damages it, and breaks several of her ribs. Dorothea finally recognizes the ghost in her dreams as a former self. She does not want to repeat his refusal to become involved and decides to help the Cantus. She persuades them to surrender peacefully and then tries to convince the authorities not to punish them harshly.

Because of Roberto's damage to her artwork, Dorothea is able to move beyond her obsession with it and show it at last. Ricky, believing he has done what he was called to Taos to do, leaves to take care of other unfinished business before his death.

Analysis: *Dorothea Dreams*, Suzy McKee Charnas' fifth novel, contains several fantasy elements—the ghost, the odd connection between Dorothea and Ricky, and the mysterious power of Dorothea's wall collage. Ricky believes that Dorothea's finishing of the collage drew both him and the ghost to her. Only Dorothea sees the ghost, mostly in her dreams, but she needs Ricky's help to understand the ghost's messages. At one point Dorothea speculates that the ghost is one of Ricky's ancestors who is trying to send a message to Ricky through her. Only after seeing the ghost's face does she recognize herself and realize that the ghost is an incarnation of herself in an earlier life. When Dorothea draws an inkwell the ghost used in her dreams, Ricky recognizes it as one he saw in France, a country Dorothea has never visited, at a museum too small to have a catalog. Except for this striking inkwell, it might be possible to dismiss the ghost as the product of a particularly vivid imagination.

The novel, then, subverts the conventional ghost story. In a sense, Dorothea is haunted by her own ghost, an unusual plot twist. Although he means well, the ghost is pitifully inept. He is quite surprised to learn that Dorothea is not, in fact, his son, and he gives terrible advice.

The parallel story of the Cantu family raises the issues of Chicano identity and community. Roberto feels alienated from white culture to the extent that he quit school, and he resents Pinto Street residents, such as his cousin Robbie's family, who leave for the more affluent, and mostly white, Heights. The media attention that results from Roberto's hostage-taking leads to an investigation that reveals that his sense of victimization is warranted. The real estate developers were trying to take advantage of the poor residents, and the police behaved improperly when they opened fire at the wedding reception.

At the same time, the novel sensitively portrays the plight of Roberto's younger sister, Blanca. Blanca recognizes the limited possibilities for an intelligent but poor and seriously asthmatic girl in a place like Pinto Street. Her goal is to escape, even if it means being a fugitive with Roberto. In a letter sent after she and Ricky become friends during the hostage ordeal, Ricky tells her that he will leave her money when he dies so that she can travel. He particularly encourages her to seek friends on her journeys who are her "heart's kindred." Blanca rereads this letter until it becomes illegible. The novel does not attempt to resolve the tension between protecting one's ethnic identity and seeking alternatives through education and travel.

Typical of Charnas' fiction, especially her Motherlines series (including *Walk to the End of the World*, 1974; *Motherlines*, 1978; and *The Furies*, 1994), the novel has a strong feminist slant. Dorothea left her husband once her children were grown to pursue her artistic career, but even so had wondered if the children had drained away all of her creative energy. The novel ends with her accepting acclaim as a prominent role model for other female artists.

—Joan Hope

DOUBLE STAR

An actor, recruited to impersonate a powerful politician kidnapped by extremists opposed to the man's policy of cooperation with nonhuman races, is forced to confront his own prejudices and to make a fundamental decision about his future

Author: Robert A. Heinlein (1907-1988)
Genre: Science fiction—extrapolatory
Type of work: Novel
Time of plot: The near future
Location: Earth, Mars, the Moon, and various spaceships
First published: 1956

The Plot: Hoping for a free meal or even a loan, down-on-his-luck actor Lorenzo Smythe buys a drink for Dak Broadbent, a spaceship captain trying to pretend he is something else. Broadbent offers more than Smythe could have hoped for, an acting job at a good salary. Before the final arrangements can be made, however, they are attacked by a human and a Martian, a race Smythe cannot tolerate, partly because of their smell. Smythe finds himself an accomplice in the deaths of the two attackers and the disposal of their bodies.

The acting job is revealed to be the impersonation of John Joseph Bonforte, one of the most important politicians in the empire and leader of the opposition Expansionist coalition, whose political philosophy, based on equality of humans and nonhumans, is at odds with Smythe's prejudices. It is suspected that terrorists with links to the ruling Humanity Party have kidnapped Bonforte to keep him from taking part in an adoption ceremony at a Martian nest, an act that would further cement human-Martian relations. Because Martian society is based on rigid rules of protocol, should Bonforte not attend for any reason except death, relations between Martians and humans would be so badly ruptured that a massacre of humans—which would result in a human war against the Martians—would likely result, and Bonforte's policy of coexistence would fall apart.

The plot follows Smythe as he prepares for his role with the help of those closest to Bonforte: personal secretary Penelope Russell, physician Dr. Capek, pilot Dak Broadbent, political operative Roger Clifton, and press liaison Bill Corpsman. As Smythe watches tapes of Bonforte, he begins to understand him. With the help of hypnosis, he is able to conquer his negative emotional reaction to the Martian race. Increasingly, he speaks, acts, and even thinks like Bonforte.

The adoption ceremony goes smoothly, but a new problem develops. Bonforte is found but has been drugged so heavily that he will be unable to appear in public for some time. Smythe agrees to continue the charade while Bonforte recovers. As the days pass, Smythe begins to make decisions as Bonforte. Corpsman resents Smythe's actions, and tension between the two escalates.

Smythe as Bonforte, gives a passionate speech, beamed throughout the solar system, defending "his" political philosophy. The impact is so strong that the Humanity Party government resigns. Emperor Willem summons the false Bonforte to the capital to form a caretaker government. During the audience, Smythe discovers that Bonforte and the emperor, a constitutional monarch with limited power, are longtime friends. The emperor in turn discovers that Smythe is not the real Bonforte but tells him to carry on with the impersonation until the ailing leader recovers.

As the election campaign gets under way, the conflict between Smythe and Corpsman comes to a head. When Corpsman is struck off the list of candidates for the Grand Assembly at Smythe's behest, he quits and sets out to expose the ongoing charade. He is defeated, however, when fingerprints taken from Smythe are found to match those on file for Bonforte.

The Expansionists win the election, but Bonforte suddenly dies from the effects of his kidnapping and drugging. Now Smythe must make the choice of his life—will he continue to be Bonforte forever?

In the last chapter, it is revealed that the entire book is a journal written by Smythe twenty-five years earlier while he struggled to retain his sanity while pretending to be Bonforte. Now married to Russell, he muses about the person he was and the person he has become as he lives Bonforte's political life.

Analysis: This Hugo Award-winning novel is one of Robert Heinlein's best. It is shorter and less strident than some of his later works. The book blends good story-telling, an interesting futuristic setting, and political and social ideas in a balanced whole.

The Humanity Party's platform of human domination over nonhumans is an easily understood metaphor for any hate group of any time or place. The Expansionist Party is the moral stand-in for all, throughout history, who have argued for the equality of all people.

The book was written in the 1950's, when women's roles were more sharply defined and limited and when the Civil Rights movement was only emerging. Some language that might have seemed innocuous when written may grate on the ears of later readers. For example, Bonforte's chief clerk, Jimmy Washington, the only member of the inner circle who has almost no role in the story, is described as "a spare, elderly mulatto." Russell, who has a master's degree and is a member of the Grand Assembly, is sometimes referred to as "hon" or "honey chile" by Broadbent and Smythe. When she gets angry at Smythe, Broadbent tells her, "Stow it, Penny, or I'll spank your round fanny." Such dated references are rare, and they pale beside the strong central message of equality and individual dignity that is at the center of the book. Smythe explains the key to the Expansionist policy: "freedom and equal rights must run with the Imperial banner. . . . The human race must never again make the mistakes that the white subrace had made in Africa and Asia." It was a timely message in 1956, but it is also a timeless message presented well.

—Paul Joseph

DOWNBELOW STATION

Damon Konstantin struggles to preserve Pell station's autonomy and populace in the face of rival Fleets

Author: C. J. Cherryh (Carolyn Janice Cherry, 1942-   )
Genre: Science fiction—future war
Type of work: Novel
Time of plot: 2352-2353
Location: Pell's Planet and nearby systems
First published: 1981

The Plot: *Downbelow Station* begins with an overview of the years 2005-2352, during which time Earth falls under the dominion of the Company, a politico-commercial entity that invests in interstellar exploration. This investment results in dominion over known space that is uncontested until a rival power emerges from the distant colony worlds located in a region of space known as The Beyond. This power, the Union, grows swiftly, fueled by a mass eugenics program that creates a burgeoning population of laboratory-born soldiers and workers.

Friction between Earth and the Union causes Earth to establish the Fleet, an interstellar flotilla that protects Company interests in interstellar space. The decline of Earth and the Company leads to retrenchment and neglect, leaving the Fleet without support, save that which it can beg, borrow, or steal from the Company space stations, which are the most important assets in colonized space.

The story begins on Pell station. Captain Signy Mallory, in command of the fleet-carrier *Norway*, demands docking privileges in order to complete the evacuation of refugees from Mariner station, which has been destroyed by the Union. Mallory, a good leader whose basic honesty is offset by ruthlessness and a considerable ego, also deposits a Union prisoner on Pell station. This prisoner, test-tube born Josh Talley, elects to have his memories erased rather than to recall the horrors of his service to the Union and of his sexual enslavement to Mallory.

The influx of refugees compels Damon Konstantin, the son of station chief Angelo Konstantin, to accept increasingly dangerous positions of authority as the station's resources are pushed to the breaking point. His wife, Elene Quen, discovers that her entire family has been killed by the Union at Mariner. Filled with a desire for vengeance, Elene does not immediately accept Damon's caretaking friendship for the now amnesiac and forlorn Josh Talley.

On Pell's Planet, the mostly habitable world that Pell station orbits, Damon's brother Emilio is forced to dismiss security personnel who are still loyal to Jon Lukas, the previous overseer of the planetside operations. Lukas, a longtime rival of the Konstantins, decides to seek covert means of toppling Angelo and his sons from power. The Konstantin hold on the planetside activities—a collection of multipurpose bases known collectively as Downbelow station—is reinforced by the rapport between the Konstantin family and the Downers, an indigenous humanoid species who are gentle and usually trusting. Many of the Downers are relocated to Pell station to help with maintenance and cargo handling. Emilio sends up a particularly clever and loyal pair of mated Downers, Satin and Bluetooth.

Mallory, having departed from Pell station, makes a rendezvous with the rest of the Fleet, which is massing for a strike at Union-held Viking station. Fleet commander Mazian aborts the assault at the last second, fleeing the vicinity of Viking. Mallory is at first dismayed by, and then suspicious of, Mazian's action.

As the Fleet reapproaches Pell station, Jon Lukas, with the help of a Union agent, kills Angelo Konstantin and takes control of the station. His treachery is uncovered by Mazian, and he is forced to act as the Fleet's puppet administrator in charge of both Pell station and Downbelow station.

Elene Quen manages to escape the occupation by the Fleet and sets out to unify the nomadic merchanters into a cohesive political and military force, using the name Quen—that of her martyred merchanter family—as a rallying cry. Her husband, Damon, is forced to go into hiding, along with Josh, who has begun to remember that he was more than a Union computer expert; he was a saboteur who helped destroy Mariner station.

The Fleet occupation of the station draws the Union forces closer. They hope to engage and destroy Mazian at Pell. Meanwhile, Mallory confirms that Mazian never meant to assault Viking; that operation was merely an excuse to reunite the Fleet for the conquest of Earth itself. Mazian's heavy-handed rule causes Downbelow station to revolt. Emilio and his forces are aided by the Downers, who offer sanctuary to the humans after they break for freedom.

This sanctuary turns out to be unnecessary. Aided by Satin and Bluetooth, Damon and Josh avoid capture by Fleet forces long enough to be seized by Mallory's troops, not Mazian's. Mallory learns from Josh that Mazian has concealed the fact that Jon Lukas was not merely a murderer but a traitor for the Union. Still loyal to the Company and Earth—and disgusted by Mazian's duplicity and egomania—Mallory breaks away from the station and, in order to ruin the Fleet's attempt at Earth conquest, leads the Union forces toward Pell. Mazian is forced to disperse his fleet.

Before the Union can seize the station, Elene Quen arrives with a sizable armada of merchanter vessels, which declare an alliance to Pell station and declare it neutral ground. The station is left unmolested, Damon is placed in charge, and Mallory's *Norway* becomes the core of its new Fleet.

Analysis: *Downbelow Station*'s sprawling scope is typical of space operas; however, various structural properties work to create a serious tone that is uncharacteristic of the space opera subgenre. Whereas space operas are often likened to "Westerns in space," *Downbelow Station* reads more like a high-quality political thriller.

Despite extraordinary numbers of characters, points of view, and rapid scene changes, C. J. Cherryh employs a gritty and direct prose that gives the narrative the tenor of reportage, rather than of high adventure. Similarly, the motivations of both characters and governments are consistent and believable. Hackneyed good-versus-evil tropes are absent, replaced by an almost brutal presentation of the realpolitik that drives persons who hold tremendous power and responsibility. Each chapter is headed by a dateline/location indicator, another structural nuance that serves to vest the narrative with an illusion of historicity. These various features combine to create a narrative structure that exudes an aura of plausibility, thereby placing *Downbelow Station* in the same domain occupied by extrapolative political or war thrillers such as Tom Clancy's *Red Storm Rising* (1986) or Fletcher Knebel and Charles Bailey II's *Seven Days in May* (1962). *Downbelow Station* won the 1982 Hugo Award, one of science fiction's top honors.

—*Charles Gannon*

DOWNWARD TO THE EARTH

An earthling returns to the alien world where he was colonial administrator and finds salvation through the natives he once despised

Author: Robert Silverberg (1935-   )
Genre: Science fiction—alien civilization
Type of work: Novel
Time of plot: The distant future
Location: The planet Belzagor
First published: 1970 (serial form, *Galaxy*, 1969)

The Plot: Earthling Edmund Gundersen returns as a tourist to the planet Belzagor. It had been a colony of Earth known as Holman's World, and Gundersen had been its administrator, but it was relinquished to the dominant indigenous species, elephant-like creatures known as "nildoror" (singular, "nildor"). The nildoror have no written language, but they have a culture. They undergo rebirth and identify themselves by how many births they have had. They coexisted with the earthlings and allowed themselves to be used as beasts of burden. They share the planet with the less-sentient anthropoid species called "sulidoror" (singular, "sulidor").

In a conversation with his former assistant, Van Beneker, who has remained on Belzagor, Gundersen reveals that he has always thought of the nildoror as animals. He is nevertheless fascinated by their culture.

The next day, he sets out on a journey into the jungle, seeking the mist country where the nildoror undergo rebirth, riding on a nildor named Srin'gahar. He revisits a place where he and fellow earthling Jeff Kurtz had shared a drink of the venom of local serpents with several nildoror, giving him a feeling of becoming a nildor. Afterward, he felt ashamed and never repeated the experiment.

Srin'gahar takes him to a group of nildoror. He overcomes earthling squeamishness to join in their food and dance, and he is granted permission to visit the mist country, on the condition that he bring back an earthling named Cedric Cullen, who has offended the nildoror in some way they will not explain. He agrees.

After a discussion with Srin'gahar in which the nildor raises the possibility that the elephants of Earth have souls, Gundersen re-encounters Van Beneker and the earthlings with whom he traveled to the planet. The earthlings consider the nildoror to be savages or animals, and Gundersen finds himself defending them. In the course of the conversation, he reveals the sin he hopes to expiate: Faced with a threat of property damage from flooding, he forced seven nildoror who were on their way to rebirth to give up their journey and work for him.

Further on, he encounters his former lover, Seena, now married to Kurtz. She reveals that the serpent venom is used by the nildoror in their rebirth ceremony, so Kurtz's recreational use of it with them constituted blasphemy in their minds. Kurtz eventually underwent the rebirth ceremony and has become a misshapen thing, babbling incoherently.

Finally Gundersen meets Cullen, who is dying of cancer, which is now curable by Earth medicine. He offers to take Cullen back, but Cullen refuses to go lest he fall into the hands of the nildoror. He reveals that the nildoror want him because he had inadvertently witnessed a part of their rebirth ceremony in which they frenziedly trample and eat other animals. Gundersen is ambivalent about bringing Cullen back, but the dilemma is resolved the next morning, when he finds Cullen dead.

Finally Gundersen reaches the place of rebirth and undergoes the ceremony. He learns that rebirth transforms the nildoror into sulidoror, and vice versa: They are one species, telepathically linked. He learns that Srin'gahar was one of the nildoror he had denied rebirth to but that Srin'gahar has forgiven him. He communes with the tortured spirit of Kurtz. He is transformed, and he prepares to return to transform first Kurtz and then any other earthlings willing to listen.

Analysis: This work first appeared, in serial form, in 1969, a time of changes for Robert Silverberg himself and for the field of science fiction. After years as an unusually prolific hack, Silverberg stopped writing science fiction in the early 1960's. He returned a few years later to write more serious science fiction, with more attention to the literary virtues of characterization and prose style and with a willingness to look to the so-called "mainstream" for examples. Along with such books as *Tower of Glass* (1970), *The Book of Skulls* (1971), and *Dying Inside* (1972), *Downward to the Earth* represented this sort of literary ambition. The field as a whole was undergoing similar changes, sometimes referred to as the "New Wave."

The book contains a number of references to Joseph Conrad's well-known treatment of the theme of clash between European and "primitive" cultures, *Heart of Darkness* (1902), most notably the name of Kurtz. It employs one of Silverberg's most frequent themes, redemption and rebirth, as well as treating an issue that was much in the news at that time, colonization and the return to native rule. Some saw the natives as less than human; others saw them as having an enviable connectedness to the land and to other life. Silverberg extended this in science-fictional manner by making the nildoror nonhuman in appearance but intelligent in their own way and even telepathic.

This did not represent a simple concession to current political fashion on Silverberg's part. Indeed, as far back as *Invaders from Earth* (1958) and *Collision Course* (1961), he had been suggesting that the alien races Earth might meet could be wiser or more clever than humanity. This approach put him on a collision course with dominant forces in the field of science fiction, most notably John W. Campbell, Jr. Since then, the idea of alien cultures as different, rather than inferior, has shown up in many books, including Ursula K. Le Guin's *The Word for World Is Forest* (1976) and Barry B. Longyear's *Manifest Destiny* (1980).

With its lavish descriptions of alien landscapes, its rich development of characters both alien and human, and its striking presentations of altered states of consciousness, *Downward to the Earth* is generally considered one of Silverberg's best novels, at least by those who do not prefer the simple adventures of his early work.

—*Arthur D. Hlavaty*

DRACULA

Count Dracula, a vampire, moves to England from his native Transylvania in search of new blood

Author: Bram Stoker (1847-1912)
Genre: Fantasy—cautionary
Type of work: Novel
Time of plot: The end of the nineteenth century
Location: Transylvania and England
First published: 1897

The Plot: Jonathan Harker, an English solicitor, visits Count Dracula in Transylvania. He finds death's aura and aroma surrounding Dracula. Harker is attacked by three female vampires, who are warded off by Dracula. Harker is his; they are given a baby to feed on. When Harker demands to be released, Dracula obliges, but a pack of wolves surrounds the castle entrance. The next day, Harker awakes, weak and sick, with a wound on his throat. Dracula leaves Harker at the castle as a prisoner.

In England, Harker's fiancée, Mina Murray, visits her friend, Lucy Westenra, a "New Woman" who plans to marry nobleman Arthur Holmwood. During Mina's visit, a ship runs aground in Whitby. The only living creature aboard is a gray wolf, which escapes into the countryside.

Lucy begins to sleepwalk. Mina follows her and sees a tall, thin man bending over Lucy in a churchyard. The man disappears when Mina approaches. Lucy grows so ill that Mina is forced to call Dr. Seward, Lucy's former suitor. While Lucy improves, Mina receives word that Harker, who had been reported missing, has been found near Budapest. Mina goes there and marries Harker.

Lucy's condition worsens, and Seward calls Dr. Van Helsing from Amsterdam. Van Helsing notices two puncture wounds on Lucy's throat. Lucy is given transfusions directly from the men, who guard her by night. Seward falls asleep while guarding Lucy and finds her more ill when he awakes. More transfusions ensue, and Van Helsing insists that Lucy wear a necklace of garlic every night.

One night, a wolf crashes through the window, the necklace slips off, and Lucy is further victimized. Van Helsing tells Holmwood that Lucy is near death. Holmwood kisses Lucy, who fastens her teeth to his neck. Lucy dies. Several neighborhood children are discovered far from home, alive but with their throats punctured. They say they followed a pretty lady in white.

Harker returns to England. Van Helsing suggests that Lucy is a vampire's victim. By night, Holmwood, Seward, Van Helsing, and Quincey P. Morris visit Lucy's tomb and find it empty. At daybreak, Lucy returns, and they drive a stake through her heart, cut off her head, and stuff garlic in her mouth.

Mina is vampirized by Dracula. The men track Dracula in London, but he escapes. By hypnotizing Mina, they learn that Dracula is at sea. They follow him to Castle Dracula. Wolves encircle the men and Mina, who gather safely within a "magic" circle Van Helsing traces. The men overtake the cart carrying Dracula's coffin. As the sun sets, Harker slashes Dracula's throat with his Kukri knife and Morris gouges Dracula's heart with his Bowie knife.

Analysis: Interest in vampires, like the creature itself, never dies. Bram Stoker's novel focuses on the victimization of women. Stoker's view is opposed to that of the "New Woman," a feminist construct of the late nineteenth century. Stoker makes references to the New Woman in *Dracula* through Mina, characterizing her as a well-informed woman of the 1890's. Mina sets herself above the New Woman, rejecting the concept for its sexual openness. The overall structure of *Dracula* indicates that Stoker employs Mina to reject the concept of the New Woman, represented by the female vampire as energized and aggressive female sexuality.

The first half of the novel presents woman as vampire. Stoker focuses on the female vampire by introducing the three female vampires who live in Dracula's castle, then centering on Lucy, Dracula's first English victim. In the second half, the focus of the story is the fight to save Mina, shifting away from the presentation of woman as vampire. The focus becomes the fight against vampirism, and, metaphorically, against energized female sexuality or the New Woman.

Lucy, the primary female focus of the first half of the novel, is turned by Dracula into one of "those awful women." The New Woman exists in her personality, however latent, surfacing when Lucy is vampirized by Dracula. In her vampirized state, she no longer suppresses her desire. Van Helsing takes it upon himself to protect men from the evils of the vampire, and, hence, the evils of the New Woman. Lucy, confronted by the men in her crypt, takes on the full-blown characteristics of the New Woman, preying on a child and speaking of her wanton desire for Holmwood. By calling Holmwood to her side, Lucy suggests that he break with the patriarchy. This does not happen because Lucy is summarily destroyed by the men; the vampire/New Woman is destroyed by the patriarchy.

The scourge of vampirism/New Womanhood also calls at Mina's door. Mina represents traditional Victorian womanhood but also feels the effects of vampirism/New Womanhood. Dracula seduces her, forcing her to drink his blood from his breast while her husband sleeps in the same bed. The patriarchy comes to Mina's rescue. As the vampire's, or New Woman's, influence over Mina grows, Dr. Seward metaphorically sees the New Woman overcoming the traditional woman. The role of Stoker's male characters is to prevent the acceptance of the New Woman by keeping women in their place, and, hence, the patriarchy in order. To do this, the men must destroy Dracula. Van Helsing chooses to fight the vampire to save the patriarchy.

At the novel's end, by destroying Dracula, Van Helsing and the men destroy vampirism and, metaphorically, the New Woman, preserving the sanctity of womanhood and the patriarchal order. Stoker's novel is therefore anti-New Woman and antifeminist. It came at a reactionary time when literary England was up in arms against the very idea of the New Woman.

—Thomas D. Petitjean, Jr.

THE DRACULA SERIES

Count Dracula's adventures are revealed from his own perspective and from the perspectives of those closely associated with him

Author: Fred Saberhagen (1930-   )
Genre: Fantasy—alternate history
Type of work: Novels
Time of plot: Primarily contemporary
Location: Various locations throughout Europe and the United States
First published: *The Dracula Tape* (1975), *The Holmes-Dracula File* (1978), *An Old Friend of the Family* (1979), *Thorn* (1980), *Dominion* (1982), *A Matter of Taste* (1990), *A Question of Time* (1992), and *Séance for a Vampire* (1994)

The Plot: *The Dracula Tape*, the first and perhaps best novel in the series, retells the story found in Bram Stoker's *Dracula* (1897) from the point of view of Count Dracula himself. The novel, supposedly dictated to descendants of the Harkers, is a brilliant reexamination of the events surrounding Dracula, Jonathan Harker, Mina, Lucy, Renfield, and the horrid Van Helsing. Fred Saberhagen's retelling has the feel of accuracy as he points out the faults in the accounts of the witnesses in Stoker's novel and reveals a much more logical tale wherein Dracula points out, for example, the improbability of uncovering him in his coffin in the middle of the night and Van Helsing's cruelty in attempting transfusions without the aid of blood-type matching.

The Holmes-Dracula File links distant cousins Sherlock Holmes and Count Dracula to solve a series of crimes involving a trail of bloodless corpses as well as a criminal group's threat of plague-infested rats. The novel provides Saberhagen's brilliant insight into the personalities of Dracula, Holmes, and Watson.

Dracula's loyalty is the main thrust of the novel *An Old Friend of the Family*. The Southerland family, living in Chicago, invokes an ancient ritual supplied by the count himself for the descendants of the Harker family, to be used only in a dire emergency. Clarissa Southerland, granddaughter of Wilhelmina Harker, is not sure what to expect when Dr. Emile Corday (Dracula) arrives, claiming to be an old friend of the family. He proves to be very resourceful in aiding the family to recapture a daughter embraced by one of the nosferatu and a son kidnapped and tortured, as well as in punishing those responsible for these atrocities, including the evil Morgan La Fey.

In *Thorn*, Saberhagen elaborates on some of the historical activities in the life of Vlad Tepes, weaving a dramatic story of a powerful love and intertwining it with a modern attempt to recover the lost portrait of his lover. In telling this story, Saberhagen adeptly parallels the lives of the then-mortal count and the modern king of the vampires.

Dominion tells the tale of an ancient struggle for an item of tremendous magical power, rekindled in modern Chicago and its surrounding areas. The presence of several bloodless bodies attracts the attention of Detective Joe Keogh. He has married into the Southerland family and therefore is acquainted with the count, but only recently has he begun to trust him. The struggle for power eventually involves Dracula and several powerful magicians from the past, including the great Merlin.

The rescuers' roles are reversed in *A Matter of Taste* as the Southerland family must battle half a millennia of the count's enemies to save him. Again Saberhagen interlaces past and present, narrating the events surrounding Vlad Tepes' assassination and initial years as a vampire and connecting these to the enemies of the present who wish to destroy him. John Southerland, now grown and engaged, and Joe Keogh, both of whom are now experienced with vampires, head the forces attempting to free the count.

A Question of Time may be the most unusual novel of the entire series, as time becomes completely nonlinear. A nosferatu sculptor named Edgar Tyrell is conducting experiments, mining the very fabrics of time and reality from deep within the ancient rocks of the Grand Canyon. In 1935, a Conservation Corps worker, Jake Rezner, is lured into working for Tyrell by his attraction for Camilla, a beautiful woman trapped by Tyrell in 1965. In 1991, Cathy Brainard, supposedly the niece of the famous sculptor but actually his daughter, winds up missing. Joe Keogh (now the head of his own investigative agency specializing in the supernatural), John Southerland, and Mr. Strangeways (Dracula) are called in to find her. All the tales eventually overlap, with Tyrell's mining threatening the lives and reality of the major characters.

Dracula, Holmes, and Watson are reunited in *Séance for a Vampire* as they attempt to decipher the bizarre events surrounding the Altamont household. The eldest daughter has drowned under mysterious circumstances. A mischievous confidence game pulled off by two false mediums trying to turn the family's misfortune into their own profit unexpectedly brings back the daughter, with a message about a stolen treasure that must be returned. This treasure was stolen by the Russian pirate Kulakov, who was embraced as a vampire to escape death by hanging in 1765. Kulakov believes that the Altamonts have his lost treasure and is terrorizing the family to ensure its return. Holmes and Dracula team up again to solve this baffling crime and battle the supernatural forces masterminding it.

Analysis: In this excellent series, Saberhagen brings a personality and fullness to the character of Dracula that perhaps goes beyond any treatment in the vampire genre. Saberhagen's Dracula seems much more plausible than the one described in Bram Stoker's novel, and his portrayal quickly engages readers, who find themselves identifying with the count and even cheering for his success.

Using historical accounts of Vlad Tepes and remaining true to most of the details in Stoker's skeletal description, Saberhagen constructs a believable personality profile of a misunderstood, loyal, complicated, human Dracula. The fanatical sense of honesty and integrity he possesses, for example, does not permit him to cover up his own faults and is responsible for much of his introspection but is also the motivation for impaling thieves when he rules in his mortal court. Many readers may be surprised to witness the wonderful, sometimes almost childlike humor and wonder the count can feel. Throughout the series, readers come to know the deep sense of honor and contentment in Dracula's character but also remain aware of the tension and power seething underneath his calm, cold mask.

Several recurring characters, in addition to Dracula, provide continuity and contrast in the novels. Sherlock Holmes and Dr. Watson appear in two of the novels, and readers also become familiar over the course of several novels with Judy Southerland, Kate Southerland Keogh, Joe Keogh, and John Southerland, all descendants of the Harker family. As readers interact with each new novel in the series, they see the striking contrast between the growth and aging of these characters and the timelessness of Dracula. Although Dracula frequently adopts new names, he otherwise remains almost unchanging throughout his mortal and immortal existence.

Saberhagen is especially sensitive to the feelings and expectations the novels create in the minds of his readers. Early in the series, Saberhagen attempts to keep the reader in suspense about the identity of the count, almost as a sly joke between the author and his readers as well as to present the feeling of what other characters experience around the count, both a sense of familiarity and a distant strangeness. This works well in *The Holmes-Dracula File* because the count is hit on the head in the beginning of the book and suffers a short amnesia. In *An Old Friend of the Family*, Saberhagen uses the strategy to mirror the sense of familiarity and distant strangeness the members of the Southerland family feel for their visitor. In each case, readers begin to suspect early the veiled identity of the count, but through the process of discovery, combined with the historical unfolding of the count's history, Saberhagen reveals Dracula to his readers.

—*Paul J. Baltes*

DRACULA UNBOUND

A scientist involves Bram Stoker, author of Dracula, *in a search throughout history for time-traveling vampires*

Author: Brian W. Aldiss (1925-   )
Genre: Science fiction—time travel
Type of work: Novel
Time of plot: 1896, 1999, and 2599
Location: London, England; Enterprise, Utah; and Tripoli, Libya
First published: 1991

The Plot: *Dracula Unbound* follows the efforts of Joe Bodenland to defeat the Fleet Ones, vampirish descendants of pterodactyls who intend to use time travel to enslave humanity. Bodenland has developed a method of toxic waste disposal involving time displacement. His friend, Bernard Clift, a paleontologist, has discovered in the deserts of Utah a coffin containing a humanoid corpse, buried in rock from the Cretaceous period.

When a ghastly "ghost train" appears over Clift's find, Bodenland and Clift manage to steal aboard. They discover that the train is a time-travel device from the far future, when Earth is ruled by the Fleet Ones, who hope to use the "time train" to dominate humans throughout all time. Clift is killed, but Bodenland seizes control of the train. Discovering that the train recently dropped off a vampire agent in the London of 1896, he travels there to attempt to thwart her. Upon arrival, he befriends Bram Stoker, who is writing the novel *Dracula*, and his gardener, Spinks.

Bella, the operative whom Bodenland seeks, seduces him. She confides that the vampires' leader, Lord Dracula, has called a great convocation of all vampires to plan humanity's ultimate downfall. She further confides that this gathering will take place in the Cretaceous period. The only weapon that could defeat Dracula, a superfusion bomb, can be found only in Tripoli, Libya, in the year 2599. Bodenland, Stoker, and Spinks stalk Bella and dispatch her with a stake.

Taking Bella's corpse with them, the three men board the time train for Tripoli, where they steal the bomb. Soon, however, Dracula captures Bodenland and tells him of Bella's true plans. She had been sent to Bodenland to lure him to Tripoli to steal the bomb, so that Dracula could then wrest it away from him. The Fleet Ones, though shrewd, are incapable of the sustained logical thought and powers of invention needed to retrieve the bomb from its sophisticated safeguards. Dracula also taunts Bodenland with the revelation that it is his invention that will lead to time travel, the vampires' pathway to total dominion over humans.

Stoker and Spinks rescue Bodenland, and they soon set out for the Cretaceous period. They bomb the convocation of Fleet Ones of which Bella had spoken, causing the cloud-shrouded cold and darkness that ended the age of reptiles. Bella is buried on a vast Cretaceous plain, to be discovered in 1999 by Clift. Bodenland destroys his time-displacement system.

Analysis: Within the highly regarded canon of Brian W. Aldiss' works, *Dracula Unbound* occupies a very specific slot—that of sequel to his well-received *Frankenstein Unbound* (1973). In the frequent manner of sequels,

Dracula Unbound mirrors *Frankenstein Unbound* in a number of ways. Both books feature scientists who travel to the 1800's to encounter famous writers of speculative fiction and characters from those authors' works. Most readers will probably agree with the majority of critics that the earlier work is the better of the two.

As *Frankenstein Unbound* takes Mary Shelley's theme of the ethical and unethical uses of science, *Dracula Unbound* borrows Bram Stoker's theme of good versus evil. The concept of absolute evil in a science-fiction framework poses some problems. Whereas many readers can readily accept Dracula as the personification of absolute evil in Stoker's Victorian horror novel, they may have problems with Aldiss' rationale for the utter evil of Dracula and his minions: their reptilian brains. Bodenland finds that the vampires' vileness is predicated on their lack of a neocortex. In short, the creatures are biologically predisposed to unmitigated evil. The ethical implications of such a discovery are vast: Are "good" and "evil" then universally based on genetics? As repulsive as the Fleet Ones are, are they responsible for their actions? Few of Aldiss' characters ponder these issues for very long. Furthermore, how the absence of a neocortex affects morality is never clearly explained.

The novel gives dubious scientific explanations for other bits of vampiriana. Vampires' fear of sunlight is given its genesis in the great bomb blast that killed the dinosaurs. Is this inherited racial memory, as the gardener Spinks suggests? The explanation for the bloodsuckers' fear of Christian symbolism is especially murky: The Fleet Ones seem to view the cross as some sort of emblem of human individuality, which they, with their more primitive brains, cannot understand. These explanations are nebulous.

The novel provides some real pleasures. Aldiss depicts instances of the ironies of time travel that fans of this subgenre savor. In Libya, Bodenland, seeing the time train overhead, realizes that he is inside it, at some other point in his adventure. The novel opens with the discovery of Bella's grave, which Bodenland digs at novel's end. Also, Aldiss devises a new extension of the vampire as metaphor. The Fleet Ones are incapable of scientific inquiry and invention; therefore, they must tap into the inventiveness of other species and siphon away their creative vitality. Because the novel opens with Bodenland and Clift worrying about the reaction to their research in academia, government, and business, it is easy to see the novel as a wry satire of the way in which industry and government appropriate and make use of

the discoveries and inventions of men and women of science, work that others cannot accomplish on their own and cannot fully appreciate beyond their potential for exploitation. Finally, perhaps the novel's greatest feat of imagination is the Fleet Ones themselves. In them, Aldiss has interwoven three subjects that have been dear to writers and readers of fantasy and science fiction for decades: dinosaurs, vampires, and time travel.

—*Thomas DuBose*

THE DRAGON IN THE SEA

While a submarine is engaged in pirating crude oil from enemy undersea wells, a psychologist attempts to discover which of its crew members is an enemy spy

Author: Frank Herbert (1920-1986)
Genre: Science fiction—extrapolatory
Type of work: Novel
Time of plot: Early in the twenty-first century
Location: The sub-tug *Fenian Ram*
First published: 1956 (serial form, "Under Pressure," *Astounding Science-Fiction*, 1955)

The Plot: As a result of a long-running war, the world is starved for petroleum products. In response, using "sub-tugs," the United States has been taking crude oil from an undersea well operated by the enemy powers. In similar missions, twenty sister submarines have been lost to enemy action. U.S. Navy experts believe that the *Fenian Ram* has a good chance for success.

Ensign John Ramsey, an electronics officer and psychologist trained in the Bureau of Psychology, becomes a member of the closely knit crew of the *Fenian Ram*. His mission is to ferret out the enemy spy among the other three members of the crew to ensure the success of this critical mission.

Nothing about the mission augurs well. A corpse is discovered in the shielded atomic drive room, hidden electronic devices signal the sub's location, and a silk wiper rag threatens to cause an explosion from static electricity. As the obstacles to success slowly are overcome, Ramsey comes no nearer to determining the identity of the unknown spy, even though he has studied the personalities of the three other crew members intensely, both ashore and on board the ship.

Each of the other crew members has distinct individual qualities as well as potential tragic flaws. Captain Sparrow is extremely competent and has earned the nickname "Savvy" for his superior ability. He is also an apparent religious fanatic, fond of quoting Scripture, yet a man of immense personal emotional control. He is a virtual father to the crew, a commanding presence who can sense or intuit problems before they occur.

Les Bonnett, the first officer, and José Garcia, the engineering officer, react to both the captain and Ramsey, the newcomer, in different ways. Both men, defensive in their protection of the crew and its mission, view Ramsey as an interloper who must prove himself before acceptance. They view the captain as an indispensable, completely sane source of safety and security in the insane undersea world they inhabit during a war, the ultimate insanity.

As the mission proceeds, the ship and crew are threatened by incident after incident of increasing danger and tension. Ramsey, the psychologist, suffers two severe mental breakdowns. The first occurs when he realizes and fully accepts the incredible dangers of this mission, in the coldest depths of the Atlantic, more than nine thousand feet below the surface. He is saved from the second breakdown, which takes the form of catatonic immobility, by the fatherly compassion of Captain Sparrow, who had seemed to Ramsey to embody the latent insanity of the crew and its mission, as well as the insane war and insane mission in which both are engaged. Sparrow maintains that sanity is the ability to swim and survival is sanity. The Bible-quoting Sparrow also provides the ominous citation from Isaiah that gives the book its title: "In that day the Lord with his . . . great and strong sword shall punish leviathan the piercing serpent, even leviathan the crooked serpent; and he shall slay the dragon that is in the sea."

Numerous scenes drenched with both action and tension gradually reveal that Garcia, fearful for the safety of his wife and children, who are under the control of the enemy powers, is the hidden spy. It is Garcia, however, in an act of sacrificial self-immolation, who saves the ship and crew from an atomic flare-up. In effect, he redeems himself by literally laying down his life for his friends.

As the tub returns to its home port through a long undersea tunnel, Ramsey notices that the tunnel resembles the birth canal and that the ship and its crew are returning from "death in water" to "life in water." Nurtured by the umbilical cord of shared dangers and experience, the ship and the crew emerge from the darkness and dangers of the depths of the sea into the light of life. Ramsey convinces the Bureau of Security that its passion for secrecy and "security" is dangerous, that there can be no security in a world filled with war, hatred, and suspicion. Submarine crews should be publicly decorated and

their incredibly dangerous missions honored as a first step toward sanity and truth.

Analysis: It is difficult to believe that *The Dragon in the Sea* is Frank Herbert's first novel. It is a mature work, populated with well-drawn characters and filled with convincing action. It remains one of Herbert's most satisfying books. It succeeds not merely on its own terms but also in the many ways it anticipates *Dune* (1965) and its five sequels, not only for its action-filled plot but also for its reliance on the tools of psychology and humane understanding to advance that plot. Moreover, in the same way that *Dune* later provided a commentary on the extent to which people will go to obtain a substance of incalculable value, this novel emphasizes an oil-starved future and the means to which people and nations will go to obtain that scarce commodity.

Never sermonic, Herbert is content simply to let his story speak for him. Submariners have written dozens of letters to Herbert, commenting that *The Dragon in the Sea* catches the spirit, the tension, and the pervading fear of submarine life better than anything else they have ever seen.

—*Willis E. McNelly*

THE DRAGON KNIGHT SERIES

Jim Eckert is transplanted into an alternate fourteenth century and must battle the Dark Powers as the Dragon Knight

Author: Gordon R. Dickson (1923-   )
Genre: Fantasy—heroic fantasy
Type of work: Novels
Time of plot: The fourteenth century
Location: An alternate Earth
First published: *The Dragon and the George* (1976; based on the novelette "St. Dragon and the George," *The Magazine of Fantasy and Science Fiction*, September, 1957), *The Dragon Knight* (1990), *The Dragon on the Border* (1992), *The Dragon at War* (1992), and *The Dragon, the Earl and the Troll* (1994)

The Plot: *The Dragon and the George* features Jim Eckert, a doctoral student in medieval history who is frustrated with the twentieth century. His girlfriend, Angie, is a research assistant to a scientist experimenting with astral projection and accidentally gets sent to some unknown world. Jim tries to follow, but only his mind is projected. He wakes up in the body of a dragon named

Gorbash. Angie, a "george"—as all humans are called by dragons—is captured by the dragon Bryagh. Gorbash's uncle, Smrgol, convinces the dragons to hold her for ransom and sends Jim to the magician S. Carolinus to arrange the negotiations.

Jim and Angie see Carolinus as their only hope of returning home. Jim meets the mage and reveals his situation. Before the mage can do anything, Bryagh takes Angie to the Loathly Towers, the fortress of the Dark Powers. Jim is caught in a battle between the forces of good and evil and is told that he must gather "Companions" before he rescues Angie.

Over the course of a few days, Jim meets Sir Brian Neville-Smythe, a knight; Aragh, the English Wolf; Danielle of the Wold, a woodswoman; her father, Giles of the Wold, an outlaw; and Daffyd ap Hwyel, a Welsh master bowman. They have a few adventures, then approach the Loathly Towers. They are joined by Carolinus, Smrgol, and Secoh (another dragon) to face the champions of the Dark Powers, including the evil Sir Hugh de Malencontri, Bryagh, and an ogre. Jim and his Companions win the battle and rescue Angie, though at a price. Jim and Angie decide to stay instead of returning home, and Jim is given back his human body.

The Dragon Knight takes place approximately ten months after the battle of the Loathly Towers. Jim, who is now Sir James, Baron de Bois de Malencontri, has married Angie and controls the Malencontri lands. He begins changing into a dragon: Because he is a magician and has not been using his magic, it has started to use him. Jim becomes apprenticed to Carolinus and begins practicing magic.

Meanwhile, Prince Edward of England has been captured in France, and the English knights mount a rescue force. Jim must go as part of feudal duty. He and Brian join the English forces. They meet Sir Giles, another English knight and a "silkie," a man on land and seal in the sea. They are given a special assignment to rescue the prince from the hands of the evil magician, Malvinne.

They go to France and meet Sir Raoul, a French knight who wants to save his king and country from Malvinne's machinations. After a few solo misadventures, Jim returns to his group to find that they have been joined by Aargh the Wolf (the spelling has changed from the first book) and Daffyd. The force eventually penetrates Malvinne's fortress and rescues the prince. They are then charged with taking the prince back to the English forces and stopping the battle between the English and the French. Jim uses his twentieth century cunning and four-teenth century magic to win the day, but Malvinne escapes.

Jim returns home to find his castle occupied by Malvinne and Sir Hugh de Malencontri. He duels with Sir Hugh and wins, but he has to face one last magical battle before he is returned safely to Angie's arms.

In *The Dragon on the Border*, Jim, Brian, and Daffyd head to Northumberland to visit the home of the de Mers. Besides finding their friend, they find a new menace: The Hollow Men are ghosts who inhabit armor and terrorize the area. They can be killed, but if even one survives, the rest will be resurrected in two days.

To make matters worse, word comes to the de Mers and Jim that the king of France is paying the king of Scotland to invade England. The Scots king plans on using the Hollow Men in the first attack. Jim decides that he has to destroy the Hollow Men all at once and comes up with a plan to do so, employing the help of Liseth de Mer, Snorl the wolf, a Scotsman named Lachlan MacGreggor, the Little Men, Brian, and Daffyd, as well as his magical abilities. The Dark Powers have set a trap for him, however, and he must battle a Worm to win the day. He does so, and as a reward for his success he gets a higher rating as a magician.

The Dragon at War takes place immediately after Jim's battle with the Hollow Men. Carolinus has been attacked by a mysterious mage, and Jim and Angie rescue him. Carolinus sends Jim, along with Giles and Brian, to the bottom of the sea to visit a kraken. He then sends them to France with Secoh and Daffyd to get information from the evil sorcerer Ecotti. They learn of a French attack on England using sea serpents but discover no information about the mysterious mage.

Jim and his Companions return to Jim's castle. The sea serpents, who hate dragons—especially English dragons—attack England and swarm Jim's castle. Jim engineers a plan with the help of the English and French dragons and the Sea Devil, Rrrnlf, but he is forced into a duel with the leader of the sea serpents. He wins, but the secret mage appears, and Jim has to shock Carolinus out of a depression to battle the other mage.

The Dragon, the Earl and the Troll takes place a few months after Jim defeats the sea serpents. This time, he is faced with different problems. Carolinus senses the Dark Powers at work and tells Jim and Angie that they must go to the Christmas Feast at the home of the earl of Somerset. They reluctantly agree.

On the way, they encounter a party slain by outlaws and rescue a baby. When they get to the castle, Jim discovers a set of problems. A troll is shaking the castle to pieces because he smells another troll upstairs. The earl hates the troll. More trolls have surrounded the castle. Lady Agatha Fallon, the baby's aunt, wants to be queen and will do almost anything to achieve that goal. The dragons want to come and be blessed by the prince of England. Compounding these problems, Jim is in danger of being stripped of all of his magical abilities. Once more, with the aid of Brian, Angie, and Aargh, Jim comes up with a plan. It solves his problems and creates a new type of magic. *The Dragon and the Djinn*, a continuation of the series, was scheduled to be published in 1996.

Analysis: The first book of the Dragon Knight series was published fourteen years before the second, and it was based on a short story written years earlier. *The Dragon and the George* is a slight twist on the quest and companion story found throughout folklore and fantasy, such as in J. R. R. Tolkien's work. The twist is that the hero is the dragon, or at least occupies the body of a dragon.

The story follows a traditional quest/companion formula. The hero gathers a group of Companions in order to fulfill the quest. Each Companion has an ability that is needed to defeat or conquer some trial or obstacle that the group encounters. There is a final battle, which the Companions win.

The next three books follow this same plot line, each ending with Jim fighting a duel in either dragon or human form. This formula is changed to an intellectual challenge in *The Dragon, the Earl and the Troll*. The greatest difference between the sequels and the original book is that Gordon Dickson becomes more concerned with place and setting. The later books involve more of Jim dealing with life in the fourteenth century. He has to adjust his thinking and attitudes to those of the time in which he now lives. Dickson also deals more with the history and politics of the times than in the first novel.

The novels stay consistent in format and characters. Jim's Companions reappear from novel to novel, with new ones added. There are some inconsistencies from the first book to the sequels. Aragh the Wolf becomes Aargh the Wolf, and Jim was a history student in the first novel but is sometimes referred to as an English instructor later on.

Dickson, winner of both Hugo and Nebula awards, is probably more famous for his science-fiction Childe cycle than for this fantasy series. He is a prolific writer with many published novels to his credit, the first in 1956. The Dragon Knight series, with the exception of the first book, is a fairly recent addition to his credits.

—*P. Andrew Miller*

THE DRAGON MASTERS

Reptilian aliens return to Aerlith to abduct humans to serve as breeding stock but are opposed by humans who have bred alien stock to produce dragons

Author: Jack Vance (1916-   )
Genre: Fantasy—invasion story
Type of work: Novella
Time of plot: The distant future
Location: A small region of the world of Aerlith
First published: 1962

The Plot: Unaccountably, a sacerdote is found in the inner sanctum of Joaz Banbeck, lord and master of Banbeck Vale, breeder of dragons, and direct descendant of Kergan Banbeck, who had successfully withstood a previous raid from the reptilian "basics." On the planet Aerlith, the sacerdotes are a mysterious hermetic culture living in secluded caves and bound to a creed of noninterference in human affairs. Joaz rushes to his study to find that the sacerdote has vanished through a concealed door.

The Banbecks have been vying with the Carcolo family for domination of the region for several generations. The planet is a marooned outpost of humanity, a residual of a galactic struggle that has destroyed the human empire. Ervis Carcolo, lord of the neighboring and relatively poorer Happy Valley, meets with Joaz to discuss preparations in the event of invasion. Joaz has studied history and the stars, and he believes that another attack from the basics is imminent because of the optimal proximity of one of their worlds. Ervis, a brutish and vengeful man, has spent all of his resources in attempts to breed new dragons, whereas Joaz has been diligently adding tunnels and escape routes for his people. Instead of aiding the preparations, Ervis proposes forcing the sacerdotes into service and perhaps having them reveal the secrets of star travel.

Soon after this conference, Ervis tries to launch a surprise attack on Joaz but instead is ambushed and routed. Joaz is again visited by a sacerdote, which he traps in his study. The sacerdote follows a code of conduct that forces him to precisely answer Joaz's questions but not to volunteer information; the situation is analogous to trying to get a computer to reveal the meaning of life. Through this interview, a visit to the caverns in disguise, and a dream communication, Joaz learns that the sacerdotes plan to reconquer the cosmos once the impure and impassioned humans have been wiped out by the basics.

Ervis directs another intrepid and poorly planned attack, and he is again caught off guard. During the pitched battle, the basics land a large spacecraft in Happy Valley. Ervis breaks off from near defeat and retreats to watch the basics destroy Happy Valley. He then follows the spacecraft to Joaz's Banbeck Vale.

Joaz meets the basic invasion with cool, efficient strategy and his considerable troop of dragons. The basics resort to bombardment of the craggy mountains in which the Banbeck forces are lurking. This destruction eventually reveals the sacerdotes' hidden caverns. During a lull in the fighting, Ervis determines to surprise the basics from behind with the paltry remnants of his troops and dragons. Ervis walks into the basics' trap, but the aliens are unprepared for the arrival of Joaz and his troops, who enter the ship and accidentally rescue Ervis before being repulsed. The sacerdotes respond to their dilemma by crippling the basics' ship with energy beams, but they suffer damage to their hidden spaceship. In the aftermath of the battle, the damaged ship belongs to Joaz, the sacerdotes are spurned and contemptuously return to their caves, Ervis is executed, and Joaz contemplates a future searching for remaining pockets of humanity and perhaps for a world called Eden.

Analysis: Commentary on Jack Vance's work often includes mention of arcane language and highly stylized narrative techniques. Such holds true, to a degree, for criticism of *The Dragon Masters*, winner of a 1963 Hugo in the category of short fiction. More noteworthy is the complexity of balanced ironic polarities. The humans have been breeding dragons (Blue Horrors, Termagants, massive Juggers, and others) from basic stock, while the basics have been breeding hominid mutations (Giants, burly dwarfish Heavy Troopers, long-limbed Trackers, and others) from human stock. The careful administration of Joaz Banbeck is contrasted with the autocratic bungling of Ervis Carcolo. The sacerdotes and their self-preserving sanctity invite comparison to the striving for progress that Joaz epitomizes. Vance colors the positions so that Joaz is appealing, while the noble sacerdotes seem aloof and uncaring.

As protagonist, Joaz initially seems autocratic, bookish, and a bit of an effete aesthete. In comparison to the boorish Ervis and because of his urge for a better life for his people, however, readers become enamored of him. He is reminiscent of the title character from Vance's *Rhialto, the Marvelous* (1984), a wizard and explorer of arcana who seldom is bested by his peers. The minuscule world created in this story seems marginalized, in ways similar to Vance's "Dying World" contexts.

A theme that emerges from the ironic tensions is that little separates one position from another, that values are more similar than different. The only characteristic that makes the humans seem better than the aliens, and that also makes Joaz better than Ervis, is compassion. Joaz cares about his people, and the human breeders care about their dragons. Neither Ervis nor the basics have a shred of compassion. Ervis tries to breed abominations and abuses his troops; the basics treat the human stock as expendable machinery. When the basics send mutated human stock to discuss capitulation with the unruly humans, the exchange clarifies how alien the basics' philosophy is to human norms. The importance of compassion is heightened by the issue of noninvolvement presented by the sacerdotes, who spitefully articulate it in a concluding conversation with Joaz.   —*Scott D. Vander Ploeg*

THE DRAGON WAITING

In an alternative Europe in which Christianity has not replaced earlier magical religions, four people join to support Richard III of England against a tyrannical and subtly encroaching Byzantine Empire

Author: John M. Ford (1957-   )
Genre: Science fiction—alternate history
Type of work: Novel
Time of plot: The fifteenth century
Location: Wales; Burgundy, France; Florence and
    Milan, Italy; and England
First published: 1983

The Plot: In this novel, four characters from different European countries and backgrounds live out their early lives and suffer from larger Byzantine plots and intrigues that sweep up their lives. Hywel Peredur, himself a wizard, is a descendant of a great Welsh wizard betrayed by the Byzantine Empire. Dimitrios Ducas, a mercenary, is the son of the governor of Burgundy in Gaul and the descendant of a deposed Byzantine emperor. Cynthia Ricci, a Florentine doctor in love with Lorenzo de' Medici, is killed, along with members of her family, in a Byzantine plot to gain control of Italy. Gregory Von Bayern is a German vampire who has never infected a human and never killed, though he possesses a vast knowledge of guns and explosives.

The four characters meet in Milan, Italy. While trying to unravel a mysterious murder, they discover their mutual hatred of the Byzantine Empire and their desire to halt its spread westward across Europe. They decide to focus their attention on England, which, though politically turbulent under Edward IV after the Wars of the Roses, still remains free of Byzantine domination. The country is not free of scheming Byzantine pawns, all hoping to further their individual ends by casting their lots with the overarching Byzantine conspiracy for world domination, a domination abhorrent to the four friends.

Their various skills make them instrumental in challenging various Byzantine-connected forces determined to deliver England to the empire. They first contend with the plots of Margaret of Anjou, the wife of England's former Lancastrian ruler Henry VI, to use occult arts and well-placed evil magicians to displace the Yorkist Edward IV. After Edward's suspicious death, the four support Edward's brother, Richard of Gloucester, as Lord Protector and regent of Edward's two young sons. Cynthia discovers that both sons have a rare but terminal blood disease and have been traitorously infected with vampirism.

While feuding relatives and other internal crises confront Richard, Hywel Peredur and Cynthia Ricci discover that other trouble is afoot in Wales. Byzantine forces, using magic and ancient Welsh legends, are building support for Henry Tydder. He is a descendant of the widow of England's King Henry V and is known to history as Henry VII, the founder of the Tudor dynasty and the man responsible for the defeat of Richard. Following the mysterious deaths of Edward's sons, Hywel, Dimitrios, Cynthia, and Gregory rally around Richard, now Richard III, in what will be not only the battle of his life but also a battle to end the inroads of Byzantine tyranny and treachery.

Analysis: The plot of *The Dragon Waiting* dramatically incorporates into fiction real characters of fifteenth century Europe such as Edward IV, Richard III, and members of their families and courts in England; Lorenzo de' Medici and his circle of friends and dependents in Italy; and Margaret of Anjou and her supporters at the French court of Louis XI. The fictional characters are as believable and alive as the historical characters with whom they interact. The novel likewise merges fictional and historical events, embellishes and provides credible causes for events whose details have been lost to historical annals, and freely alters occurrences that may have been different had previous underlying events not taken place or philosophical worldviews not been established.

John M. Ford has acquired a reputation as a diverse and talented writer as well as some fame as a game designer. His literary output is as varied as it is extensive. He has covered a wide range of science-fiction and fantasy subgenres. His first works were children's stories, which he wrote under an assumed name. Previous work written under his own name and published professionally includes short stories in *Isaac Asimov's Science Fiction Magazine*; his *Alternities Corporation* series of science-fiction stories (1979-1981); *Web of Angels* (1980), an early novelistic venture into cyberpunk before its conventions were established; an informative manual for potential science-fiction writers titled *On Writing Science Fiction: The Editors Strike Back!* (1981), which he coauthored with George H. Scithers and Darrell Schweitzer; and a second novel, *The Princes of the Air* (1982), a space opera noted more for its details than for its breadth. *The Dragon Waiting* was Ford's first attempt at alternate history. It represents not so much a departure from previous work as the creation of a new venue for the exploration of human struggle with apparently intractable forces.

The novel won the 1984 World Fantasy Award. These awards, familiarly known as "Howards" in imitation of the Hugo Awards for science fiction that date from the 1950's, were initiated in 1975 specifically to recognize outstanding work in fantasy. Winners are determined by a panel of critics, and the awards are presented at the World Fantasy Convention held annually in October, usually in the United States. The novel interweaves the fantasy themes of wizardry, sorcery, and magical ritual with historical events and intermingles fictional and biographical characters against a backdrop of imaginatively improvised yet plausible historical events and outcomes.

Ford has continued his varied outpouring of literary works. These include two Star Trek television tie-ins, *The Final Reflection* (1984) and *How Much for Just the Planet?* (1987); novels such as *The Scholars of Night* (1988); and a number of short stories. Some critics believe that Ford's variety in selection of genres and themes and his far-ranging imagination have damaged his career commercially. He has failed to establish a definitive mode of writing that would win him a permanent and loyal audience. Others believe that his originality and creative talent assure his readers that his writing will never become stale and predictable.

—*Christine R. Catron*

THE DRAGONBONE CHAIR

An epic fantasy quest in which Simon, a castle kitchen scullion, must search for the swords of prophecy to fight the rising evil power of the Storm King

Author: Tad Williams (1957-   )
Genre: Fantasy—heroic fantasy
Type of work: Novel
Time of plot: Undefined
Location: Osten Ard, a land resembling medieval Europe
First published: 1988

The Plot: Simon, an orphaned castle kitchen scullion, avoids his duties and spends his time dreaming of becoming a hero. He is apprenticed to Dr. Morgenes, the castle's sorcerer, in an attempt to teach him to be industrious. When Prester John, the High King, dies, his elder son, Elias, takes over the throne. Elias is increasingly influenced by the evil priest Pyrates, lackey of the vengeful Storm King. Josua, the younger son, tries with Morgenes to halt the encroaching evil. Finally, they and their allies must search for the missing swords of prophecy to restore order to Osten Ard.

Morgenes dies as he helps Josua escape from his brother. Scared and alone, Simon must follow Josua to his holding in the north. Simon wanders through the woods until hunger drives him toward a town, where he saves a humanlike creature from a hunter. The creature is Jiriki, a prince of the fairy-folk Sithi. Jiriki rewards Simon with a white arrow, a mark of debt owed.

As Simon ponders the meaning of the arrow, the troll Binabik appears to help Simon on his way. They meet up with Melachias, another castle runaway. Binabik leads the two young people to Geloë's house in the woods to rest and recuperate. She, along with Binabik, is a member of the League of the Scroll, a centuries-old group formed to gather knowledge and fight evil. Morgenes also had been a member. While at Geloë's house, Melachias reveals herself to be Marya, a serving lady to the princess. She is hurrying to Josua with an important message from the princess.

After more harrowing adventures, Simon, Marya, and Binabik reach Josua. Simon discovers that Marya is actually the princess herself and so must learn to quell his rising feelings for her. He also learns, for the first time, of the prophecy of the swords and that the sword Thorn is hoarded by an ice dragon. Simon and Binabik lead a small party into the mountains to search for it.

Meanwhile, Prester John's realm is in disarray with conspiracies and plots that Elias and Pyrates foster. Those dukes and barons loyal to Prester John's ideals are held as virtual prisoners, while others, greedy for power, curry favor with the king and his priest. The land is ravaged by plague and the weather is unusual, both ef-

fects of the Storm King's rising power.

Simon's party is captured by a group of Sithi, and only his white arrow prevents them from being killed. Jiriki vouches for them as he begins to realize there is something special about Simon. Jiriki agrees to help them hunt for Thorn. They find the sword, but they arouse the dragon guarding it. Simon, holding Thorn, kills the dragon, but he thinks the killing was more the sword's doing than his. Dragon blood spurts over a lock of Simon's hair, turning it white. Jiriki tells him that he has been marked, and he is known thereafter as Simon Snowlock.

Analysis: *The Dragonbone Chair* is the first part of the trilogy Memory, Sorrow, and Thorn. *Stone of Farewell* (1990) and *To Green Angel Tower* (1993) continue the search for the three swords and describe the eventual downfall of Elias, Pyrates, and the Storm King.

The Dragonbone Chair is very much in the tradition of heroic fantasy, akin to J. R. R. Tolkien's Lord of the Rings trilogy (1954-1955) and the epic quest fantasies that followed. *The Dragonbone Chair* is quite different from Tad Williams' first book, *Tailchaser's Song* (1986), a one-volume animal fantasy novel about the cat kingdom.

The Dragonbone Chair contains all the hallmarks of fantasy quest literature: a young boy of uncertain parentage who matures into his powers as well as his manhood, a resourceful princess whom the hero feels inadequate to love, wizards and prophecies to help the hero on his quest, a small band of companions struggling against a larger evil force, a betrayer from within who almost ruins their plans, and a land that is sickening and dying because of an ever-growing evil presence. What raises *The Dragonbone Chair* above the level of many such epic quests is the depth of characterization. Simon, Binabik, Josua, Elias, Pyrates, and the many others involved in the plot are fully realized people commanding pity, admiration, or horror. Simon is an especially riveting hero as he grows from a complaining, idling kitchen boy into the ice dragon's killer. Even the minor characters within the extensive cast are carefully drawn. The world in which they travel is varied and well detailed, creating a complete sense of reality. Williams even includes maps so the reader can follow Simon's journey. The interweaving of the different narratives as the novel moves among the many factions in the struggle keeps the story moving and engages the reader.

Motivation for the evil that the heroes fight, often ignored in quest fantasies that rely solely on adventure, is only hinted at in this first volume but is further explained in the remaining parts of the trilogy. The reasons are buried deep in Osten Ard's history, which is explained, in part, in *The Dragonbone Chair*. The reader, along with Simon, must piece together that history from dreams, snatches of old books that have somehow survived, and bits of knowledge possessed by the League of the Scroll. It is a complex history of the strife between humanity and the Sithi, and Simon learns that humans are not always in the right.

The Dragonbone Chair is an engaging beginning to a trilogy filled with unique characters, plot twists, and surprises. It serves well as an introduction to the world of Osten Ard, as well as to Simon and his friends and enemies. *The Dragonbone Chair* is well crafted, complex, and extremely imaginative, leaving the reader both satisfied and hungering for the next installment of the trilogy.   —*Marjorie Ginsberg*

THE DRAGONRIDERS OF PERN

Attacked by deadly spores called Thread, the former Earth colony Pern is protected by brave men and women and their telepathic, fire-breathing dragons

Author: Anne McCaffrey (1926-   )
Genre: Science fiction—extrasensory powers
Type of work: Novels
Time of plot: Pre-landing through the Ninth Pass
Location: Pern, an undeveloped world
First published: *Dragonflight* (1968; the opening is a revised form of "Weyr Search," *Analog*, 1967), *Dragonquest* (1971), *The White Dragon* (1978; part previously published as "A Time When," 1975), *Dragonsong* (1976), *Dragonsinger* (1977), *Dragondrums* (1979), *Moreta, Dragonlady of Pern* (1983), *Nerilka's Story* (1986), *Dragonsdawn* (1988), *The Renegades of Pern* (1989), *All the Weyrs of Pern* (1991), *Rescue Run* (1991; earlier version in *Analog*, 1991), *The Dolphins' Bell* (1993), *The Girl Who Heard Dragons* (1994), and *The Dolphins of Pern* (1994)

The Plot: In 1967, Anne McCaffrey introduced readers to the Dragonriders of Pern series with the story "Weyr Search." Pern's story begins with Earth colonists landing on an agricultural planet. All goes well for eight years, until Pern is attacked by deadly spores called Thread. The initial losses to Thread in livestock, crops, and human life are staggering. To fight Thread, the Pernese

biogenetically engineer large, telepathic, fire-breathing dragons (weyrs) and Thread-eating grubs.

A Thread attack, called a Pass, lasts fifty years; they come in Intervals of two hundred years. By the Ninth Pass, five weyrs have disappeared, Benden Weyr has fallen into disarray, and dragonriders are in disfavor. Only Benden Weyrleaders Lessa and F'lar and F'lar's half brother F'nor believe that Thread will fall again. They try to prepare Pern, but the two hundred dragons of Benden cannot defend all the settlements. Lessa discovers that the dragons can teleport between times as well as between places, and she and her queen, Ramoth, travel back in time to bring the missing five weyrs forward to aid Benden's fight with Thread.

Tensions mount because the Oldtimers resent the cultural changes in Pern. Dragonman fights dragonman as F'lar fights T'ron and later T'kul. A queen egg is stolen and then returned by the young Lord Holder Jaxom, who, against all tradition, impresses the white dragon Ruth. The male-dominated culture continues to evolve as Menolly becomes the first female harper, Mirrim impresses a green dragon, and female and male young people attend cross-crafting classes together for the first time.

Small, emphatic friends called fire lizards are discovered. They form a link among holders, craftsmen, and dragonriders. Masterharper Robinton helps to guide the development of Pern with wise counsel and carefully developed teaching ballads. Old knowledge is rediscovered, and the Pernese learn to use a distance viewer, talking wires, and an enlarger. The Lord Holders pressure the dragonriders to go to the Red Star to eliminate Thread at its source. Using the distance viewer, F'nor directs his brown dragon Canth to the Red Star, and they are nearly killed trying to land on the turbulent planet.

Ruins are discovered on the southern continent. These include the shuttles that brought the colonists to Pern and a voice-activated interactive computer. The powerful computer teaches the Pernese much of the knowledge lost over the years and helps them plan how to use the Dawn Sisters, the original starships, to get rid of Thread. Jaxom and Ruth again are instrumental in making plans that signal a new beginning for this agricultural world.

Analysis: The science-fiction elements are stronger in some Pern novels than in others. *Dragonsdawn* explains that the colonists arrive in the three transport spaceships with all the necessary technology. In fact, the dolphins who arrived at the same time had been genetically enhanced before the journey to enable them to communicate with human partners.

One important science-fiction device in this series is the biogenetic manipulation of the dragonets (later called fire lizards) into the powerful fire-breathing dragons of Pern. They fly, teleport, breath fire, and possess telepathic abilities, all as a result of genetic engineering rather than magic. In several novels, these science-fiction elements are only implied; after *Dragonsdawn*, it is not until *The White Dragon* that physical remains of the landing are discovered. At the conclusion of *The Renegades of Pern*, the Artificial Intelligence Voice Address System, or AIVAS, is discovered, and the Pernese begin to explore their scientific origins.

McCaffrey has created a world that many readers would like to visit. Pern is a place with fascinating telepathic creatures, complex and growing characters, and a strong work ethic. Although the series is science fiction, the stories largely concern relationships among people and between people and animals. Readers return to the series as new novels are published because the history of Pern is so rich and intricate. Many teachers in elementary and junior high schools require their students to read "The Smallest Dragonboy" (1982), a Pern story that is anthologized widely, and the novels of the Harper Hall trilogy (*Dragonsong*, *Dragonsinger*, and *Dragondrums*).

McCaffrey has recommended starting with the two main trilogies within the series, the Harper Hall trilogy and the adult trilogy consisting of *Dragonflight*, *Dragonquest*, and *The White Dragon*. These six novels provide an understanding of the complex social structure of weyrs, holds, and crafts that sets up the other novels. The two trilogies also contain the most exciting events of the series: Lessa's trip through time, Ramoth's Impression, F'lar's fights with Oldtimers, F'nor's attempt to reach the Red Star, the discovery of fire lizards, Ruth's Impression, the stealing of the queen egg and its return, and Robinton's heart attack. The other novels are more concerned with historical details than with character development or exciting events.

The Dragonriders of Pern series is a history of the birth and growth of this society. McCaffrey describes the birth of the colony in *Dragonsdawn*, but significant births are scattered throughout the series. In the novella *The Dolphins' Bell*, after many adventures on the voyage north, dolphin Carolina's calf, Atlanta, is born. Jaxom is born by being forcibly removed from his mother's belly after F'lar kills his father, Fax. Perhaps the more memorable and endearing of the births are the hatchings. Ramoth's birth is described in detail from the sound of the bronze dragons' hum and the cries of the golden dragonet to Lessa's feelings of admiration, respect, and uncondi-

tional love from and for her dragon. The hatchings of Hannath after Moreta's and Orlith's deaths, of Ruth torn out of the egg by Jaxom, of Menolly's fire lizards in the cave during Thread, and of Robinton's and Sebell's fire lizards all create a desire in the reader for such a loyal and magnificent companion who loves so quickly and unconditionally. Readers return to Pern to visit these creatures and their partners.

McCaffrey illustrates the growth of this male-dominated society largely through female and teenage major characters. Moreta, queen rider of Orlith and weyrwoman at Fort Weyr, flies vaccine to quarantined holds during a devastating plague. Lessa fights to protect her home from Fax and later to lead Pern into the future. Craftbred Brekke becomes a queen rider and fights to adjust her values. Menolly impresses nine fire lizards and, with Masterharper Robinton's encouragement, invades the all-male harpercraft as the teenager Mirrim impresses a green dragon against custom. Another young person, Readis, re-establishes the link with the dolphins of Pern and creates the first dolphin crafthall.

McCaffrey was the first woman to win both the Hugo Award (1968, for "Weyr Search") and the Nebula Award (1968, for "Dragonrider"), and she was one of the first science-fiction writers to have a book—*The White Dragon*—on the best-seller lists. Other awards came over the years, including the E. E. Smith Award for fantasy in 1975; the American Library Association notable book citation in 1976 for *Dragonsong* and in 1977 for *Dragonsinger*; the *Horn Book* Fanfare Citation in 1977 for *Dragonsong*; and the Ditmar Award (Australia), Gandalf Award, and Eurocon/Steso Award, all in 1979, for *The White Dragon*.

The Dragonriders of Pern series inspired three companion texts: *The Atlas of Pern* (1984) by Karen Wynn Fonstad; *The People of Pern* (1988) by Robin Wood, with text and introduction by Anne McCaffrey; and *The Dragonlover's Guide to Pern* (1989) by Jody Lynn Nye with Anne McCaffrey. McCaffrey started the Dragonriders of Pern series early in her career and has returned to it repeatedly, but it is not her only popular series. The Pegasus series, sometimes known as the Rowan Women series or Talents series, began with McCaffrey's first published short story, "Lady in the Tower" (*The Magazine of Fantasy and Science Fiction*, April, 1959). *Lyon's Pride*, the sixth novel in this series, was published in 1994. *Dinosaur Planet* (1978) and *The Crystal Singer* (1982) each begin a separate series.

Although some of the Pern novels are stronger and more popular than others, each aids in the creation of a complicated world as enduring as C. S. Lewis' Narnia, Roger Zelazny's Amber, or Marion Zimmer Bradley's Darkover. Readers will continue to enjoy the novels about the Dragonriders of Pern and their magnificent companions for years to come. —*Susan A. VanSchuyver*

DRAGONSBANE

After joining with the dragon Morkeleb to defeat the wicked Zyerne, witch Jenny Waynest must decide between the unlimited powers Morkeleb offers and the human love of John Aversin, Dragonsbane

Author: Barbara Hambly (1951-   )
Genre: Fantasy—heroic fantasy
Type of work: Novel
Time of plot: The late medieval period
Location: The Realm of the King, Winterlands, and Belmarie
First published: 1986

The Plot: Although *Dragonsbane* refers to Lord John Aversin of Alyn Hold, the only living man to have slain a dragon, the story centers on Jenny Waynest and the dilemma she faces in being both a human being and a mage. This dilemma first arose ten years before the time of the plot, when Jenny met and fell in love with John, and reaches its climax after Prince Gareth comes to the Winterlands, a province of King Urien's realm, to recruit the aid of the Dragonsbane in ridding the Deep of Ylferdun of the black dragon. Reluctantly, Jenny and John, the north country scholar with a deep brogue and a love of old wives' tales, accompany Gareth to the land of Belmarie to slay the dragon.

They soon realize that the dragon is merely a symptom of the realm's problems. The king's mistress, Zyerne, a beautiful but utterly ruthless young sorceress who places no limitations on her powers, is the disease. Jenny learns from a gnome mage, Lady Mab, that as a child Zyerne was apprenticed to the gnomes and learned their magic. While with them, Zyerne stole her way to the Stone in the heart of the Deep, the spot from which unlimited powers emanate. Zyerne's every move since has been calculated to gain her permanent access to the Stone. For that purpose, she summoned Morkeleb, the black dragon, to rid the Deep of the gnomes and now is unable to banish the greedy dragon from the gold hordes. That is where Dragonsbane comes in. Zyerne wants John to kill Morkeleb so that she can take over the Deep. She did not count on the small witch, Jenny Waynest, getting in her way.

In contrast to Zyerne's single-minded dedication to her "art," for ten years Jenny's life has been divided between her love for John and their two sons and her devotion to magic. She knows that she is no match for Zyerne and no threat to Morkeleb. When John insists that they battle the dragon to keep Zyerne from gaining ultimate power, she is distraught, having foreseen the outcome of the combat. When John stumbles back badly wounded, she decides to go into the Deep and find the places of healing to restore him to life. In so doing, she must confront Morkeleb. Also mortally wounded, Morkeleb telepathically bargains with her, offering to convey her through the intricate warrens if she will heal him. Jenny agrees, but not before she looks into the eyes of the dragon, entangling her soul with his.

After Jenny heals Morkeleb, she exacts his promise to leave and learns his true name, music that holds the essence of his soul and binds him to her. The problem is far from solved, however. By this time, Zyerne knows they are rid of the dragon and incites a mob to take over the Deep. Although Jenny's powers have increased, she has practically exhausted her abilities in holding off the mob when Morkeleb unexpectedly returns. Morkeleb and Jenny are united in the final battle with Zyerne, now indomitable because she has defiled the Stone and attained unlimited power. Jenny and Morkeleb are able to hold off the shape-shifter until John and Gareth blow up the Stone, thus killing Zyerne.

Although peace returns to the land with Zyerne's death, peace does not return to Jenny. She has tasted the freedom and magic of the dragon. Morkeleb wants her to accompany him north, as a dragon. After some deliberation, she sheds her humanness and soars into the sky, white dragon against black dragon. Even in the first glow of her freedom, though, she looks down on John Aversin and feels the sterility of this life, realizing that "the key to magic was not magic," as her master Caerdinn had asserted, but the use of magic. As her love draws her back earthward, Morkeleb's love for her allows her to go.

Analysis: *Dragonsbane* was one of the first adult fantasy novels to make the Best Books List (1986). Many of Barbara Hambly's other works, such as *The Rainbow Abyss* (1991), traverse the voids between alternate universes and time sequences. *Dragonsbane*, in contrast, is set completely within one time frame and one universe.

Common threads run throughout Hambly's various work, which includes *Star Wars* novels such as *Children of the Jedi* (1995) and fantasies from the Darwath Trilogy (*The Time of the Dark*, 1982; *The Walls of Air*, 1983;

and *The Armies of Daylight*, 1983) to *The Witches of Wenshar* (1987) to the Windrose Chronicles (*The Silent Tower*, 1986; *The Silicon Mage*, 1988; and *Dog Wizard*, 1993). Among these threads are her ability to draw memorable characters and her examination of the uses and abuses of power. *Dragonsbane*, a formula fantasy, is no exception. Critics alternately accuse Hambly of providing too much narration and too little dialogue and praise her for presenting charming vignettes of everyday life. *Dragonsbane* offers some of the best Hambly has to offer—suspenseful narration, a gritty view of late medieval life, and compelling, likable characters.

In the plain, thirty-seven-year old witch with limited powers, Jenny Waynest; the gangly scholar John Aversin, who has the audacity to kill a dragon using an axe; and even bespectacled Prince Gareth, Hambly realistically portrays antiheroes who simultaneously defy and fulfill their mythic roles. Hambly highlights the conflict between Jenny's desire for unlimited power and her humanity by presenting a major plot complication that pits the fragmented Jenny against her single-minded alter egos, evil energy-vampire Zyerne and amoral Morkeleb. Hers is a Frankensteinian view of the sterility and, sometimes, evil that ensues when one dedicates oneself totally to anything, be it art, magic, or science, without regard to universal laws or human feelings.

—*Jaquelyn W. Walsh*